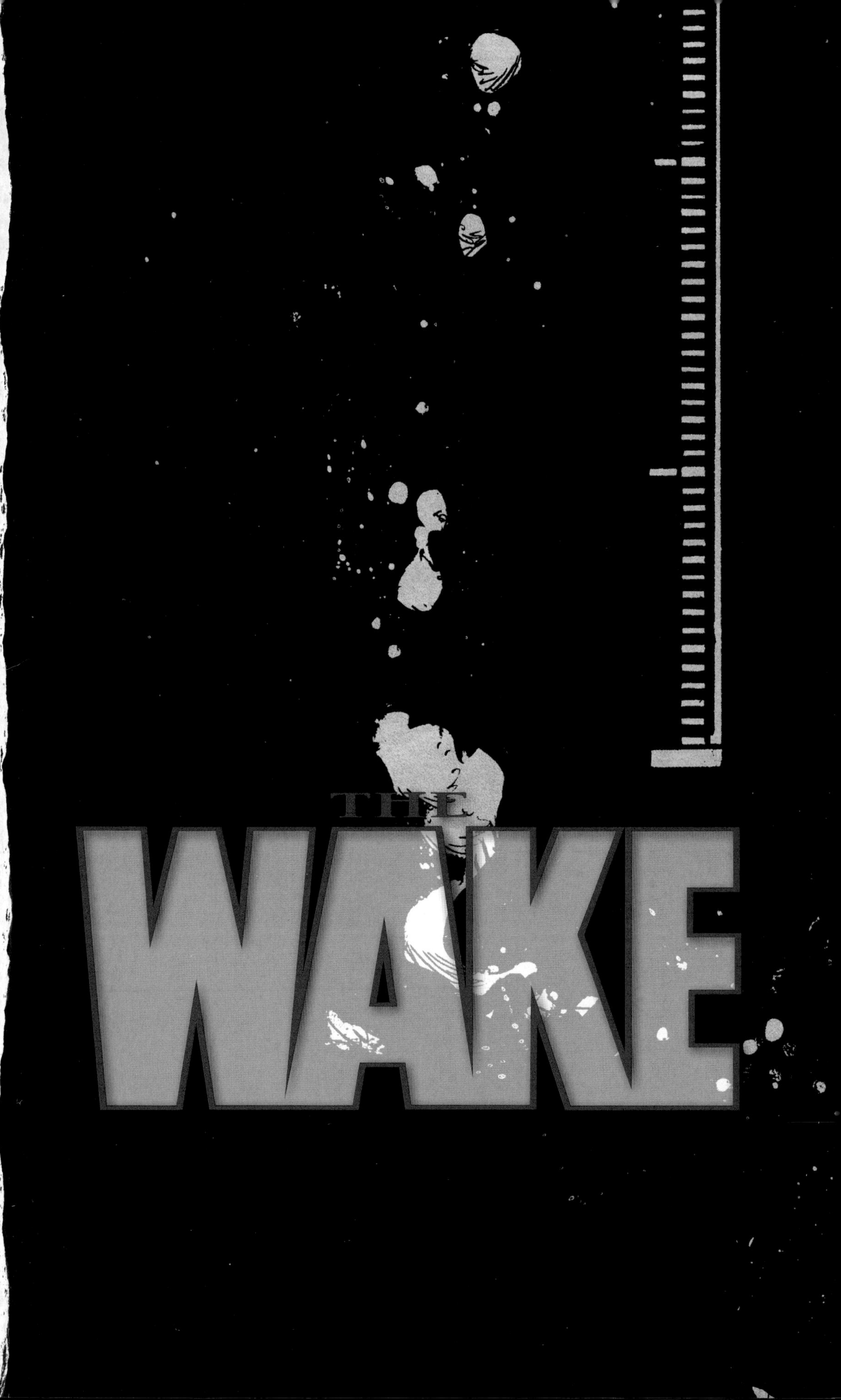
THE
WAKE

SCOTT
SNYDER
WRITER

SEAN
MURPHY
ARTIST

MATT
HOLLINGSWORTH
COLORIST

JARED K.
FLETCHER
LETTERER

SEAN MURPHY WITH
JORDIE BELLAIRE AND
ANDREW ROBINSON
ORIGINAL SERIES COVERS

SPECIAL THANKS TO
CHRISTIAN DIBARI

THE WAKE CREATED BY
SCOTT SNYDER AND
SEAN MURPHY

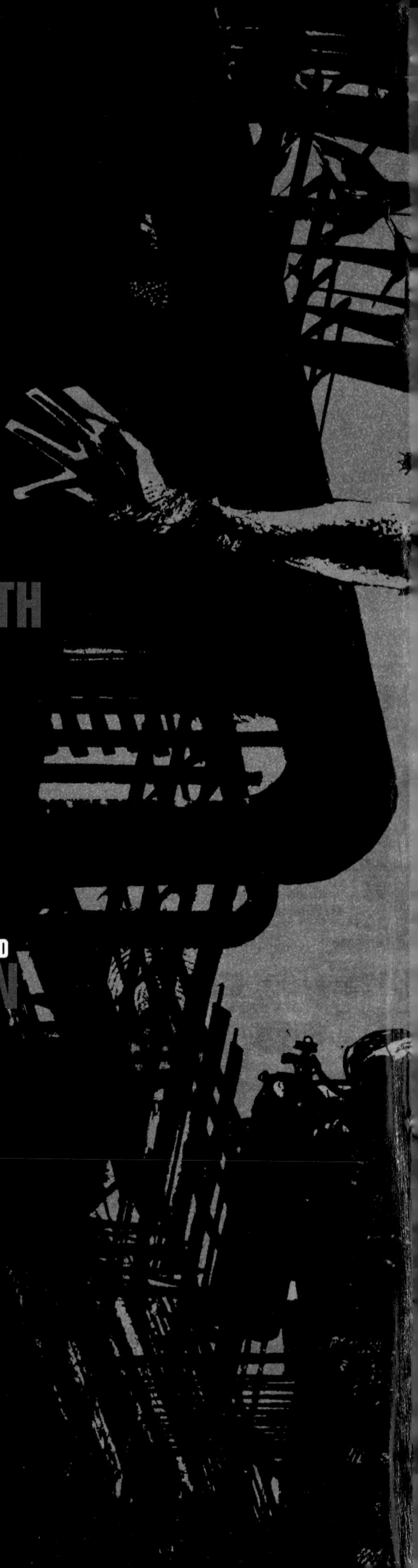

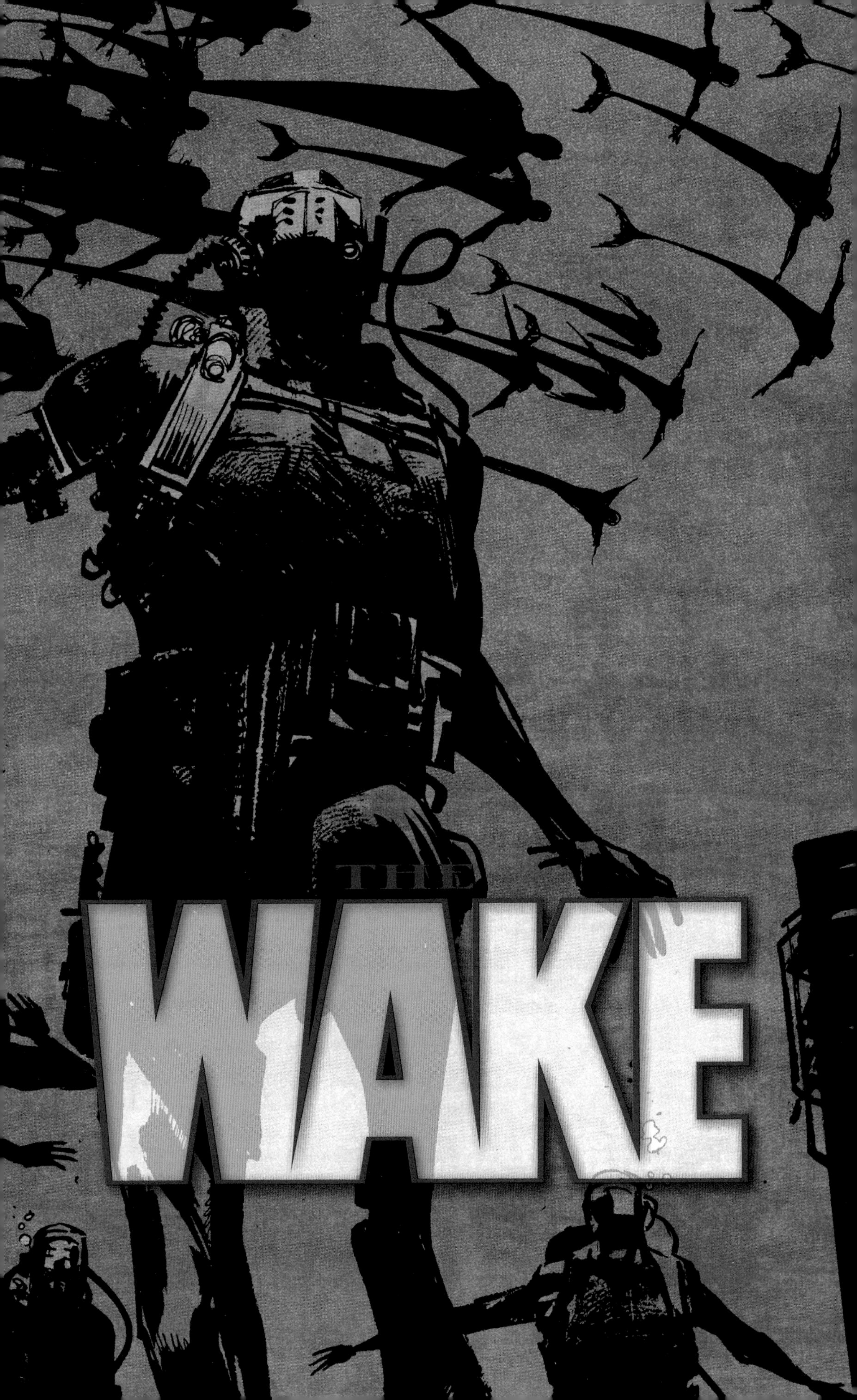
THE
WAKE

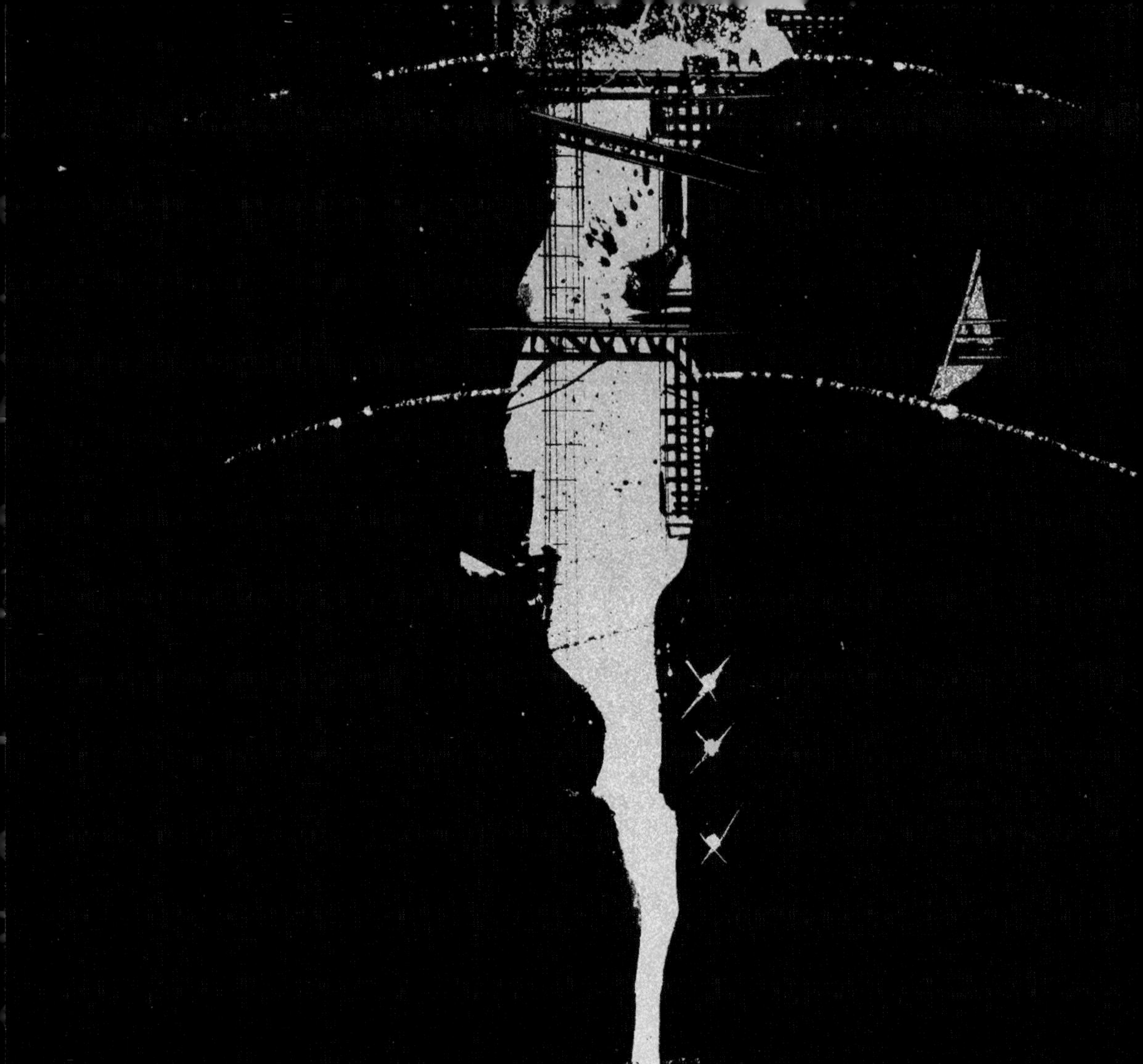

Mark Doyle Editor – Original Series
Sara Miller Assistant Editor – Original Series
Peter Hamboussi Editor
Robbin Brosterman Design Director – Books
Damian Ryland Publication Design

Shelly Bond Executive Editor – Vertigo
Hank Kanalz Senior VP – Vertigo & Integrated Publishing

Diane Nelson President
Dan DiDio and Jim Lee Co-Publishers
Geoff Johns Chief Creative Officer
Amit Desai Senior VP – Marketing & Franchise Management
Amy Genkins Senior VP – Business & Legal Affairs
Nairi Gardiner Senior VP – Finance
Jeff Boison VP – Publishing Planning
Mark Chiarello VP – Art Direction & Design
John Cunningham VP – Marketing
Terri Cunningham VP – Editorial Administration
Larry Ganem VP – Talent Relations & Services
Alison Gill Senior VP – Manufacturing & Operations
Jay Kogan VP – Business & Legal Affairs, Publishing
Jack Mahan VP – Business Affairs, Talent
Nick Napolitano VP – Manufacturing Administration
Sue Pohja VP – Book Sales
Fred Ruiz VP – Manufacturing Operations
Courtney Simmons Senior VP – Publicity
Bob Wayne Senior VP – Sales

THE WAKE

Published by DC Comics. Compilation Copyright © 2014 Scott Snyder and
Sean Murphy. All Rights Reserved.

Originally published in single magazine form as THE WAKE 1-10. Copyright
© 2013, 2014 Scott Snyder and Sean Murphy. All Rights Reserved. All
characters, their distinctive likenesses and related elements featured in
this publication are trademarks of DC Comics. VERTIGO is a trademark of DC
Comics. The stories, characters and incidents featured in this publication
are entirely fictional. DC Comics does not read or accept unsolicited
submissions of ideas, stories or artwork.

DC Comics, 1700 Broadway, New York, NY 10019
A Warner Bros. Entertainment Company.
Printed in the USA. First Printing.
ISBN: 978-1-4012-4523-8

Snyder, Scott, author.
The Wake / Scott Snyder, writer ; Sean Murphy, artist.
  pages cm
  ISBN 978-1-4012-4523-8 (hardback)
  1. Graphic novels. I. Murphy, Sean Gordon, 1980- illustrator. II. Title.

PN6727.S555W35 2014
741.5'973 — dc23
                                        2014026869

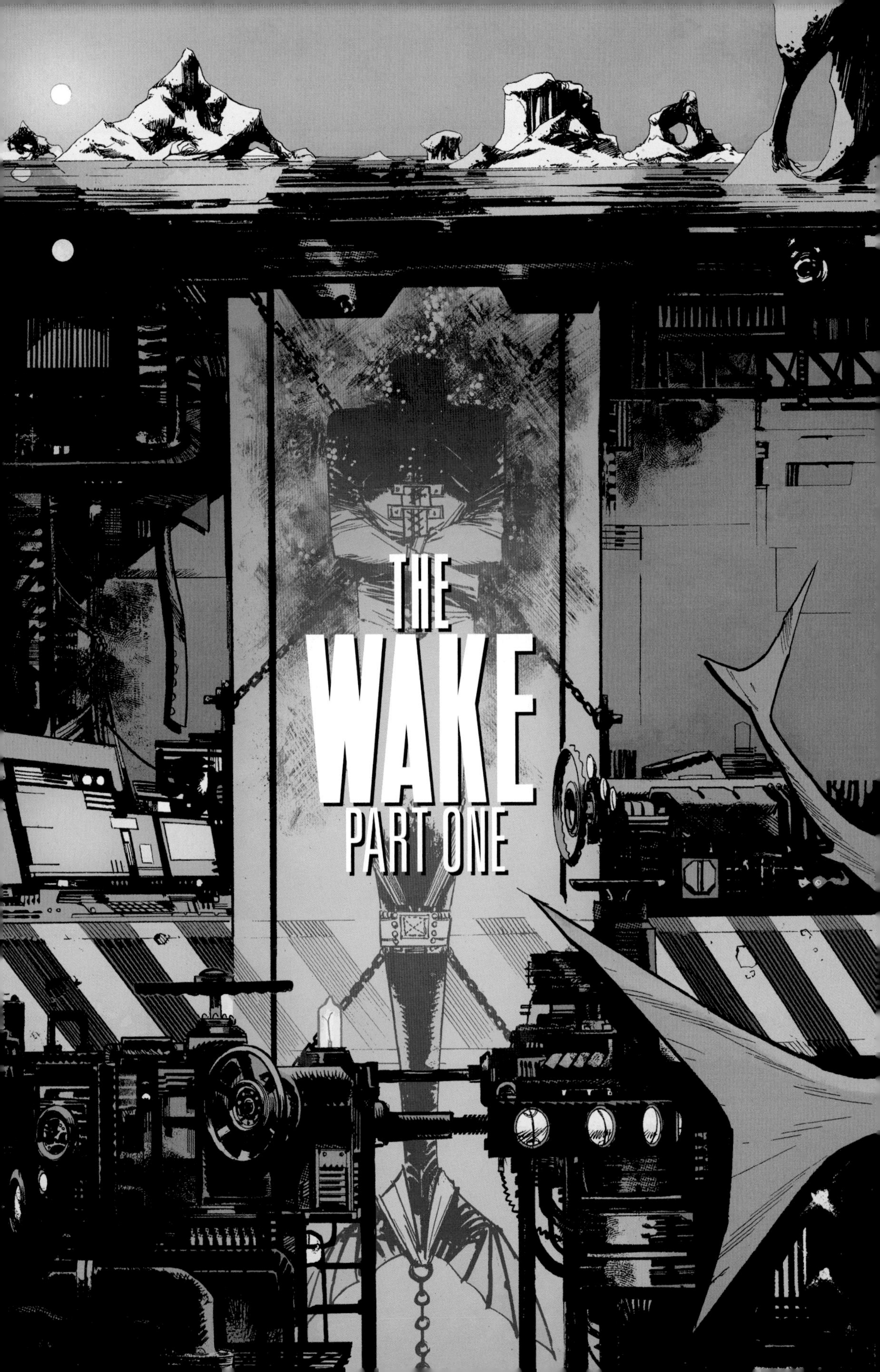
THE
WAKE
PART ONE

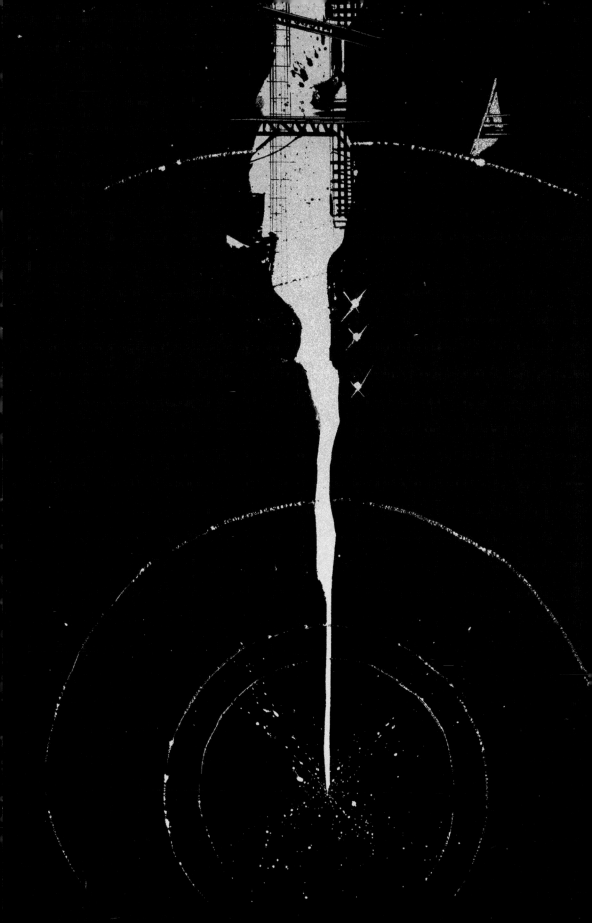

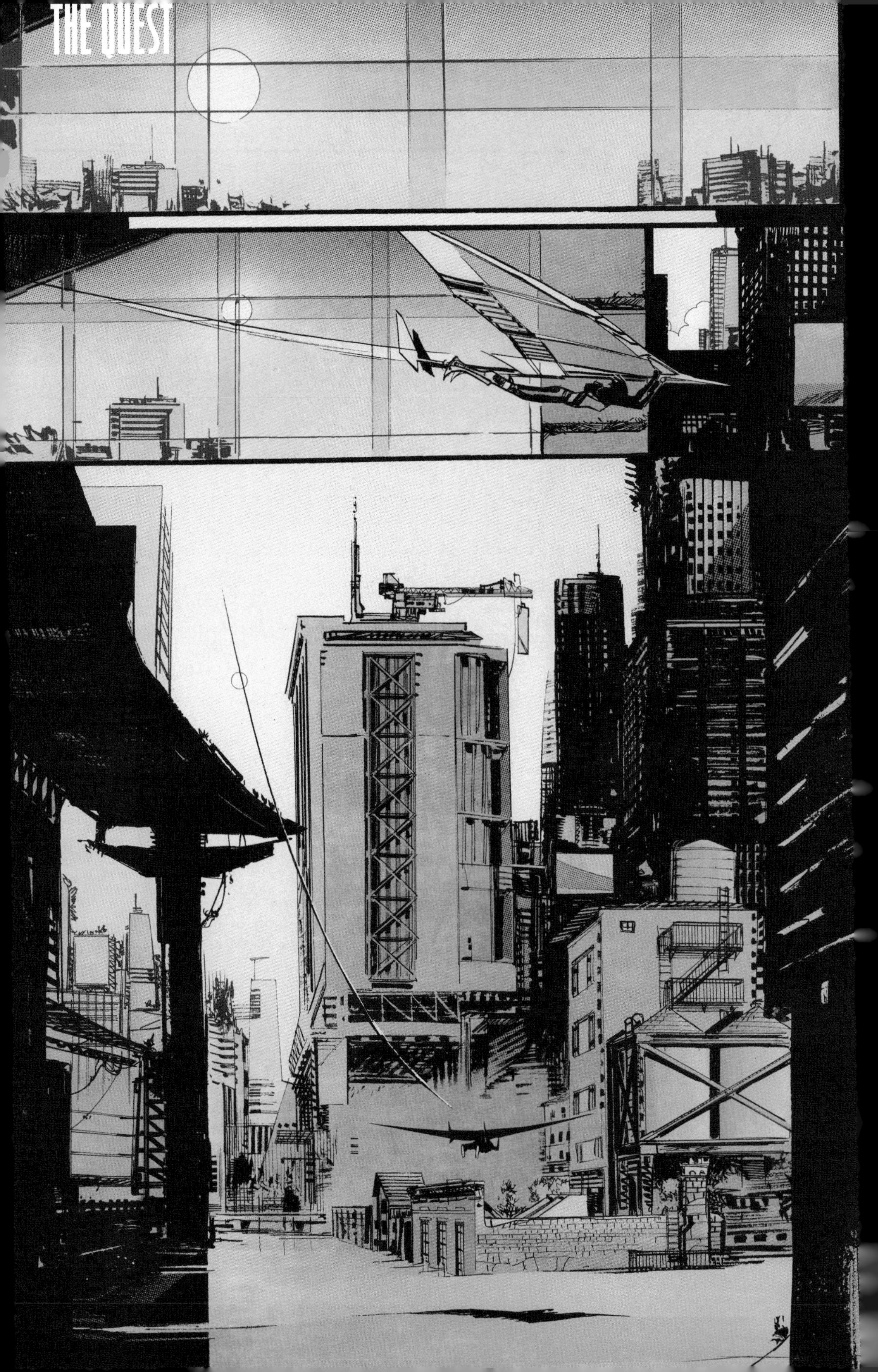

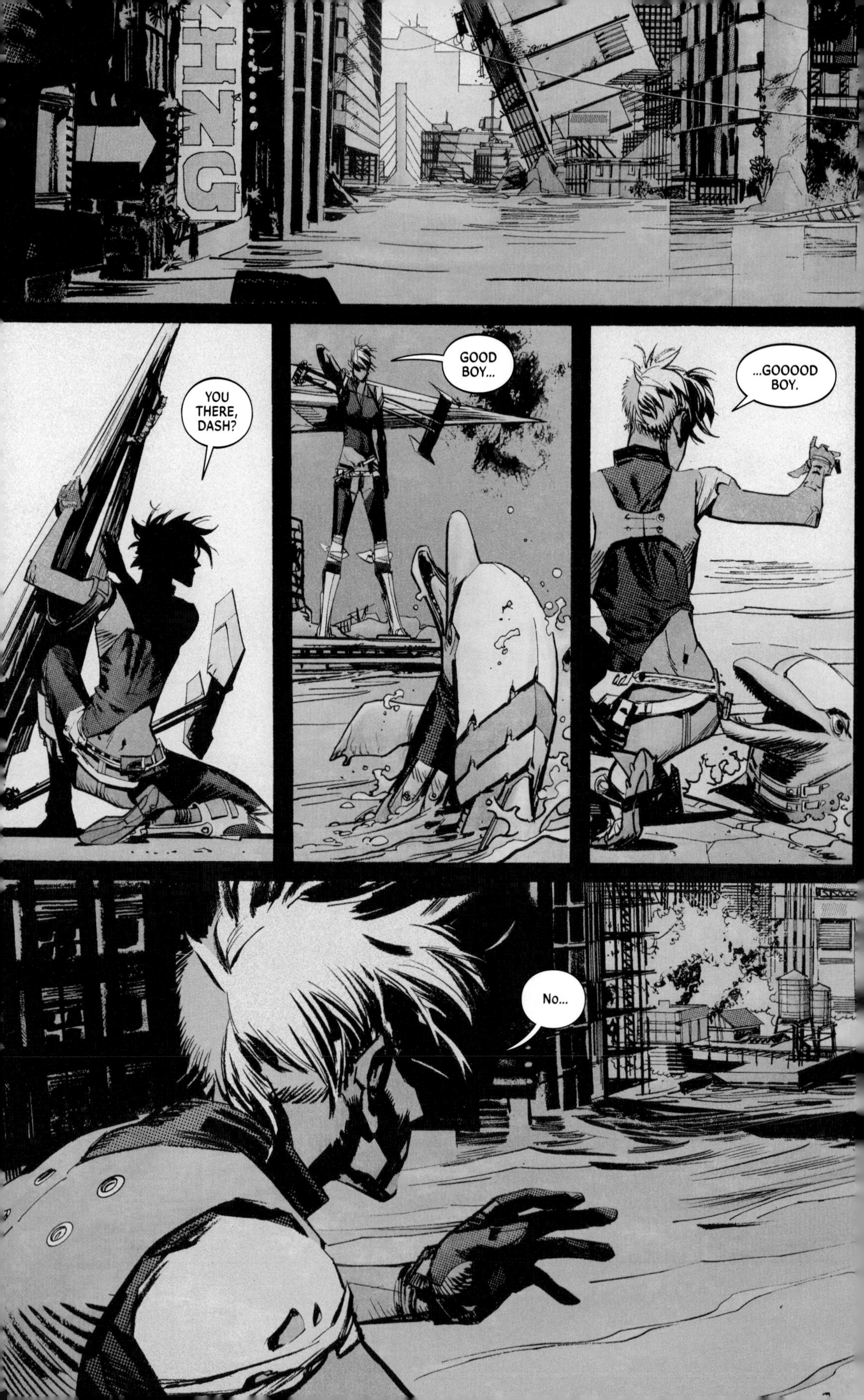
NG
YOU THERE, DASH?
GOOD BOY...
...GOOOOD BOY.
No...

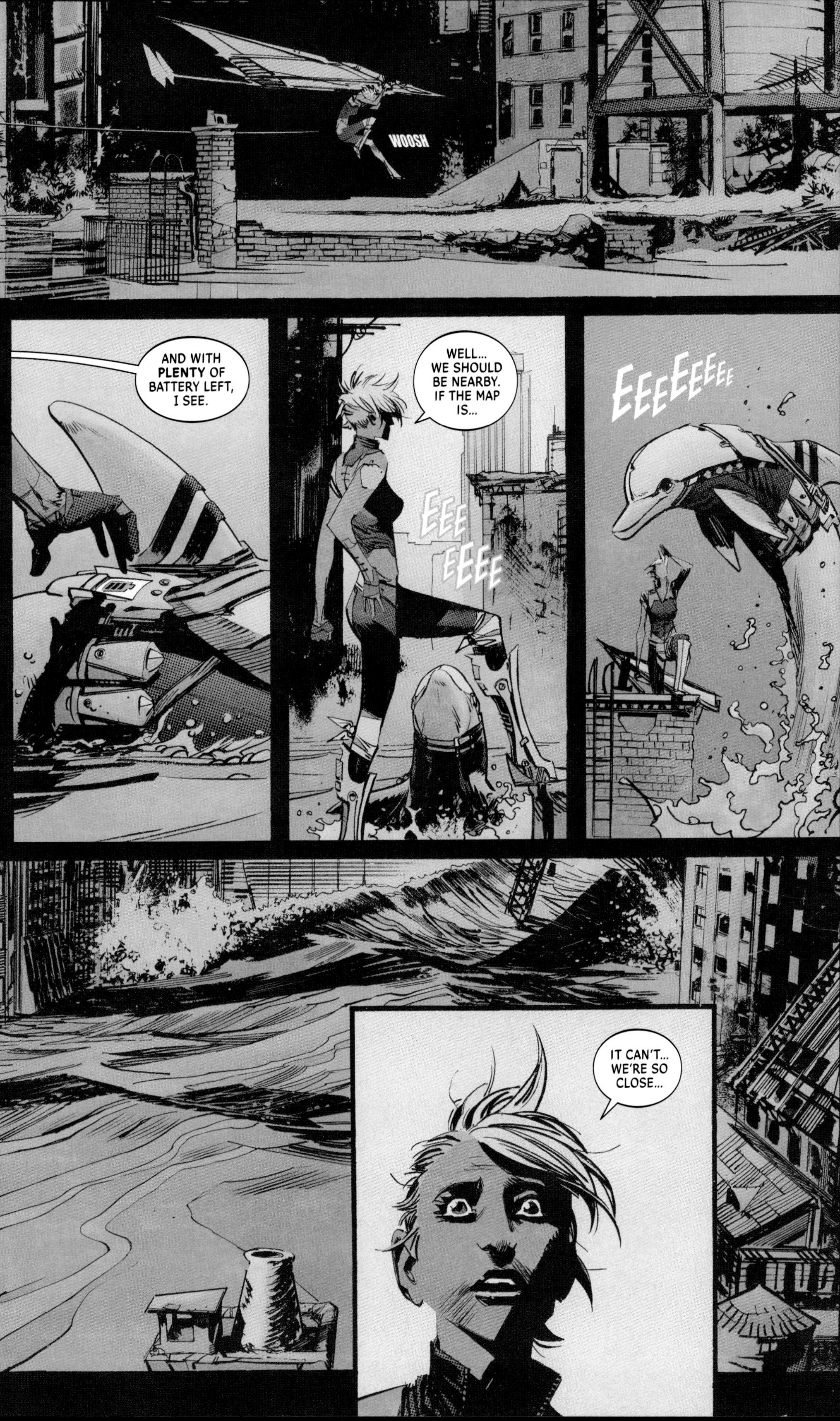
WOOSH
AND WITH **PLENTY** OF BATTERY LEFT, I SEE.
WELL... WE SHOULD BE NEARBY. IF THE MAP IS...
EEE EEEE
EEEEEEEE
IT CAN'T... WE'RE SO CLOSE...

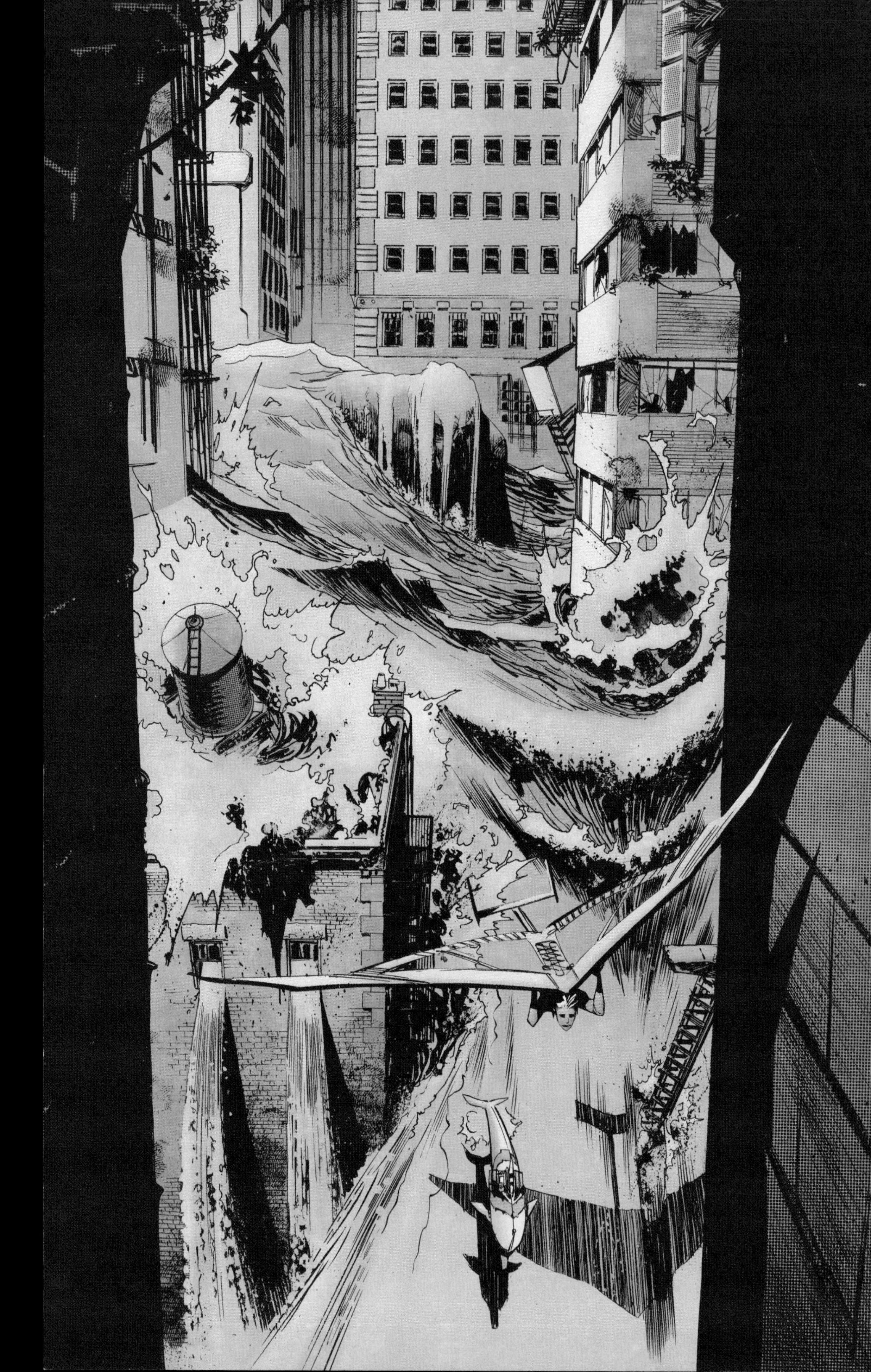

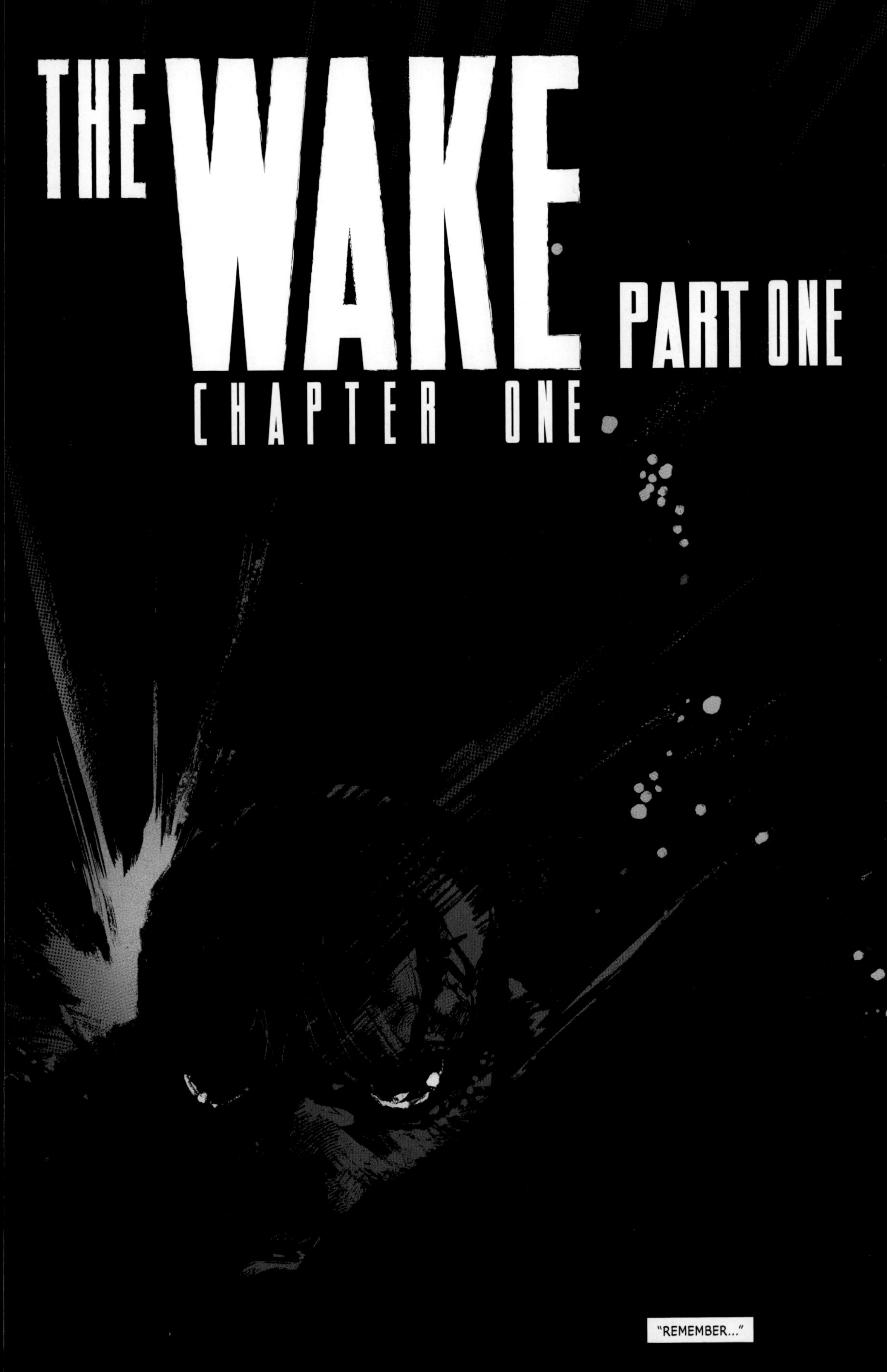
THE WAKE
PART ONE
CHAPTER ONE
"REMEMBER..."

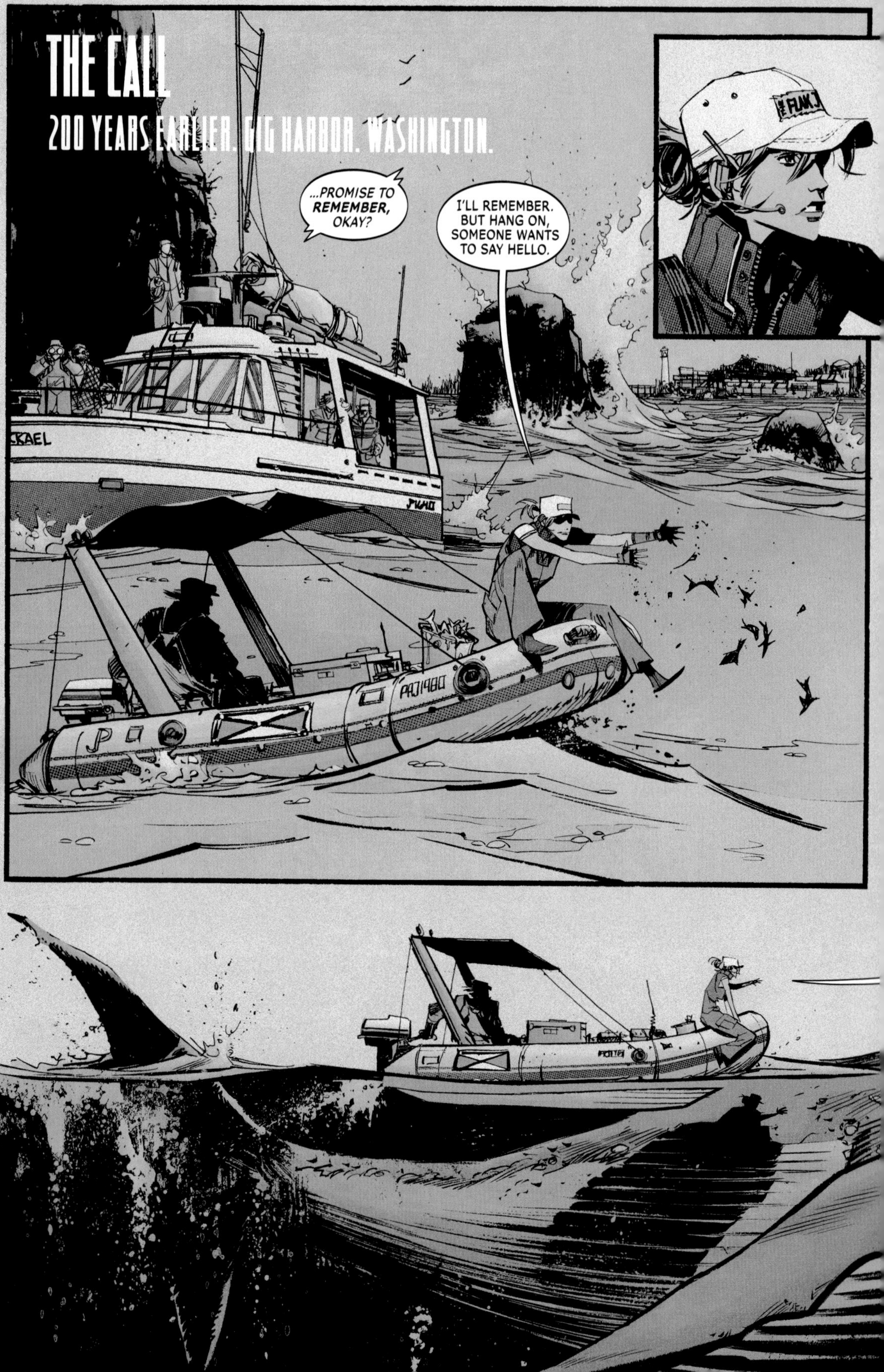
THE CALL
200 YEARS EARLIER. GIG HARBOR. WASHINGTON.
...PROMISE TO REMEMBER, OKAY?
I'LL REMEMBER. BUT HANG ON, SOMEONE WANTS TO SAY HELLO.

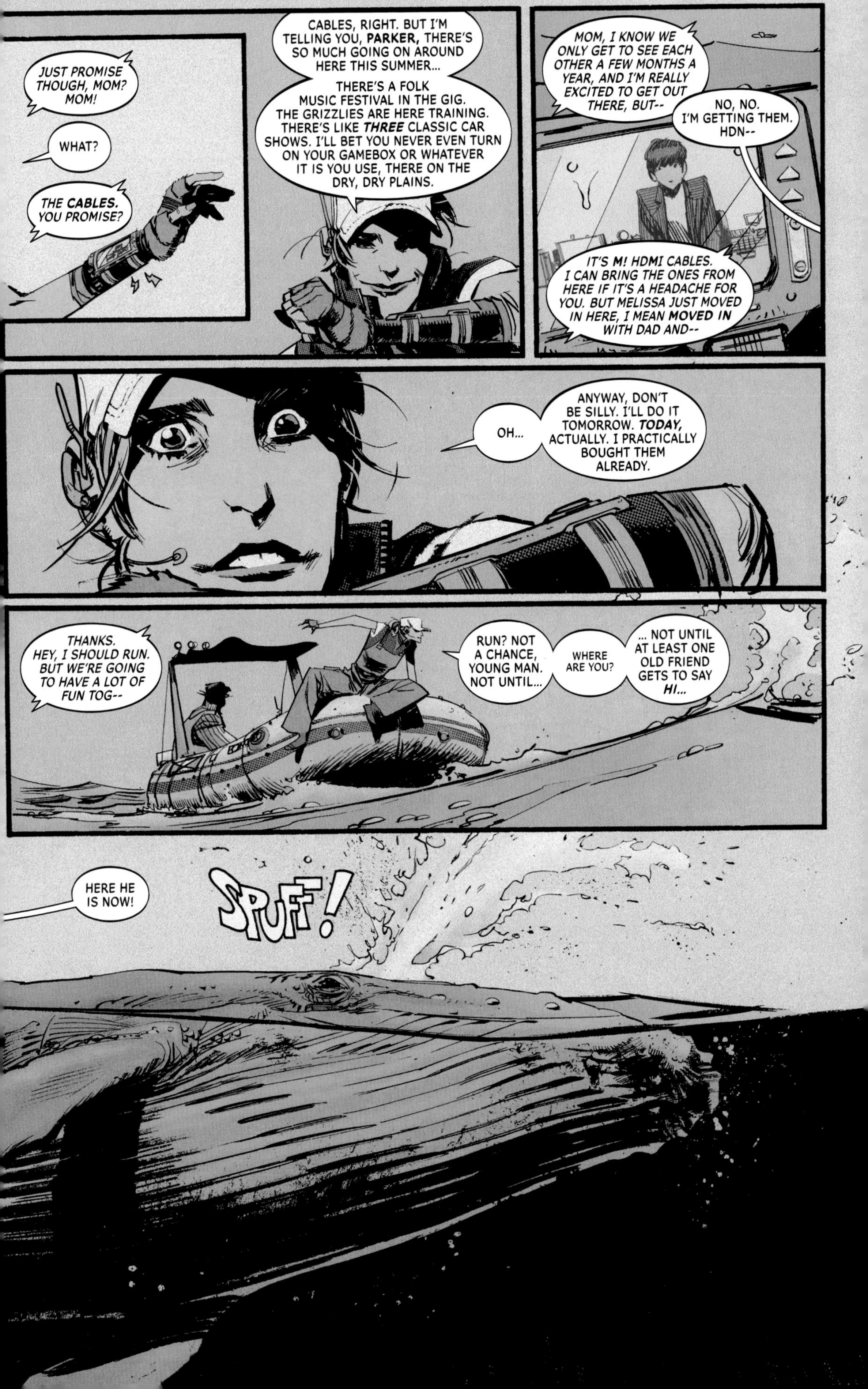
JUST PROMISE THOUGH, MOM? MOM!
WHAT?
THE CABLES. YOU PROMISE?
CABLES, RIGHT. BUT I'M TELLING YOU, PARKER, THERE'S SO MUCH GOING ON AROUND HERE THIS SUMMER...
THERE'S A FOLK MUSIC FESTIVAL IN THE GIG. THE GRIZZLIES ARE HERE TRAINING. THERE'S LIKE THREE CLASSIC CAR SHOWS. I'LL BET YOU NEVER EVEN TURN ON YOUR GAMEBOX OR WHATEVER IT IS YOU USE, THERE ON THE DRY, DRY PLAINS.
MOM, I KNOW WE ONLY GET TO SEE EACH OTHER A FEW MONTHS A YEAR, AND I'M REALLY EXCITED TO GET OUT THERE, BUT--
NO, NO. I'M GETTING THEM. HDN--
IT'S M! HDMI CABLES. I CAN BRING THE ONES FROM HERE IF IT'S A HEADACHE FOR YOU. BUT MELISSA JUST MOVED IN HERE, I MEAN MOVED IN WITH DAD AND--
OH...
ANYWAY, DON'T BE SILLY. I'LL DO IT TOMORROW. TODAY, ACTUALLY. I PRACTICALLY BOUGHT THEM ALREADY.
THANKS. HEY, I SHOULD RUN. BUT WE'RE GOING TO HAVE A LOT OF FUN TOG--
RUN? NOT A CHANCE, YOUNG MAN. NOT UNTIL...
WHERE ARE YOU?
... NOT UNTIL AT LEAST ONE OLD FRIEND GETS TO SAY HI...
HERE HE IS NOW!
SPUFF!

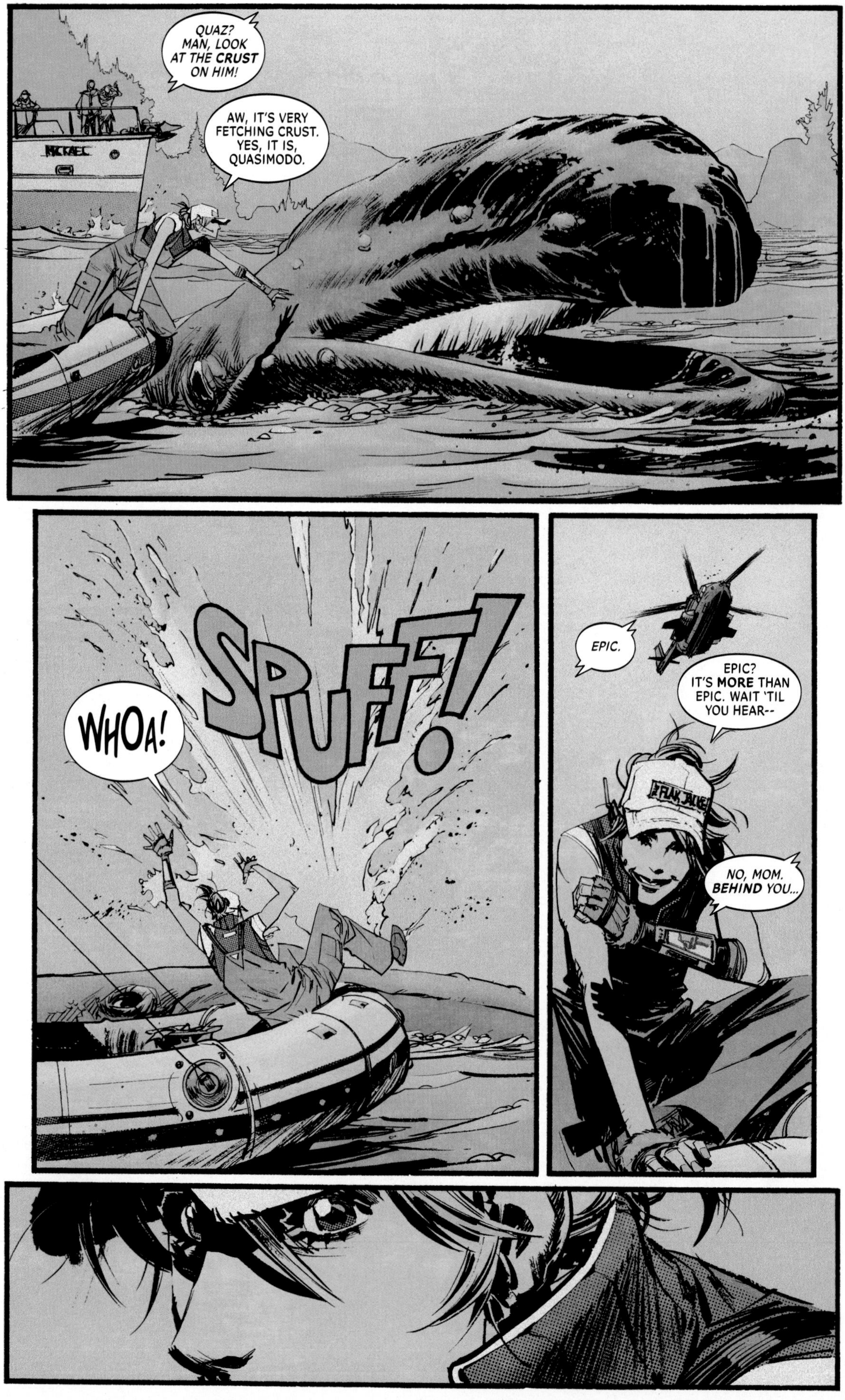
QUAZ? MAN, LOOK AT THE **CRUST** ON HIM!
AW, IT'S VERY FETCHING CRUST. YES, IT IS, QUASIMODO.
MICHAEL
WHOA!
SPUFF!
EPIC.
EPIC? IT'S **MORE** THAN EPIC. WAIT 'TIL YOU HEAR--
FLAK JACKET
NO, MOM. **BEHIND** YOU...

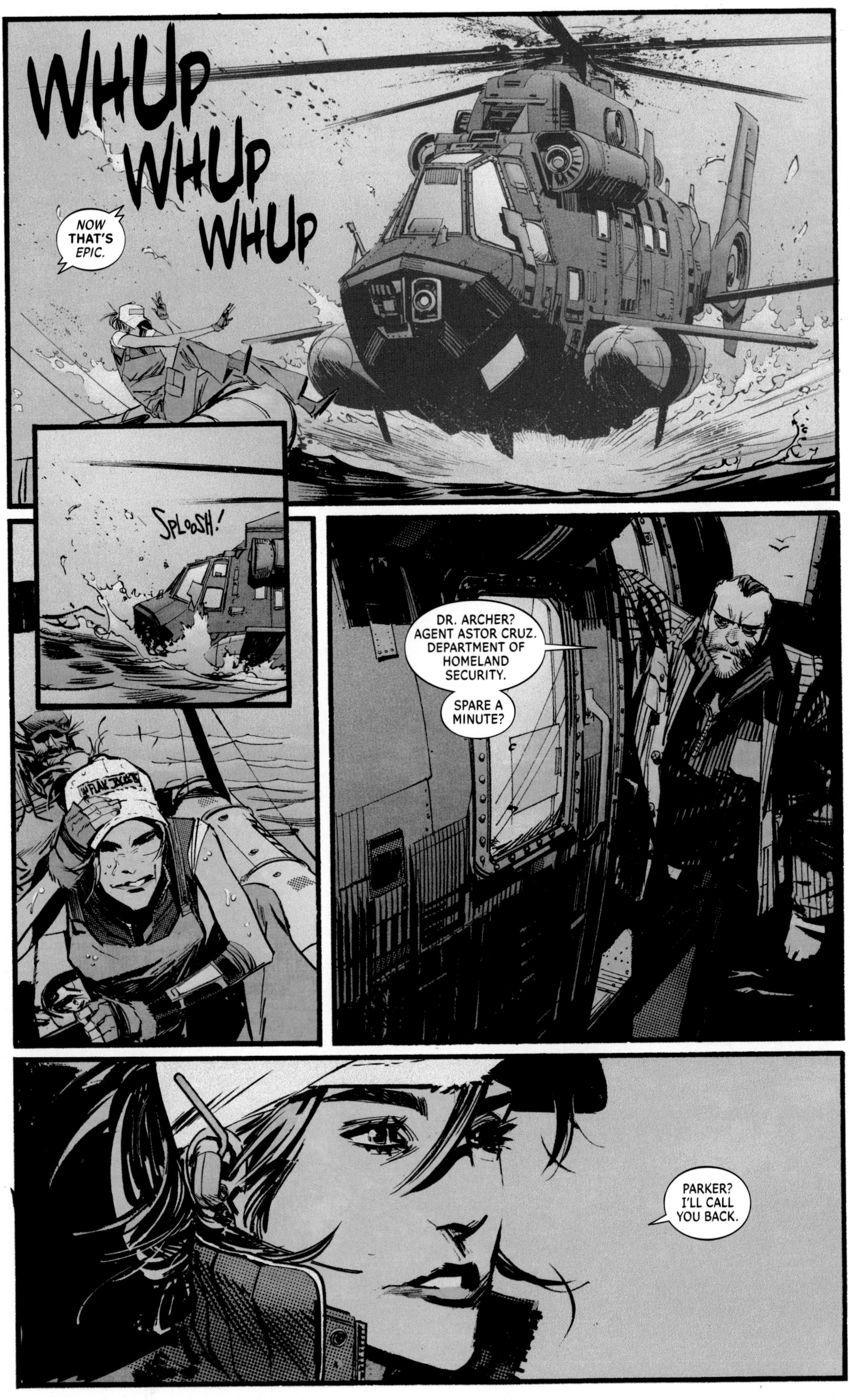
WHUP WHUP WHUP
NOW THAT'S EPIC.
SPLOOSH!
FLAK JACKET
DR. ARCHER? AGENT ASTOR CRUZ. DEPARTMENT OF HOMELAND SECURITY.
SPARE A MINUTE?
PARKER? I'LL CALL YOU BACK.

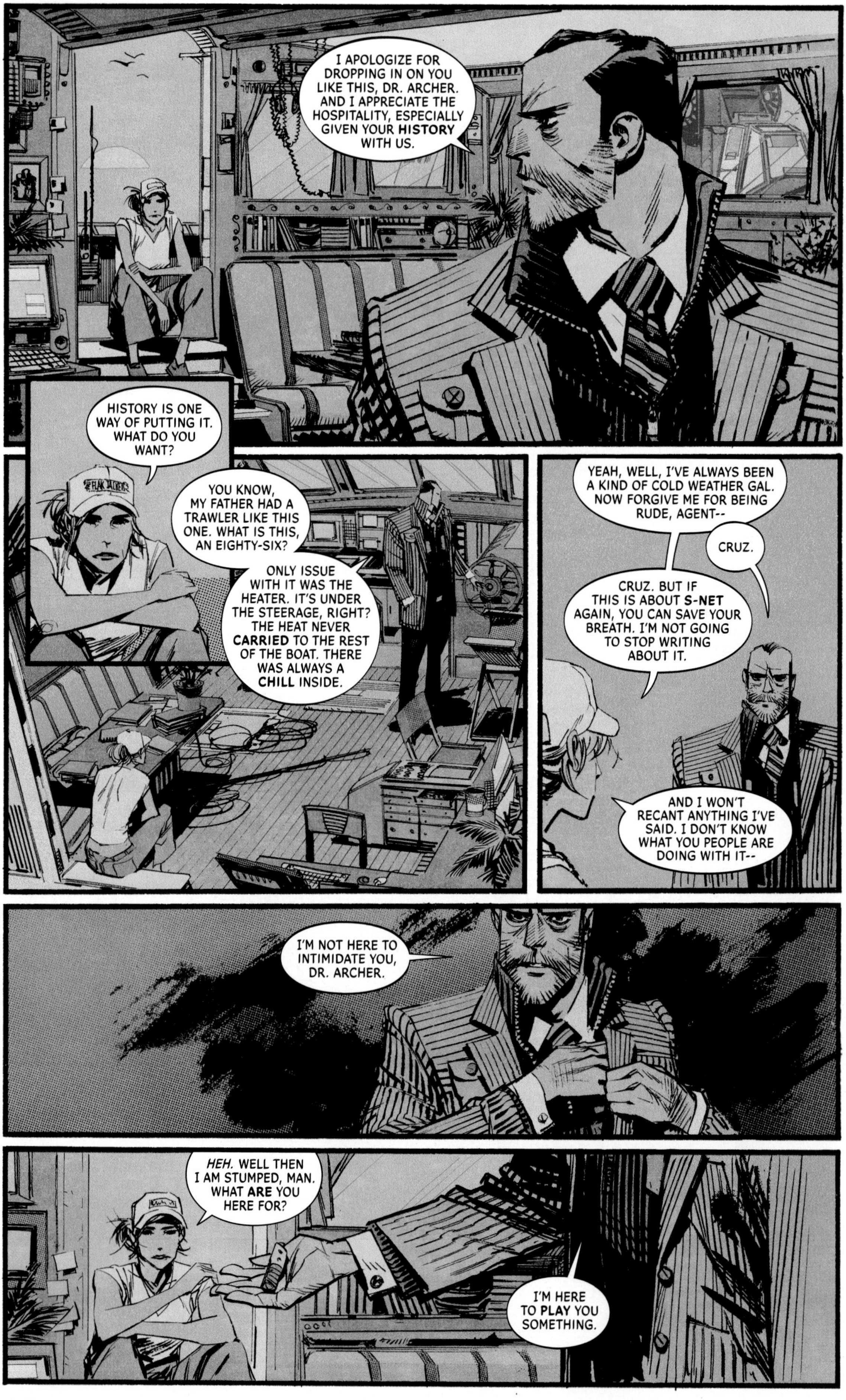
I APOLOGIZE FOR DROPPING IN ON YOU LIKE THIS, DR. ARCHER. AND I APPRECIATE THE HOSPITALITY, ESPECIALLY GIVEN YOUR **HISTORY** WITH US.
HISTORY IS ONE WAY OF PUTTING IT. WHAT DO YOU WANT?
YOU KNOW, MY FATHER HAD A TRAWLER LIKE THIS ONE. WHAT IS THIS, AN EIGHTY-SIX?
ONLY ISSUE WITH IT WAS THE HEATER. IT'S UNDER THE STEERAGE, RIGHT? THE HEAT NEVER **CARRIED** TO THE REST OF THE BOAT. THERE WAS ALWAYS A **CHILL** INSIDE.
YEAH, WELL, I'VE ALWAYS BEEN A KIND OF COLD WEATHER GAL. NOW FORGIVE ME FOR BEING RUDE, AGENT--
CRUZ.
CRUZ. BUT IF THIS IS ABOUT **S-NET** AGAIN, YOU CAN SAVE YOUR BREATH. I'M NOT GOING TO STOP WRITING ABOUT IT.
AND I WON'T RECANT ANYTHING I'VE SAID. I DON'T KNOW WHAT YOU PEOPLE ARE DOING WITH IT--
I'M NOT HERE TO INTIMIDATE YOU, DR. ARCHER.
HEH. WELL THEN I AM STUMPED, MAN. WHAT **ARE** YOU HERE FOR?
I'M HERE TO **PLAY** YOU SOMETHING.

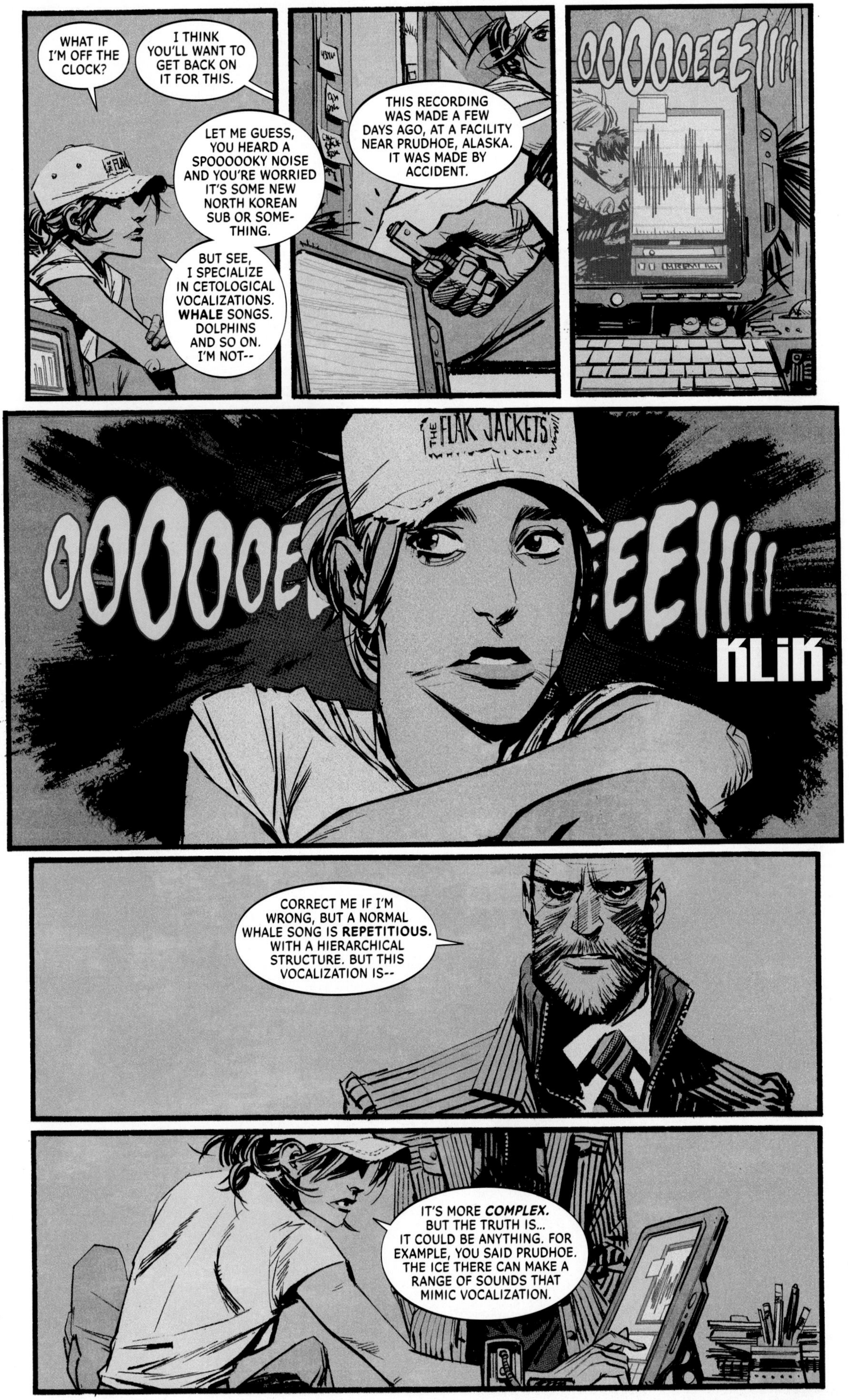
WHAT IF I'M OFF THE CLOCK?
I THINK YOU'LL WANT TO GET BACK ON IT FOR THIS.
LET ME GUESS, YOU HEARD A SPOOOOOKY NOISE AND YOU'RE WORRIED IT'S SOME NEW NORTH KOREAN SUB OR SOME-THING.
BUT SEE, I SPECIALIZE IN CETOLOGICAL VOCALIZATIONS. WHALE SONGS. DOLPHINS AND SO ON. I'M NOT--
THIS RECORDING WAS MADE A FEW DAYS AGO, AT A FACILITY NEAR PRUDHOE, ALASKA. IT WAS MADE BY ACCIDENT.
OOOOOEEEIIII
THE FLAK JACKETS
OOOOOEEEIIII
KLIK
CORRECT ME IF I'M WRONG, BUT A NORMAL WHALE SONG IS REPETITIOUS. WITH A HIERARCHICAL STRUCTURE. BUT THIS VOCALIZATION IS--
IT'S MORE COMPLEX. BUT THE TRUTH IS... IT COULD BE ANYTHING. FOR EXAMPLE, YOU SAID PRUDHOE. THE ICE THERE CAN MAKE A RANGE OF SOUNDS THAT MIMIC VOCALIZATION.

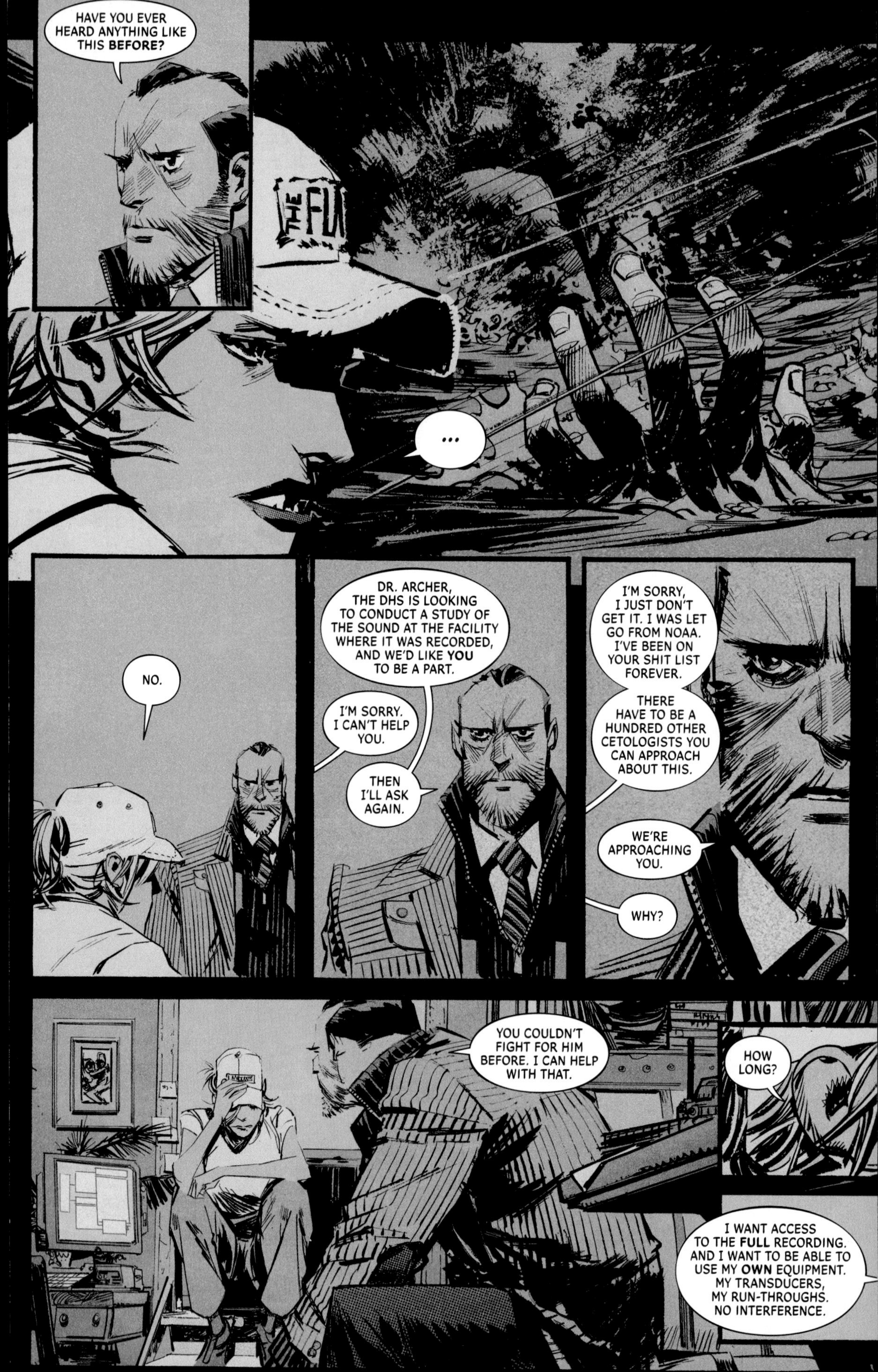
HAVE YOU EVER HEARD ANYTHING LIKE THIS BEFORE?
...
NO.
DR. ARCHER, THE DHS IS LOOKING TO CONDUCT A STUDY OF THE SOUND AT THE FACILITY WHERE IT WAS RECORDED, AND WE'D LIKE YOU TO BE A PART.
I'M SORRY. I CAN'T HELP YOU.
THEN I'LL ASK AGAIN.
I'M SORRY, I JUST DON'T GET IT. I WAS LET GO FROM NOAA. I'VE BEEN ON YOUR SHIT LIST FOREVER.
THERE HAVE TO BE A HUNDRED OTHER CETOLOGISTS YOU CAN APPROACH ABOUT THIS.
WE'RE APPROACHING YOU.
WHY?
YOU COULDN'T FIGHT FOR HIM BEFORE. I CAN HELP WITH THAT.
HOW LONG?
I WANT ACCESS TO THE FULL RECORDING. AND I WANT TO BE ABLE TO USE MY OWN EQUIPMENT. MY TRANSDUCERS, MY RUN-THROUGHS. NO INTERFERENCE.

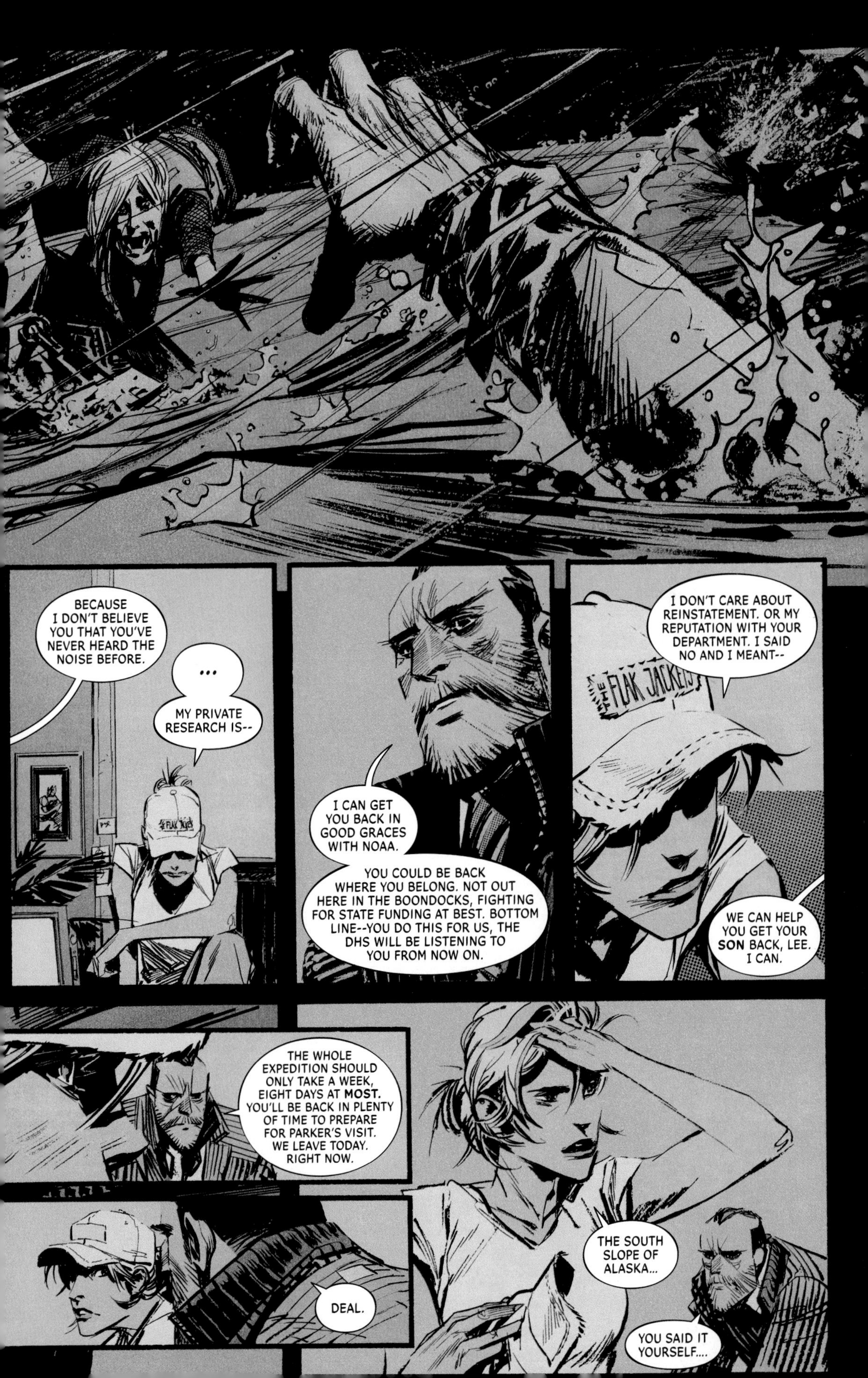
BECAUSE I DON'T BELIEVE YOU THAT YOU'VE NEVER HEARD THE NOISE BEFORE.
...
MY PRIVATE RESEARCH IS--
I CAN GET YOU BACK IN GOOD GRACES WITH NOAA.
YOU COULD BE BACK WHERE YOU BELONG. NOT OUT HERE IN THE BOONDOCKS, FIGHTING FOR STATE FUNDING AT BEST. BOTTOM LINE--YOU DO THIS FOR US, THE DHS WILL BE LISTENING TO YOU FROM NOW ON.
THE FLAK JACKETS
I DON'T CARE ABOUT REINSTATEMENT. OR MY REPUTATION WITH YOUR DEPARTMENT. I SAID NO AND I MEANT--
WE CAN HELP YOU GET YOUR **SON** BACK, LEE. I CAN.
THE WHOLE EXPEDITION SHOULD ONLY TAKE A WEEK, EIGHT DAYS AT **MOST.** YOU'LL BE BACK IN PLENTY OF TIME TO PREPARE FOR PARKER'S VISIT. WE LEAVE TODAY. RIGHT NOW.
DEAL.
THE SOUTH SLOPE OF ALASKA...
YOU SAID IT YOURSELF....

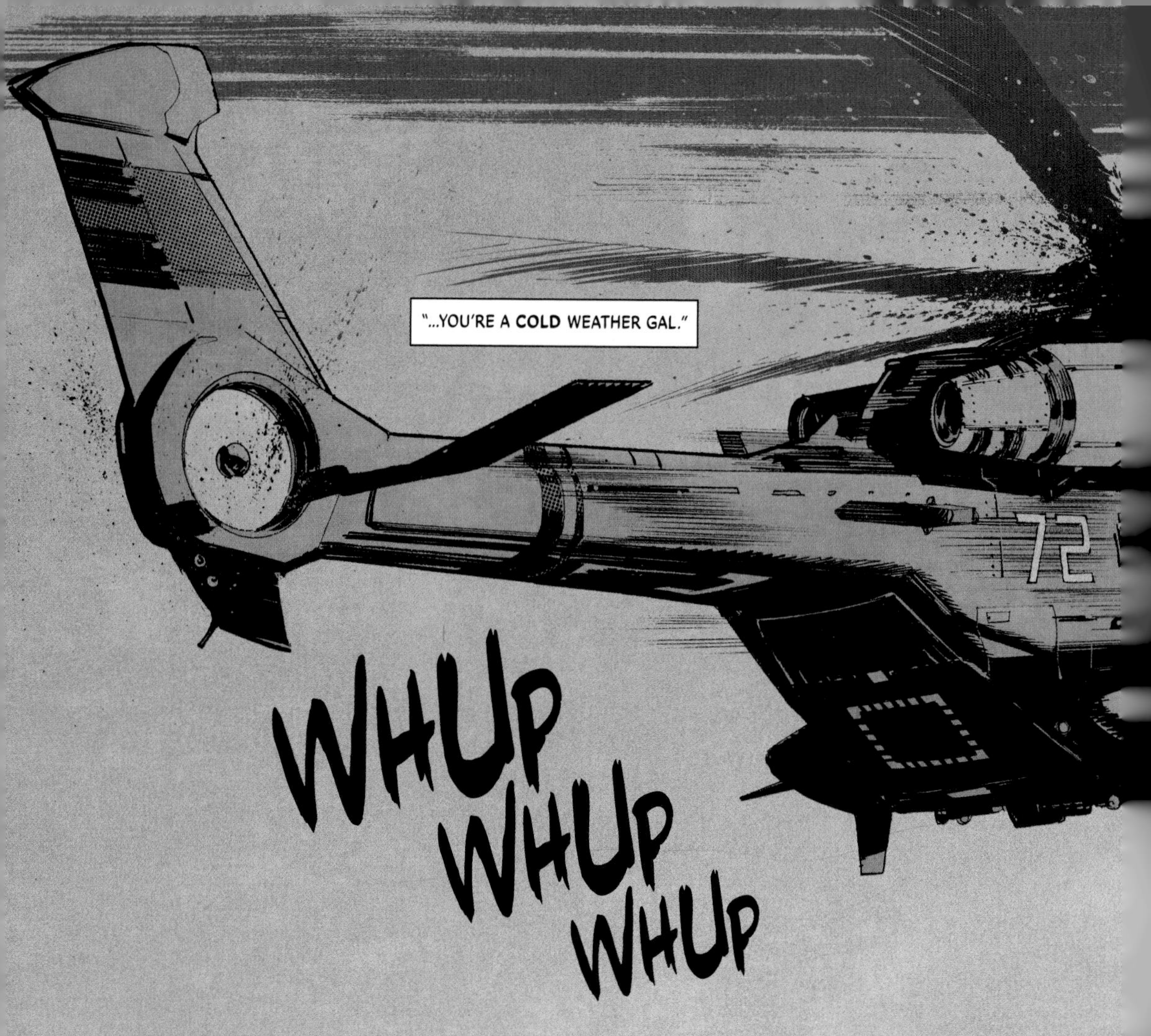
"...YOU'RE A **COLD** WEATHER GAL."
WHUP WHUP WHUP

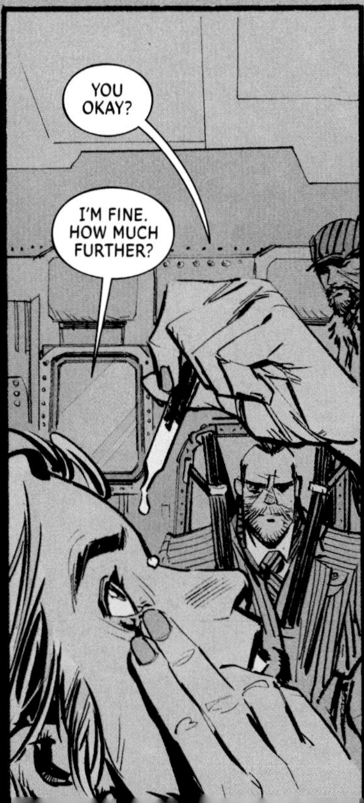
YOU OKAY?
I'M FINE. HOW MUCH FURTHER?

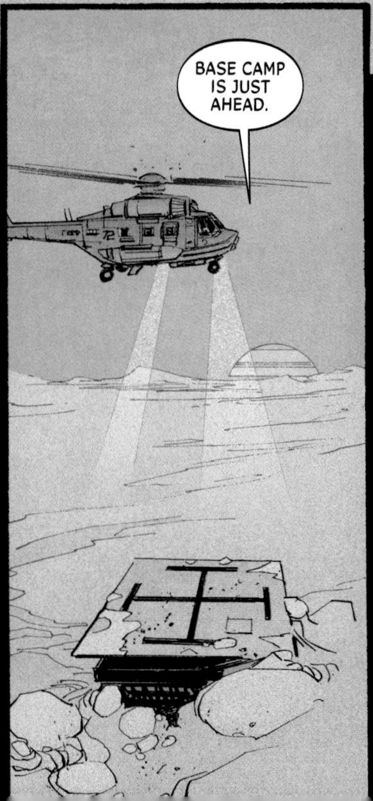
BASE CAMP IS JUST AHEAD.

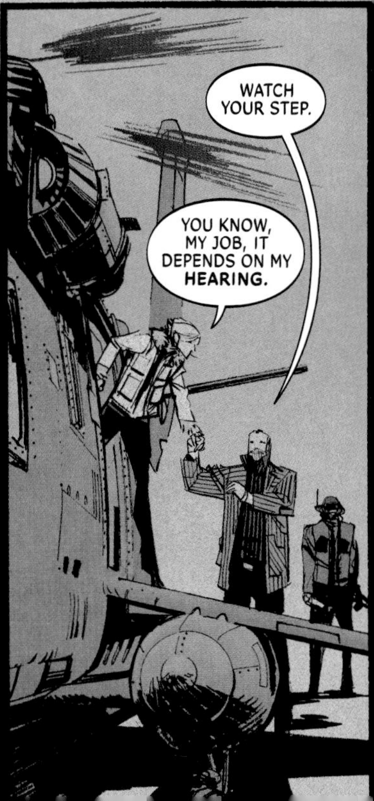
WATCH YOUR STEP.
YOU KNOW, MY JOB, IT DEPENDS ON MY **HEARING.**

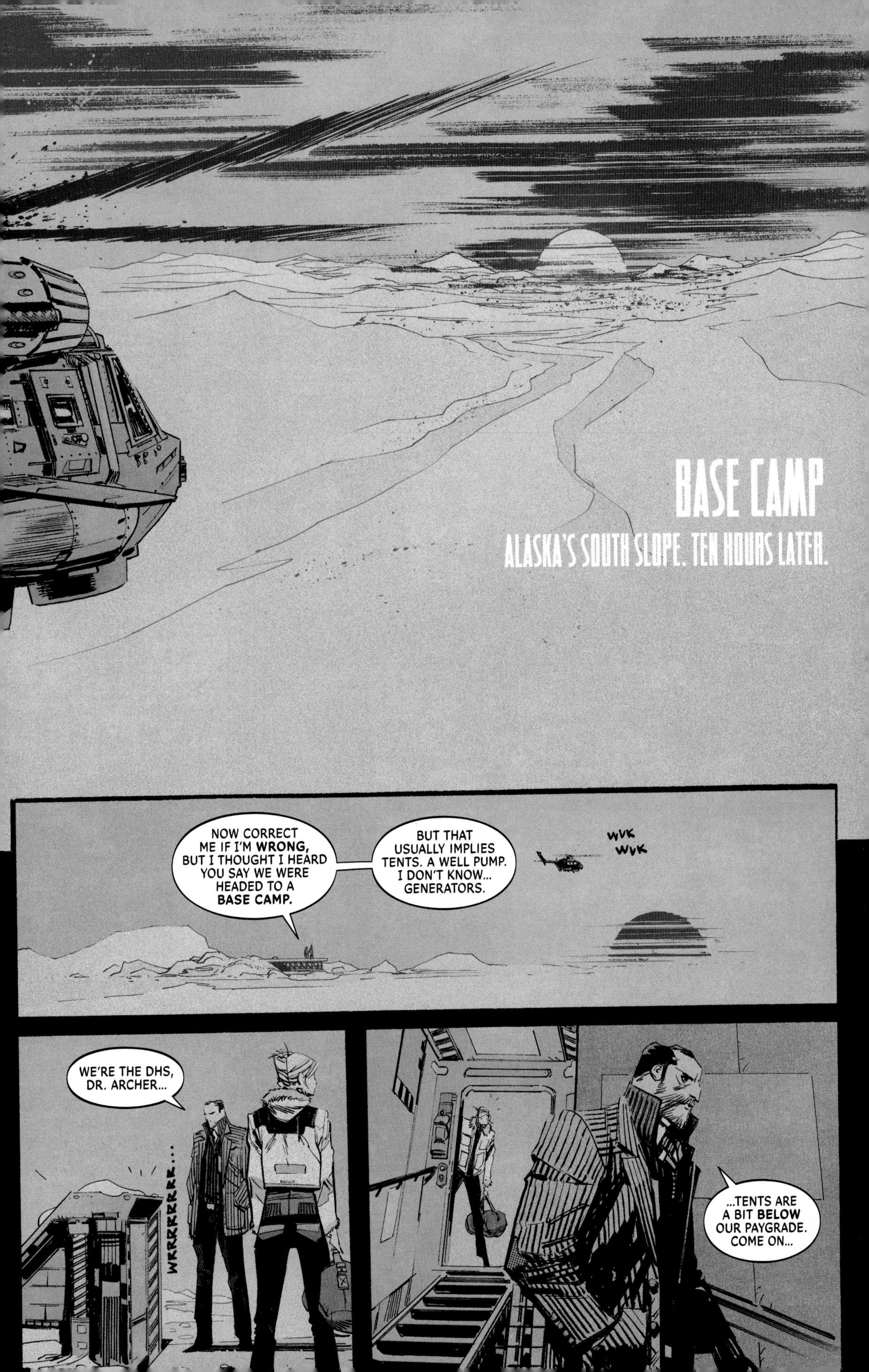
BASE CAMP
ALASKA'S SOUTH SLOPE. TEN HOURS LATER.
NOW CORRECT ME IF I'M **WRONG,** BUT I THOUGHT I HEARD YOU SAY WE WERE HEADED TO A **BASE CAMP.**
BUT THAT USUALLY IMPLIES TENTS. A WELL PUMP. I DON'T KNOW... GENERATORS.
WVK WVK
WE'RE THE DHS, DR. ARCHER...
WKRRRRRRR...
...TENTS ARE A BIT **BELOW** OUR PAYGRADE. COME ON...

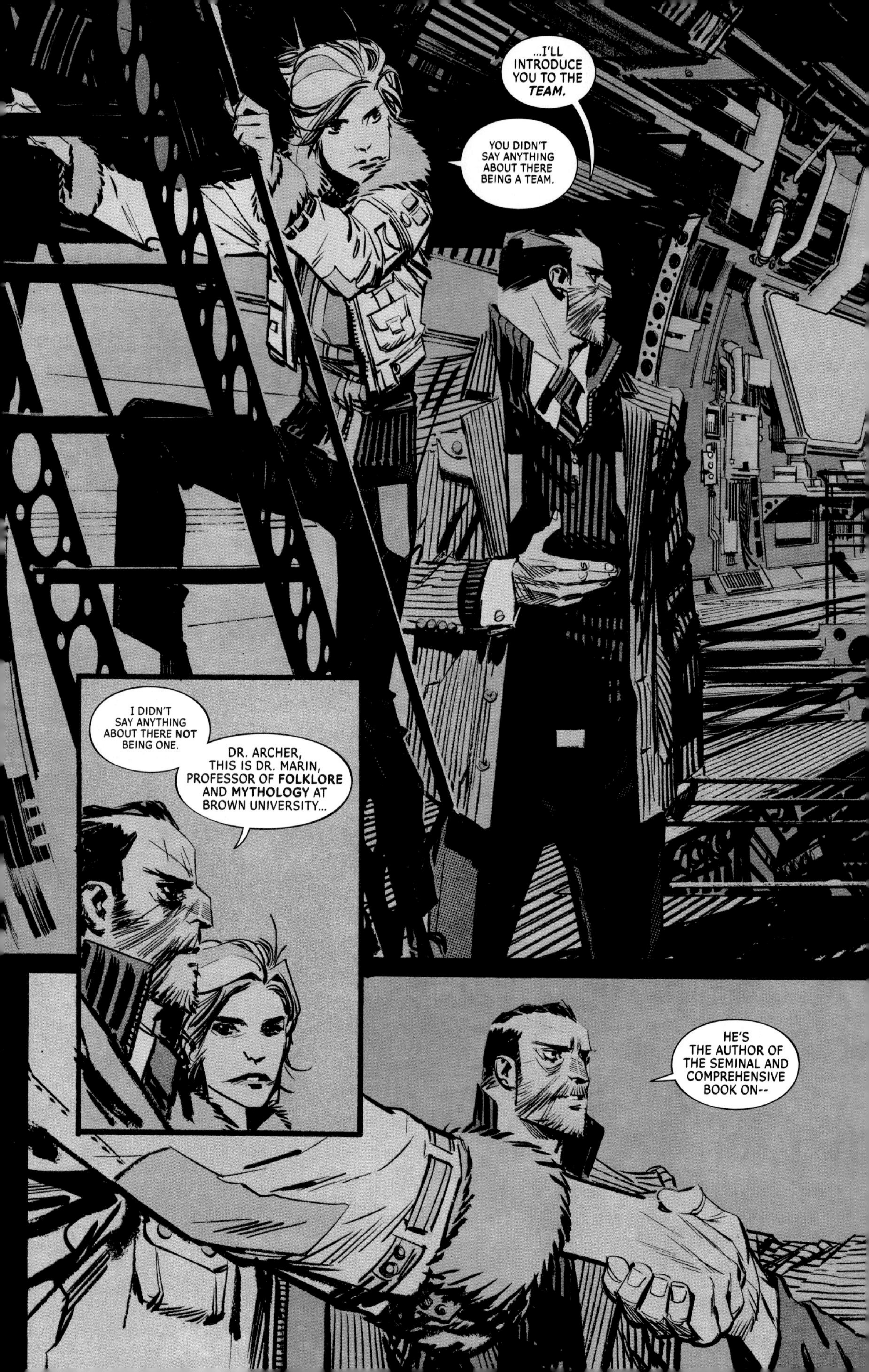
...I'LL INTRODUCE YOU TO THE TEAM.
YOU DIDN'T SAY ANYTHING ABOUT THERE BEING A TEAM.
I DIDN'T SAY ANYTHING ABOUT THERE NOT BEING ONE.
DR. ARCHER, THIS IS DR. MARIN, PROFESSOR OF FOLKLORE AND MYTHOLOGY AT BROWN UNIVERSITY...
HE'S THE AUTHOR OF THE SEMINAL AND COMPREHENSIVE BOOK ON--

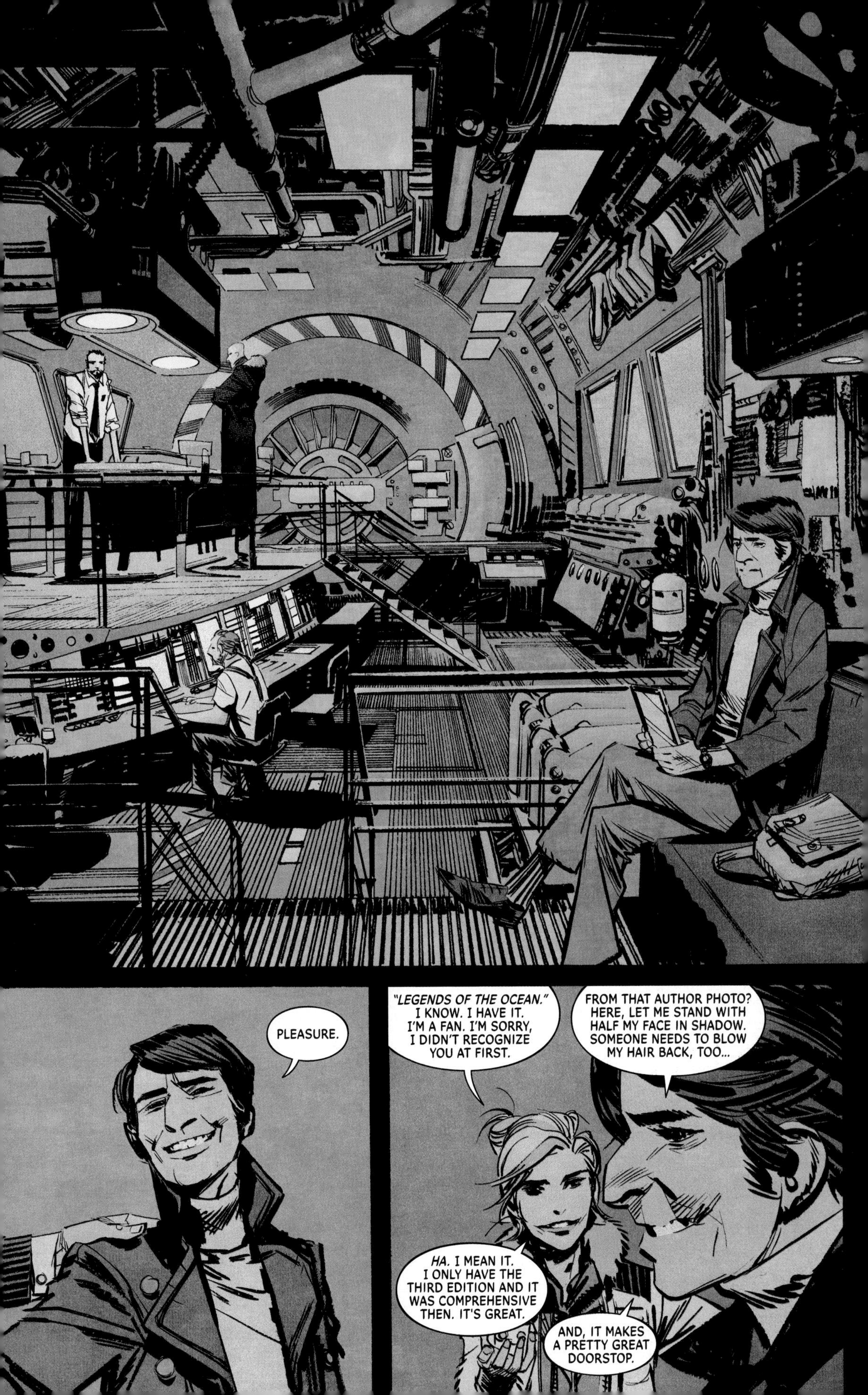
PLEASURE.
"LEGENDS OF THE OCEAN." I KNOW. I HAVE IT. I'M A FAN. I'M SORRY, I DIDN'T RECOGNIZE YOU AT FIRST.
FROM THAT AUTHOR PHOTO? HERE, LET ME STAND WITH HALF MY FACE IN SHADOW. SOMEONE NEEDS TO BLOW MY HAIR BACK, TOO...
HA. I MEAN IT. I ONLY HAVE THE THIRD EDITION AND IT WAS COMPREHENSIVE THEN. IT'S GREAT.
AND, IT MAKES A PRETTY GREAT DOORSTOP.

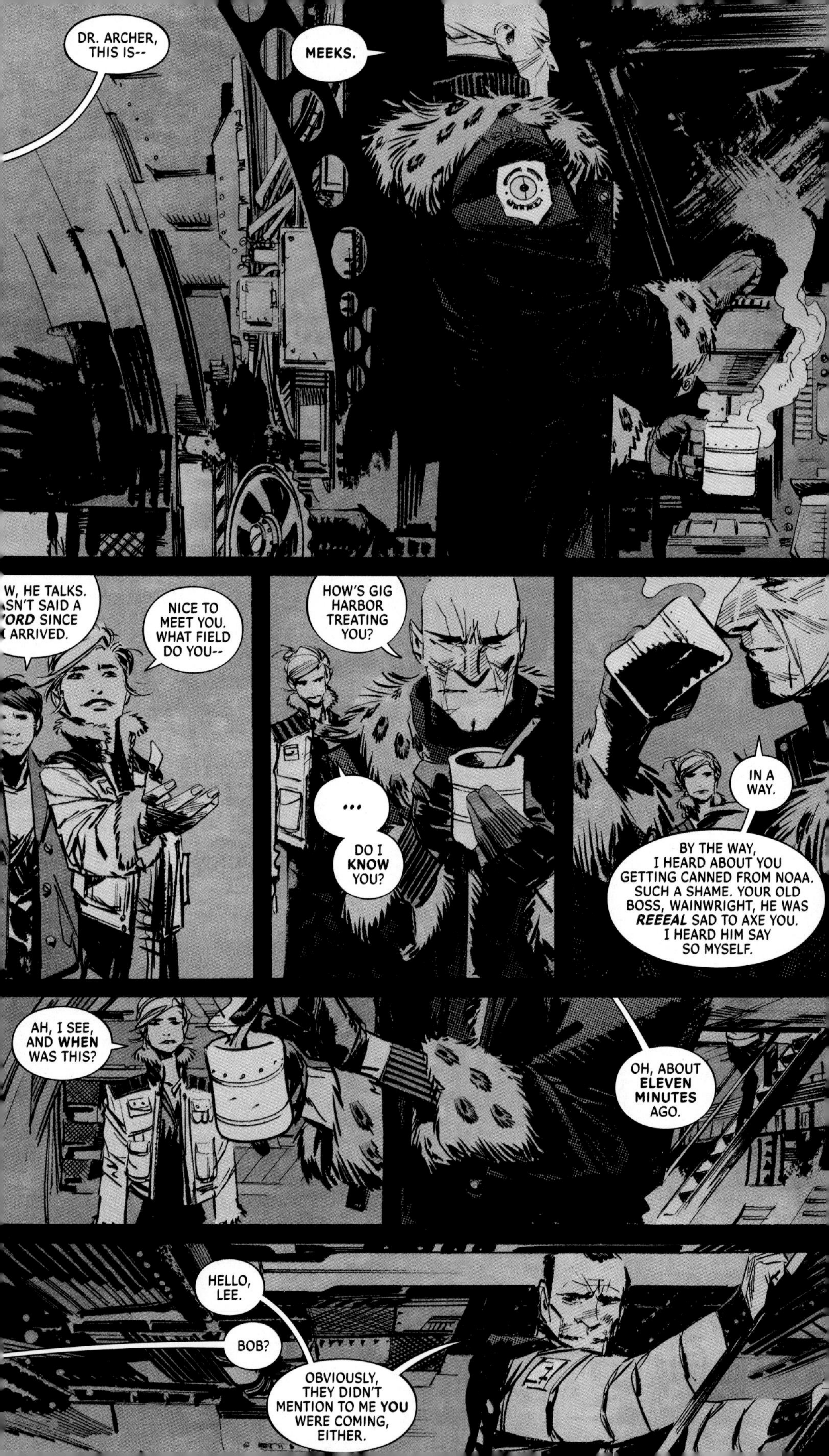

DR. ARCHER, THIS IS--
MEEKS.
W, HE TALKS. ASN'T SAID A ORD SINCE ARRIVED.
NICE TO MEET YOU. WHAT FIELD DO YOU--
HOW'S GIG HARBOR TREATING YOU?
...
DO I KNOW YOU?
IN A WAY.
BY THE WAY, I HEARD ABOUT YOU GETTING CANNED FROM NOAA. SUCH A SHAME. YOUR OLD BOSS, WAINWRIGHT, HE WAS REEEAL SAD TO AXE YOU. I HEARD HIM SAY SO MYSELF.
AH, I SEE, AND WHEN WAS THIS?
OH, ABOUT ELEVEN MINUTES AGO.
HELLO, LEE.
BOB?
OBVIOUSLY, THEY DIDN'T MENTION TO ME YOU WERE COMING, EITHER.

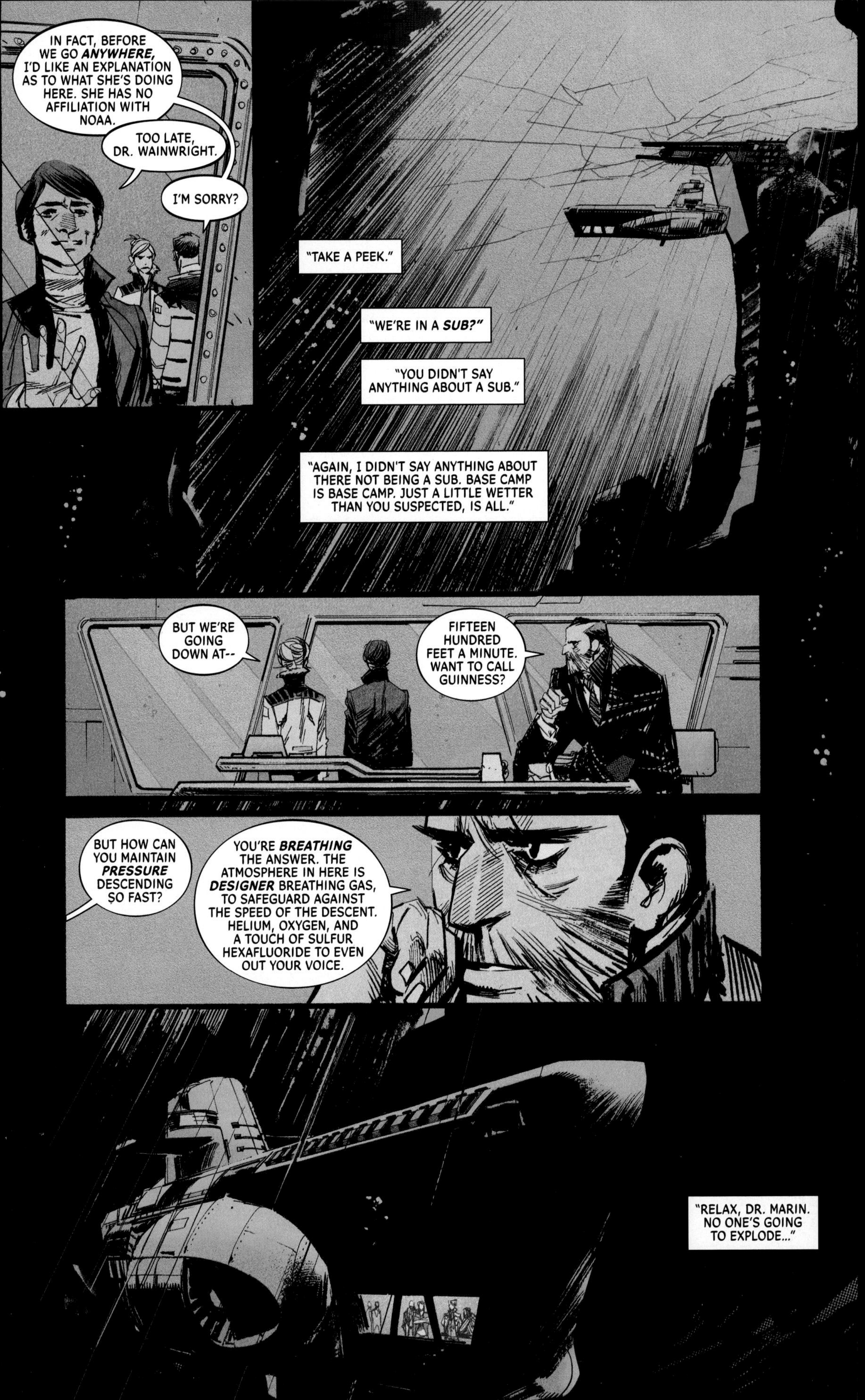
IN FACT, BEFORE WE GO ANYWHERE, I'D LIKE AN EXPLANATION AS TO WHAT SHE'S DOING HERE. SHE HAS NO AFFILIATION WITH NOAA.
TOO LATE, DR. WAINWRIGHT.
I'M SORRY?
"TAKE A PEEK."
"WE'RE IN A SUB?"
"YOU DIDN'T SAY ANYTHING ABOUT A SUB."
"AGAIN, I DIDN'T SAY ANYTHING ABOUT THERE NOT BEING A SUB. BASE CAMP IS BASE CAMP. JUST A LITTLE WETTER THAN YOU SUSPECTED, IS ALL."
BUT WE'RE GOING DOWN AT--
FIFTEEN HUNDRED FEET A MINUTE. WANT TO CALL GUINNESS?
BUT HOW CAN YOU MAINTAIN PRESSURE DESCENDING SO FAST?
YOU'RE BREATHING THE ANSWER. THE ATMOSPHERE IN HERE IS DESIGNER BREATHING GAS, TO SAFEGUARD AGAINST THE SPEED OF THE DESCENT. HELIUM, OXYGEN, AND A TOUCH OF SULFUR HEXAFLUORIDE TO EVEN OUT YOUR VOICE.
"RELAX, DR. MARIN. NO ONE'S GOING TO EXPLODE..."

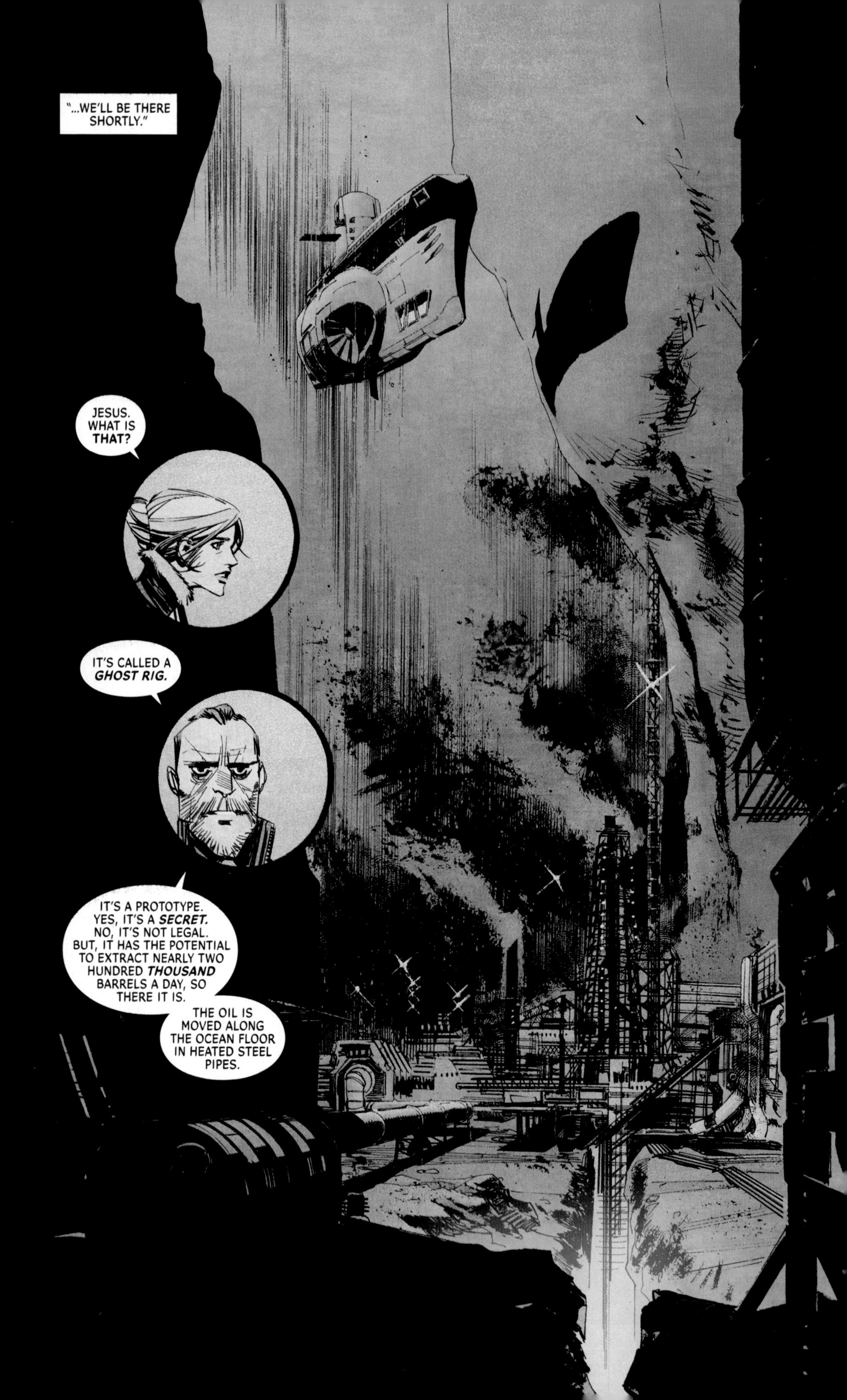

"...WE'LL BE THERE SHORTLY."
JESUS. WHAT IS **THAT?**
IT'S CALLED A ***GHOST RIG.***
IT'S A PROTOTYPE. YES, IT'S A ***SECRET.*** NO, IT'S NOT LEGAL. BUT, IT HAS THE POTENTIAL TO EXTRACT NEARLY TWO HUNDRED ***THOUSAND*** BARRELS A DAY, SO THERE IT IS.
THE OIL IS MOVED ALONG THE OCEAN FLOOR IN HEATED STEEL PIPES.

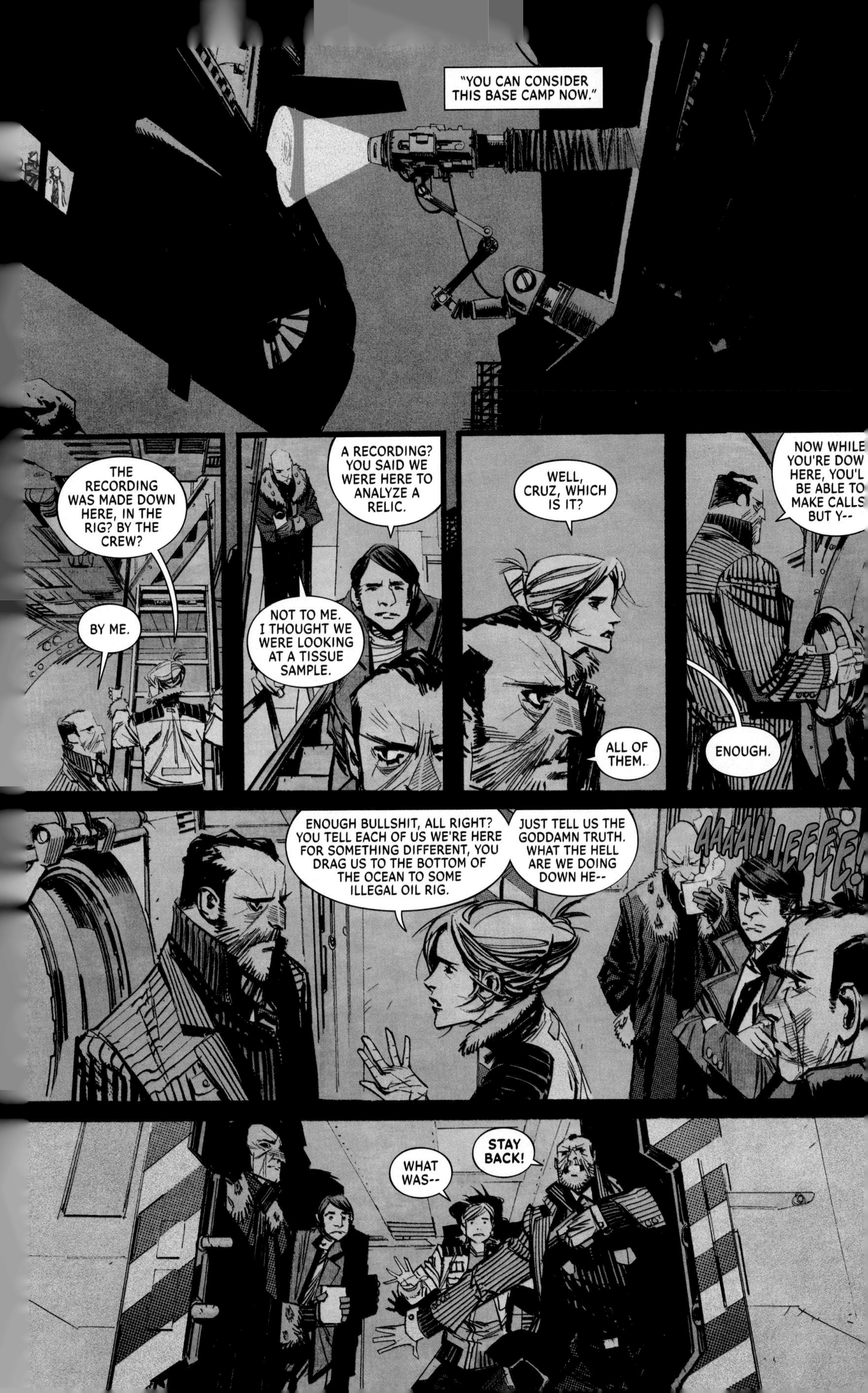
"YOU CAN CONSIDER THIS BASE CAMP NOW."
THE RECORDING WAS MADE DOWN HERE, IN THE RIG? BY THE CREW?
BY ME.
A RECORDING? YOU SAID WE WERE HERE TO ANALYZE A RELIC.
NOT TO ME. I THOUGHT WE WERE LOOKING AT A TISSUE SAMPLE.
WELL, CRUZ, WHICH IS IT?
ALL OF THEM.
NOW WHILE YOU'RE DOW HERE, YOU'L BE ABLE TO MAKE CALLS BUT Y--
ENOUGH.
ENOUGH BULLSHIT, ALL RIGHT? YOU TELL EACH OF US WE'RE HERE FOR SOMETHING DIFFERENT, YOU DRAG US TO THE BOTTOM OF THE OCEAN TO SOME ILLEGAL OIL RIG.
JUST TELL US THE GODDAMN TRUTH. WHAT THE HELL ARE WE DOING DOWN HE--
AAAAIIIEEEEE!
WHAT WAS--
STAY BACK!

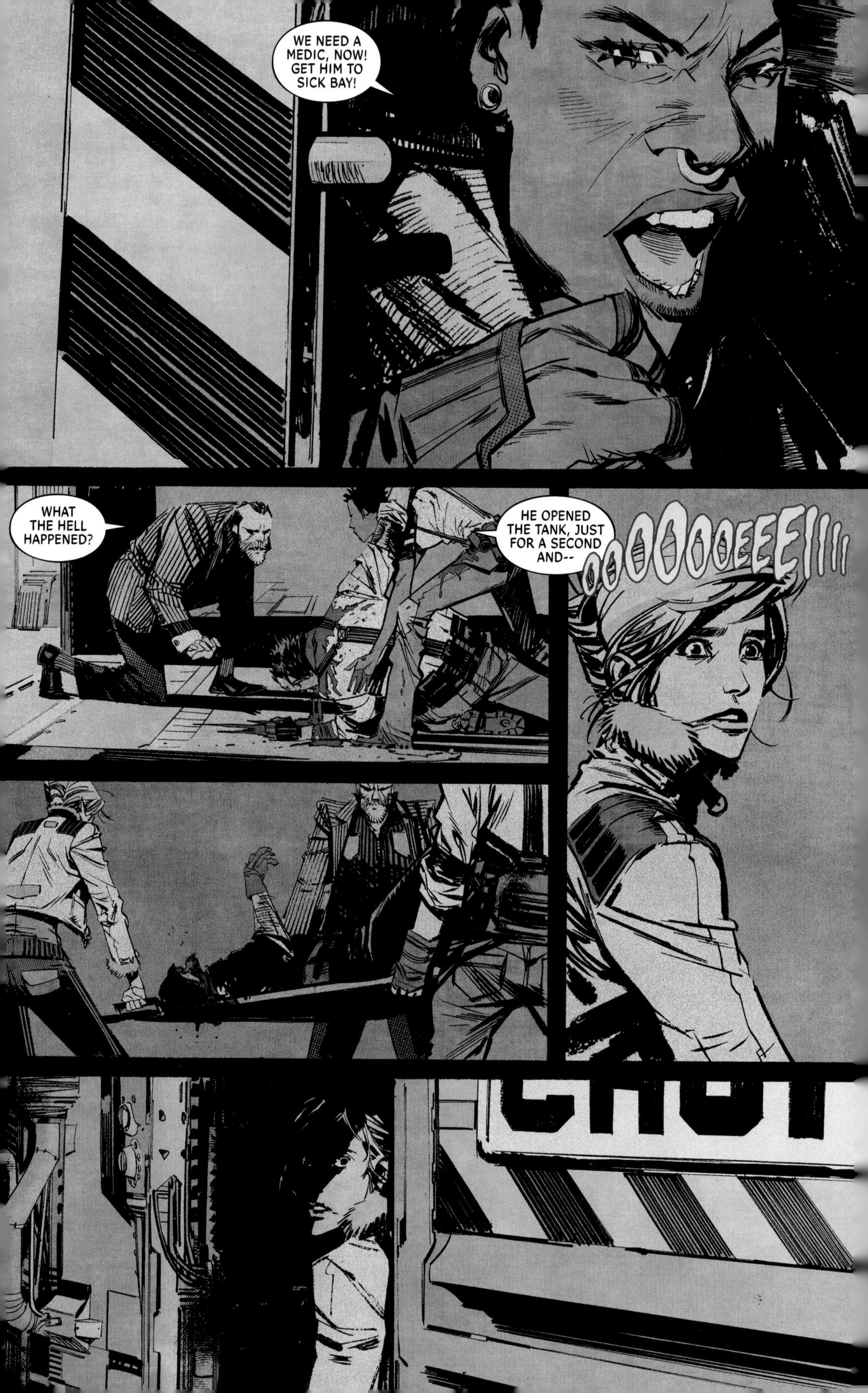

WE NEED A MEDIC, NOW! GET HIM TO SICK BAY!
WHAT THE HELL HAPPENED?
HE OPENED THE TANK, JUST FOR A SECOND AND--
OOOOOOEEEIIII

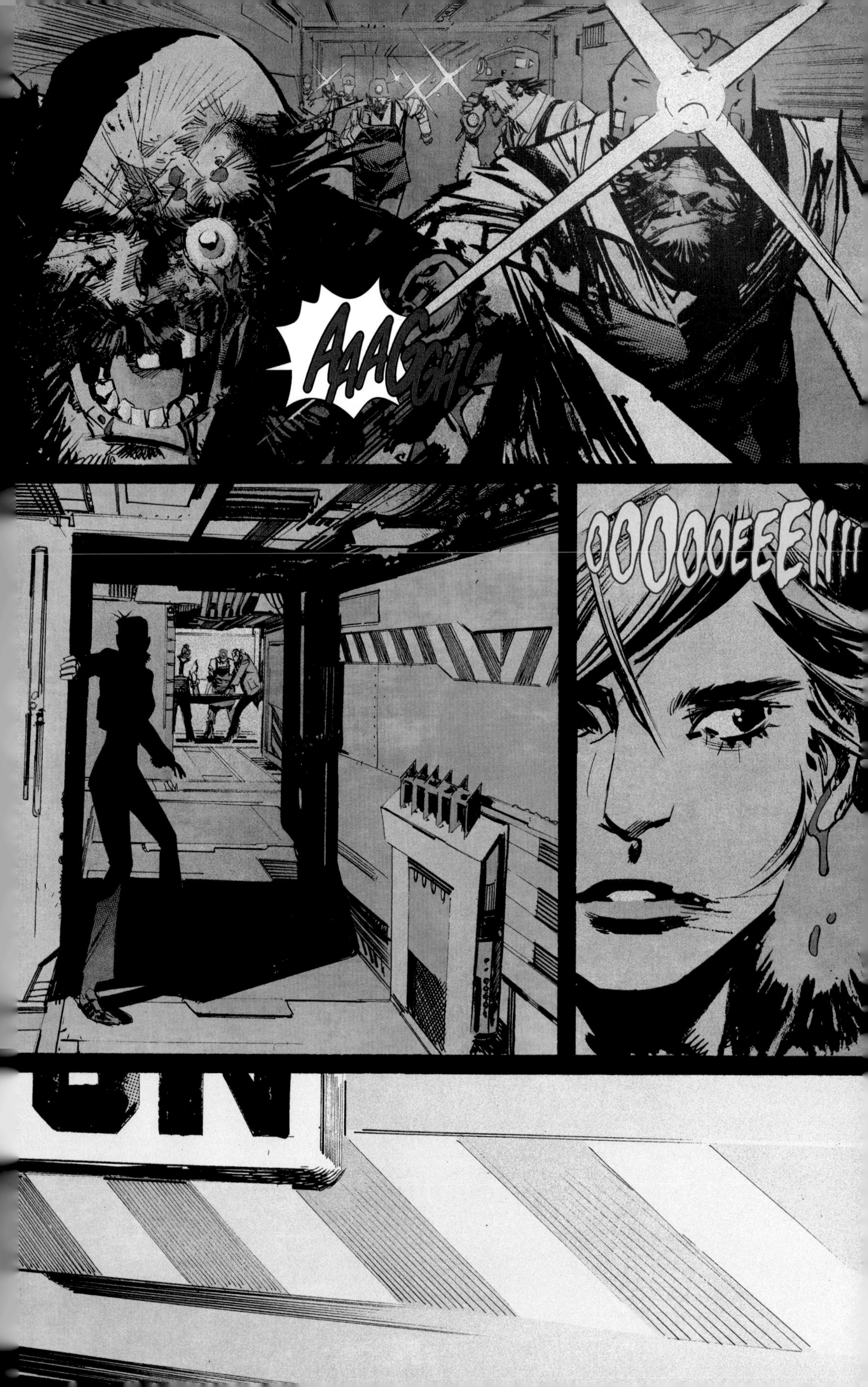
AAAGGH!!
OOOOOOEEEII!!!

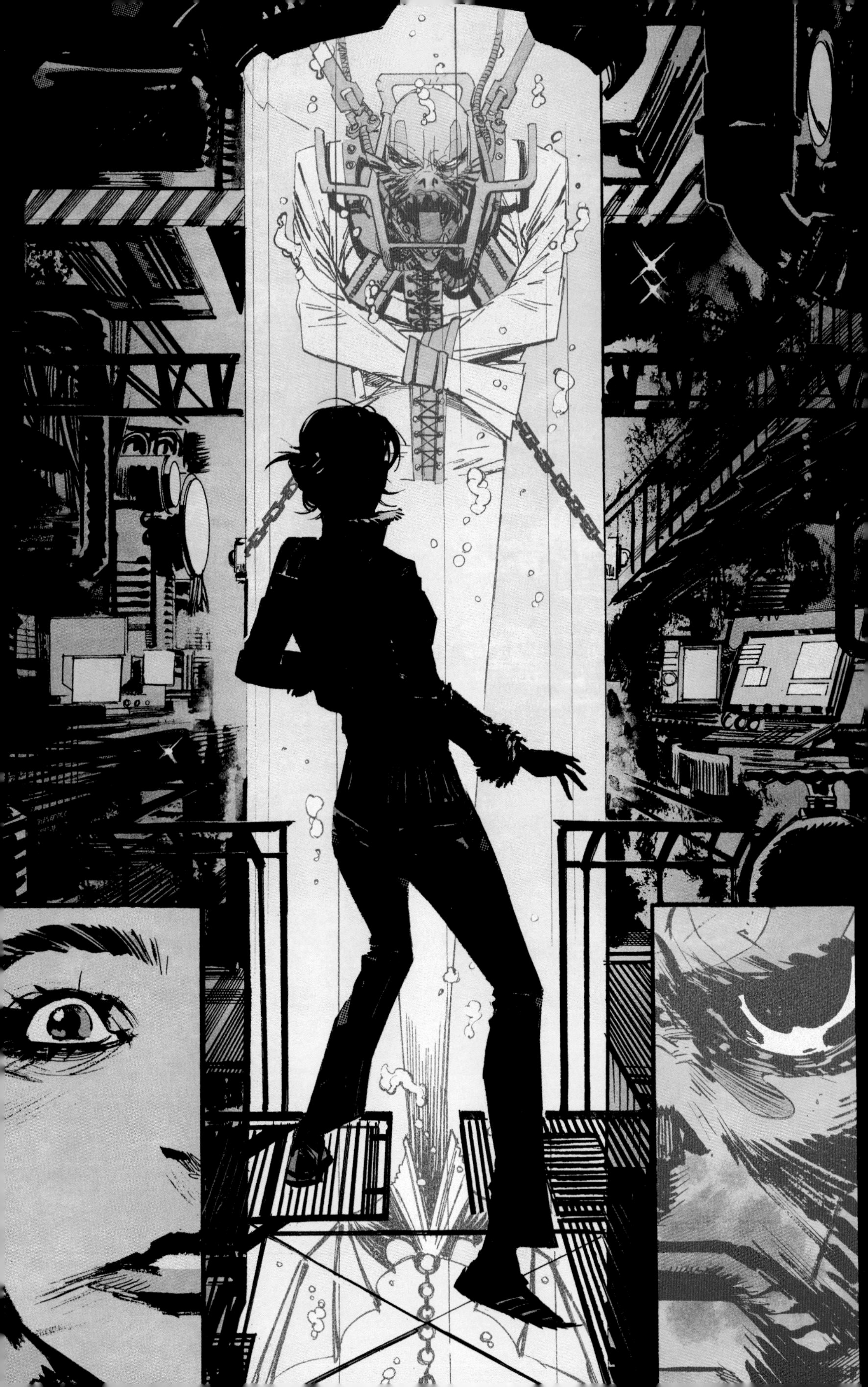

THE STORYTELLER

100,000 YEARS AGO.

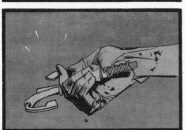

AAAGGH!

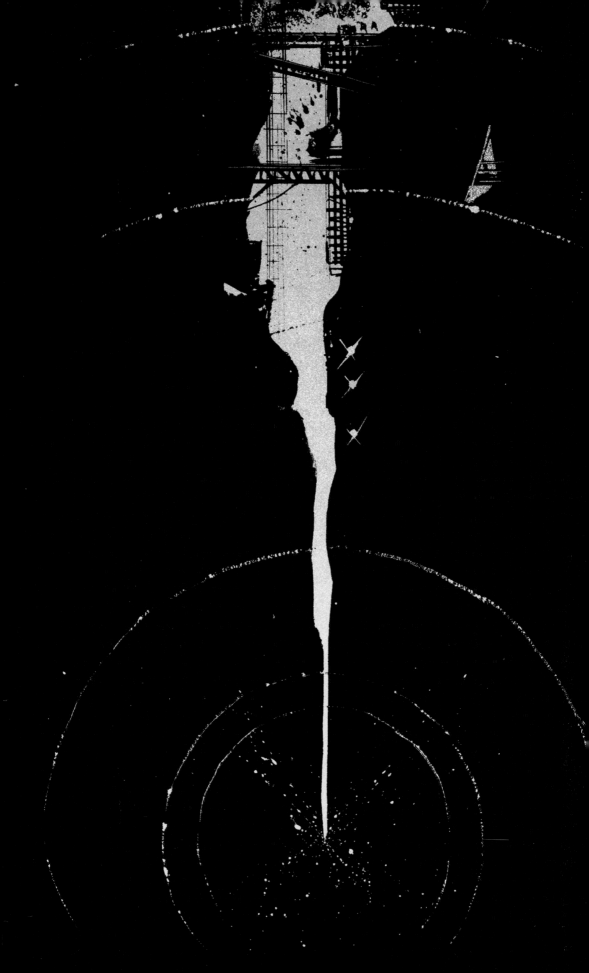

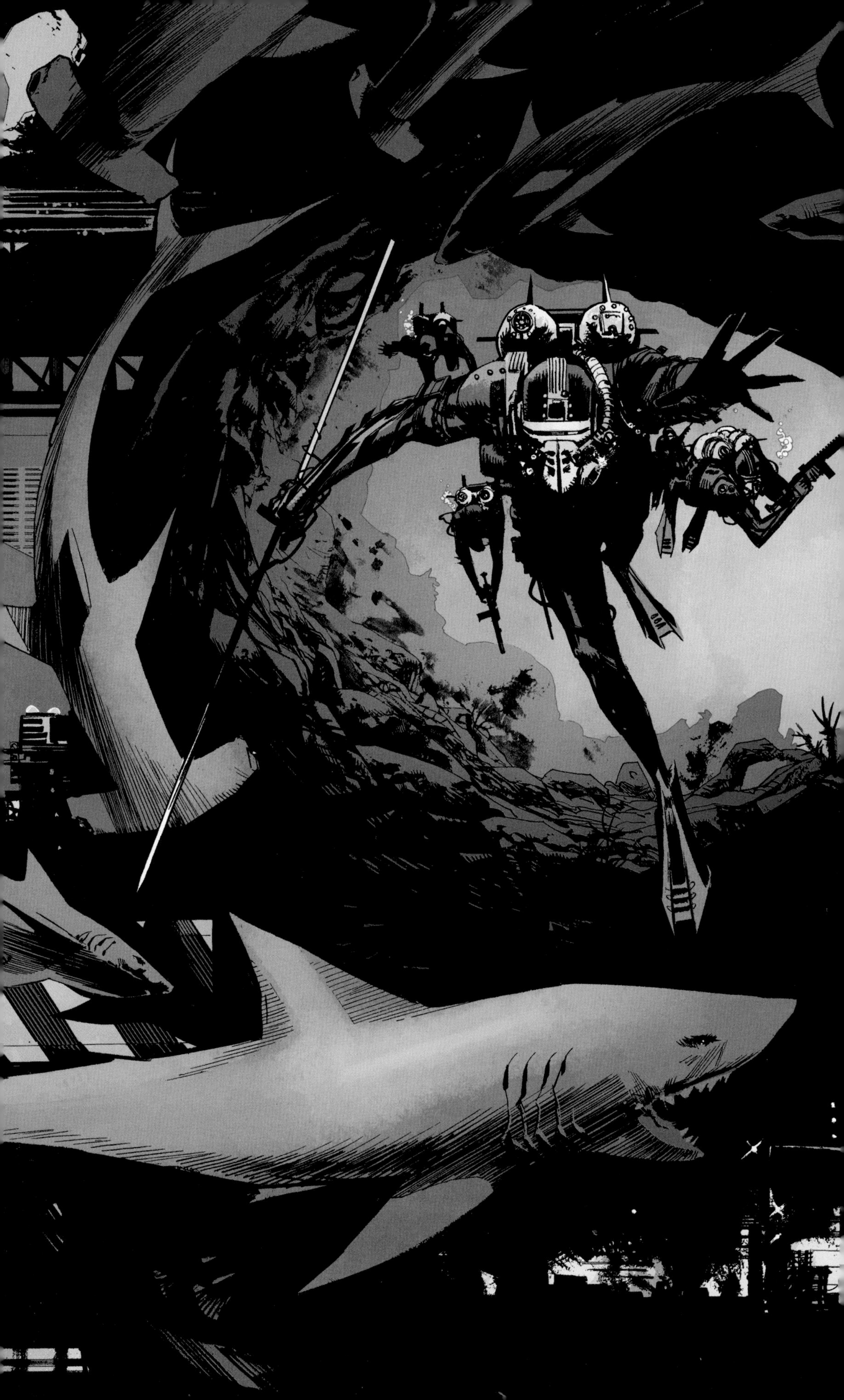

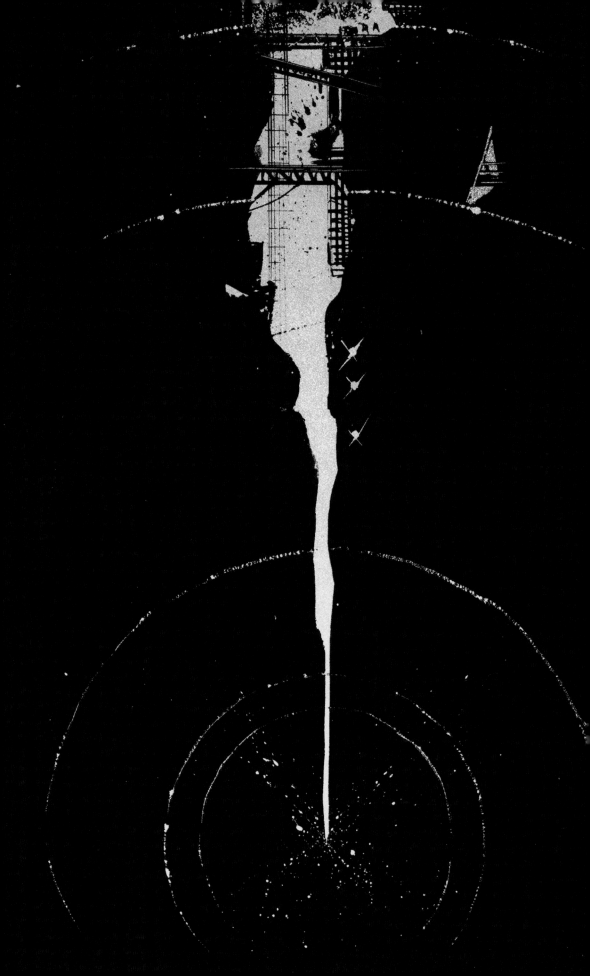

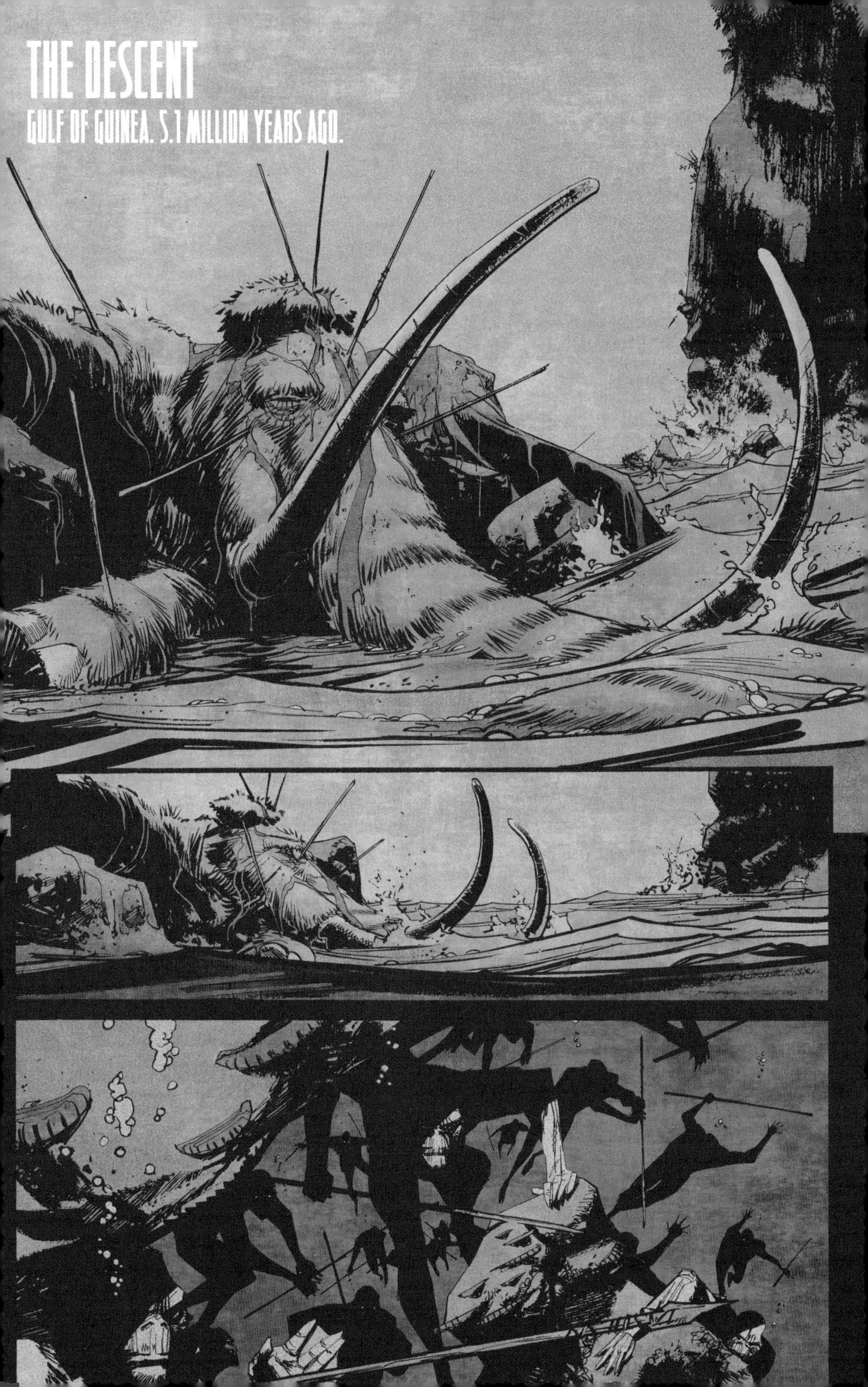
THE DESCENT
GULF OF GUINEA. 5.1 MILLION YEARS AGO.

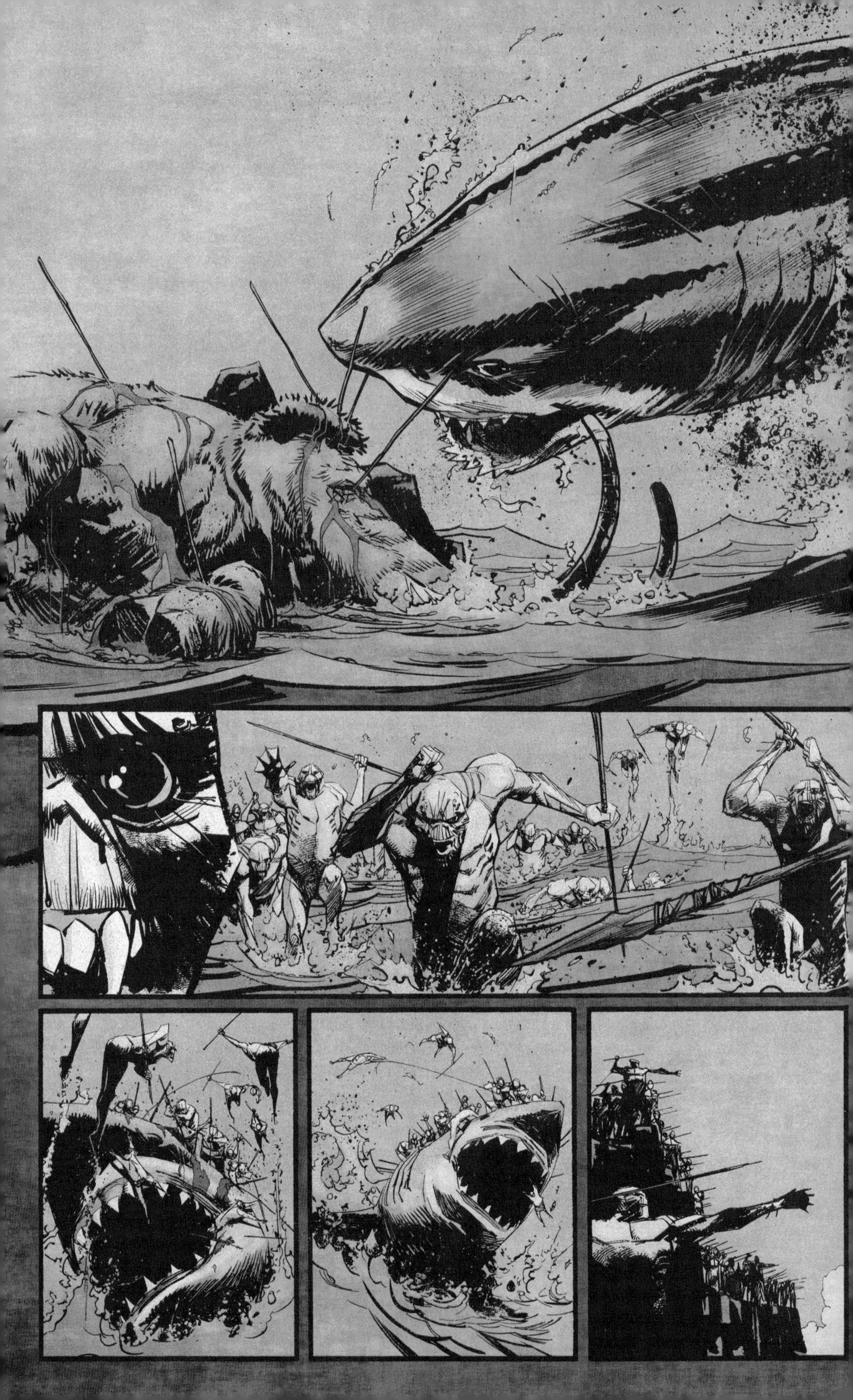

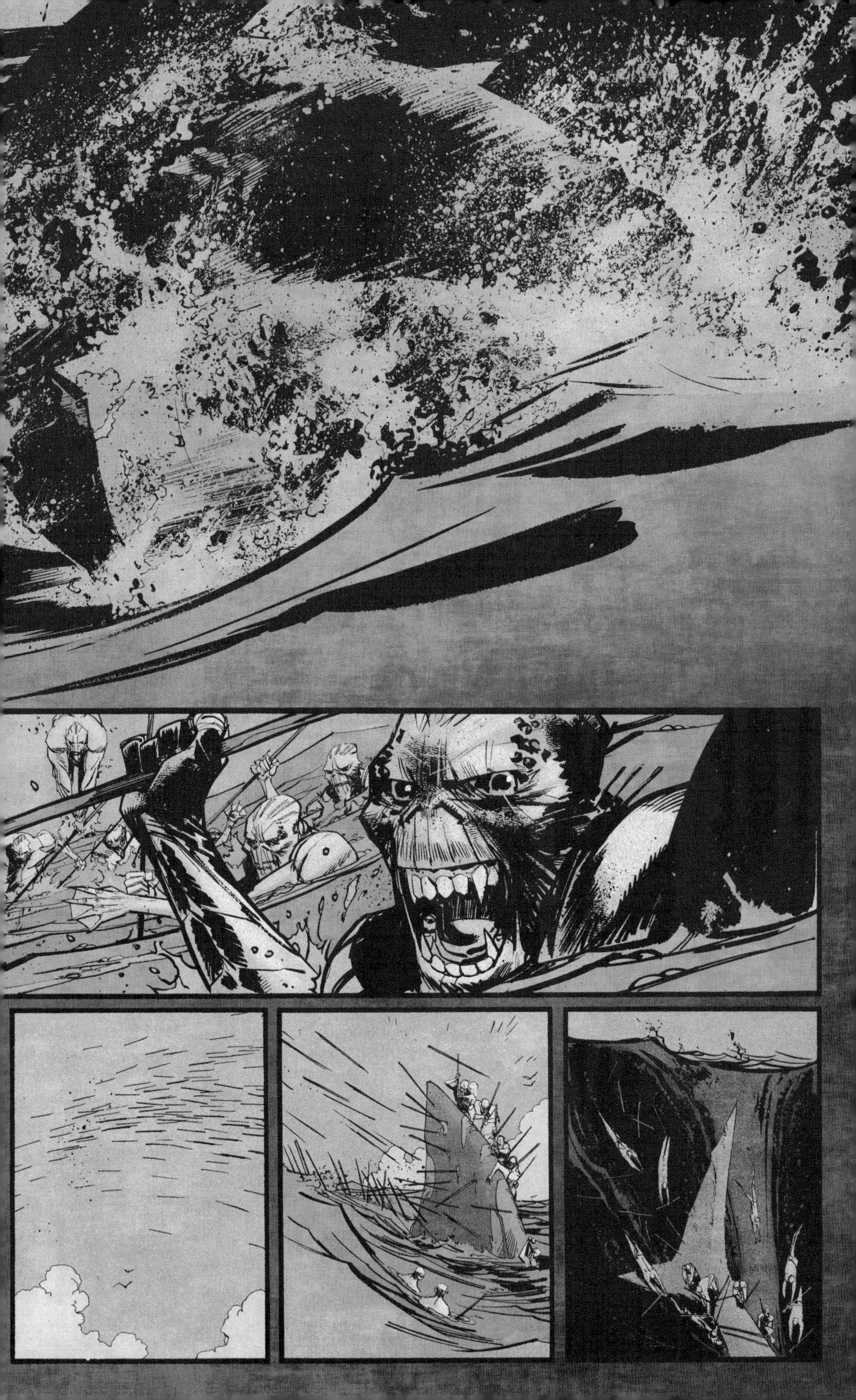

THE WAKE

CHAPTER TWO

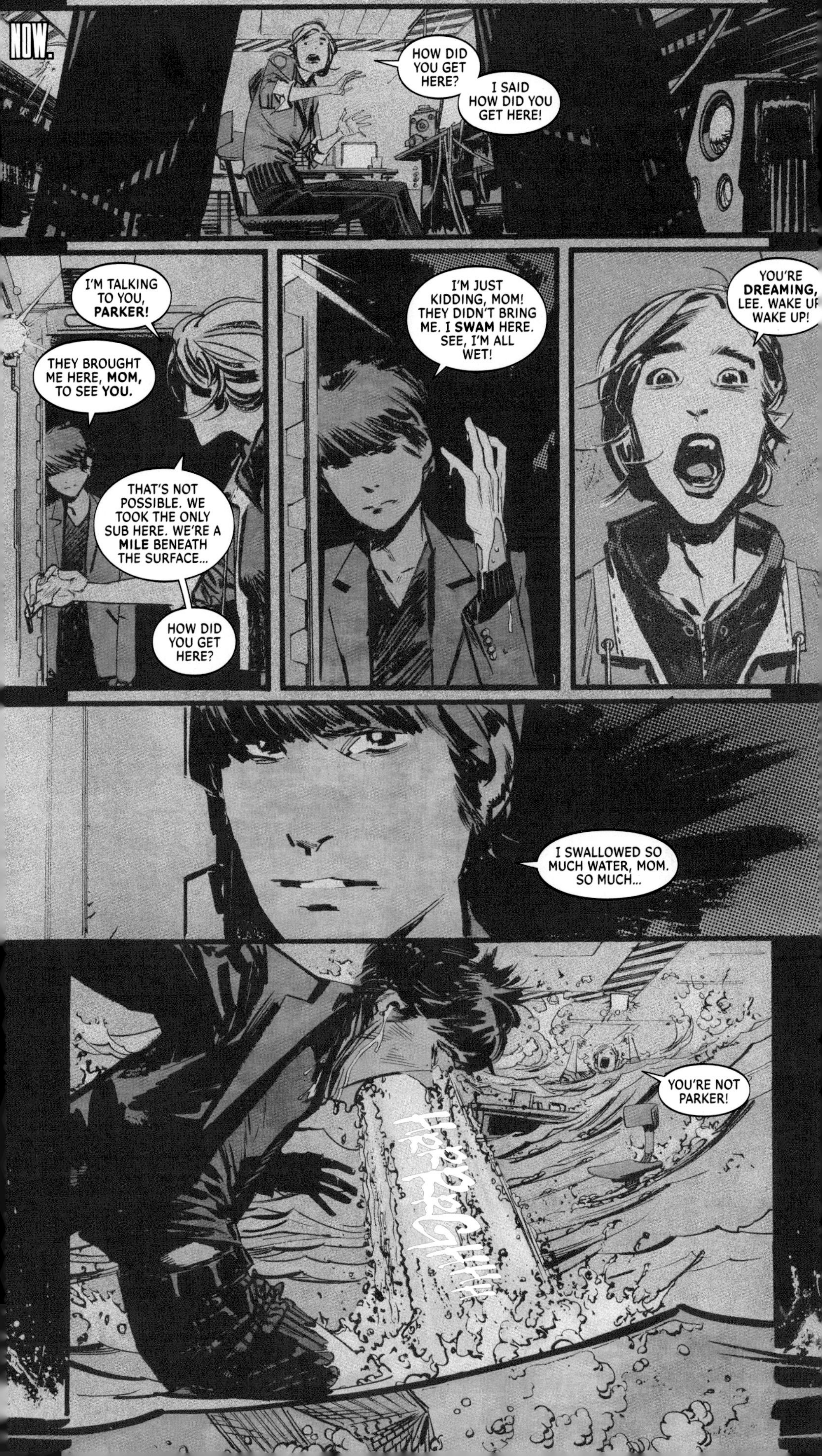

NOW.
HOW DID YOU GET HERE?
I SAID HOW DID YOU GET HERE!
I'M TALKING TO YOU, **PARKER!**
THEY BROUGHT ME HERE, **MOM,** TO SEE **YOU.**
THAT'S NOT POSSIBLE. WE TOOK THE ONLY SUB HERE. WE'RE A **MILE** BENEATH THE SURFACE...
HOW DID YOU GET HERE?
I'M JUST KIDDING, MOM! THEY DIDN'T BRING ME. I **SWAM** HERE. SEE, I'M ALL WET!
YOU'RE **DREAMING,** LEE. WAKE UP WAKE UP!
I SWALLOWED SO MUCH WATER, MOM. SO MUCH...
YOU'RE NOT PARKER!
HRRRGHHHH

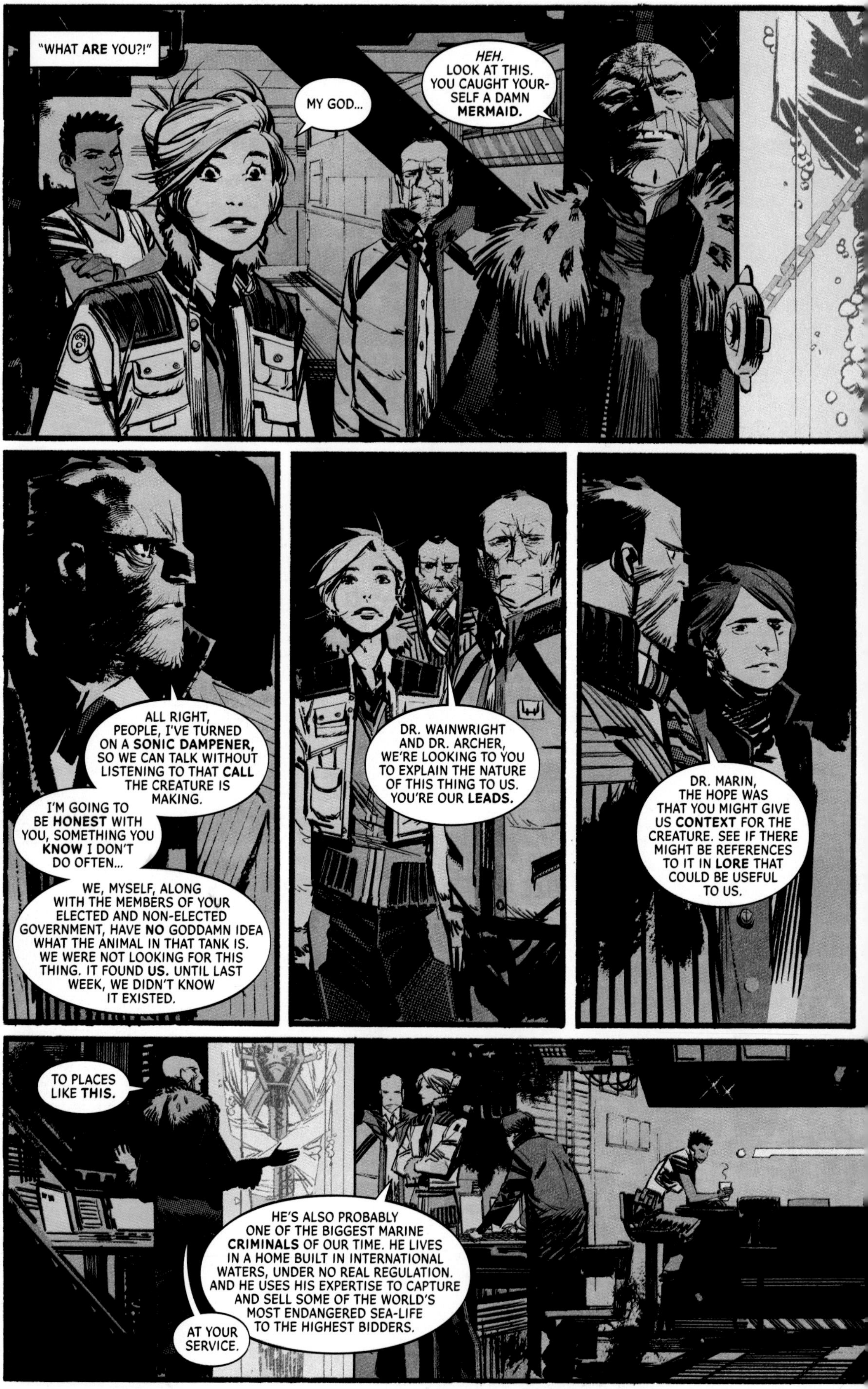
"WHAT ARE YOU?!"
MY GOD...
HEH. LOOK AT THIS. YOU CAUGHT YOURSELF A DAMN MERMAID.
ALL RIGHT, PEOPLE, I'VE TURNED ON A SONIC DAMPENER, SO WE CAN TALK WITHOUT LISTENING TO THAT CALL THE CREATURE IS MAKING.
I'M GOING TO BE HONEST WITH YOU, SOMETHING YOU KNOW I DON'T DO OFTEN...
WE, MYSELF, ALONG WITH THE MEMBERS OF YOUR ELECTED AND NON-ELECTED GOVERNMENT, HAVE NO GODDAMN IDEA WHAT THE ANIMAL IN THAT TANK IS. WE WERE NOT LOOKING FOR THIS THING. IT FOUND US. UNTIL LAST WEEK, WE DIDN'T KNOW IT EXISTED.
DR. WAINWRIGHT AND DR. ARCHER, WE'RE LOOKING TO YOU TO EXPLAIN THE NATURE OF THIS THING TO US. YOU'RE OUR LEADS.
DR. MARIN, THE HOPE WAS THAT YOU MIGHT GIVE US CONTEXT FOR THE CREATURE. SEE IF THERE MIGHT BE REFERENCES TO IT IN LORE THAT COULD BE USEFUL TO US.
TO PLACES LIKE THIS.
HE'S ALSO PROBABLY ONE OF THE BIGGEST MARINE CRIMINALS OF OUR TIME. HE LIVES IN A HOME BUILT IN INTERNATIONAL WATERS, UNDER NO REAL REGULATION. AND HE USES HIS EXPERTISE TO CAPTURE AND SELL SOME OF THE WORLD'S MOST ENDANGERED SEA-LIFE TO THE HIGHEST BIDDERS.
AT YOUR SERVICE.

INDEED. MAYBE AN ASHRAY...

MEEKS, YOU'RE HERE TO--

KILL IT.

CONTAIN IT.

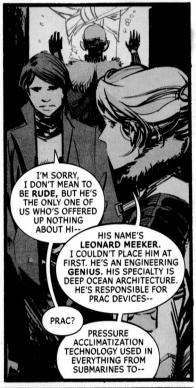

I'M SORRY, I DON'T MEAN TO BE RUDE, BUT HE'S THE ONLY ONE OF US WHO'S OFFERED UP NOTHING ABOUT HI--

HIS NAME'S LEONARD MEEKER. I COULDN'T PLACE HIM AT FIRST. HE'S AN ENGINEERING GENIUS. HIS SPECIALTY IS DEEP OCEAN ARCHITECTURE. HE'S RESPONSIBLE FOR PRAC DEVICES--

PRAC?

PRESSURE ACCLIMATIZATION TECHNOLOGY USED IN EVERYTHING FROM SUBMARINES TO--

LIKE YOU SAID, MEEKS IS HERE BECAUSE HE KNOWS HOW TO CONTAIN AND EXTRICATE DEEP SEA LIFE BETTER THAN ANYONE ON EARTH.

BUT BACK TO THE POINT. EACH OF YOU HAS SOMETHING TO TELL ME ABOUT THE CREATURE IN THIS TANK...

...AND I'M ALL EARS.

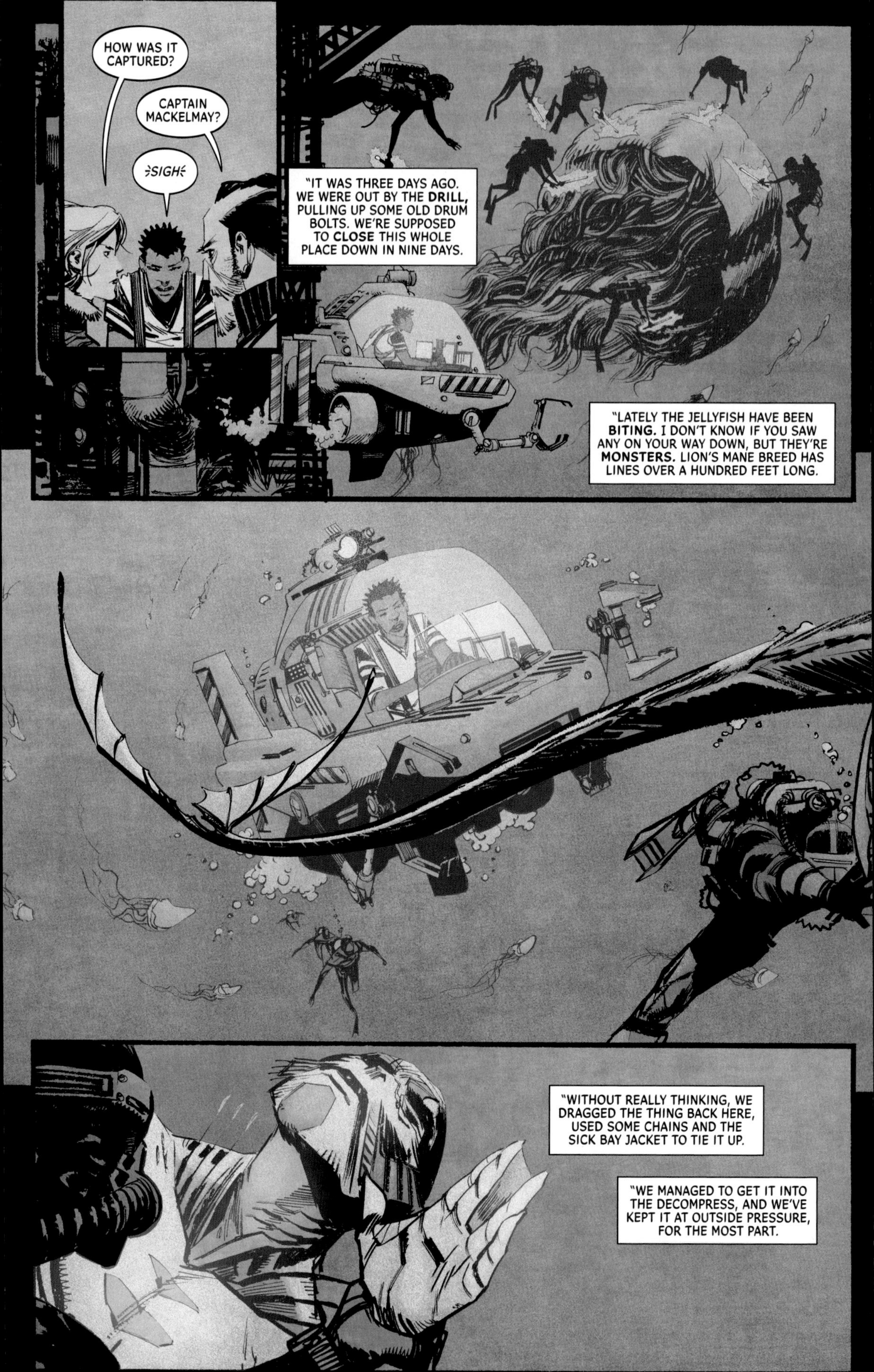
HOW WAS IT CAPTURED?
CAPTAIN MACKELMAY?
SIGH
"IT WAS THREE DAYS AGO. WE WERE OUT BY THE DRILL, PULLING UP SOME OLD DRUM BOLTS. WE'RE SUPPOSED TO CLOSE THIS WHOLE PLACE DOWN IN NINE DAYS.
"LATELY THE JELLYFISH HAVE BEEN BITING. I DON'T KNOW IF YOU SAW ANY ON YOUR WAY DOWN, BUT THEY'RE MONSTERS. LION'S MANE BREED HAS LINES OVER A HUNDRED FEET LONG.
"WITHOUT REALLY THINKING, WE DRAGGED THE THING BACK HERE, USED SOME CHAINS AND THE SICK BAY JACKET TO TIE IT UP.
"WE MANAGED TO GET IT INTO THE DECOMPRESS, AND WE'VE KEPT IT AT OUTSIDE PRESSURE, FOR THE MOST PART.

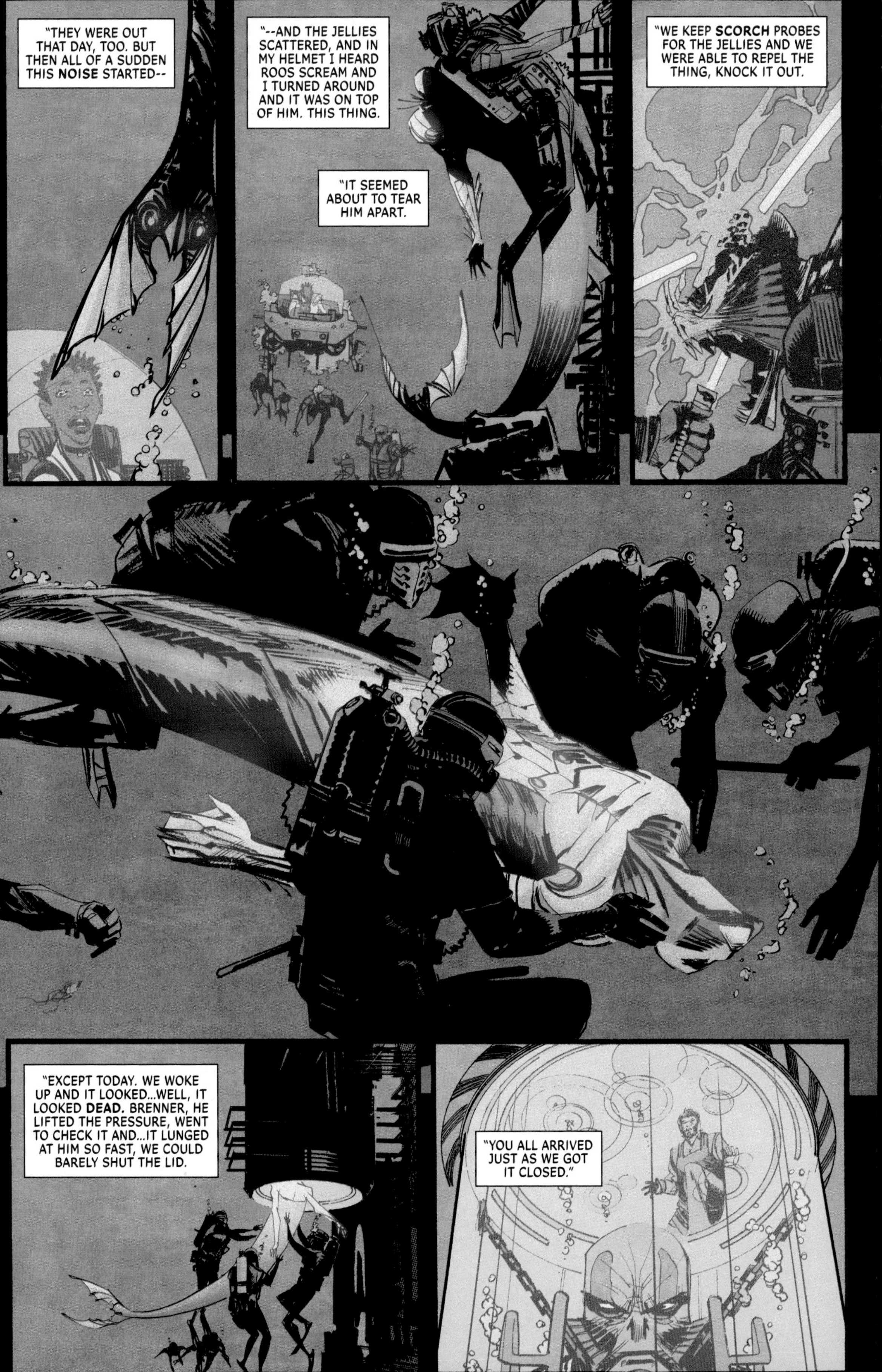
"THEY WERE OUT THAT DAY, TOO. BUT THEN ALL OF A SUDDEN THIS NOISE STARTED--
"--AND THE JELLIES SCATTERED, AND IN MY HELMET I HEARD ROOS SCREAM AND I TURNED AROUND AND IT WAS ON TOP OF HIM. THIS THING.
"IT SEEMED ABOUT TO TEAR HIM APART.
"WE KEEP SCORCH PROBES FOR THE JELLIES AND WE WERE ABLE TO REPEL THE THING, KNOCK IT OUT.
"EXCEPT TODAY. WE WOKE UP AND IT LOOKED...WELL, IT LOOKED DEAD. BRENNER, HE LIFTED THE PRESSURE, WENT TO CHECK IT AND...IT LUNGED AT HIM SO FAST, WE COULD BARELY SHUT THE LID.
"YOU ALL ARRIVED JUST AS WE GOT IT CLOSED."

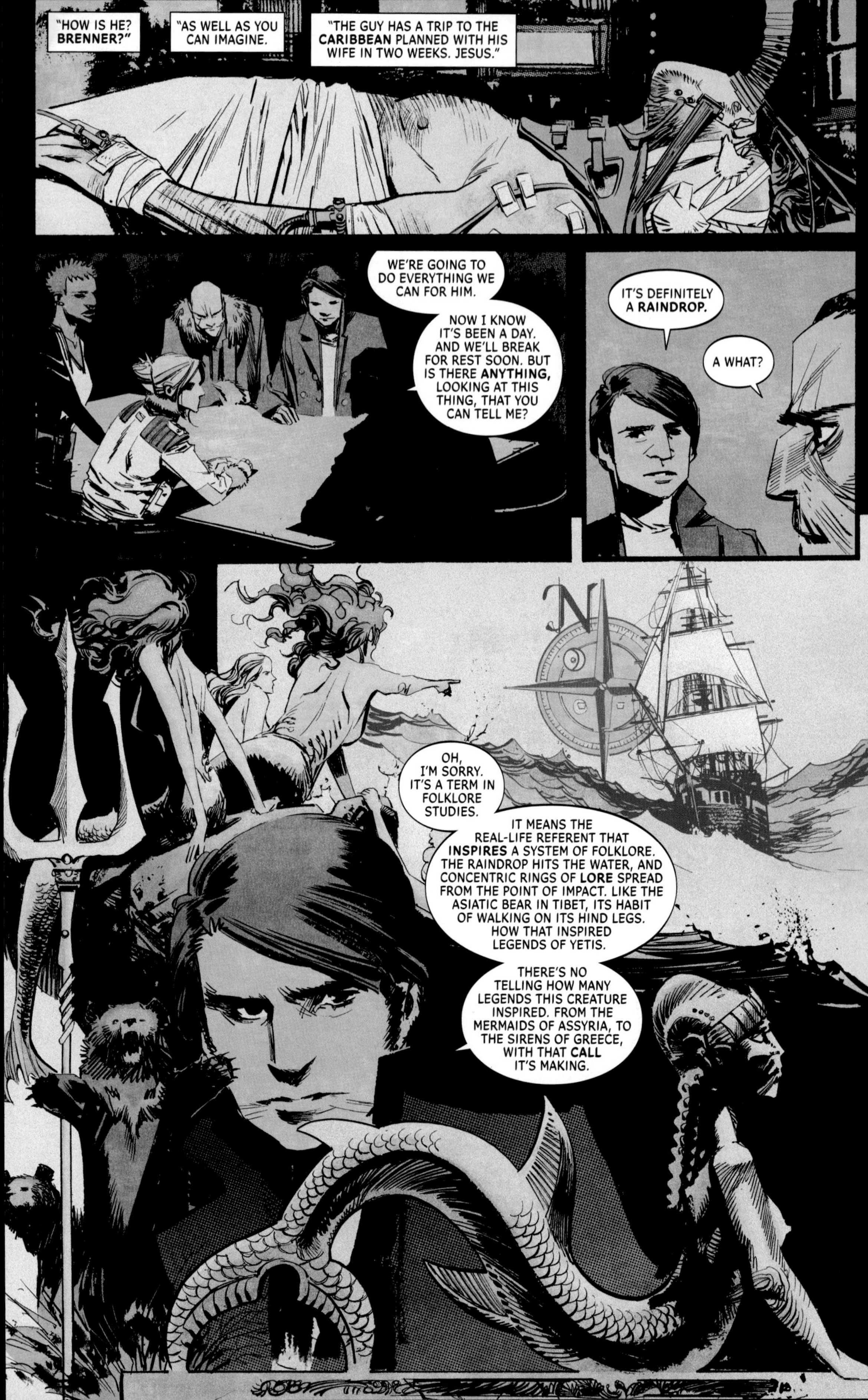
"HOW IS HE? BRENNER?"
"AS WELL AS YOU CAN IMAGINE.
"THE GUY HAS A TRIP TO THE CARIBBEAN PLANNED WITH HIS WIFE IN TWO WEEKS. JESUS."
WE'RE GOING TO DO EVERYTHING WE CAN FOR HIM.
NOW I KNOW IT'S BEEN A DAY. AND WE'LL BREAK FOR REST SOON. BUT IS THERE ANYTHING, LOOKING AT THIS THING, THAT YOU CAN TELL ME?
IT'S DEFINITELY A RAINDROP.
A WHAT?
OH, I'M SORRY. IT'S A TERM IN FOLKLORE STUDIES.
IT MEANS THE REAL-LIFE REFERENT THAT INSPIRES A SYSTEM OF FOLKLORE. THE RAINDROP HITS THE WATER, AND CONCENTRIC RINGS OF LORE SPREAD FROM THE POINT OF IMPACT. LIKE THE ASIATIC BEAR IN TIBET, ITS HABIT OF WALKING ON ITS HIND LEGS. HOW THAT INSPIRED LEGENDS OF YETIS.
THERE'S NO TELLING HOW MANY LEGENDS THIS CREATURE INSPIRED. FROM THE MERMAIDS OF ASSYRIA, TO THE SIRENS OF GREECE, WITH THAT CALL IT'S MAKING.

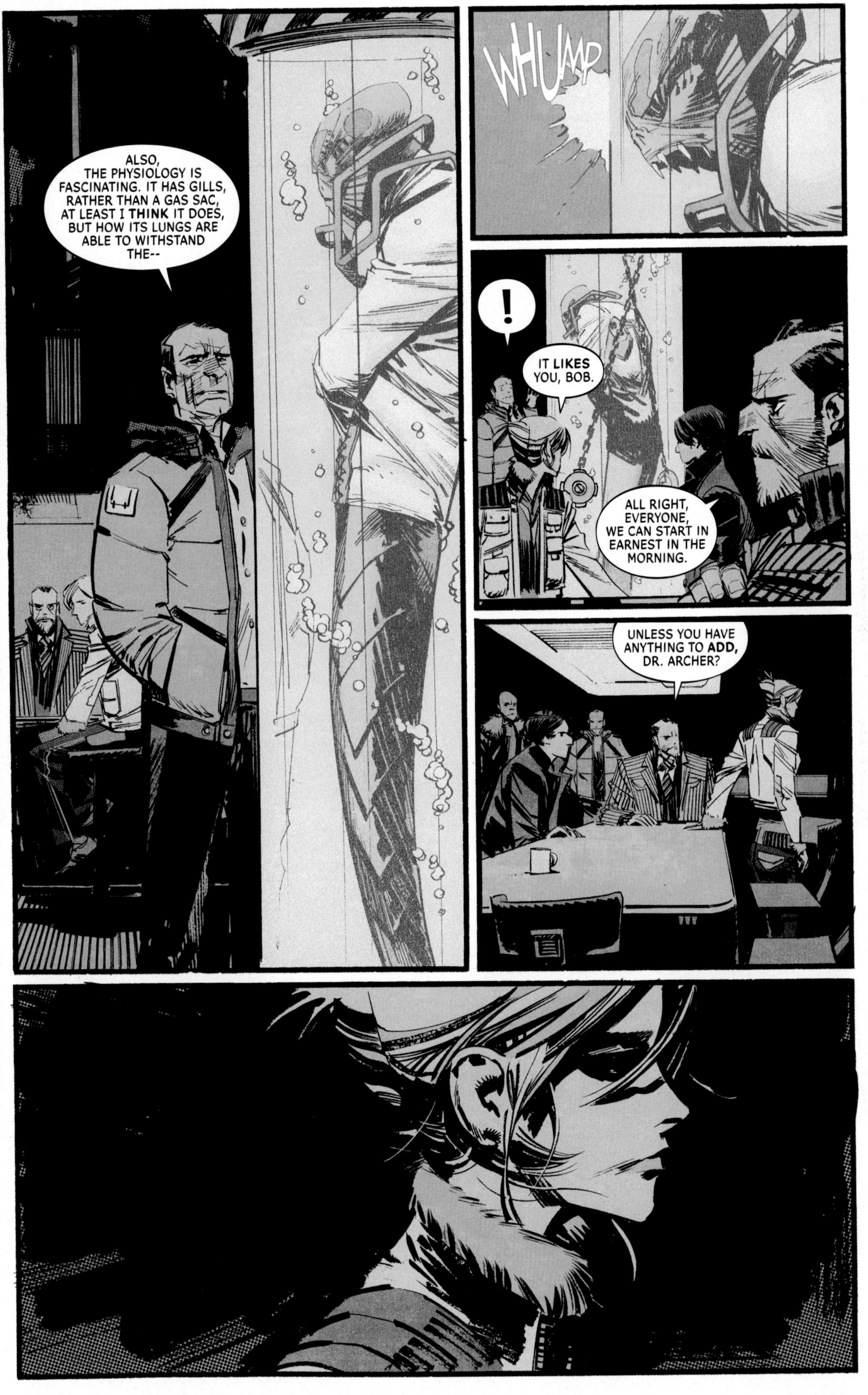
ALSO, THE PHYSIOLOGY IS FASCINATING. IT HAS GILLS, RATHER THAN A GAS SAC, AT LEAST I THINK IT DOES, BUT HOW ITS LUNGS ARE ABLE TO WITHSTAND THE--
WHUMP
!
IT LIKES YOU, BOB.
ALL RIGHT, EVERYONE, WE CAN START IN EARNEST IN THE MORNING.
UNLESS YOU HAVE ANYTHING TO ADD, DR. ARCHER?

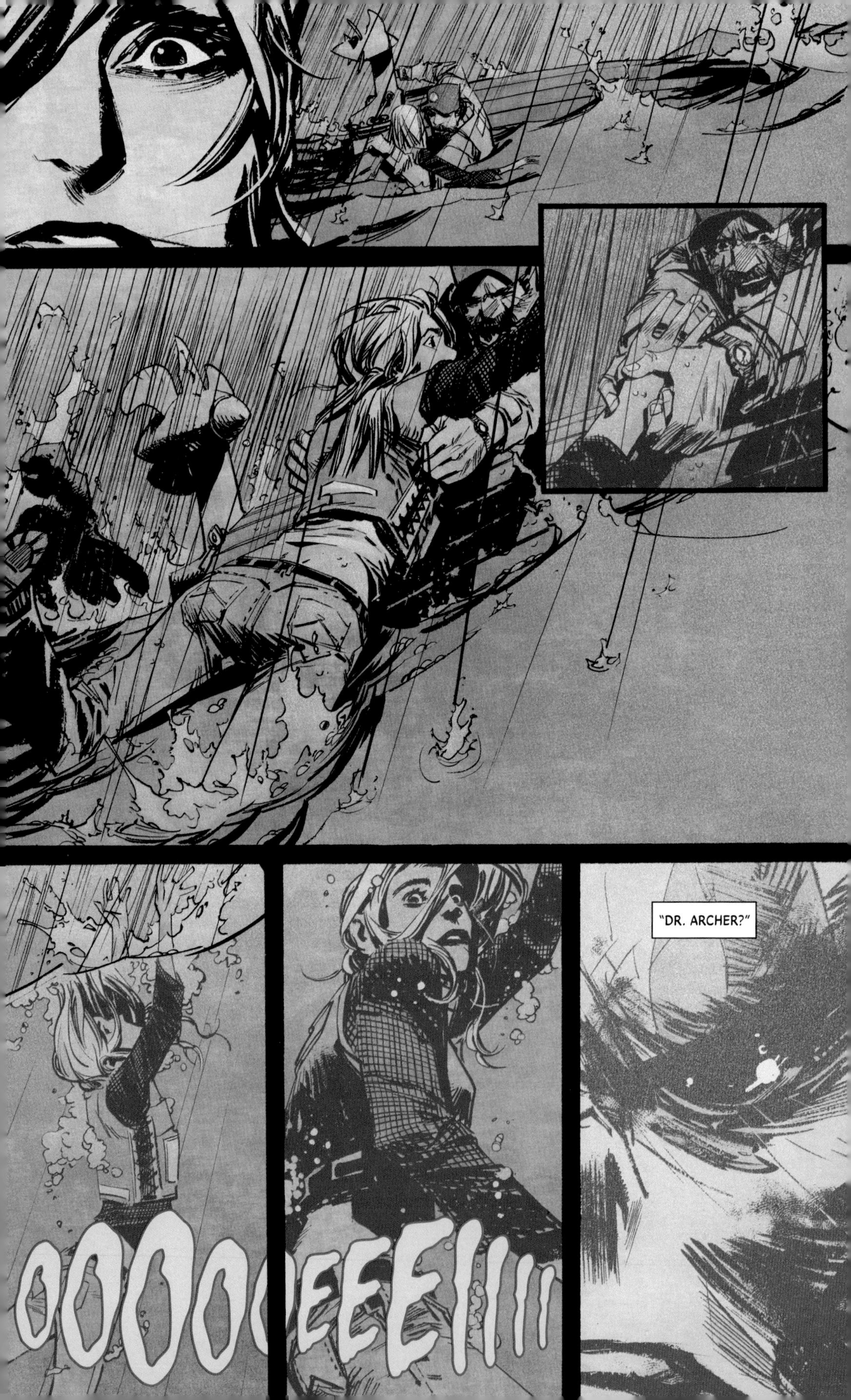
OOOOEEEIIII
"DR. ARCHER?"

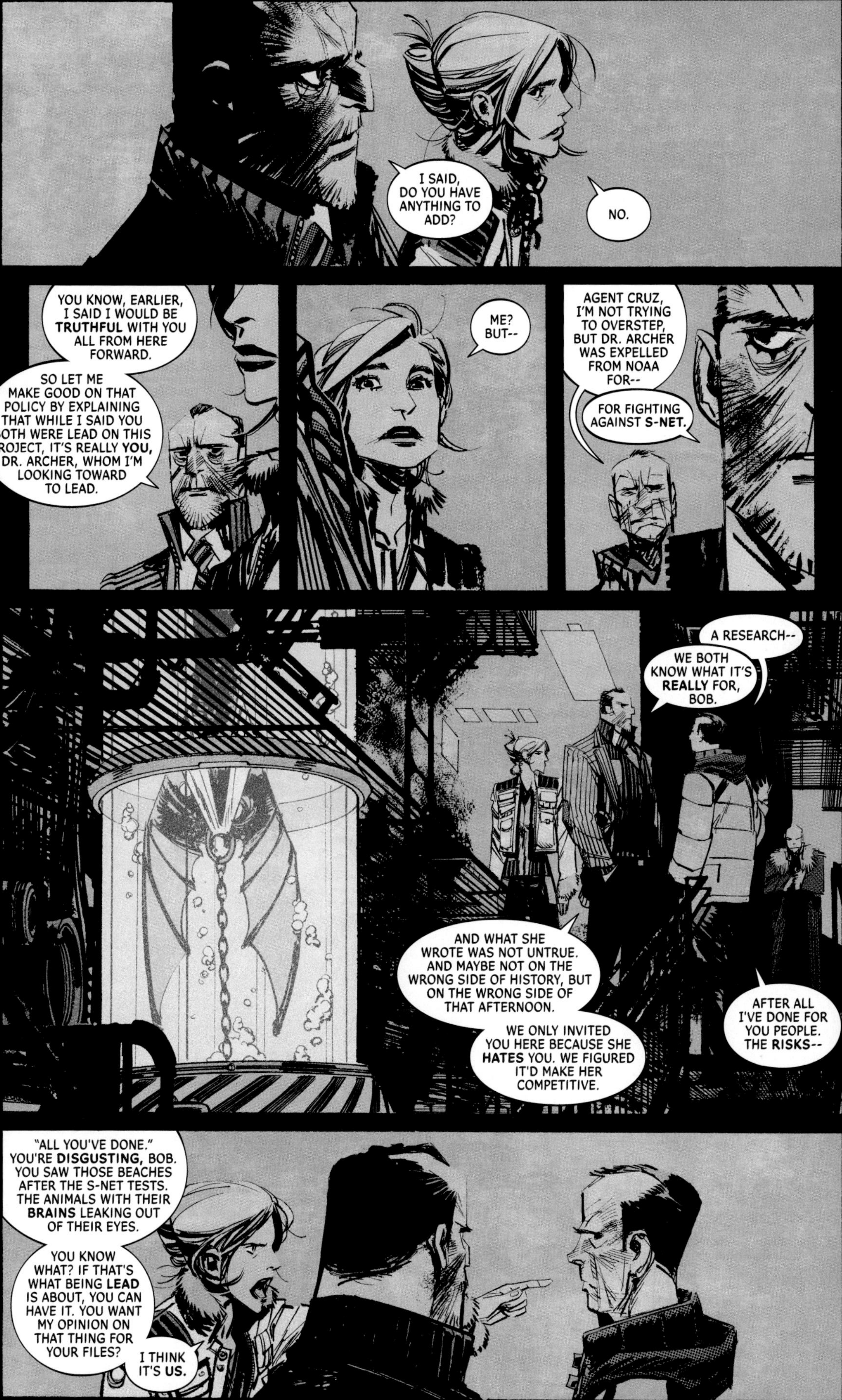
I SAID, DO YOU HAVE ANYTHING TO ADD?
NO.
YOU KNOW, EARLIER, I SAID I WOULD BE **TRUTHFUL** WITH YOU ALL FROM HERE FORWARD.
SO LET ME MAKE GOOD ON THAT POLICY BY EXPLAINING THAT WHILE I SAID YOU BOTH WERE LEAD ON THIS PROJECT, IT'S REALLY **YOU,** DR. ARCHER, WHOM I'M LOOKING TOWARD TO LEAD.
ME? BUT--
AGENT CRUZ, I'M NOT TRYING TO OVERSTEP, BUT DR. ARCHER WAS EXPELLED FROM NOAA FOR--
FOR FIGHTING AGAINST **S-NET.**
A RESEARCH--
WE BOTH KNOW WHAT IT'S **REALLY** FOR, BOB.
AND WHAT SHE WROTE WAS NOT UNTRUE. AND MAYBE NOT ON THE WRONG SIDE OF HISTORY, BUT ON THE WRONG SIDE OF THAT AFTERNOON.
WE ONLY INVITED YOU HERE BECAUSE SHE **HATES** YOU. WE FIGURED IT'D MAKE HER COMPETITIVE.
AFTER ALL I'VE DONE FOR YOU PEOPLE. THE **RISKS**--
"ALL YOU'VE DONE." YOU'RE **DISGUSTING,** BOB. YOU SAW THOSE BEACHES AFTER THE S-NET TESTS. THE ANIMALS WITH THEIR **BRAINS** LEAKING OUT OF THEIR EYES.
YOU KNOW WHAT? IF THAT'S WHAT BEING **LEAD** IS ABOUT, YOU CAN HAVE IT. YOU WANT MY OPINION ON THAT THING FOR YOUR FILES?
I THINK IT'S **US.**

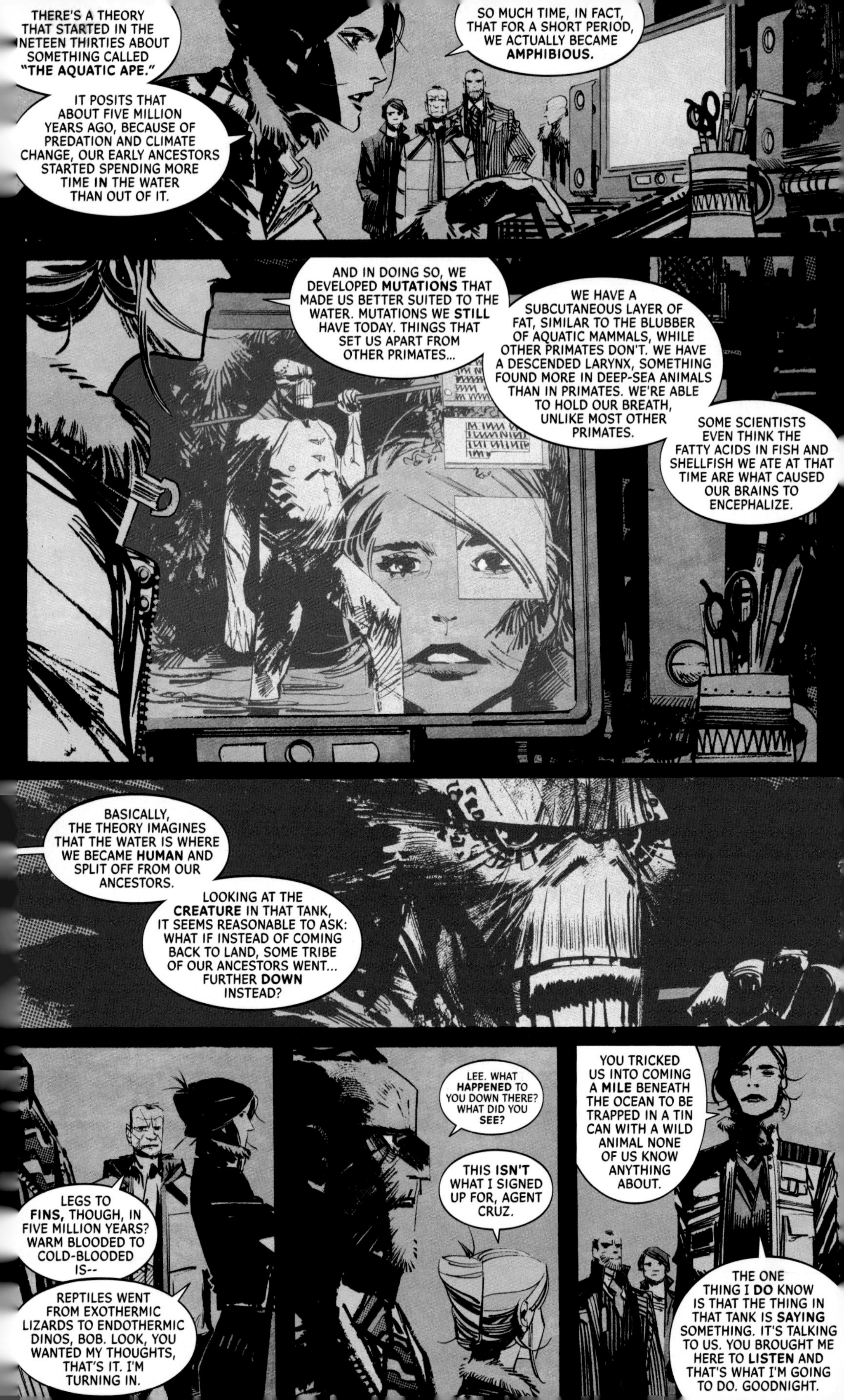
THERE'S A THEORY THAT STARTED IN THE NETEEN THIRTIES ABOUT SOMETHING CALLED "THE AQUATIC APE."
IT POSITS THAT ABOUT FIVE MILLION YEARS AGO, BECAUSE OF PREDATION AND CLIMATE CHANGE, OUR EARLY ANCESTORS STARTED SPENDING MORE TIME IN THE WATER THAN OUT OF IT.
SO MUCH TIME, IN FACT, THAT FOR A SHORT PERIOD, WE ACTUALLY BECAME AMPHIBIOUS.
AND IN DOING SO, WE DEVELOPED MUTATIONS THAT MADE US BETTER SUITED TO THE WATER. MUTATIONS WE STILL HAVE TODAY. THINGS THAT SET US APART FROM OTHER PRIMATES...
WE HAVE A SUBCUTANEOUS LAYER OF FAT, SIMILAR TO THE BLUBBER OF AQUATIC MAMMALS, WHILE OTHER PRIMATES DON'T. WE HAVE A DESCENDED LARYNX, SOMETHING FOUND MORE IN DEEP-SEA ANIMALS THAN IN PRIMATES. WE'RE ABLE TO HOLD OUR BREATH, UNLIKE MOST OTHER PRIMATES.
SOME SCIENTISTS EVEN THINK THE FATTY ACIDS IN FISH AND SHELLFISH WE ATE AT THAT TIME ARE WHAT CAUSED OUR BRAINS TO ENCEPHALIZE.
BASICALLY, THE THEORY IMAGINES THAT THE WATER IS WHERE WE BECAME HUMAN AND SPLIT OFF FROM OUR ANCESTORS.
LOOKING AT THE CREATURE IN THAT TANK, IT SEEMS REASONABLE TO ASK: WHAT IF INSTEAD OF COMING BACK TO LAND, SOME TRIBE OF OUR ANCESTORS WENT... FURTHER DOWN INSTEAD?
LEGS TO FINS, THOUGH, IN FIVE MILLION YEARS? WARM BLOODED TO COLD-BLOODED IS--
REPTILES WENT FROM EXOTHERMIC LIZARDS TO ENDOTHERMIC DINOS, BOB. LOOK, YOU WANTED MY THOUGHTS, THAT'S IT. I'M TURNING IN.
LEE. WHAT HAPPENED TO YOU DOWN THERE? WHAT DID YOU SEE?
THIS ISN'T WHAT I SIGNED UP FOR, AGENT CRUZ.
YOU TRICKED US INTO COMING A MILE BENEATH THE OCEAN TO BE TRAPPED IN A TIN CAN WITH A WILD ANIMAL NONE OF US KNOW ANYTHING ABOUT.
THE ONE THING I DO KNOW IS THAT THE THING IN THAT TANK IS SAYING SOMETHING. IT'S TALKING TO US. YOU BROUGHT ME HERE TO LISTEN AND THAT'S WHAT I'M GOING TO DO. GOODNIGHT.

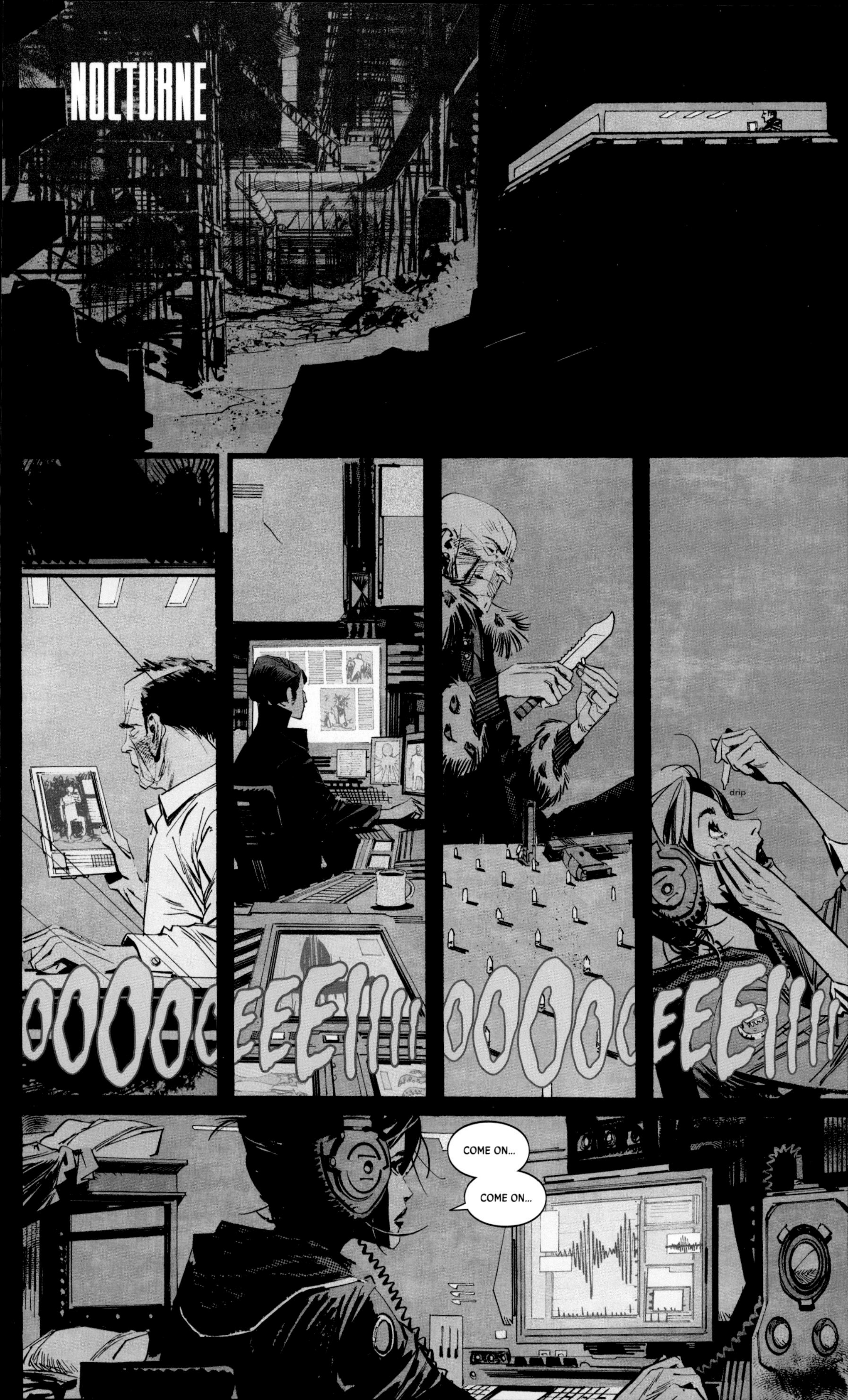
NOCTURNE
drip
OOOOEEEIIII OOOOEEEIIII
COME ON...
COME ON...

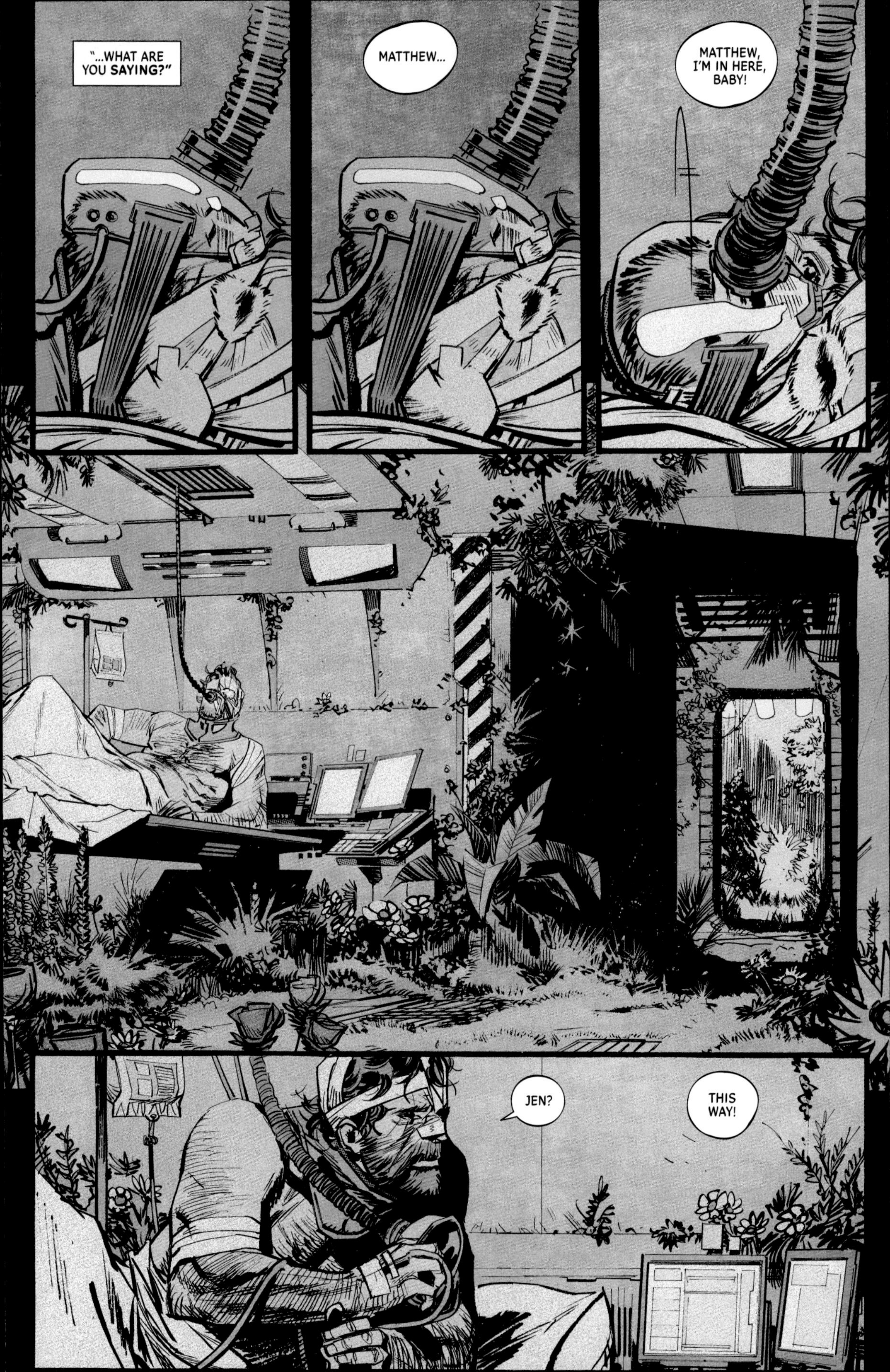
"...WHAT ARE YOU SAYING?"
MATTHEW...
MATTHEW, I'M IN HERE, BABY!
JEN?
THIS WAY!

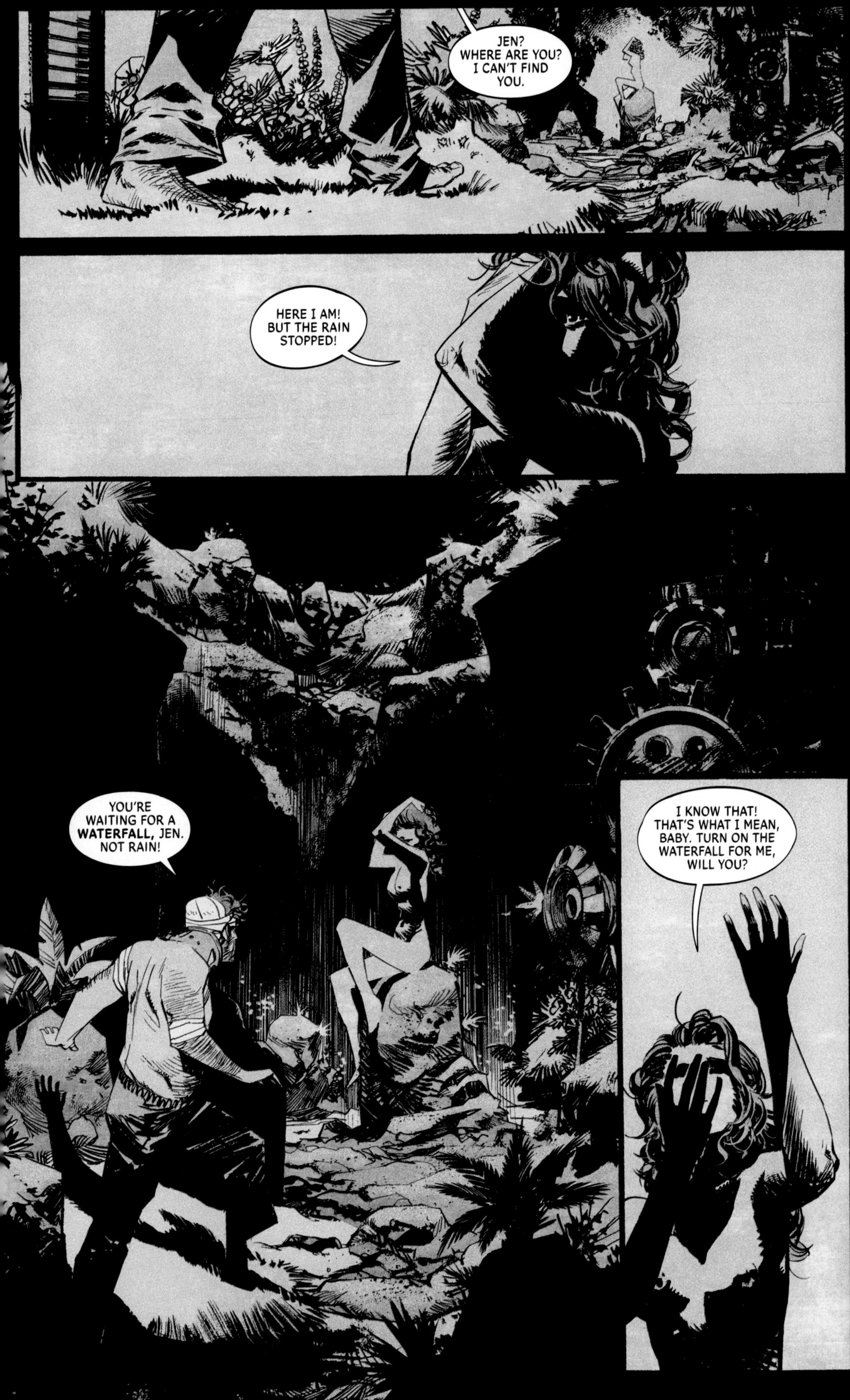
JEN? WHERE ARE YOU? I CAN'T FIND YOU.
HERE I AM! BUT THE RAIN STOPPED!
YOU'RE WAITING FOR A **WATERFALL,** JEN. NOT RAIN!
I KNOW THAT! THAT'S WHAT I MEAN, BABY. TURN ON THE WATERFALL FOR ME, WILL YOU?

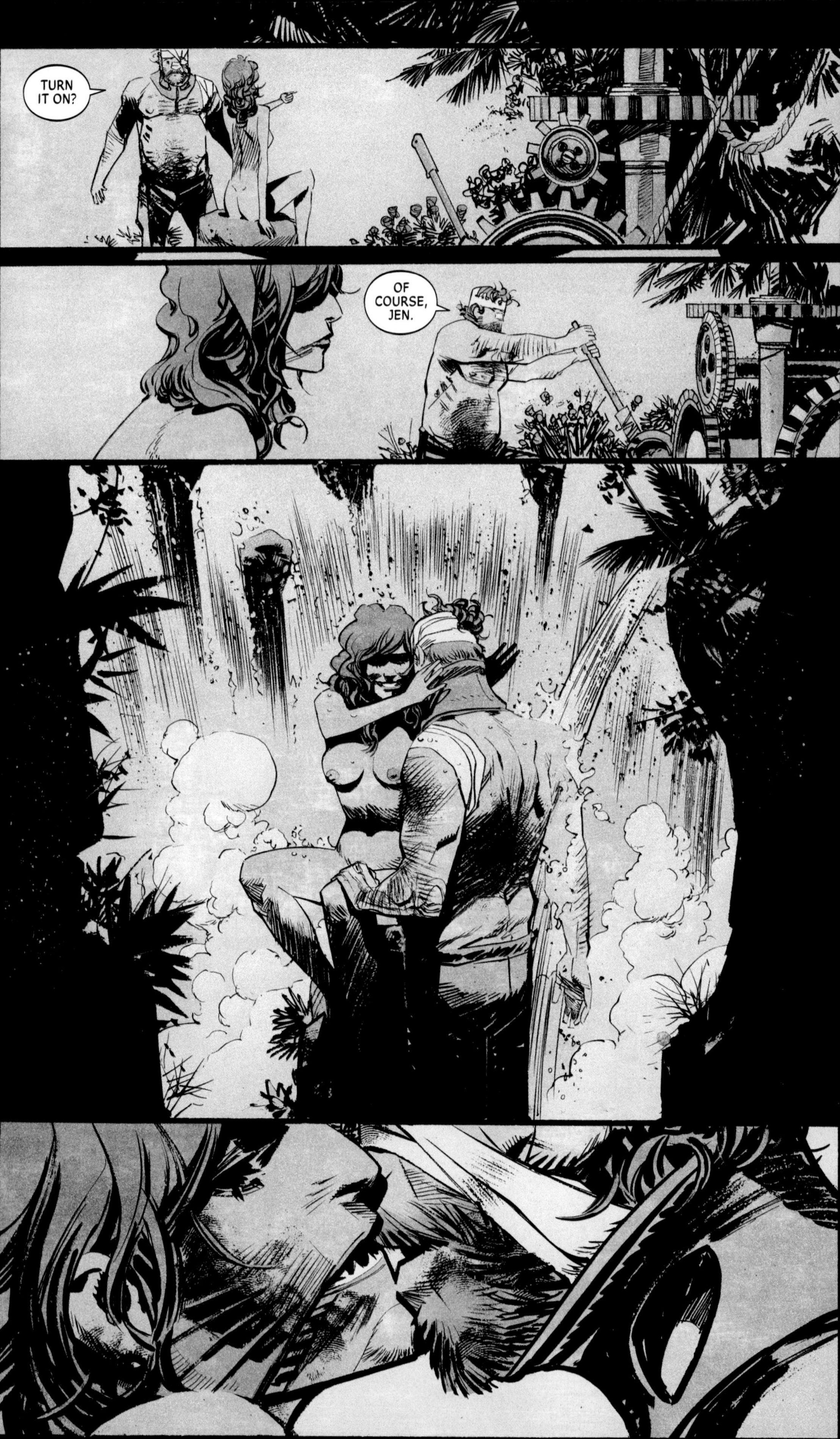
TURN IT ON?
OF COURSE, JEN.

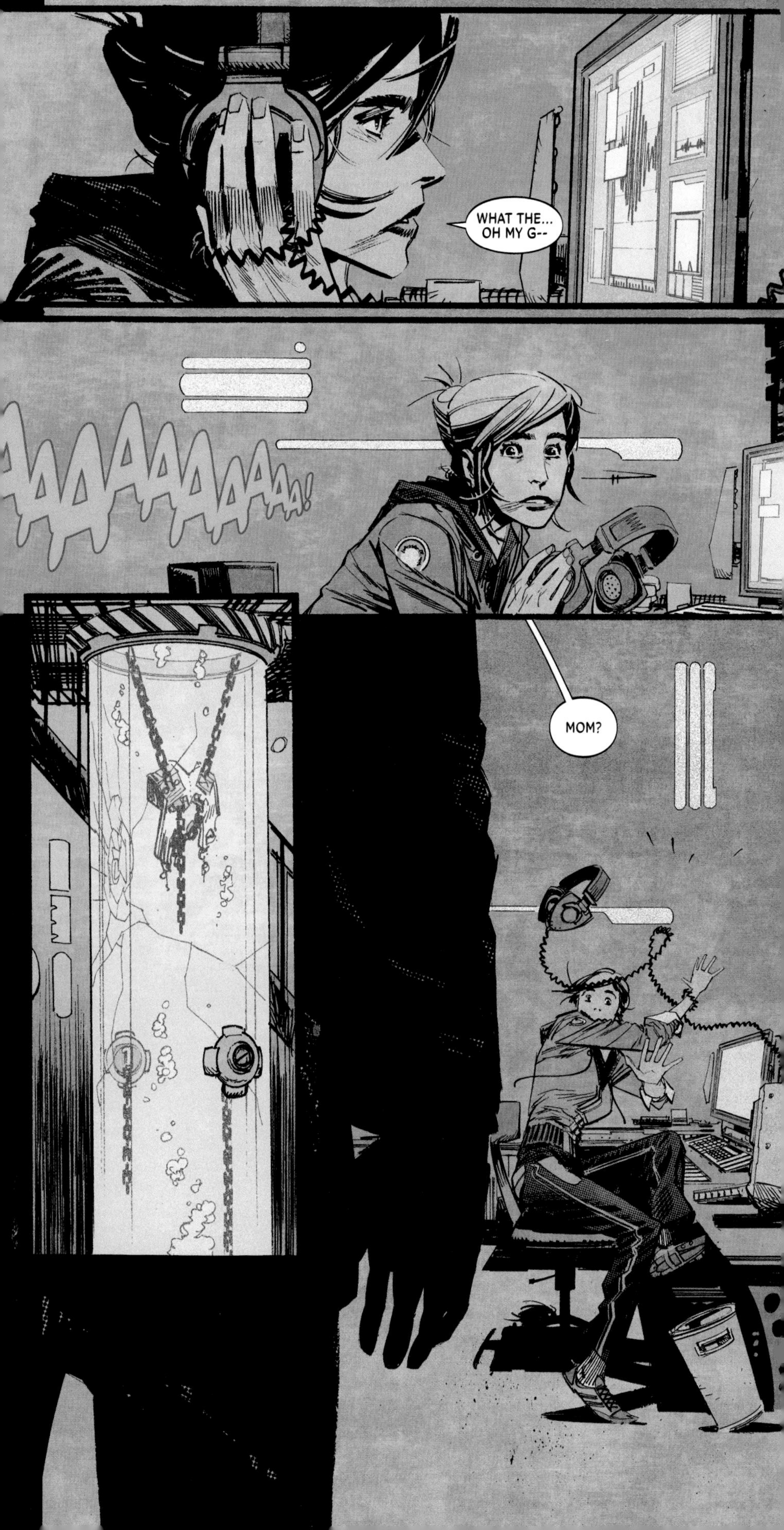
WHAT THE... OH MY G--
AAAAAAAAAAA!
MOM?

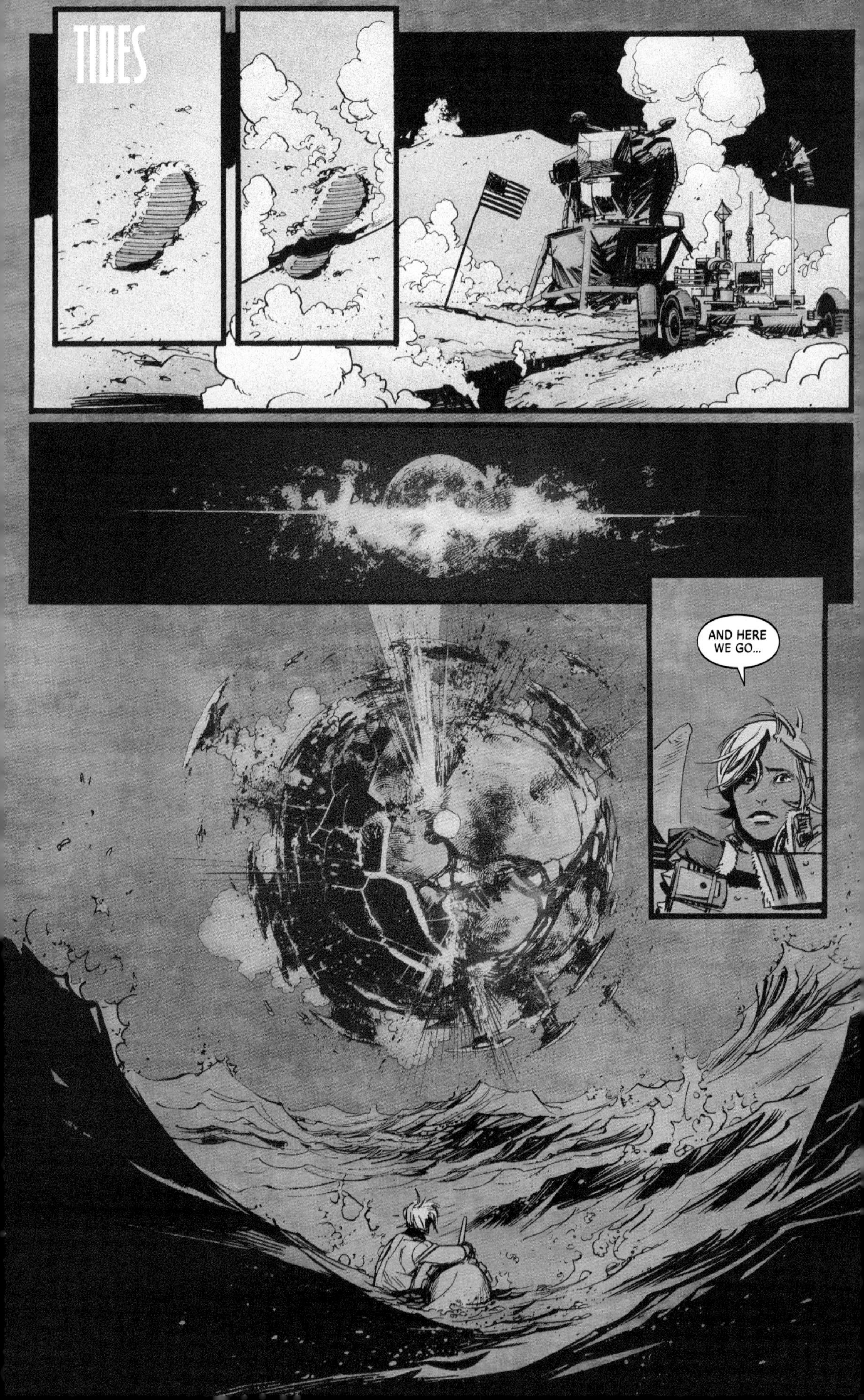
TIDES
AND HERE WE GO...

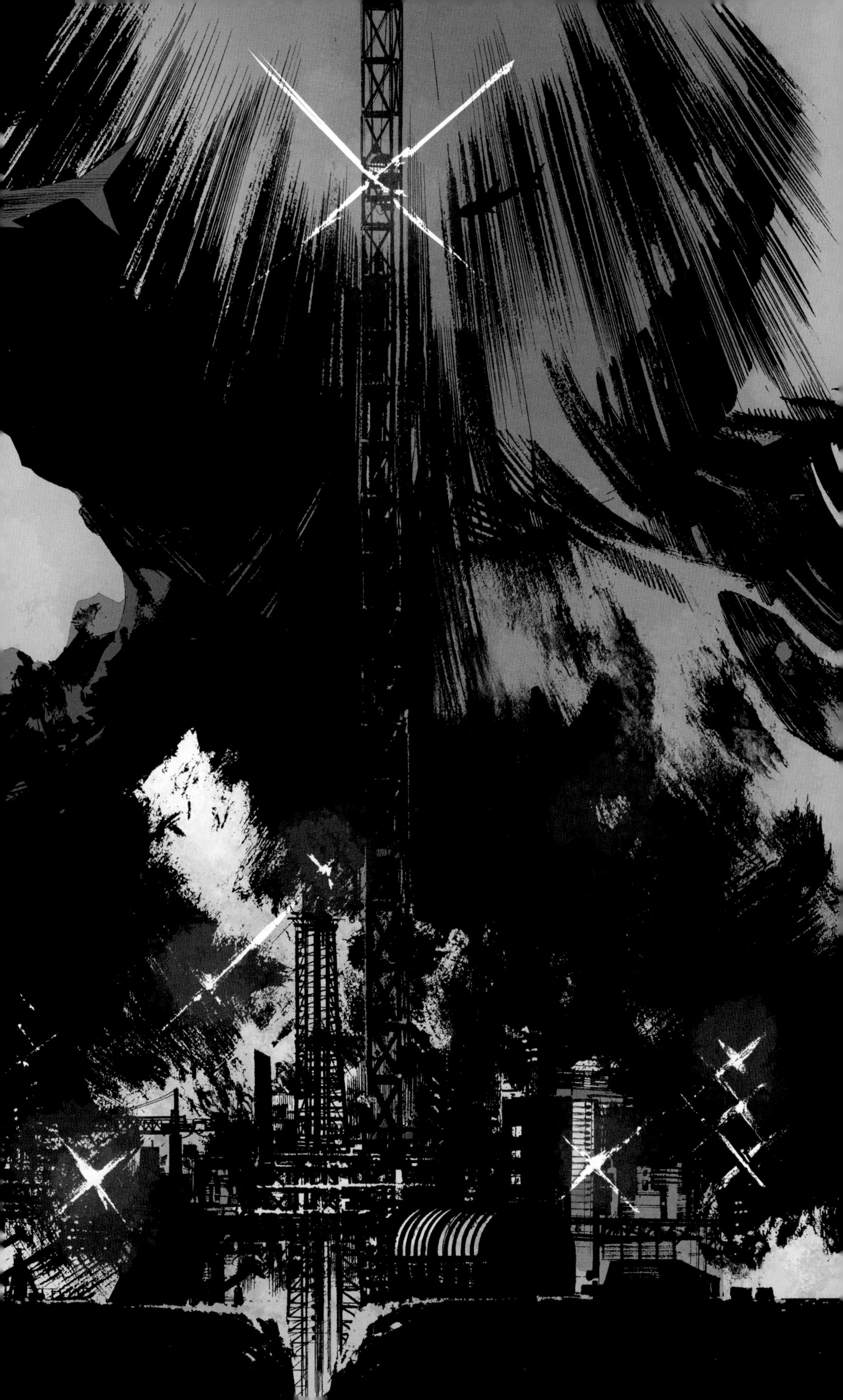

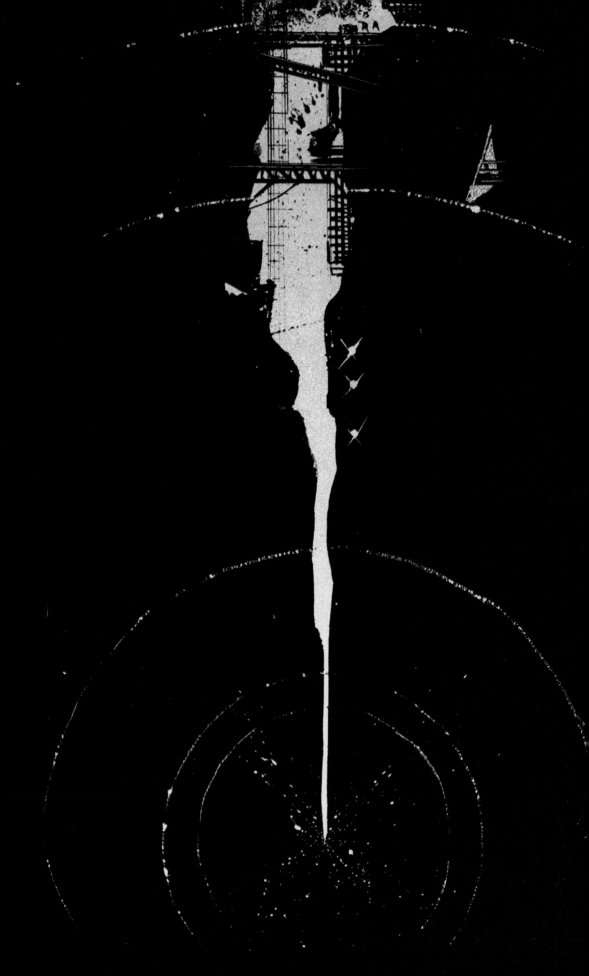

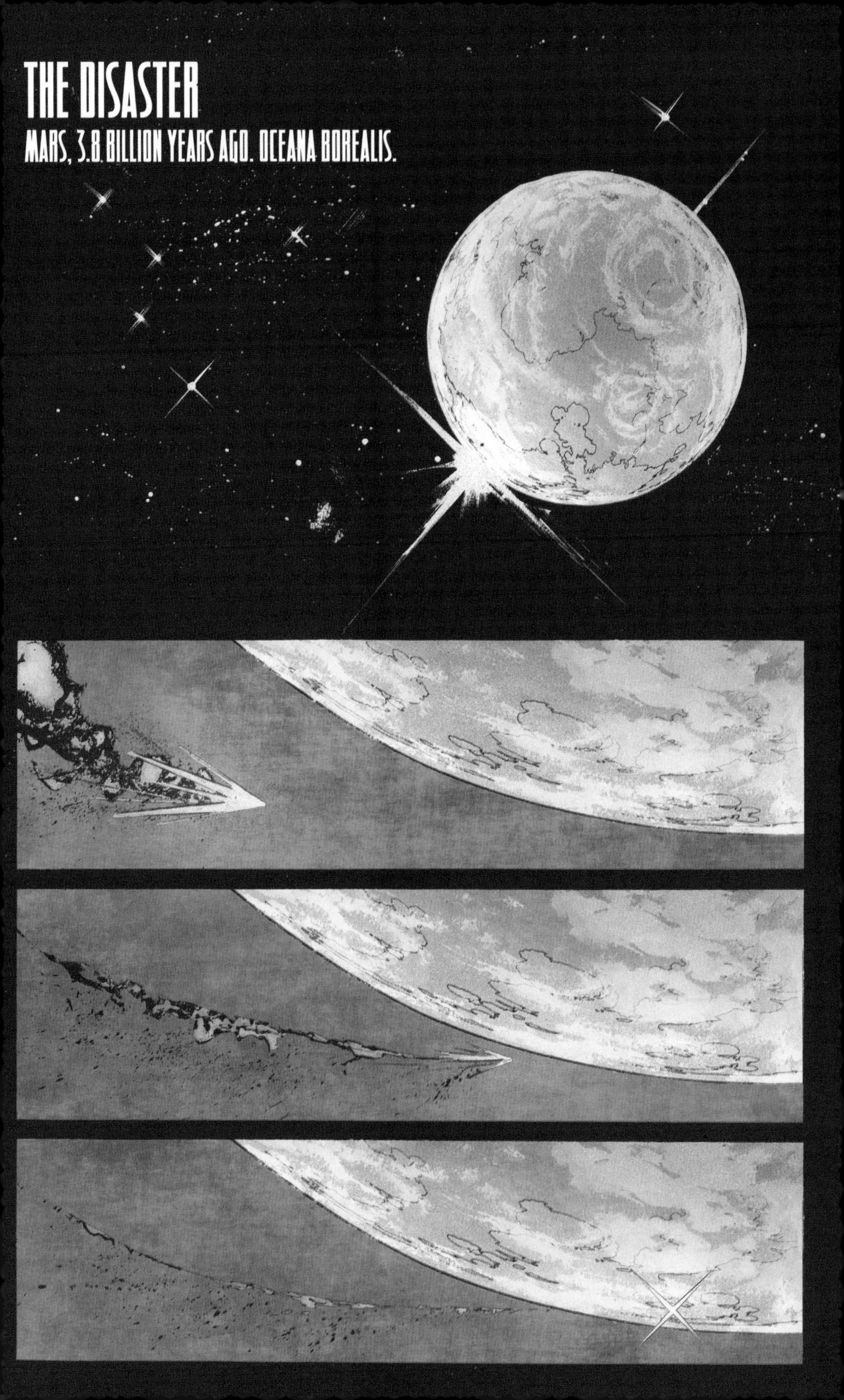
THE DISASTER
MARS, 3.8 BILLION YEARS AGO. OCEANA BOREALIS.

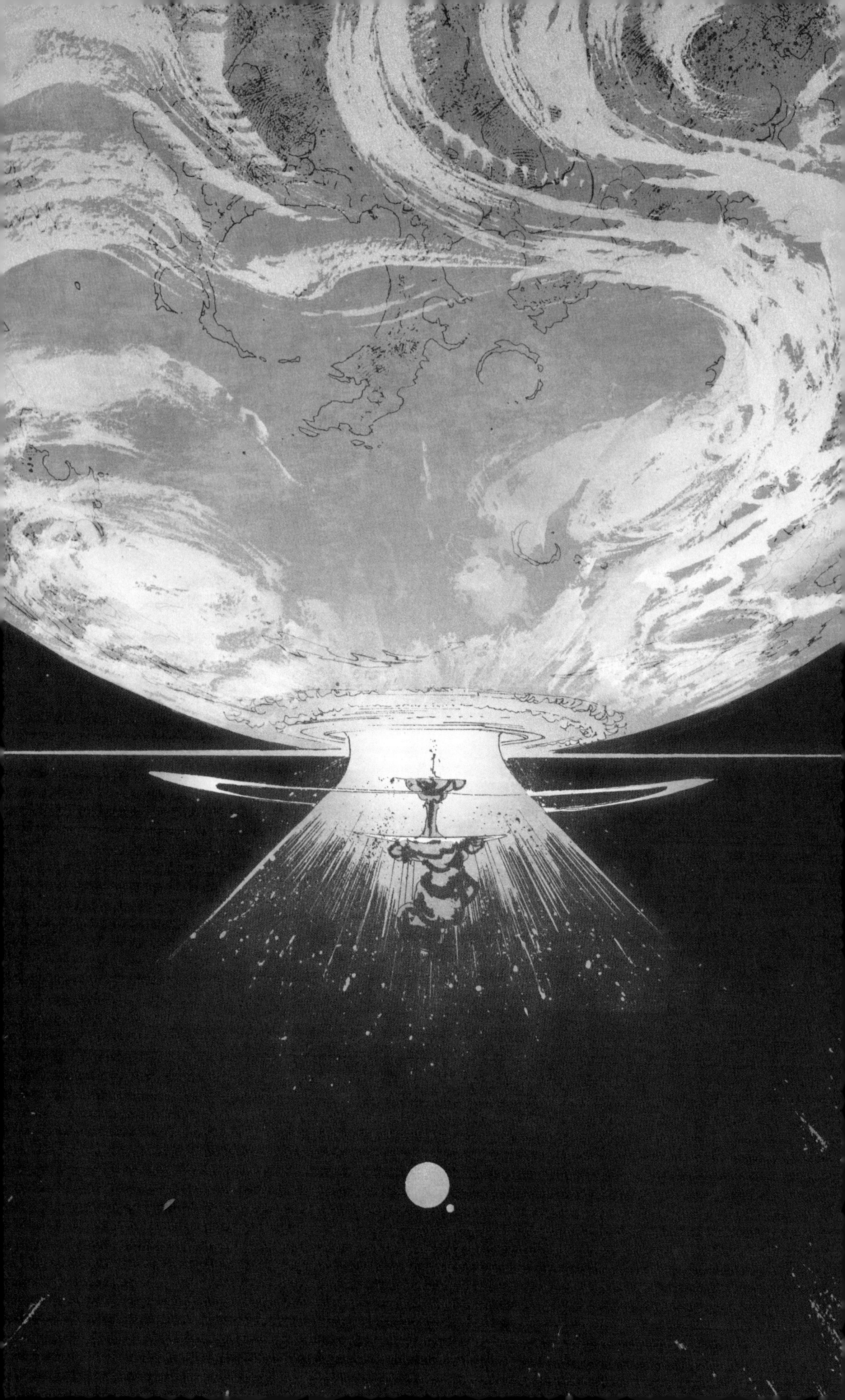

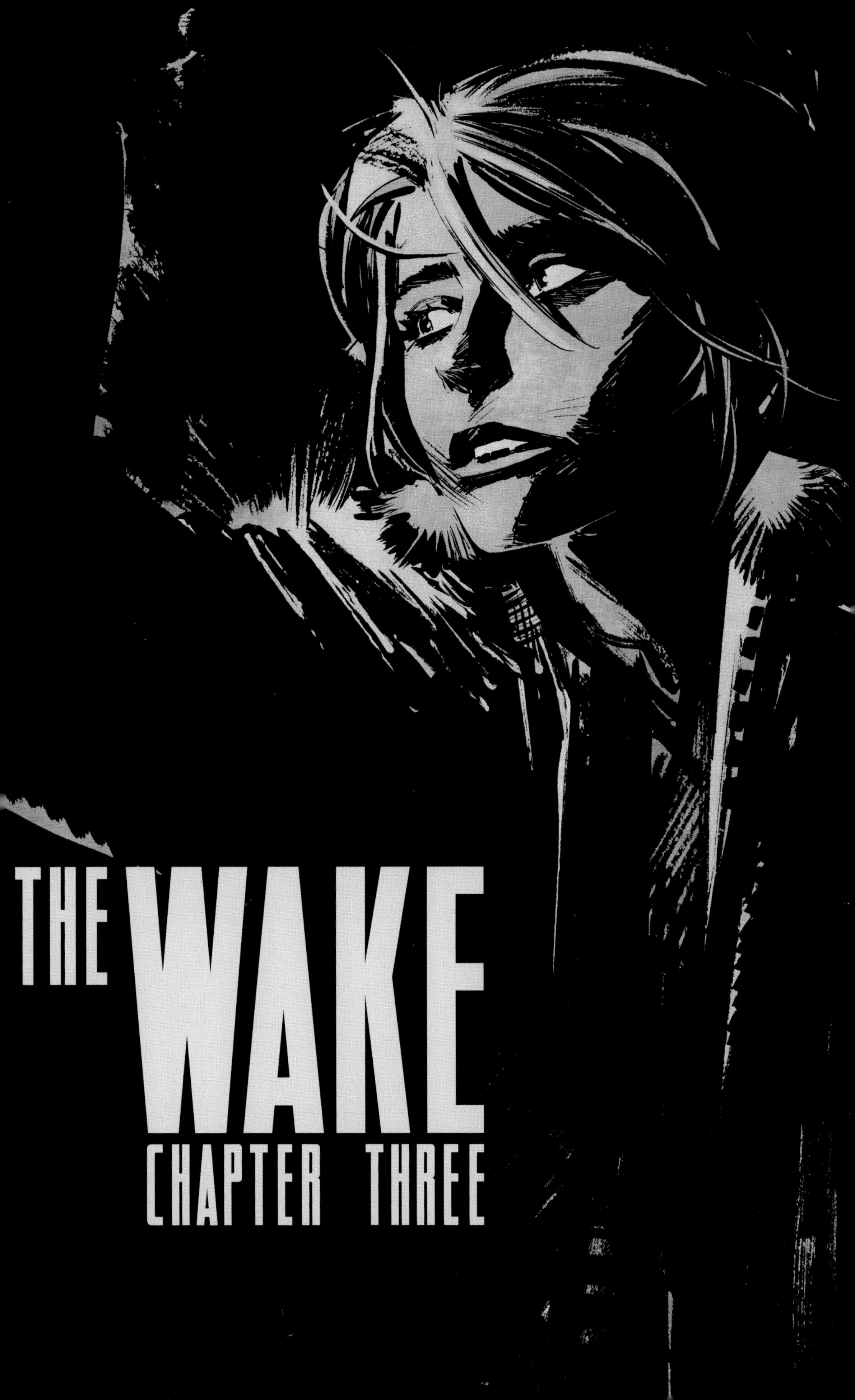
THE WAKE
CHAPTER THREE

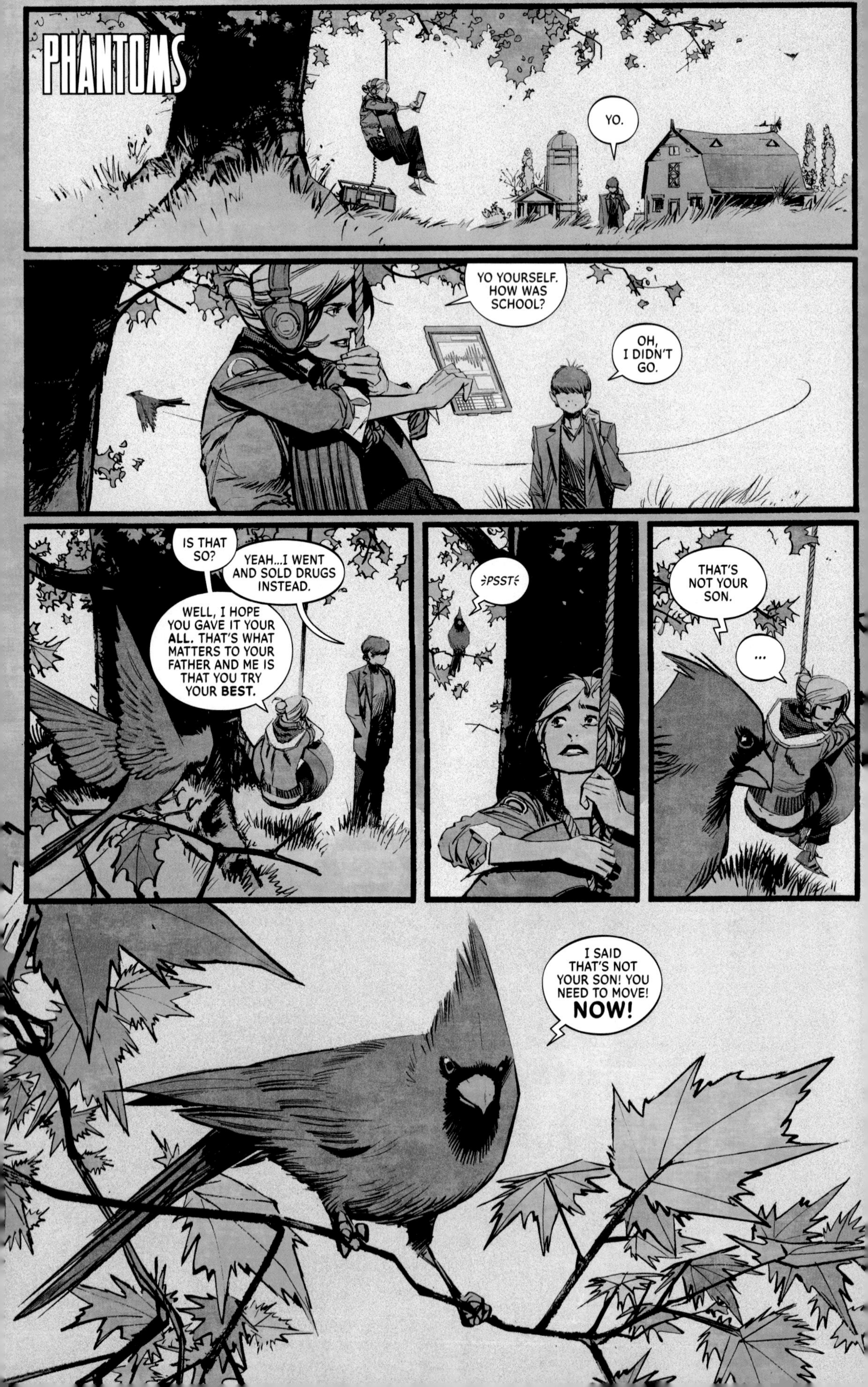
PHANTOMS
YO.
YO YOURSELF. HOW WAS SCHOOL?
OH, I DIDN'T GO.
IS THAT SO?
YEAH...I WENT AND SOLD DRUGS INSTEAD.
WELL, I HOPE YOU GAVE IT YOUR ALL. THAT'S WHAT MATTERS TO YOUR FATHER AND ME IS THAT YOU TRY YOUR BEST.
PSST
THAT'S NOT YOUR SON.
...
I SAID THAT'S NOT YOUR SON! YOU NEED TO MOVE! NOW!

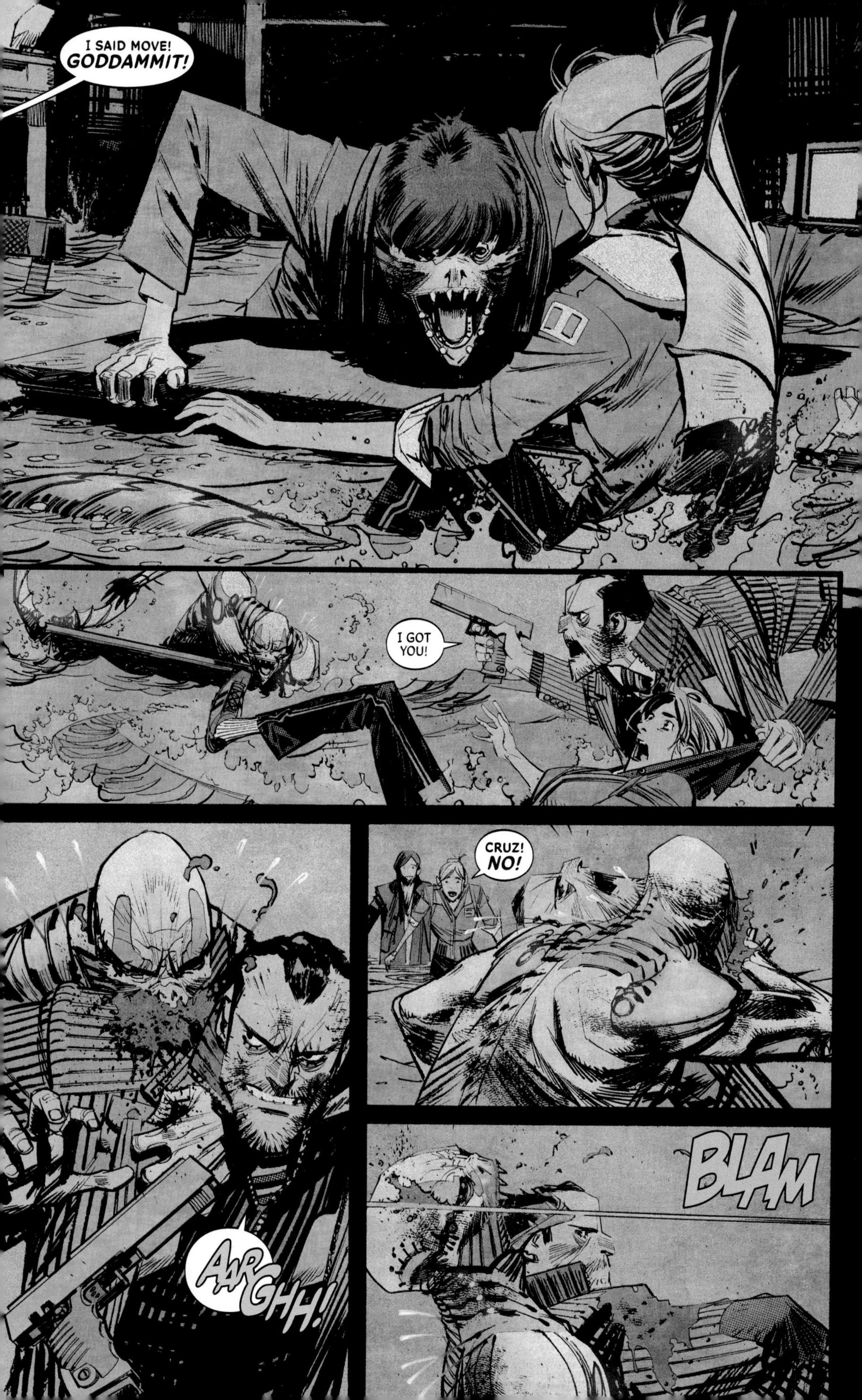
I SAID MOVE! GODDAMMIT!
I GOT YOU!
AARGHH!
CRUZ! NO!
BLAM

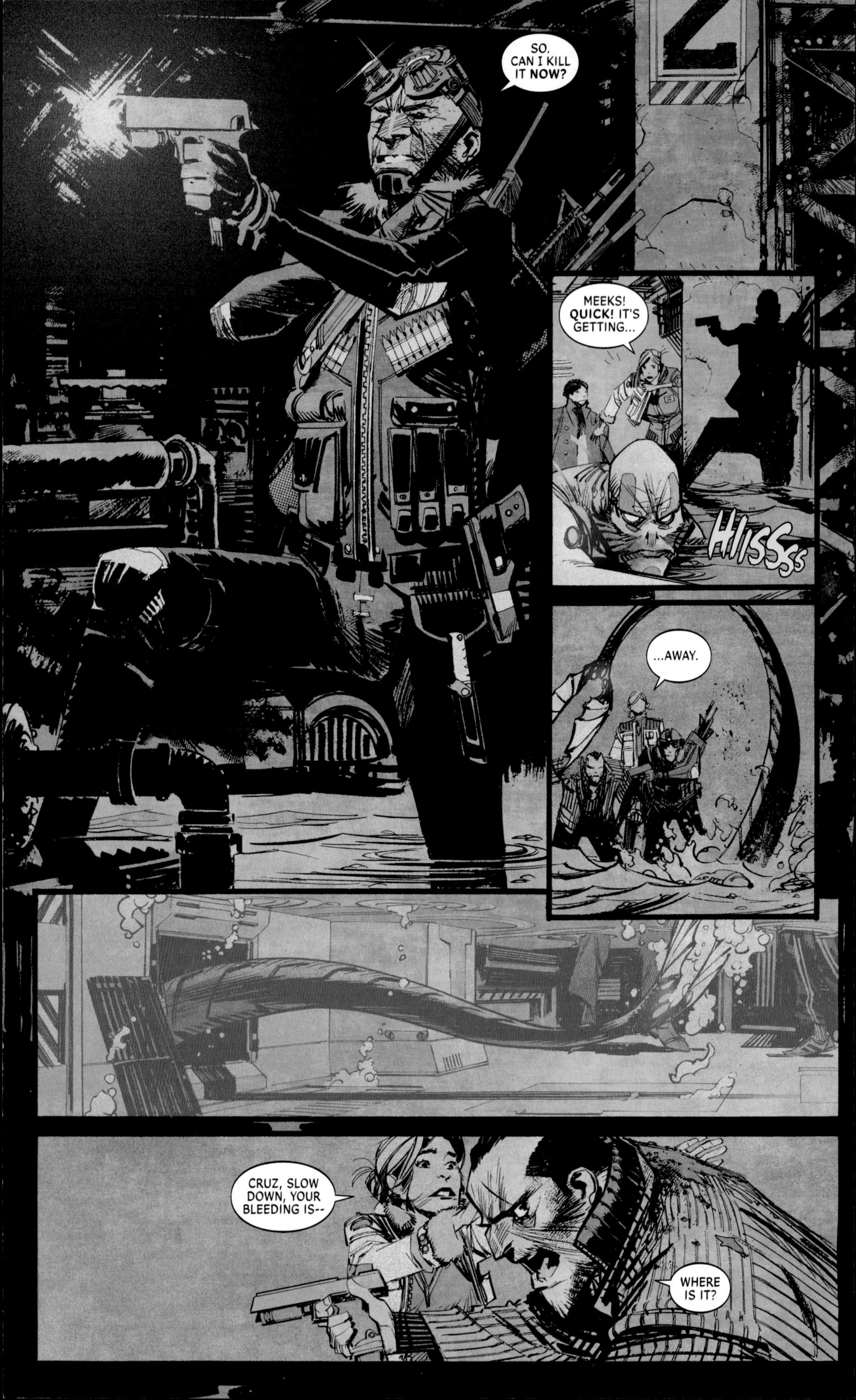
SO. CAN I KILL IT NOW?
MEEKS! QUICK! IT'S GETTING...
HIISSss
...AWAY.
CRUZ, SLOW DOWN, YOUR BLEEDING IS--
WHERE IS IT?

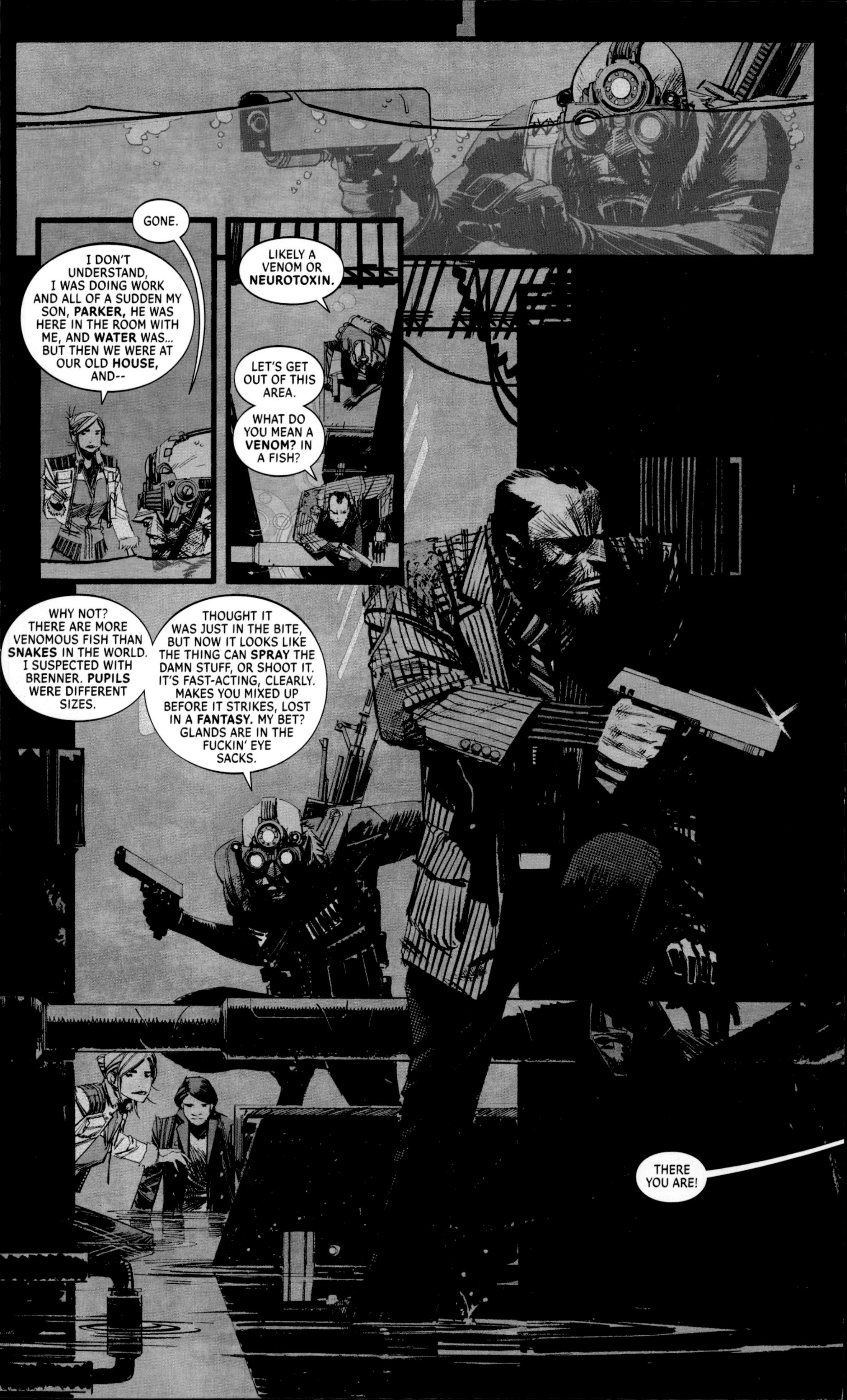
GONE.
I DON'T UNDERSTAND, I WAS DOING WORK AND ALL OF A SUDDEN MY SON, PARKER, HE WAS HERE IN THE ROOM WITH ME, AND WATER WAS... BUT THEN WE WERE AT OUR OLD HOUSE, AND--
LIKELY A VENOM OR NEUROTOXIN.
LET'S GET OUT OF THIS AREA.
WHAT DO YOU MEAN A VENOM? IN A FISH?
WHY NOT? THERE ARE MORE VENOMOUS FISH THAN SNAKES IN THE WORLD. I SUSPECTED WITH BRENNER. PUPILS WERE DIFFERENT SIZES.
THOUGHT IT WAS JUST IN THE BITE, BUT NOW IT LOOKS LIKE THE THING CAN SPRAY THE DAMN STUFF, OR SHOOT IT. IT'S FAST-ACTING, CLEARLY. MAKES YOU MIXED UP BEFORE IT STRIKES, LOST IN A FANTASY. MY BET? GLANDS ARE IN THE FUCKIN' EYE SACKS.
THERE YOU ARE!

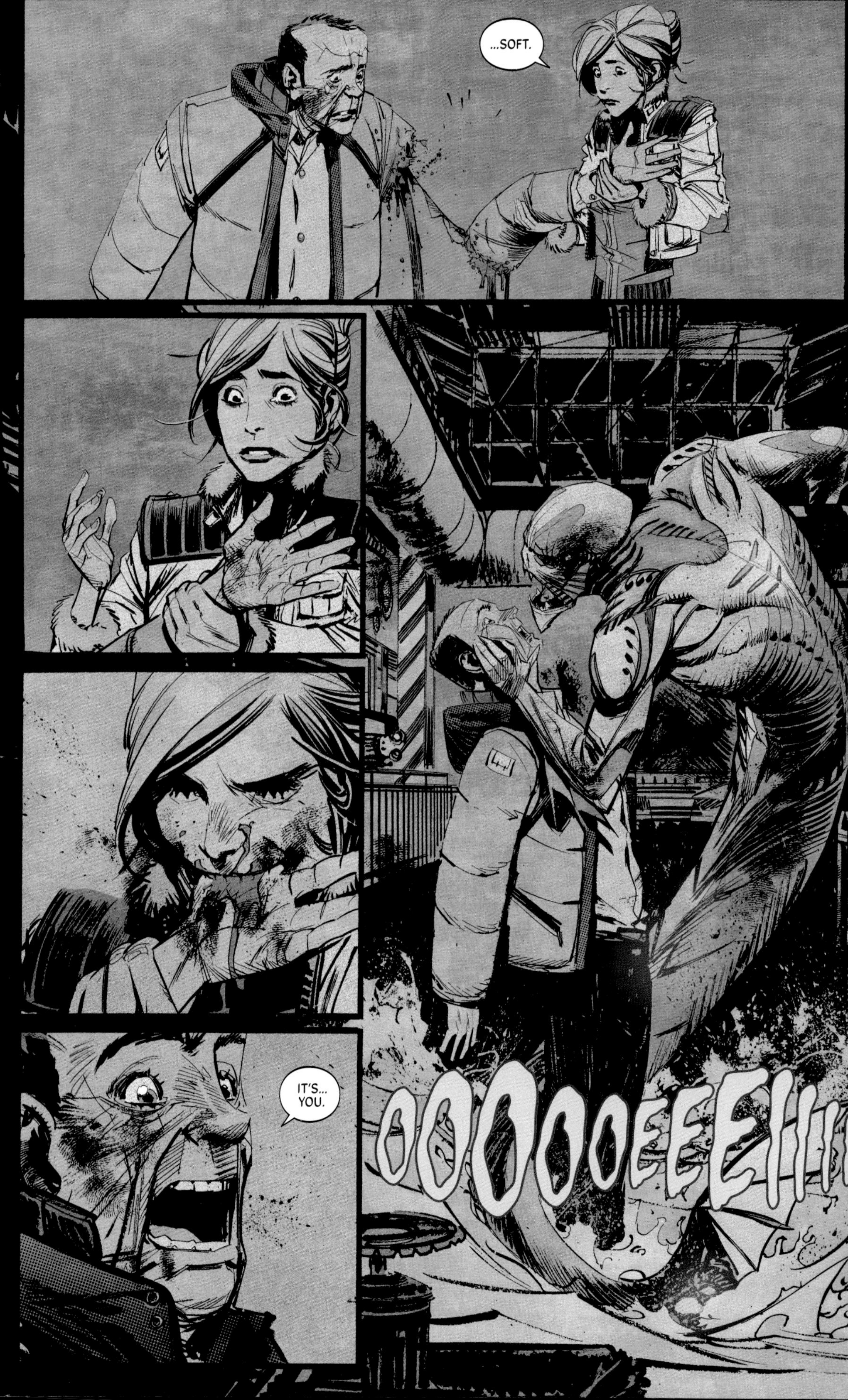

...SOFT.
IT'S... YOU.
OOOOOEEEIIII

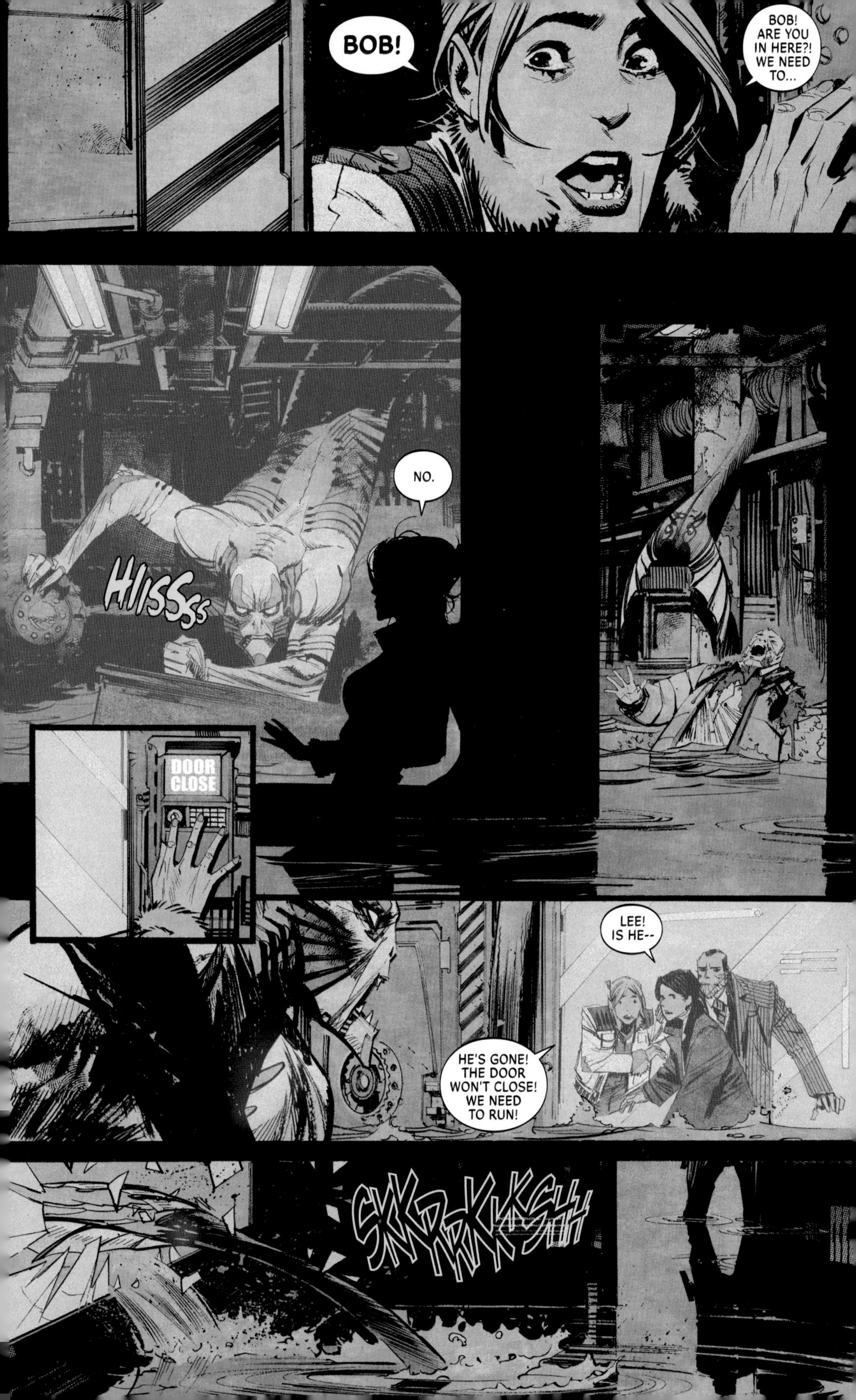
BOB!
BOB! ARE YOU IN HERE?! WE NEED TO...
NO.
HIISSsss
DOOR CLOSE
LEE! IS HE--
HE'S GONE! THE DOOR WON'T CLOSE! WE NEED TO RUN!
SKKDRRKKKSHH

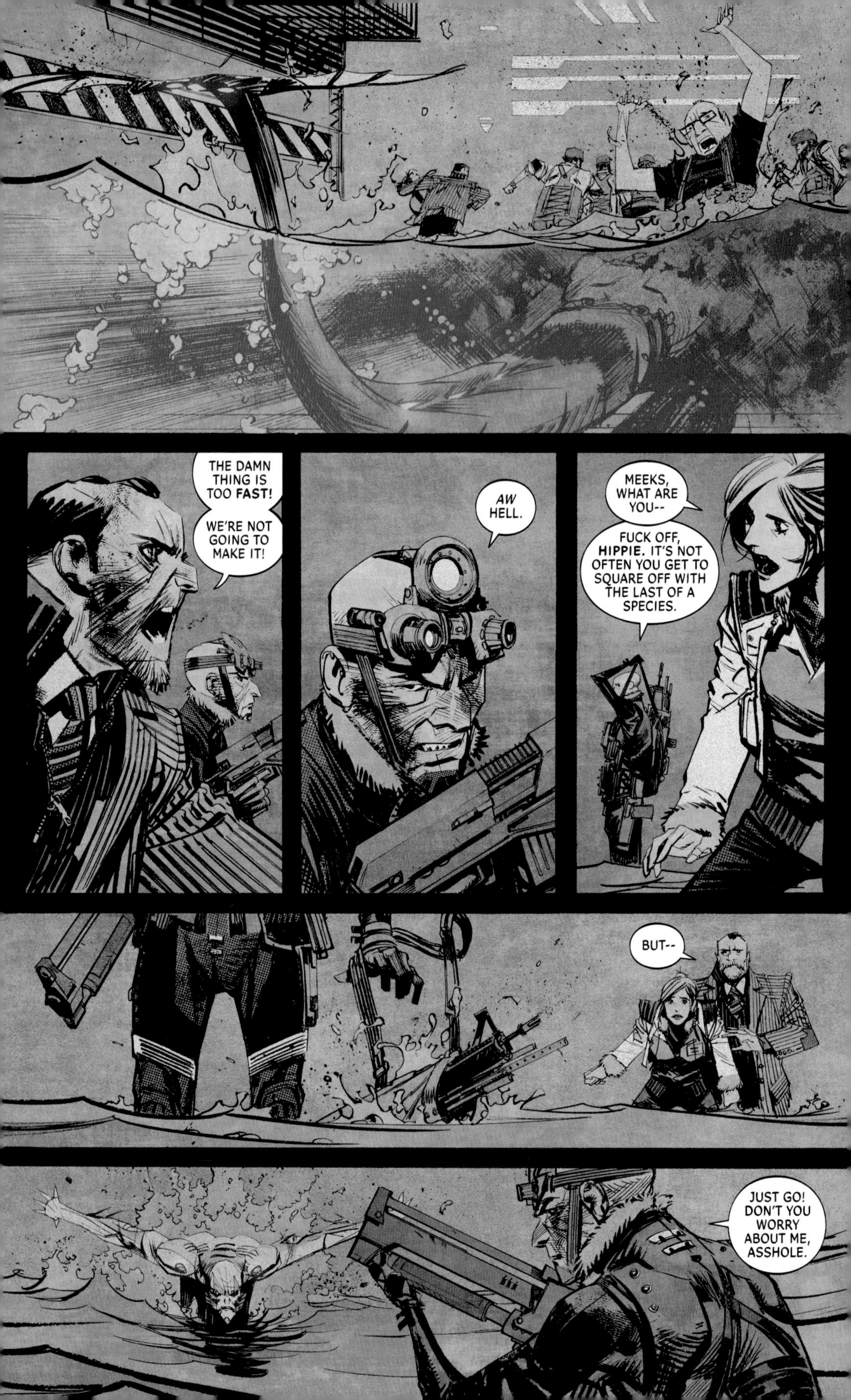
THE DAMN THING IS TOO FAST!
WE'RE NOT GOING TO MAKE IT!
AW HELL.
MEEKS, WHAT ARE YOU--
FUCK OFF, HIPPIE. IT'S NOT OFTEN YOU GET TO SQUARE OFF WITH THE LAST OF A SPECIES.
BUT--
JUST GO! DON'T YOU WORRY ABOUT ME, ASSHOLE.

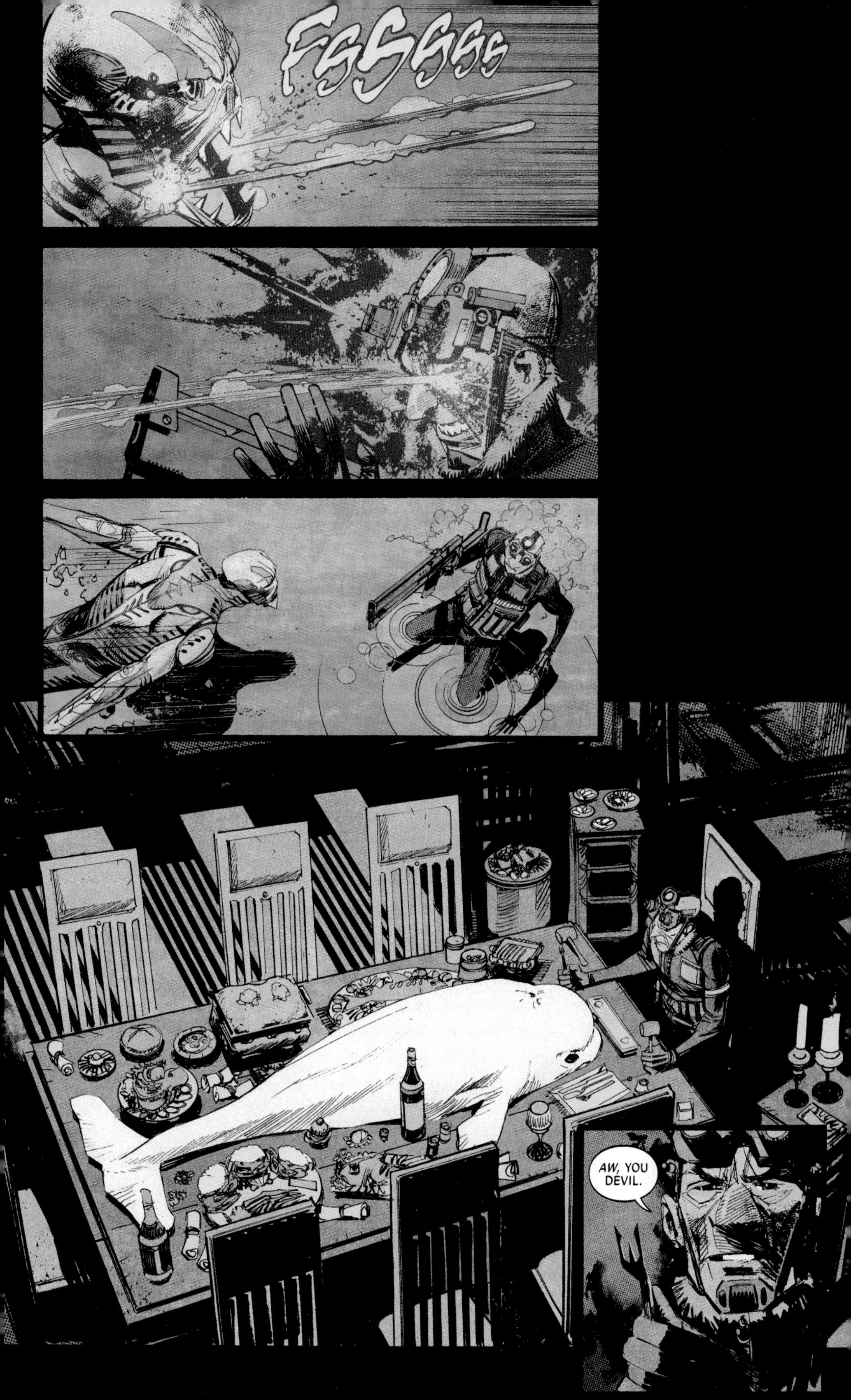
FSSSSS
AW, YOU DEVIL.

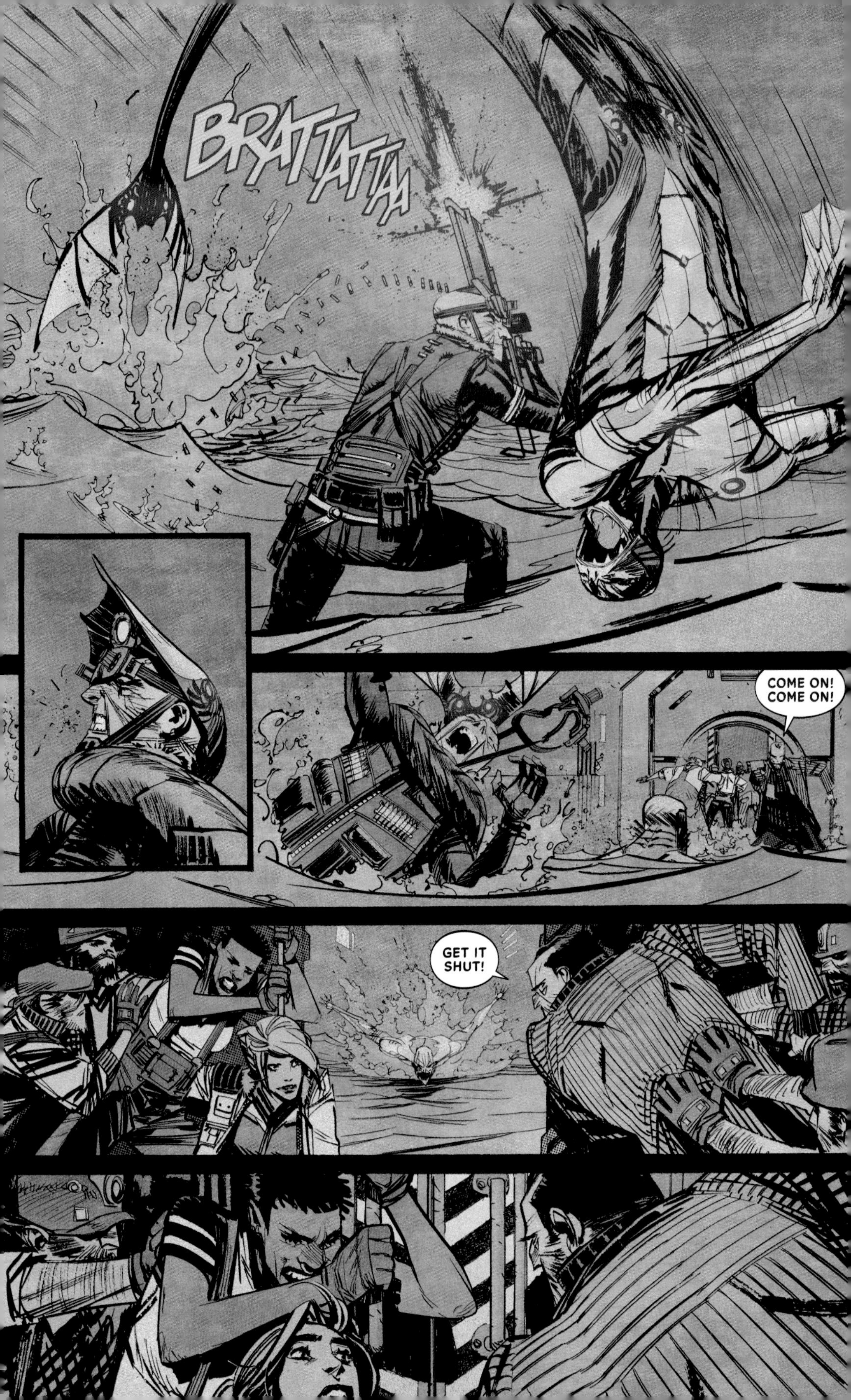
BRATTATTAA
COME ON! COME ON!
GET IT SHUT!

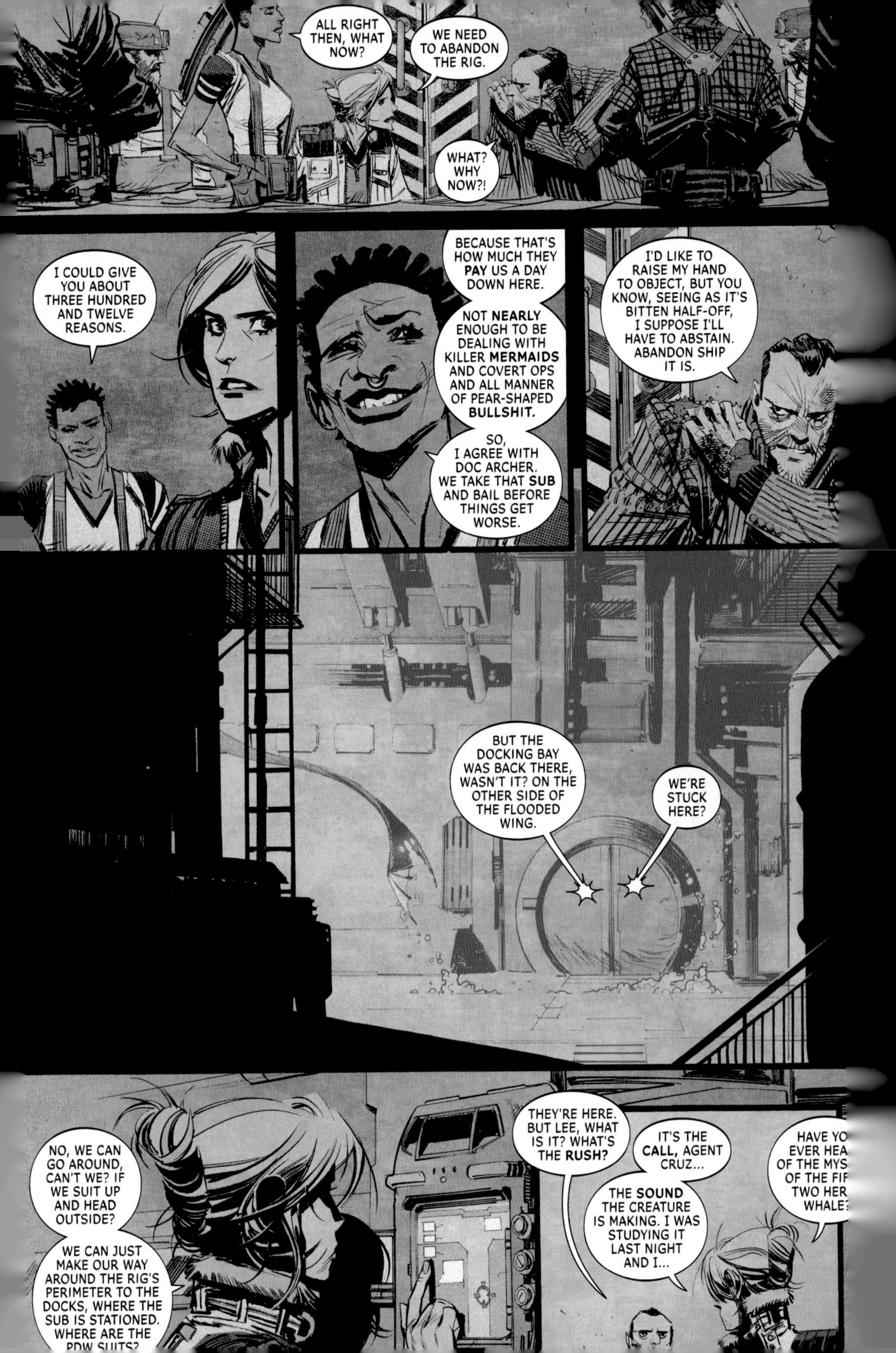
ALL RIGHT THEN, WHAT NOW?
WE NEED TO ABANDON THE RIG.
WHAT? WHY NOW?!
I COULD GIVE YOU ABOUT THREE HUNDRED AND TWELVE REASONS.
BECAUSE THAT'S HOW MUCH THEY PAY US A DAY DOWN HERE.
NOT NEARLY ENOUGH TO BE DEALING WITH KILLER MERMAIDS AND COVERT OPS AND ALL MANNER OF PEAR-SHAPED BULLSHIT.
SO, I AGREE WITH DOC ARCHER. WE TAKE THAT SUB AND BAIL BEFORE THINGS GET WORSE.
I'D LIKE TO RAISE MY HAND TO OBJECT, BUT YOU KNOW, SEEING AS IT'S BITTEN HALF-OFF, I SUPPOSE I'LL HAVE TO ABSTAIN. ABANDON SHIP IT IS.
BUT THE DOCKING BAY WAS BACK THERE, WASN'T IT? ON THE OTHER SIDE OF THE FLOODED WING.
WE'RE STUCK HERE?
NO, WE CAN GO AROUND, CAN'T WE? IF WE SUIT UP AND HEAD OUTSIDE?
WE CAN JUST MAKE OUR WAY AROUND THE RIG'S PERIMETER TO THE DOCKS, WHERE THE SUB IS STATIONED. WHERE ARE THE PDW SUITS?
THEY'RE HERE. BUT LEE, WHAT IS IT? WHAT'S THE RUSH?
IT'S THE CALL, AGENT CRUZ...
THE SOUND THE CREATURE IS MAKING. I WAS STUDYING IT LAST NIGHT AND I...

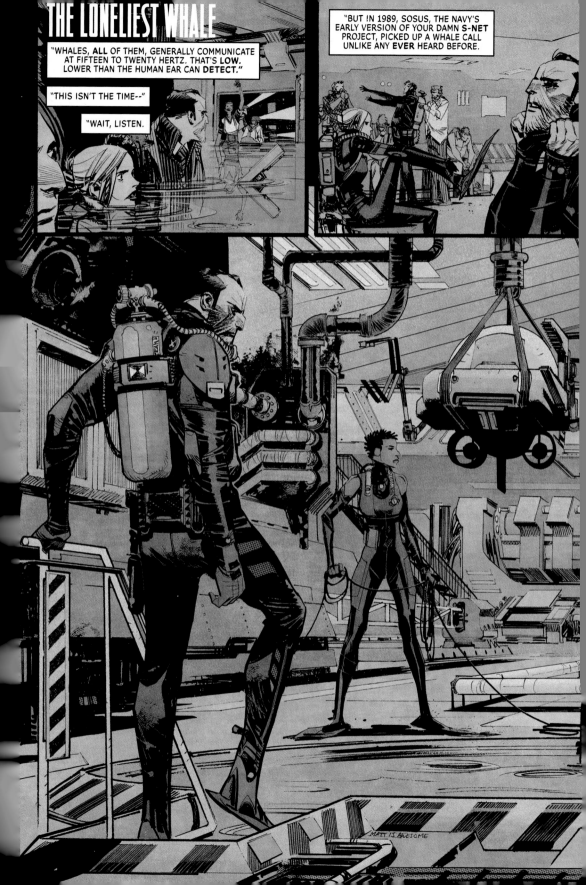

THE LONELIEST WHALE

"WHALES, **ALL** OF THEM, GENERALLY COMMUNICATE AT FIFTEEN TO TWENTY HERTZ. THAT'S **LOW.** LOWER THAN THE HUMAN EAR CAN **DETECT.**"

"THIS ISN'T THE TIME--"

"WAIT, LISTEN."

"BUT IN 1989, SOSUS, THE NAVY'S EARLY VERSION OF YOUR DAMN **S-NET** PROJECT, PICKED UP A WHALE CALL UNLIKE ANY **EVER** HEARD BEFORE."

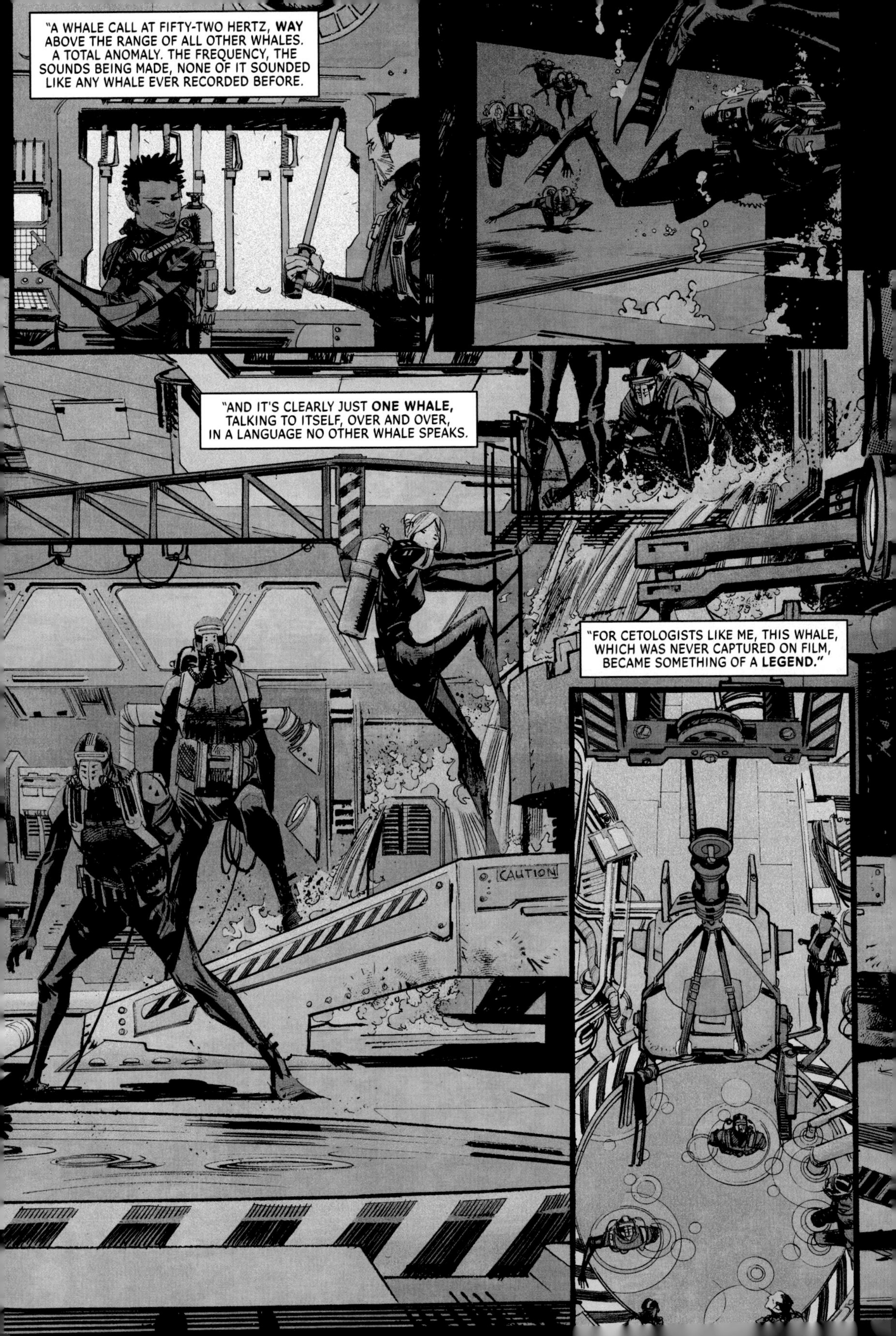
"A WHALE CALL AT FIFTY-TWO HERTZ, **WAY** ABOVE THE RANGE OF ALL OTHER WHALES. A TOTAL ANOMALY. THE FREQUENCY, THE SOUNDS BEING MADE, NONE OF IT SOUNDED LIKE ANY WHALE EVER RECORDED BEFORE.
"AND IT'S CLEARLY JUST **ONE WHALE,** TALKING TO ITSELF, OVER AND OVER, IN A LANGUAGE NO OTHER WHALE SPEAKS.
CAUTION
"FOR CETOLOGISTS LIKE ME, THIS WHALE, WHICH WAS NEVER CAPTURED ON FILM, BECAME SOMETHING OF A **LEGEND.**"

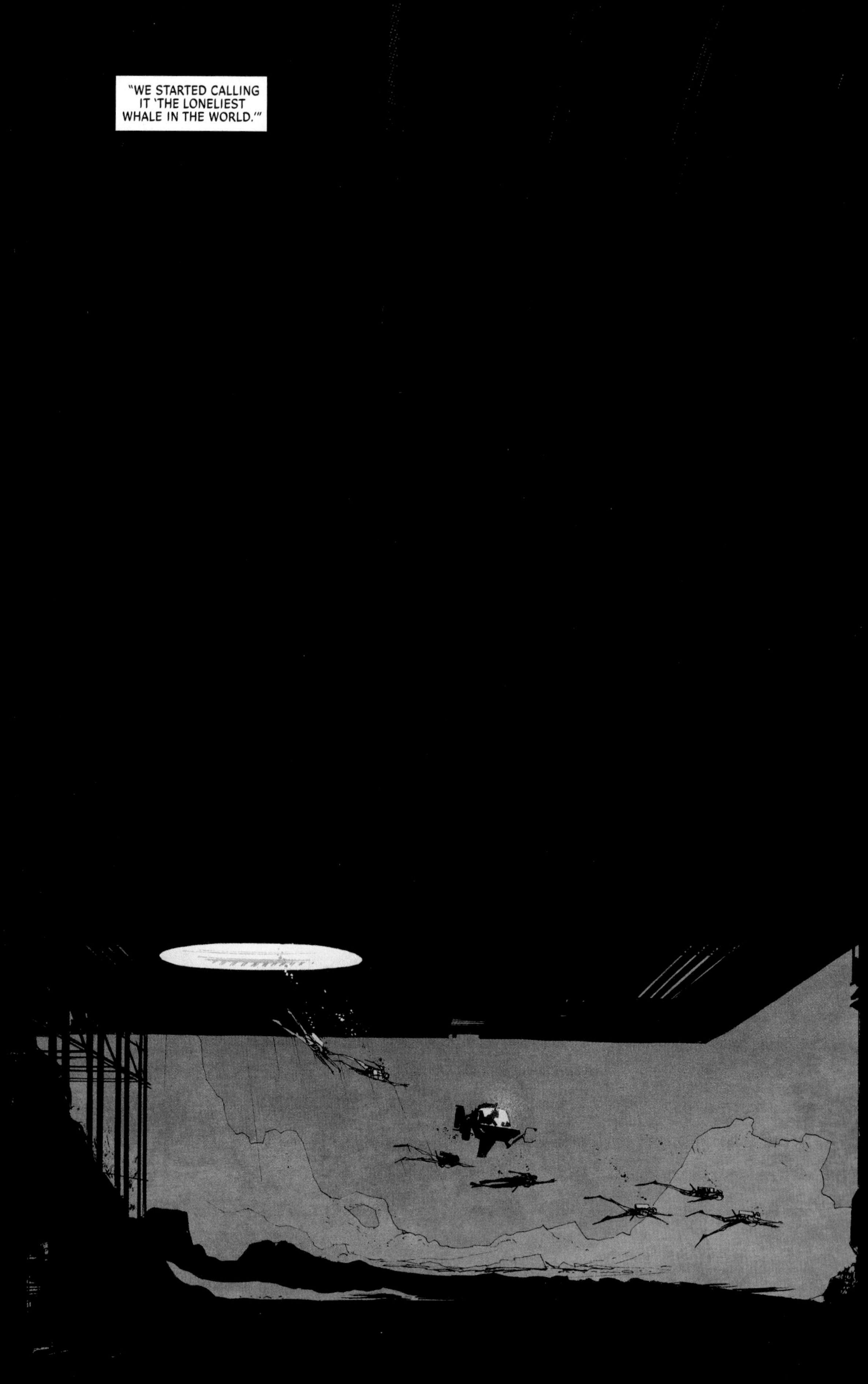
"WE STARTED CALLING IT 'THE LONELIEST WHALE IN THE WORLD.'"

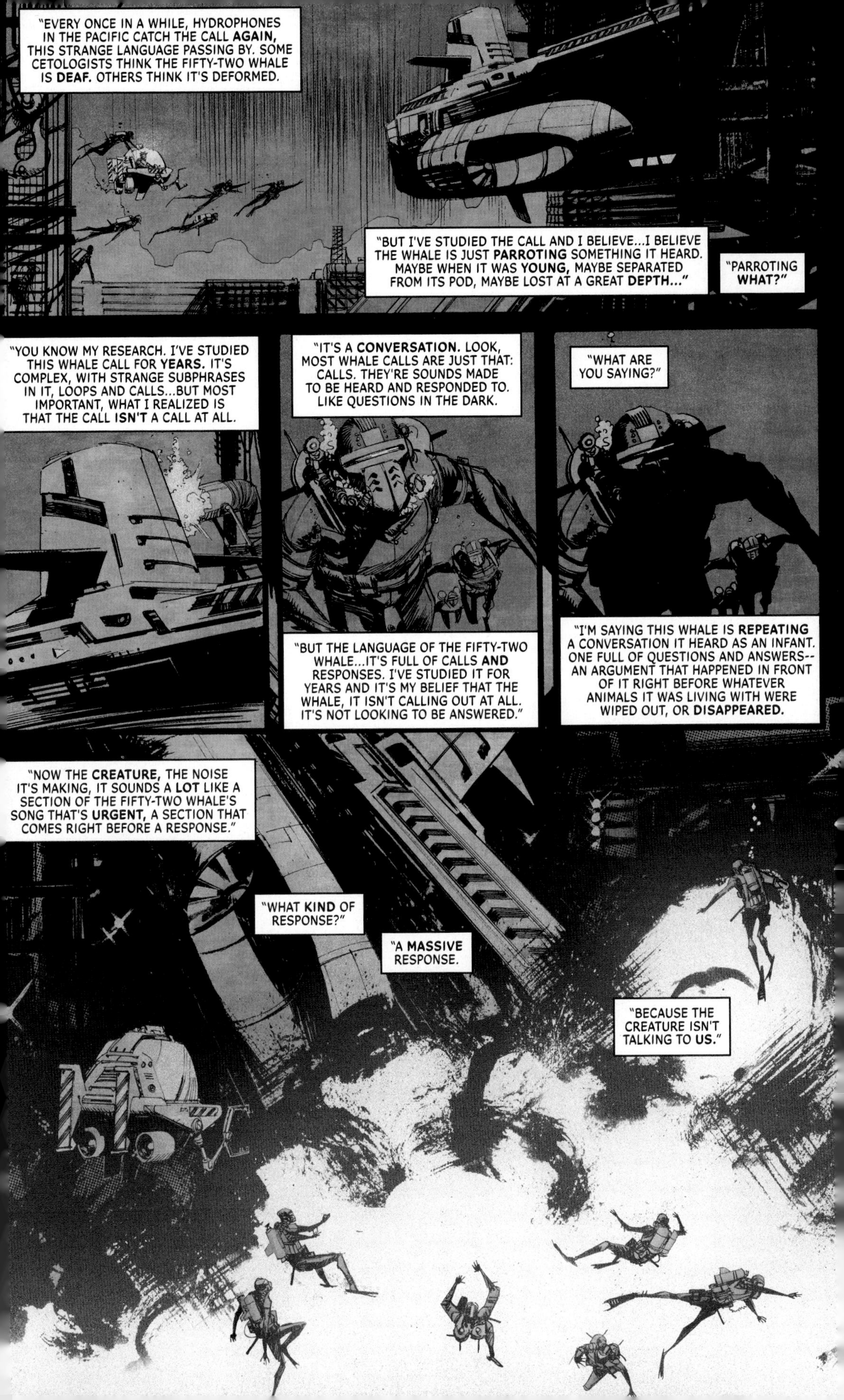
"EVERY ONCE IN A WHILE, HYDROPHONES IN THE PACIFIC CATCH THE CALL AGAIN, THIS STRANGE LANGUAGE PASSING BY. SOME CETOLOGISTS THINK THE FIFTY-TWO WHALE IS DEAF. OTHERS THINK IT'S DEFORMED.
"BUT I'VE STUDIED THE CALL AND I BELIEVE...I BELIEVE THE WHALE IS JUST PARROTING SOMETHING IT HEARD. MAYBE WHEN IT WAS YOUNG, MAYBE SEPARATED FROM ITS POD, MAYBE LOST AT A GREAT DEPTH..."
"PARROTING WHAT?"
"YOU KNOW MY RESEARCH. I'VE STUDIED THIS WHALE CALL FOR YEARS. IT'S COMPLEX, WITH STRANGE SUBPHRASES IN IT, LOOPS AND CALLS...BUT MOST IMPORTANT, WHAT I REALIZED IS THAT THE CALL ISN'T A CALL AT ALL.
"IT'S A CONVERSATION. LOOK, MOST WHALE CALLS ARE JUST THAT: CALLS. THEY'RE SOUNDS MADE TO BE HEARD AND RESPONDED TO. LIKE QUESTIONS IN THE DARK.
"BUT THE LANGUAGE OF THE FIFTY-TWO WHALE...IT'S FULL OF CALLS AND RESPONSES. I'VE STUDIED IT FOR YEARS AND IT'S MY BELIEF THAT THE WHALE, IT ISN'T CALLING OUT AT ALL. IT'S NOT LOOKING TO BE ANSWERED."
"WHAT ARE YOU SAYING?"
"I'M SAYING THIS WHALE IS REPEATING A CONVERSATION IT HEARD AS AN INFANT. ONE FULL OF QUESTIONS AND ANSWERS--AN ARGUMENT THAT HAPPENED IN FRONT OF IT RIGHT BEFORE WHATEVER ANIMALS IT WAS LIVING WITH WERE WIPED OUT, OR DISAPPEARED.
"NOW THE CREATURE, THE NOISE IT'S MAKING, IT SOUNDS A LOT LIKE A SECTION OF THE FIFTY-TWO WHALE'S SONG THAT'S URGENT, A SECTION THAT COMES RIGHT BEFORE A RESPONSE."
"WHAT KIND OF RESPONSE?"
"A MASSIVE RESPONSE.
"BECAUSE THE CREATURE ISN'T TALKING TO US."

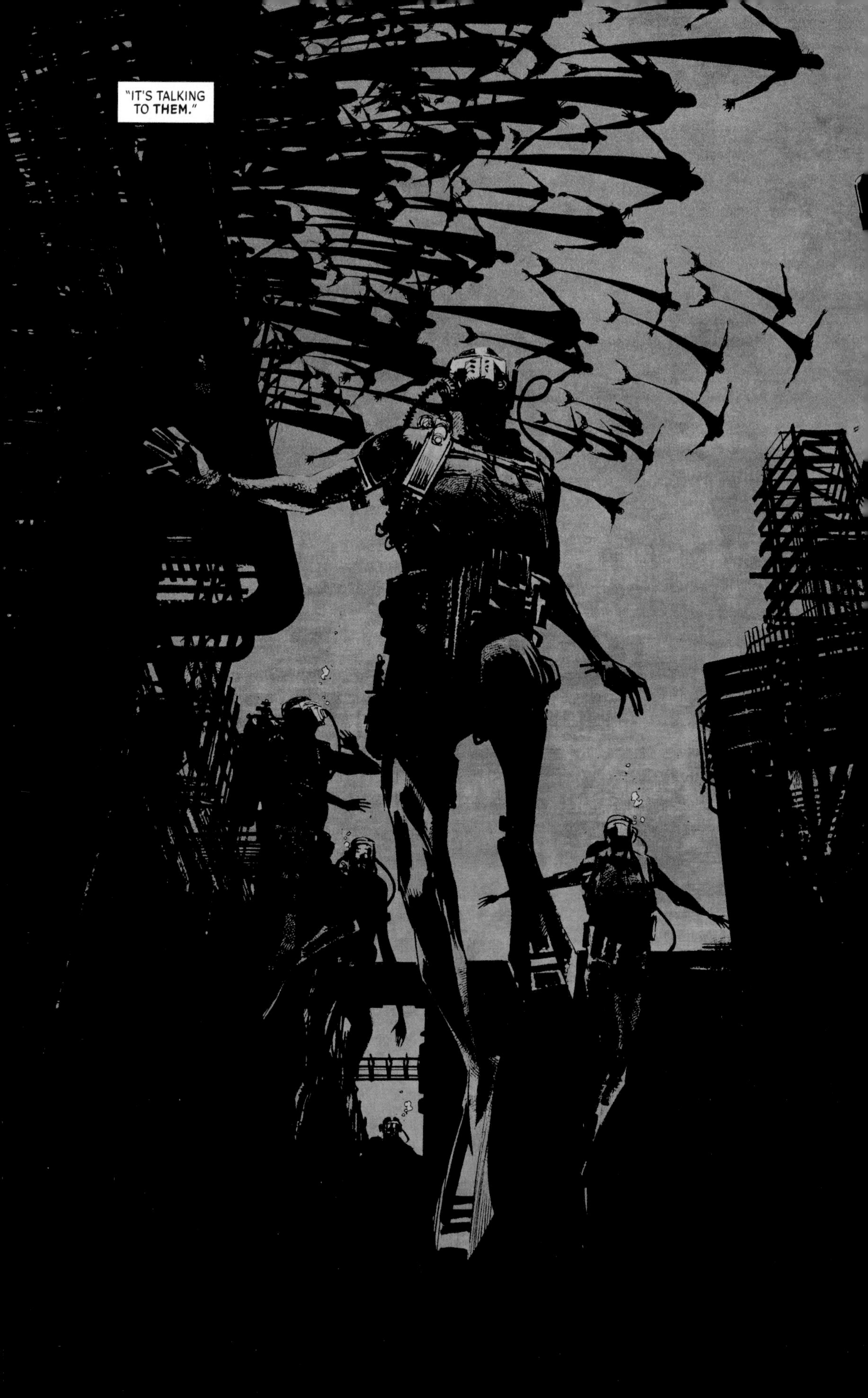
"IT'S TALKING TO THEM."

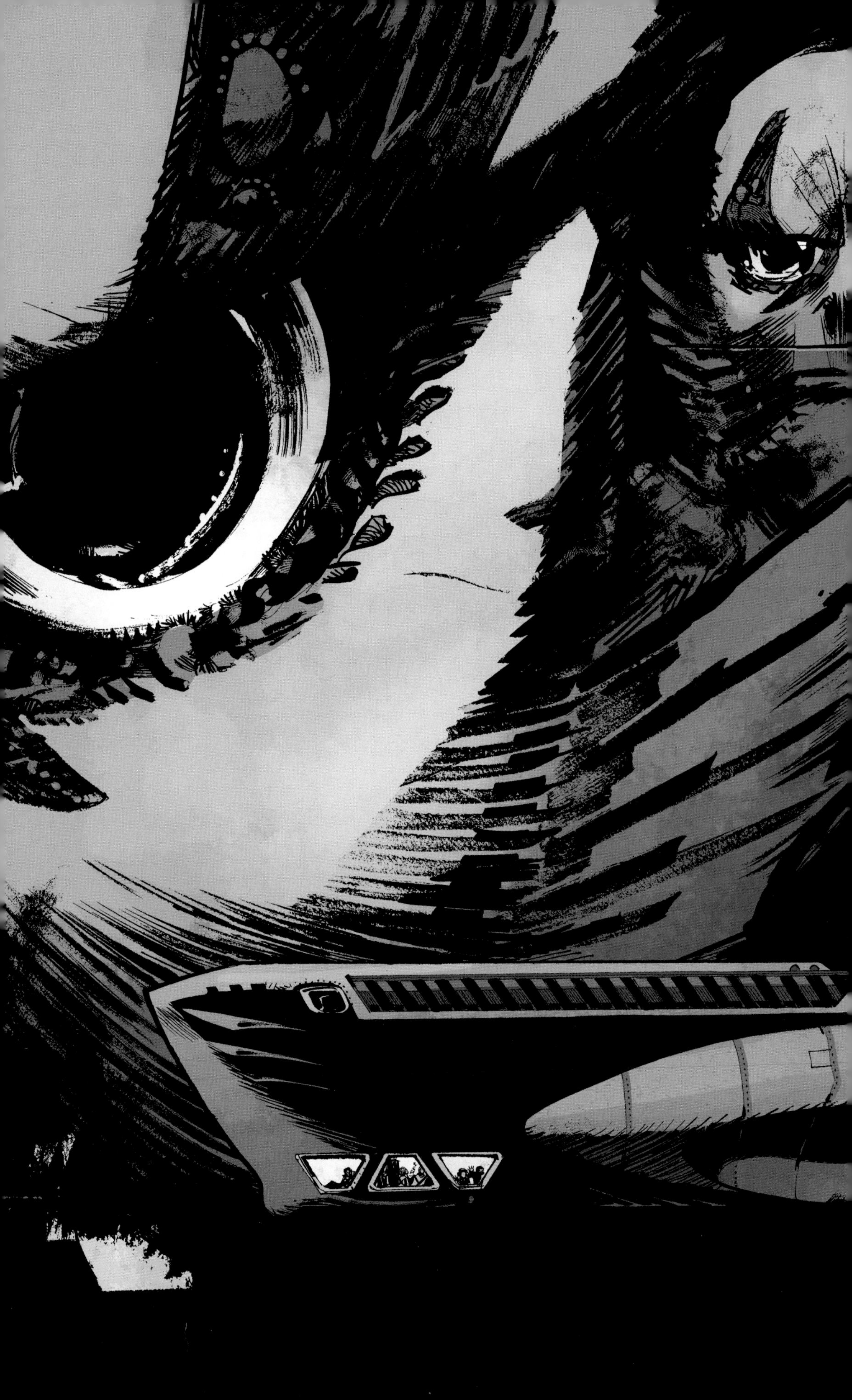

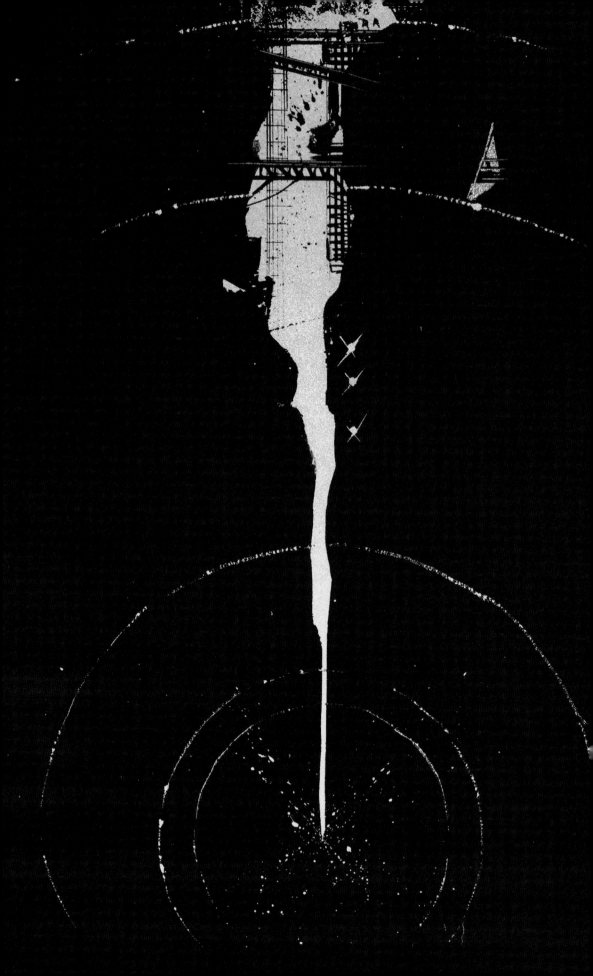

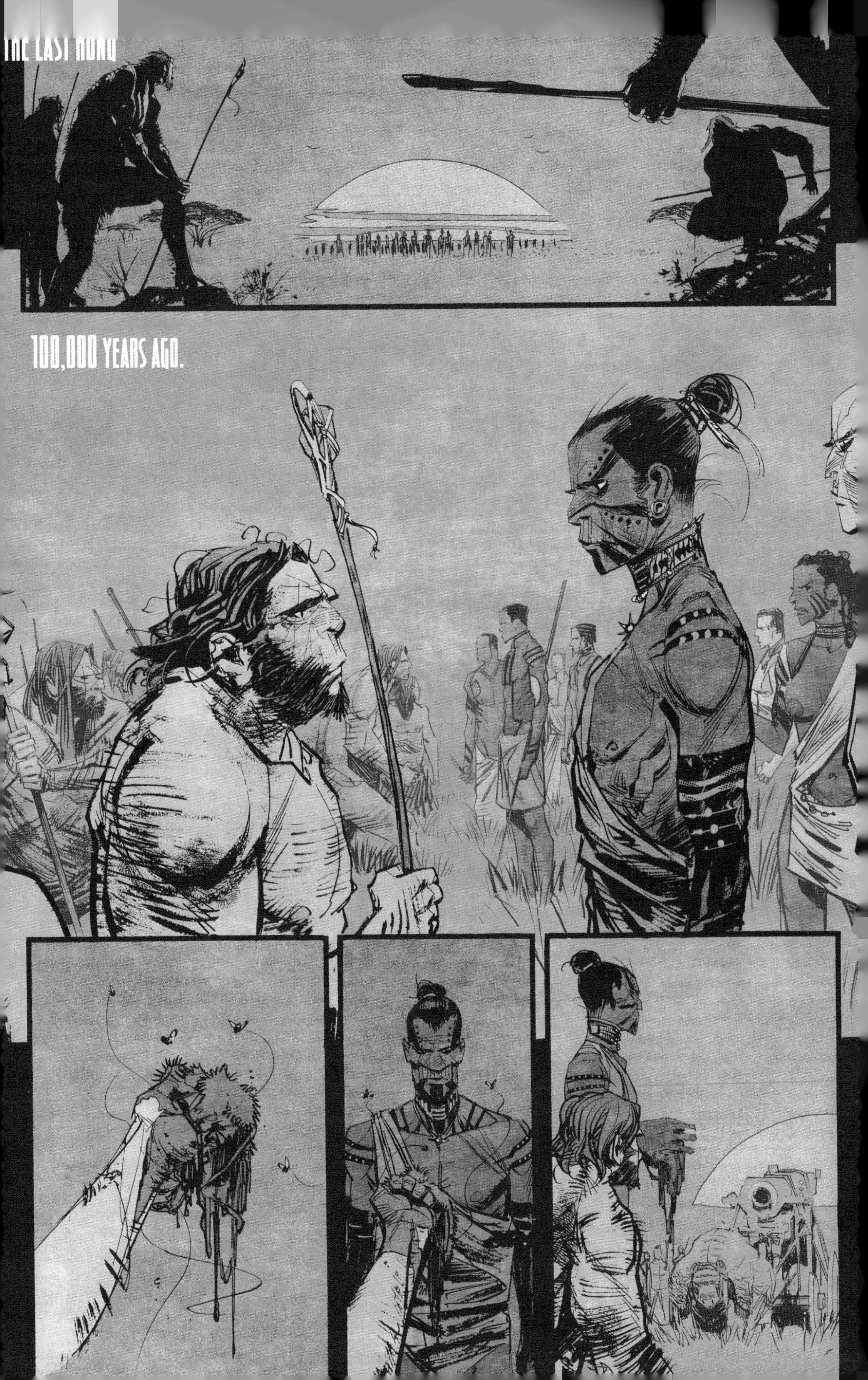
THE LAST RONIN
100,000 YEARS AGO.

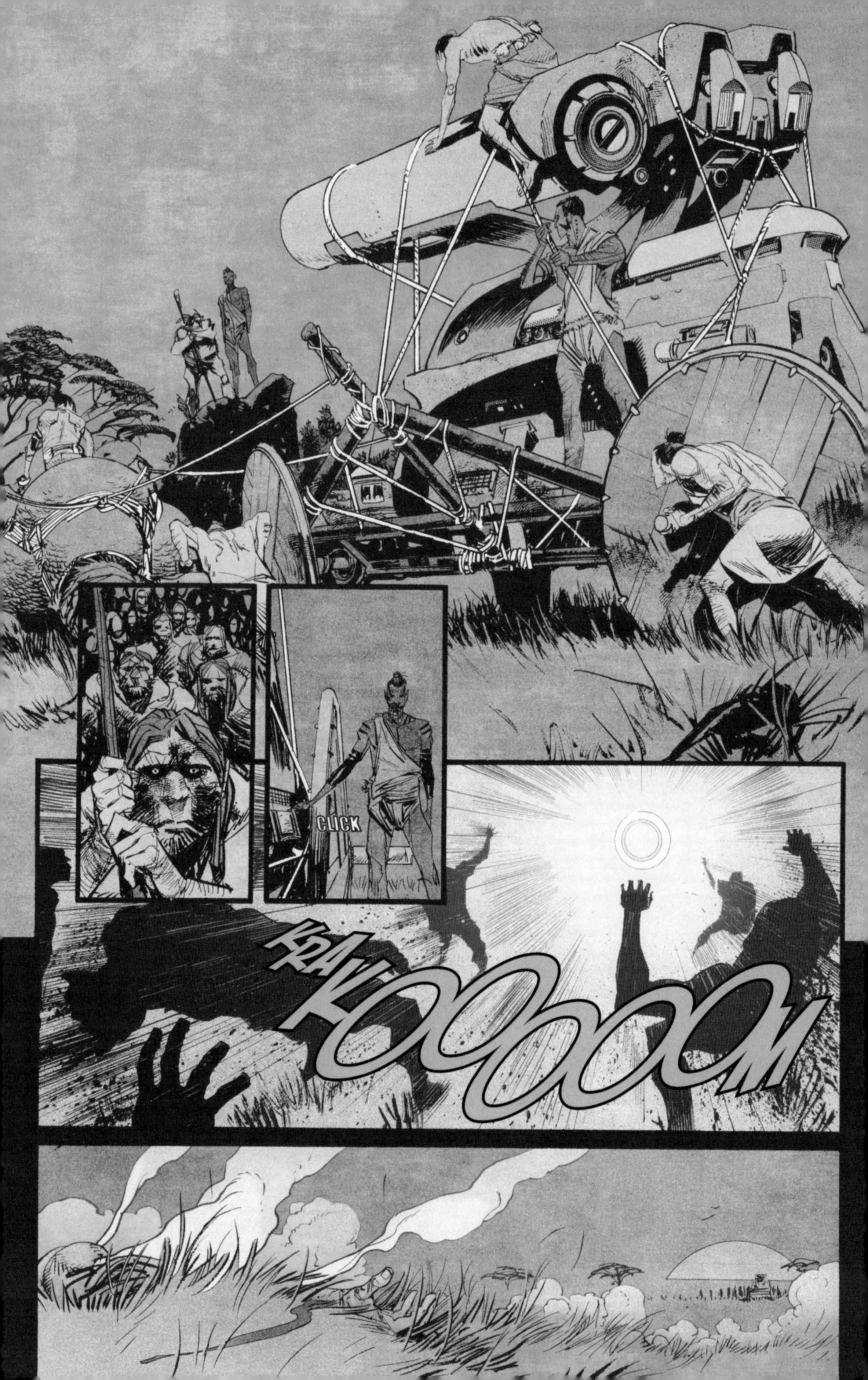
CLICK
KRA-KOOOOOM

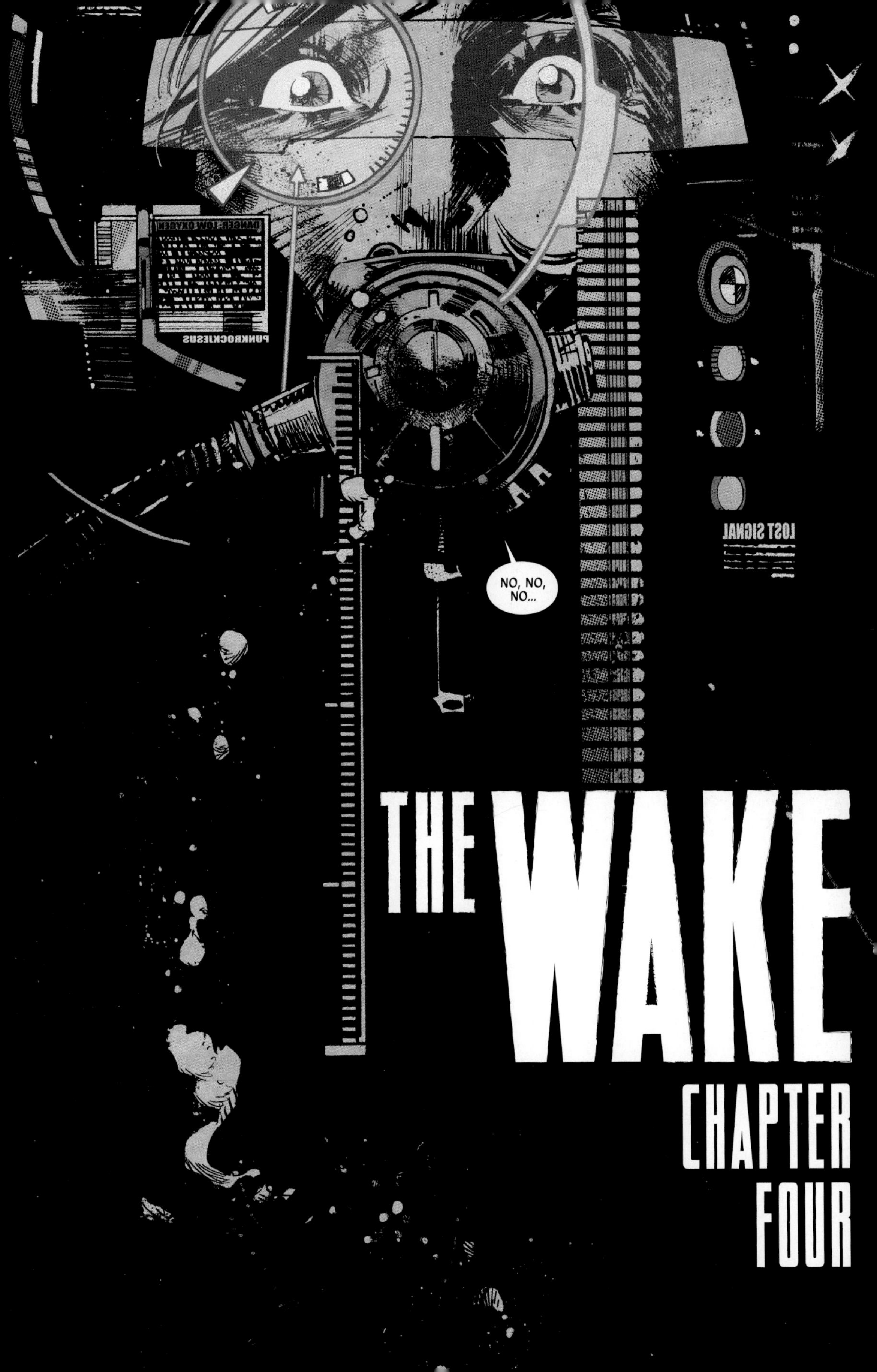
DANGER: LOW OXYGEN
PUNKROCKJESUS
LOST SIGNAL
NO, NO, NO...
THE WAKE
CHAPTER FOUR

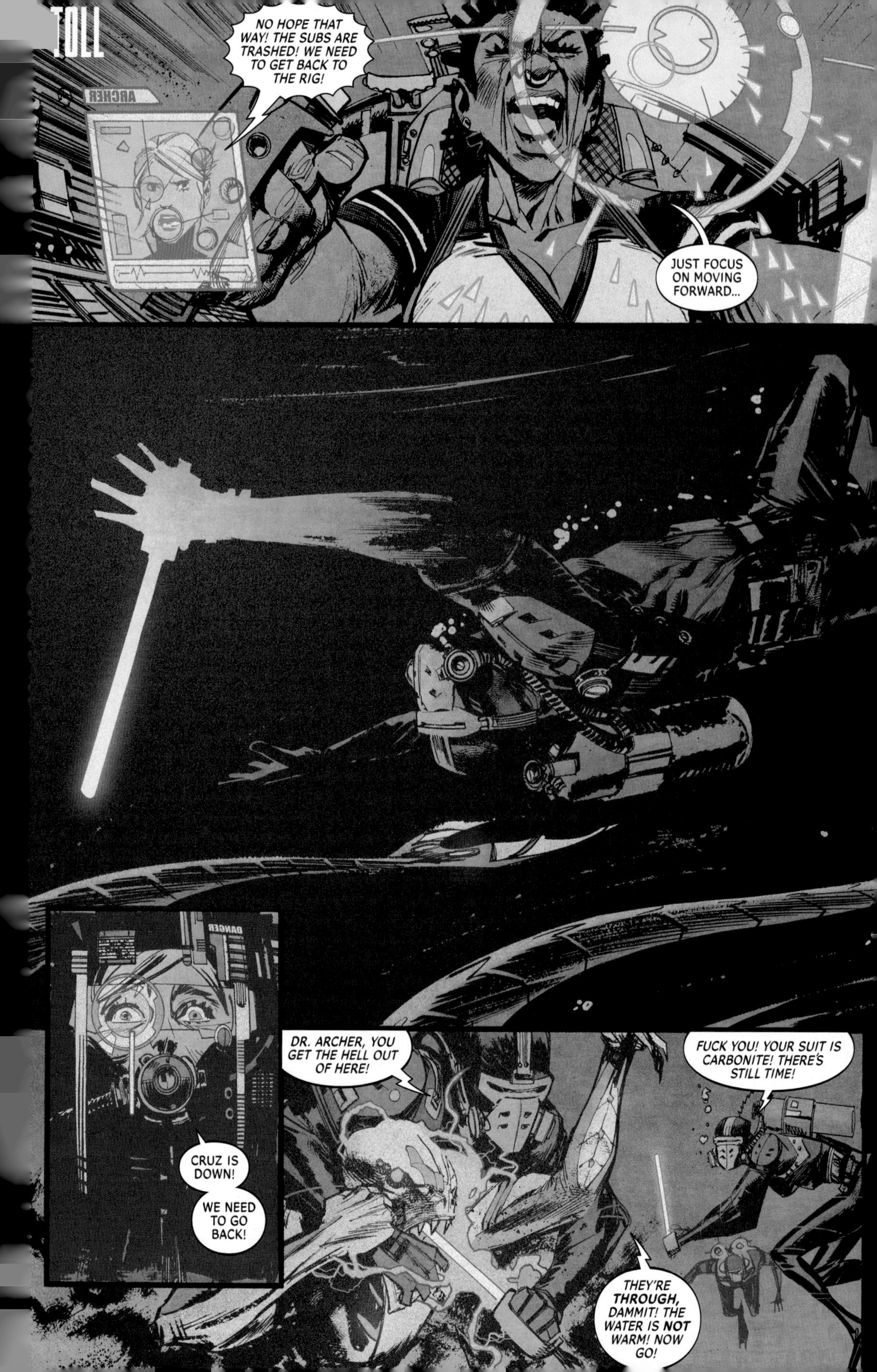
NO HOPE THAT WAY! THE SUBS ARE TRASHED! WE NEED TO GET BACK TO THE RIG!
JUST FOCUS ON MOVING FORWARD...
CRUZ IS DOWN!
WE NEED TO GO BACK!
DR. ARCHER, YOU GET THE HELL OUT OF HERE!
FUCK YOU! YOUR SUIT IS CARBONITE! THERE'S STILL TIME!
THEY'RE **THROUGH,** DAMMIT! THE WATER IS **NOT** WARM! NOW GO!

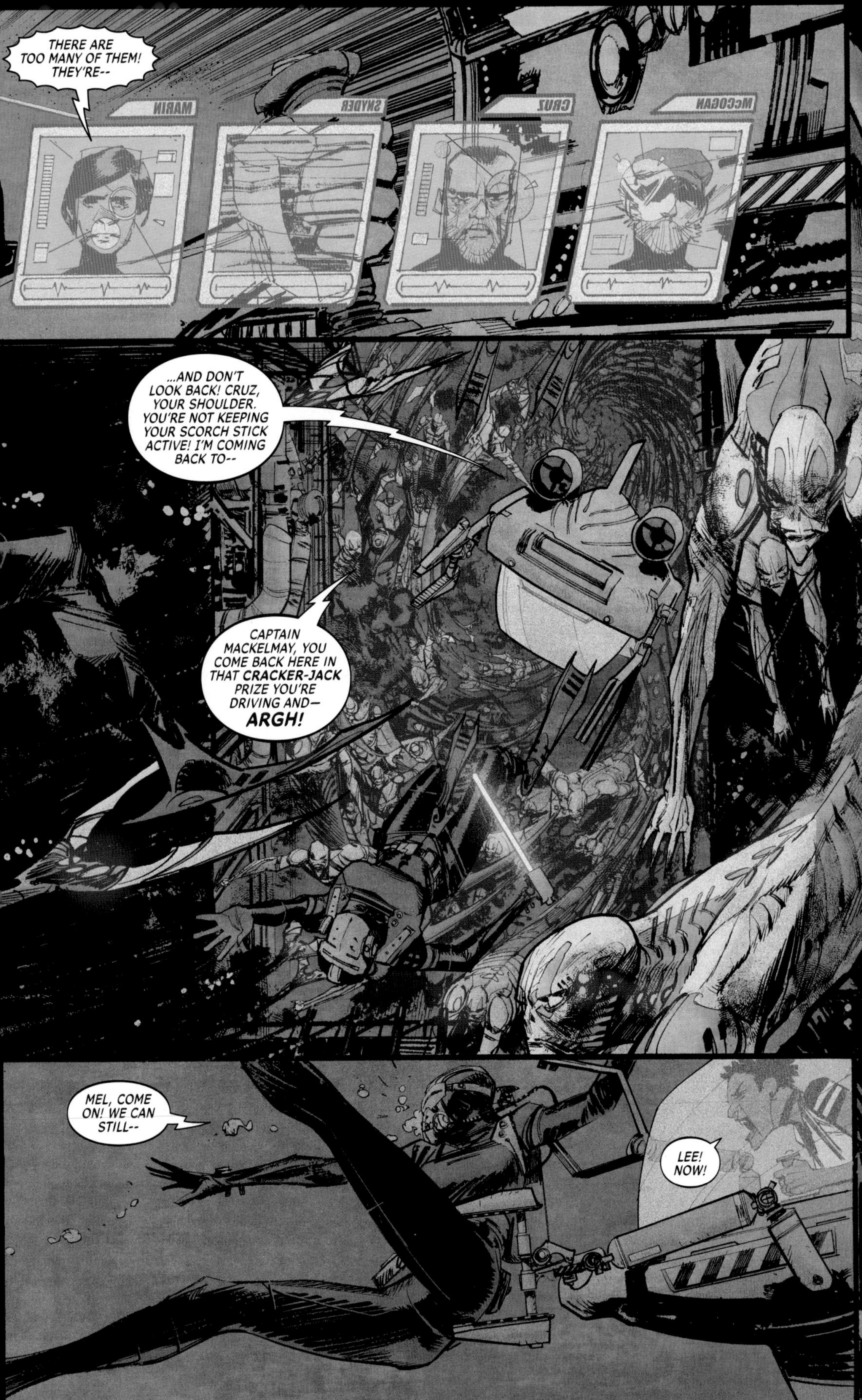
THERE ARE TOO MANY OF THEM! THEY'RE--
MARIN
SNYDER
CRUZ
McCOGAN
...AND DON'T LOOK BACK! CRUZ, YOUR SHOULDER. YOU'RE NOT KEEPING YOUR SCORCH STICK ACTIVE! I'M COMING BACK TO--
CAPTAIN MACKELMAY, YOU COME BACK HERE IN THAT CRACKER-JACK PRIZE YOU'RE DRIVING AND— ARGH!
MEL, COME ON! WE CAN STILL--
LEE! NOW!

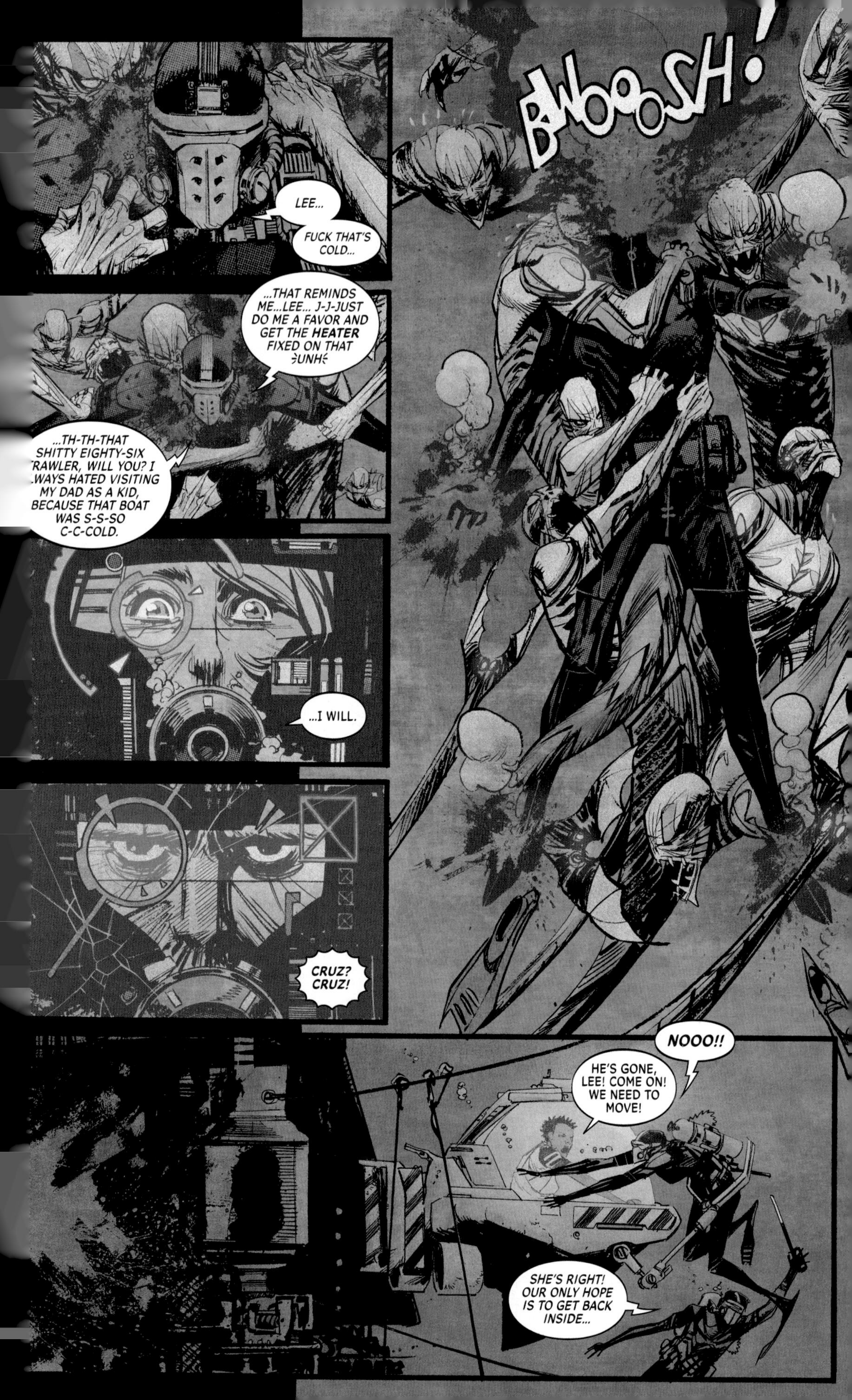
LEE...
FUCK THAT'S COLD...
...THAT REMINDS ME...LEE... J-J-JUST DO ME A FAVOR AND GET THE HEATER FIXED ON THAT -UNH-
...TH-TH-THAT SHITTY EIGHTY-SIX RAWLER, WILL YOU? I WAYS HATED VISITING MY DAD AS A KID, BECAUSE THAT BOAT WAS S-S-SO C-C-COLD.
...I WILL.
CRUZ? CRUZ!
BWOOOSH!
NOOO!!
HE'S GONE, LEE! COME ON! WE NEED TO MOVE!
SHE'S RIGHT! OUR ONLY HOPE IS TO GET BACK INSIDE...

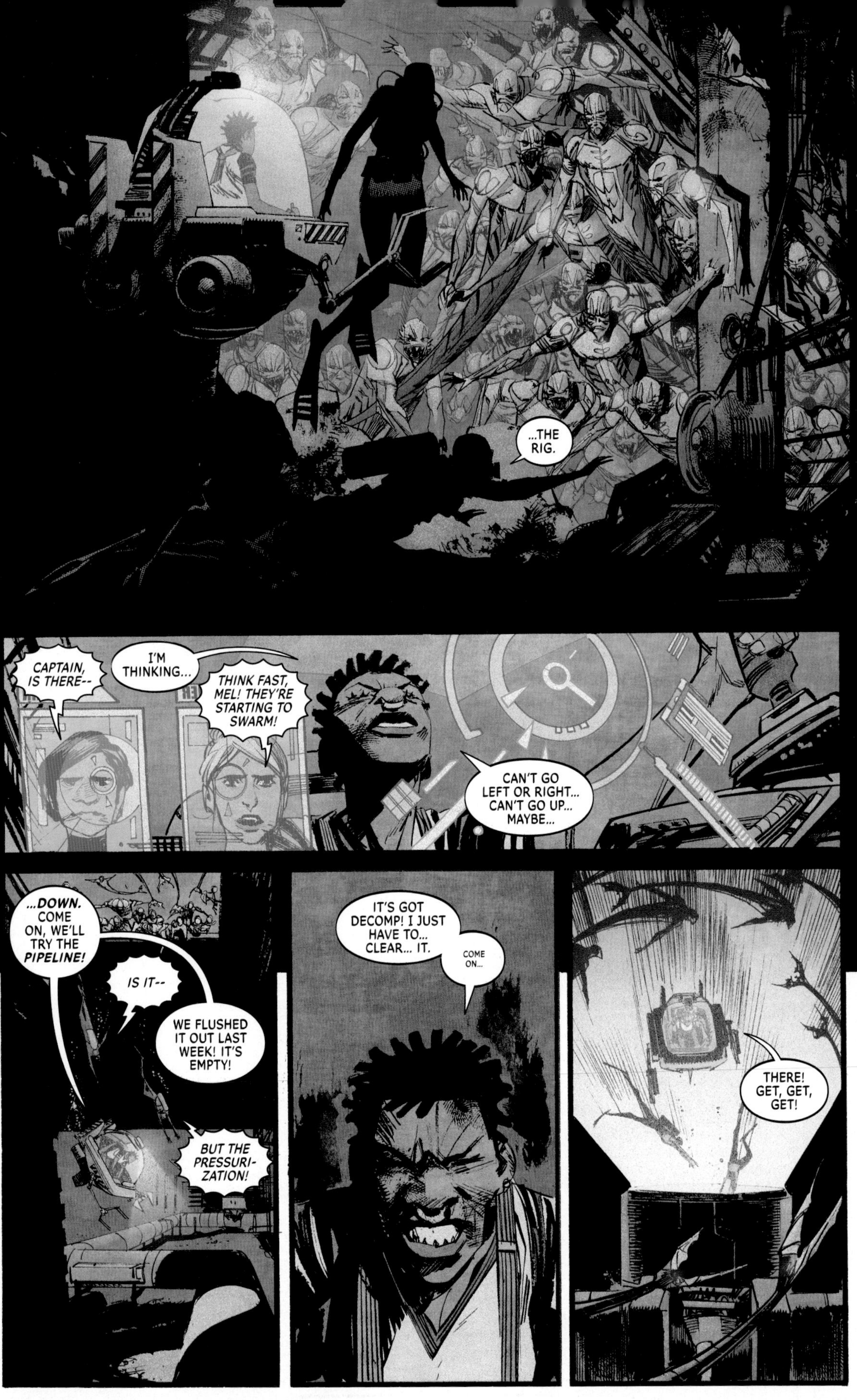
...THE RIG.
CAPTAIN, IS THERE--
I'M THINKING...
THINK FAST, MEL! THEY'RE STARTING TO SWARM!
CAN'T GO LEFT OR RIGHT... CAN'T GO UP... MAYBE...
...DOWN. COME ON, WE'LL TRY THE PIPELINE!
IS IT--
WE FLUSHED IT OUT LAST WEEK! IT'S EMPTY!
BUT THE PRESSURI-ZATION!
IT'S GOT DECOMP! I JUST HAVE TO... CLEAR... IT.
COME ON...
THERE! GET, GET, GET!

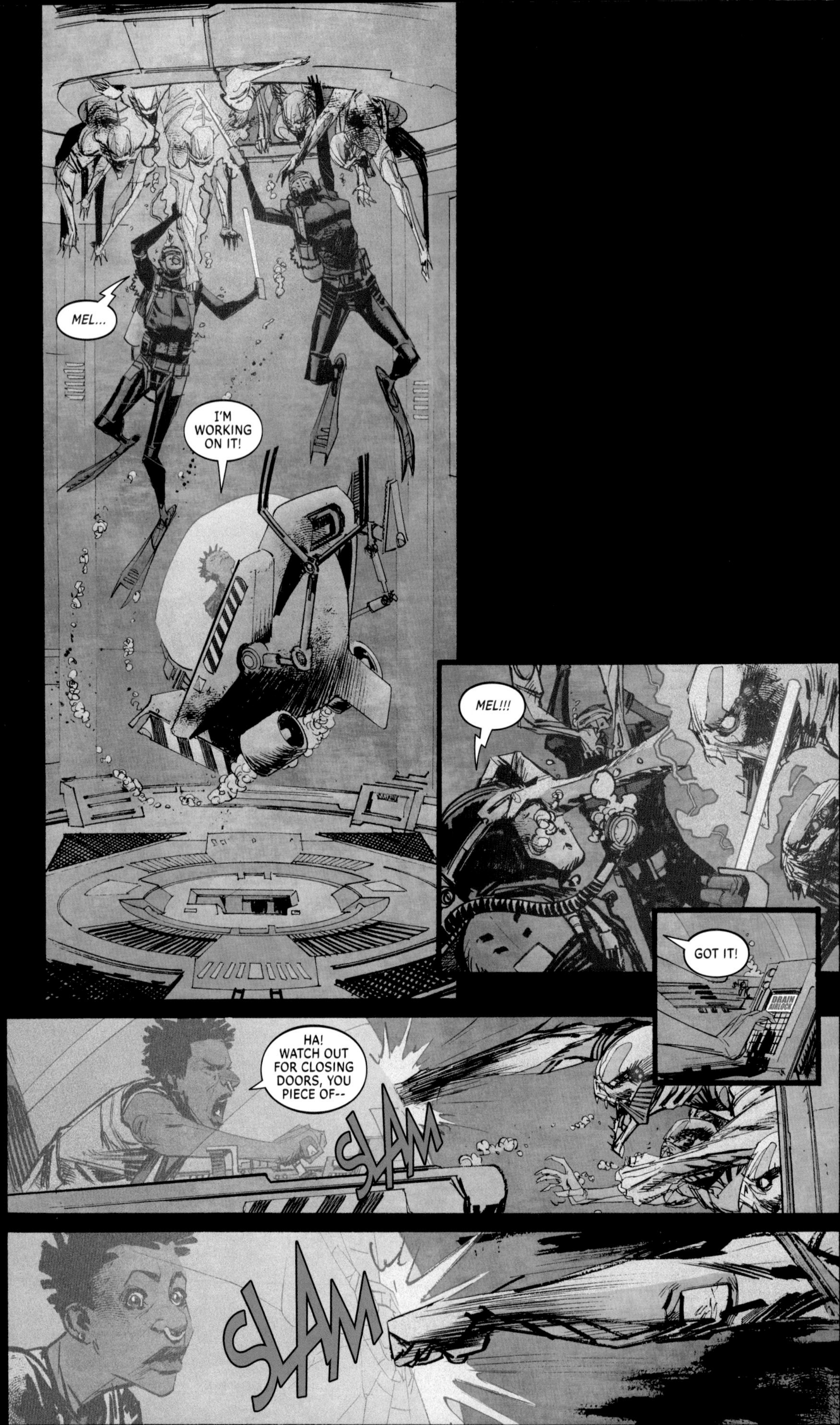
MEL...
I'M WORKING ON IT!
MEL!!!
GOT IT!
DRAIN AIRLOCK
HA! WATCH OUT FOR CLOSING DOORS, YOU PIECE OF--
SLAM
SLAM

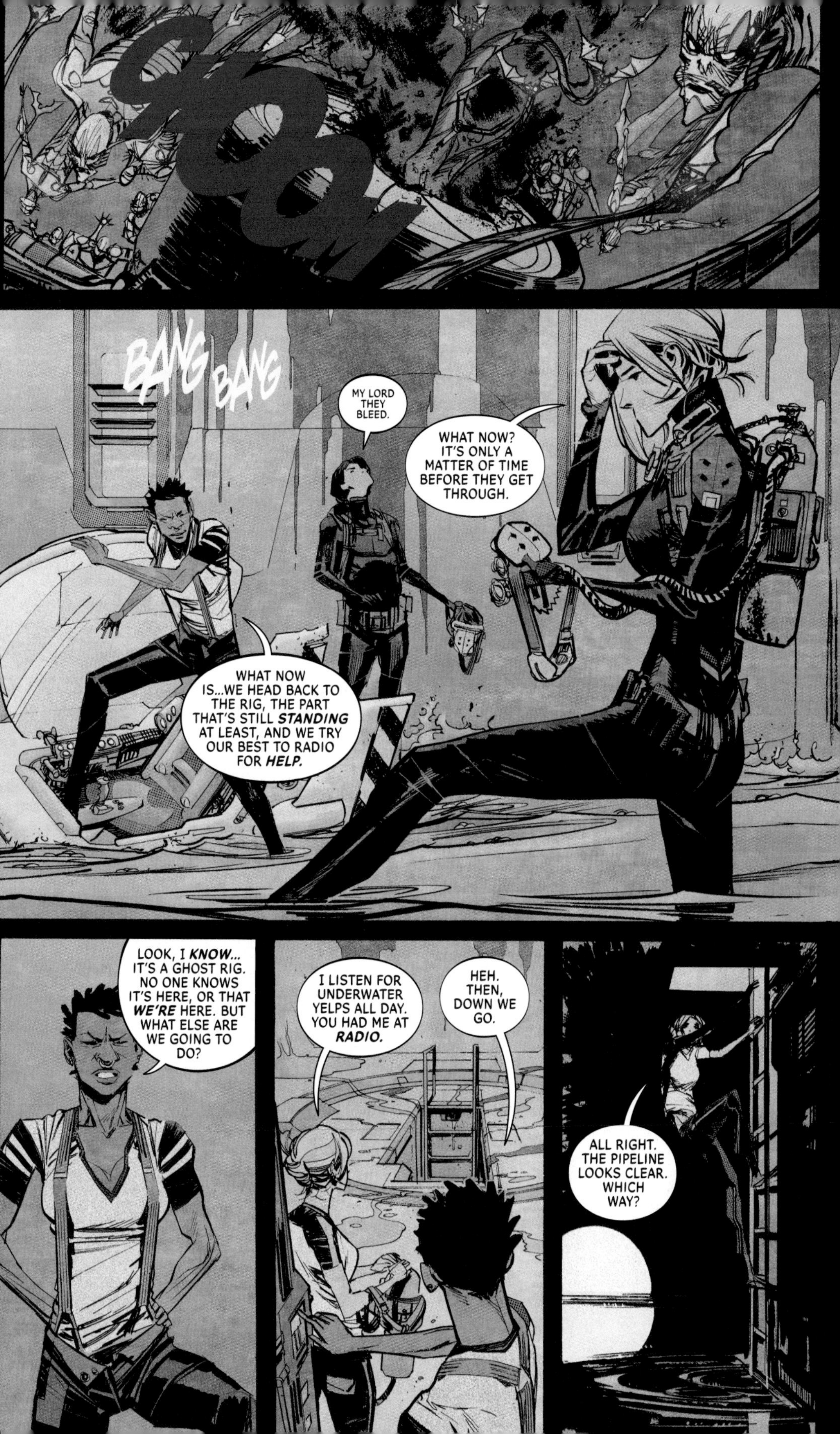

BANG BANG
MY LORD THEY BLEED.
WHAT NOW? IT'S ONLY A MATTER OF TIME BEFORE THEY GET THROUGH.
WHAT NOW IS...WE HEAD BACK TO THE RIG, THE PART THAT'S STILL ***STANDING*** AT LEAST, AND WE TRY OUR BEST TO RADIO FOR ***HELP.***
LOOK, I ***KNOW...*** IT'S A GHOST RIG. NO ONE KNOWS IT'S HERE, OR THAT ***WE'RE*** HERE. BUT WHAT ELSE ARE WE GOING TO DO?
I LISTEN FOR UNDERWATER YELPS ALL DAY. YOU HAD ME AT ***RADIO.***
HEH. THEN, DOWN WE GO.
ALL RIGHT. THE PIPELINE LOOKS CLEAR. WHICH WAY?

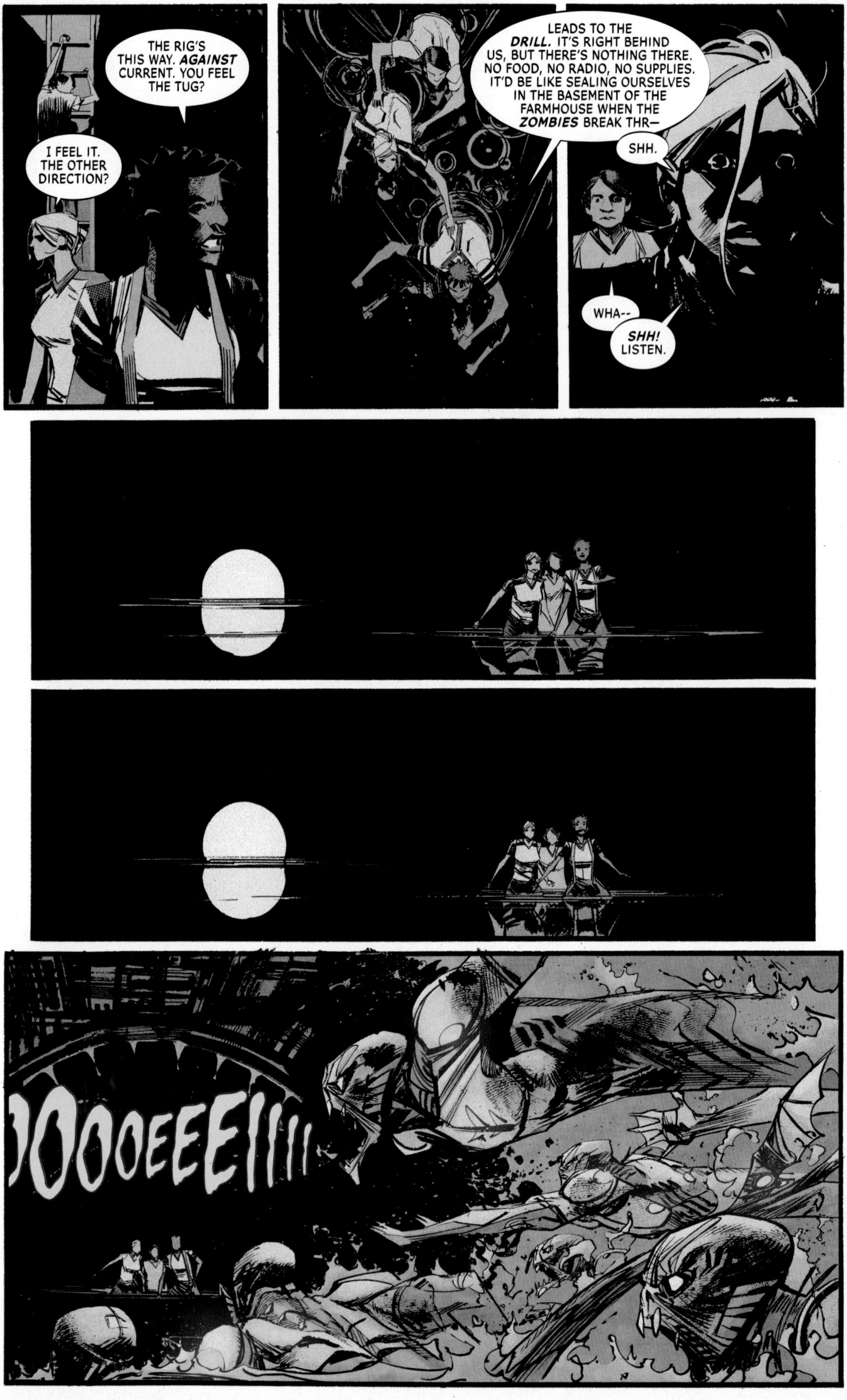
THE RIG'S THIS WAY. *AGAINST* CURRENT. YOU FEEL THE TUG?
I FEEL IT. THE OTHER DIRECTION?
LEADS TO THE *DRILL.* IT'S RIGHT BEHIND US, BUT THERE'S NOTHING THERE. NO FOOD, NO RADIO, NO SUPPLIES. IT'D BE LIKE SEALING OURSELVES IN THE BASEMENT OF THE FARMHOUSE WHEN THE *ZOMBIES* BREAK THR—
SHH.
WHA--
SHH! LISTEN.
OOOEEEIIII

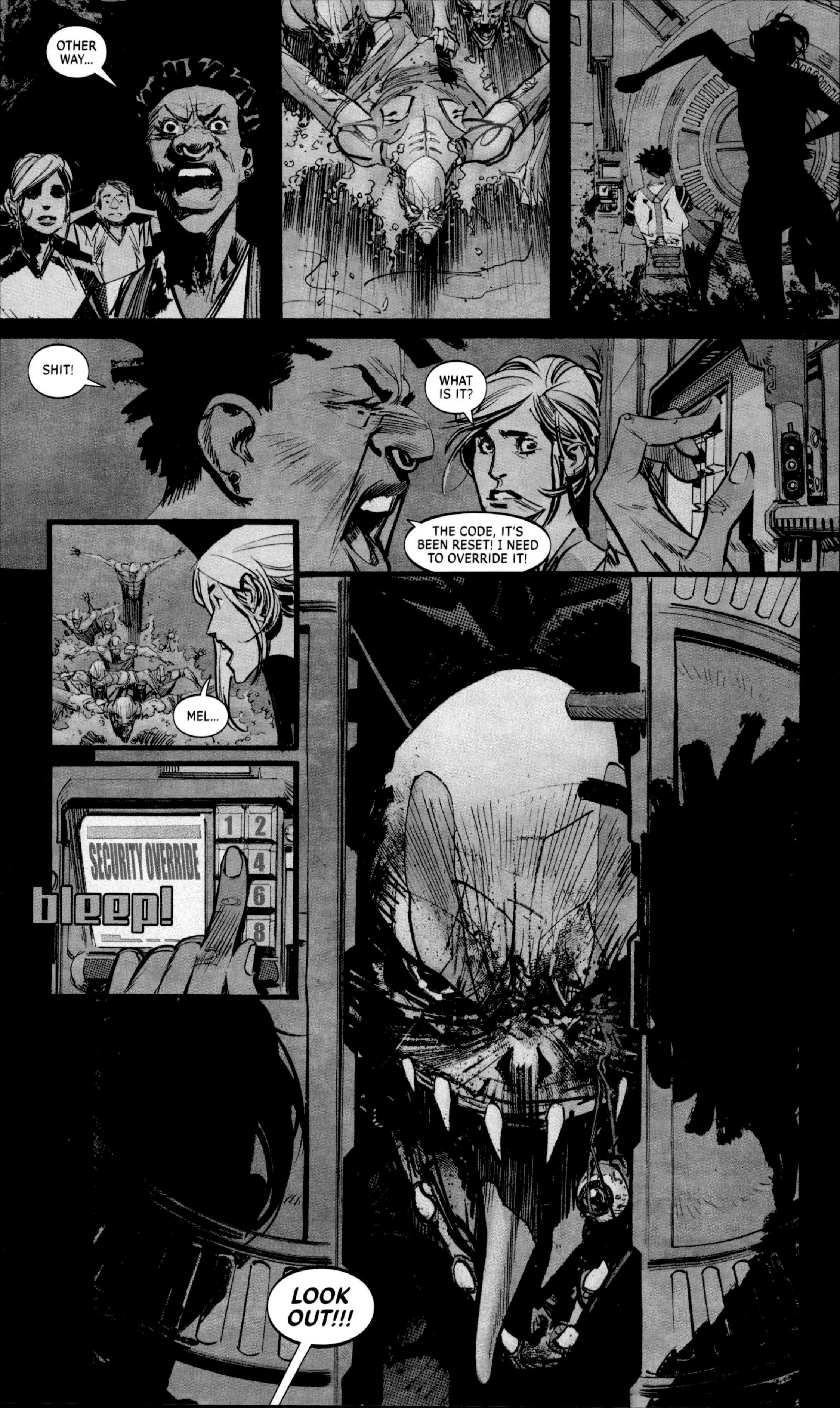
OTHER WAY...
SHIT!
WHAT IS IT?
THE CODE, IT'S BEEN RESET! I NEED TO OVERRIDE IT!
MEL...
SECURITY OVERRIDE
bleep!
LOOK OUT!!!

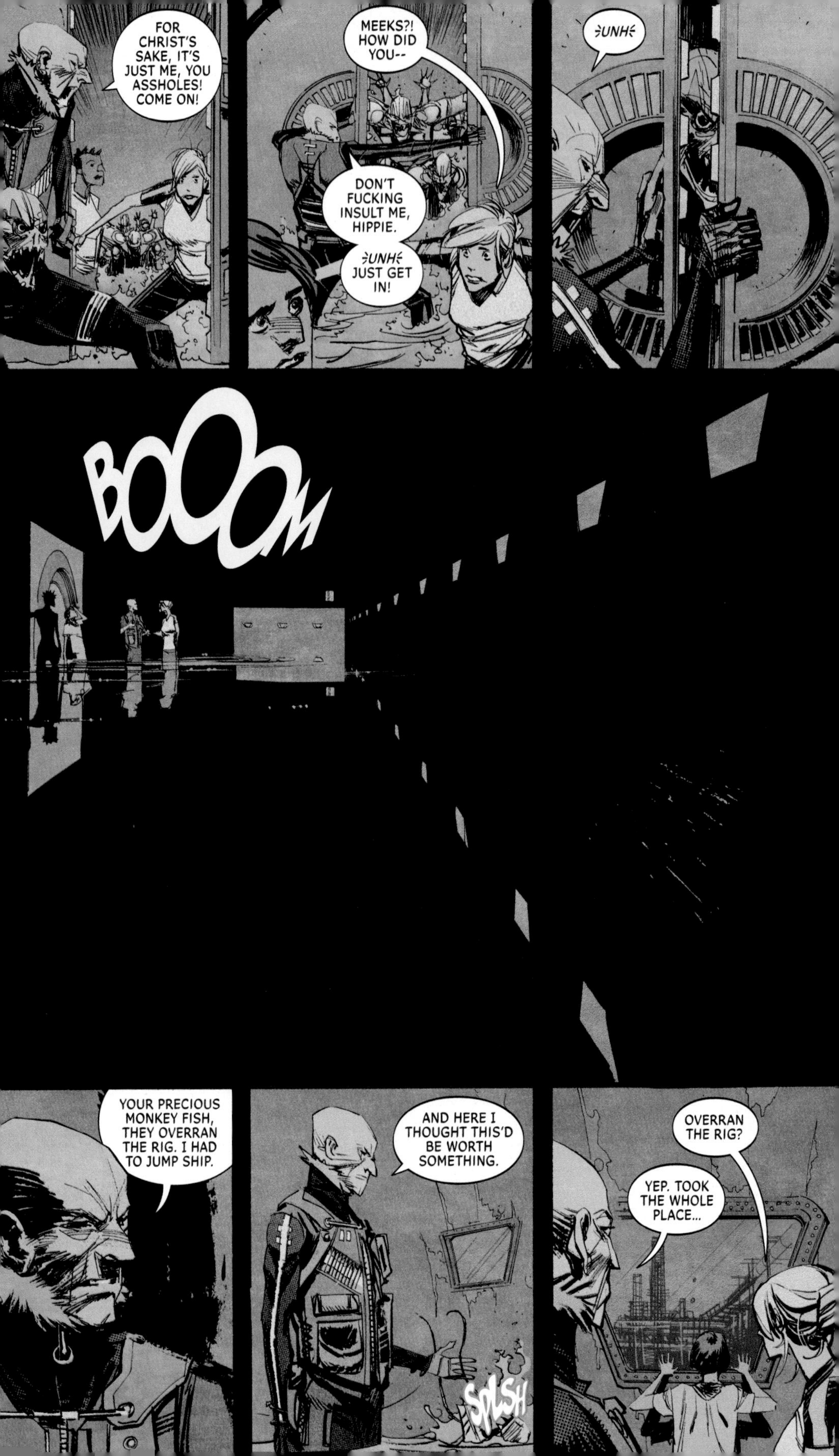
FOR CHRIST'S SAKE, IT'S JUST ME, YOU ASSHOLES! COME ON!
MEEKS?! HOW DID YOU--
DON'T FUCKING INSULT ME, HIPPIE.
UNH JUST GET IN!
UNH
BOOOM
YOUR PRECIOUS MONKEY FISH, THEY OVERRAN THE RIG. I HAD TO JUMP SHIP.
AND HERE I THOUGHT THIS'D BE WORTH SOMETHING.
SPLSH
OVERRAN THE RIG?
YEP. TOOK THE WHOLE PLACE...

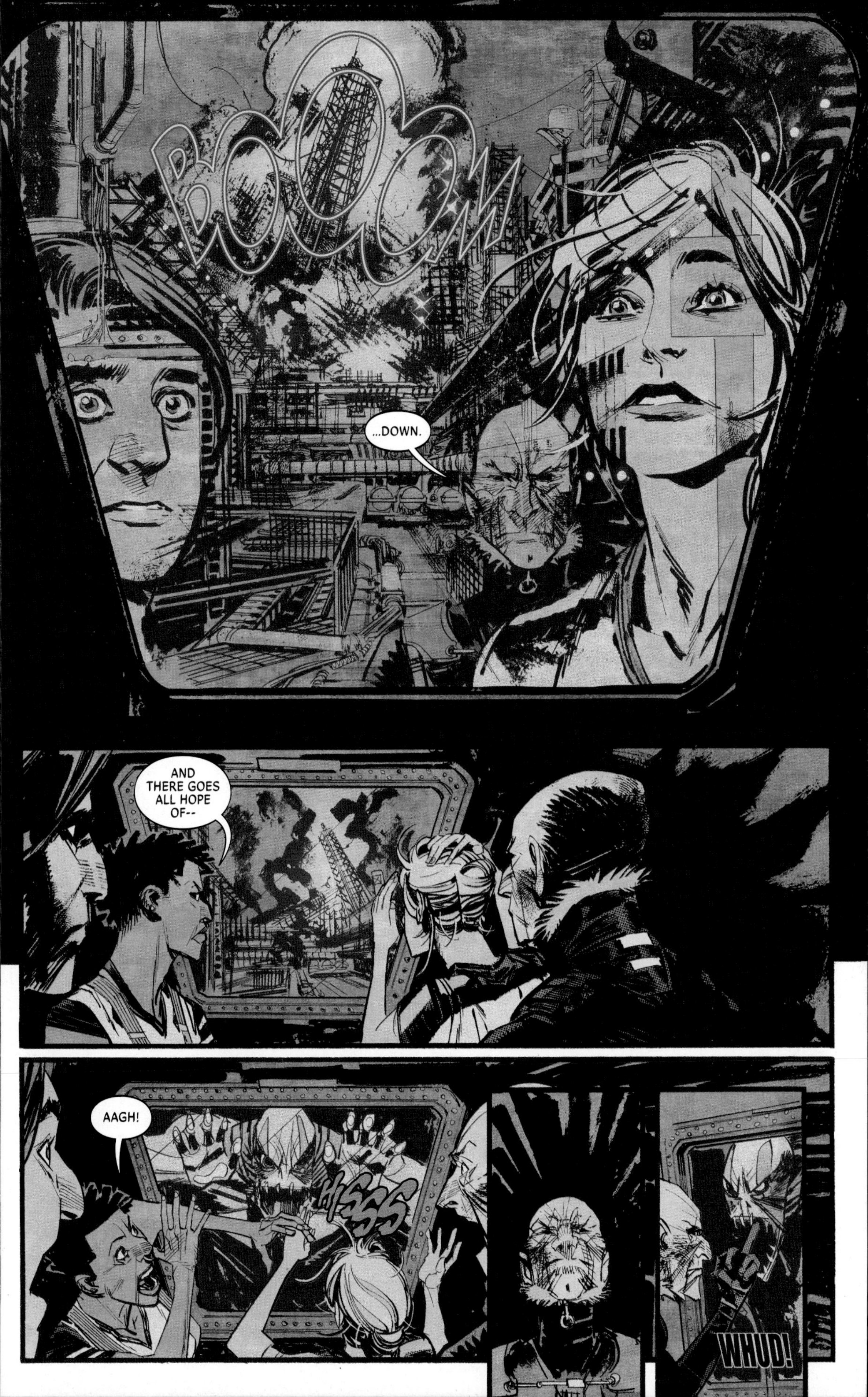
BOOOM
...DOWN.
AND THERE GOES ALL HOPE OF--
AAGH!
HISSS
WHUD!

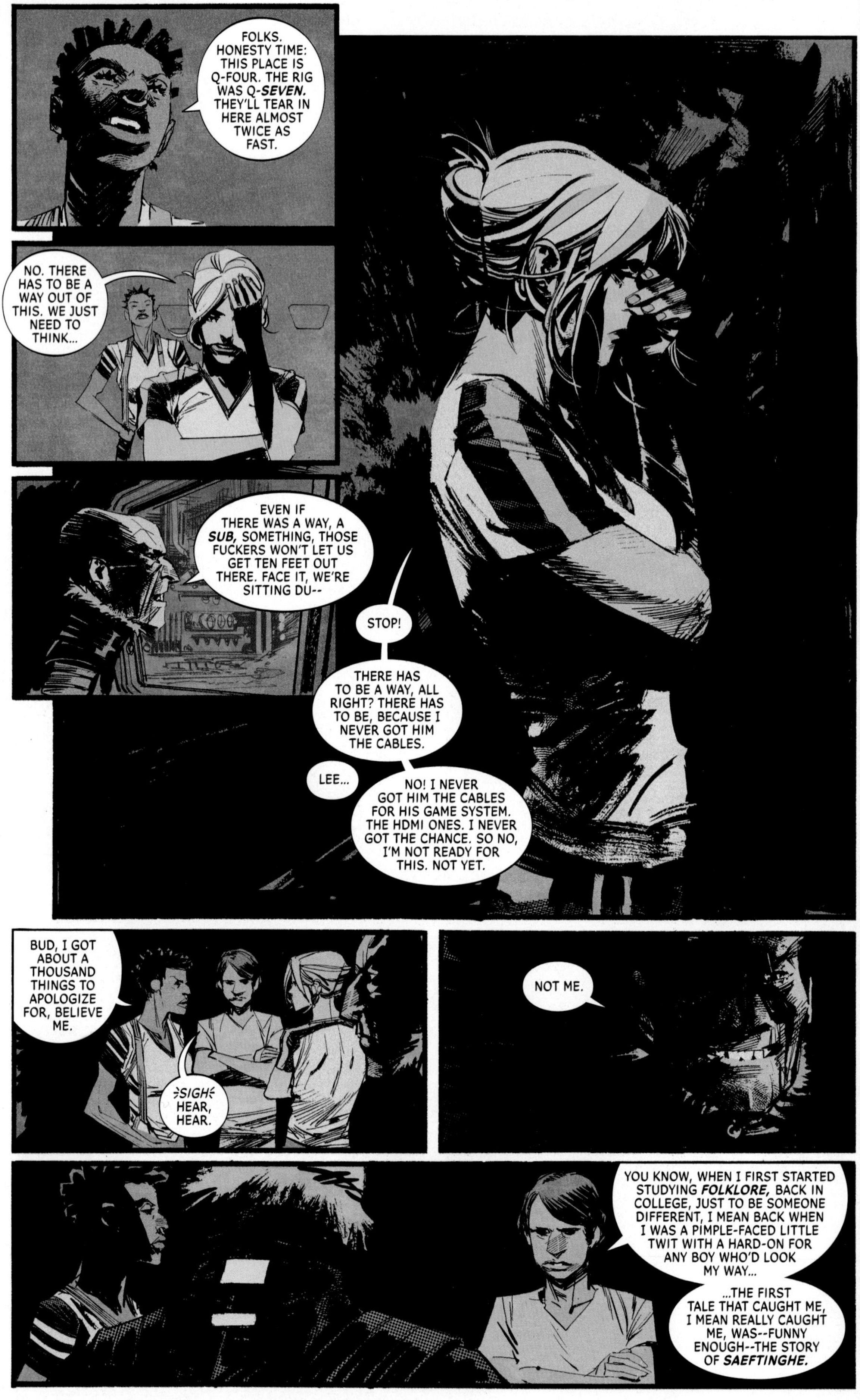
FOLKS. HONESTY TIME: THIS PLACE IS Q-FOUR. THE RIG WAS Q-*SEVEN.* THEY'LL TEAR IN HERE ALMOST TWICE AS FAST.
NO. THERE HAS TO BE A WAY OUT OF THIS. WE JUST NEED TO THINK...
EVEN IF THERE WAS A WAY, A *SUB,* SOMETHING, THOSE FUCKERS WON'T LET US GET TEN FEET OUT THERE. FACE IT, WE'RE SITTING DU--
STOP!
THERE HAS TO BE A WAY, ALL RIGHT? THERE HAS TO BE, BECAUSE I NEVER GOT HIM THE CABLES.
LEE...
NO! I NEVER GOT HIM THE CABLES FOR HIS GAME SYSTEM. THE HDMI ONES. I NEVER GOT THE CHANCE. SO NO, I'M NOT READY FOR THIS. NOT YET.
BUD, I GOT ABOUT A THOUSAND THINGS TO APOLOGIZE FOR, BELIEVE ME.
SIGH HEAR, HEAR.
NOT ME.
YOU KNOW, WHEN I FIRST STARTED STUDYING *FOLKLORE,* BACK IN COLLEGE, JUST TO BE SOMEONE DIFFERENT, I MEAN BACK WHEN I WAS A PIMPLE-FACED LITTLE TWIT WITH A HARD-ON FOR ANY BOY WHO'D LOOK MY WAY...
...THE FIRST TALE THAT CAUGHT ME, I MEAN REALLY CAUGHT ME, WAS--FUNNY ENOUGH--THE STORY OF *SAEFTINGHE.*

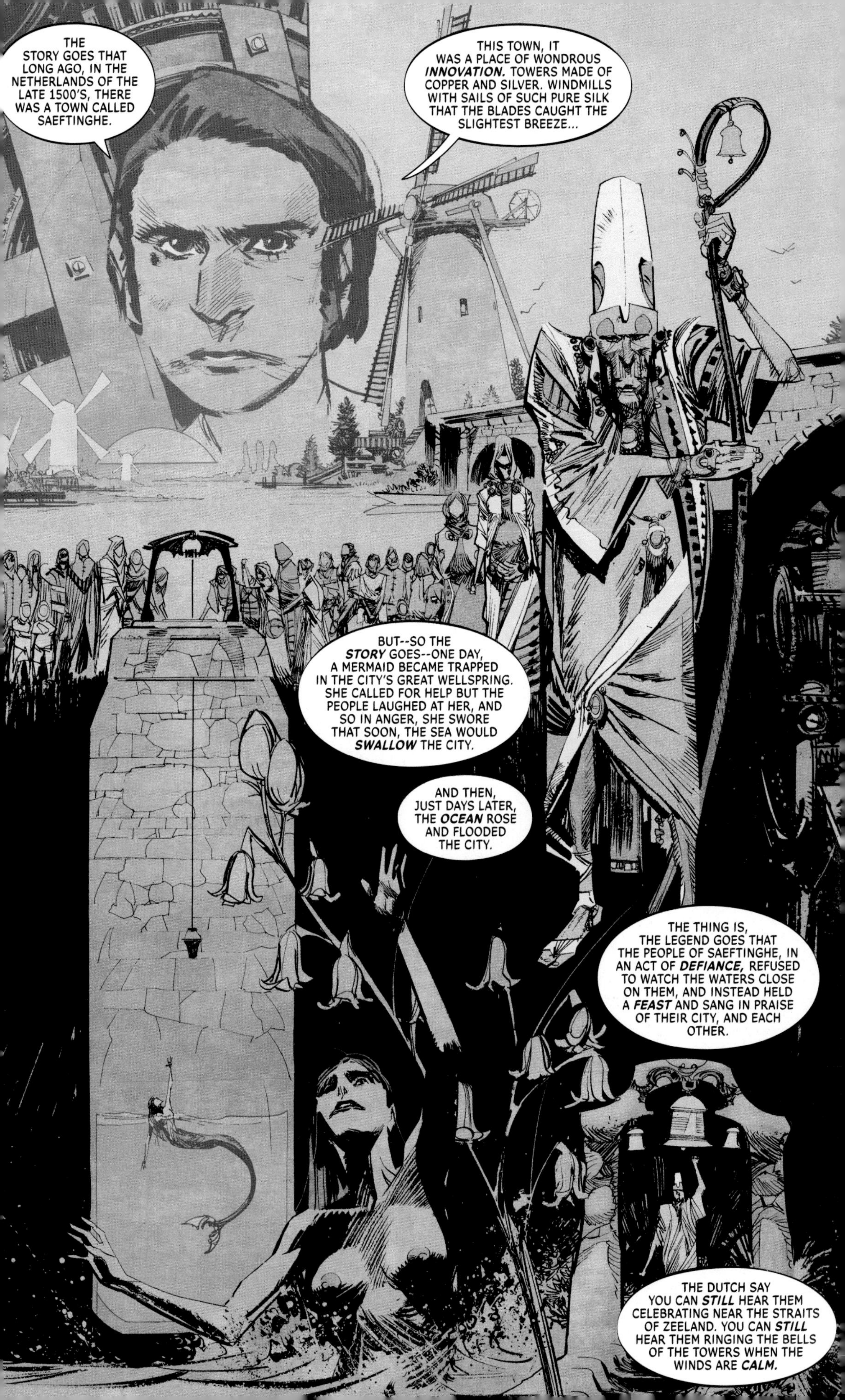
THE STORY GOES THAT LONG AGO, IN THE NETHERLANDS OF THE LATE 1500'S, THERE WAS A TOWN CALLED SAEFTINGHE.
THIS TOWN, IT WAS A PLACE OF WONDROUS INNOVATION. TOWERS MADE OF COPPER AND SILVER. WINDMILLS WITH SAILS OF SUCH PURE SILK THAT THE BLADES CAUGHT THE SLIGHTEST BREEZE...
BUT--SO THE STORY GOES--ONE DAY, A MERMAID BECAME TRAPPED IN THE CITY'S GREAT WELLSPRING. SHE CALLED FOR HELP BUT THE PEOPLE LAUGHED AT HER, AND SO IN ANGER, SHE SWORE THAT SOON, THE SEA WOULD SWALLOW THE CITY.
AND THEN, JUST DAYS LATER, THE OCEAN ROSE AND FLOODED THE CITY.
THE THING IS, THE LEGEND GOES THAT THE PEOPLE OF SAEFTINGHE, IN AN ACT OF DEFIANCE, REFUSED TO WATCH THE WATERS CLOSE ON THEM, AND INSTEAD HELD A FEAST AND SANG IN PRAISE OF THEIR CITY, AND EACH OTHER.
THE DUTCH SAY YOU CAN STILL HEAR THEM CELEBRATING NEAR THE STRAITS OF ZEELAND. YOU CAN STILL HEAR THEM RINGING THE BELLS OF THE TOWERS WHEN THE WINDS ARE CALM.

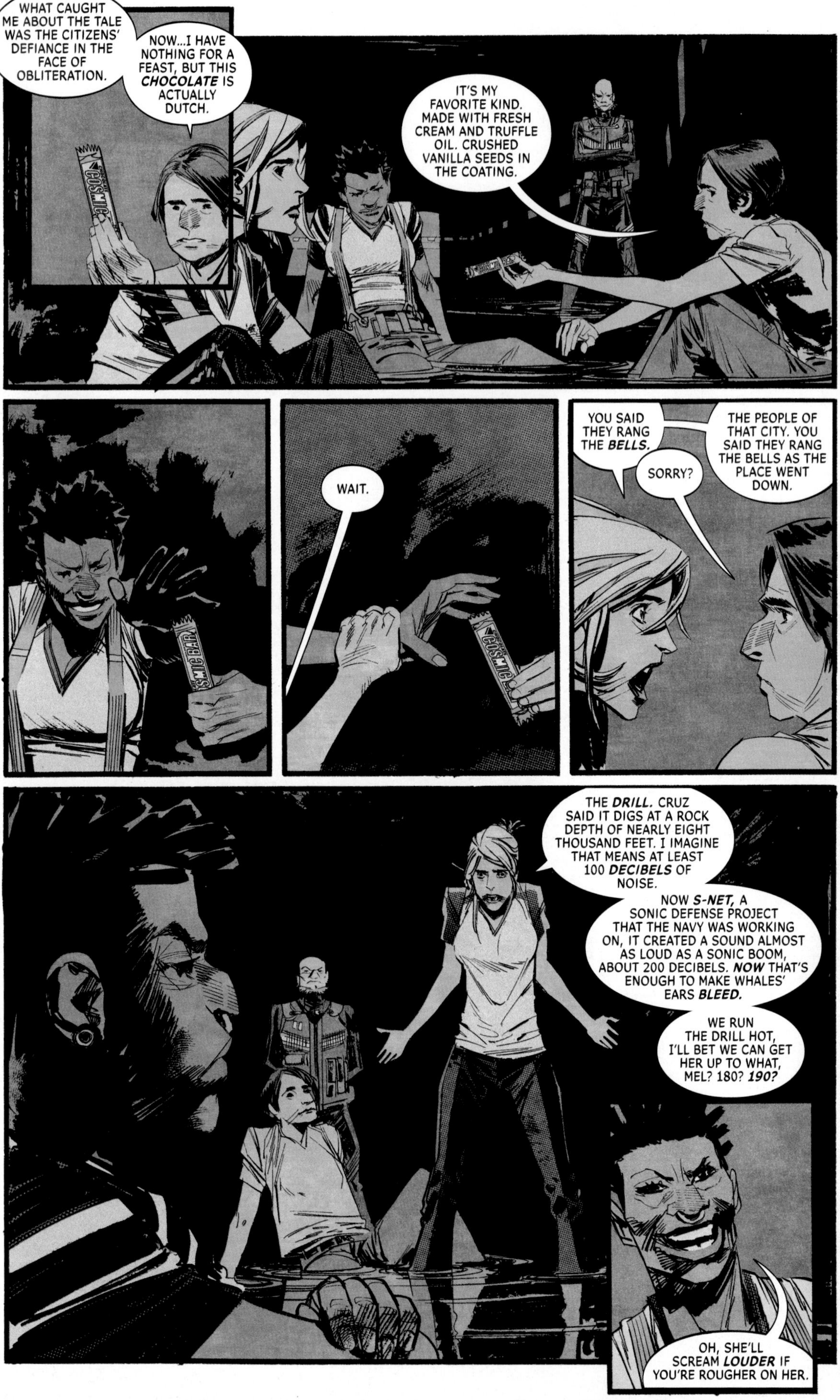
WHAT CAUGHT ME ABOUT THE TALE WAS THE CITIZENS' DEFIANCE IN THE FACE OF OBLITERATION.
NOW...I HAVE NOTHING FOR A FEAST, BUT THIS CHOCOLATE IS ACTUALLY DUTCH.
COSMIC
IT'S MY FAVORITE KIND. MADE WITH FRESH CREAM AND TRUFFLE OIL. CRUSHED VANILLA SEEDS IN THE COATING.
SMIC BAR
WAIT.
COSMIC
YOU SAID THEY RANG THE BELLS.
SORRY?
THE PEOPLE OF THAT CITY. YOU SAID THEY RANG THE BELLS AS THE PLACE WENT DOWN.
THE DRILL. CRUZ SAID IT DIGS AT A ROCK DEPTH OF NEARLY EIGHT THOUSAND FEET. I IMAGINE THAT MEANS AT LEAST 100 DECIBELS OF NOISE.
NOW S-NET, A SONIC DEFENSE PROJECT THAT THE NAVY WAS WORKING ON, IT CREATED A SOUND ALMOST AS LOUD AS A SONIC BOOM, ABOUT 200 DECIBELS. NOW THAT'S ENOUGH TO MAKE WHALES' EARS BLEED.
WE RUN THE DRILL HOT, I'LL BET WE CAN GET HER UP TO WHAT, MEL? 180? 190?
OH, SHE'LL SCREAM LOUDER IF YOU'RE ROUGHER ON HER.

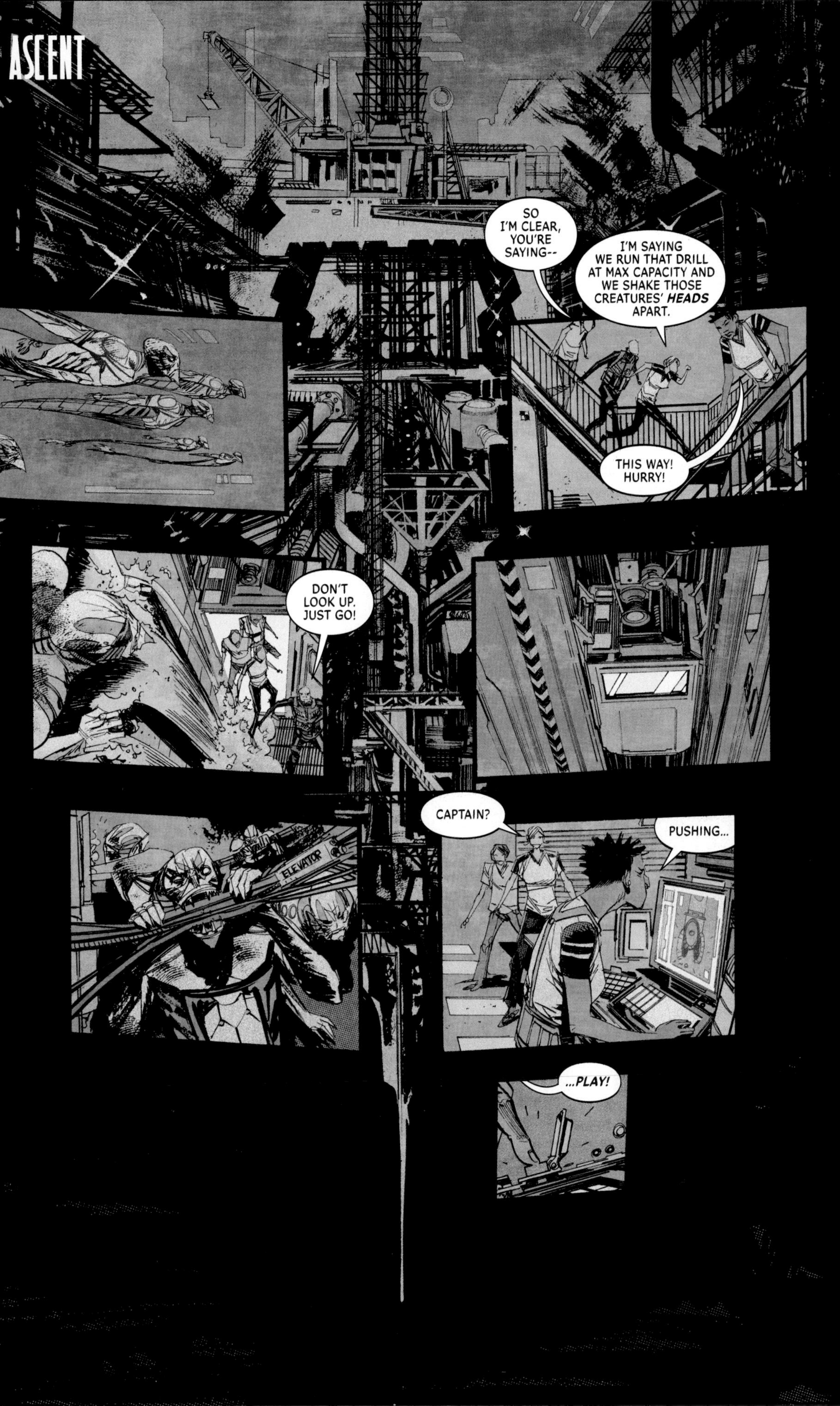
ASCENT
SO I'M CLEAR, YOU'RE SAYING--
I'M SAYING WE RUN THAT DRILL AT MAX CAPACITY AND WE SHAKE THOSE CREATURES' **HEADS** APART.
THIS WAY! HURRY!
DON'T LOOK UP. JUST GO!
ELEVATOR
CAPTAIN?
PUSHING...
...PLAY!

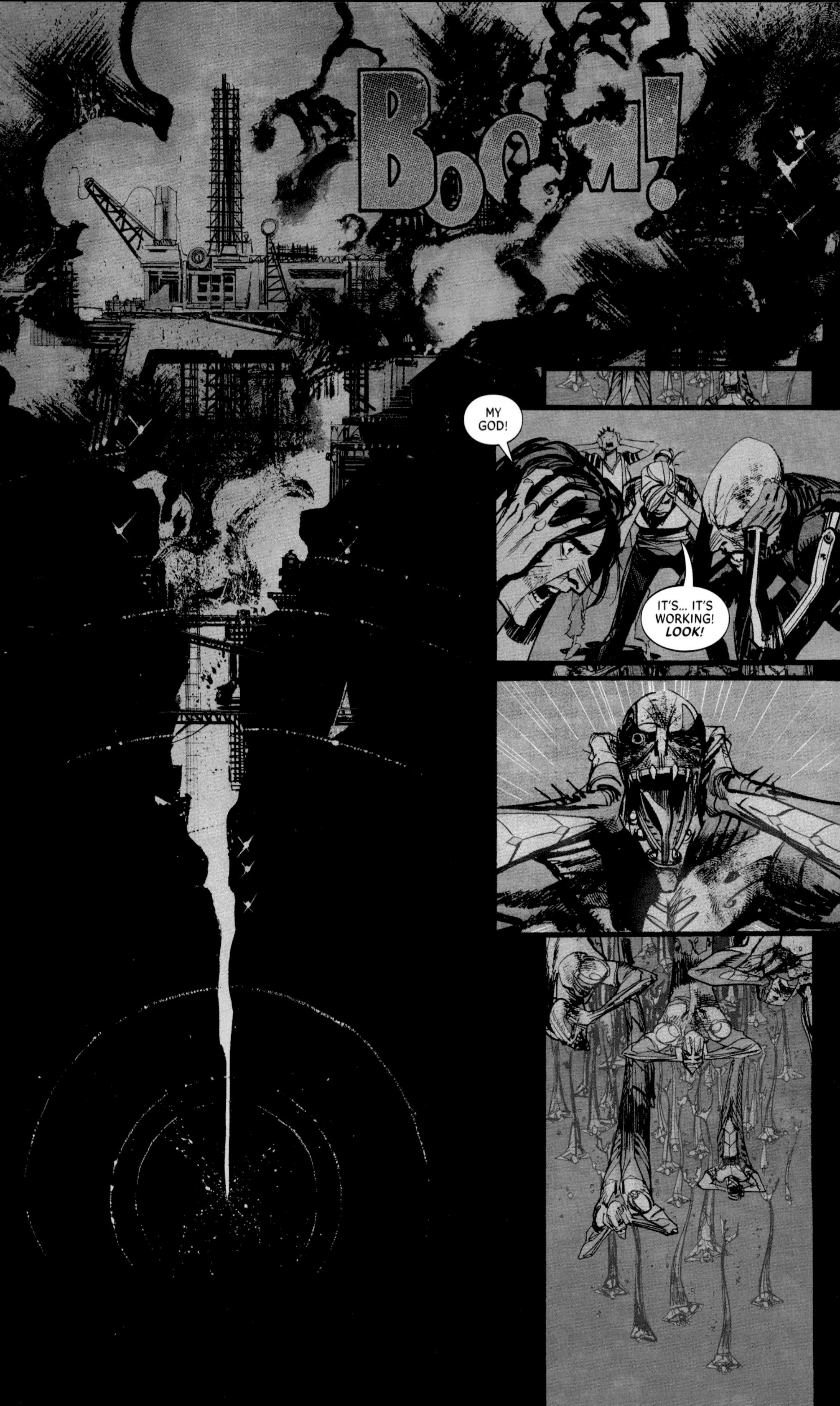
BOOM!
MY GOD!
IT'S... IT'S WORKING! LOOK!

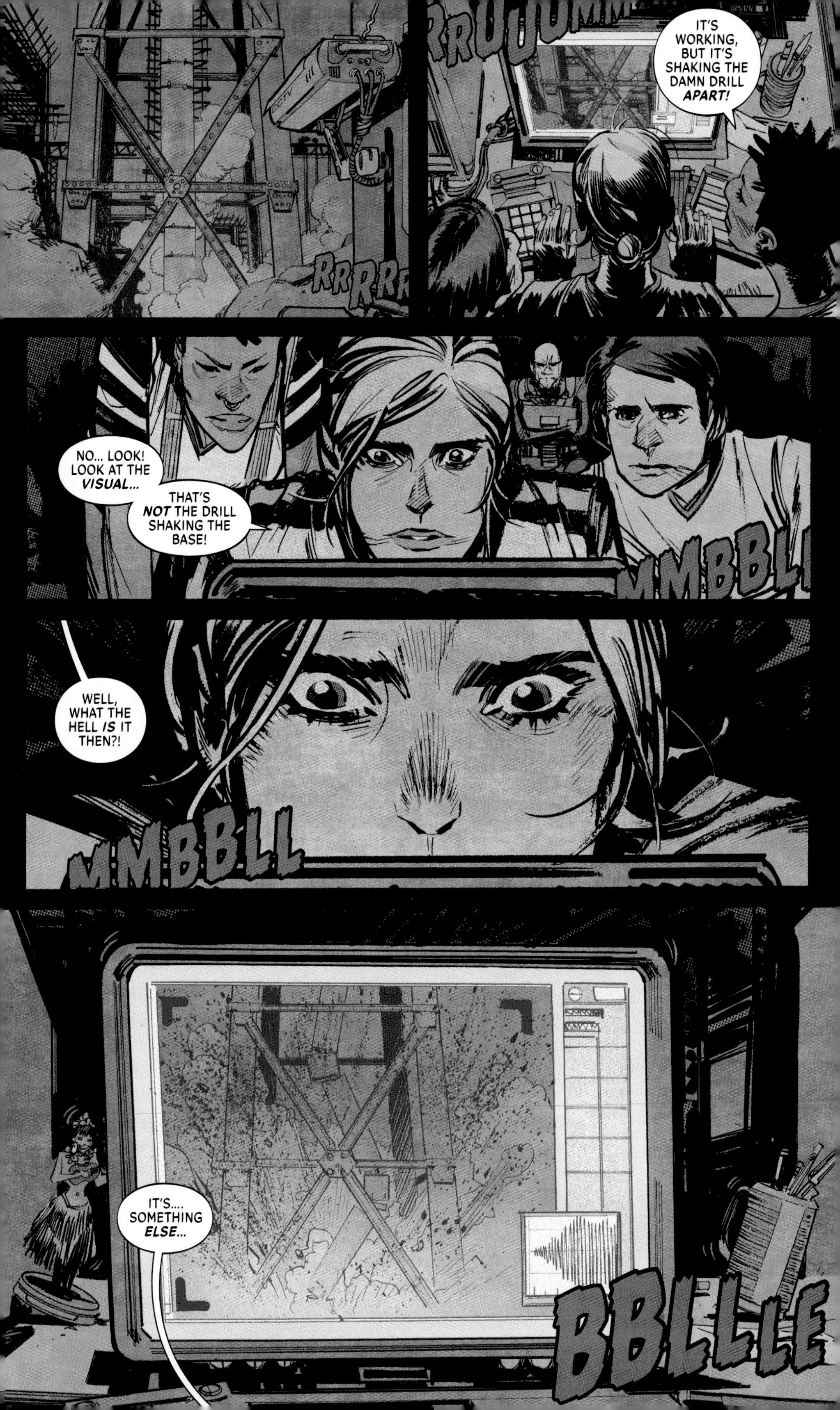
RRUUUMM
RRRRR
IT'S WORKING, BUT IT'S SHAKING THE DAMN DRILL APART!
NO... LOOK! LOOK AT THE VISUAL...
THAT'S NOT THE DRILL SHAKING THE BASE!
MMBBLL
WELL, WHAT THE HELL IS IT THEN?!
MMBBLL
IT'S.... SOMETHING ELSE...
BBLLLE

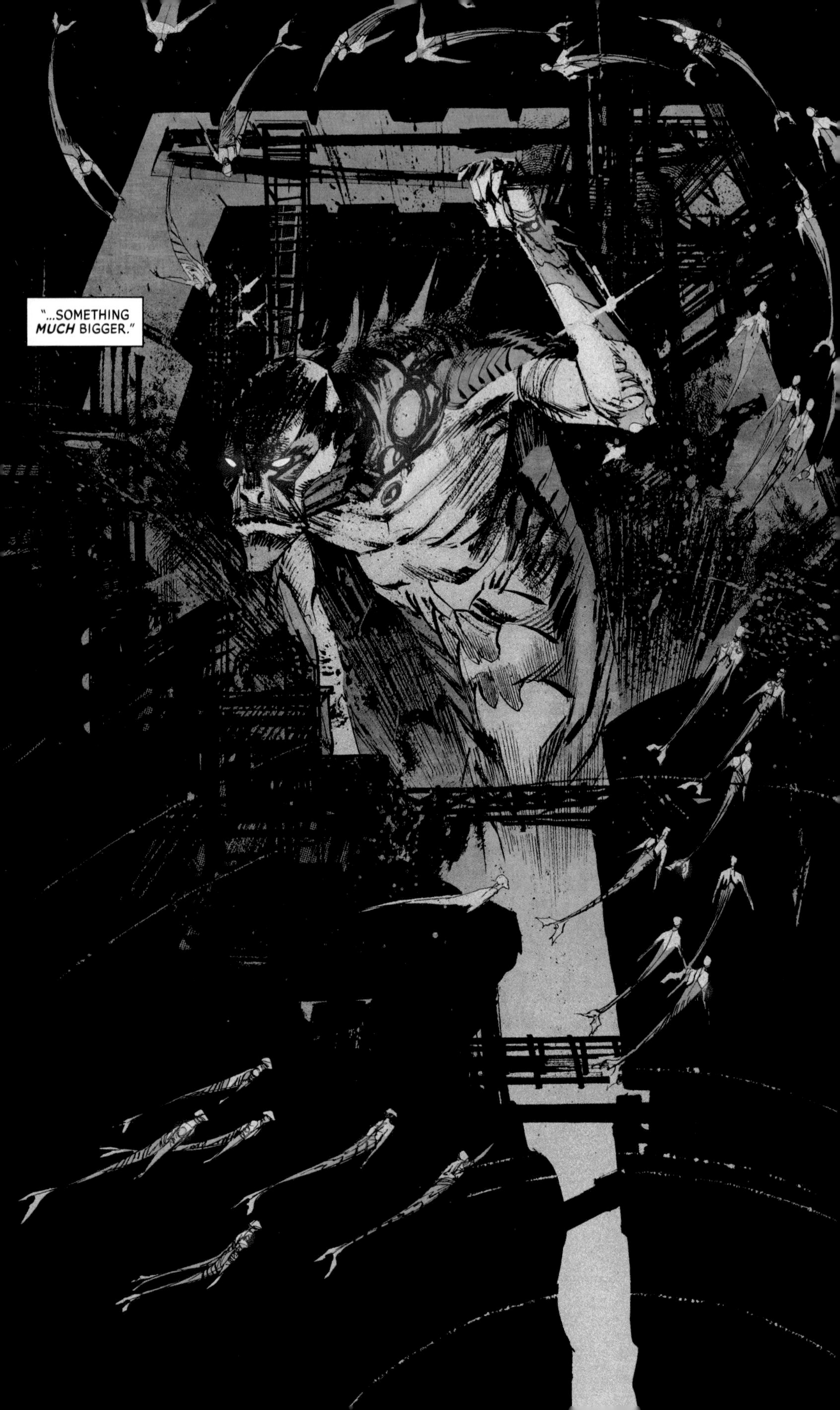
"...SOMETHING MUCH BIGGER."

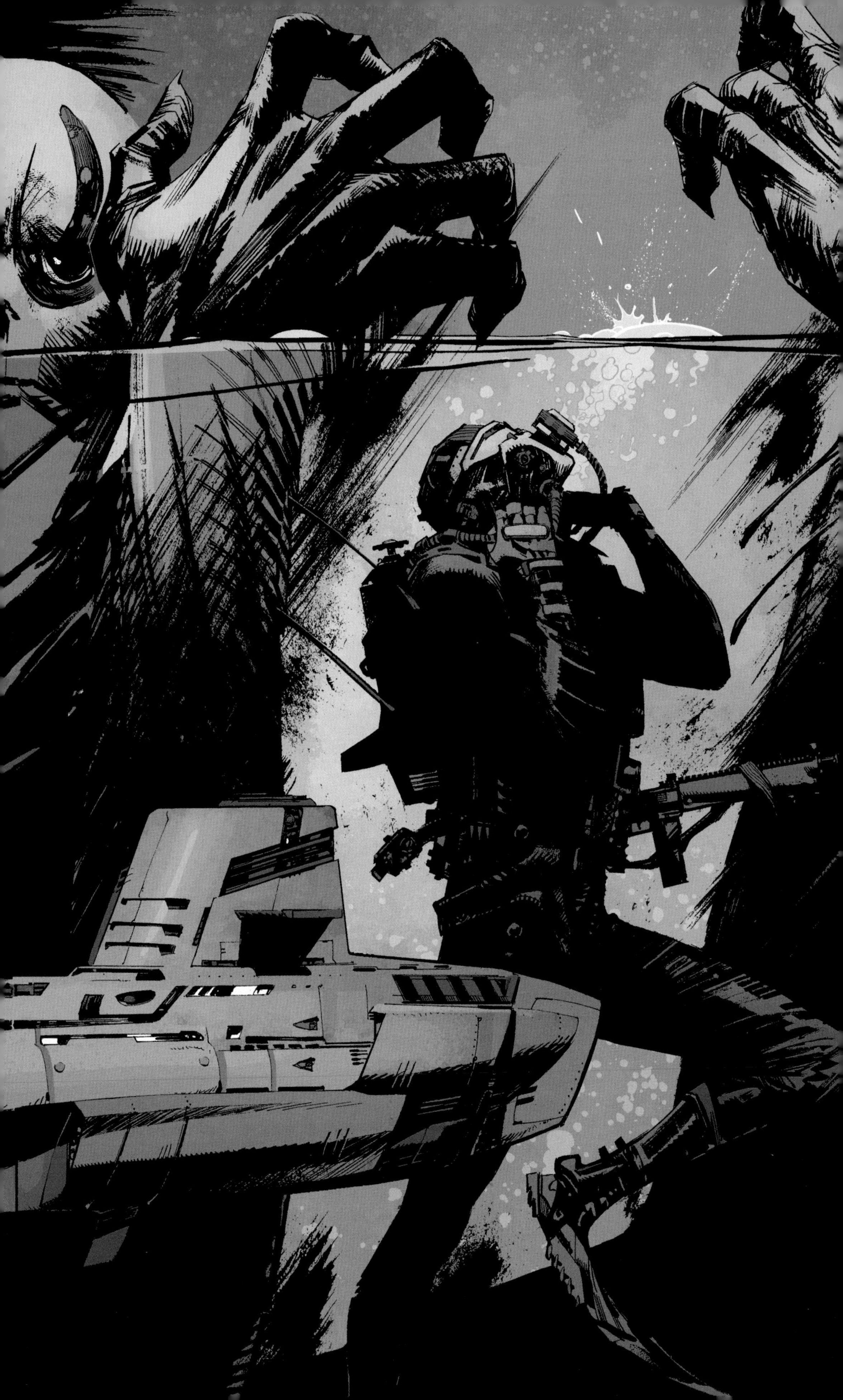

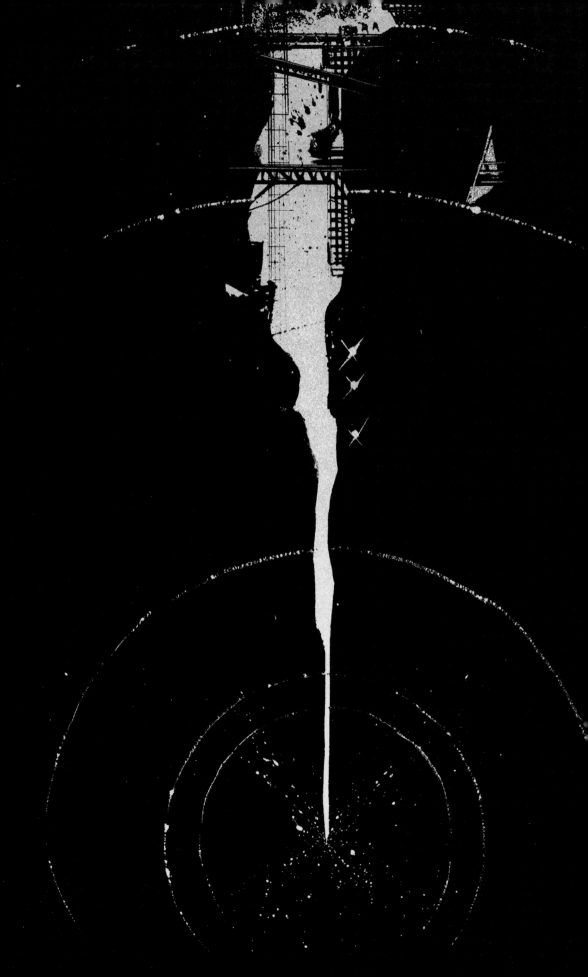

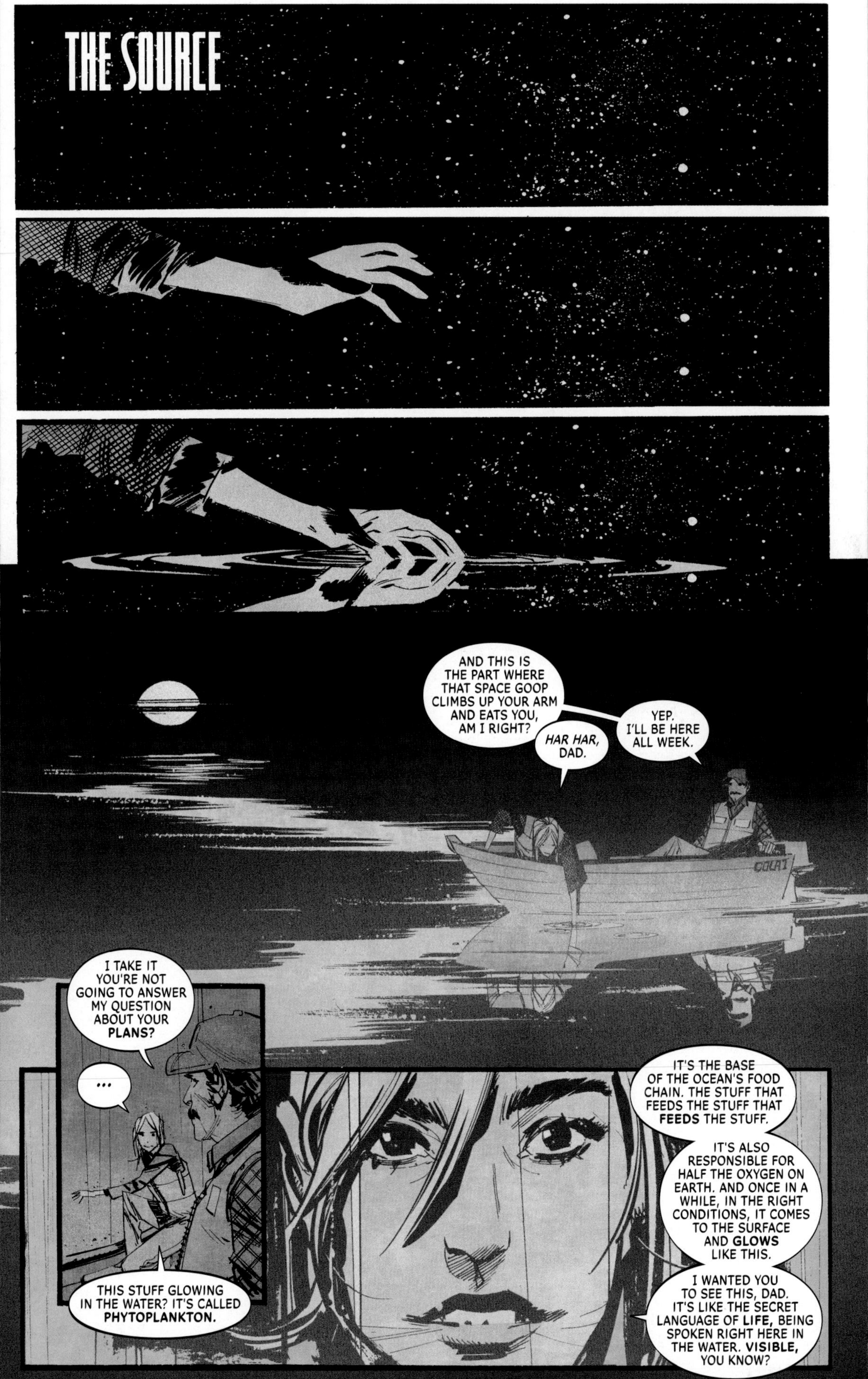
THE SOURCE
AND THIS IS THE PART WHERE THAT SPACE GOOP CLIMBS UP YOUR ARM AND EATS YOU, AM I RIGHT?
HAR HAR, DAD.
YEP. I'LL BE HERE ALL WEEK.
I TAKE IT YOU'RE NOT GOING TO ANSWER MY QUESTION ABOUT YOUR PLANS?
...
THIS STUFF GLOWING IN THE WATER? IT'S CALLED PHYTOPLANKTON.
IT'S THE BASE OF THE OCEAN'S FOOD CHAIN. THE STUFF THAT FEEDS THE STUFF THAT FEEDS THE STUFF.
IT'S ALSO RESPONSIBLE FOR HALF THE OXYGEN ON EARTH. AND ONCE IN A WHILE, IN THE RIGHT CONDITIONS, IT COMES TO THE SURFACE AND GLOWS LIKE THIS.
I WANTED YOU TO SEE THIS, DAD. IT'S LIKE THE SECRET LANGUAGE OF LIFE, BEING SPOKEN RIGHT HERE IN THE WATER. VISIBLE, YOU KNOW?

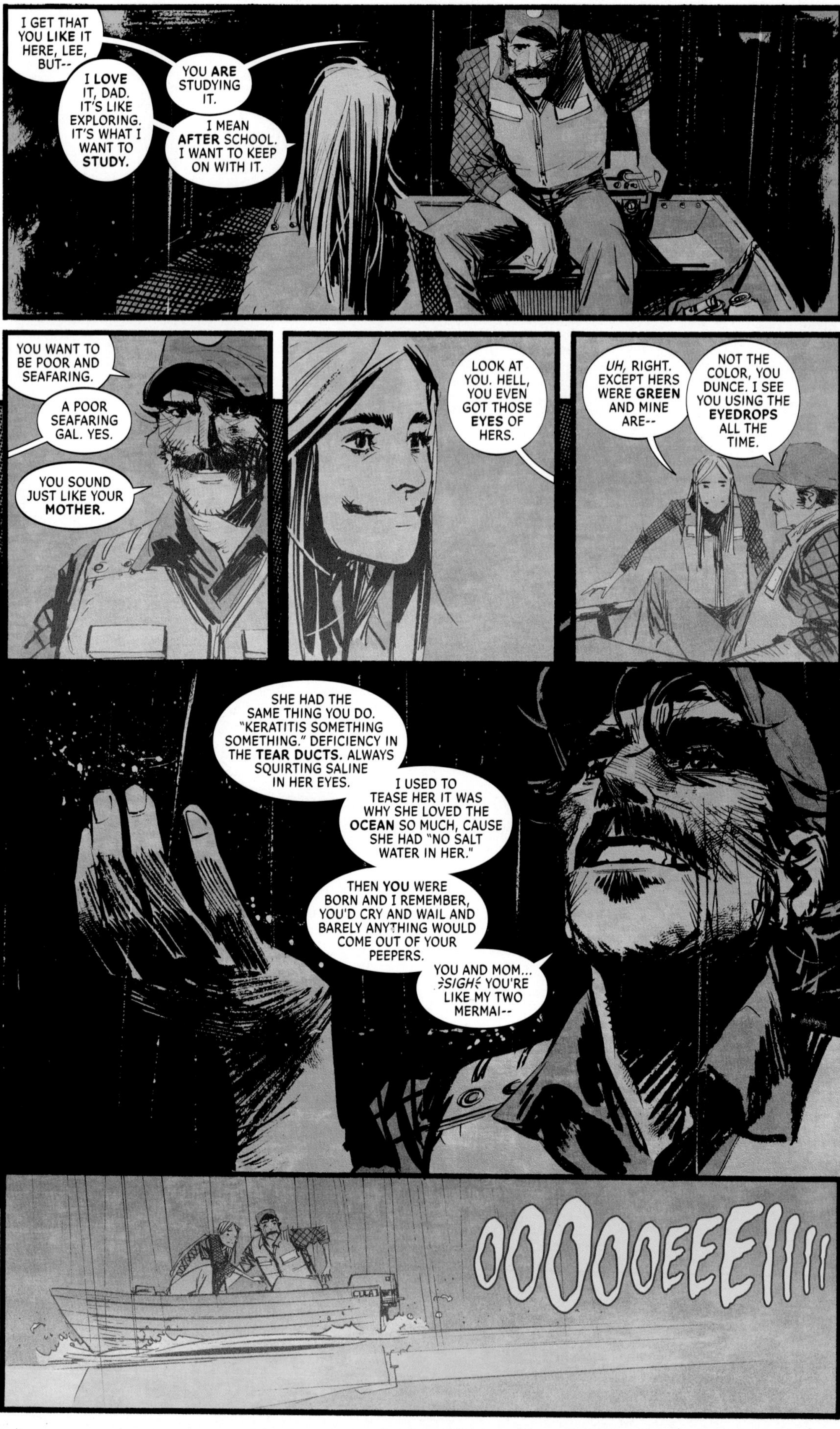
I GET THAT YOU LIKE IT HERE, LEE, BUT--
I LOVE IT, DAD. IT'S LIKE EXPLORING. IT'S WHAT I WANT TO STUDY.
YOU ARE STUDYING IT.
I MEAN AFTER SCHOOL. I WANT TO KEEP ON WITH IT.
YOU WANT TO BE POOR AND SEAFARING.
A POOR SEAFARING GAL. YES.
YOU SOUND JUST LIKE YOUR MOTHER.
LOOK AT YOU. HELL, YOU EVEN GOT THOSE EYES OF HERS.
UH, RIGHT. EXCEPT HERS WERE GREEN AND MINE ARE--
NOT THE COLOR, YOU DUNCE. I SEE YOU USING THE EYEDROPS ALL THE TIME.
SHE HAD THE SAME THING YOU DO. "KERATITIS SOMETHING SOMETHING." DEFICIENCY IN THE TEAR DUCTS. ALWAYS SQUIRTING SALINE IN HER EYES.
I USED TO TEASE HER IT WAS WHY SHE LOVED THE OCEAN SO MUCH, CAUSE SHE HAD "NO SALT WATER IN HER."
THEN YOU WERE BORN AND I REMEMBER, YOU'D CRY AND WAIL AND BARELY ANYTHING WOULD COME OUT OF YOUR PEEPERS.
YOU AND MOM... SIGH YOU'RE LIKE MY TWO MERMAI--
OOOOOEEEIIII

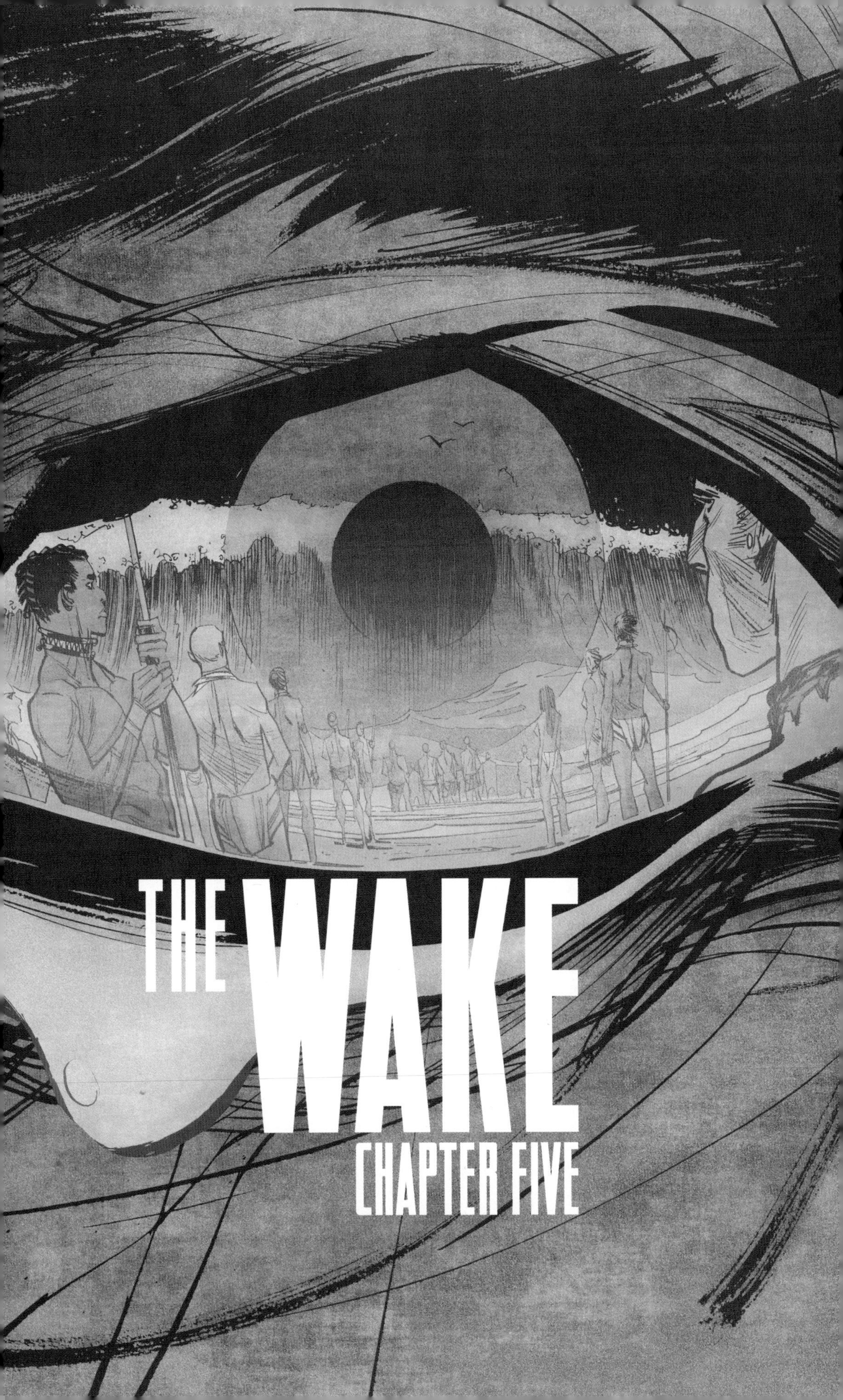
THE WAKE
CHAPTER FIVE

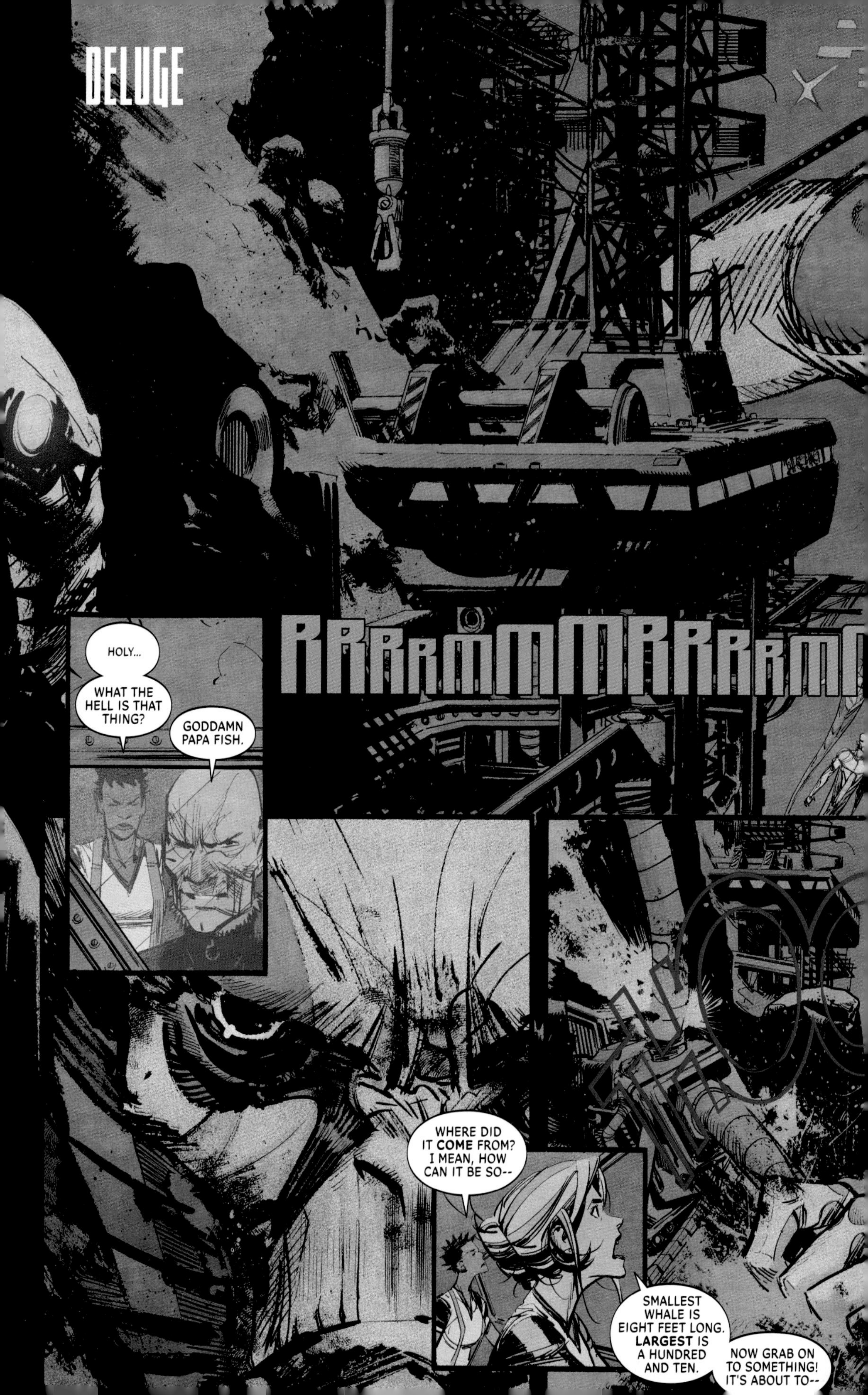
DELUGE
HOLY...
WHAT THE HELL IS THAT THING?
GODDAMN PAPA FISH.
RRRRMMMRRRRRM
WHERE DID IT COME FROM? I MEAN, HOW CAN IT BE SO--
SMALLEST WHALE IS EIGHT FEET LONG. LARGEST IS A HUNDRED AND TEN.
NOW GRAB ON TO SOMETHING! IT'S ABOUT TO--

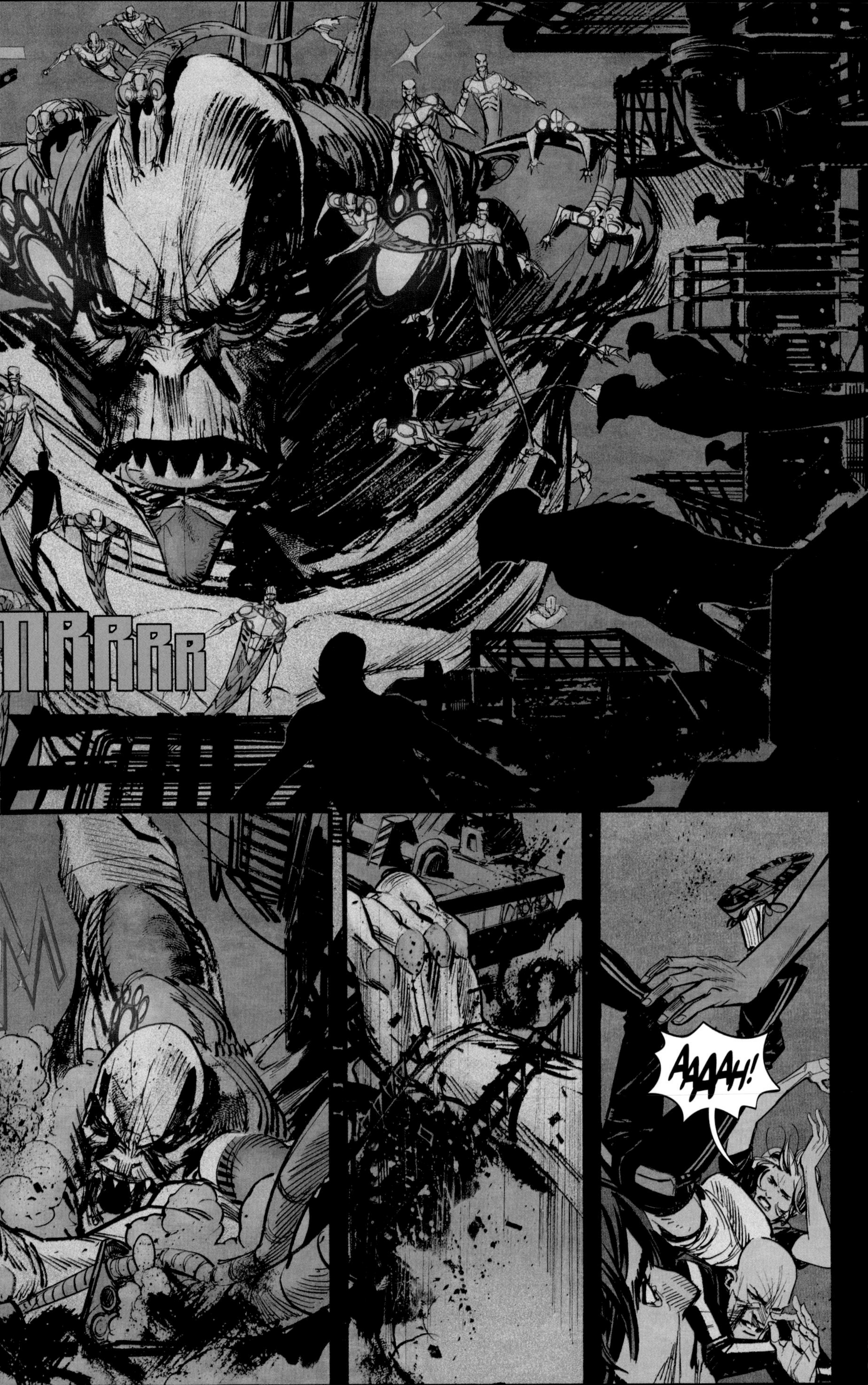
RRRR
AAAAH!

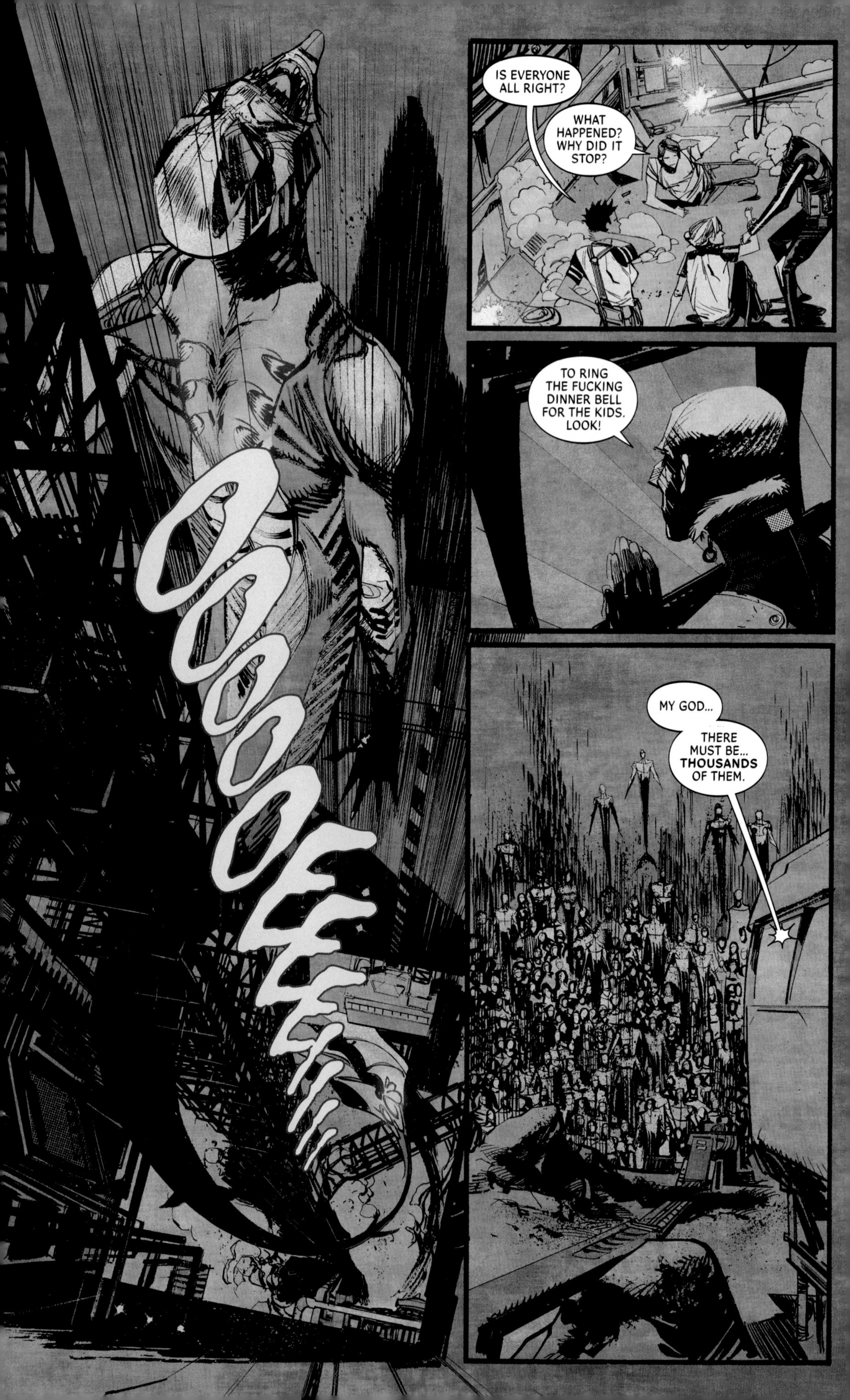
OOOOOEEEE!!!!
IS EVERYONE ALL RIGHT?
WHAT HAPPENED? WHY DID IT STOP?
TO RING THE FUCKING DINNER BELL FOR THE KIDS. LOOK!
MY GOD...
THERE MUST BE... **THOUSANDS** OF THEM.

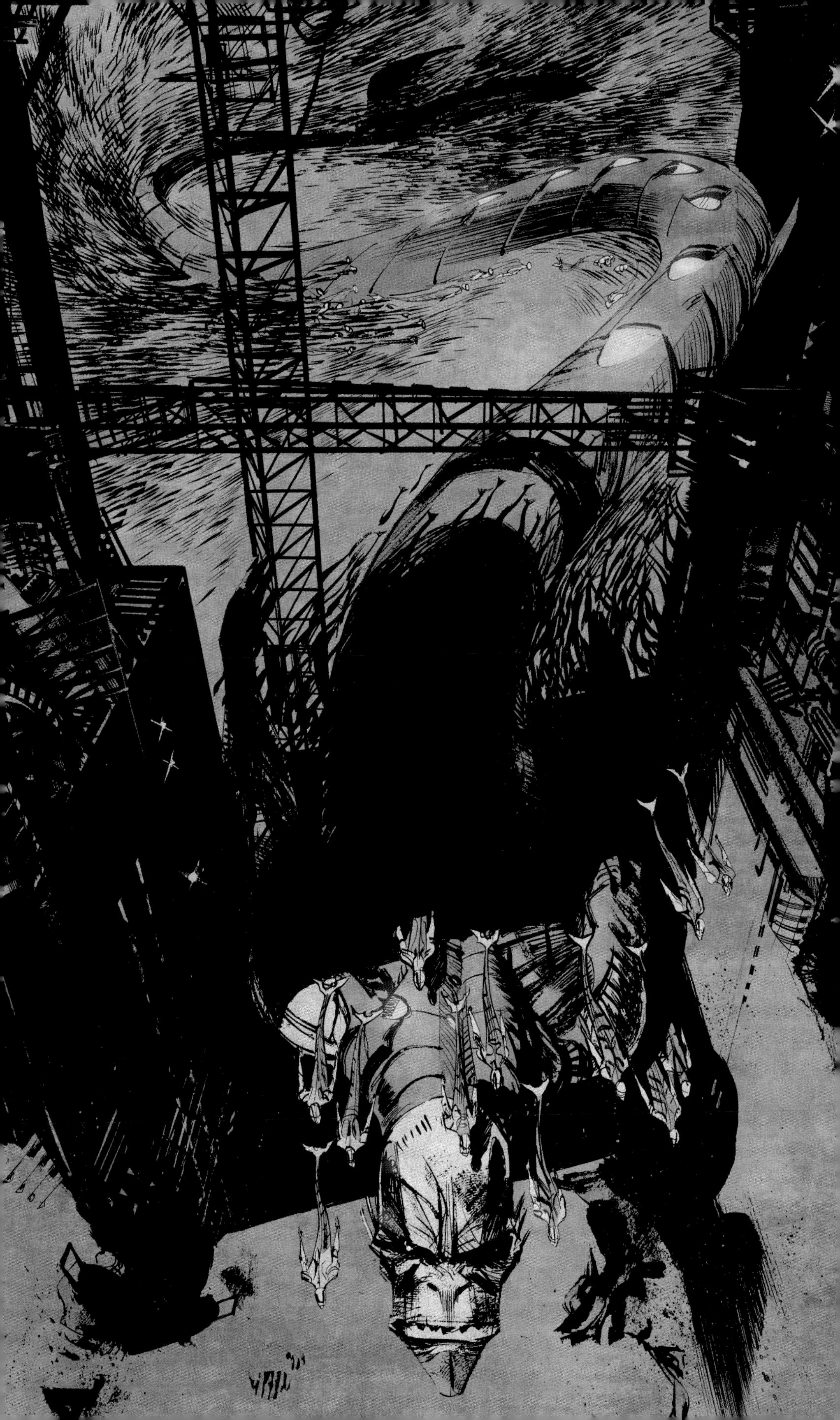

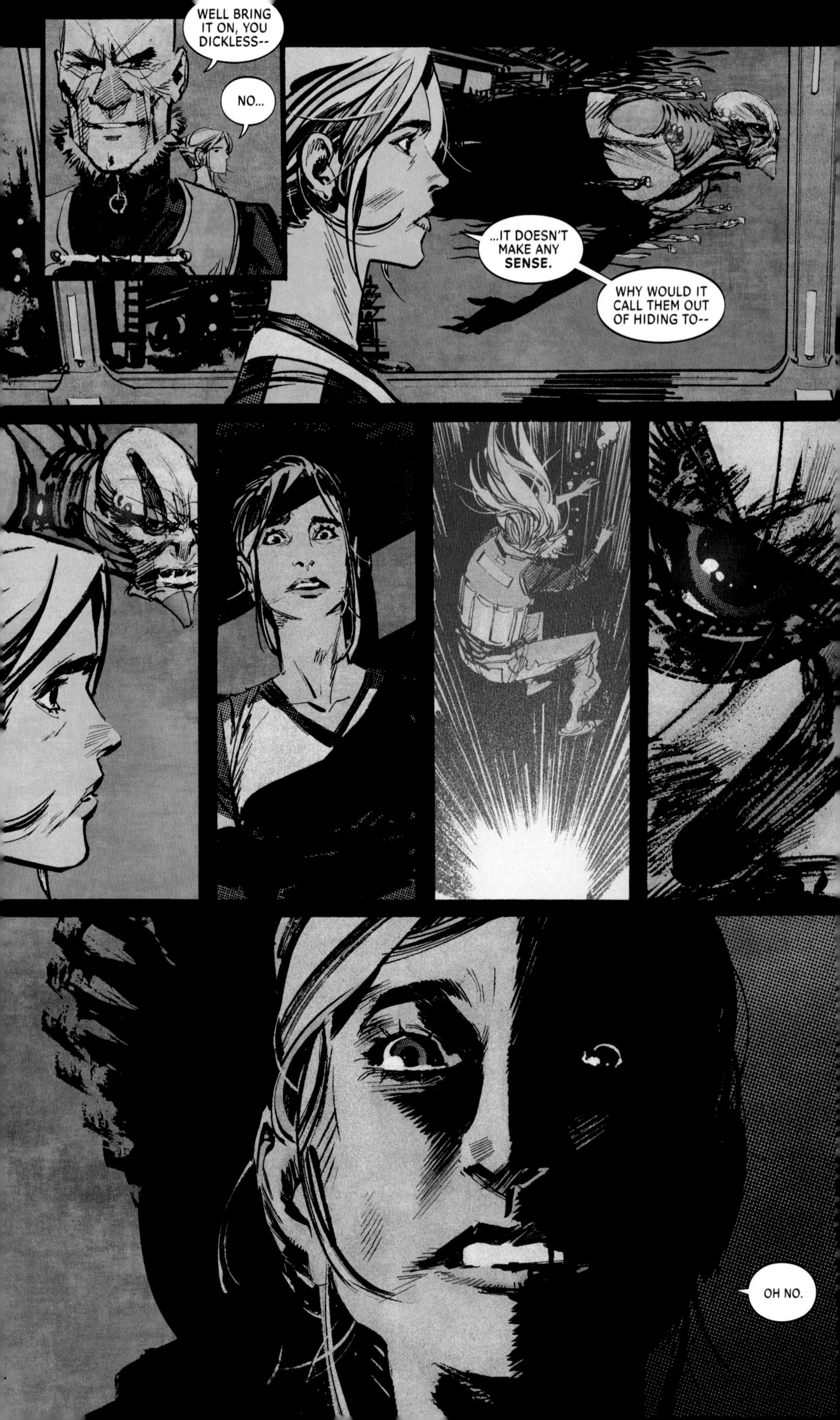
WELL BRING IT ON, YOU DICKLESS--
NO...
...IT DOESN'T MAKE ANY SENSE.
WHY WOULD IT CALL THEM OUT OF HIDING TO--
OH NO.

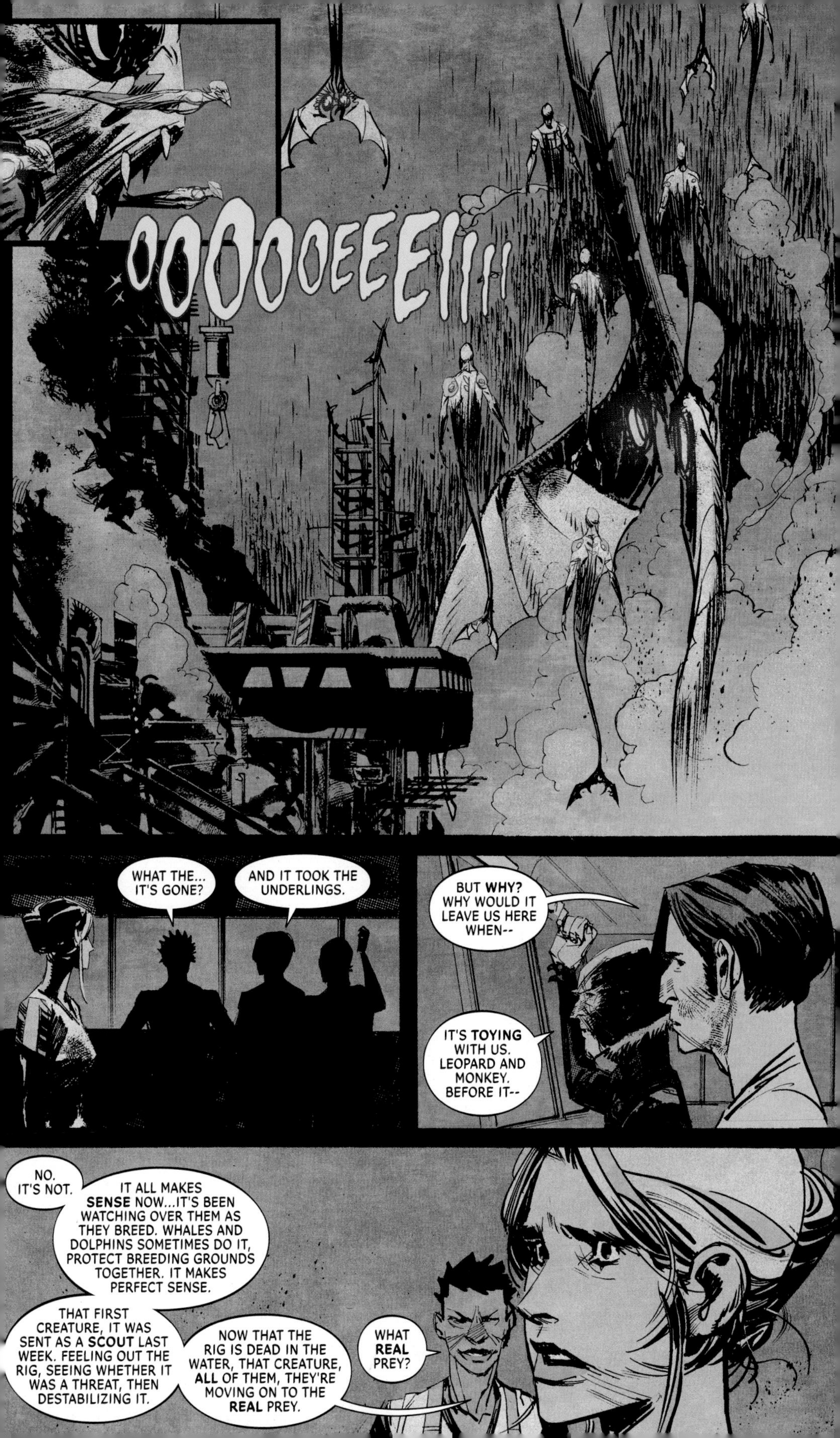
OOOOOEEEIIII
WHAT THE... IT'S GONE?
AND IT TOOK THE UNDERLINGS.
BUT **WHY?** WHY WOULD IT LEAVE US HERE WHEN--
IT'S **TOYING** WITH US. LEOPARD AND MONKEY. BEFORE IT--
NO. IT'S NOT.
IT ALL MAKES **SENSE** NOW...IT'S BEEN WATCHING OVER THEM AS THEY BREED. WHALES AND DOLPHINS SOMETIMES DO IT, PROTECT BREEDING GROUNDS TOGETHER. IT MAKES PERFECT SENSE.
THAT FIRST CREATURE, IT WAS SENT AS A **SCOUT** LAST WEEK. FEELING OUT THE RIG, SEEING WHETHER IT WAS A THREAT, THEN DESTABILIZING IT.
NOW THAT THE RIG IS DEAD IN THE WATER, THAT CREATURE, **ALL** OF THEM, THEY'RE MOVING ON TO THE **REAL** PREY.
WHAT **REAL** PREY?

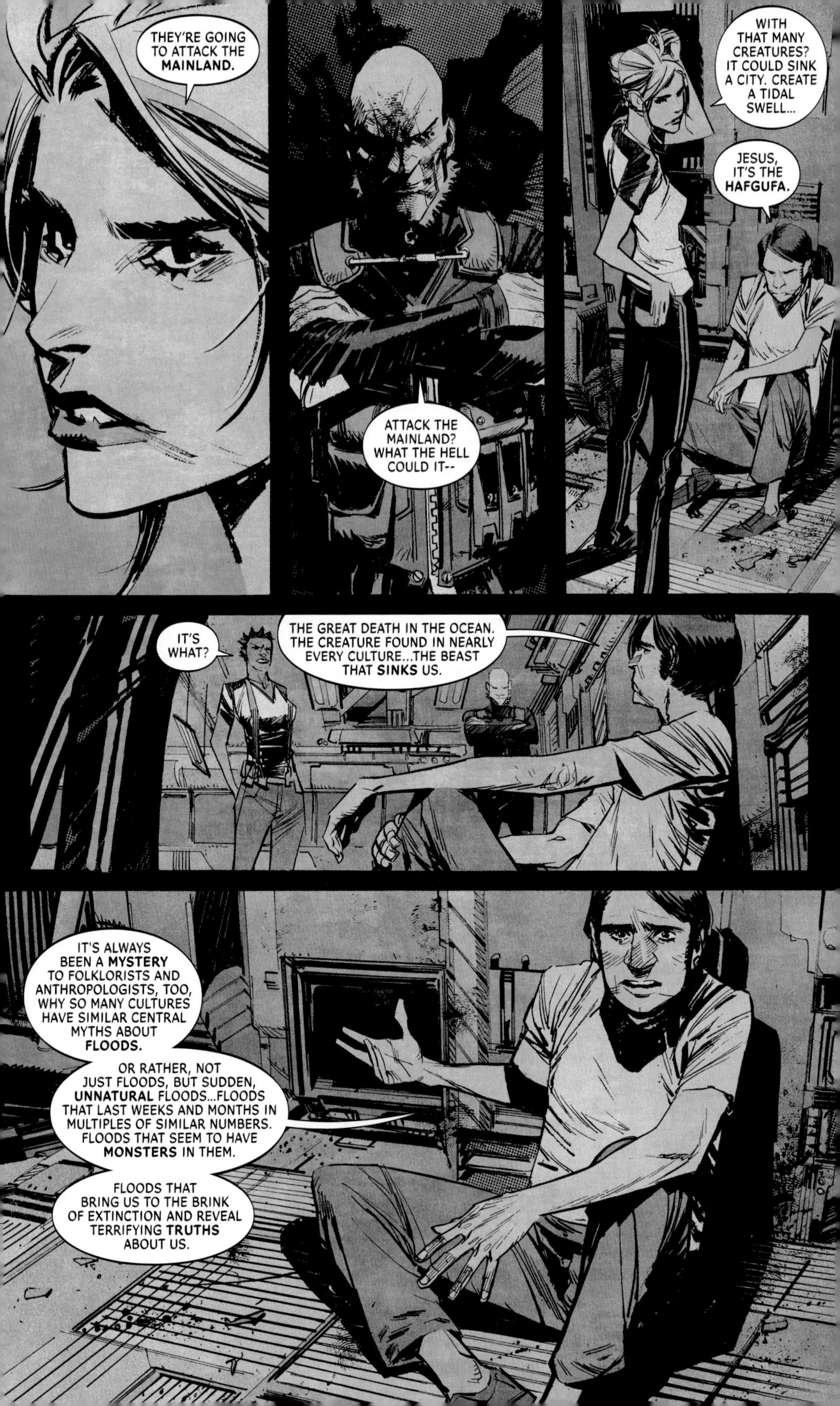

THEY'RE GOING TO ATTACK THE **MAINLAND.**
ATTACK THE MAINLAND? WHAT THE HELL COULD IT--
WITH THAT MANY CREATURES? IT COULD SINK A CITY. CREATE A TIDAL SWELL...
JESUS, IT'S THE **HAFGUFA.**
IT'S WHAT?
THE GREAT DEATH IN THE OCEAN. THE CREATURE FOUND IN NEARLY EVERY CULTURE...THE BEAST THAT **SINKS** US.
IT'S ALWAYS BEEN A **MYSTERY** TO FOLKLORISTS AND ANTHROPOLOGISTS, TOO, WHY SO MANY CULTURES HAVE SIMILAR CENTRAL MYTHS ABOUT **FLOODS.**
OR RATHER, NOT JUST FLOODS, BUT SUDDEN, **UNNATURAL** FLOODS...FLOODS THAT LAST WEEKS AND MONTHS IN MULTIPLES OF SIMILAR NUMBERS. FLOODS THAT SEEM TO HAVE **MONSTERS** IN THEM.
FLOODS THAT BRING US TO THE BRINK OF EXTINCTION AND REVEAL TERRIFYING **TRUTHS** ABOUT US.

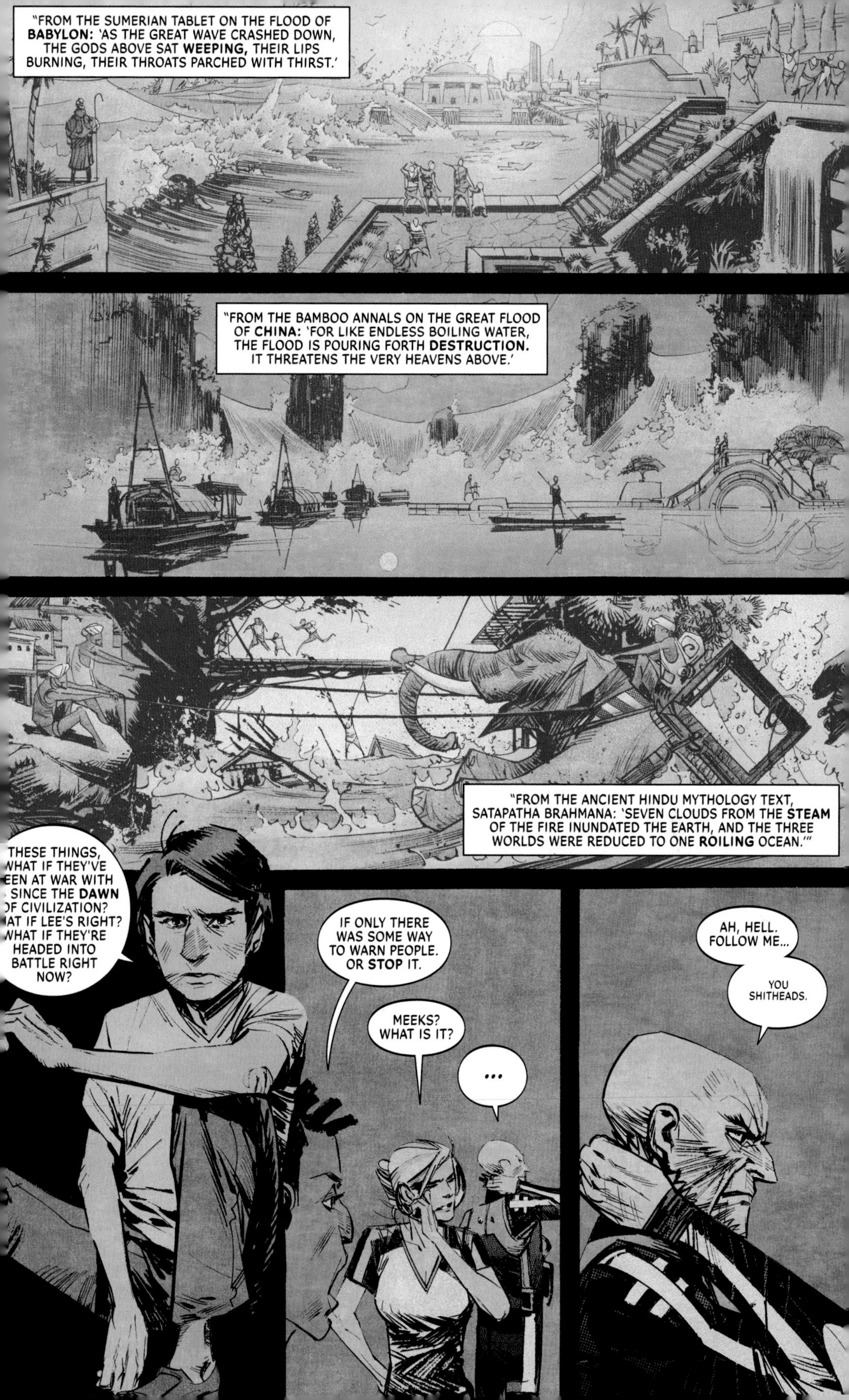
"FROM THE SUMERIAN TABLET ON THE FLOOD OF BABYLON: 'AS THE GREAT WAVE CRASHED DOWN, THE GODS ABOVE SAT WEEPING, THEIR LIPS BURNING, THEIR THROATS PARCHED WITH THIRST.'
"FROM THE BAMBOO ANNALS ON THE GREAT FLOOD OF CHINA: 'FOR LIKE ENDLESS BOILING WATER, THE FLOOD IS POURING FORTH DESTRUCTION. IT THREATENS THE VERY HEAVENS ABOVE.'
"FROM THE ANCIENT HINDU MYTHOLOGY TEXT, SATAPATHA BRAHMANA: 'SEVEN CLOUDS FROM THE STEAM OF THE FIRE INUNDATED THE EARTH, AND THE THREE WORLDS WERE REDUCED TO ONE ROILING OCEAN.'"
THESE THINGS, WHAT IF THEY'VE EEN AT WAR WITH SINCE THE DAWN OF CIVILIZATION? AT IF LEE'S RIGHT? WHAT IF THEY'RE HEADED INTO BATTLE RIGHT NOW?
IF ONLY THERE WAS SOME WAY TO WARN PEOPLE. OR STOP IT.
MEEKS? WHAT IS IT?
...
AH, HELL. FOLLOW ME...
YOU SHITHEADS.

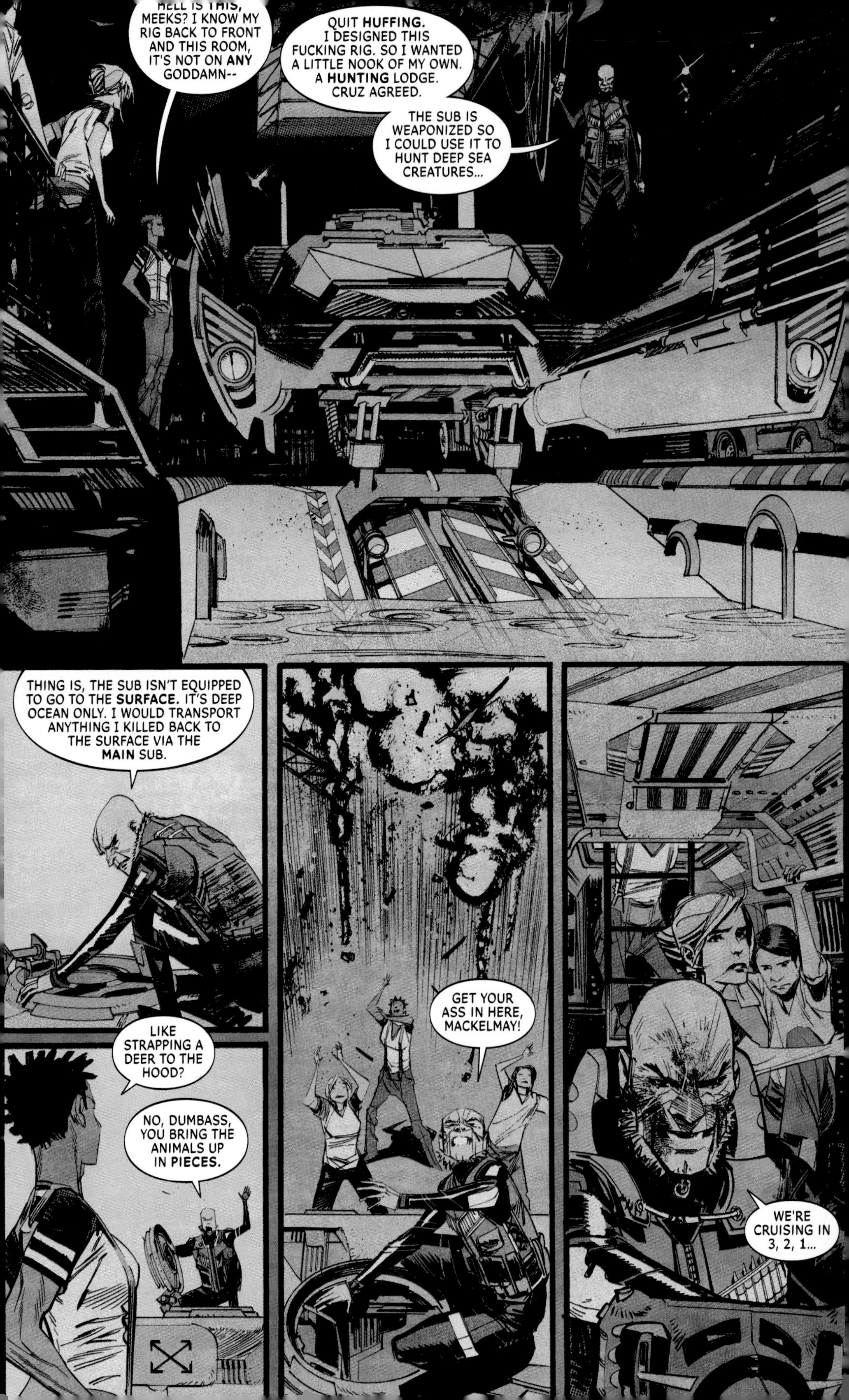
HELL IS THIS, MEEKS? I KNOW MY RIG BACK TO FRONT AND THIS ROOM, IT'S NOT ON ANY GODDAMN--
QUIT HUFFING. I DESIGNED THIS FUCKING RIG. SO I WANTED A LITTLE NOOK OF MY OWN. A HUNTING LODGE. CRUZ AGREED.
THE SUB IS WEAPONIZED SO I COULD USE IT TO HUNT DEEP SEA CREATURES...
THING IS, THE SUB ISN'T EQUIPPED TO GO TO THE SURFACE. IT'S DEEP OCEAN ONLY. I WOULD TRANSPORT ANYTHING I KILLED BACK TO THE SURFACE VIA THE MAIN SUB.
LIKE STRAPPING A DEER TO THE HOOD?
NO, DUMBASS, YOU BRING THE ANIMALS UP IN PIECES.
GET YOUR ASS IN HERE, MACKELMAY!
WE'RE CRUISING IN 3, 2, 1...

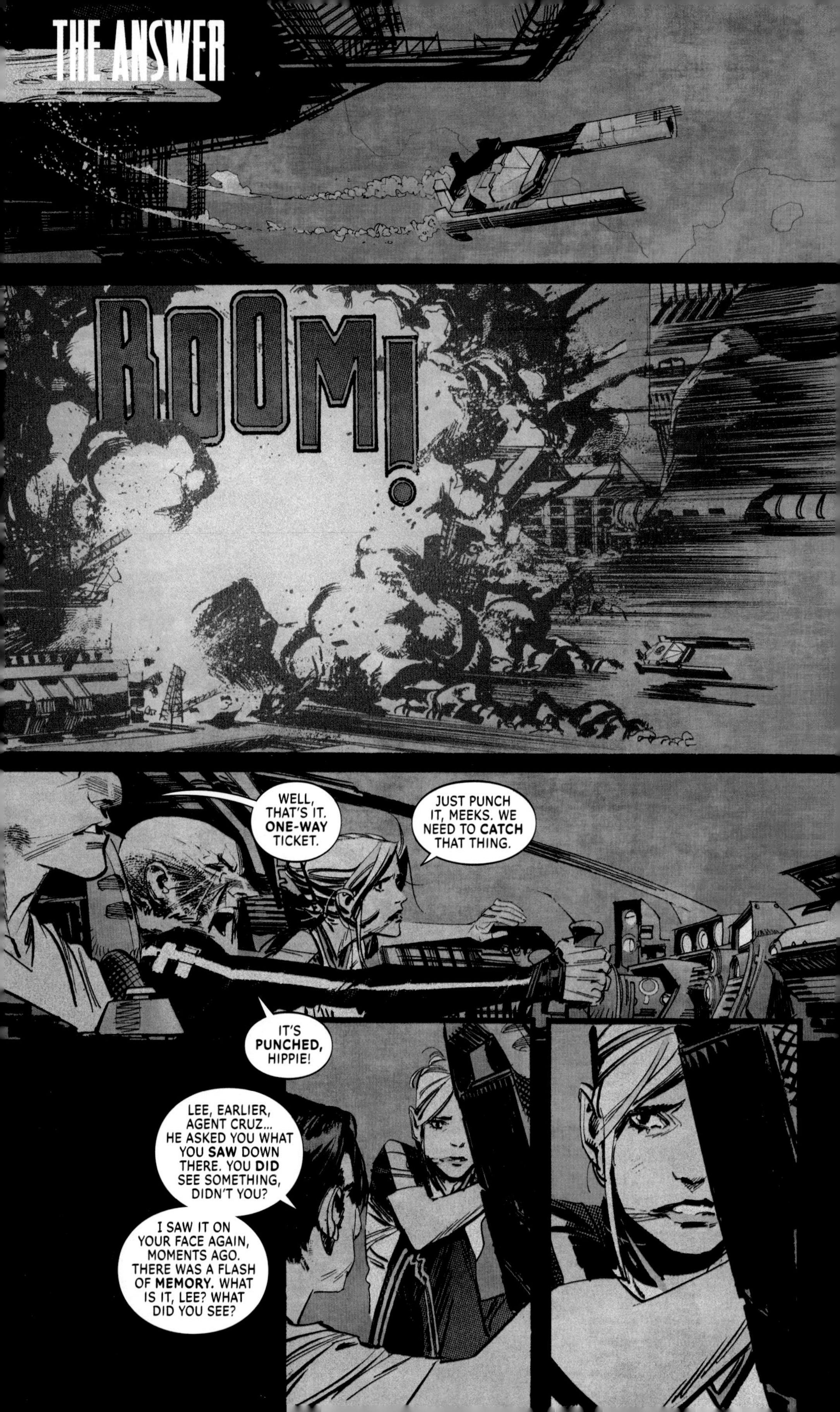
THE ANSWER
BOOM!
WELL, THAT'S IT. ONE-WAY TICKET.
JUST PUNCH IT, MEEKS. WE NEED TO CATCH THAT THING.
IT'S PUNCHED, HIPPIE!
LEE, EARLIER, AGENT CRUZ... HE ASKED YOU WHAT YOU SAW DOWN THERE. YOU DID SEE SOMETHING, DIDN'T YOU?
I SAW IT ON YOUR FACE AGAIN, MOMENTS AGO. THERE WAS A FLASH OF MEMORY. WHAT IS IT, LEE? WHAT DID YOU SEE?

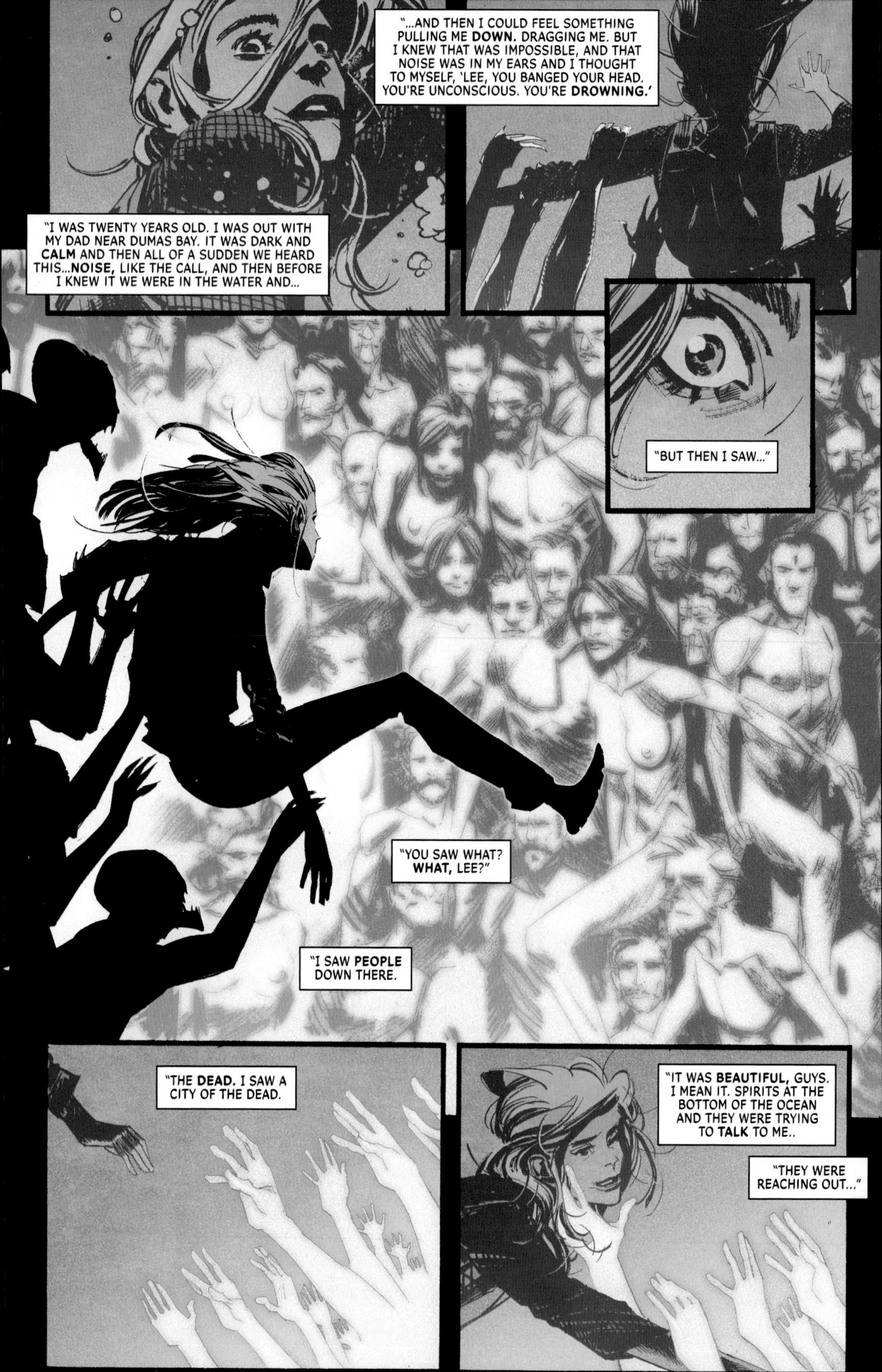
"...AND THEN I COULD FEEL SOMETHING PULLING ME DOWN. DRAGGING ME. BUT I KNEW THAT WAS IMPOSSIBLE, AND THAT NOISE WAS IN MY EARS AND I THOUGHT TO MYSELF, 'LEE, YOU BANGED YOUR HEAD. YOU'RE UNCONSCIOUS. YOU'RE DROWNING.'
"I WAS TWENTY YEARS OLD. I WAS OUT WITH MY DAD NEAR DUMAS BAY. IT WAS DARK AND CALM AND THEN ALL OF A SUDDEN WE HEARD THIS...NOISE, LIKE THE CALL, AND THEN BEFORE I KNEW IT WE WERE IN THE WATER AND...
"BUT THEN I SAW..."
"YOU SAW WHAT? WHAT, LEE?"
"I SAW PEOPLE DOWN THERE.
"THE DEAD. I SAW A CITY OF THE DEAD.
"IT WAS BEAUTIFUL, GUYS. I MEAN IT. SPIRITS AT THE BOTTOM OF THE OCEAN AND THEY WERE TRYING TO TALK TO ME..
"THEY WERE REACHING OUT..."

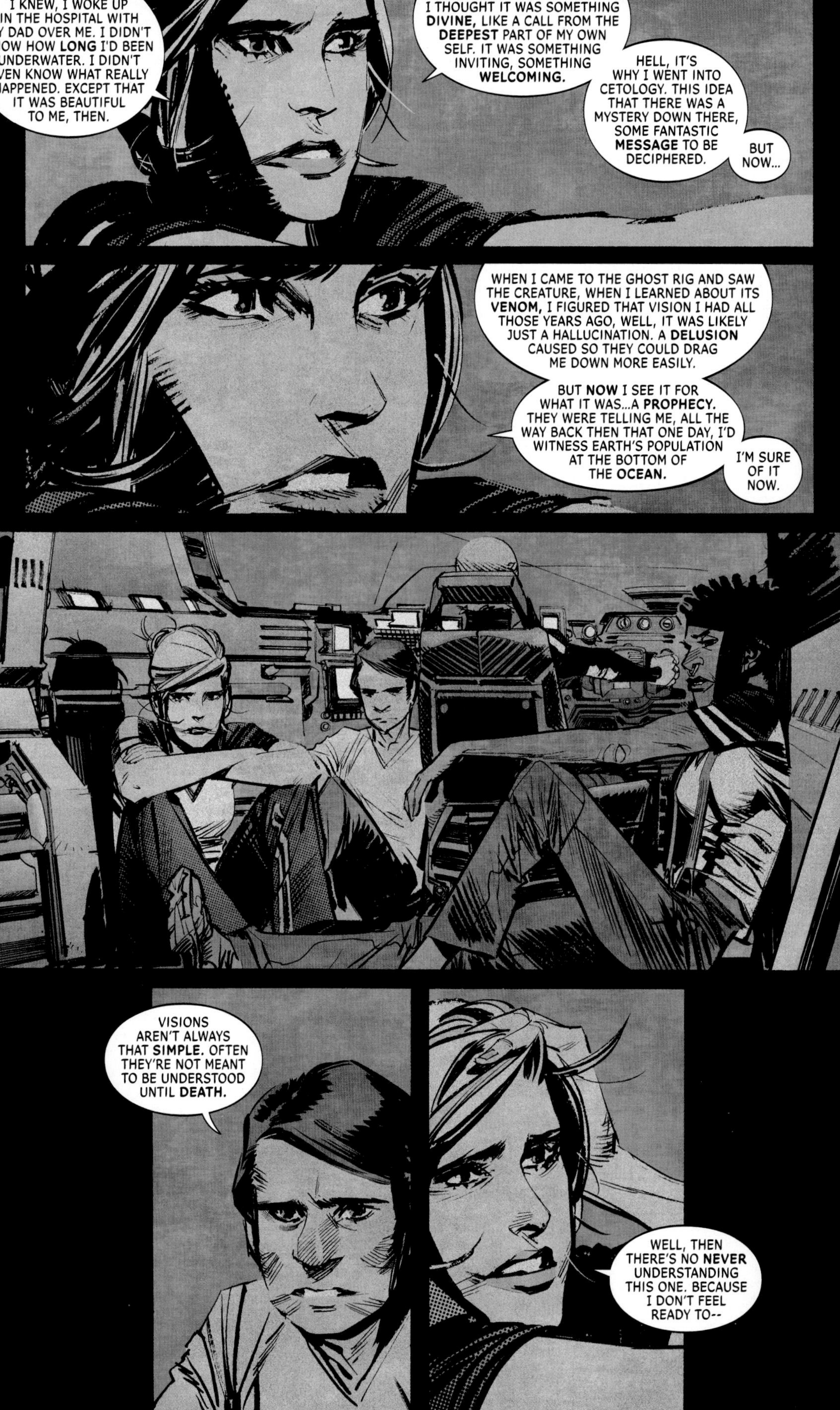
I KNEW, I WOKE UP IN THE HOSPITAL WITH MY DAD OVER ME. I DIDN'T KNOW HOW LONG I'D BEEN UNDERWATER. I DIDN'T EVEN KNOW WHAT REALLY HAPPENED. EXCEPT THAT IT WAS BEAUTIFUL TO ME, THEN.
I THOUGHT IT WAS SOMETHING DIVINE, LIKE A CALL FROM THE DEEPEST PART OF MY OWN SELF. IT WAS SOMETHING INVITING, SOMETHING WELCOMING.
HELL, IT'S WHY I WENT INTO CETOLOGY. THIS IDEA THAT THERE WAS A MYSTERY DOWN THERE, SOME FANTASTIC MESSAGE TO BE DECIPHERED.
BUT NOW...
WHEN I CAME TO THE GHOST RIG AND SAW THE CREATURE, WHEN I LEARNED ABOUT ITS VENOM, I FIGURED THAT VISION I HAD ALL THOSE YEARS AGO, WELL, IT WAS LIKELY JUST A HALLUCINATION. A DELUSION CAUSED SO THEY COULD DRAG ME DOWN MORE EASILY.
BUT NOW I SEE IT FOR WHAT IT WAS...A PROPHECY. THEY WERE TELLING ME, ALL THE WAY BACK THEN THAT ONE DAY, I'D WITNESS EARTH'S POPULATION AT THE BOTTOM OF THE OCEAN.
I'M SURE OF IT NOW.
VISIONS AREN'T ALWAYS THAT SIMPLE. OFTEN THEY'RE NOT MEANT TO BE UNDERSTOOD UNTIL DEATH.
WELL, THEN THERE'S NO NEVER UNDERSTANDING THIS ONE. BECAUSE I DON'T FEEL READY TO--

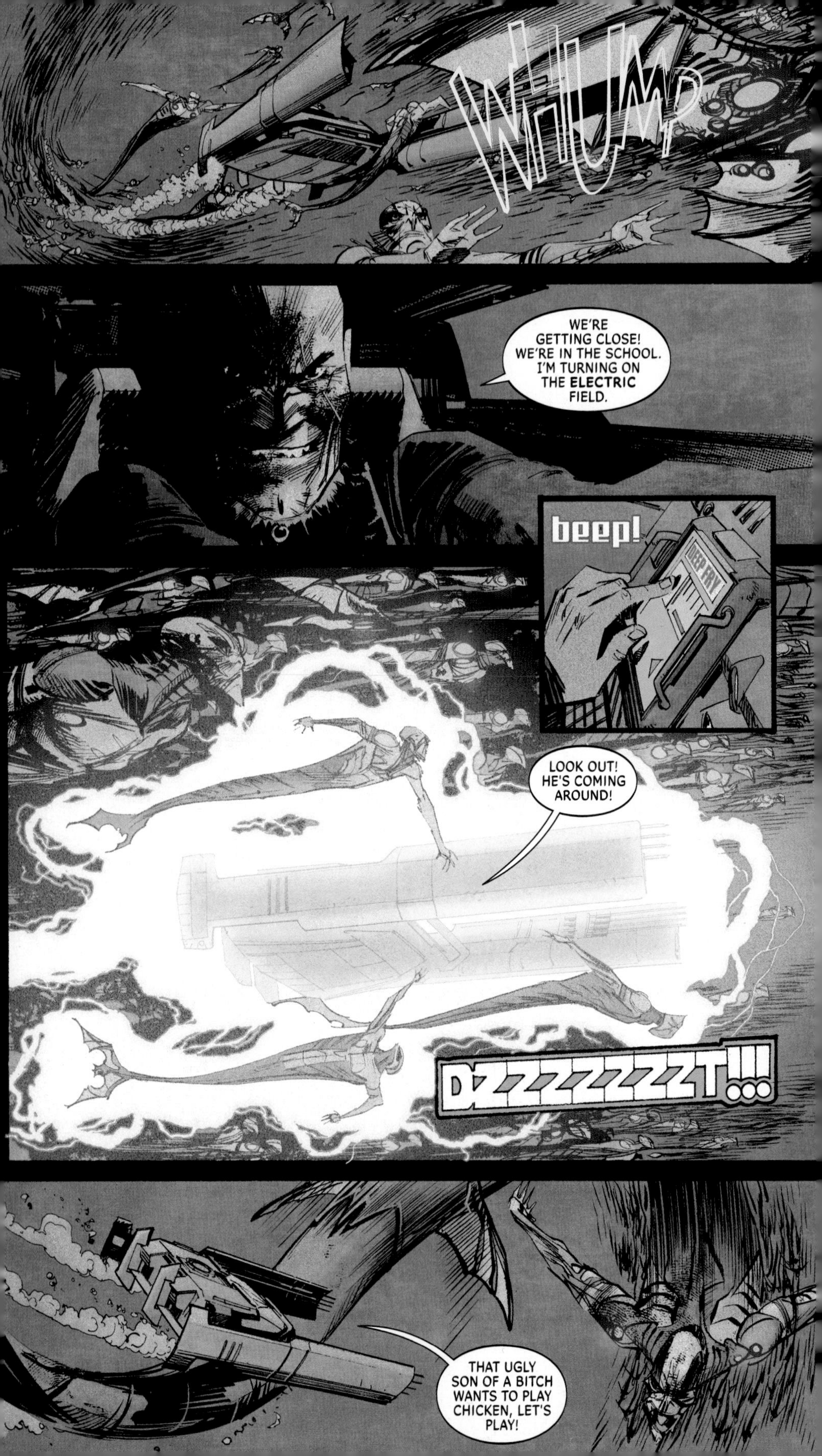
WHUMP
WE'RE GETTING CLOSE! WE'RE IN THE SCHOOL. I'M TURNING ON THE ELECTRIC FIELD.
beep!
DEEP FRY
LOOK OUT! HE'S COMING AROUND!
DZZZZZZZZT!!!
THAT UGLY SON OF A BITCH WANTS TO PLAY CHICKEN, LET'S PLAY!

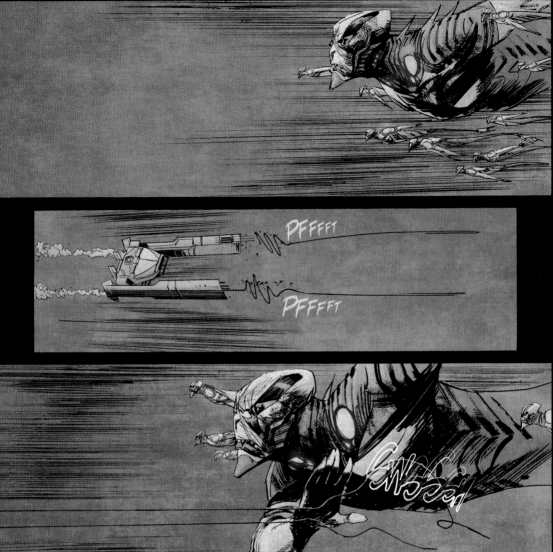

PFFFFT

PFFFFT

GNOSSE

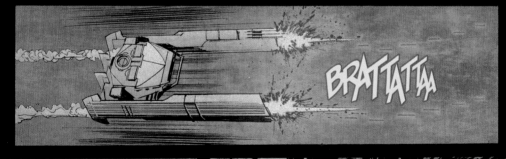

BRATTATTAA

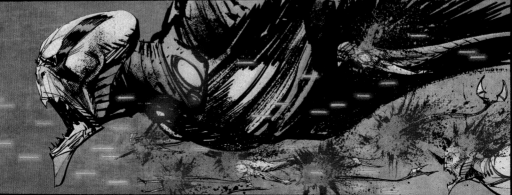

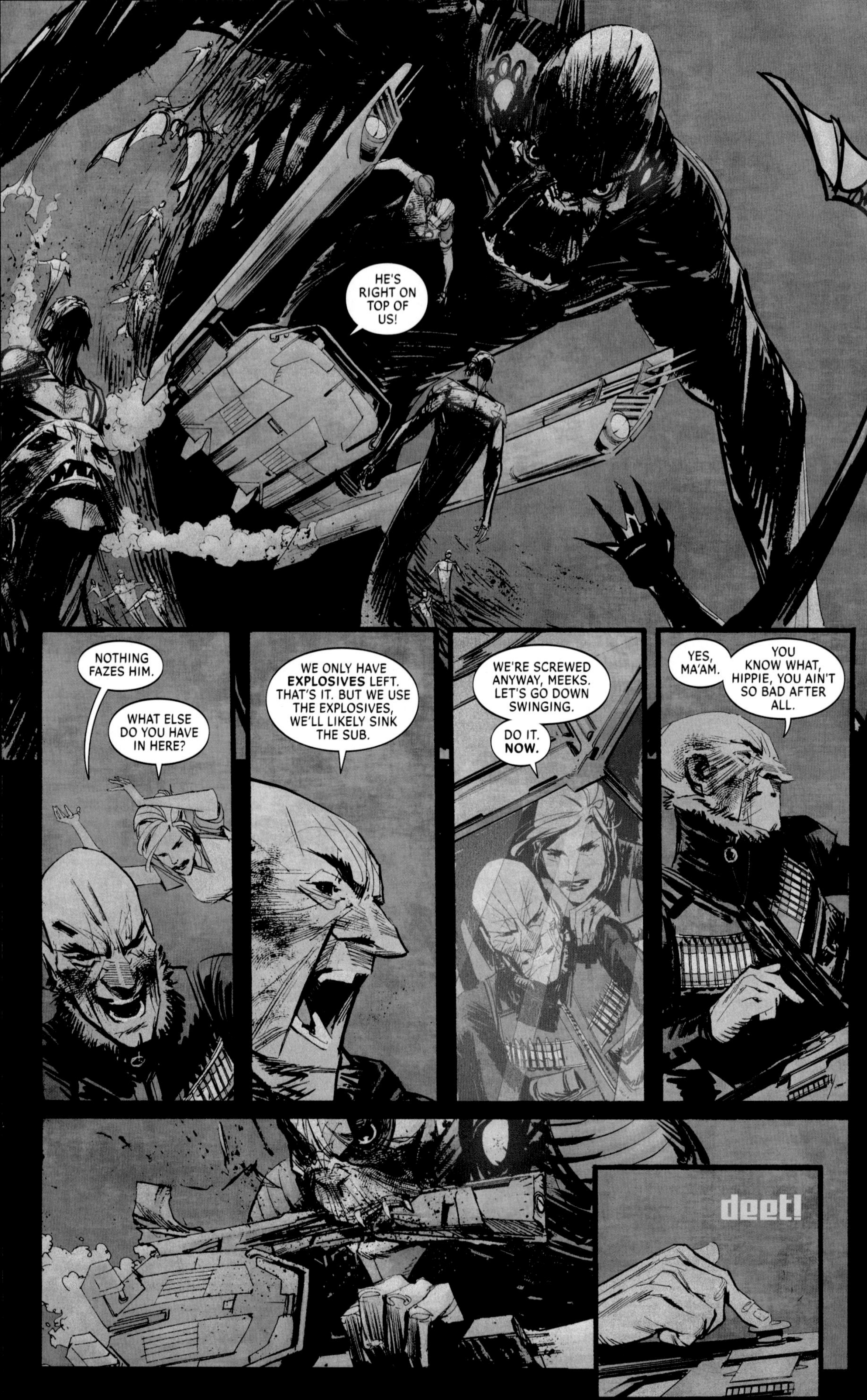
HE'S RIGHT ON TOP OF US!
NOTHING FAZES HIM.
WHAT ELSE DO YOU HAVE IN HERE?
WE ONLY HAVE **EXPLOSIVES** LEFT. THAT'S IT. BUT WE USE THE EXPLOSIVES, WE'LL LIKELY SINK THE SUB.
WE'RE SCREWED ANYWAY, MEEKS. LET'S GO DOWN SWINGING.
DO IT. **NOW.**
YES, MA'AM.
YOU KNOW WHAT, HIPPIE, YOU AIN'T SO BAD AFTER ALL.
deet!

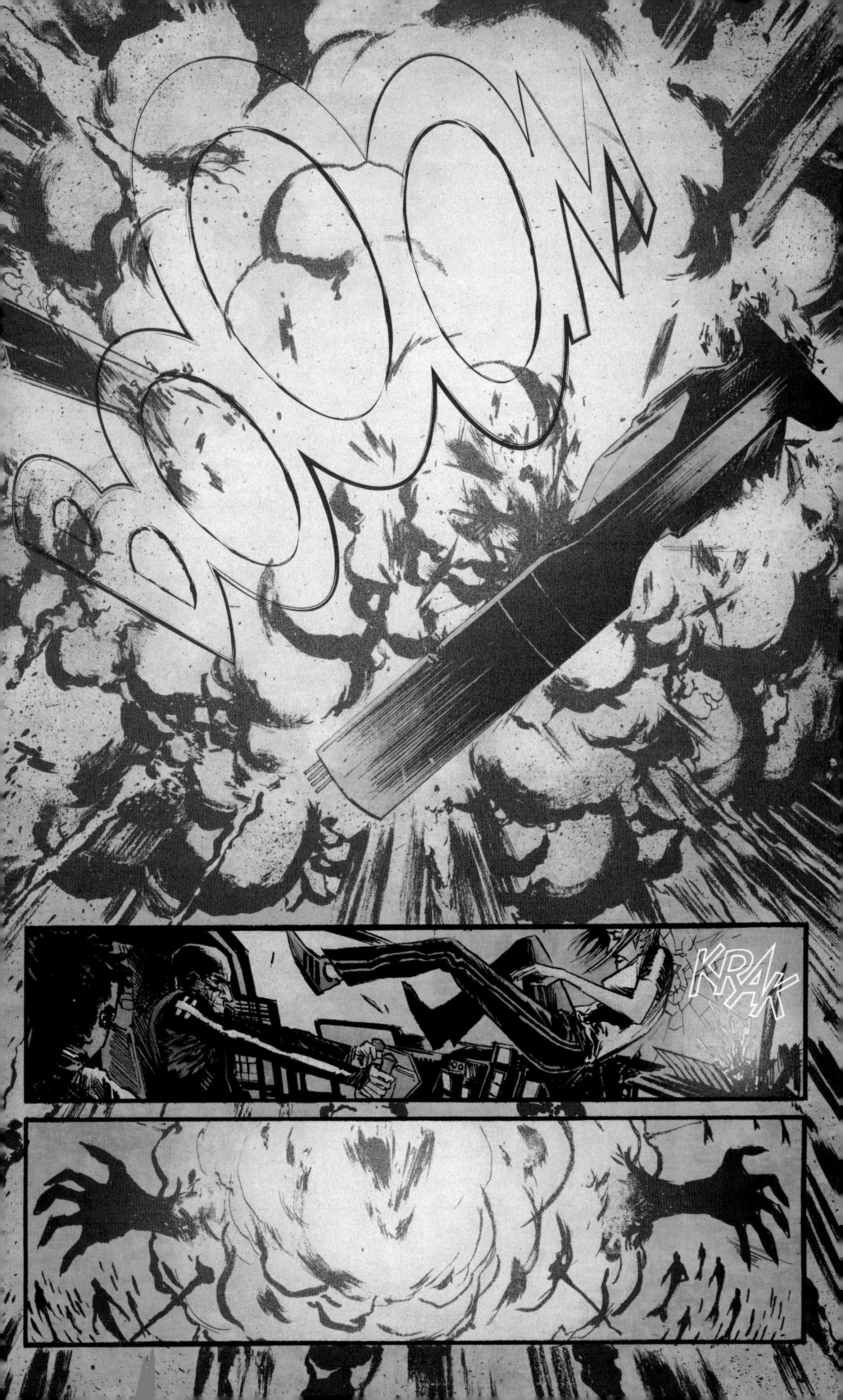
BOOOOM
KRAK

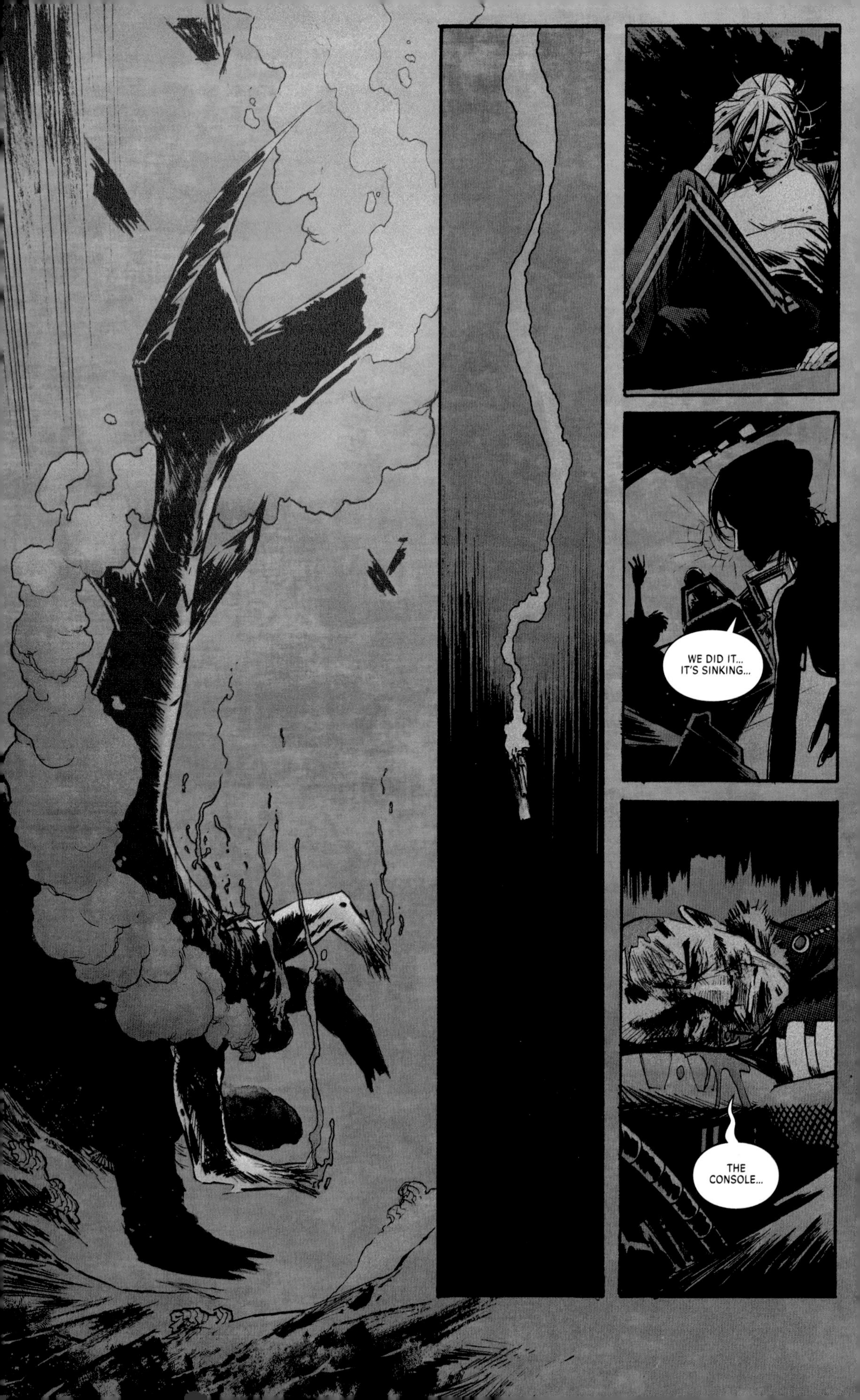
WE DID IT...
IT'S SINKING...
THE CONSOLE...

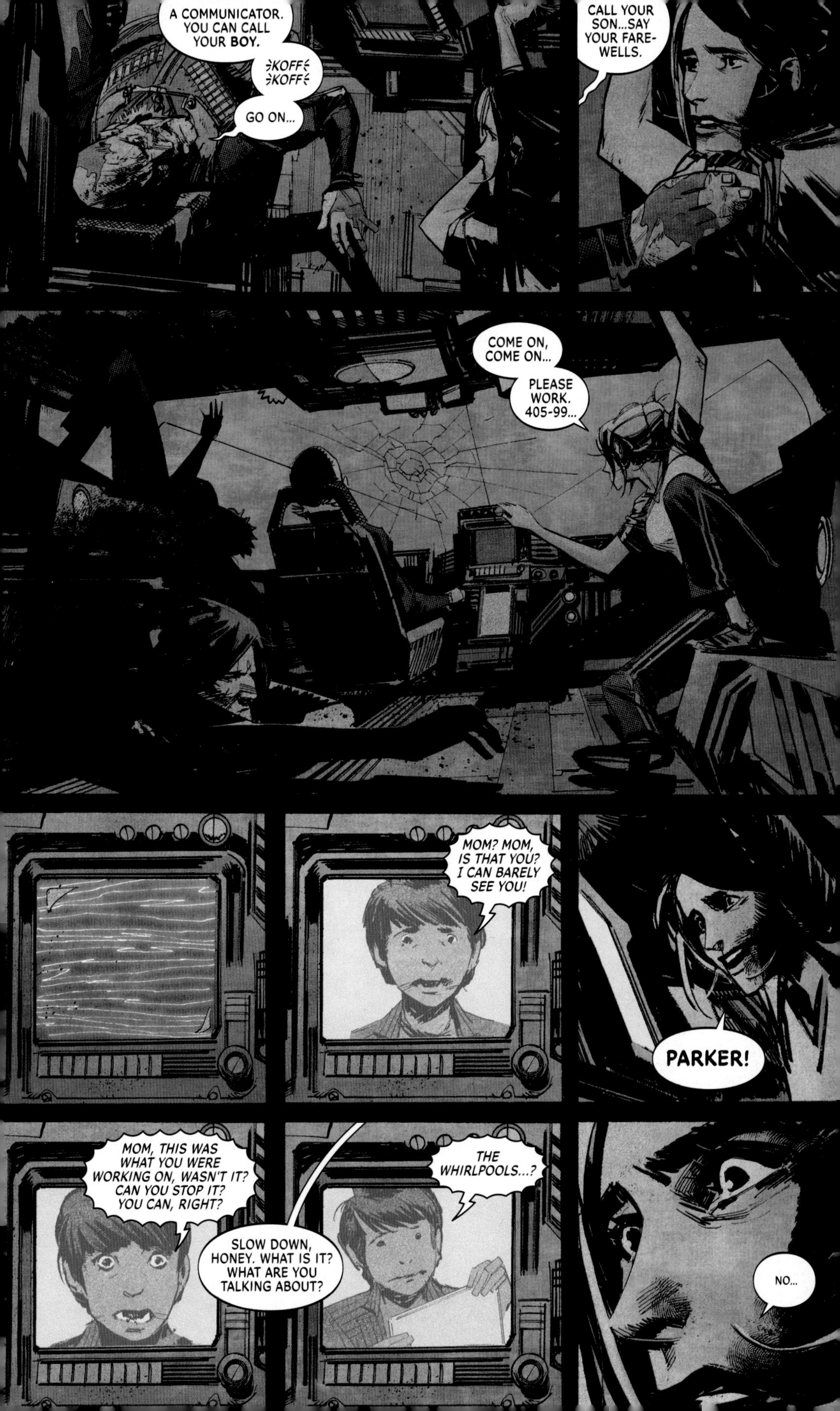
A COMMUNICATOR. YOU CAN CALL YOUR BOY.
KOFF KOFF
GO ON...
CALL YOUR SON...SAY YOUR FARE-WELLS.
COME ON, COME ON...
PLEASE WORK. 405-99...
MOM? MOM, IS THAT YOU? I CAN BARELY SEE YOU!
PARKER!
MOM, THIS WAS WHAT YOU WERE WORKING ON, WASN'T IT? CAN YOU STOP IT? YOU CAN, RIGHT?
SLOW DOWN, HONEY. WHAT IS IT? WHAT ARE YOU TALKING ABOUT?
THE WHIRLPOOLS...?
NO...

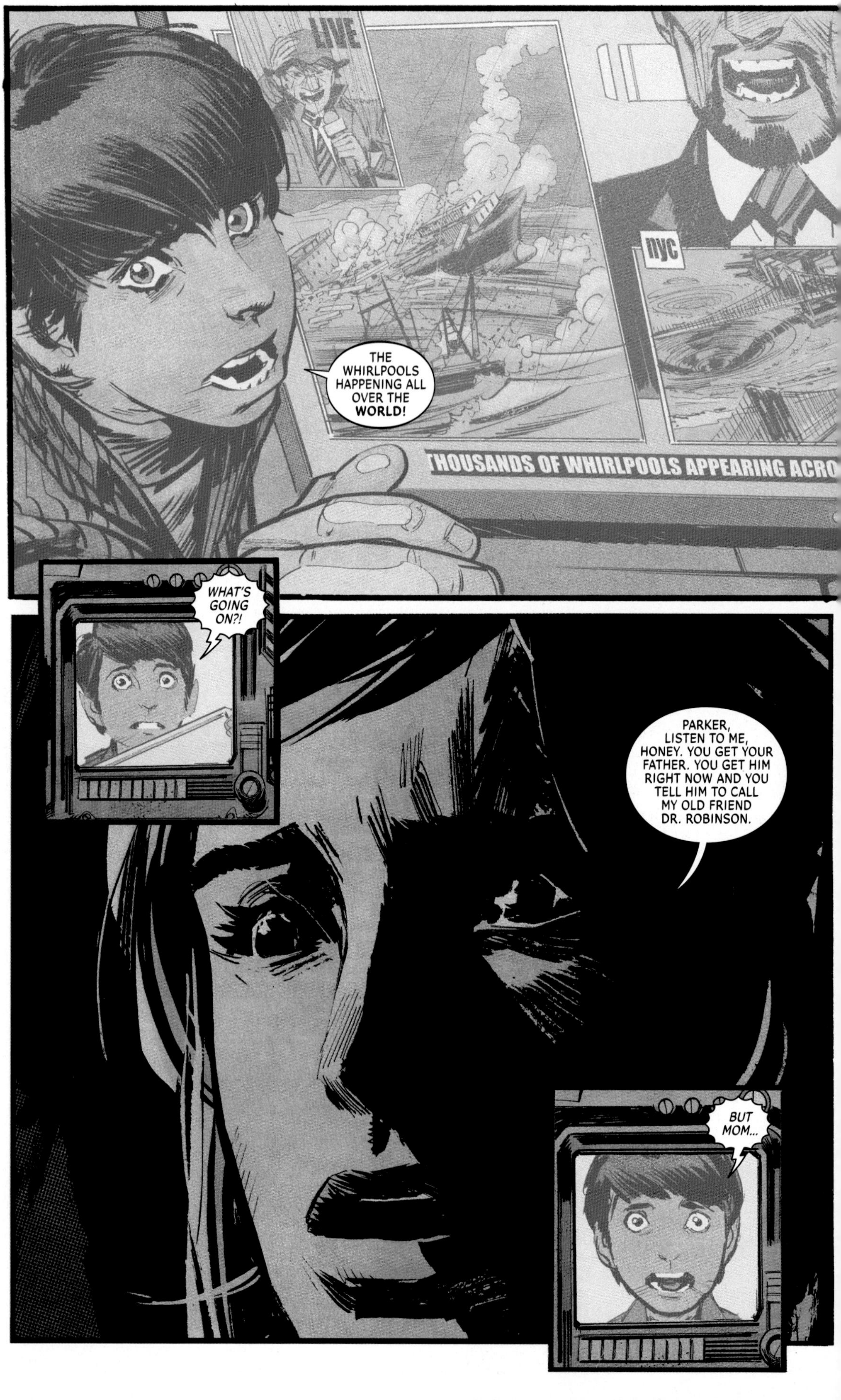

LIVE
nyc
THE WHIRLPOOLS HAPPENING ALL OVER THE **WORLD**!
THOUSANDS OF WHIRLPOOLS APPEARING ACRO
WHAT'S GOING ON?!
PARKER, LISTEN TO ME, HONEY. YOU GET YOUR FATHER. YOU GET HIM RIGHT NOW AND YOU TELL HIM TO CALL MY OLD FRIEND DR. ROBINSON.
BUT MOM...

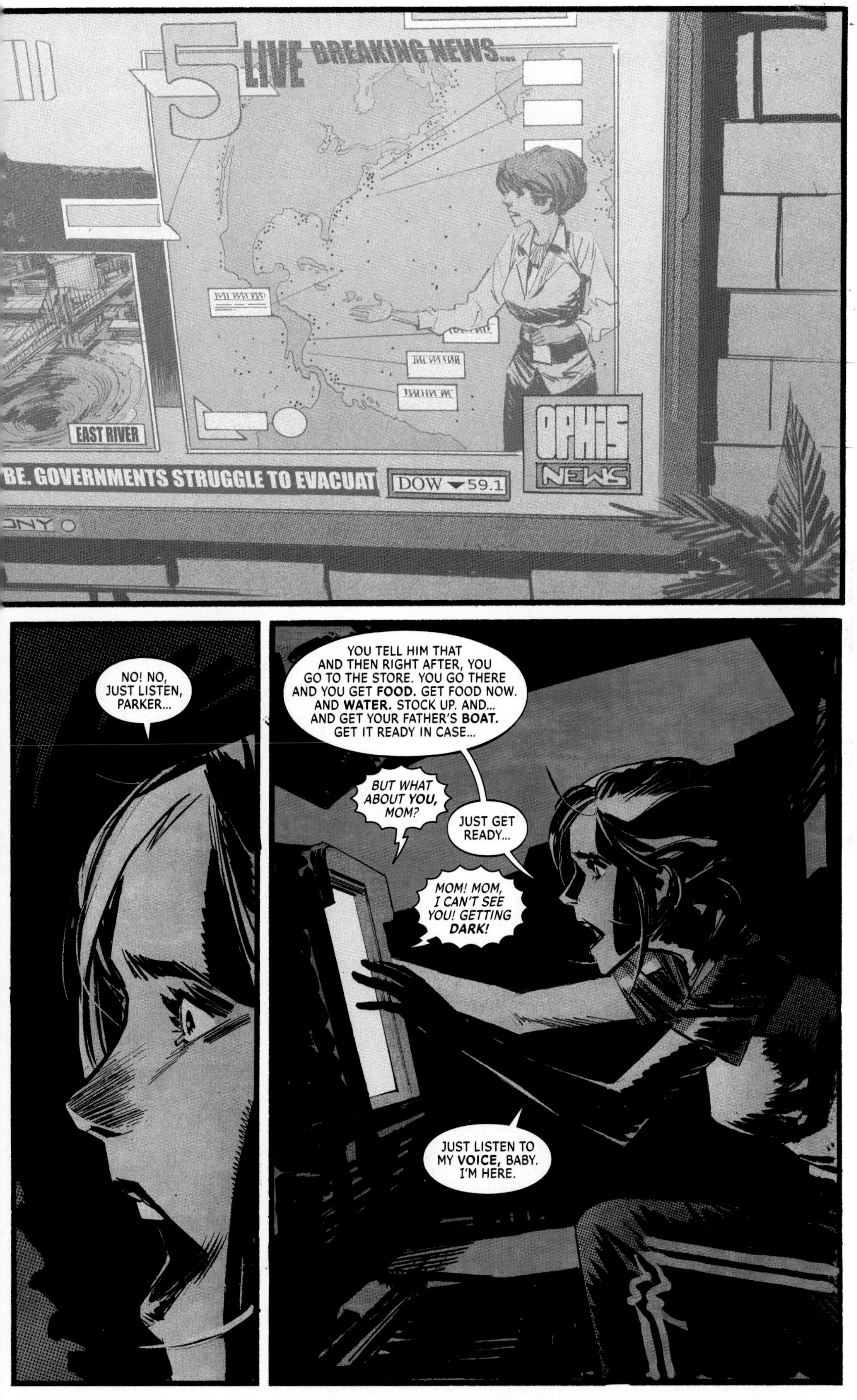

5 LIVE BREAKING NEWS...
EAST RIVER
BE. GOVERNMENTS STRUGGLE TO EVACUAT
DOW 59.1
OPHIS NEWS
NO! NO, JUST LISTEN, PARKER...
YOU TELL HIM THAT AND THEN RIGHT AFTER, YOU GO TO THE STORE. YOU GO THERE AND YOU GET FOOD. GET FOOD NOW. AND WATER. STOCK UP. AND... AND GET YOUR FATHER'S BOAT. GET IT READY IN CASE...
BUT WHAT ABOUT YOU, MOM?
JUST GET READY...
MOM! MOM, I CAN'T SEE YOU! GETTING DARK!
JUST LISTEN TO MY VOICE, BABY. I'M HERE.

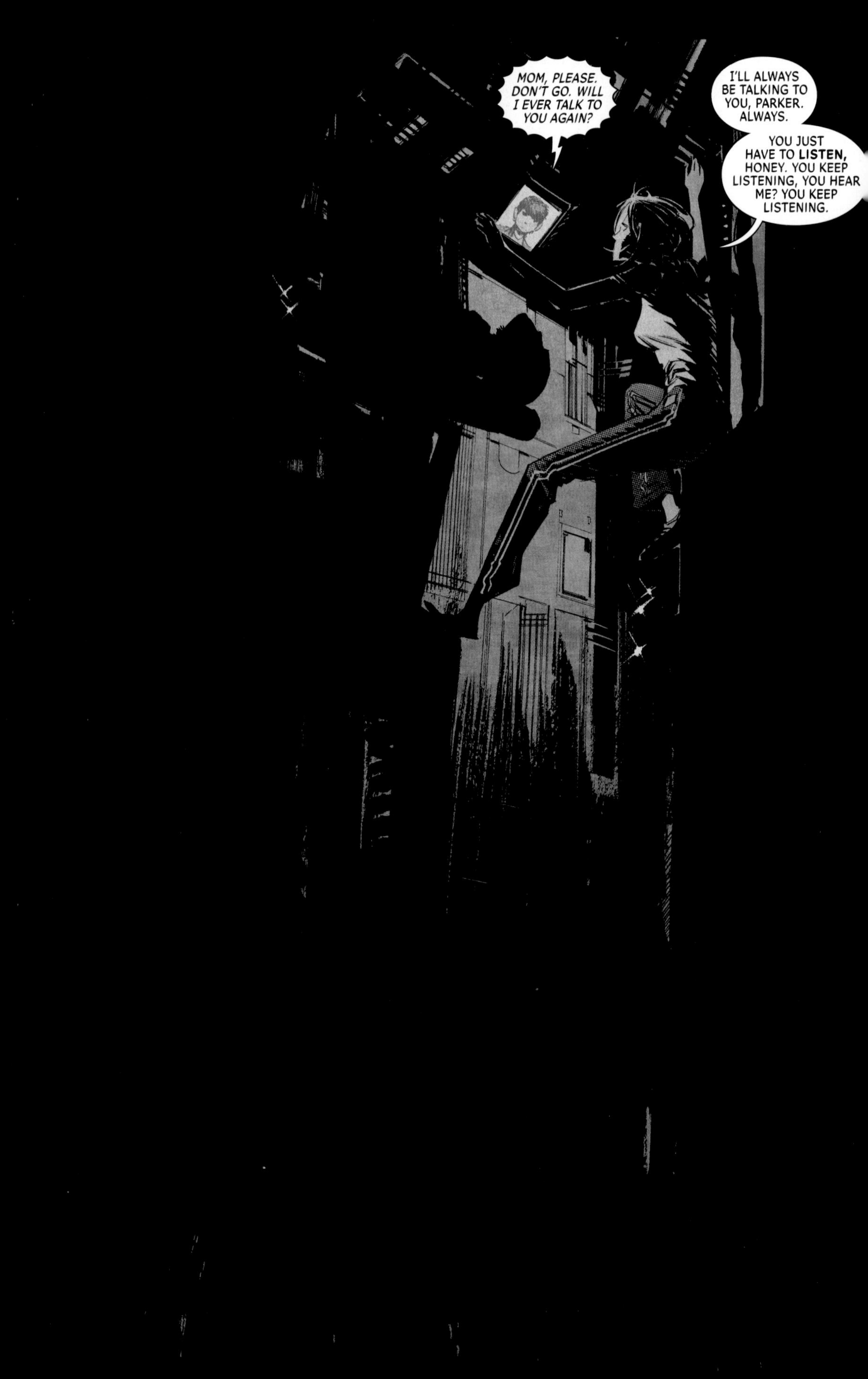
MOM, PLEASE. DON'T GO. WILL I EVER TALK TO YOU AGAIN?
I'LL ALWAYS BE TALKING TO YOU, PARKER. ALWAYS.
YOU JUST HAVE TO LISTEN, HONEY. YOU KEEP LISTENING, YOU HEAR ME? YOU KEEP LISTENING.

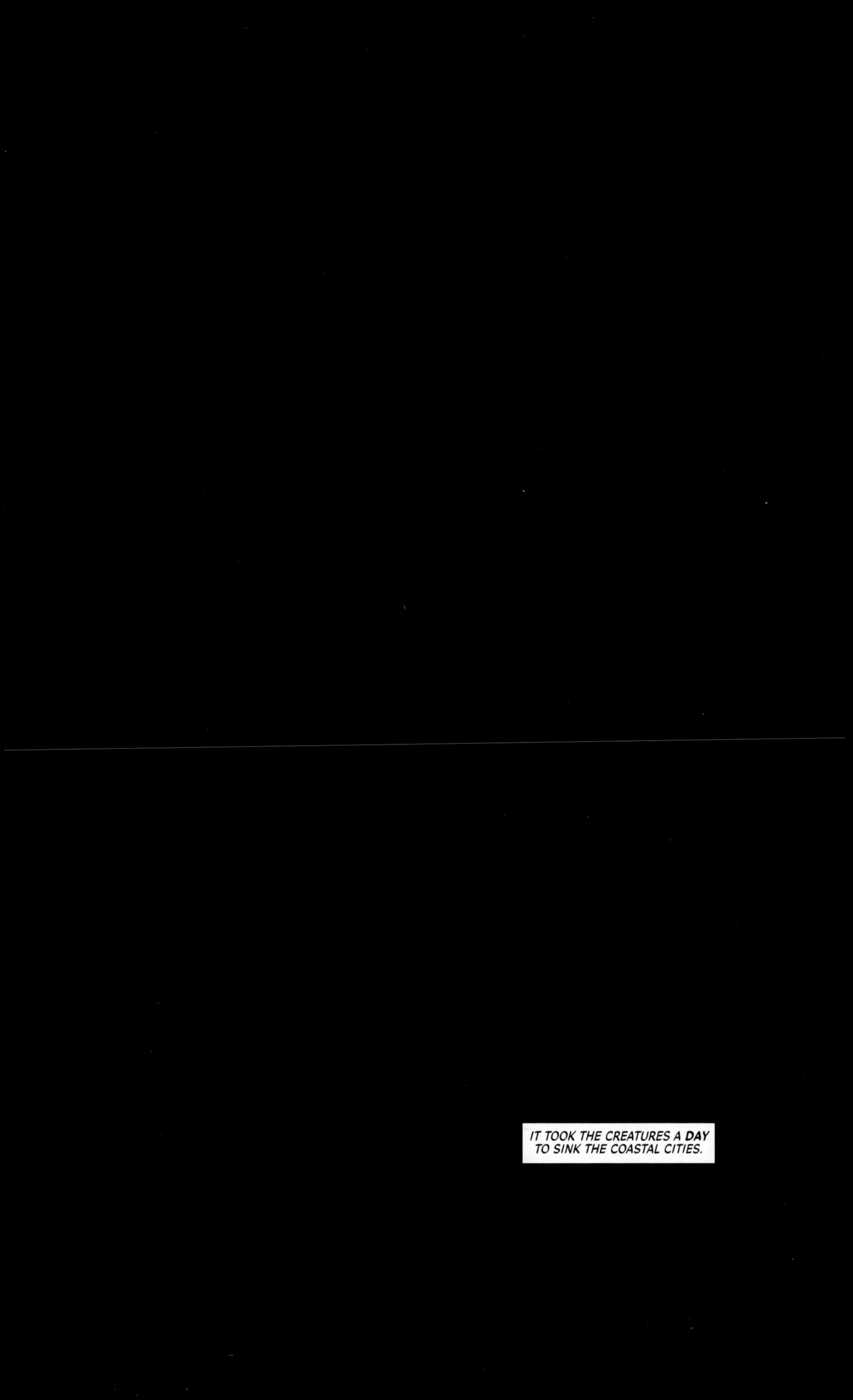
IT TOOK THE CREATURES A **DAY** TO SINK THE COASTAL CITIES.

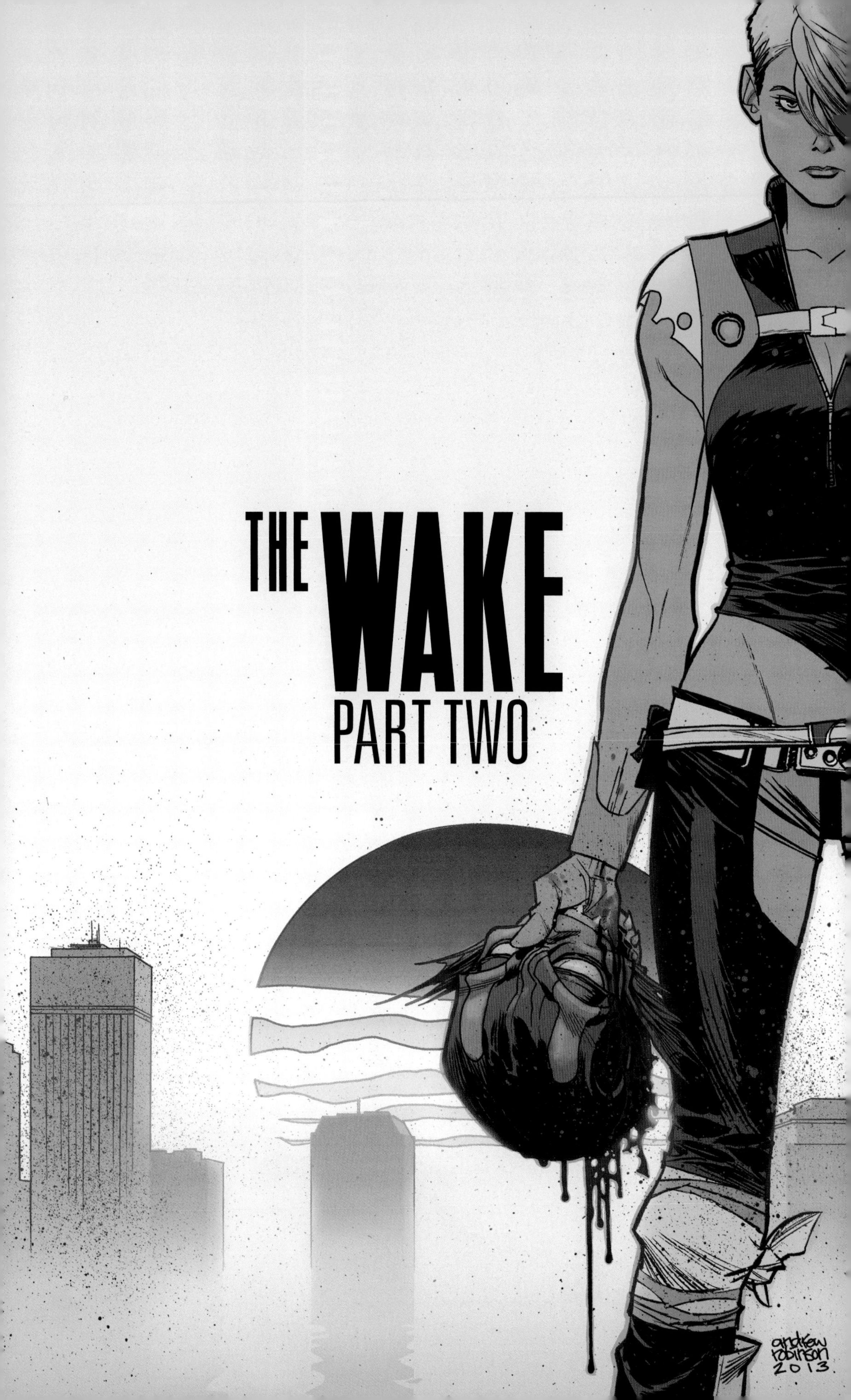
THE WAKE
PART TWO
andrew robinson 2013

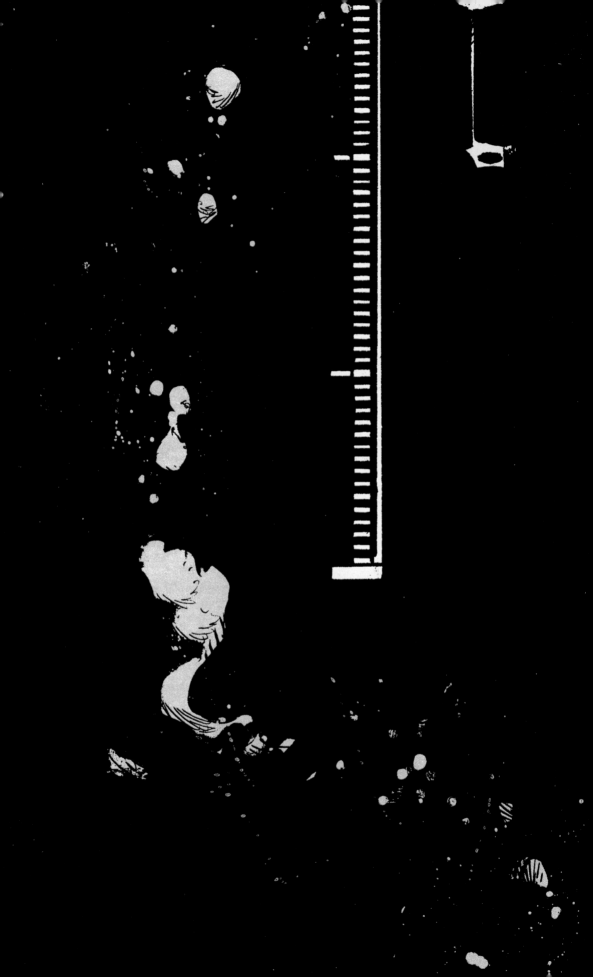

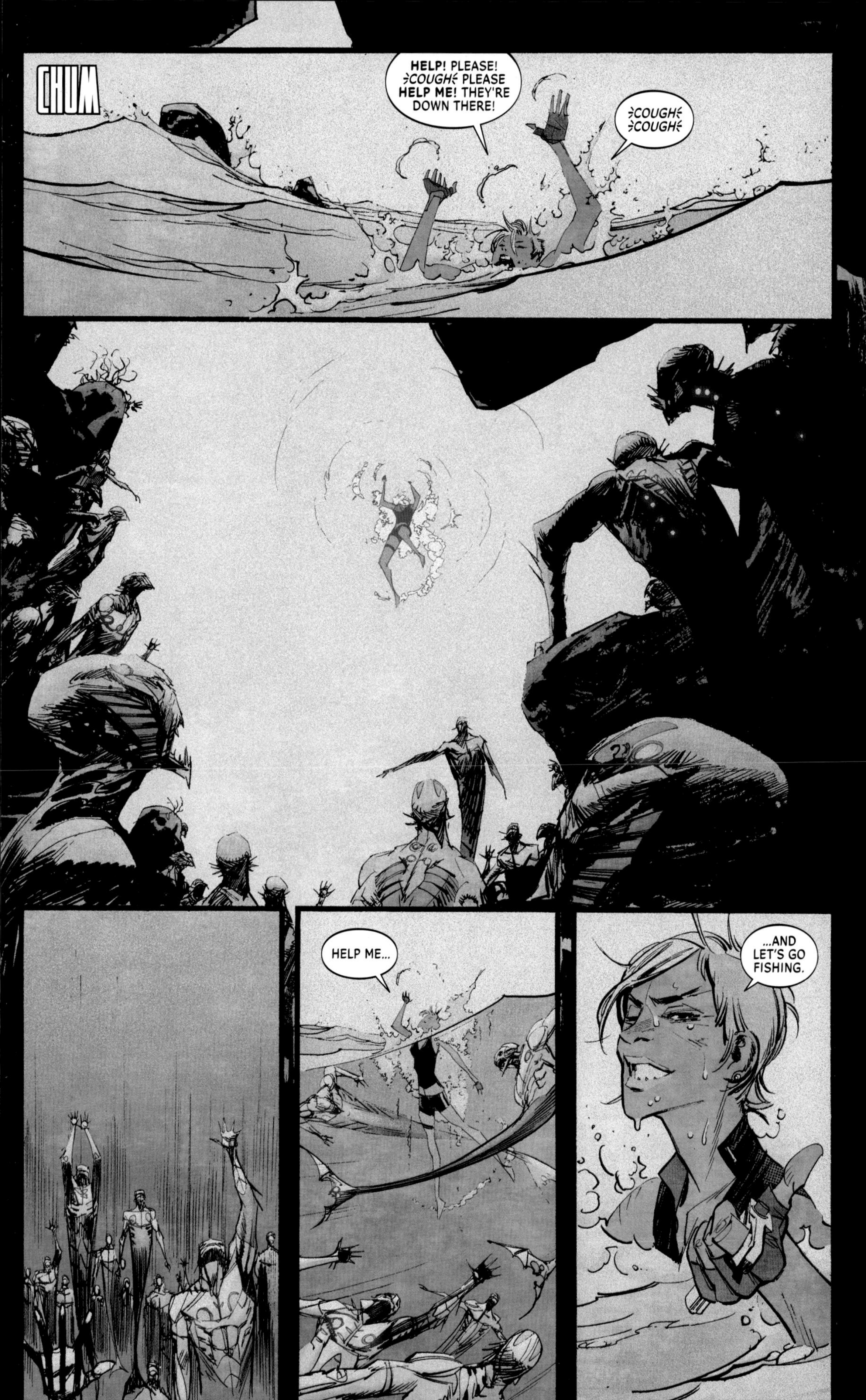
CHUM
HELP! PLEASE! *COUGH* PLEASE HELP ME! THEY'RE DOWN THERE!
COUGH *COUGH*
HELP ME...
...AND LET'S GO FISHING.

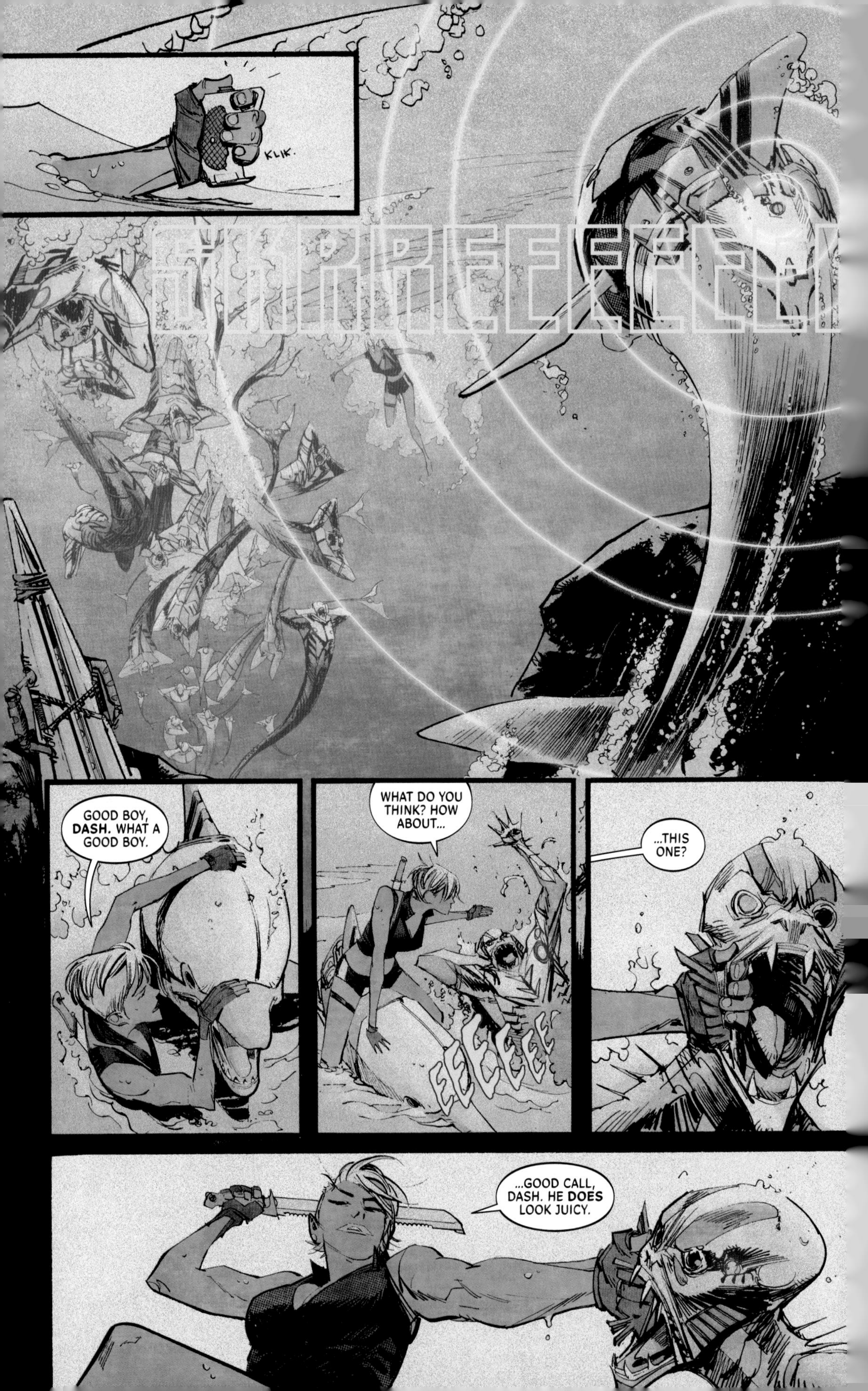
KLIK.
SKRREEEEE
GOOD BOY, **DASH.** WHAT A GOOD BOY.
WHAT DO YOU THINK? HOW ABOUT...
EEEEEE
...THIS ONE?
...GOOD CALL, DASH. HE **DOES** LOOK JUICY.

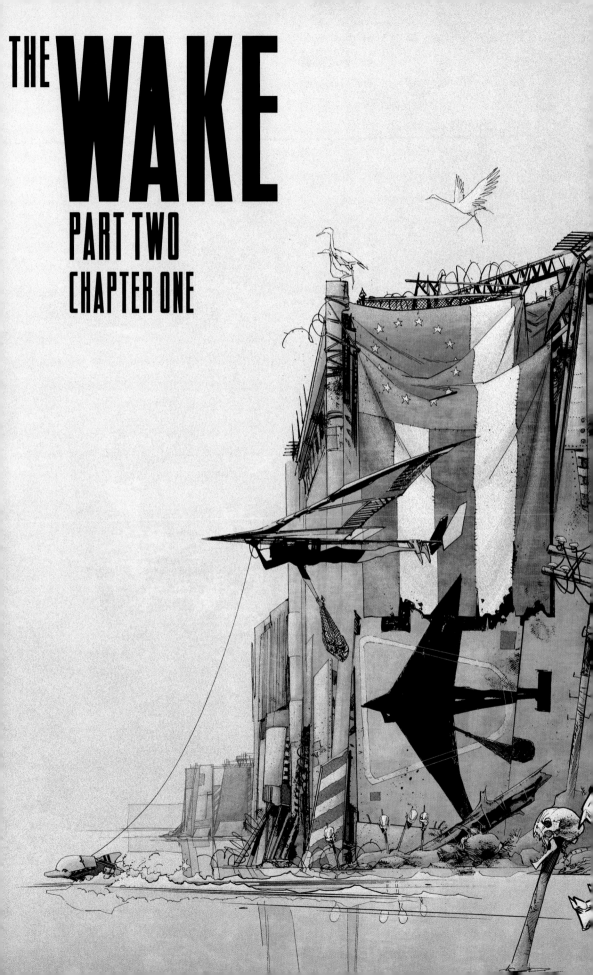

THE WAKE

PART TWO
CHAPTER ONE

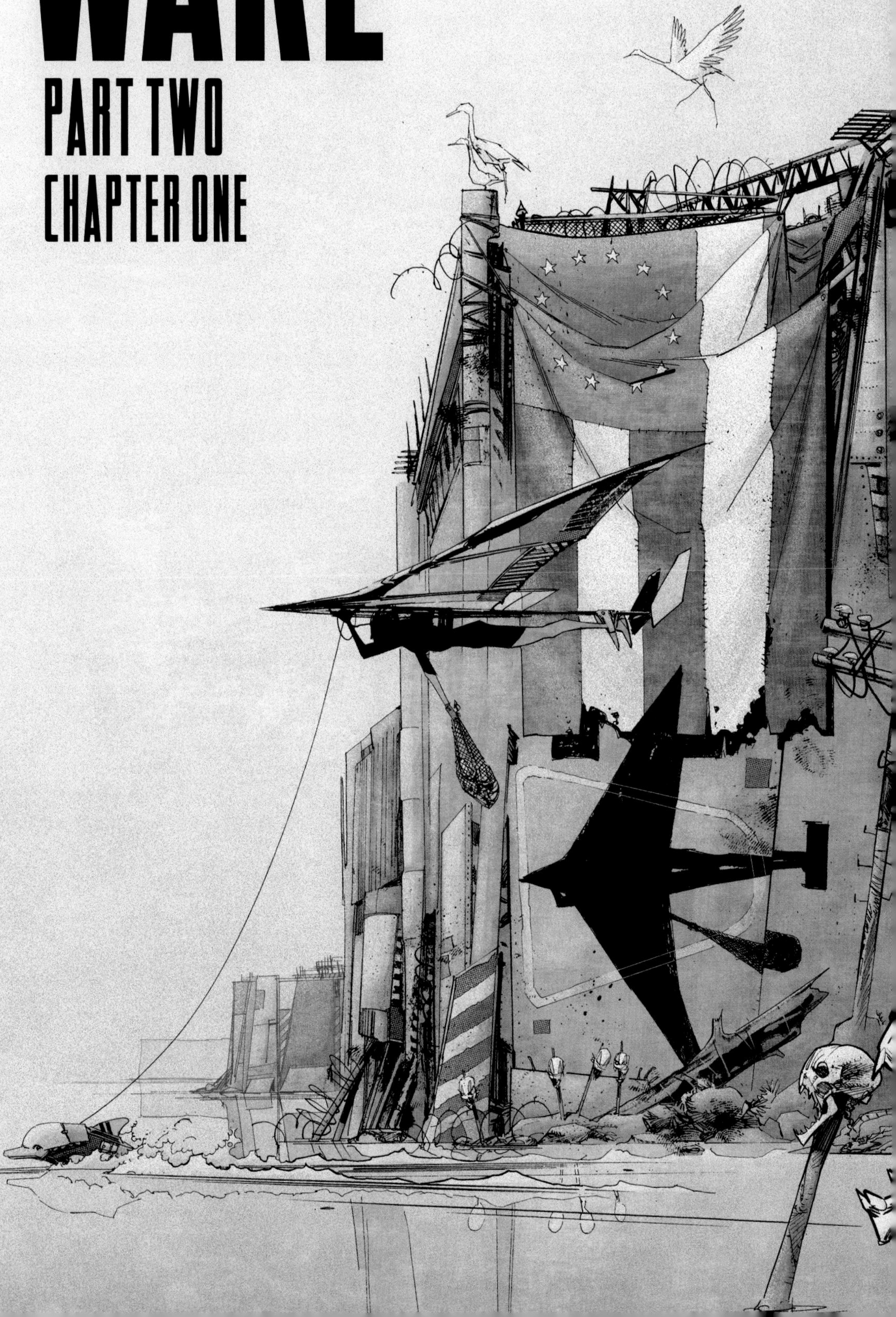

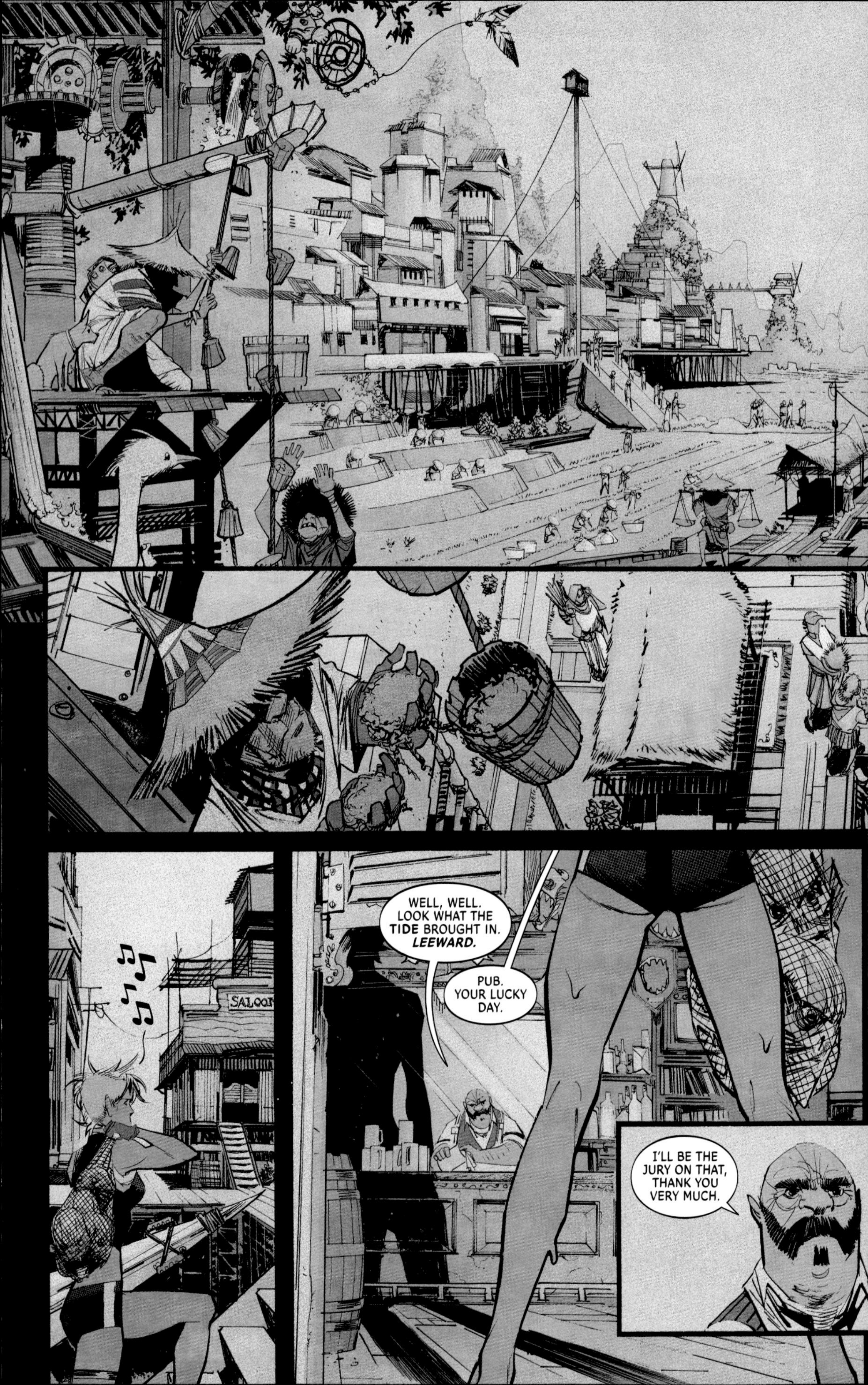
SALOON
WELL, WELL. LOOK WHAT THE TIDE BROUGHT IN. LEEWARD.
PUB. YOUR LUCKY DAY.
I'LL BE THE JURY ON THAT, THANK YOU VERY MUCH.

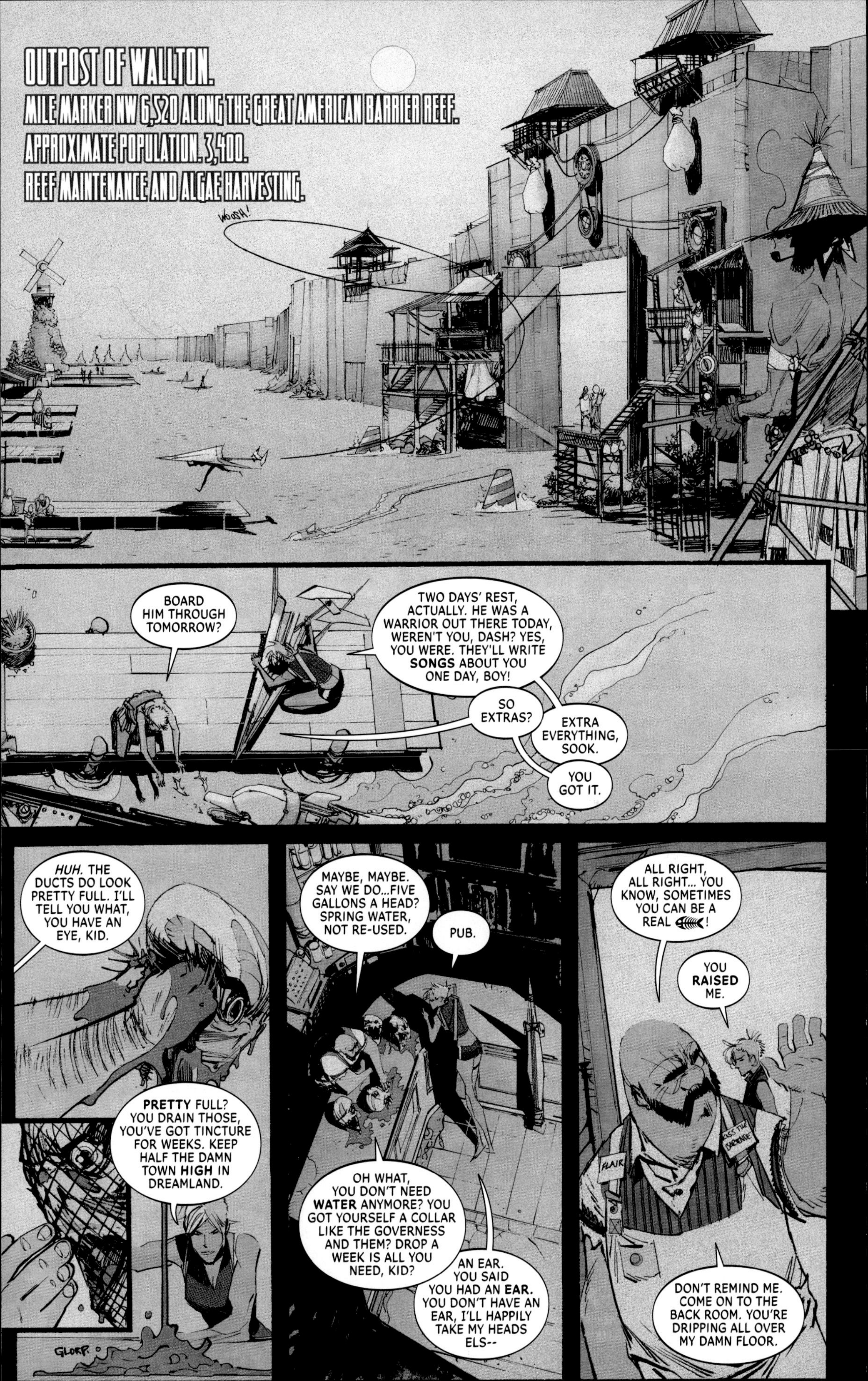
OUTPOST OF WALLTON.
MILE MARKER NW 6,520 ALONG THE GREAT AMERICAN BARRIER REEF.
APPROXIMATE POPULATION. 3,400.
REEF MAINTENANCE AND ALGAE HARVESTING.
WOOSH!
BOARD HIM THROUGH TOMORROW?
TWO DAYS' REST, ACTUALLY. HE WAS A WARRIOR OUT THERE TODAY, WEREN'T YOU, DASH? YES, YOU WERE. THEY'LL WRITE **SONGS** ABOUT YOU ONE DAY, BOY!
SO EXTRAS?
EXTRA EVERYTHING, SOOK.
YOU GOT IT.
HUH. THE DUCTS DO LOOK PRETTY FULL. I'LL TELL YOU WHAT, YOU HAVE AN EYE, KID.
PRETTY FULL? YOU DRAIN THOSE, YOU'VE GOT TINCTURE FOR WEEKS. KEEP HALF THE DAMN TOWN **HIGH** IN DREAMLAND.
GLORP.
MAYBE, MAYBE. SAY WE DO...FIVE GALLONS A HEAD? SPRING WATER, NOT RE-USED.
PUB.
OH WHAT, YOU DON'T NEED **WATER** ANYMORE? YOU GOT YOURSELF A COLLAR LIKE THE GOVERNESS AND THEM? DROP A WEEK IS ALL YOU NEED, KID?
AN EAR. YOU SAID YOU HAD AN **EAR.** YOU DON'T HAVE AN EAR, I'LL HAPPILY TAKE MY HEADS ELS--
ALL RIGHT, ALL RIGHT... YOU KNOW, SOMETIMES YOU CAN BE A REAL !
YOU **RAISED** ME.
FLAIR
DON'T REMIND ME. COME ON TO THE BACK ROOM. YOU'RE DRIPPING ALL OVER MY DAMN FLOOR.

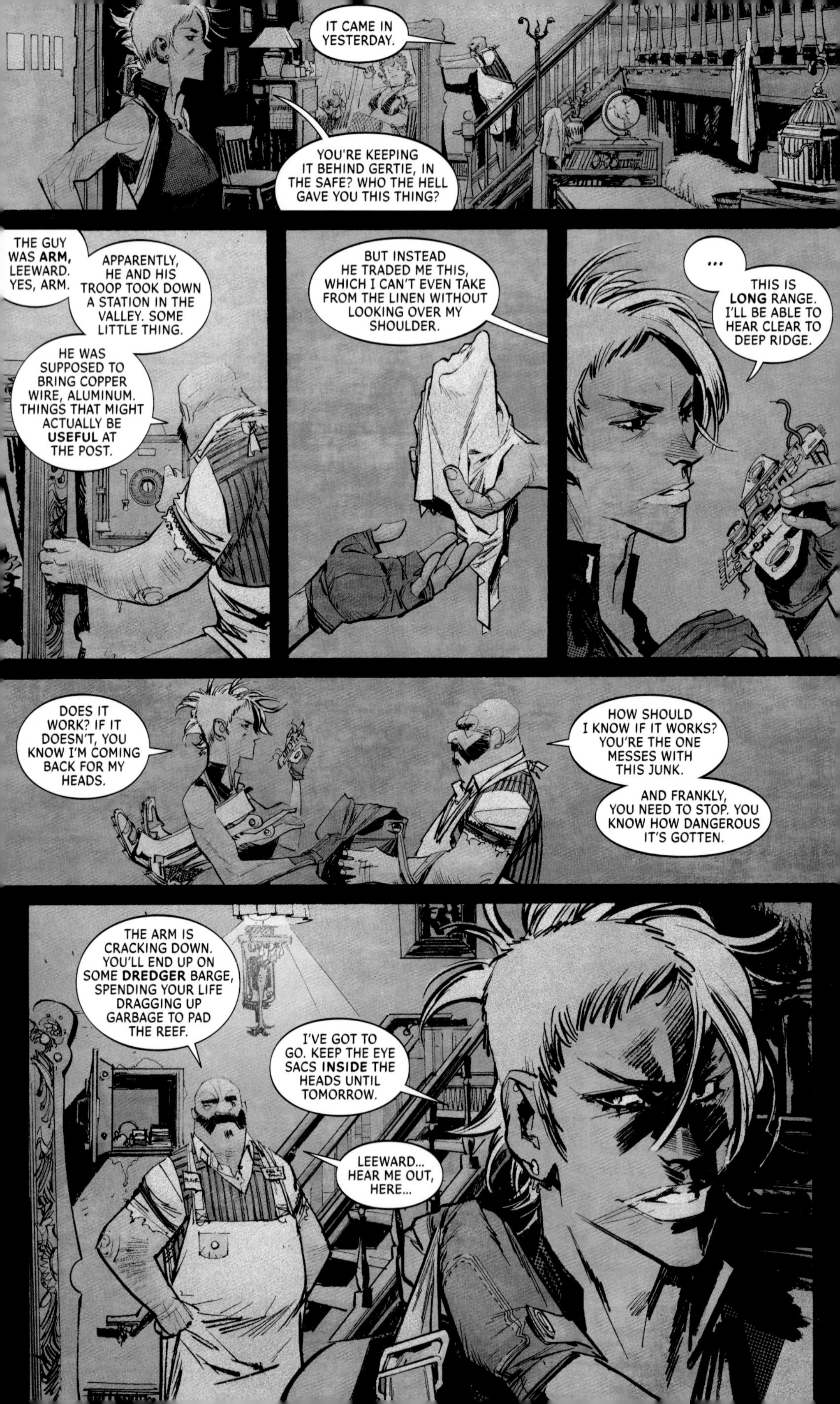
IT CAME IN YESTERDAY.
YOU'RE KEEPING IT BEHIND GERTIE, IN THE SAFE? WHO THE HELL GAVE YOU THIS THING?
THE GUY WAS **ARM**, LEEWARD. YES, ARM.
APPARENTLY, HE AND HIS TROOP TOOK DOWN A STATION IN THE VALLEY. SOME LITTLE THING.
HE WAS SUPPOSED TO BRING COPPER WIRE, ALUMINUM. THINGS THAT MIGHT ACTUALLY BE **USEFUL** AT THE POST.
BUT INSTEAD HE TRADED ME THIS, WHICH I CAN'T EVEN TAKE FROM THE LINEN WITHOUT LOOKING OVER MY SHOULDER.
...
THIS IS **LONG** RANGE. I'LL BE ABLE TO HEAR CLEAR TO DEEP RIDGE.
DOES IT WORK? IF IT DOESN'T, YOU KNOW I'M COMING BACK FOR MY HEADS.
HOW SHOULD I KNOW IF IT WORKS? YOU'RE THE ONE MESSES WITH THIS JUNK.
AND FRANKLY, YOU NEED TO STOP. YOU KNOW HOW DANGEROUS IT'S GOTTEN.
THE ARM IS CRACKING DOWN. YOU'LL END UP ON SOME **DREDGER** BARGE, SPENDING YOUR LIFE DRAGGING GARBAGE UP TO PAD THE REEF.
I'VE GOT TO GO. KEEP THE EYE SACS **INSIDE** THE HEADS UNTIL TOMORROW.
LEEWARD... HEAR ME OUT, HERE...

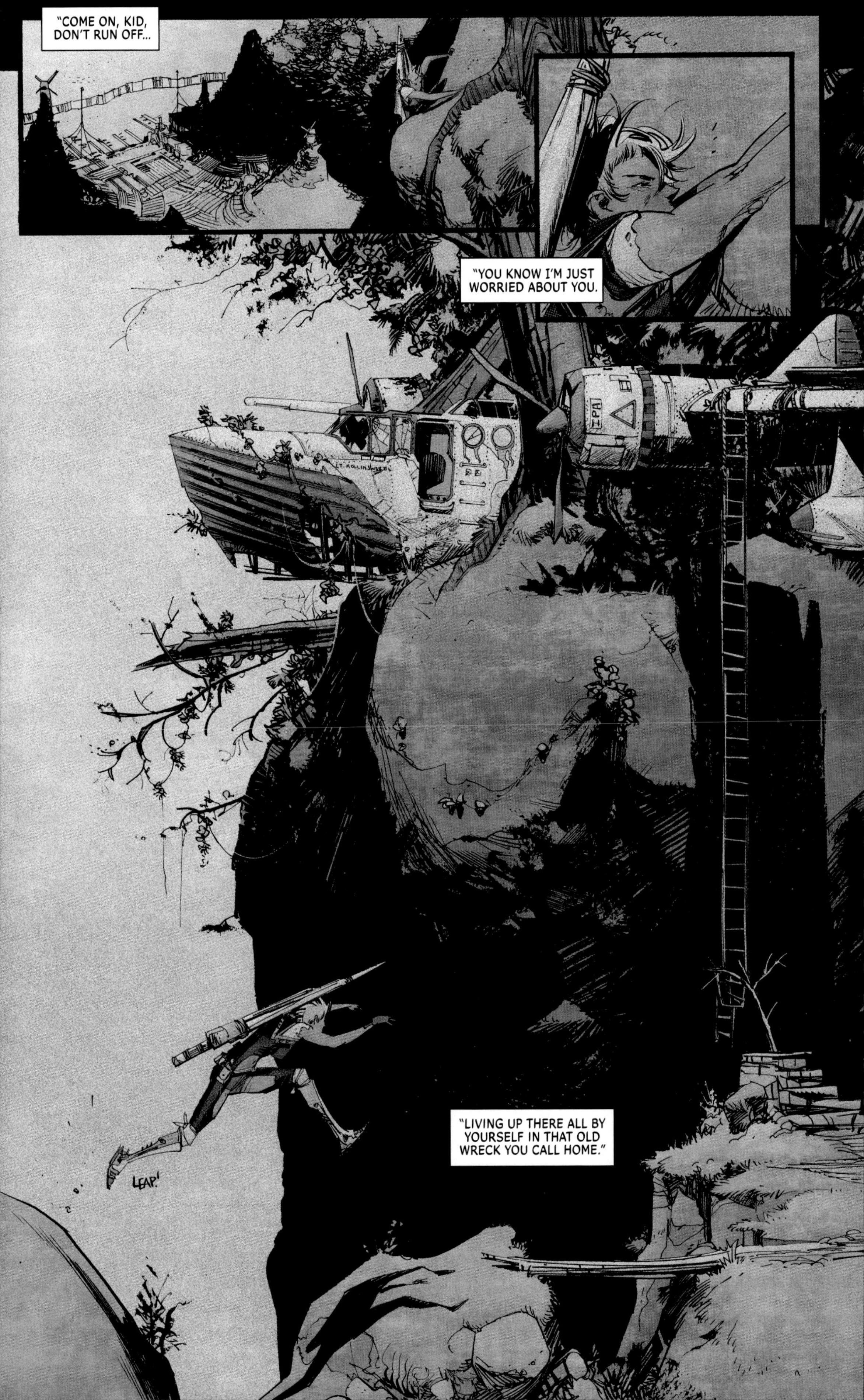
"COME ON, KID, DON'T RUN OFF...
"YOU KNOW I'M JUST WORRIED ABOUT YOU.
"LIVING UP THERE ALL BY YOURSELF IN THAT OLD WRECK YOU CALL HOME."
LEAP!

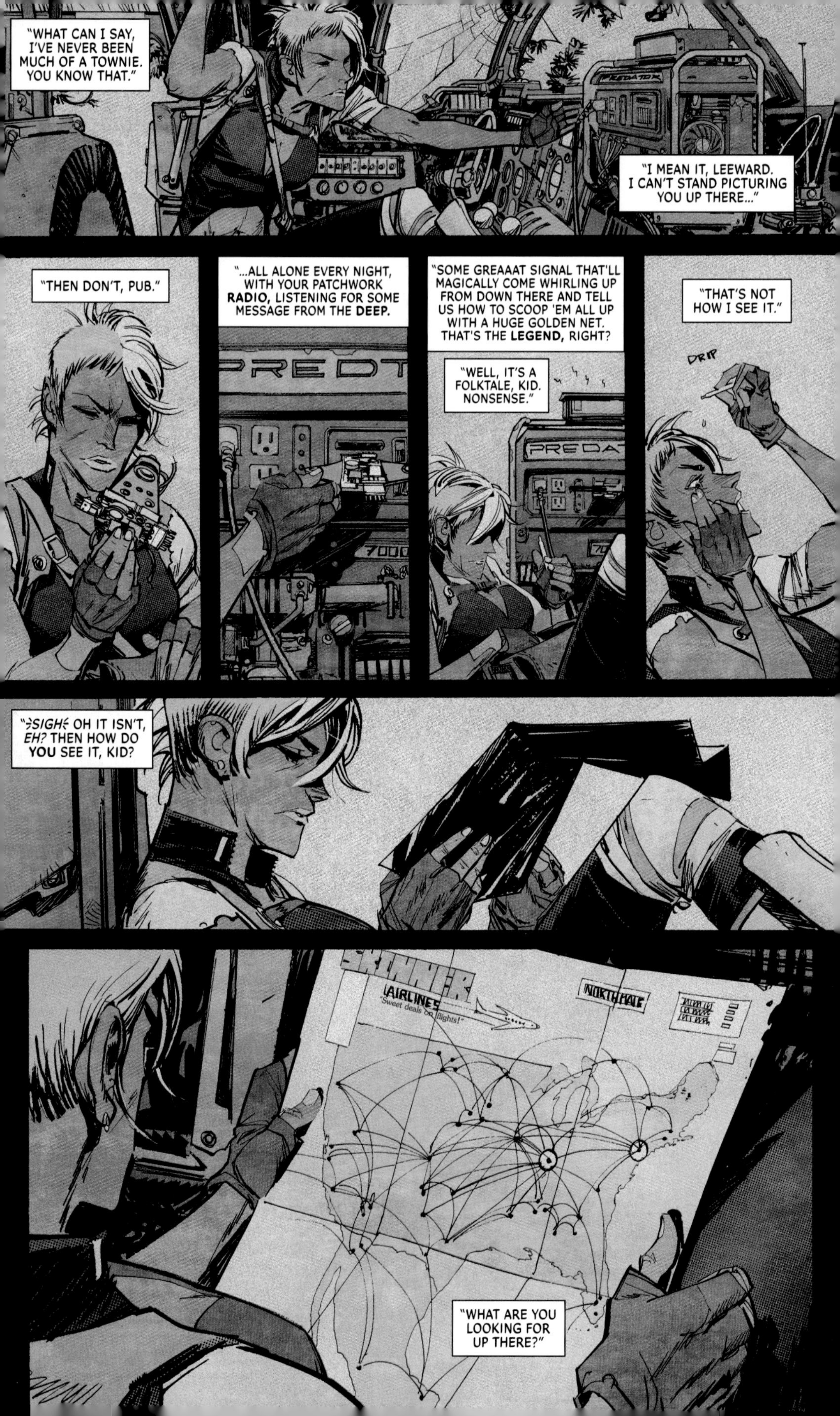
"WHAT CAN I SAY, I'VE NEVER BEEN MUCH OF A TOWNIE. YOU KNOW THAT."
"I MEAN IT, LEEWARD. I CAN'T STAND PICTURING YOU UP THERE..."
"THEN DON'T, PUB."
"...ALL ALONE EVERY NIGHT, WITH YOUR PATCHWORK RADIO, LISTENING FOR SOME MESSAGE FROM THE DEEP.
PREDT
"SOME GREAAAT SIGNAL THAT'LL MAGICALLY COME WHIRLING UP FROM DOWN THERE AND TELL US HOW TO SCOOP 'EM ALL UP WITH A HUGE GOLDEN NET. THAT'S THE LEGEND, RIGHT?
"WELL, IT'S A FOLKTALE, KID. NONSENSE."
PREDA
"THAT'S NOT HOW I SEE IT."
DRIP
"SIGH OH IT ISN'T, EH? THEN HOW DO YOU SEE IT, KID?
AIRLINES
"Sweet deals on flights!"
NORTH
"WHAT ARE YOU LOOKING FOR UP THERE?"

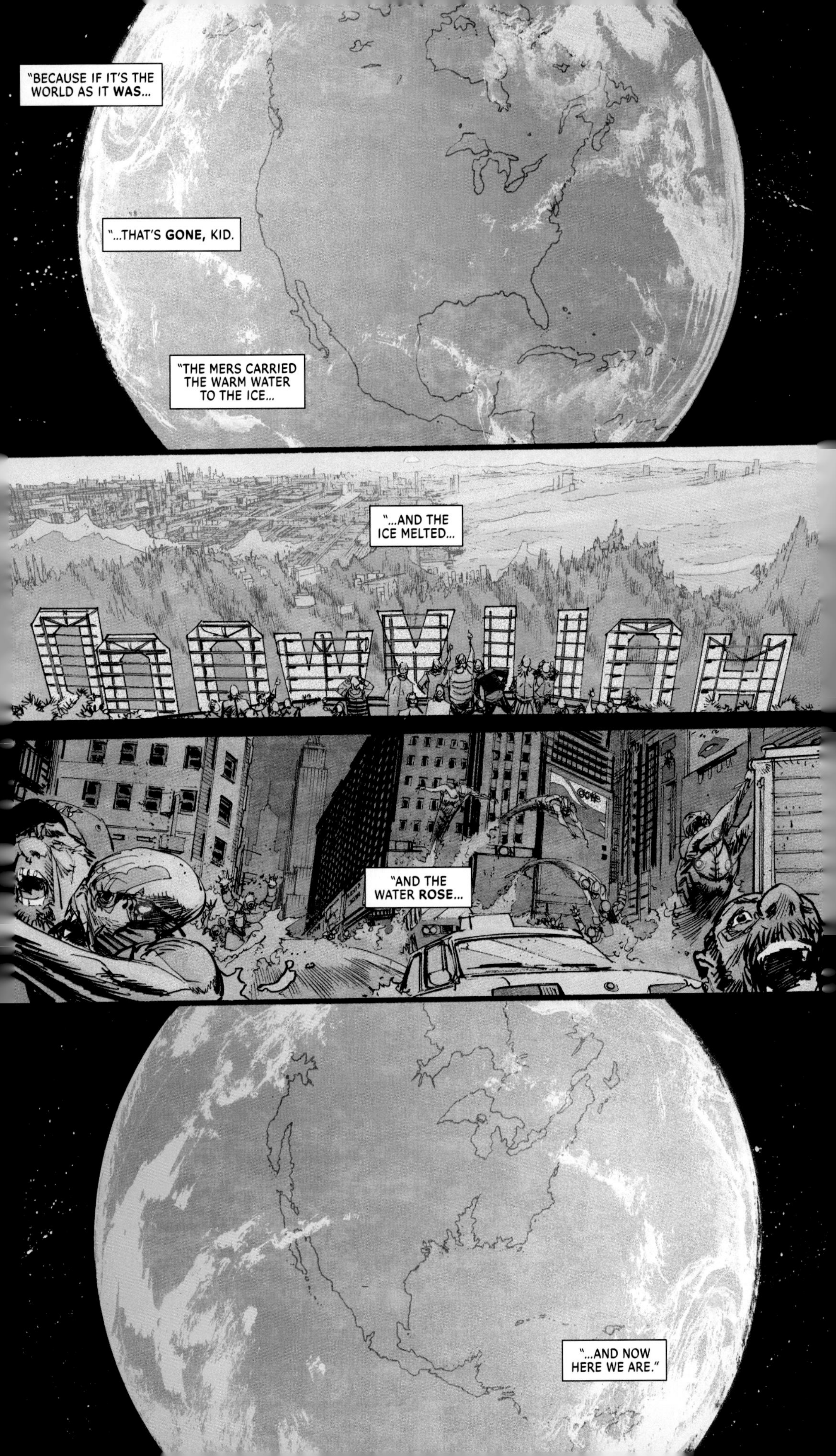
"BECAUSE IF IT'S THE WORLD AS IT WAS...
"...THAT'S GONE, KID.
"THE MERS CARRIED THE WARM WATER TO THE ICE...
"...AND THE ICE MELTED...
"AND THE WATER ROSE...
"...AND NOW HERE WE ARE."

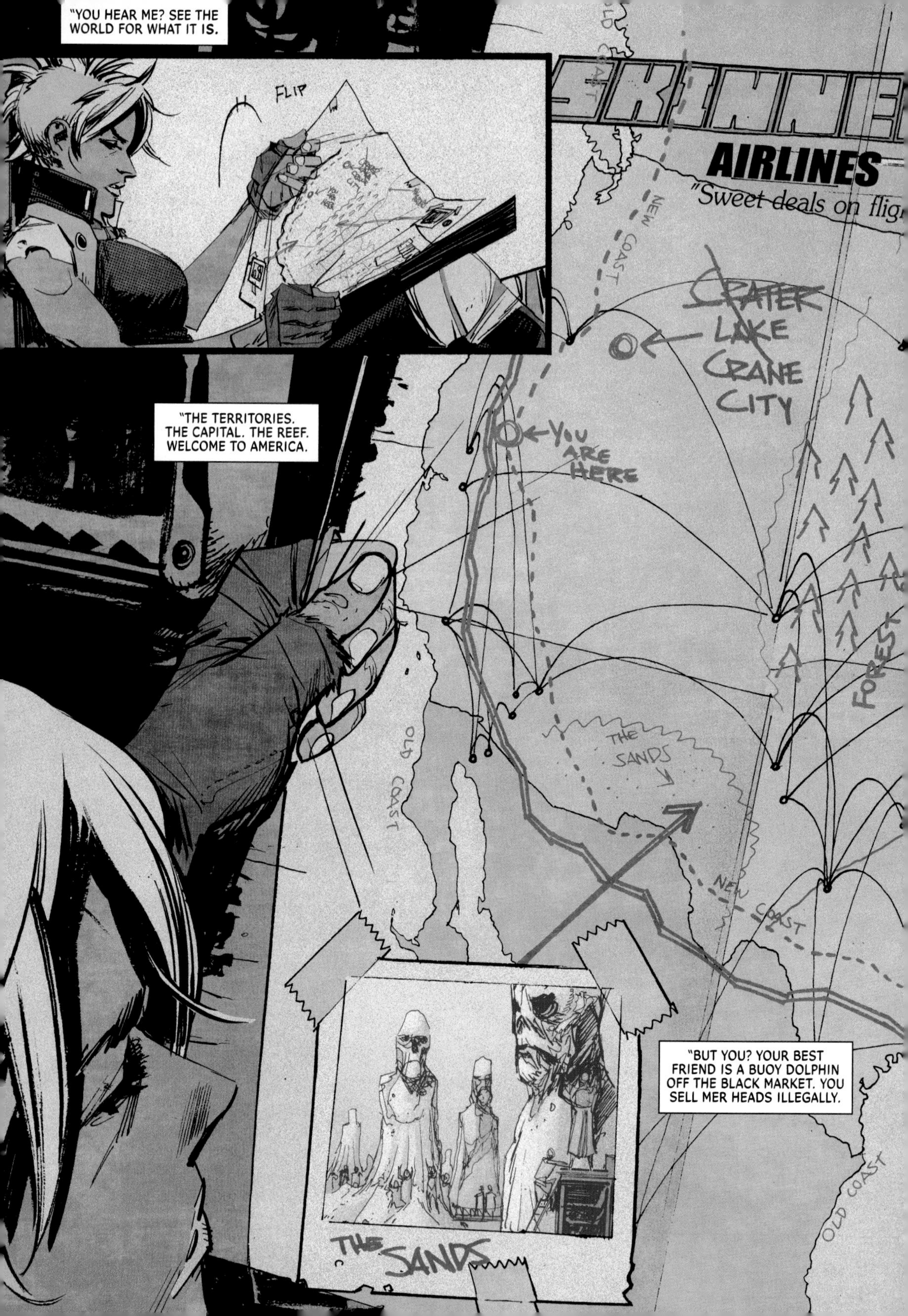

"YOU HEAR ME? SEE THE WORLD FOR WHAT IT IS.
FLIP
SKINNER
AIRLINES
"Sweet deals on flig
NEW COAST
CRATER LAKE
CRANE CITY
"THE TERRITORIES. THE CAPITAL. THE REEF. WELCOME TO AMERICA.
YOU ARE HERE
FOREST
OLD COAST
THE SANDS
NEW COAST
"BUT YOU? YOUR BEST FRIEND IS A BUOY DOLPHIN OFF THE BLACK MARKET. YOU SELL MER HEADS ILLEGALLY.
THE SANDS
OLD COAST

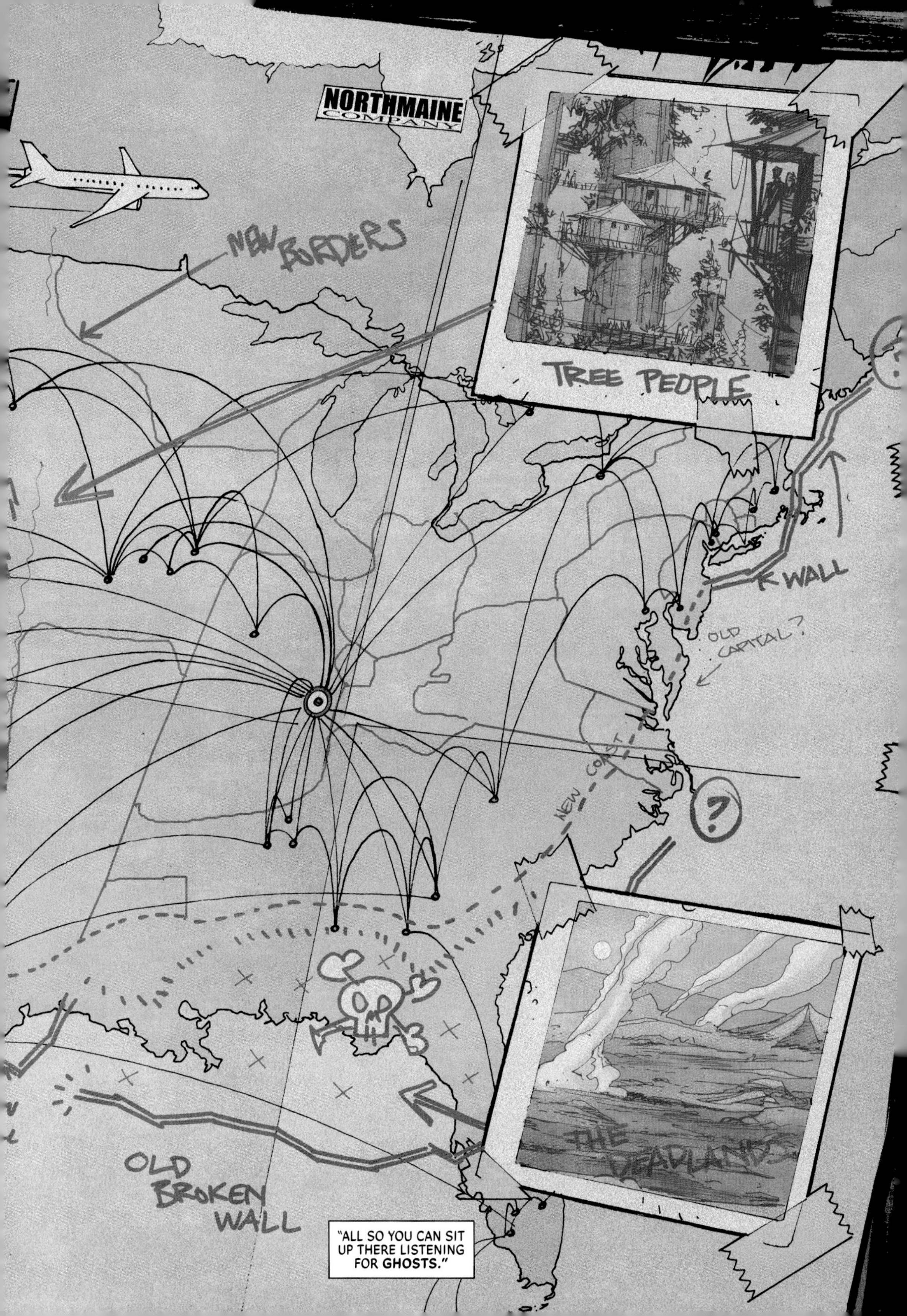

NORTHMAINE COMPANY
NEW BORDERS
TREE PEOPLE
WALL
OLD CAPITAL?
NEW COAST
?
THE DEADLANDS
OLD BROKEN WALL
"ALL SO YOU CAN SIT UP THERE LISTENING FOR GHOSTS."

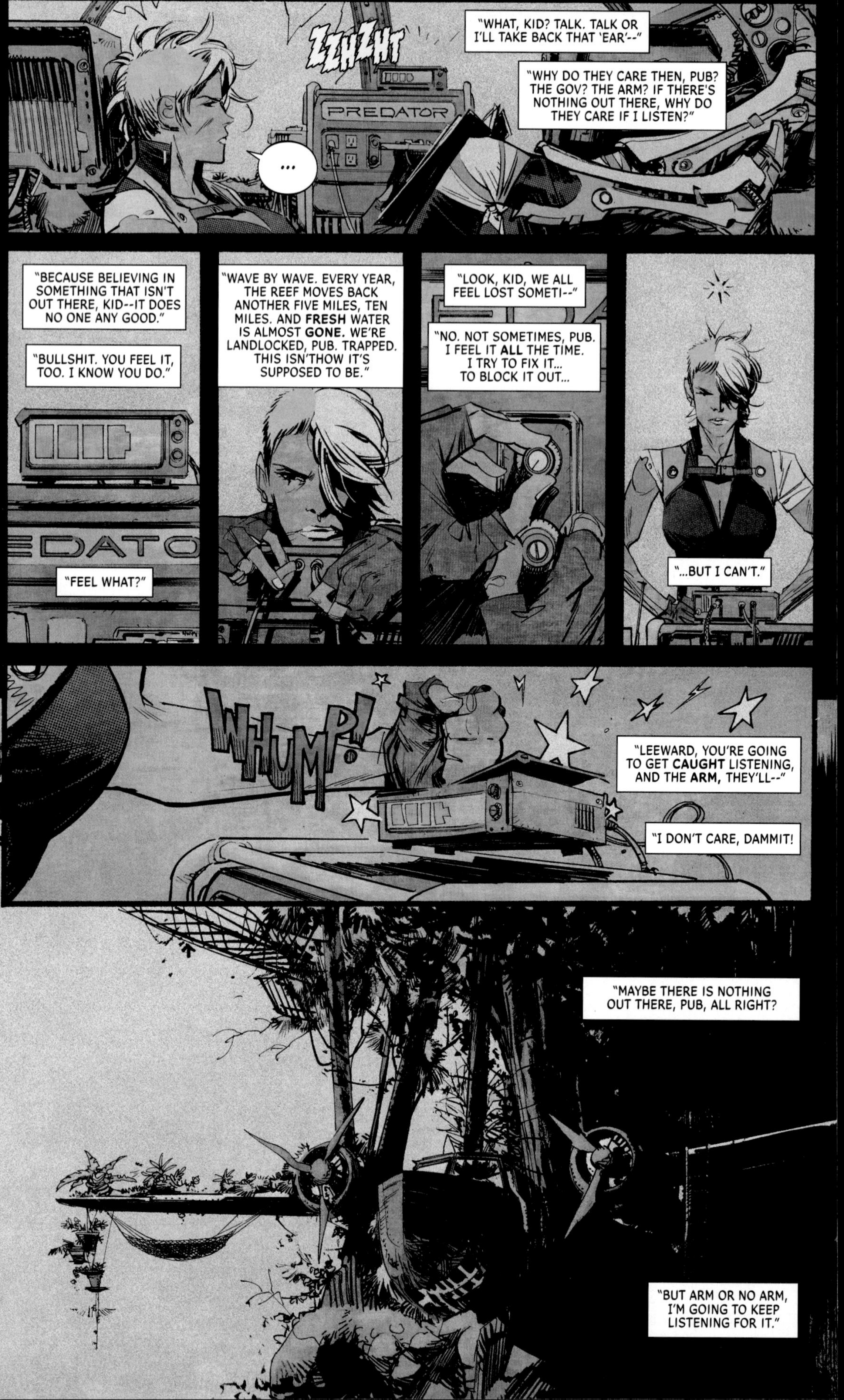
ZZHZHT
"WHAT, KID? TALK. TALK OR I'LL TAKE BACK THAT 'EAR'--"
...
"WHY DO THEY CARE THEN, PUB? THE GOV? THE ARM? IF THERE'S NOTHING OUT THERE, WHY DO THEY CARE IF I LISTEN?"
PREDATOR
"BECAUSE BELIEVING IN SOMETHING THAT ISN'T OUT THERE, KID--IT DOES NO ONE ANY GOOD."
"BULLSHIT. YOU FEEL IT, TOO. I KNOW YOU DO."
"FEEL WHAT?"
"WAVE BY WAVE. EVERY YEAR, THE REEF MOVES BACK ANOTHER FIVE MILES, TEN MILES. AND FRESH WATER IS ALMOST GONE. WE'RE LANDLOCKED, PUB. TRAPPED. THIS ISN'THOW IT'S SUPPOSED TO BE."
"LOOK, KID, WE ALL FEEL LOST SOMETI--"
"NO. NOT SOMETIMES, PUB. I FEEL IT ALL THE TIME. I TRY TO FIX IT... TO BLOCK IT OUT...
"...BUT I CAN'T."
WHUMP!
"LEEWARD, YOU'RE GOING TO GET CAUGHT LISTENING, AND THE ARM, THEY'LL--"
"I DON'T CARE, DAMMIT!
"MAYBE THERE IS NOTHING OUT THERE, PUB, ALL RIGHT?
"BUT ARM OR NO ARM, I'M GOING TO KEEP LISTENING FOR IT."

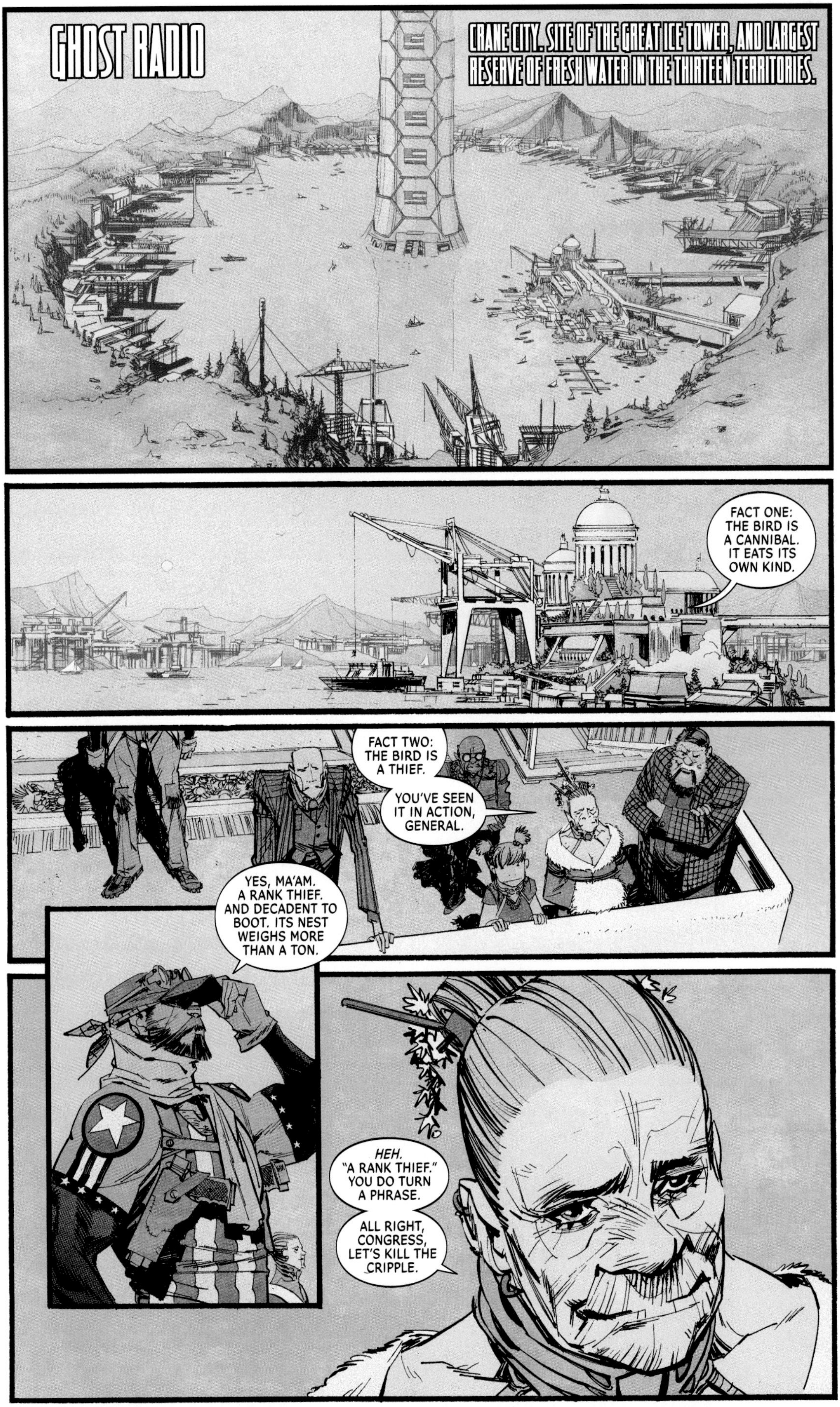
GHOST RADIO
CRANE CITY. SITE OF THE GREAT ICE TOWER, AND LARGEST RESERVE OF FRESH WATER IN THE THIRTEEN TERRITORIES.
FACT ONE: THE BIRD IS A CANNIBAL. IT EATS ITS OWN KIND.
FACT TWO: THE BIRD IS A THIEF.
YOU'VE SEEN IT IN ACTION, GENERAL.
YES, MA'AM. A RANK THIEF. AND DECADENT TO BOOT. ITS NEST WEIGHS MORE THAN A TON.
HEH. "A RANK THIEF." YOU DO TURN A PHRASE.
ALL RIGHT, CONGRESS, LET'S KILL THE CRIPPLE.

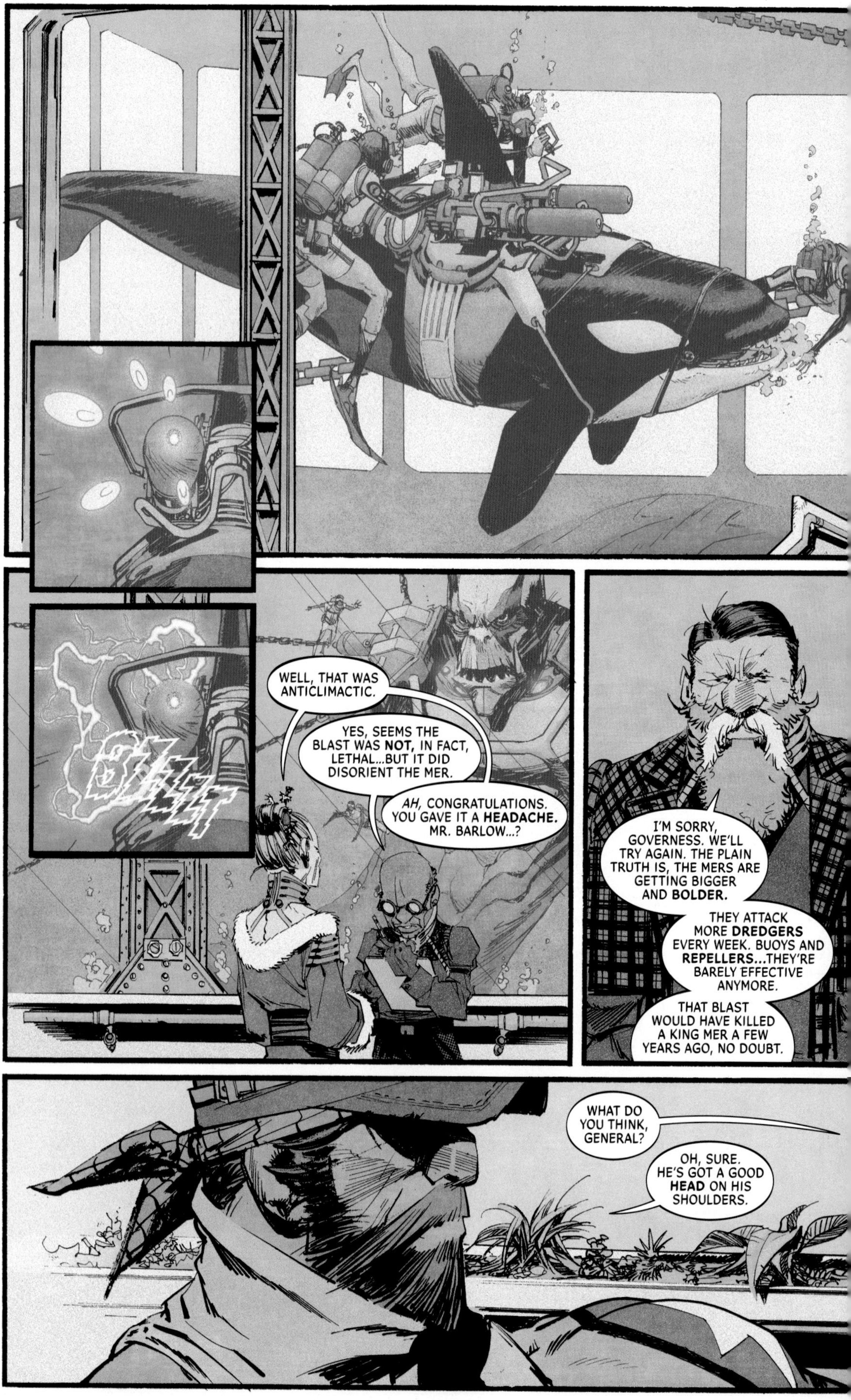
WELL, THAT WAS ANTICLIMACTIC.
YES, SEEMS THE BLAST WAS **NOT,** IN FACT, LETHAL...BUT IT DID DISORIENT THE MER.
AH, CONGRATULATIONS. YOU GAVE IT A **HEADACHE.** MR. BARLOW...?
I'M SORRY, GOVERNESS. WE'LL TRY AGAIN. THE PLAIN TRUTH IS, THE MERS ARE GETTING BIGGER AND **BOLDER.**
THEY ATTACK MORE **DREDGERS** EVERY WEEK. BUOYS AND **REPELLERS...**THEY'RE BARELY EFFECTIVE ANYMORE.
THAT BLAST WOULD HAVE KILLED A KING MER A FEW YEARS AGO, NO DOUBT.
WHAT DO YOU THINK, GENERAL?
OH, SURE. HE'S GOT A GOOD **HEAD** ON HIS SHOULDERS.

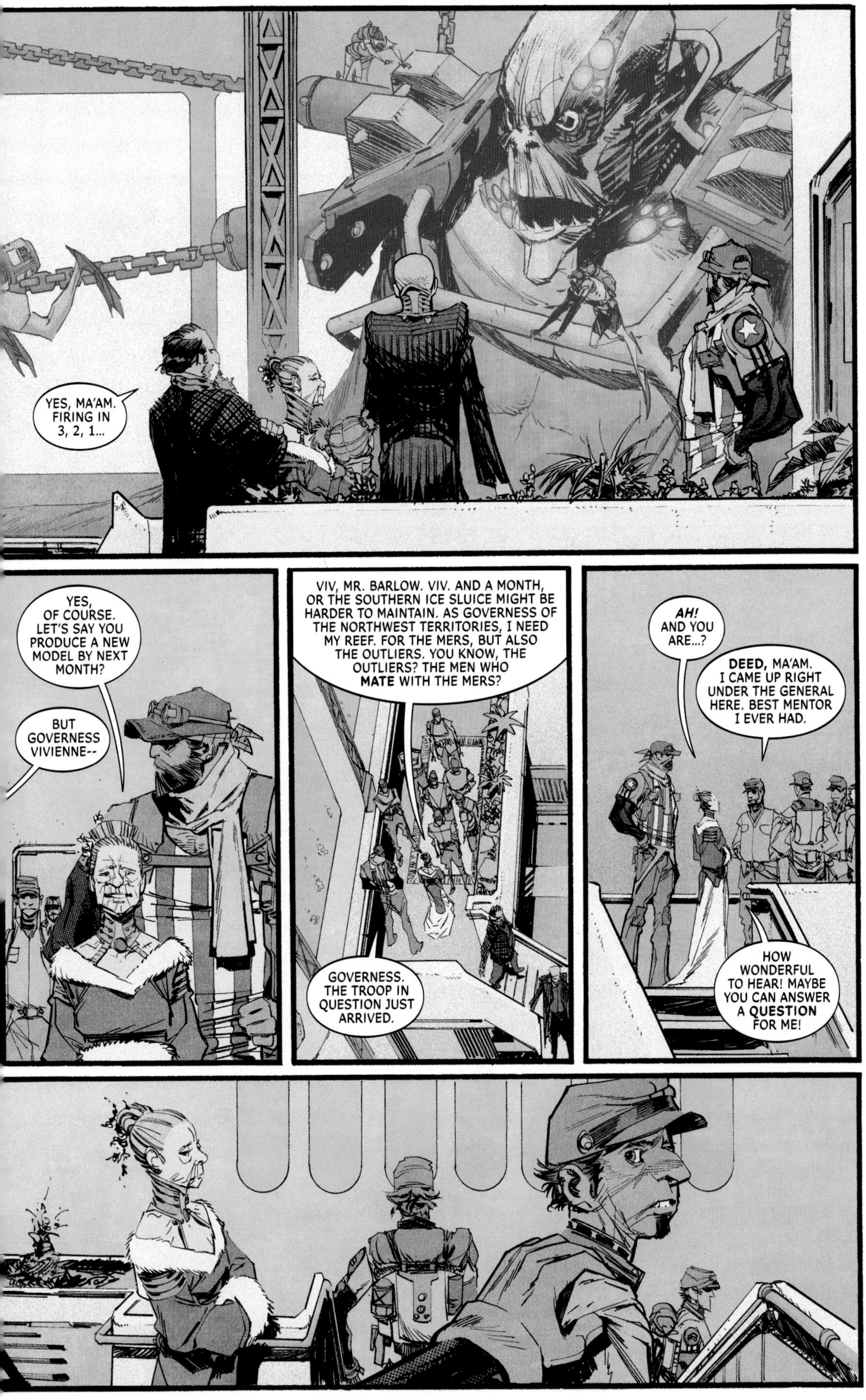

YES, MA'AM. FIRING IN 3, 2, 1...
YES, OF COURSE. LET'S SAY YOU PRODUCE A NEW MODEL BY NEXT MONTH?
BUT GOVERNESS VIVIENNE--
VIV, MR. BARLOW. VIV. AND A MONTH, OR THE SOUTHERN ICE SLUICE MIGHT BE HARDER TO MAINTAIN. AS GOVERNESS OF THE NORTHWEST TERRITORIES, I NEED MY REEF. FOR THE MERS, BUT ALSO THE OUTLIERS. YOU KNOW, THE OUTLIERS? THE MEN WHO MATE WITH THE MERS?
GOVERNESS. THE TROOP IN QUESTION JUST ARRIVED.
AH! AND YOU ARE...?
DEED, MA'AM. I CAME UP RIGHT UNDER THE GENERAL HERE. BEST MENTOR I EVER HAD.
HOW WONDERFUL TO HEAR! MAYBE YOU CAN ANSWER A QUESTION FOR ME!

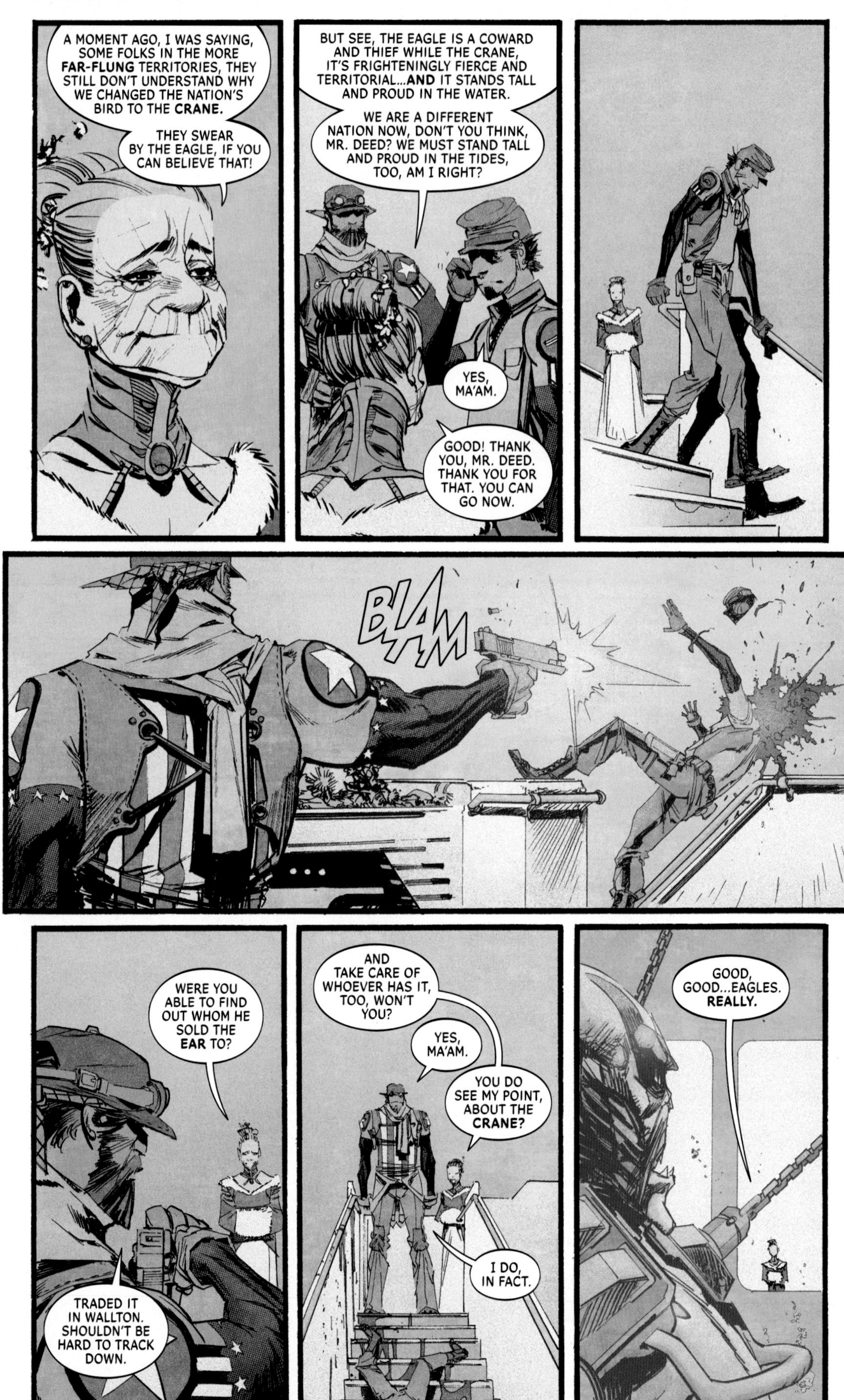
A MOMENT AGO, I WAS SAYING, SOME FOLKS IN THE MORE **FAR-FLUNG** TERRITORIES, THEY STILL DON'T UNDERSTAND WHY WE CHANGED THE NATION'S BIRD TO THE **CRANE.**
THEY SWEAR BY THE EAGLE, IF YOU CAN BELIEVE THAT!
BUT SEE, THE EAGLE IS A COWARD AND THIEF WHILE THE CRANE, IT'S FRIGHTENINGLY FIERCE AND TERRITORIAL...**AND** IT STANDS TALL AND PROUD IN THE WATER.
WE ARE A DIFFERENT NATION NOW, DON'T YOU THINK, MR. DEED? WE MUST STAND TALL AND PROUD IN THE TIDES, TOO, AM I RIGHT?
YES, MA'AM.
GOOD! THANK YOU, MR. DEED. THANK YOU FOR THAT. YOU CAN GO NOW.
BLAM
WERE YOU ABLE TO FIND OUT WHOM HE SOLD THE **EAR** TO?
TRADED IT IN WALLTON. SHOULDN'T BE HARD TO TRACK DOWN.
AND TAKE CARE OF WHOEVER HAS IT, TOO, WON'T YOU?
YES, MA'AM.
YOU DO SEE MY POINT, ABOUT THE **CRANE?**
I DO, IN FACT.
GOOD, GOOD...EAGLES. **REALLY.**

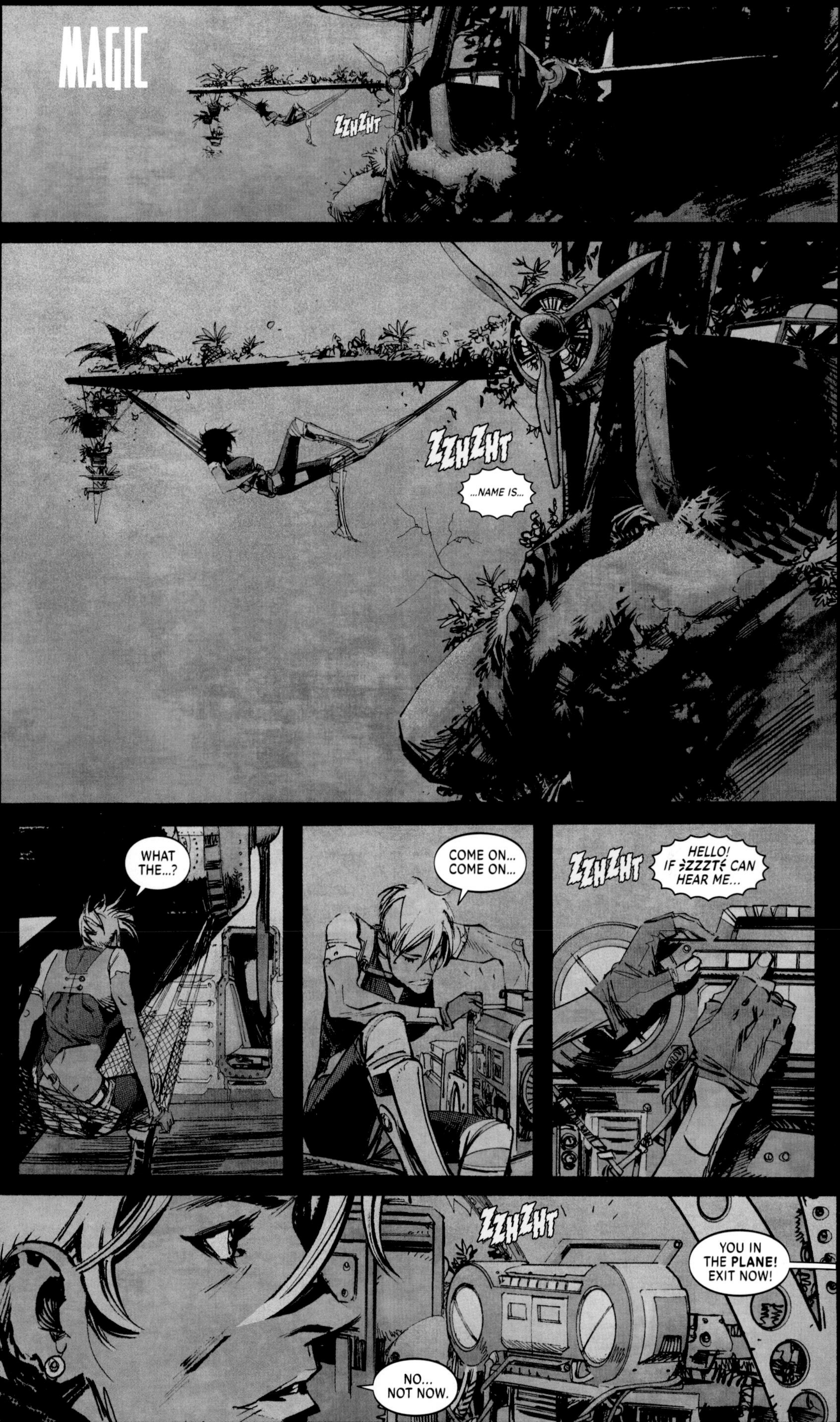
MAGIC
ZZHZHT
ZZHZHT
...NAME IS...
WHAT THE...?
COME ON... COME ON...
ZZHZHT
HELLO! IF ≯ZZZT≮ CAN HEAR ME...
ZZHZHT
YOU IN THE PLANE! EXIT NOW!
NO... NOT NOW.

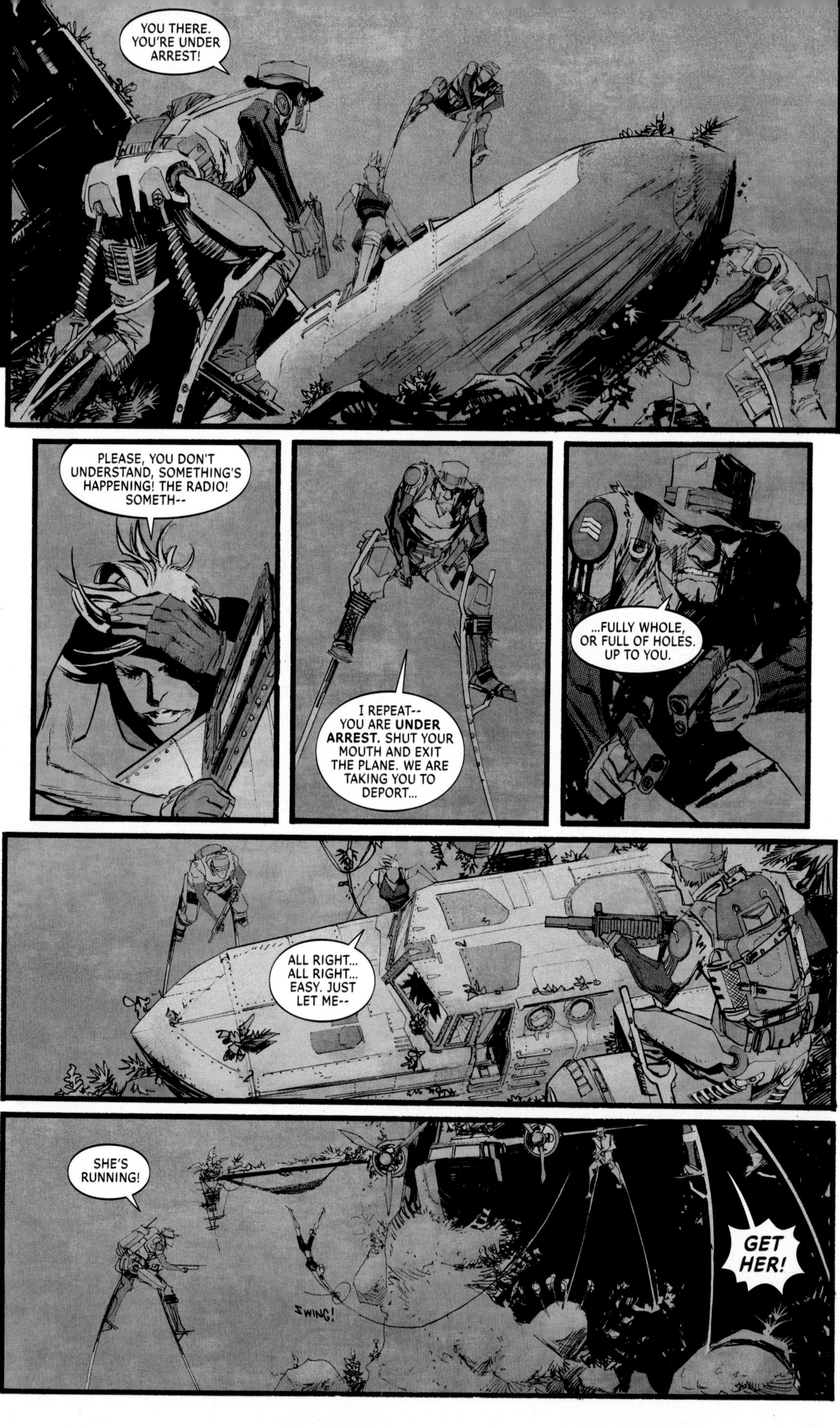
YOU THERE. YOU'RE UNDER ARREST!
PLEASE, YOU DON'T UNDERSTAND, SOMETHING'S HAPPENING! THE RADIO! SOMETH--
I REPEAT-- YOU ARE **UNDER ARREST.** SHUT YOUR MOUTH AND EXIT THE PLANE. WE ARE TAKING YOU TO DEPORT...
...FULLY WHOLE, OR FULL OF HOLES. UP TO YOU.
ALL RIGHT... ALL RIGHT... EASY. JUST LET ME--
SHE'S RUNNING!
SWING!
GET HER!

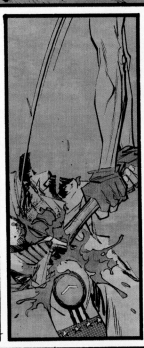

DAMMIT! IF YOU SHITS WOULD JUST LISTEN!

GOT HER!

...LISTEN ⁄UNH⁄ FOR ONE... MINUTE!

ZZHZHT

...NAME IS...

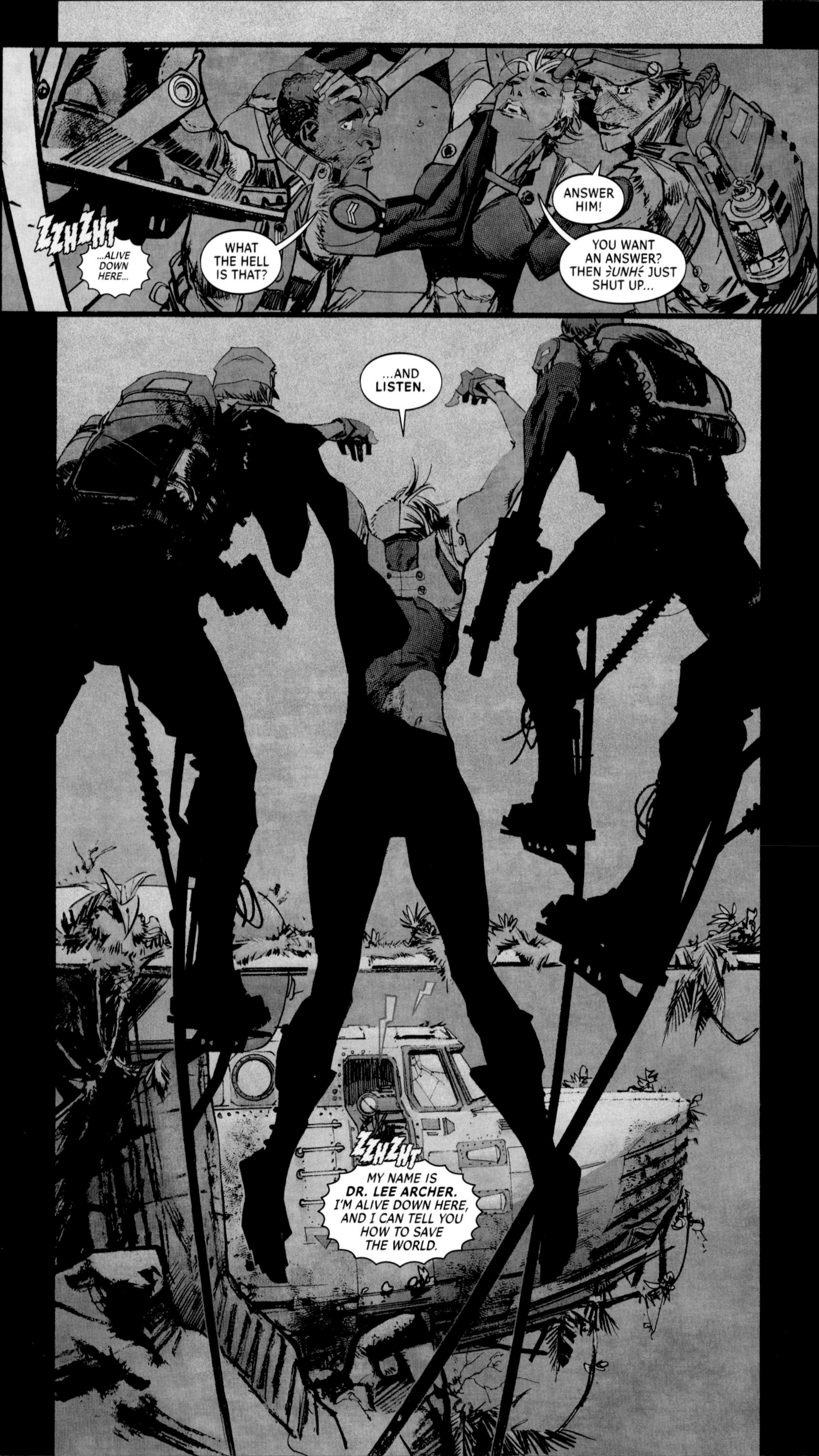
ZZHZHT
...ALIVE DOWN HERE...
WHAT THE HELL IS THAT?
ANSWER HIM!
YOU WANT AN ANSWER? THEN ≠UNH≠ JUST SHUT UP...
...AND LISTEN.
ZZHZHT
MY NAME IS DR. LEE ARCHER. I'M ALIVE DOWN HERE, AND I CAN TELL YOU HOW TO SAVE THE WORLD.

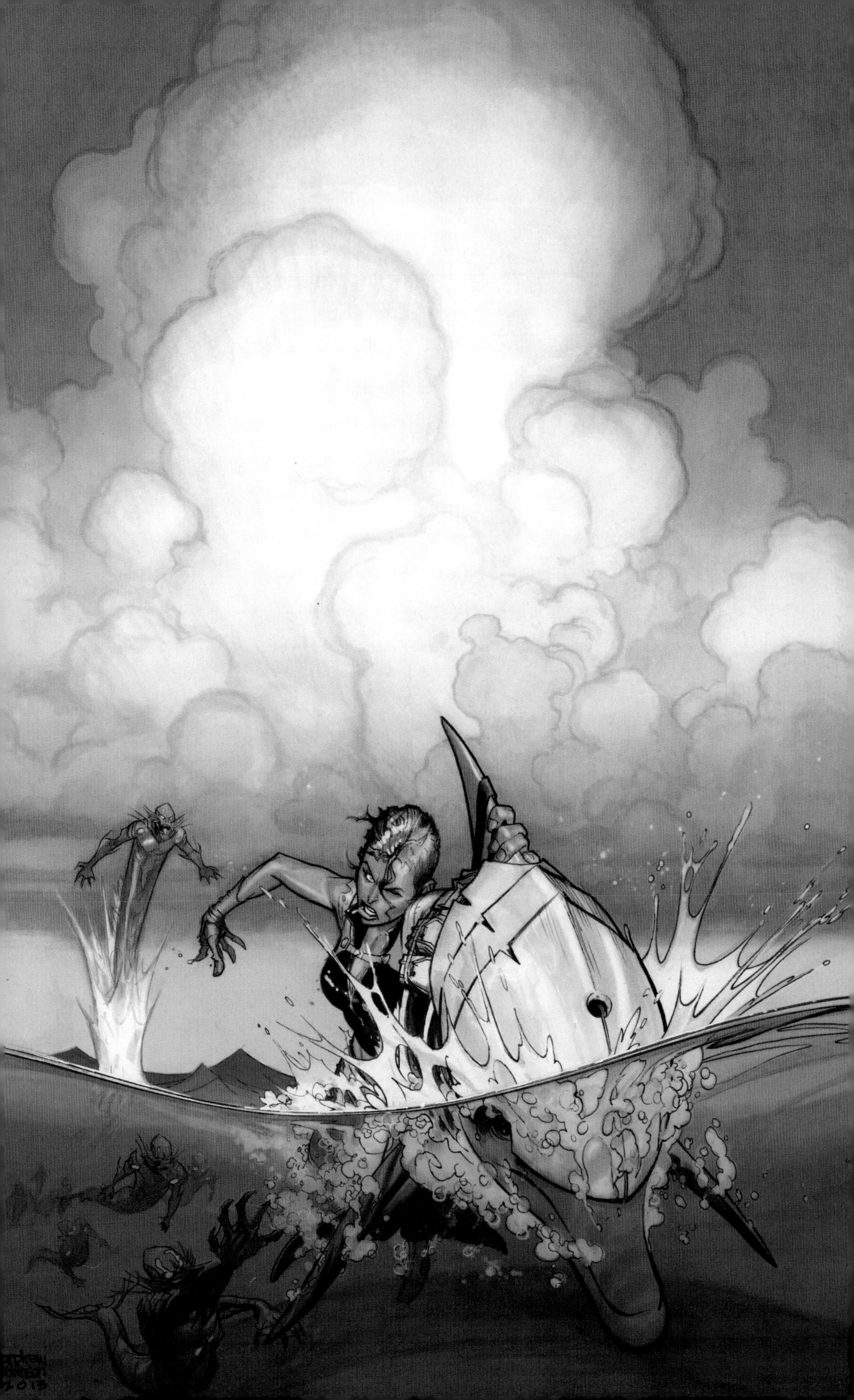

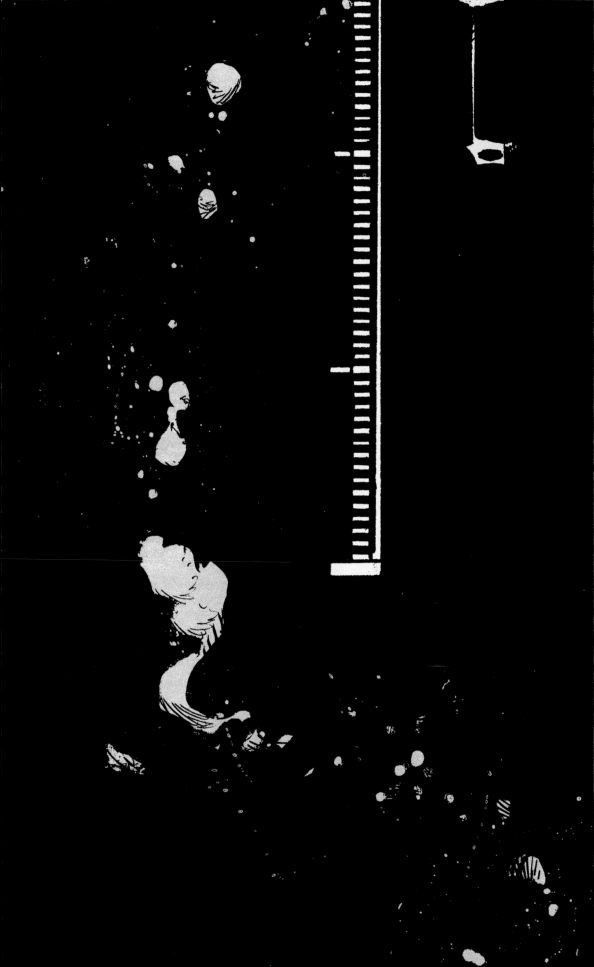

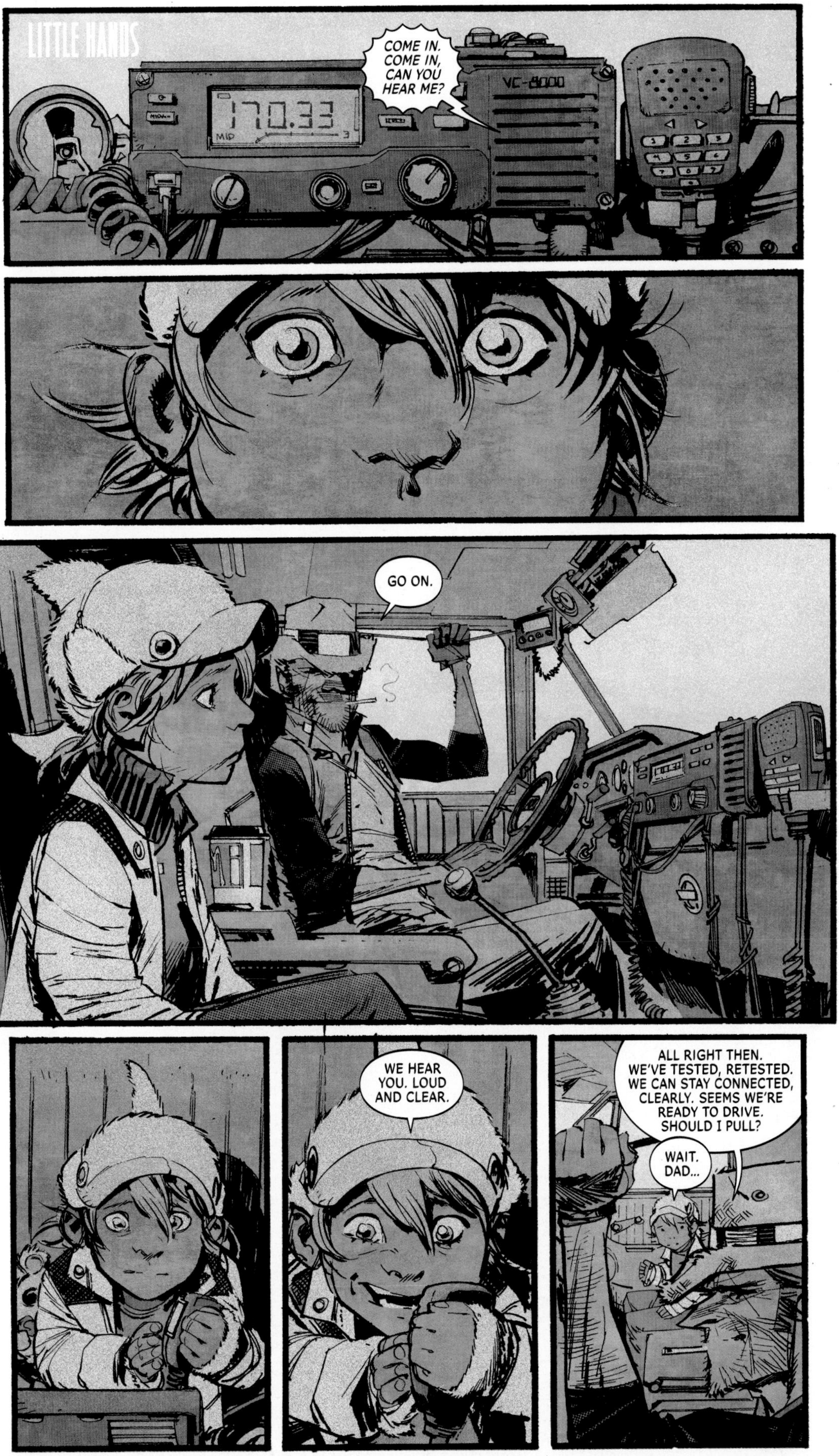
LITTLE HANDS
COME IN. COME IN, CAN YOU HEAR ME?
VC-8000
170.33
GO ON.
WE HEAR YOU. LOUD AND CLEAR.
ALL RIGHT THEN. WE'VE TESTED, RETESTED. WE CAN STAY CONNECTED, CLEARLY. SEEMS WE'RE READY TO DRIVE. SHOULD I PULL?
WAIT. DAD...

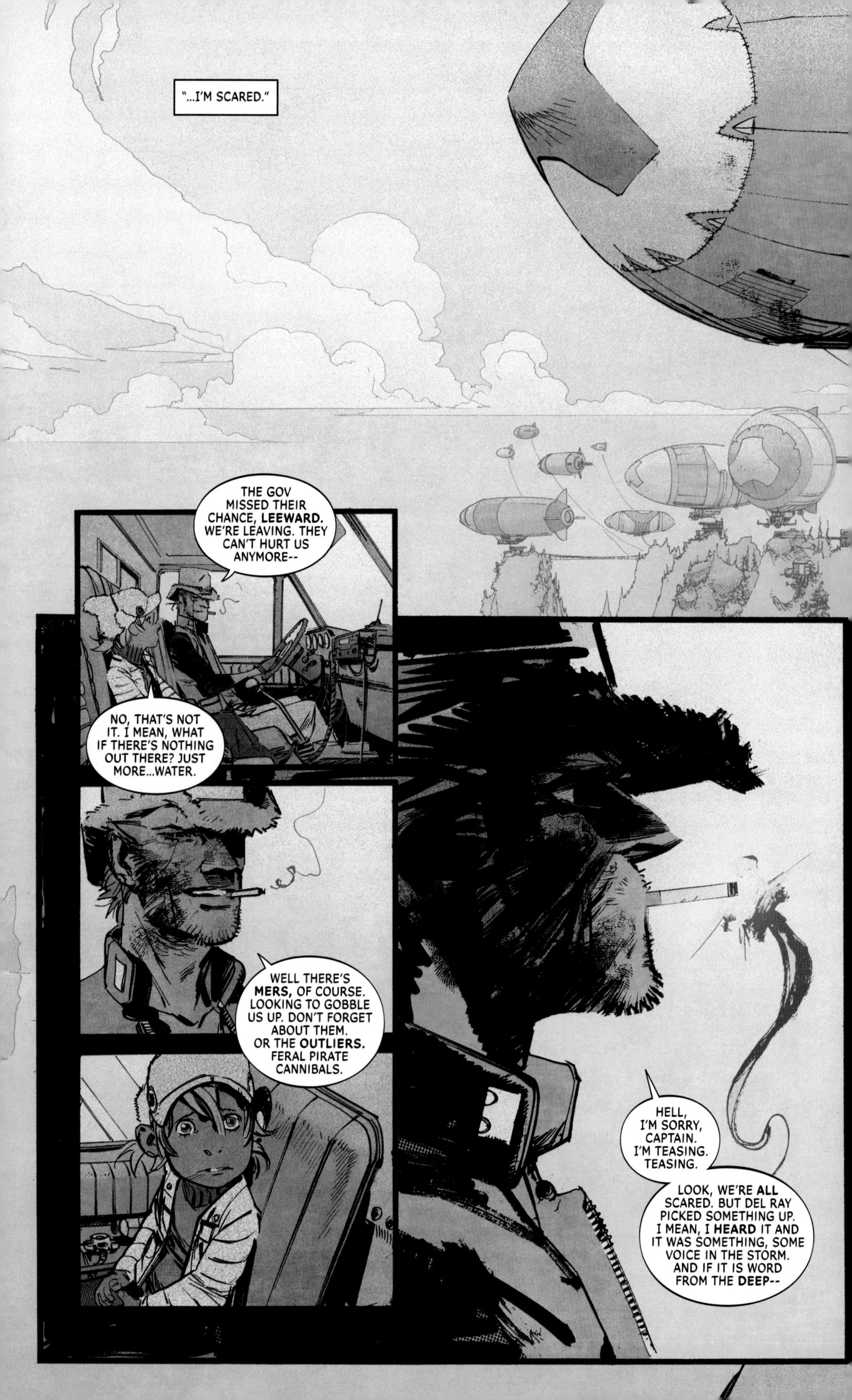
"...I'M SCARED."
THE GOV MISSED THEIR CHANCE, LEEWARD. WE'RE LEAVING. THEY CAN'T HURT US ANYMORE--
NO, THAT'S NOT IT. I MEAN, WHAT IF THERE'S NOTHING OUT THERE? JUST MORE...WATER.
WELL THERE'S MERS, OF COURSE. LOOKING TO GOBBLE US UP. DON'T FORGET ABOUT THEM. OR THE OUTLIERS. FERAL PIRATE CANNIBALS.
HELL, I'M SORRY, CAPTAIN. I'M TEASING. TEASING.
LOOK, WE'RE ALL SCARED. BUT DEL RAY PICKED SOMETHING UP. I MEAN, I HEARD IT AND IT WAS SOMETHING, SOME VOICE IN THE STORM. AND IF IT IS WORD FROM THE DEEP--

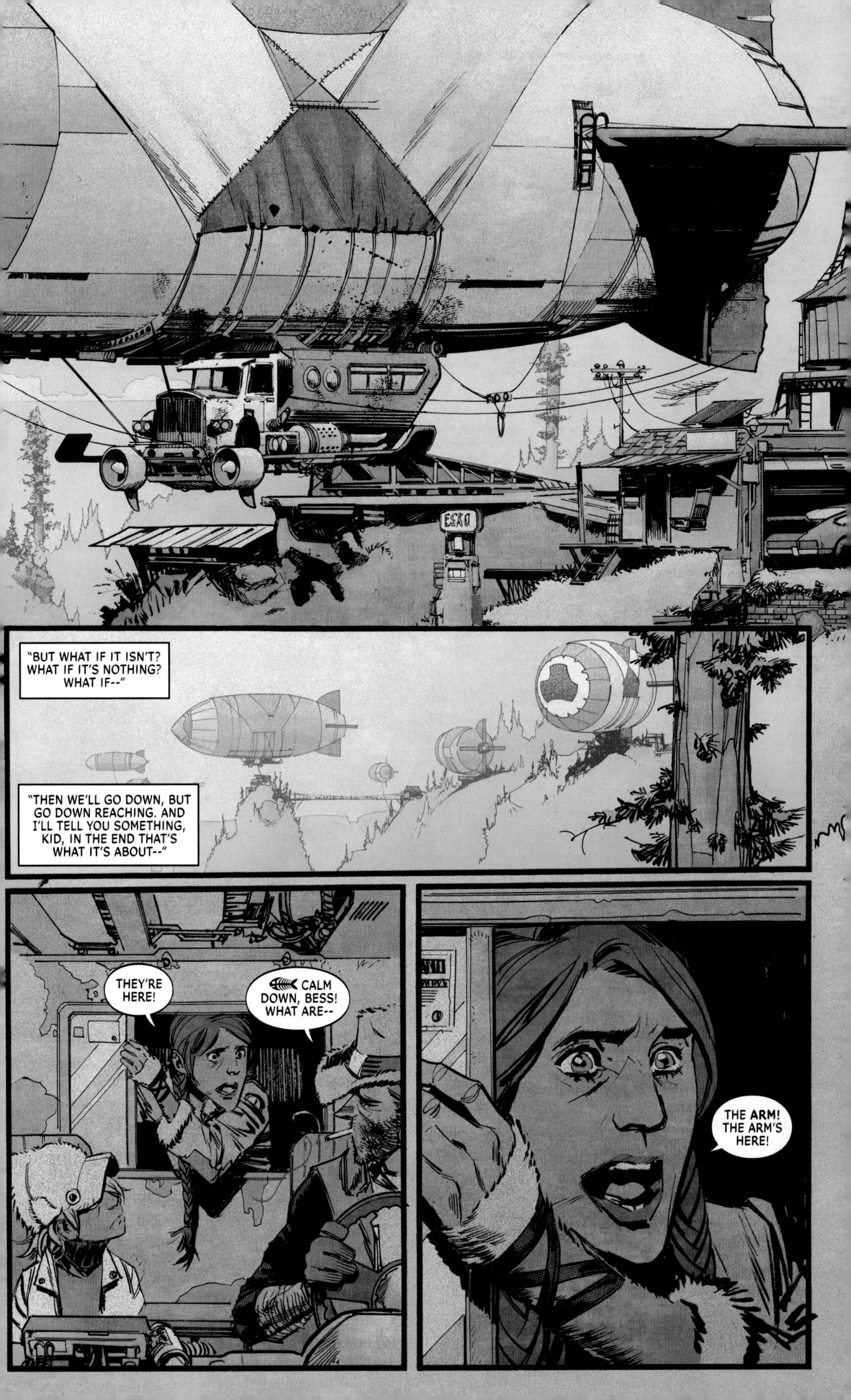
ESKO
"BUT WHAT IF IT ISN'T? WHAT IF IT'S NOTHING? WHAT IF--"
"THEN WE'LL GO DOWN, BUT GO DOWN REACHING. AND I'LL TELL YOU SOMETHING, KID, IN THE END THAT'S WHAT IT'S ABOUT--"
THEY'RE HERE!
CALM DOWN, BESS! WHAT ARE--
THE **ARM**! THE ARM'S HERE!

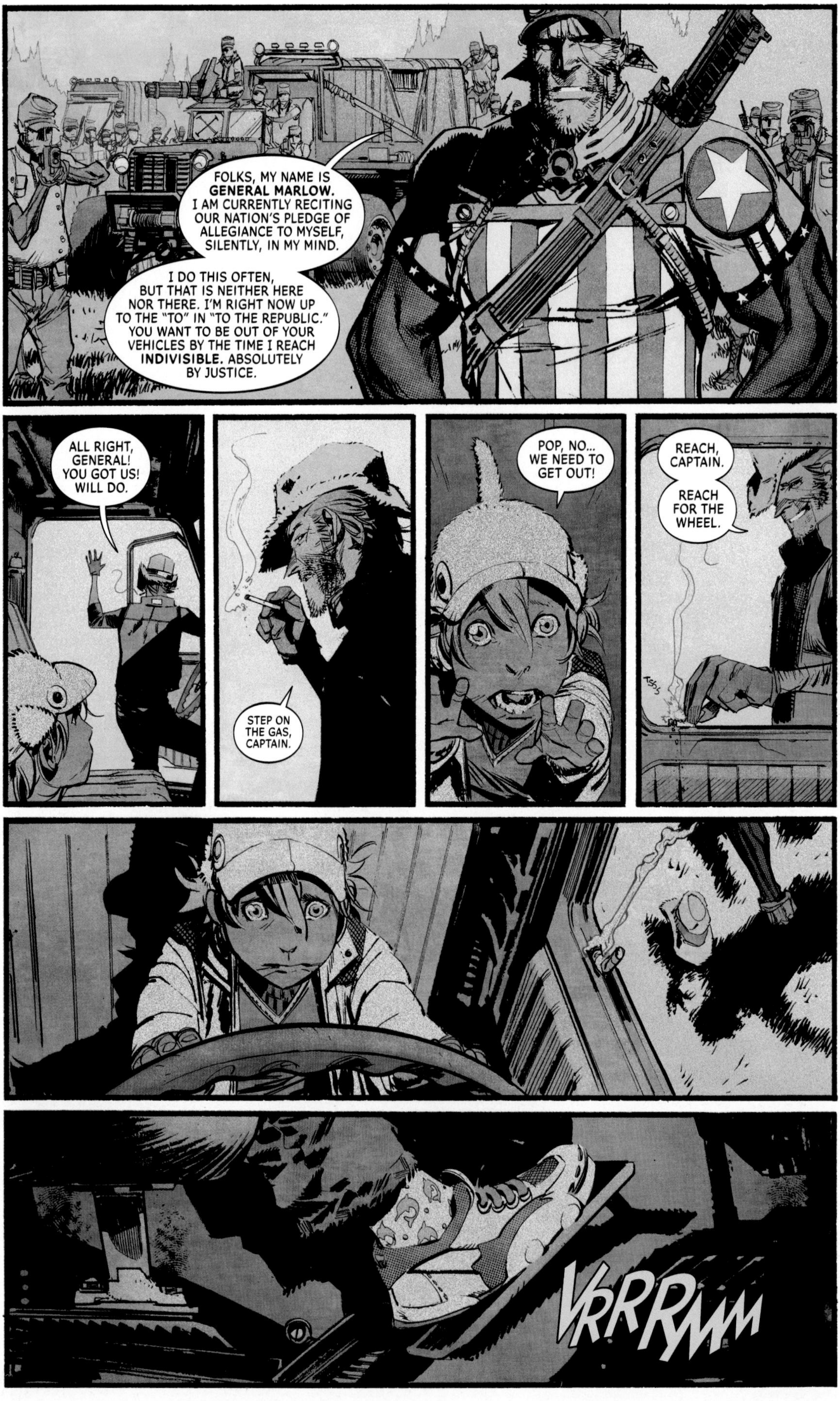
FOLKS, MY NAME IS **GENERAL MARLOW.** I AM CURRENTLY RECITING OUR NATION'S PLEDGE OF ALLEGIANCE TO MYSELF, SILENTLY, IN MY MIND.
I DO THIS OFTEN, BUT THAT IS NEITHER HERE NOR THERE. I'M RIGHT NOW UP TO THE "TO" IN "TO THE REPUBLIC." YOU WANT TO BE OUT OF YOUR VEHICLES BY THE TIME I REACH **INDIVISIBLE.** ABSOLUTELY BY JUSTICE.
ALL RIGHT, GENERAL! YOU GOT US! WILL DO.
STEP ON THE GAS, CAPTAIN.
POP, NO... WE NEED TO GET OUT!
REACH, CAPTAIN.
REACH FOR THE WHEEL.
VRRRMM

THE WAKE
CHAPTER TWO

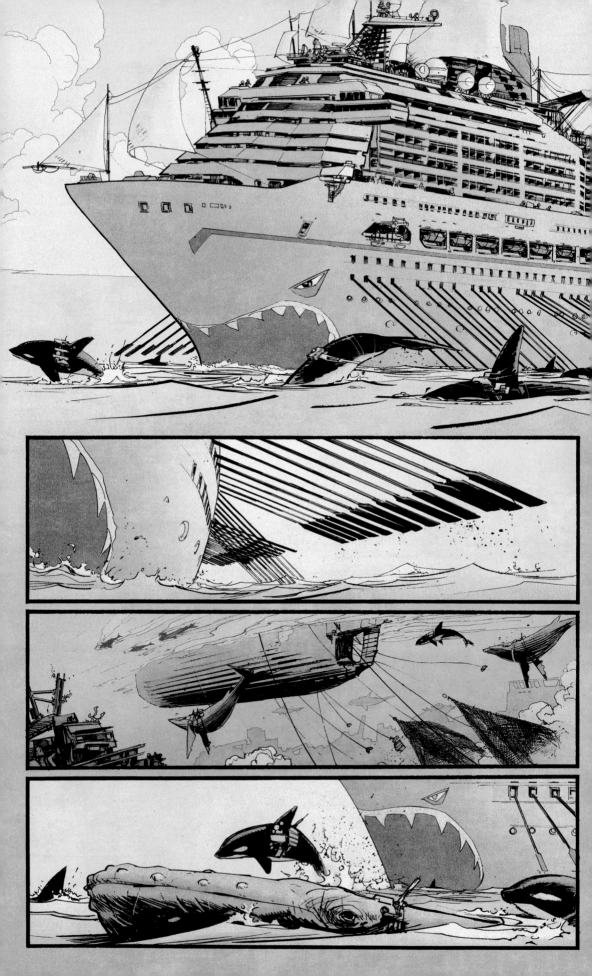

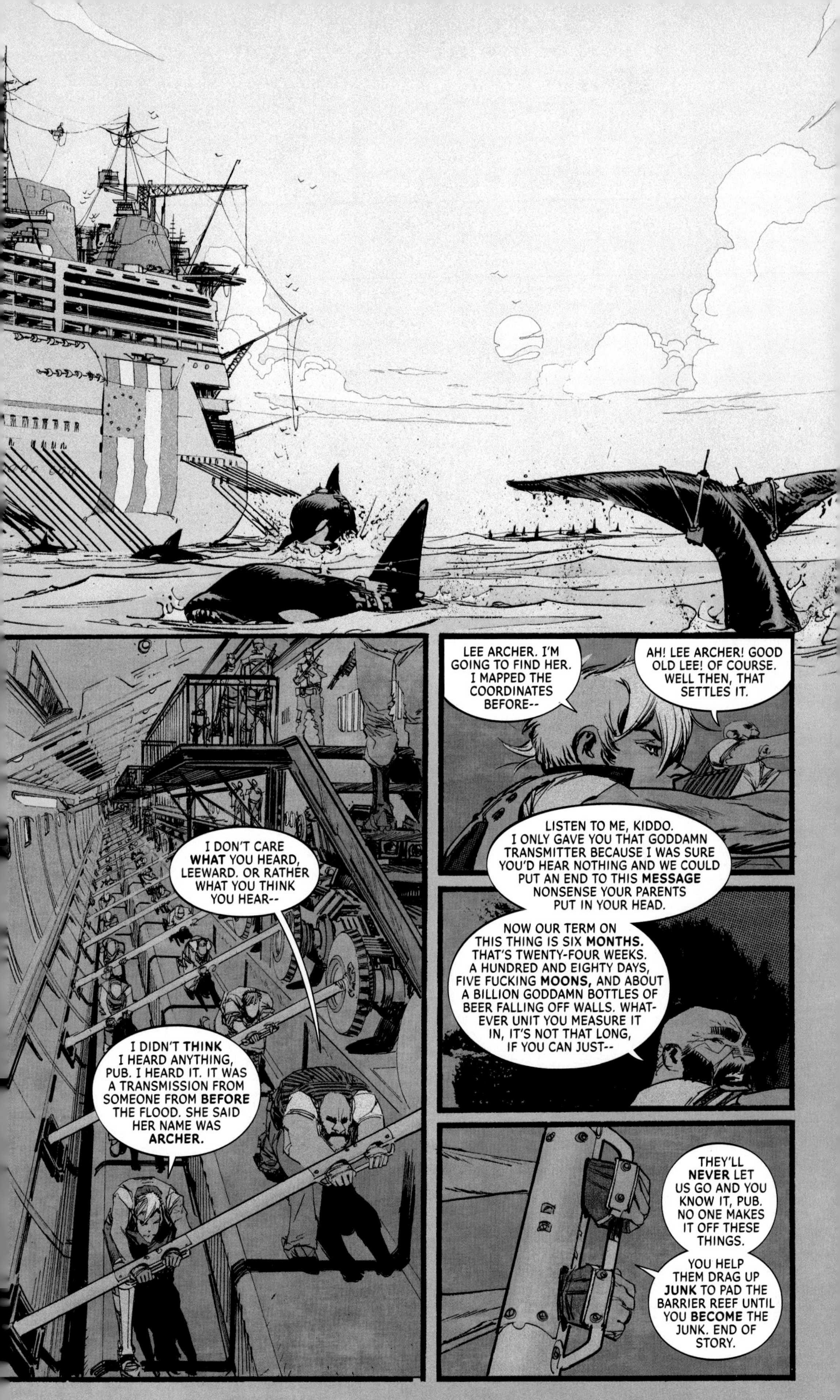
I DON'T CARE WHAT YOU HEARD, LEEWARD. OR RATHER WHAT YOU THINK YOU HEAR--
I DIDN'T THINK I HEARD ANYTHING, PUB. I HEARD IT. IT WAS A TRANSMISSION FROM SOMEONE FROM BEFORE THE FLOOD. SHE SAID HER NAME WAS ARCHER.
LEE ARCHER. I'M GOING TO FIND HER. I MAPPED THE COORDINATES BEFORE--
AH! LEE ARCHER! GOOD OLD LEE! OF COURSE. WELL THEN, THAT SETTLES IT.
LISTEN TO ME, KIDDO. I ONLY GAVE YOU THAT GODDAMN TRANSMITTER BECAUSE I WAS SURE YOU'D HEAR NOTHING AND WE COULD PUT AN END TO THIS MESSAGE NONSENSE YOUR PARENTS PUT IN YOUR HEAD.
NOW OUR TERM ON THIS THING IS SIX MONTHS. THAT'S TWENTY-FOUR WEEKS. A HUNDRED AND EIGHTY DAYS, FIVE FUCKING MOONS, AND ABOUT A BILLION GODDAMN BOTTLES OF BEER FALLING OFF WALLS. WHATEVER UNIT YOU MEASURE IT IN, IT'S NOT THAT LONG, IF YOU CAN JUST--
THEY'LL NEVER LET US GO AND YOU KNOW IT, PUB. NO ONE MAKES IT OFF THESE THINGS.
YOU HELP THEM DRAG UP JUNK TO PAD THE BARRIER REEF UNTIL YOU BECOME THE JUNK. END OF STORY.

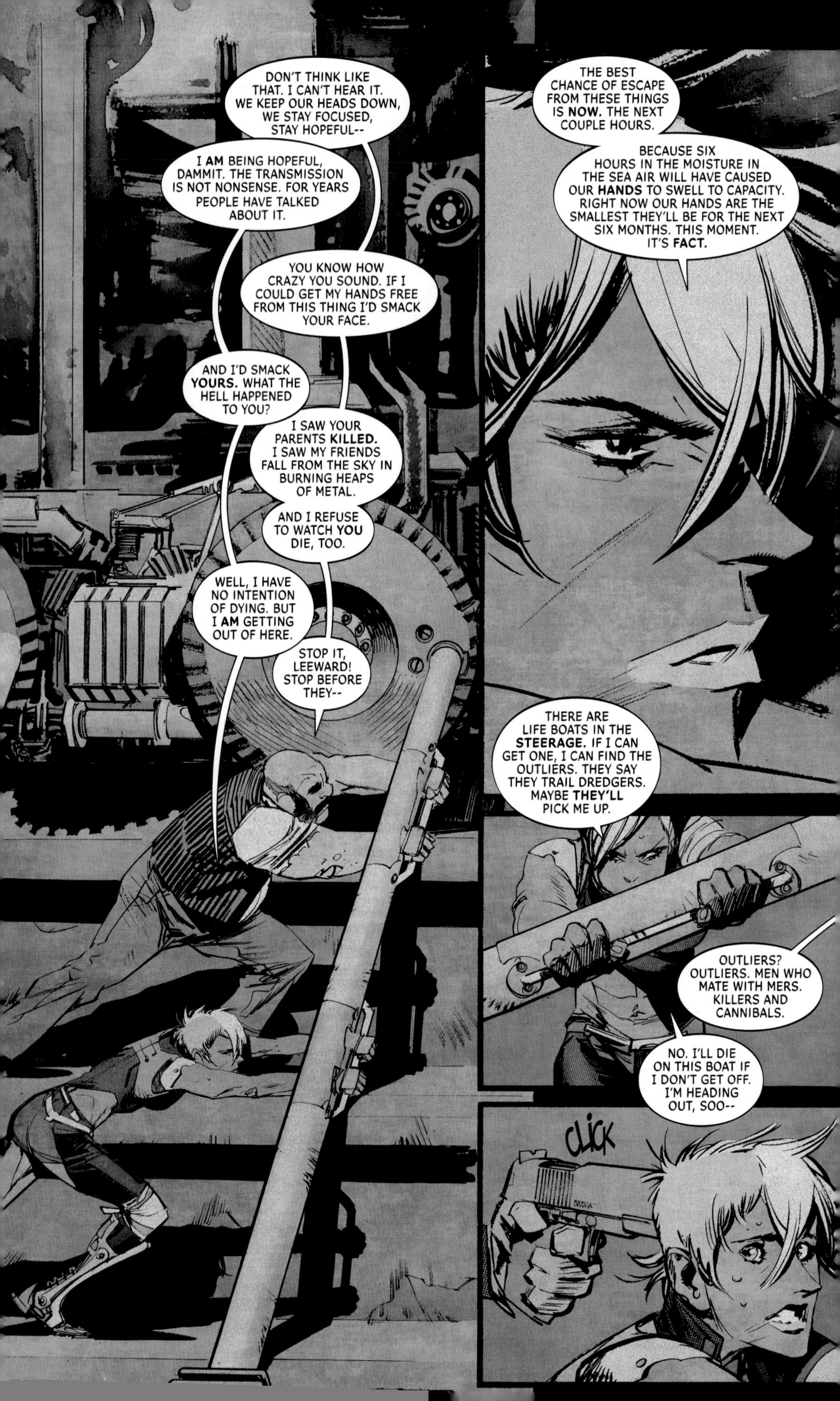
DON'T THINK LIKE THAT. I CAN'T HEAR IT. WE KEEP OUR HEADS DOWN, WE STAY FOCUSED, STAY HOPEFUL--
I AM BEING HOPEFUL, DAMMIT. THE TRANSMISSION IS NOT NONSENSE. FOR YEARS PEOPLE HAVE TALKED ABOUT IT.
YOU KNOW HOW CRAZY YOU SOUND. IF I COULD GET MY HANDS FREE FROM THIS THING I'D SMACK YOUR FACE.
AND I'D SMACK YOURS. WHAT THE HELL HAPPENED TO YOU?
I SAW YOUR PARENTS KILLED. I SAW MY FRIENDS FALL FROM THE SKY IN BURNING HEAPS OF METAL.
AND I REFUSE TO WATCH YOU DIE, TOO.
WELL, I HAVE NO INTENTION OF DYING. BUT I AM GETTING OUT OF HERE.
STOP IT, LEEWARD! STOP BEFORE THEY--
THE BEST CHANCE OF ESCAPE FROM THESE THINGS IS NOW. THE NEXT COUPLE HOURS.
BECAUSE SIX HOURS IN THE MOISTURE IN THE SEA AIR WILL HAVE CAUSED OUR HANDS TO SWELL TO CAPACITY. RIGHT NOW OUR HANDS ARE THE SMALLEST THEY'LL BE FOR THE NEXT SIX MONTHS. THIS MOMENT. IT'S FACT.
THERE ARE LIFE BOATS IN THE STEERAGE. IF I CAN GET ONE, I CAN FIND THE OUTLIERS. THEY SAY THEY TRAIL DREDGERS. MAYBE THEY'LL PICK ME UP.
OUTLIERS? OUTLIERS. MEN WHO MATE WITH MERS. KILLERS AND CANNIBALS.
NO. I'LL DIE ON THIS BOAT IF I DON'T GET OFF. I'M HEADING OUT, SOO--
CLICK

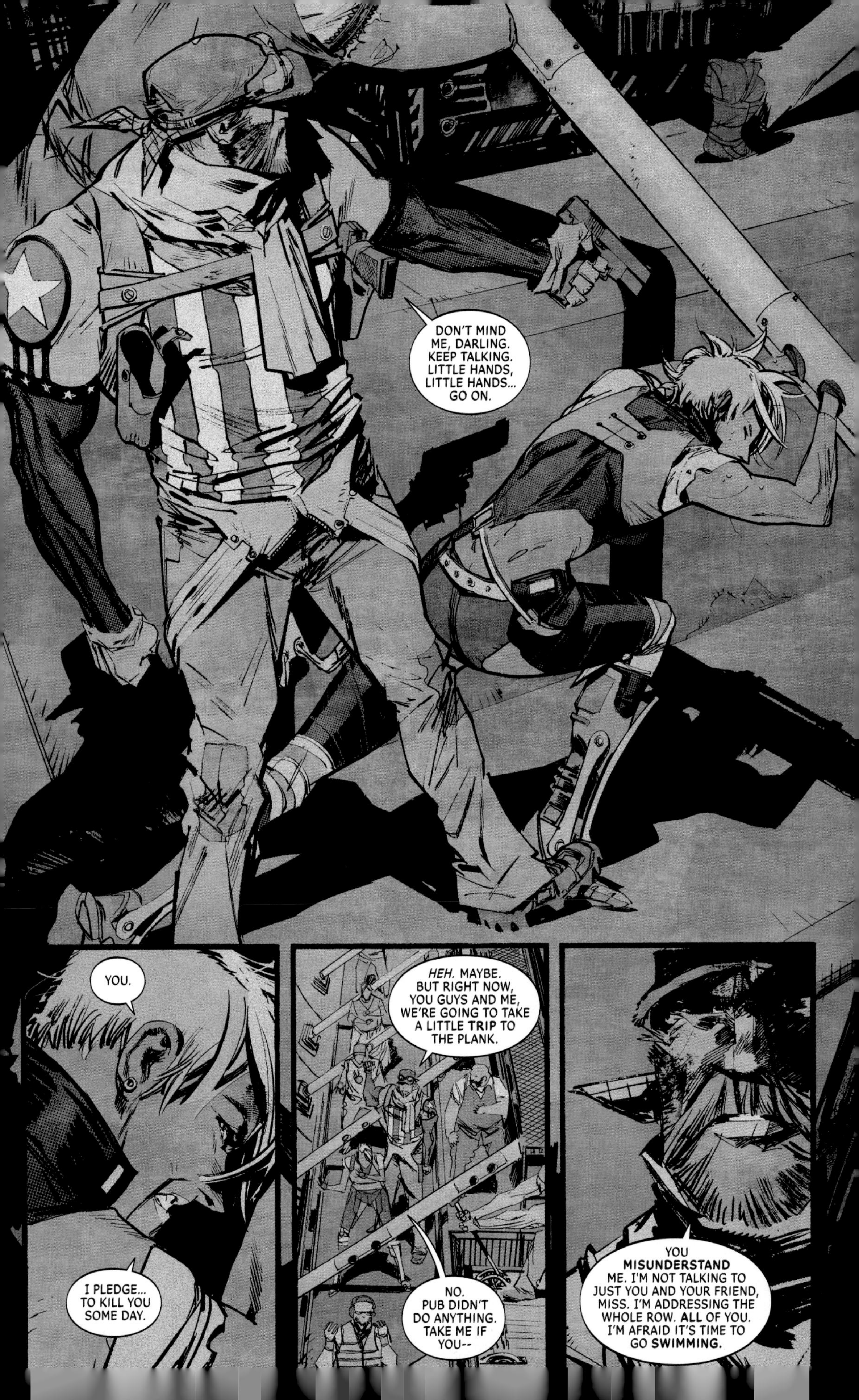

DON'T MIND ME, DARLING. KEEP TALKING. LITTLE HANDS, LITTLE HANDS... GO ON.
YOU.
I PLEDGE... TO KILL YOU SOME DAY.
HEH. MAYBE. BUT RIGHT NOW, YOU GUYS AND ME, WE'RE GOING TO TAKE A LITTLE **TRIP** TO THE PLANK.
NO. PUB DIDN'T DO ANYTHING. TAKE ME IF YOU--
YOU **MISUNDERSTAND** ME. I'M NOT TALKING TO JUST YOU AND YOUR FRIEND, MISS. I'M ADDRESSING THE WHOLE ROW. **ALL** OF YOU. I'M AFRAID IT'S TIME TO GO **SWIMMING.**

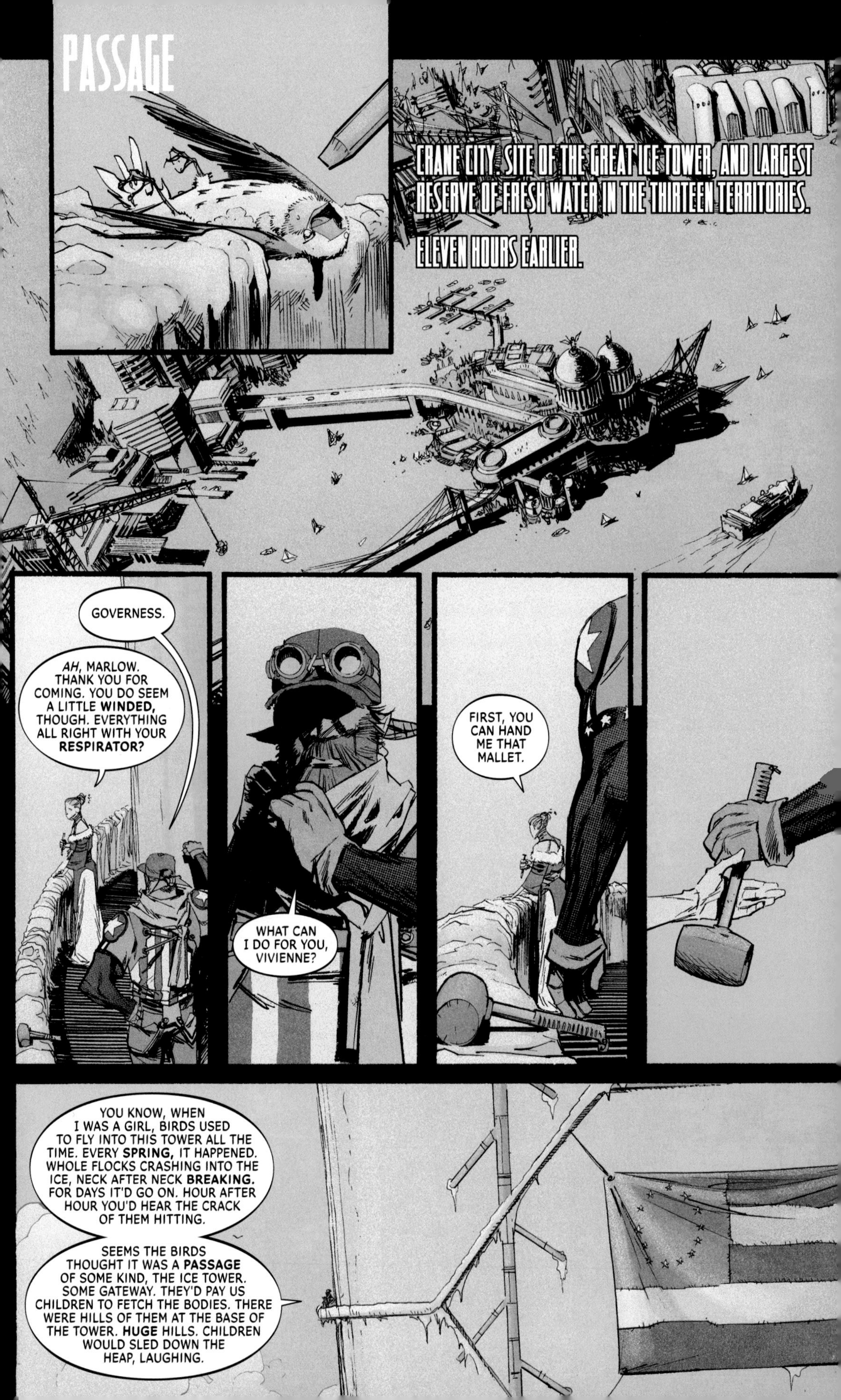
PASSAGE
CRANE CITY. SITE OF THE GREAT ICE TOWER, AND LARGEST RESERVE OF FRESH WATER IN THE THIRTEEN TERRITORIES.
ELEVEN HOURS EARLIER.
GOVERNESS.
AH, MARLOW. THANK YOU FOR COMING. YOU DO SEEM A LITTLE WINDED, THOUGH. EVERYTHING ALL RIGHT WITH YOUR RESPIRATOR?
WHAT CAN I DO FOR YOU, VIVIENNE?
FIRST, YOU CAN HAND ME THAT MALLET.
YOU KNOW, WHEN I WAS A GIRL, BIRDS USED TO FLY INTO THIS TOWER ALL THE TIME. EVERY SPRING, IT HAPPENED. WHOLE FLOCKS CRASHING INTO THE ICE, NECK AFTER NECK BREAKING. FOR DAYS IT'D GO ON. HOUR AFTER HOUR YOU'D HEAR THE CRACK OF THEM HITTING.
SEEMS THE BIRDS THOUGHT IT WAS A PASSAGE OF SOME KIND, THE ICE TOWER. SOME GATEWAY. THEY'D PAY US CHILDREN TO FETCH THE BODIES. THERE WERE HILLS OF THEM AT THE BASE OF THE TOWER. HUGE HILLS. CHILDREN WOULD SLED DOWN THE HEAP, LAUGHING.

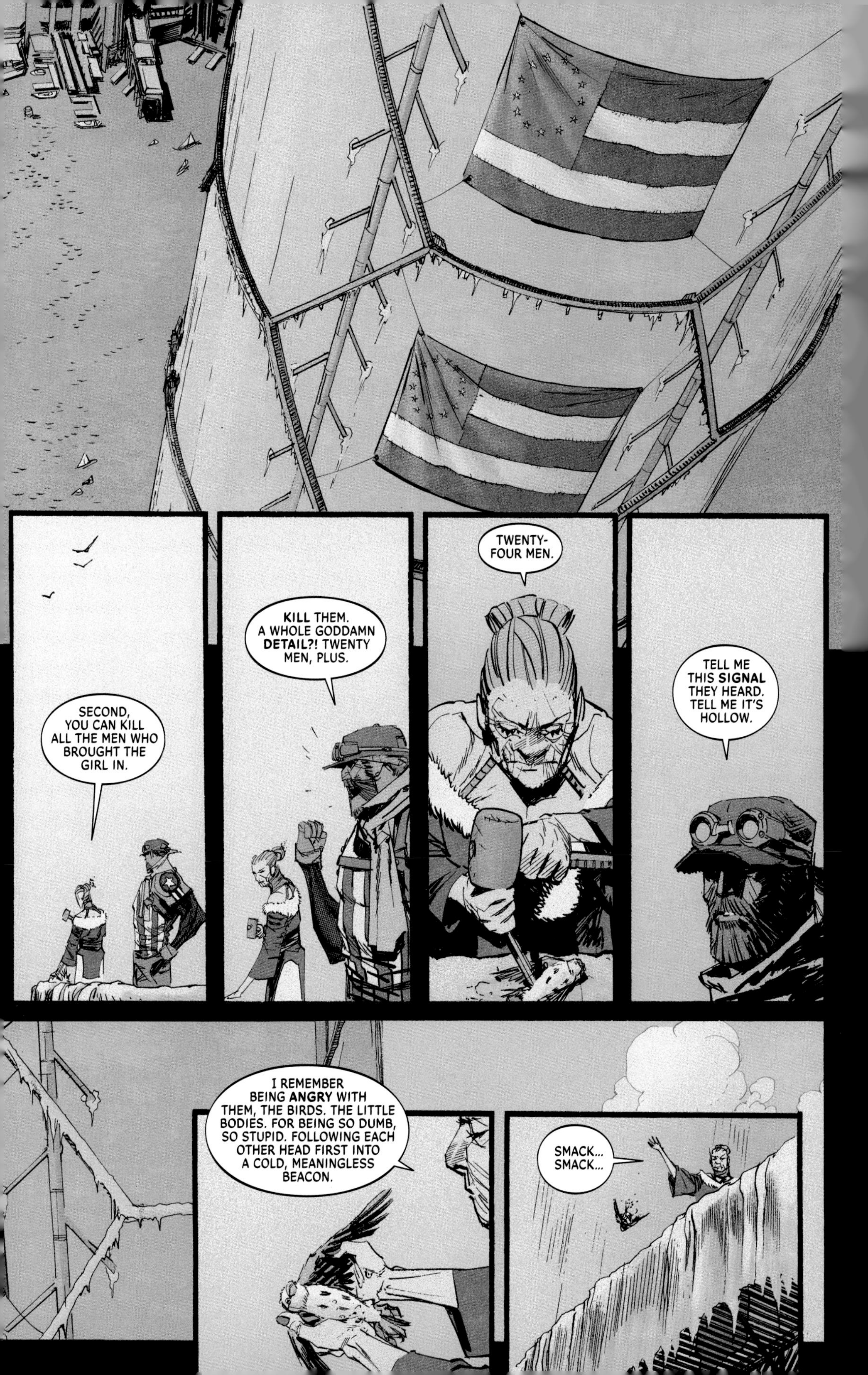
SECOND, YOU CAN KILL ALL THE MEN WHO BROUGHT THE GIRL IN.
KILL THEM. A WHOLE GODDAMN DETAIL?! TWENTY MEN, PLUS.
TWENTY-FOUR MEN.
TELL ME THIS SIGNAL THEY HEARD. TELL ME IT'S HOLLOW.
I REMEMBER BEING ANGRY WITH THEM, THE BIRDS. THE LITTLE BODIES. FOR BEING SO DUMB, SO STUPID. FOLLOWING EACH OTHER HEAD FIRST INTO A COLD, MEANINGLESS BEACON.
SMACK... SMACK...

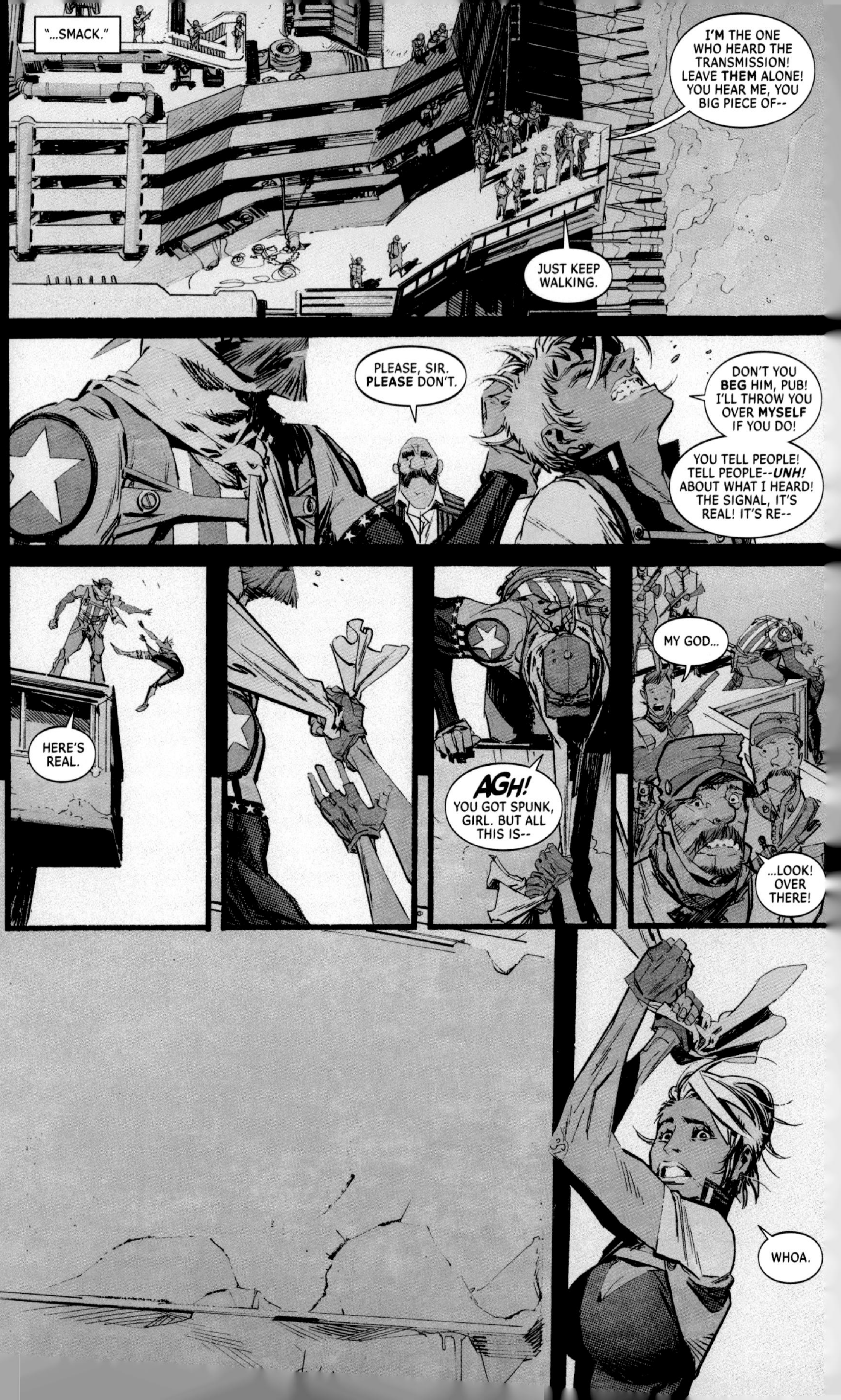
"...SMACK."
I'M THE ONE WHO HEARD THE TRANSMISSION! LEAVE THEM ALONE! YOU HEAR ME, YOU BIG PIECE OF--
JUST KEEP WALKING.
PLEASE, SIR. PLEASE DON'T.
DON'T YOU BEG HIM, PUB! I'LL THROW YOU OVER MYSELF IF YOU DO!
YOU TELL PEOPLE! TELL PEOPLE--UNH! ABOUT WHAT I HEARD! THE SIGNAL, IT'S REAL! IT'S RE--
HERE'S REAL.
AGH!
YOU GOT SPUNK, GIRL. BUT ALL THIS IS--
MY GOD...
...LOOK! OVER THERE!
WHOA.

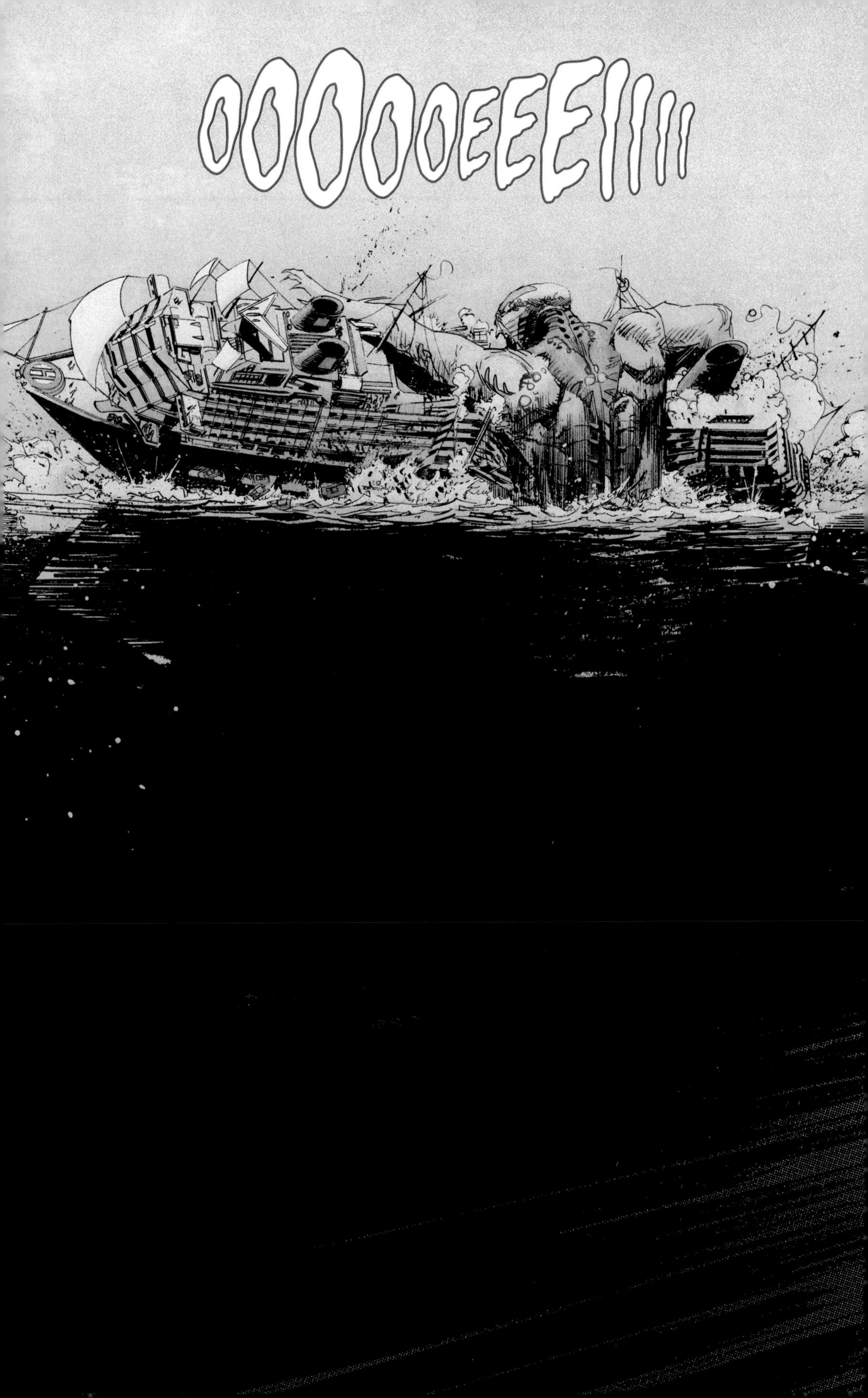
OOOOOEEEIIII

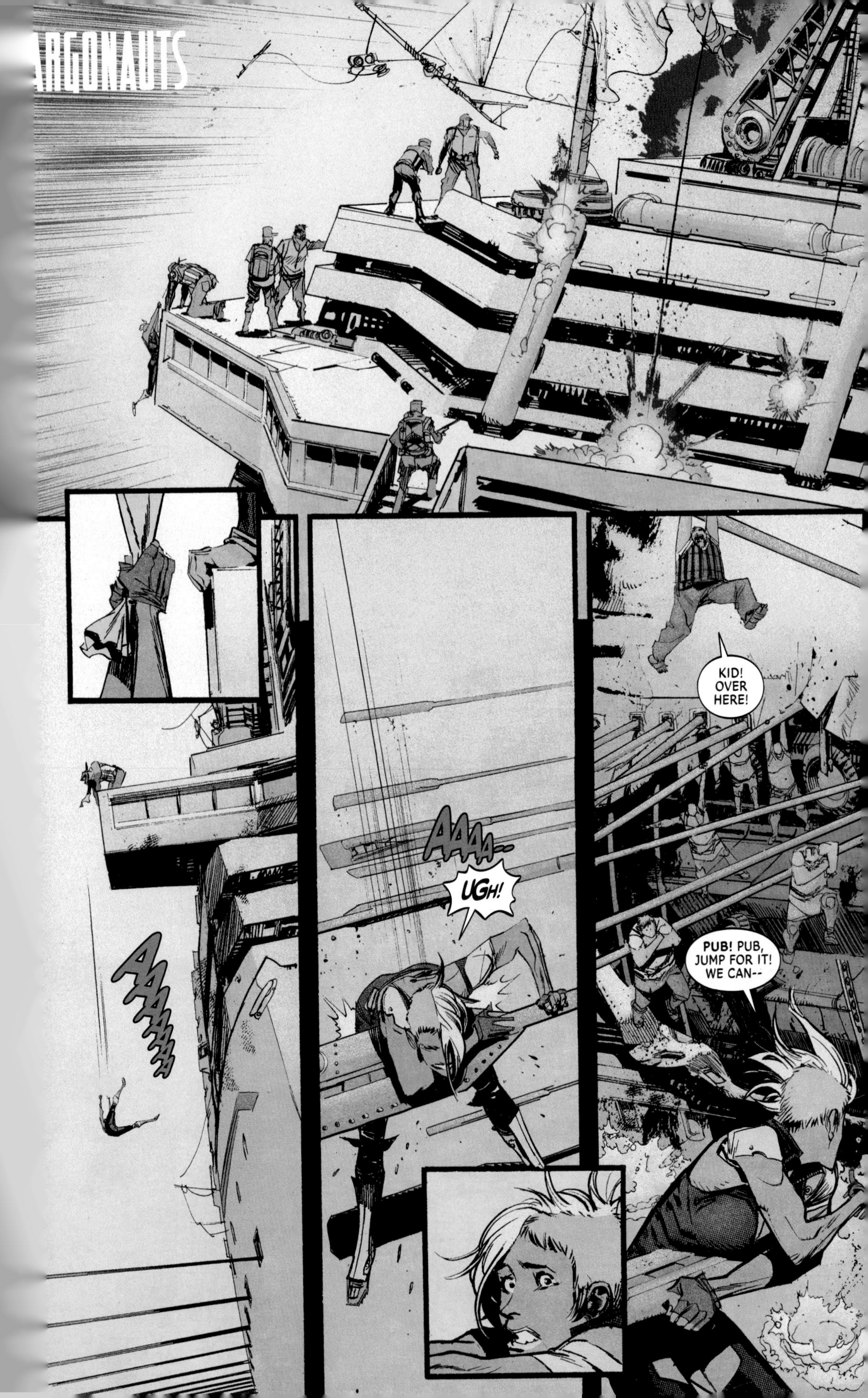
ARGONAUTS
KID! OVER HERE!
AAAA--
UGH!
AAAAAAAA
PUB! PUB, JUMP FOR IT! WE CAN--

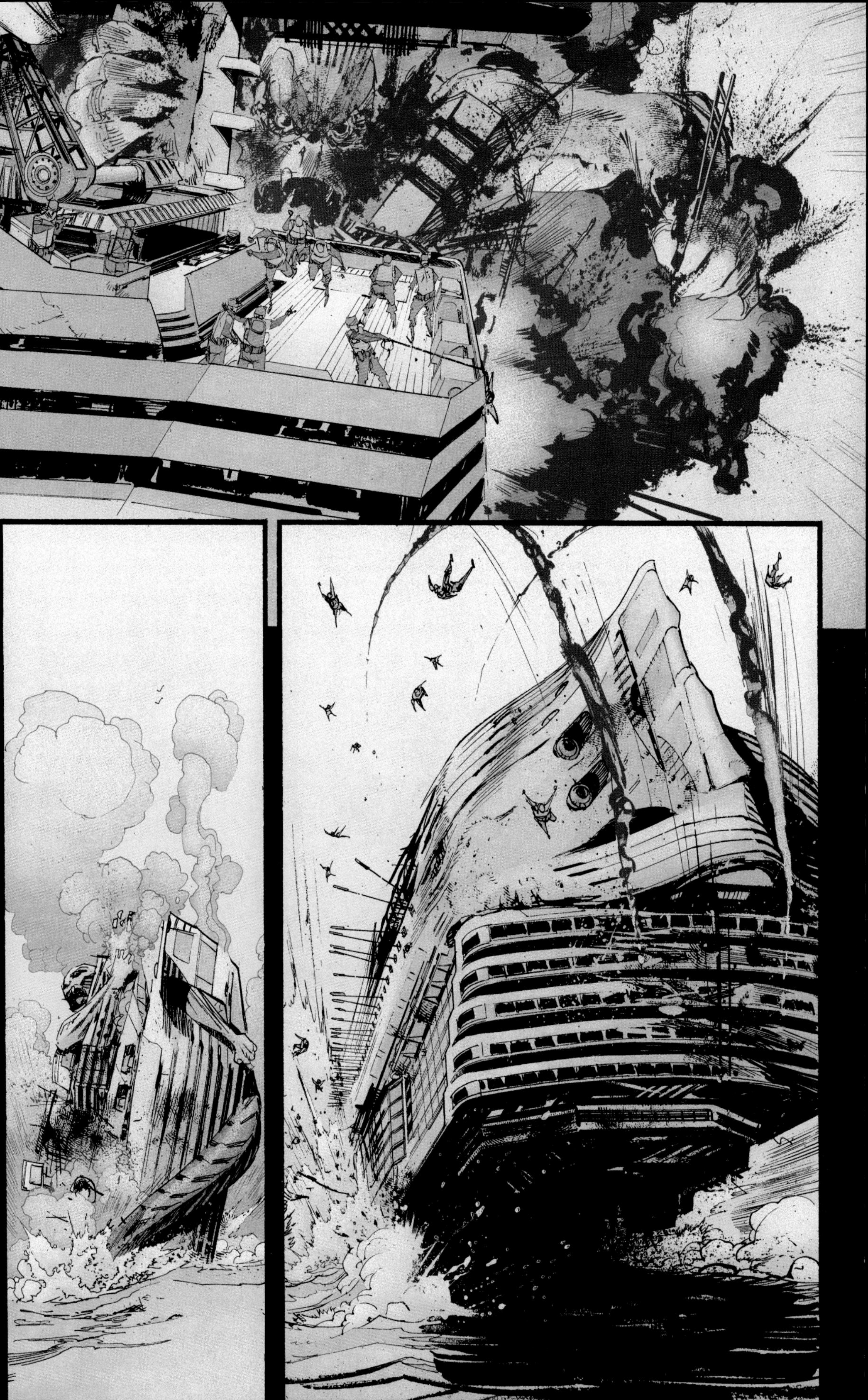

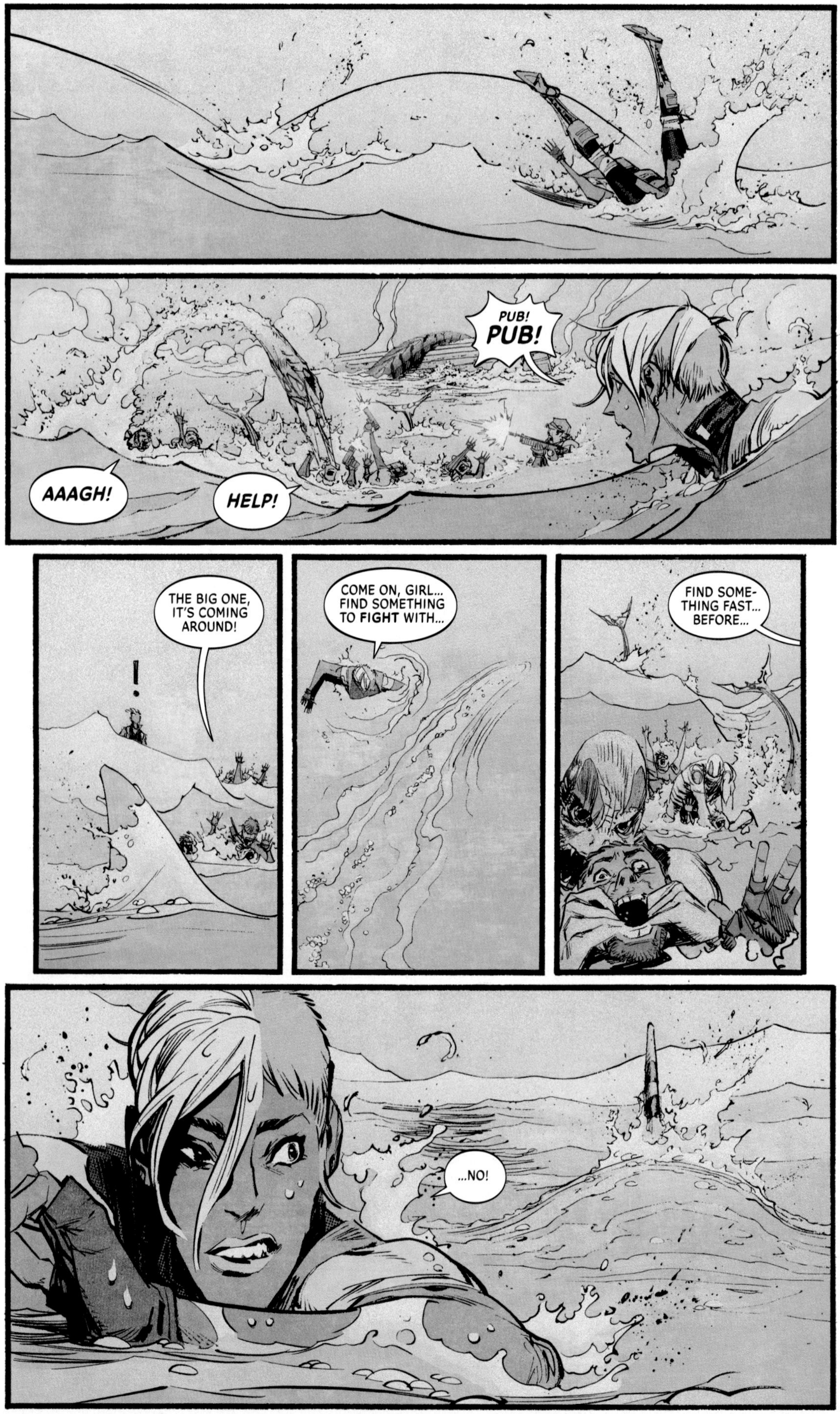
PUB!
PUB!
AAAGH!
HELP!
THE BIG ONE, IT'S COMING AROUND!
!
COME ON, GIRL... FIND SOMETHING TO **FIGHT** WITH...
FIND SOME-THING FAST... BEFORE...
...NO!

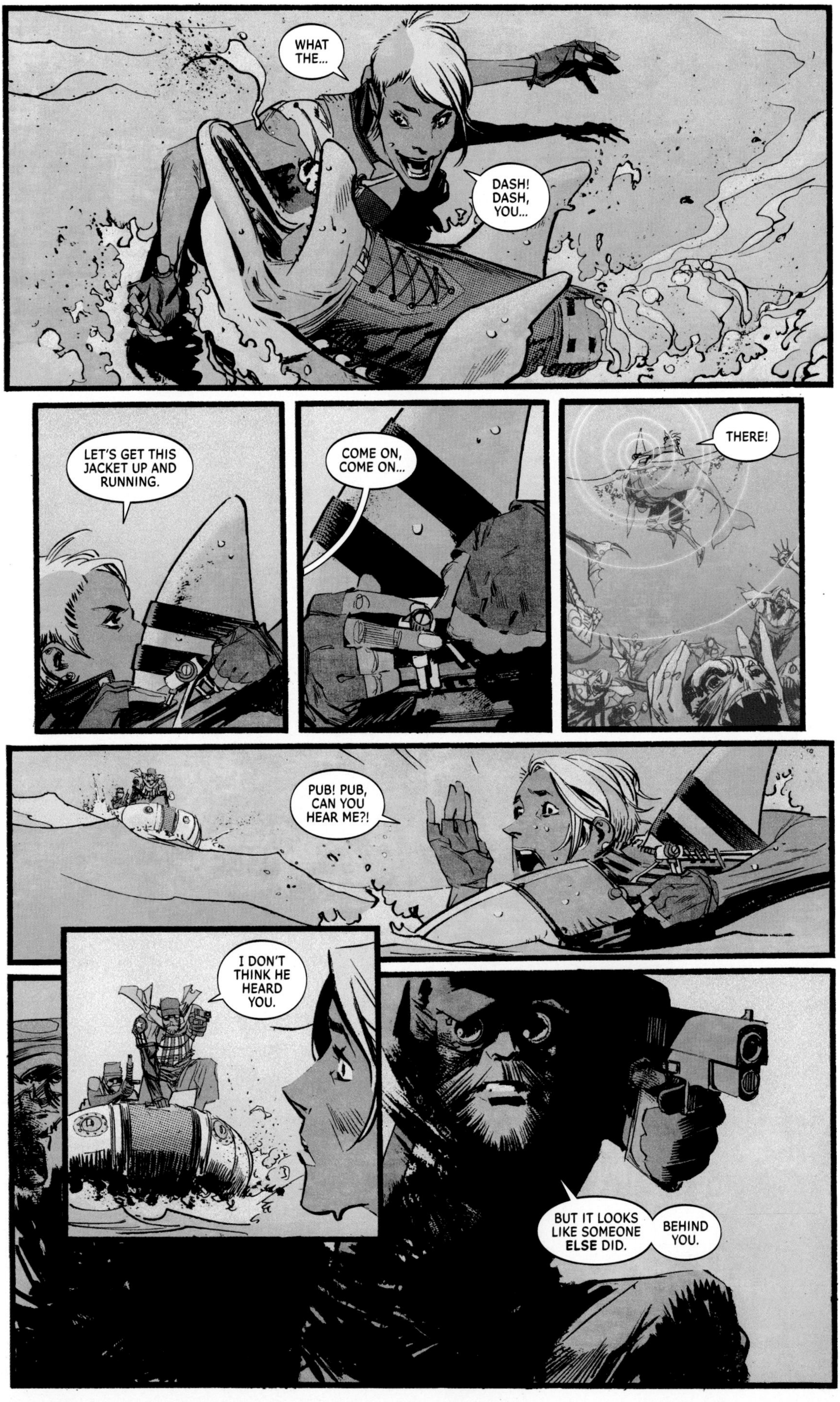
WHAT THE...
DASH! DASH, YOU...
LET'S GET THIS JACKET UP AND RUNNING.
COME ON, COME ON...
THERE!
PUB! PUB, CAN YOU HEAR ME?!
I DON'T THINK HE HEARD YOU.
BUT IT LOOKS LIKE SOMEONE **ELSE** DID.
BEHIND YOU.

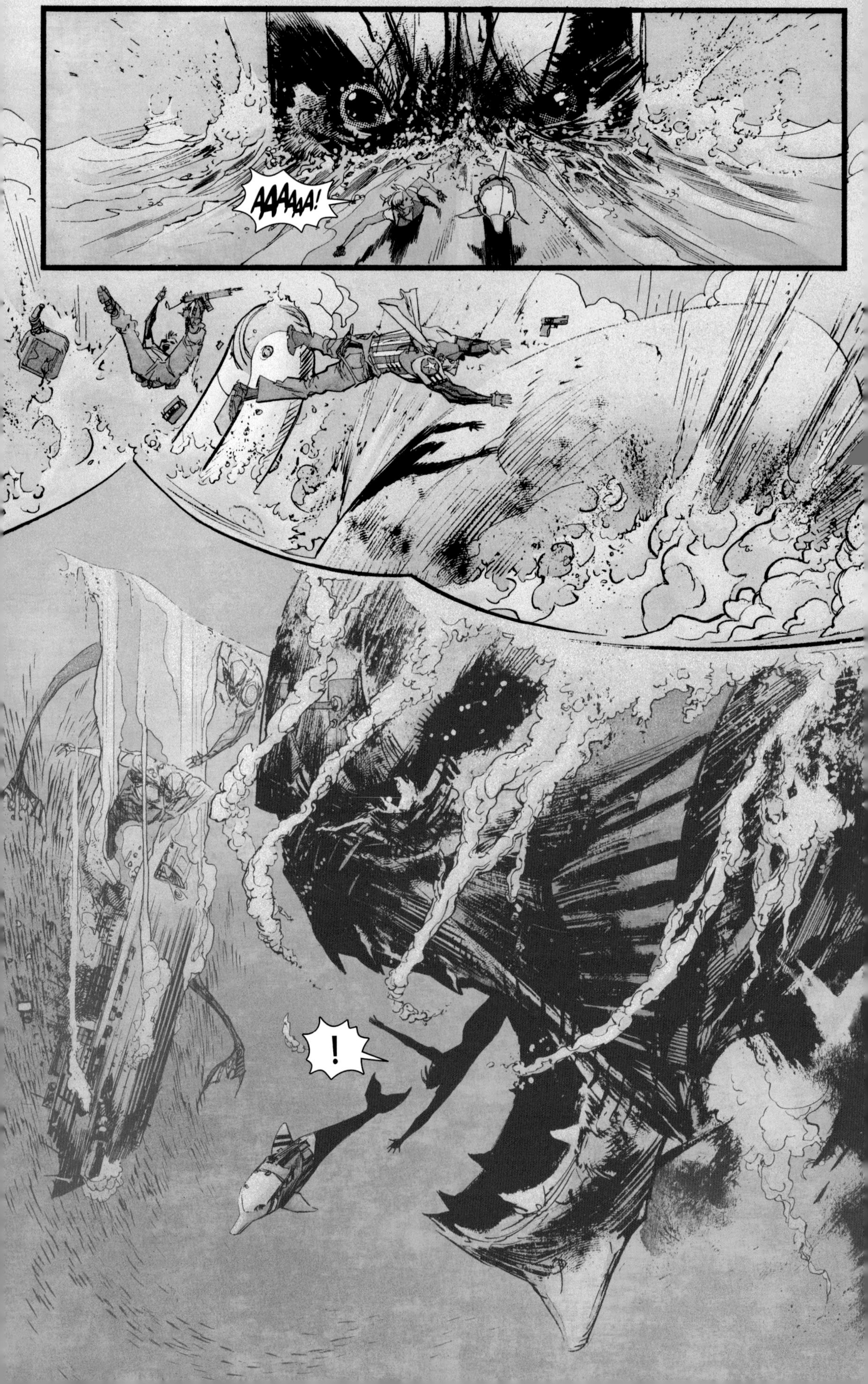
AAAAAA!
!

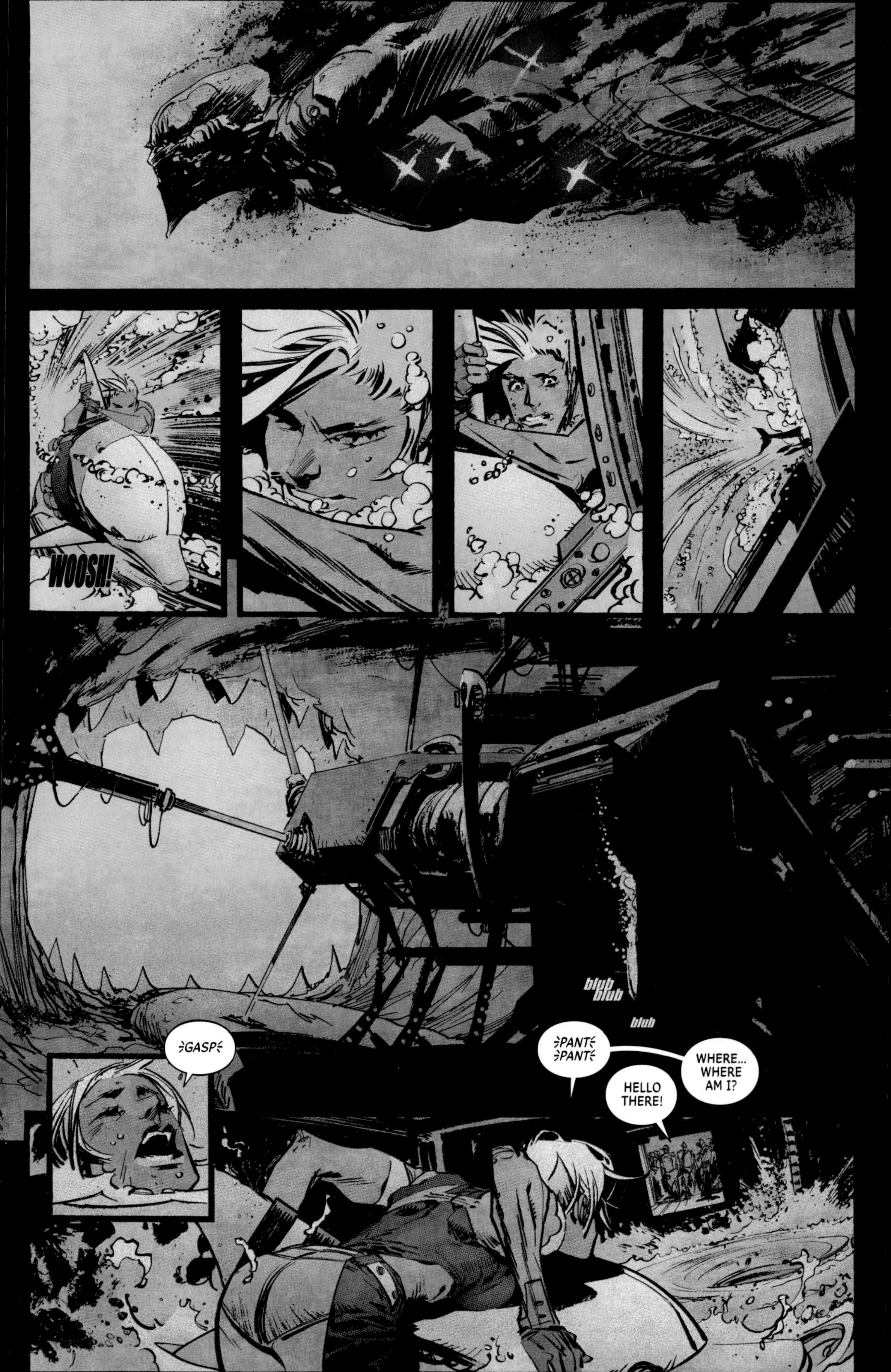
WOOSH!
blub
blub
blub
GASP
PANT PANT
WHERE... WHERE AM I?
HELLO THERE!

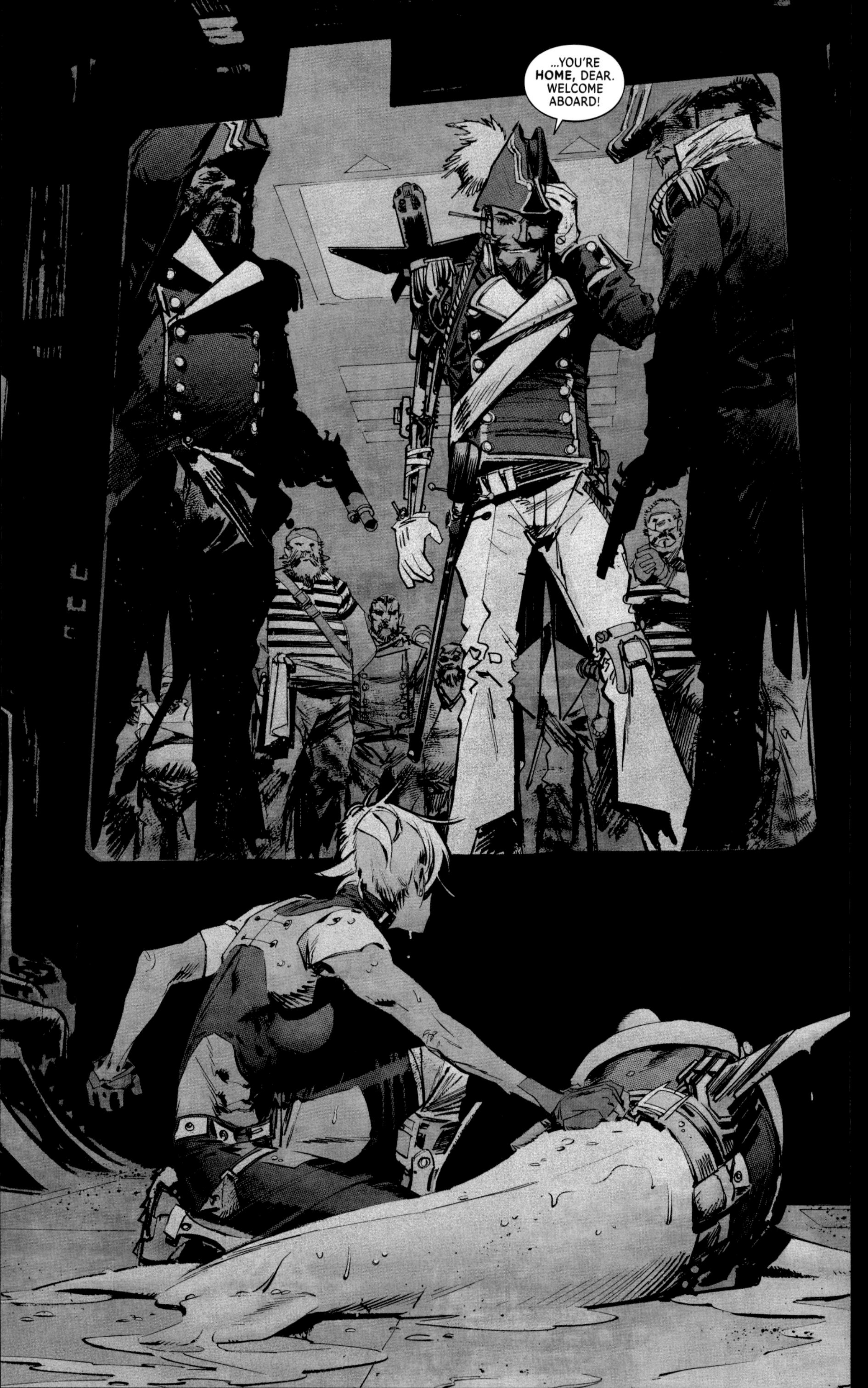
...YOU'RE HOME, DEAR. WELCOME ABOARD!

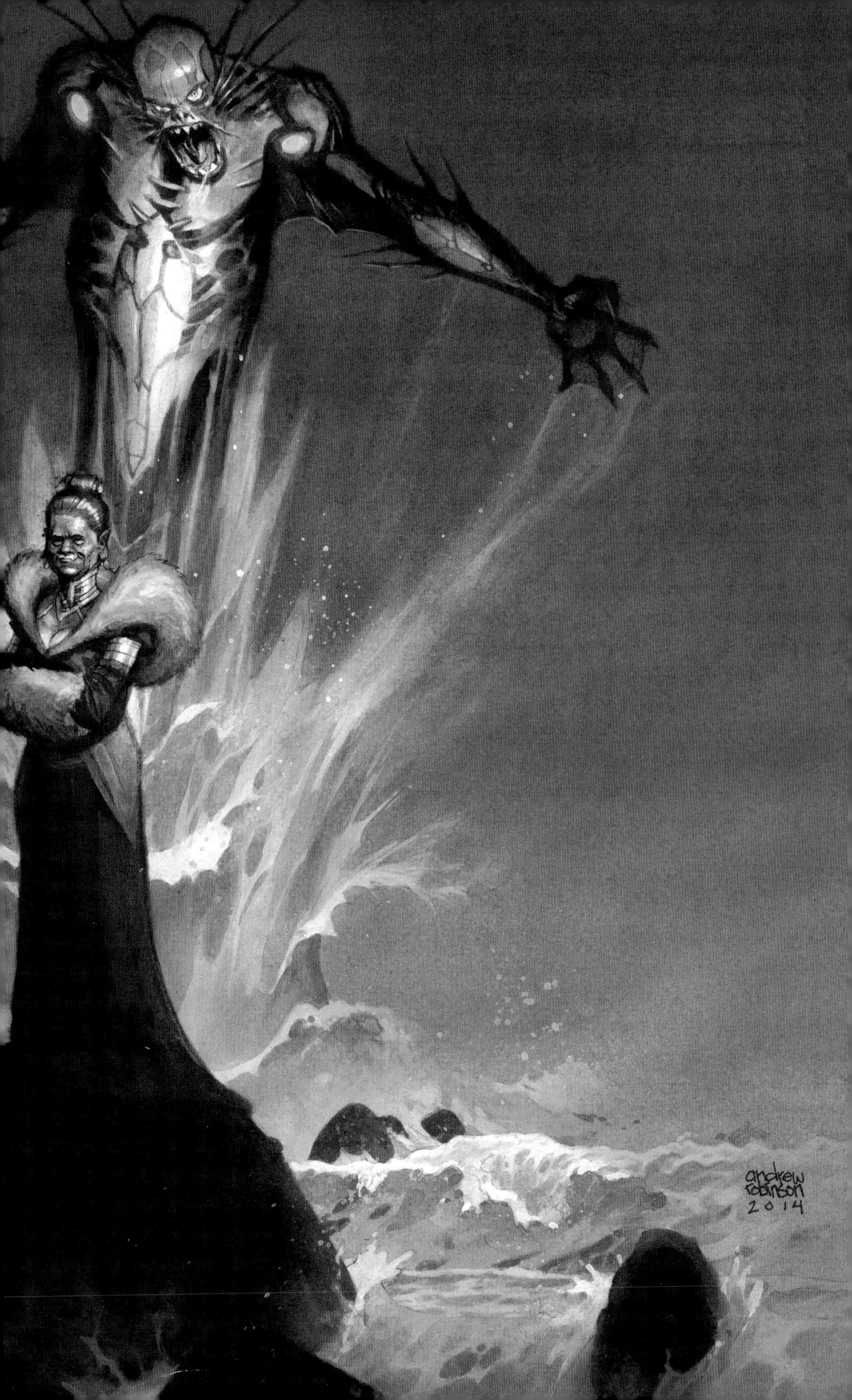
andrew
robinson
2014

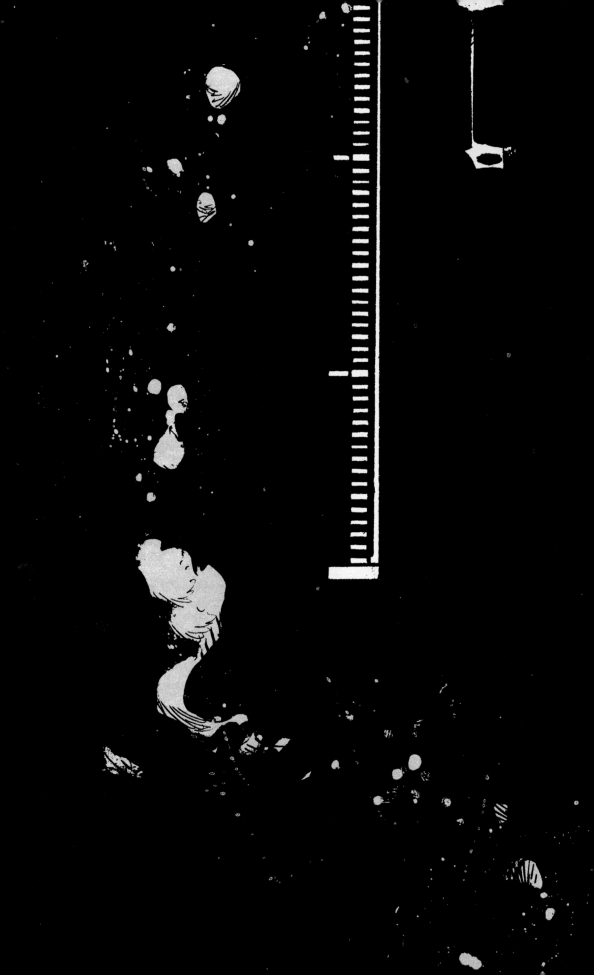

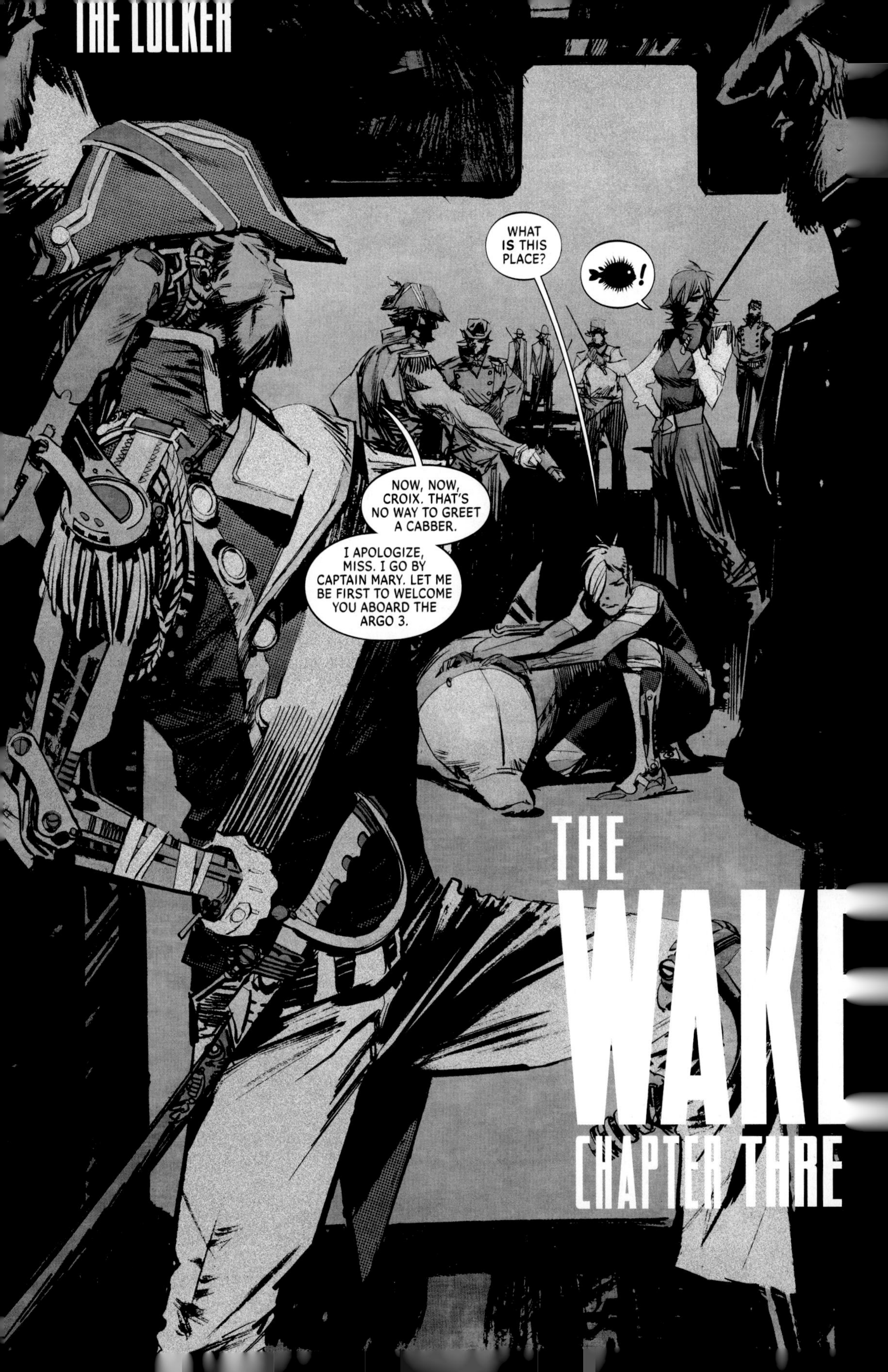
THE LOCKER
WHAT IS THIS PLACE?
!
NOW, NOW, CROIX. THAT'S NO WAY TO GREET A CABBER.
I APOLOGIZE, MISS. I GO BY CAPTAIN MARY. LET ME BE FIRST TO WELCOME YOU ABOARD THE ARGO 3.
THE WAKE
CHAPTER THRE

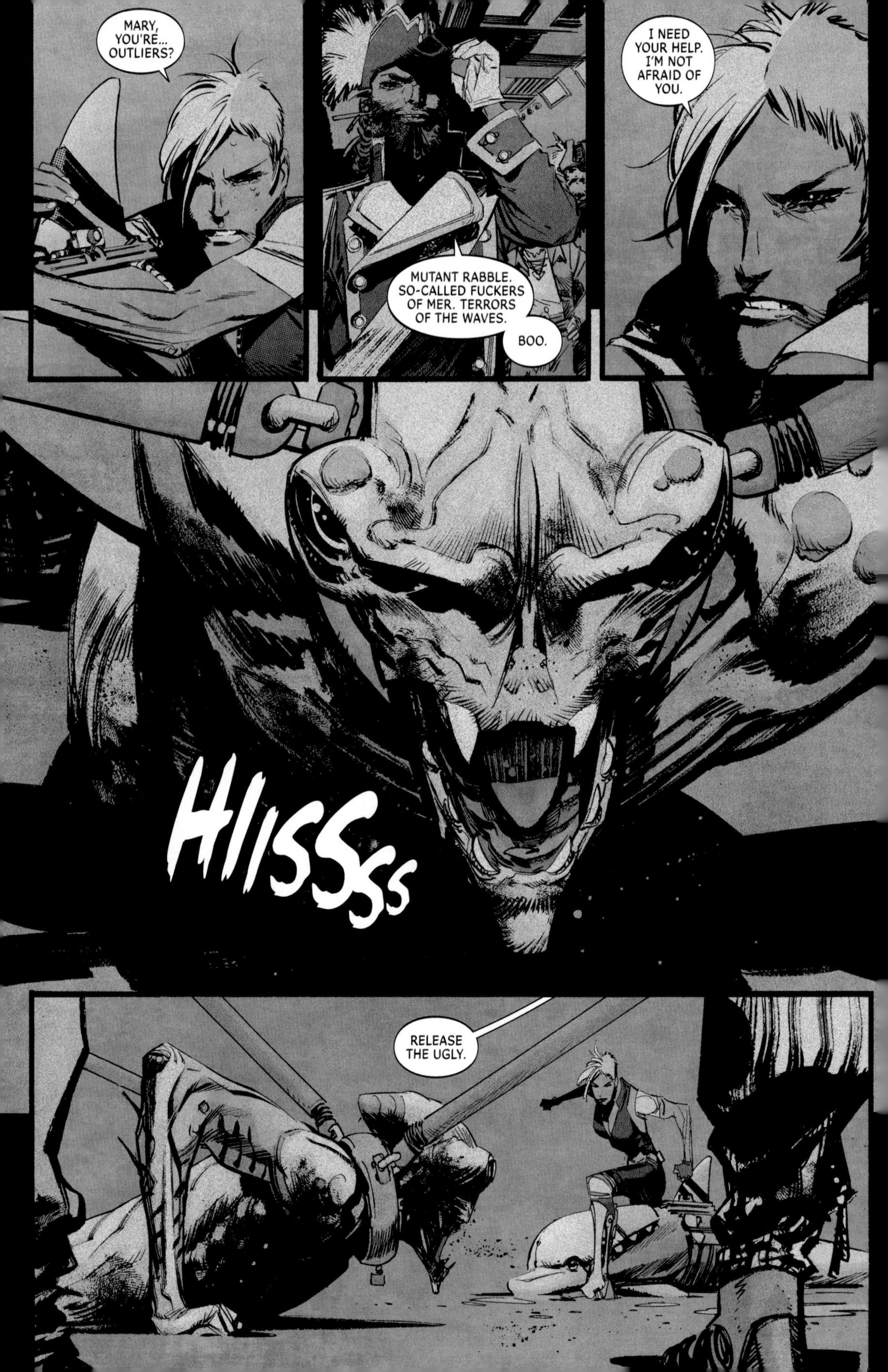
MARY, YOU'RE... OUTLIERS?
MUTANT RABBLE. SO-CALLED FUCKERS OF MER. TERRORS OF THE WAVES.
BOO.
I NEED YOUR HELP. I'M NOT AFRAID OF YOU.
HIISSsss
RELEASE THE UGLY.

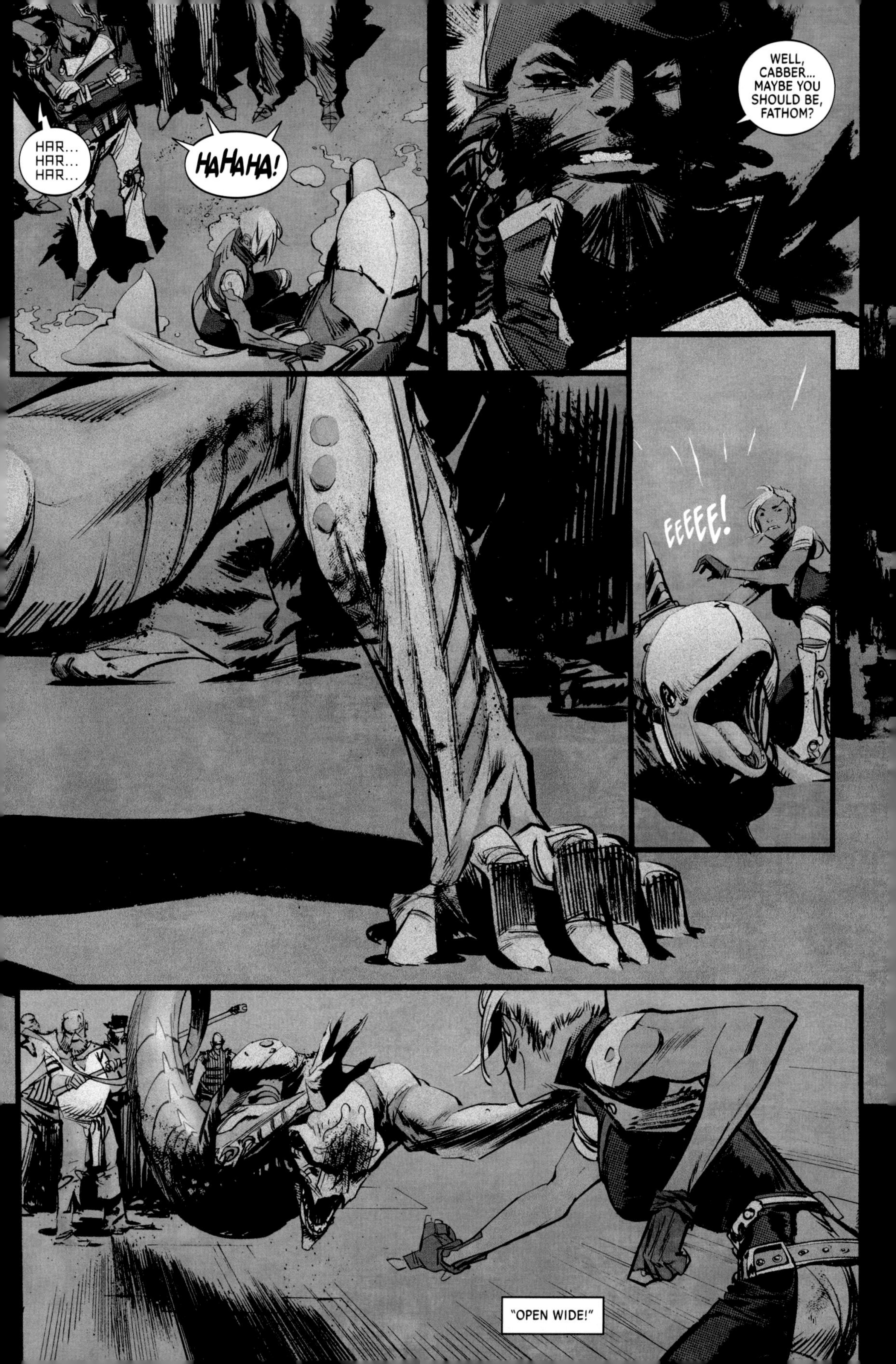
HAR...
HAR...
HAR...
HAHAHA!
WELL, CABBER... MAYBE YOU SHOULD BE, FATHOM?
EEEEE!
"OPEN WIDE!"

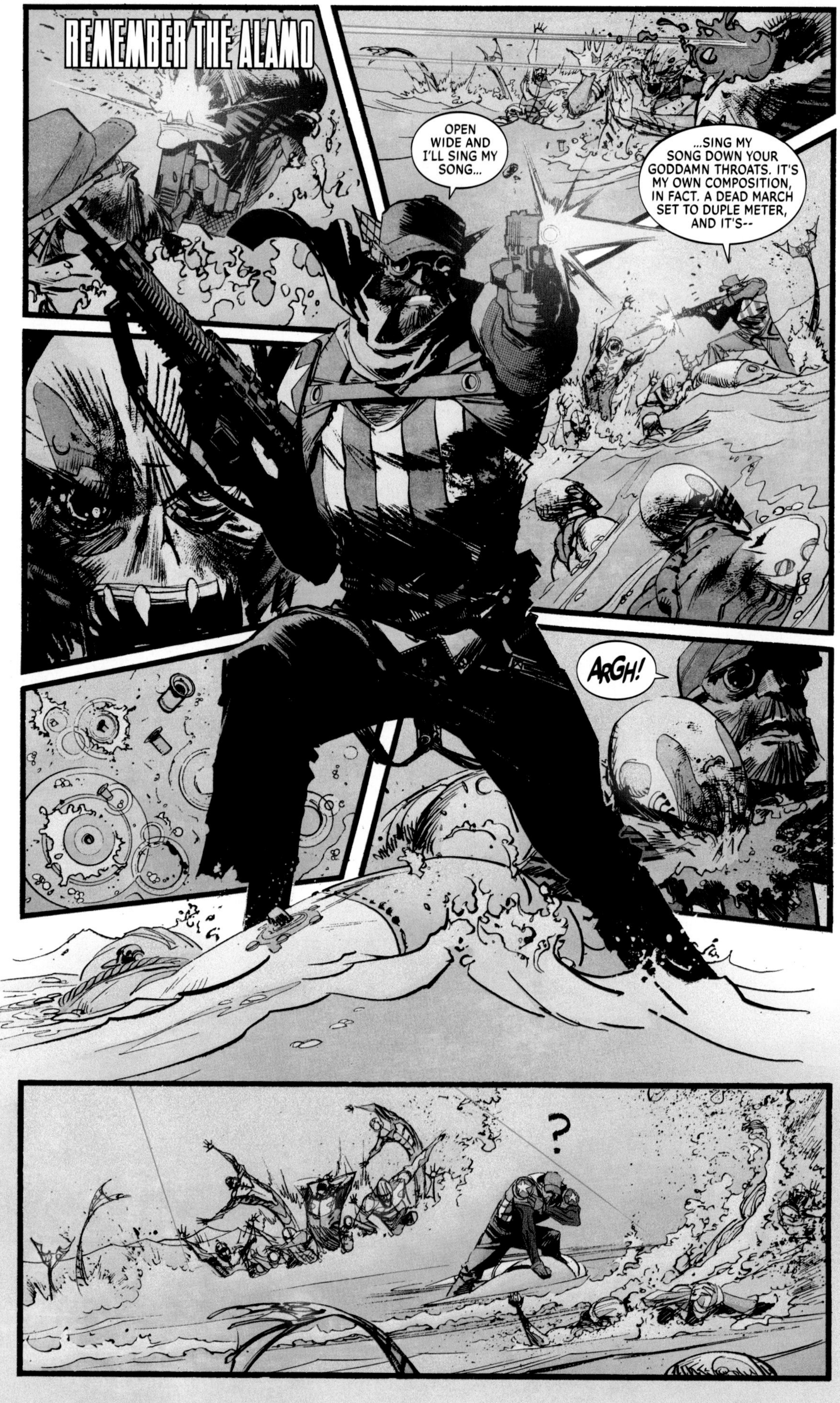
REMEMBER THE ALAMO
OPEN WIDE AND I'LL SING MY SONG...
...SING MY SONG DOWN YOUR GODDAMN THROATS. IT'S MY OWN COMPOSITION, IN FACT. A DEAD MARCH SET TO DUPLE METER, AND IT'S--
ARGH!
?

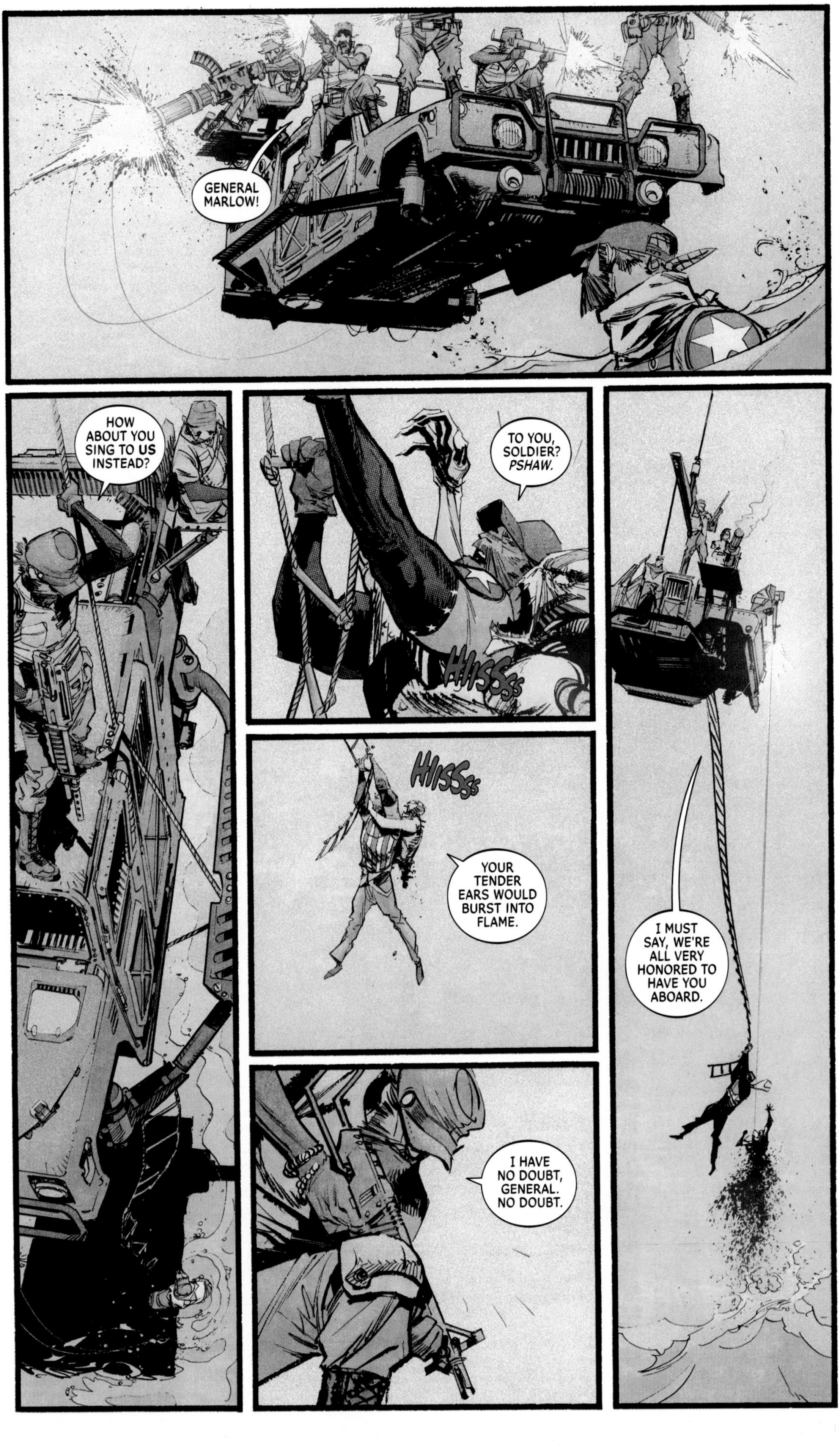
GENERAL MARLOW!
HOW ABOUT YOU SING TO **US** INSTEAD?
TO YOU, SOLDIER? *PSHAW.*
HIISSss
HIISSss
YOUR TENDER EARS WOULD BURST INTO FLAME.
I HAVE NO DOUBT, GENERAL. NO DOUBT.
I MUST SAY, WE'RE ALL VERY HONORED TO HAVE YOU ABOARD.

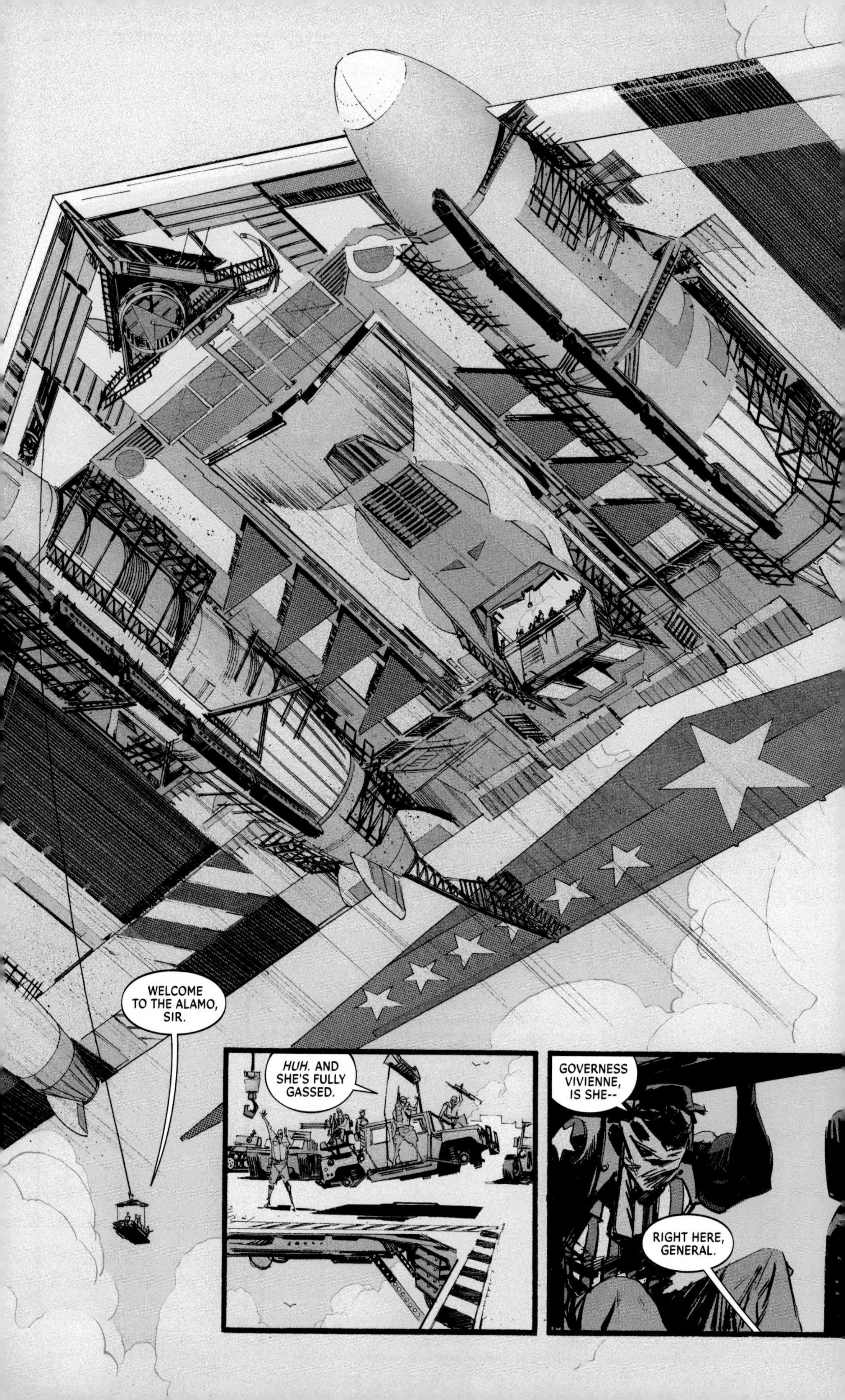
WELCOME TO THE ALAMO, SIR.
HUH. AND SHE'S FULLY GASSED.
GOVERNESS VIVIENNE, IS SHE--
RIGHT HERE, GENERAL.

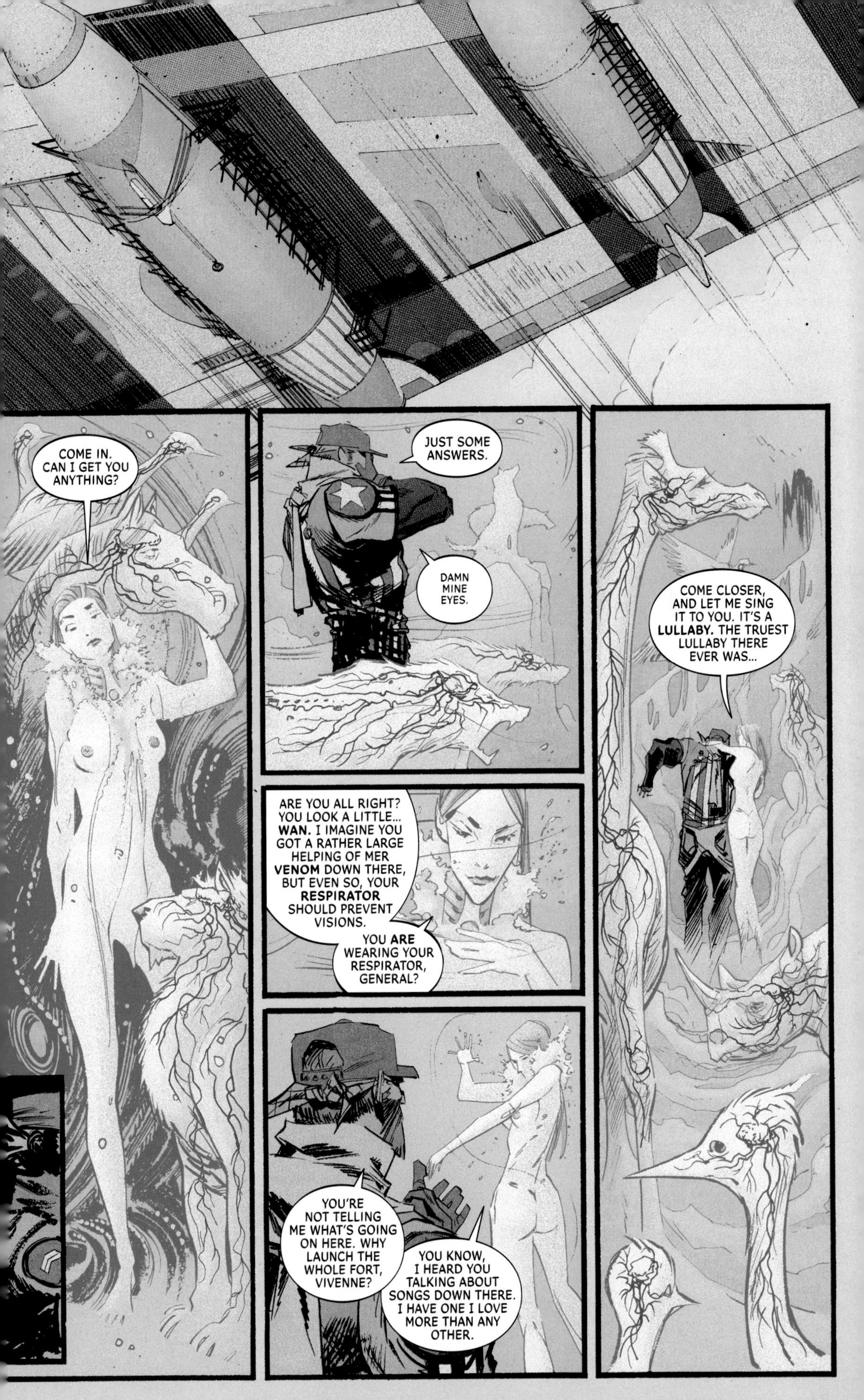
COME IN. CAN I GET YOU ANYTHING?
JUST SOME ANSWERS.
DAMN MINE EYES.
ARE YOU ALL RIGHT? YOU LOOK A LITTLE... WAN. I IMAGINE YOU GOT A RATHER LARGE HELPING OF MER VENOM DOWN THERE, BUT EVEN SO, YOUR RESPIRATOR SHOULD PREVENT VISIONS.
YOU ARE WEARING YOUR RESPIRATOR, GENERAL?
YOU'RE NOT TELLING ME WHAT'S GOING ON HERE. WHY LAUNCH THE WHOLE FORT, VIVENNE?
YOU KNOW, I HEARD YOU TALKING ABOUT SONGS DOWN THERE. I HAVE ONE I LOVE MORE THAN ANY OTHER.
COME CLOSER, AND LET ME SING IT TO YOU. IT'S A LULLABY. THE TRUEST LULLABY THERE EVER WAS...

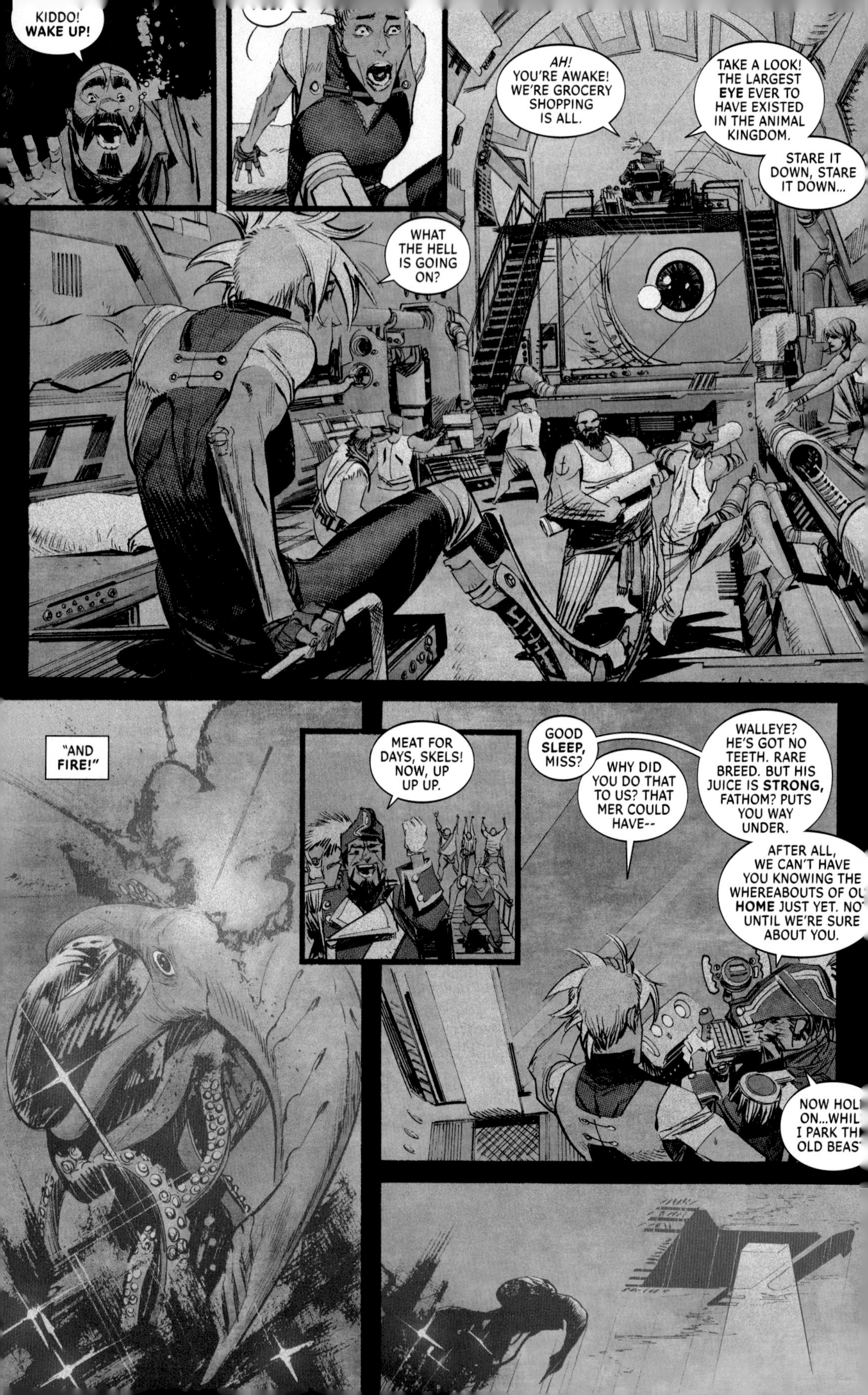
KIDDO! WAKE UP!
AH! YOU'RE AWAKE! WE'RE GROCERY SHOPPING IS ALL.
TAKE A LOOK! THE LARGEST EYE EVER TO HAVE EXISTED IN THE ANIMAL KINGDOM.
STARE IT DOWN, STARE IT DOWN...
WHAT THE HELL IS GOING ON?
"AND FIRE!"
MEAT FOR DAYS, SKELS! NOW, UP UP UP.
GOOD SLEEP, MISS?
WHY DID YOU DO THAT TO US? THAT MER COULD HAVE--
WALLEYE? HE'S GOT NO TEETH. RARE BREED. BUT HIS JUICE IS STRONG, FATHOM? PUTS YOU WAY UNDER.
AFTER ALL, WE CAN'T HAVE YOU KNOWING THE WHEREABOUTS OF OU HOME JUST YET. NO UNTIL WE'RE SURE ABOUT YOU.
NOW HOL ON...WHIL I PARK TH OLD BEAS

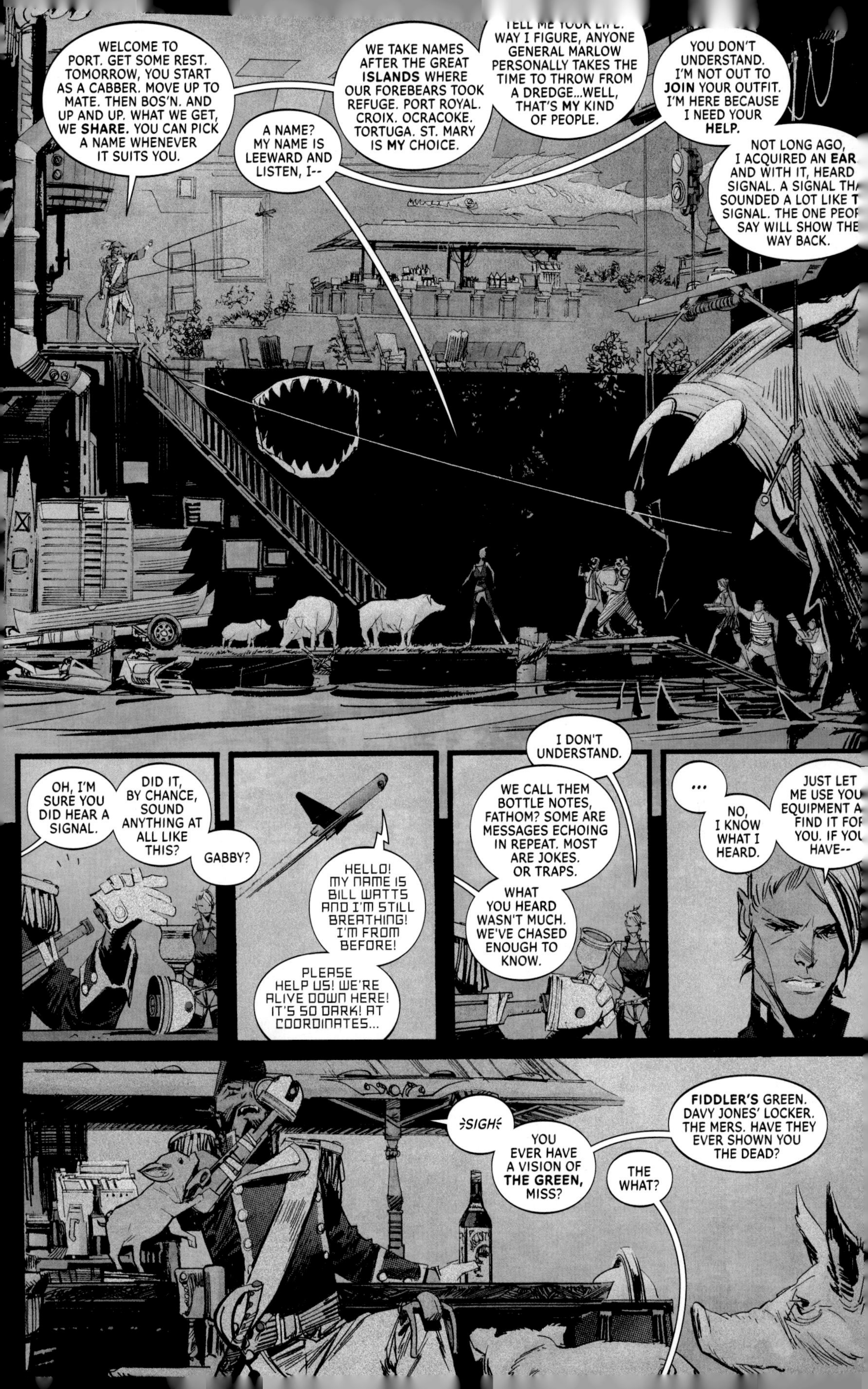

WELCOME TO PORT. GET SOME REST. TOMORROW, YOU START AS A CABBER. MOVE UP TO MATE. THEN BOS'N. AND UP AND UP. WHAT WE GET, WE **SHARE.** YOU CAN PICK A NAME WHENEVER IT SUITS YOU.
A NAME? MY NAME IS LEEWARD AND LISTEN, I--
WE TAKE NAMES AFTER THE GREAT **ISLANDS** WHERE OUR FOREBEARS TOOK REFUGE. PORT ROYAL. CROIX. OCRACOKE. TORTUGA. ST. MARY IS **MY** CHOICE.
WAY I FIGURE, ANYONE GENERAL MARLOW PERSONALLY TAKES THE TIME TO THROW FROM A DREDGE...WELL, THAT'S **MY** KIND OF PEOPLE.
YOU DON'T UNDERSTAND. I'M NOT OUT TO **JOIN** YOUR OUTFIT. I'M HERE BECAUSE I NEED YOUR **HELP.**
NOT LONG AGO, I ACQUIRED AN AND WITH IT, HEARD SIGNAL. A SIGNAL SOUNDED A LOT LIKE SIGNAL. THE ONE SAY WILL SHOW THE WAY BACK.
OH, I'M SURE YOU DID HEAR A SIGNAL.
DID IT, BY CHANCE, SOUND ANYTHING AT ALL LIKE THIS?
GABBY?
HELLO! MY NAME IS BILL WATTS AND I'M STILL BREATHING! I'M FROM BEFORE!
PLEASE HELP US! WE'RE ALIVE DOWN HERE! IT'S SO DARK! AT COORDINATES...
I DON'T UNDERSTAND.
WE CALL THEM BOTTLE NOTES, FATHOM? SOME ARE MESSAGES ECHOING IN REPEAT. MOST ARE JOKES. OR TRAPS.
WHAT YOU HEARD WASN'T MUCH. WE'VE CHASED ENOUGH TO KNOW.
...
NO, I KNOW WHAT I HEARD.
JUST LET ME USE YOU EQUIPMENT A FIND IT FOR YOU. IF YO HAVE--
SIGH
YOU EVER HAVE A VISION OF **THE GREEN,** MISS?
THE WHAT?
FIDDLER'S GREEN. DAVY JONES' LOCKER. THE MERS. HAVE THEY EVER SHOWN YOU THE DEAD?

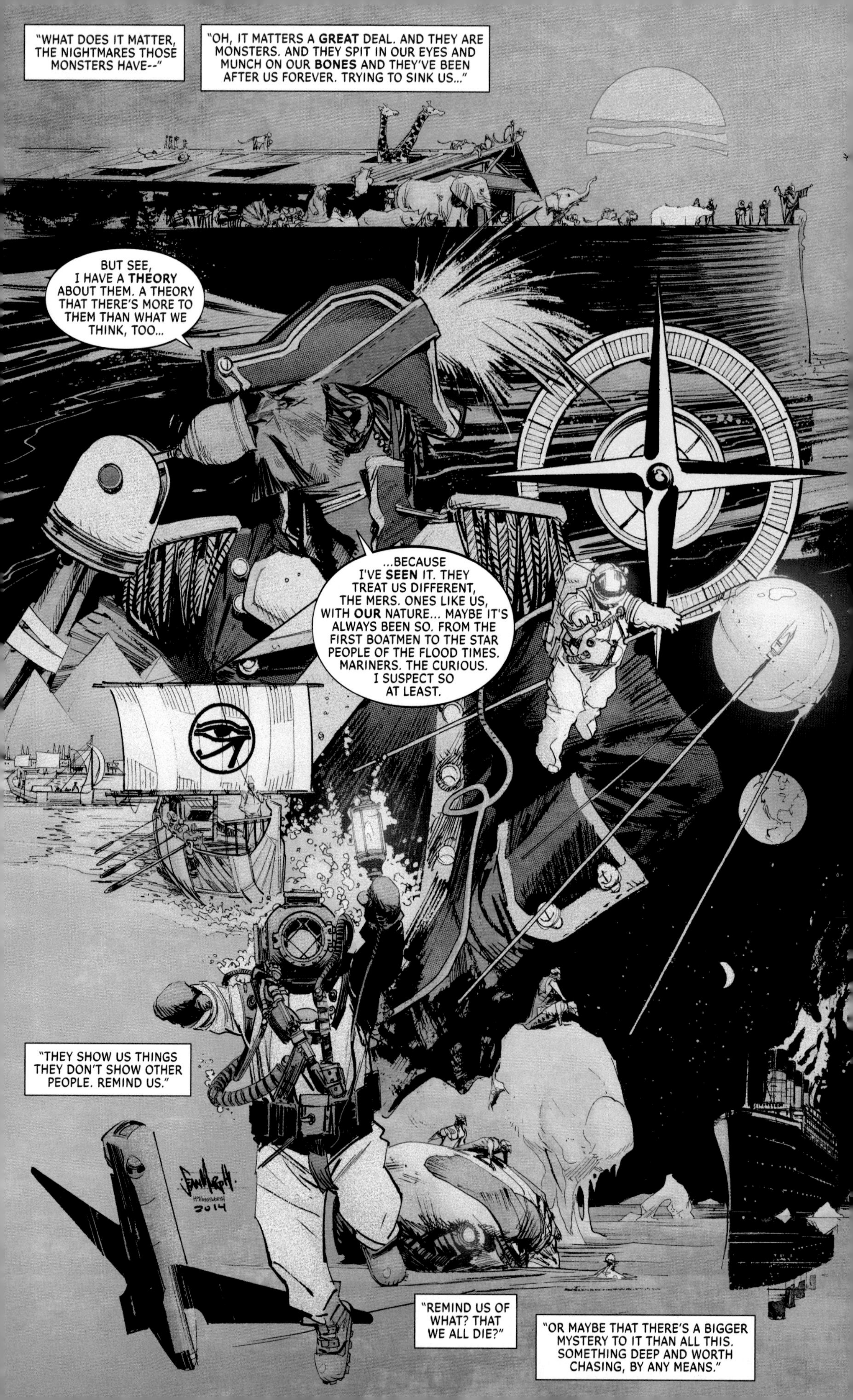
"WHAT DOES IT MATTER, THE NIGHTMARES THOSE MONSTERS HAVE--"
"OH, IT MATTERS A **GREAT** DEAL. AND THEY ARE MONSTERS. AND THEY SPIT IN OUR EYES AND MUNCH ON OUR **BONES** AND THEY'VE BEEN AFTER US FOREVER. TRYING TO SINK US..."
BUT SEE, I HAVE A **THEORY** ABOUT THEM. A THEORY THAT THERE'S MORE TO THEM THAN WHAT WE THINK, TOO...
...BECAUSE I'VE **SEEN** IT. THEY TREAT US DIFFERENT, THE MERS. ONES LIKE US, WITH **OUR** NATURE... MAYBE IT'S ALWAYS BEEN SO. FROM THE FIRST BOATMEN TO THE STAR PEOPLE OF THE FLOOD TIMES. MARINERS. THE CURIOUS. I SUSPECT SO AT LEAST.
"THEY SHOW US THINGS THEY DON'T SHOW OTHER PEOPLE. REMIND US."
"REMIND US OF WHAT? THAT WE ALL DIE?"
"OR MAYBE THAT THERE'S A BIGGER MYSTERY TO IT THAN ALL THIS. SOMETHING DEEP AND WORTH CHASING, BY ANY MEANS."

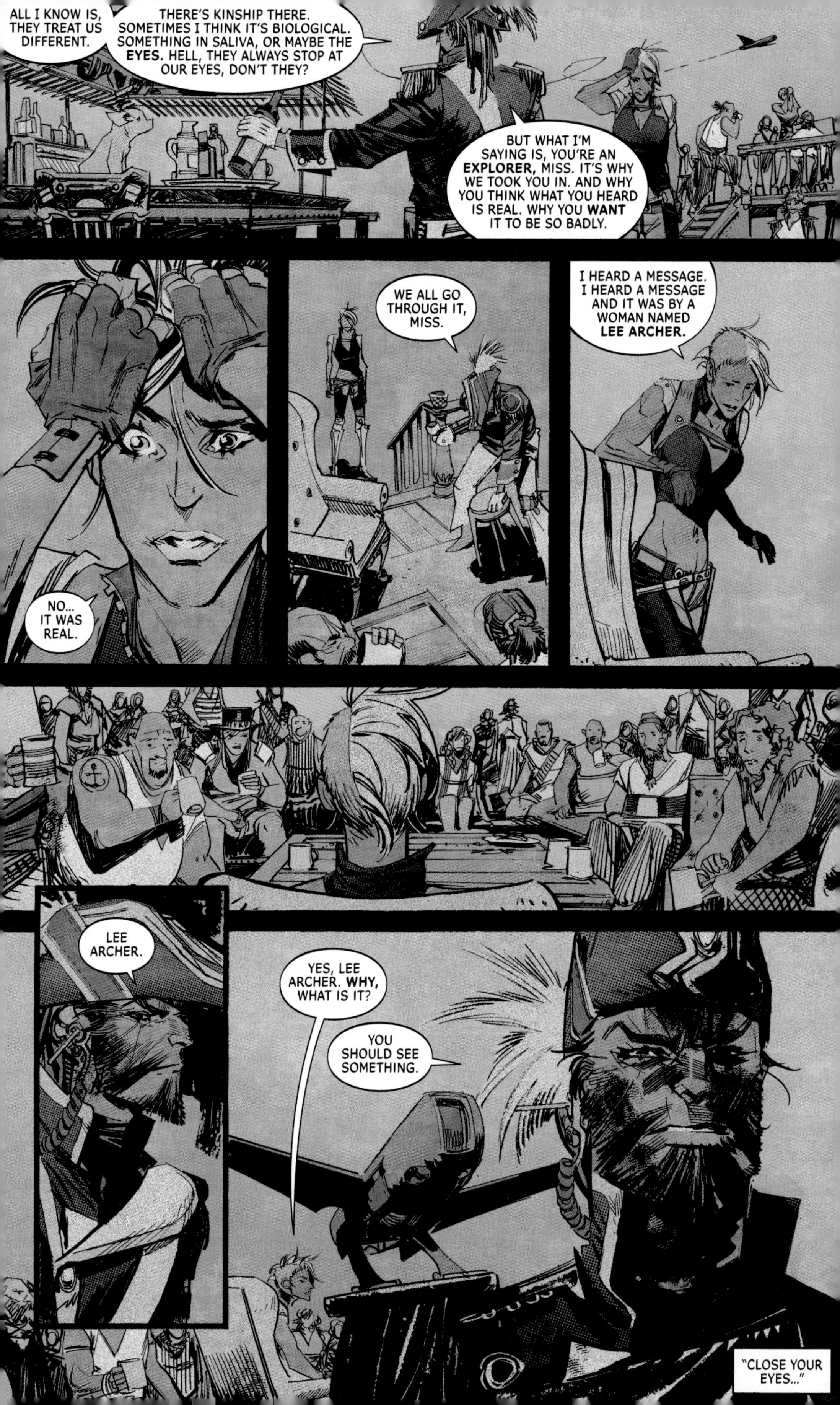

ALL I KNOW IS, THEY TREAT US DIFFERENT.
THERE'S KINSHIP THERE. SOMETIMES I THINK IT'S BIOLOGICAL. SOMETHING IN SALIVA, OR MAYBE THE **EYES.** HELL, THEY ALWAYS STOP AT OUR EYES, DON'T THEY?
BUT WHAT I'M SAYING IS, YOU'RE AN **EXPLORER,** MISS. IT'S WHY WE TOOK YOU IN. AND WHY YOU THINK WHAT YOU HEARD IS REAL. WHY YOU **WANT** IT TO BE SO BADLY.
NO... IT WAS REAL.
WE ALL GO THROUGH IT, MISS.
I HEARD A MESSAGE. I HEARD A MESSAGE AND IT WAS BY A WOMAN NAMED **LEE ARCHER.**
LEE ARCHER.
YES, LEE ARCHER. **WHY,** WHAT IS IT?
YOU SHOULD SEE SOMETHING.
"CLOSE YOUR EYES..."

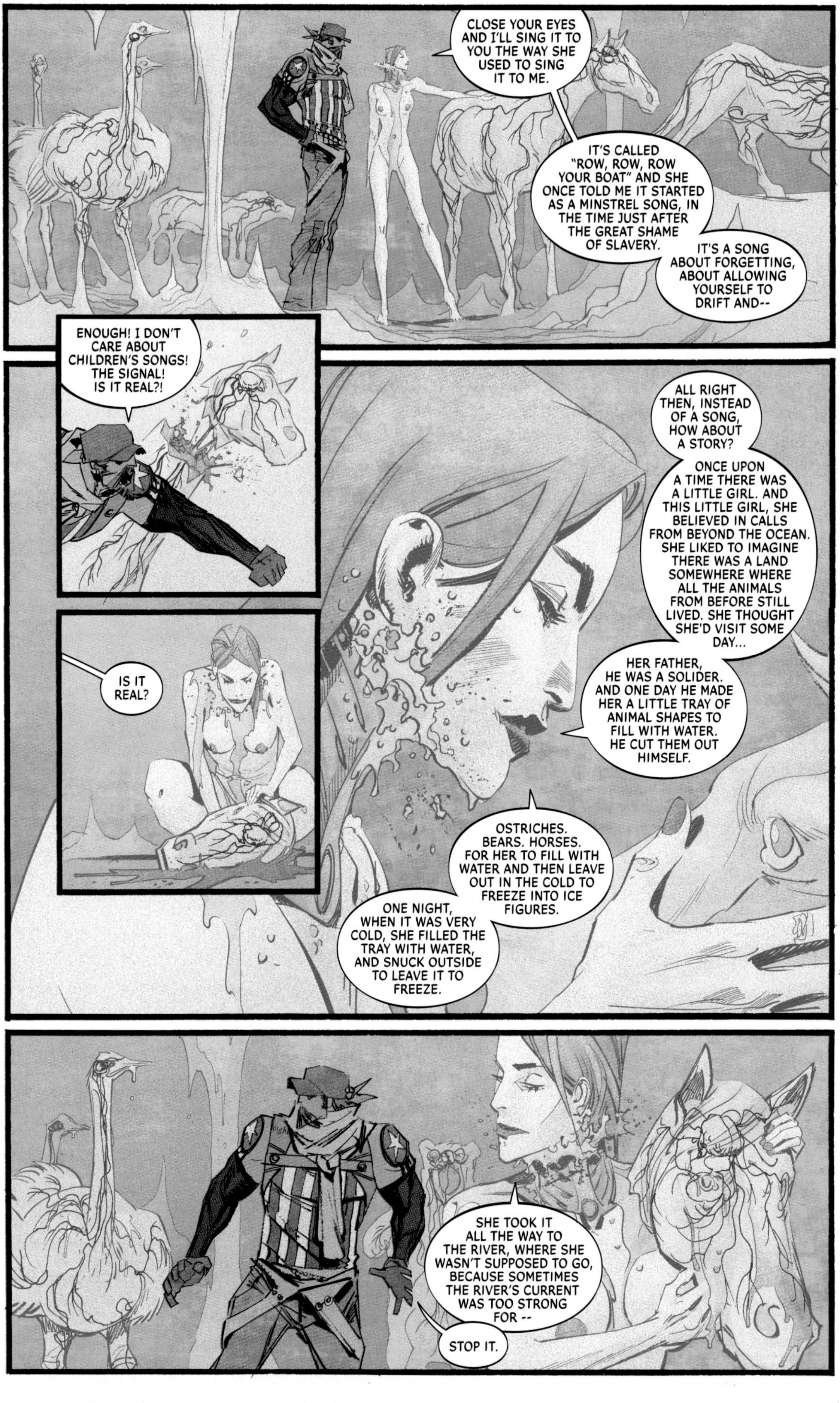
CLOSE YOUR EYES AND I'LL SING IT TO YOU THE WAY SHE USED TO SING IT TO ME.
IT'S CALLED "ROW, ROW, ROW YOUR BOAT" AND SHE ONCE TOLD ME IT STARTED AS A MINSTREL SONG, IN THE TIME JUST AFTER THE GREAT SHAME OF SLAVERY.
IT'S A SONG ABOUT FORGETTING, ABOUT ALLOWING YOURSELF TO DRIFT AND--
ENOUGH! I DON'T CARE ABOUT CHILDREN'S SONGS! THE SIGNAL! IS IT REAL?!
IS IT REAL?
ALL RIGHT THEN, INSTEAD OF A SONG, HOW ABOUT A STORY?
ONCE UPON A TIME THERE WAS A LITTLE GIRL. AND THIS LITTLE GIRL, SHE BELIEVED IN CALLS FROM BEYOND THE OCEAN. SHE LIKED TO IMAGINE THERE WAS A LAND SOMEWHERE WHERE ALL THE ANIMALS FROM BEFORE STILL LIVED. SHE THOUGHT SHE'D VISIT SOME DAY...
HER FATHER, HE WAS A SOLIDER. AND ONE DAY HE MADE HER A LITTLE TRAY OF ANIMAL SHAPES TO FILL WITH WATER. HE CUT THEM OUT HIMSELF.
OSTRICHES. BEARS. HORSES. FOR HER TO FILL WITH WATER AND THEN LEAVE OUT IN THE COLD TO FREEZE INTO ICE FIGURES.
ONE NIGHT, WHEN IT WAS VERY COLD, SHE FILLED THE TRAY WITH WATER, AND SNUCK OUTSIDE TO LEAVE IT TO FREEZE.
SHE TOOK IT ALL THE WAY TO THE RIVER, WHERE SHE WASN'T SUPPOSED TO GO, BECAUSE SOMETIMES THE RIVER'S CURRENT WAS TOO STRONG FOR --
STOP IT.

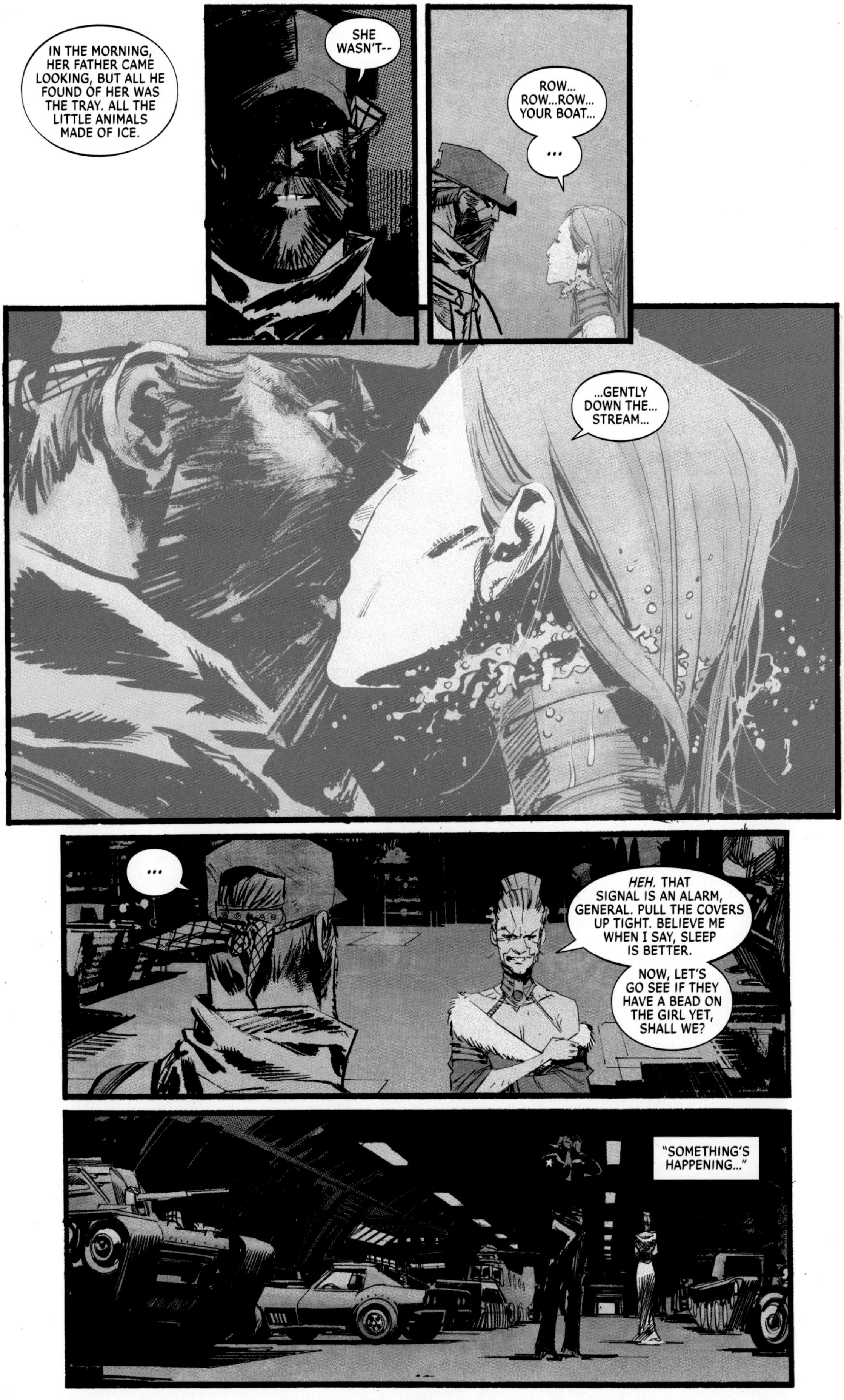
IN THE MORNING, HER FATHER CAME LOOKING, BUT ALL HE FOUND OF HER WAS THE TRAY. ALL THE LITTLE ANIMALS MADE OF ICE.
SHE WASN'T--
ROW... ROW...ROW... YOUR BOAT...
...
...GENTLY DOWN THE... STREAM...
...
HEH. THAT SIGNAL IS AN ALARM, GENERAL. PULL THE COVERS UP TIGHT. BELIEVE ME WHEN I SAY, SLEEP IS BETTER.
NOW, LET'S GO SEE IF THEY HAVE A BEAD ON THE GIRL YET, SHALL WE?
"SOMETHING'S HAPPENING..."

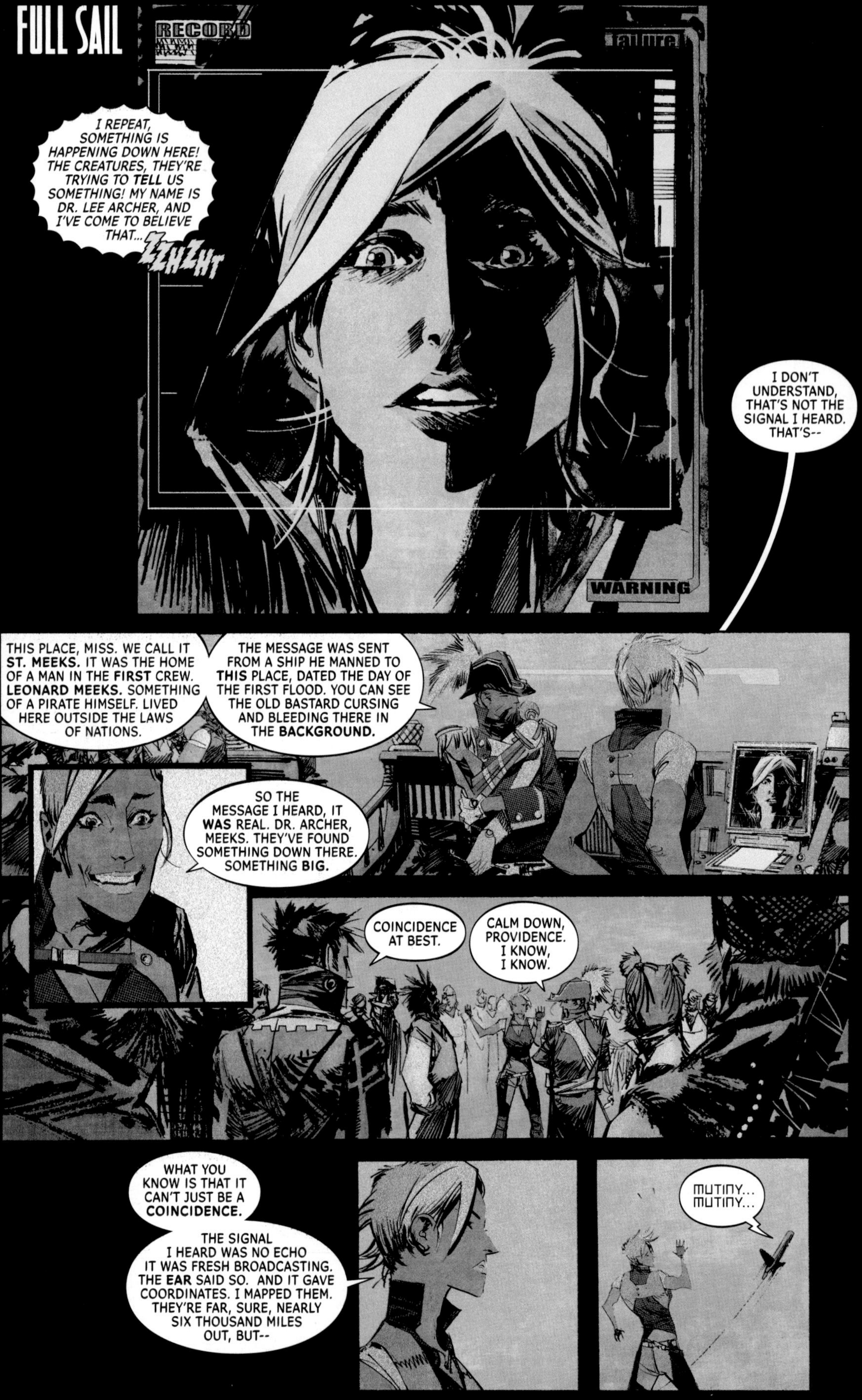
FULL SAIL
RECORD
WARNING
I REPEAT, SOMETHING IS HAPPENING DOWN HERE! THE CREATURES, THEY'RE TRYING TO TELL US SOMETHING! MY NAME IS DR. LEE ARCHER, AND I'VE COME TO BELIEVE THAT...
ZZHZHT
I DON'T UNDERSTAND, THAT'S NOT THE SIGNAL I HEARD. THAT'S--
THIS PLACE, MISS. WE CALL IT ST. MEEKS. IT WAS THE HOME OF A MAN IN THE FIRST CREW. LEONARD MEEKS. SOMETHING OF A PIRATE HIMSELF. LIVED HERE OUTSIDE THE LAWS OF NATIONS.
THE MESSAGE WAS SENT FROM A SHIP HE MANNED TO THIS PLACE, DATED THE DAY OF THE FIRST FLOOD. YOU CAN SEE THE OLD BASTARD CURSING AND BLEEDING THERE IN THE BACKGROUND.
SO THE MESSAGE I HEARD, IT WAS REAL. DR. ARCHER, MEEKS. THEY'VE FOUND SOMETHING DOWN THERE. SOMETHING BIG.
COINCIDENCE AT BEST.
CALM DOWN, PROVIDENCE. I KNOW, I KNOW.
WHAT YOU KNOW IS THAT IT CAN'T JUST BE A COINCIDENCE.
THE SIGNAL I HEARD WAS NO ECHO IT WAS FRESH BROADCASTING. THE EAR SAID SO. AND IT GAVE COORDINATES. I MAPPED THEM. THEY'RE FAR, SURE, NEARLY SIX THOUSAND MILES OUT, BUT--
MUTINY... MUTINY...

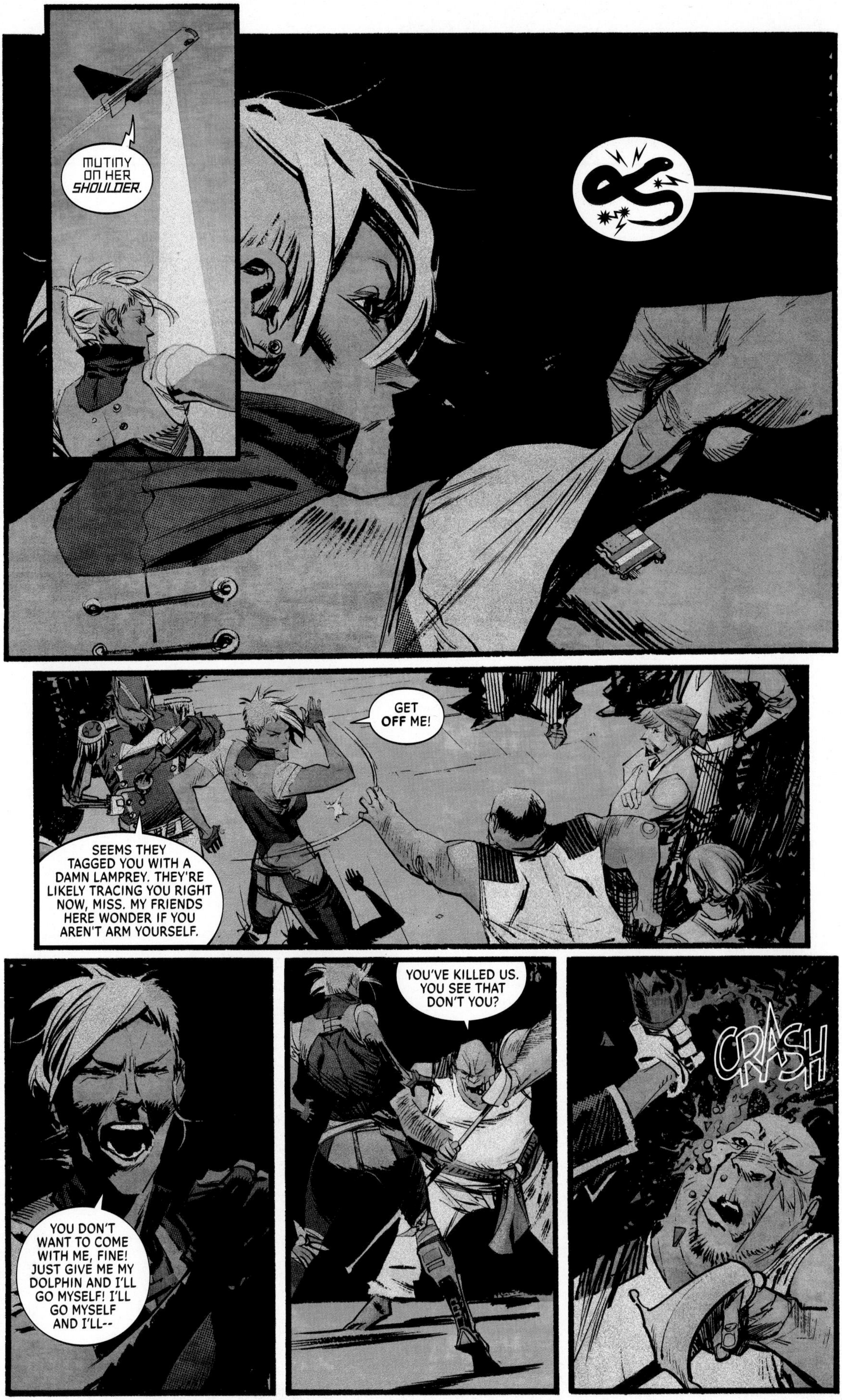

MUTINY ON HER SHOULDER.
GET OFF ME!
SEEMS THEY TAGGED YOU WITH A DAMN LAMPREY. THEY'RE LIKELY TRACING YOU RIGHT NOW, MISS. MY FRIENDS HERE WONDER IF YOU AREN'T ARM YOURSELF.
YOU DON'T WANT TO COME WITH ME, FINE! JUST GIVE ME MY DOLPHIN AND I'LL GO MYSELF! I'LL GO MYSELF AND I'LL--
YOU'VE KILLED US. YOU SEE THAT DON'T YOU?
CRASH

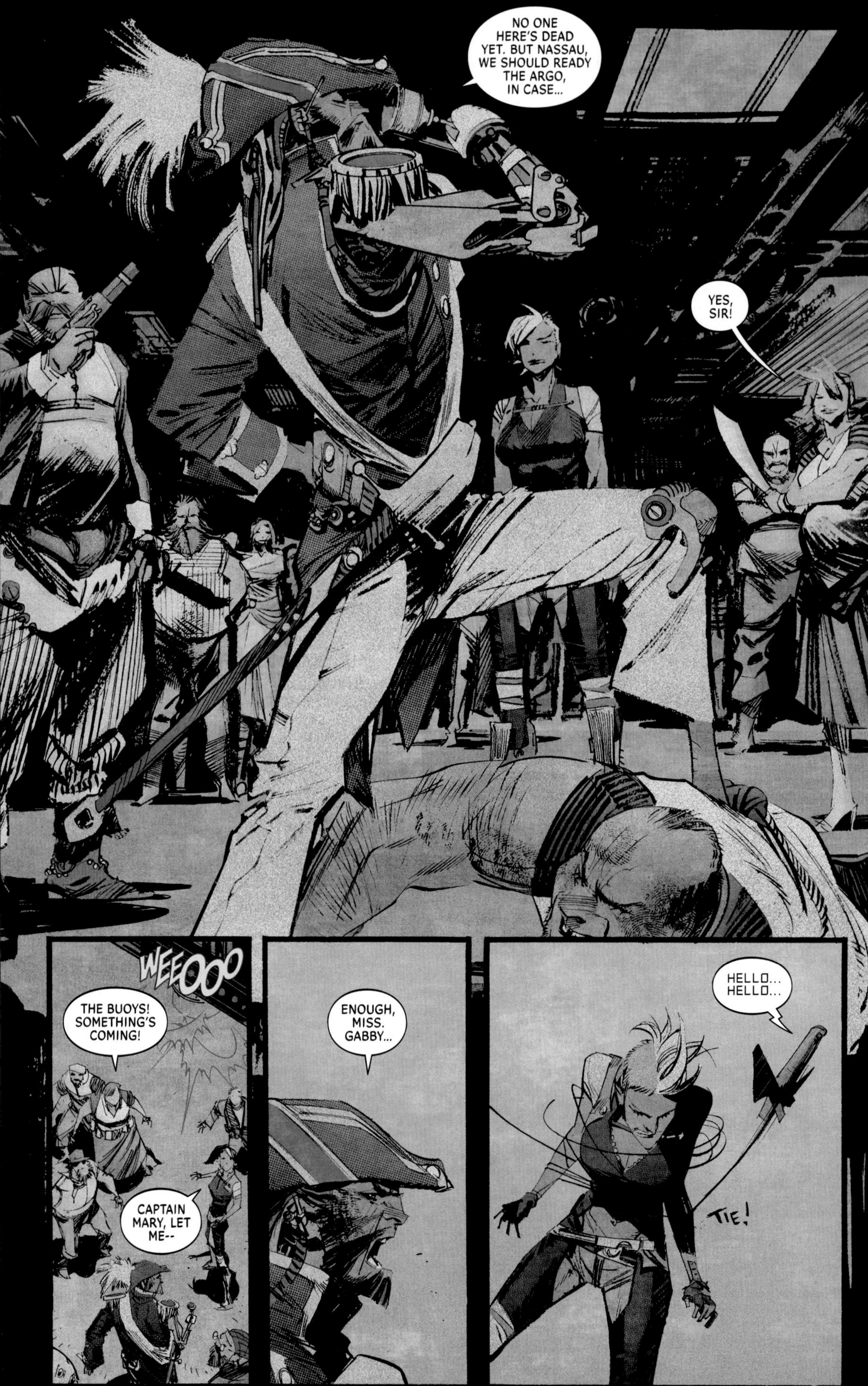
NO ONE HERE'S DEAD YET. BUT NASSAU, WE SHOULD READY THE ARGO, IN CASE...
YES, SIR!
WEEOOO
THE BUOYS! SOMETHING'S COMING!
CAPTAIN MARY, LET ME--
ENOUGH, MISS. GABBY...
HELLO... HELLO...
TIE!

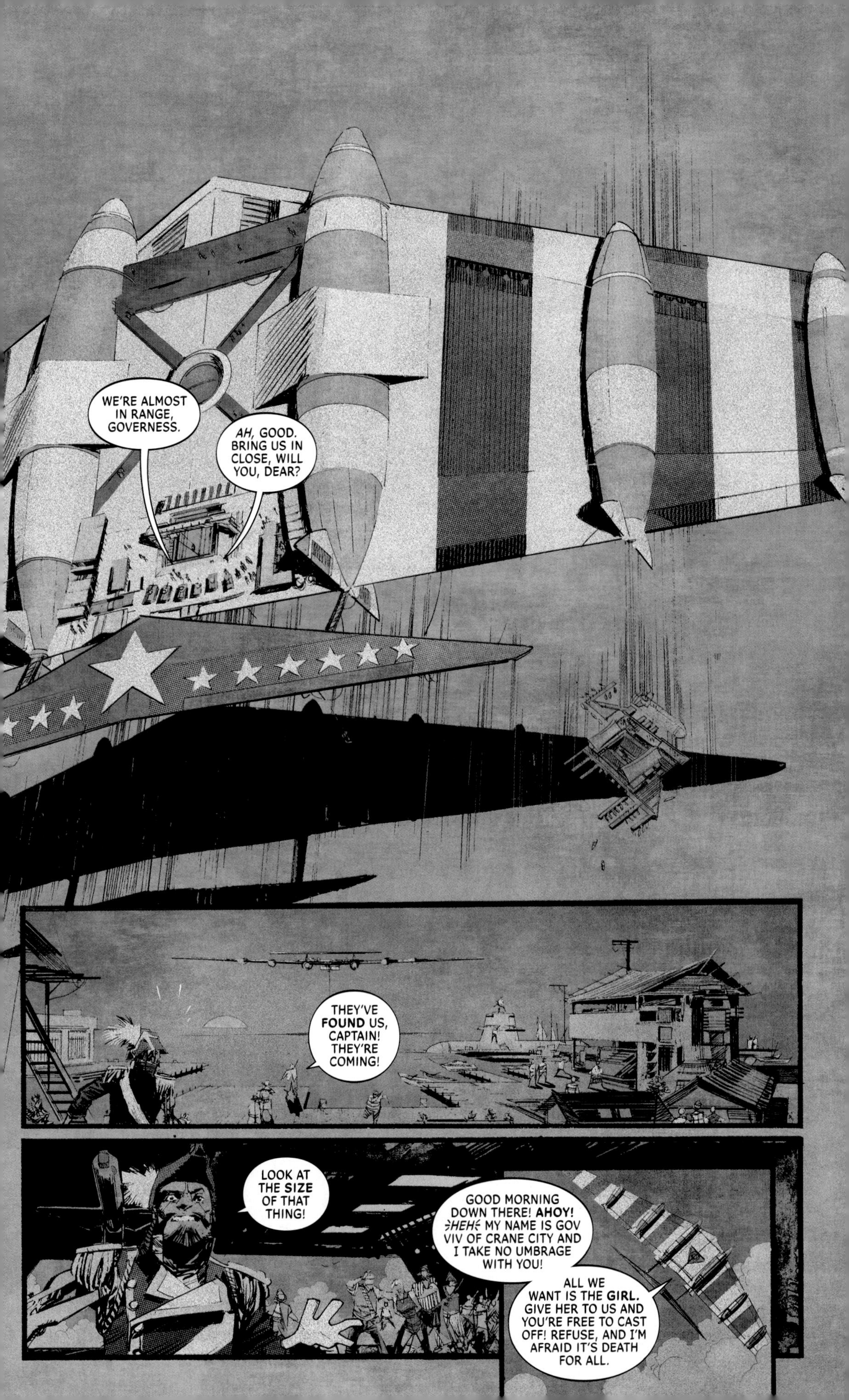
WE'RE ALMOST IN RANGE, GOVERNESS.
AH, GOOD. BRING US IN CLOSE, WILL YOU, DEAR?
THEY'VE **FOUND** US, CAPTAIN! THEY'RE COMING!
LOOK AT THE **SIZE** OF THAT THING!
GOOD MORNING DOWN THERE! **AHOY!** *HEH* MY NAME IS GOV VIV OF CRANE CITY AND I TAKE NO UMBRAGE WITH YOU!
ALL WE WANT IS THE **GIRL.** GIVE HER TO US AND YOU'RE FREE TO CAST OFF! REFUSE, AND I'M AFRAID IT'S DEATH FOR ALL.

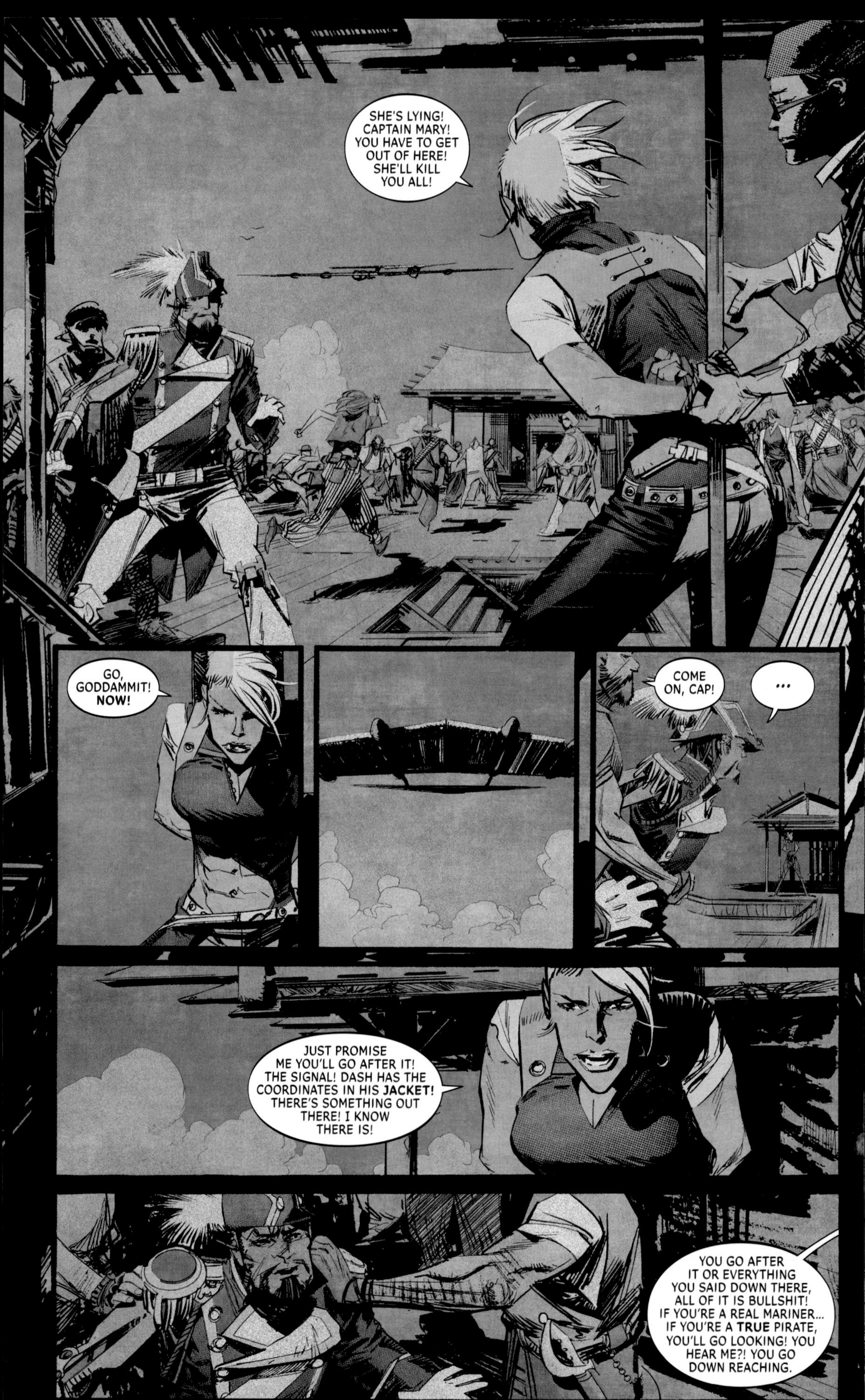
SHE'S LYING! CAPTAIN MARY! YOU HAVE TO GET OUT OF HERE! SHE'LL KILL YOU ALL!
GO, GODDAMMIT! **NOW!**
COME ON, CAP!
...
JUST PROMISE ME YOU'LL GO AFTER IT! THE SIGNAL! DASH HAS THE COORDINATES IN HIS **JACKET!** THERE'S SOMETHING OUT THERE! I KNOW THERE IS!
YOU GO AFTER IT OR EVERYTHING YOU SAID DOWN THERE, ALL OF IT IS BULLSHIT! IF YOU'RE A REAL MARINER... IF YOU'RE A **TRUE** PIRATE, YOU'LL GO LOOKING! YOU HEAR ME?! YOU GO DOWN REACHING.

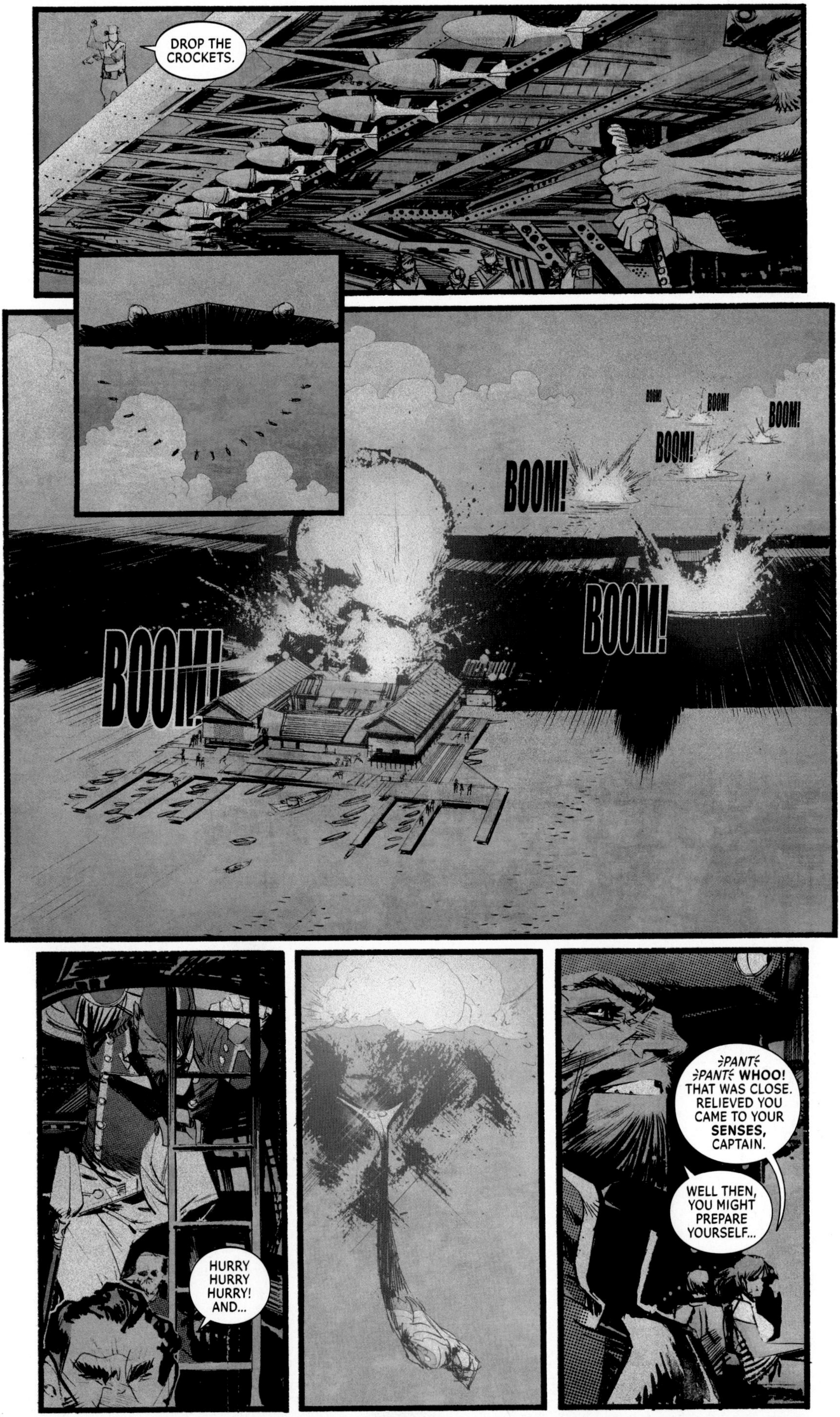
DROP THE CROCKETS.
BOOM!
BOOM!
BOOM!
BOOM!
BOOM!
BOOM!
BOOM!
HURRY HURRY HURRY! AND...
PANT *PANT* WHOO! THAT WAS CLOSE. RELIEVED YOU CAME TO YOUR SENSES, CAPTAIN.
WELL THEN, YOU MIGHT PREPARE YOURSELF...

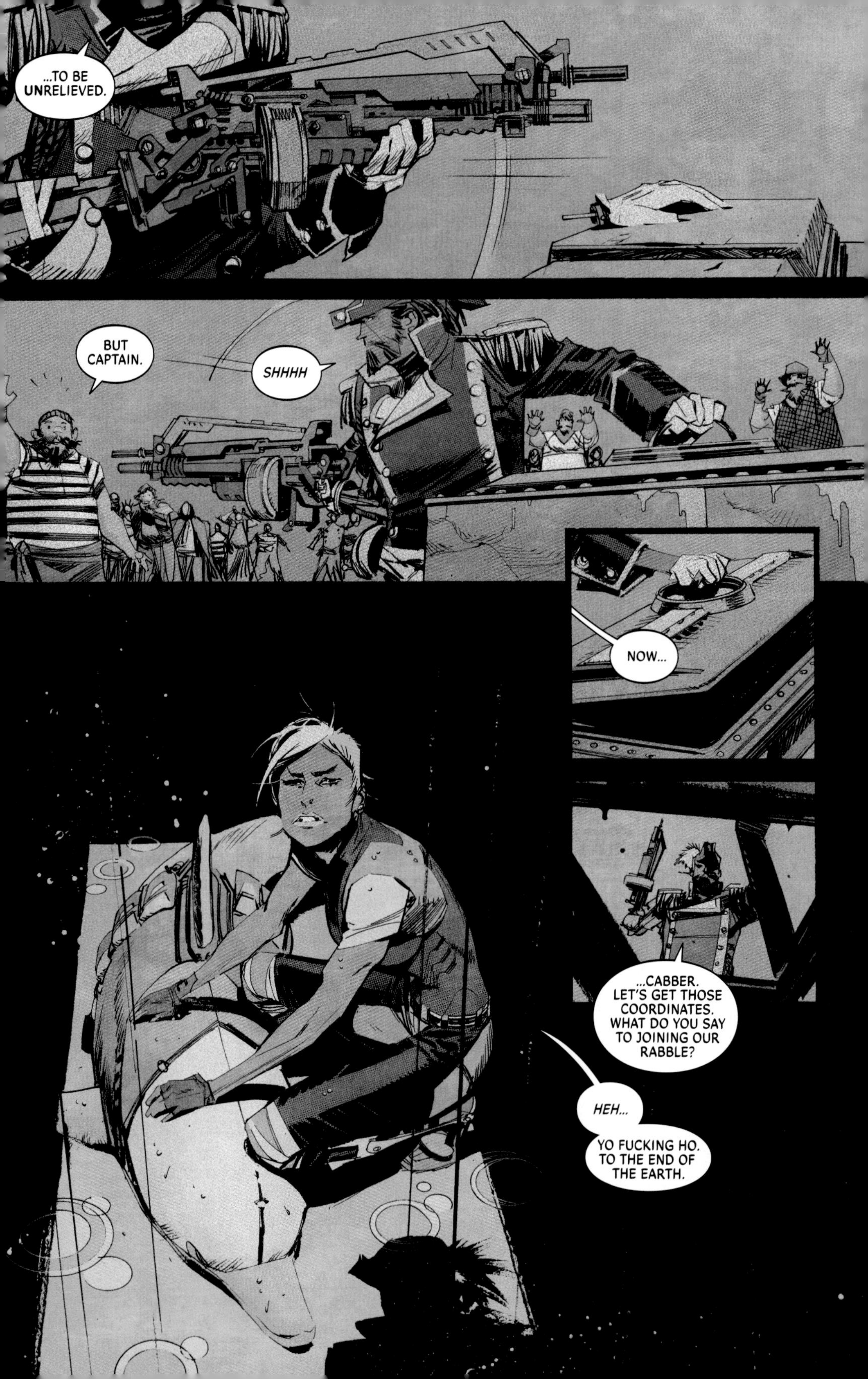
...TO BE UNRELIEVED.
BUT CAPTAIN.
SHHHH
NOW...
...CABBER. LET'S GET THOSE COORDINATES. WHAT DO YOU SAY TO JOINING OUR RABBLE?
HEH...
YO FUCKING HO. TO THE END OF THE EARTH.

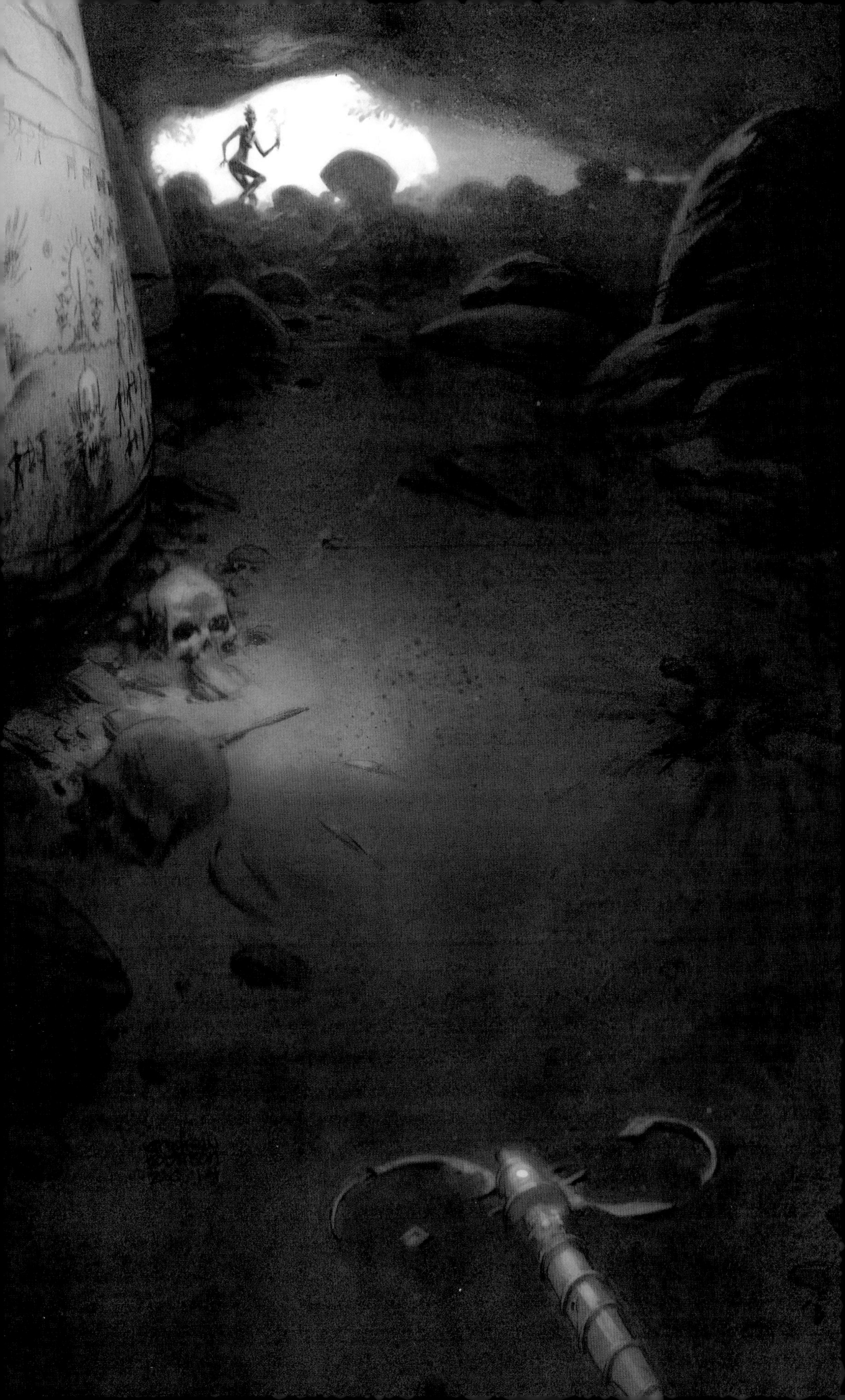

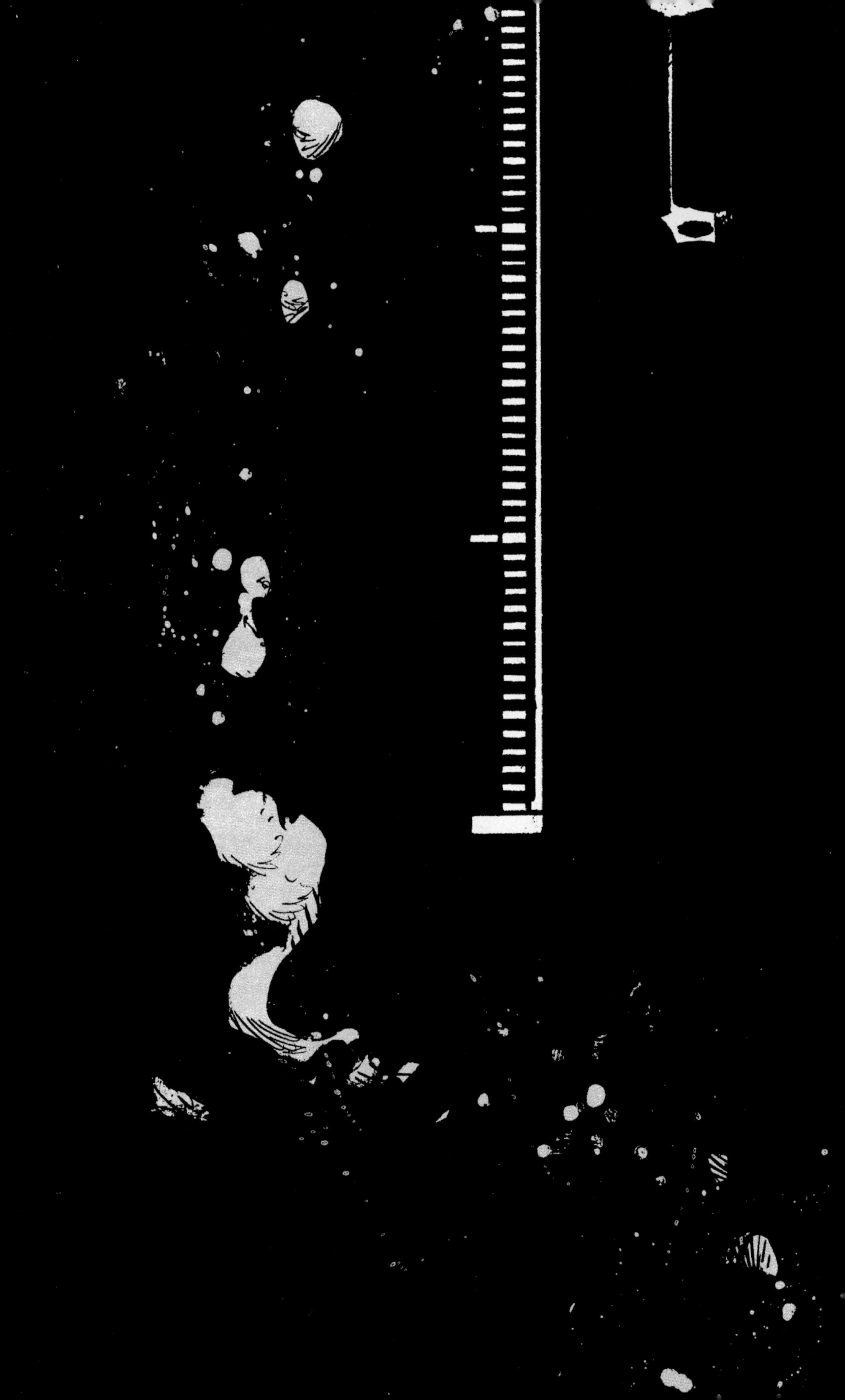

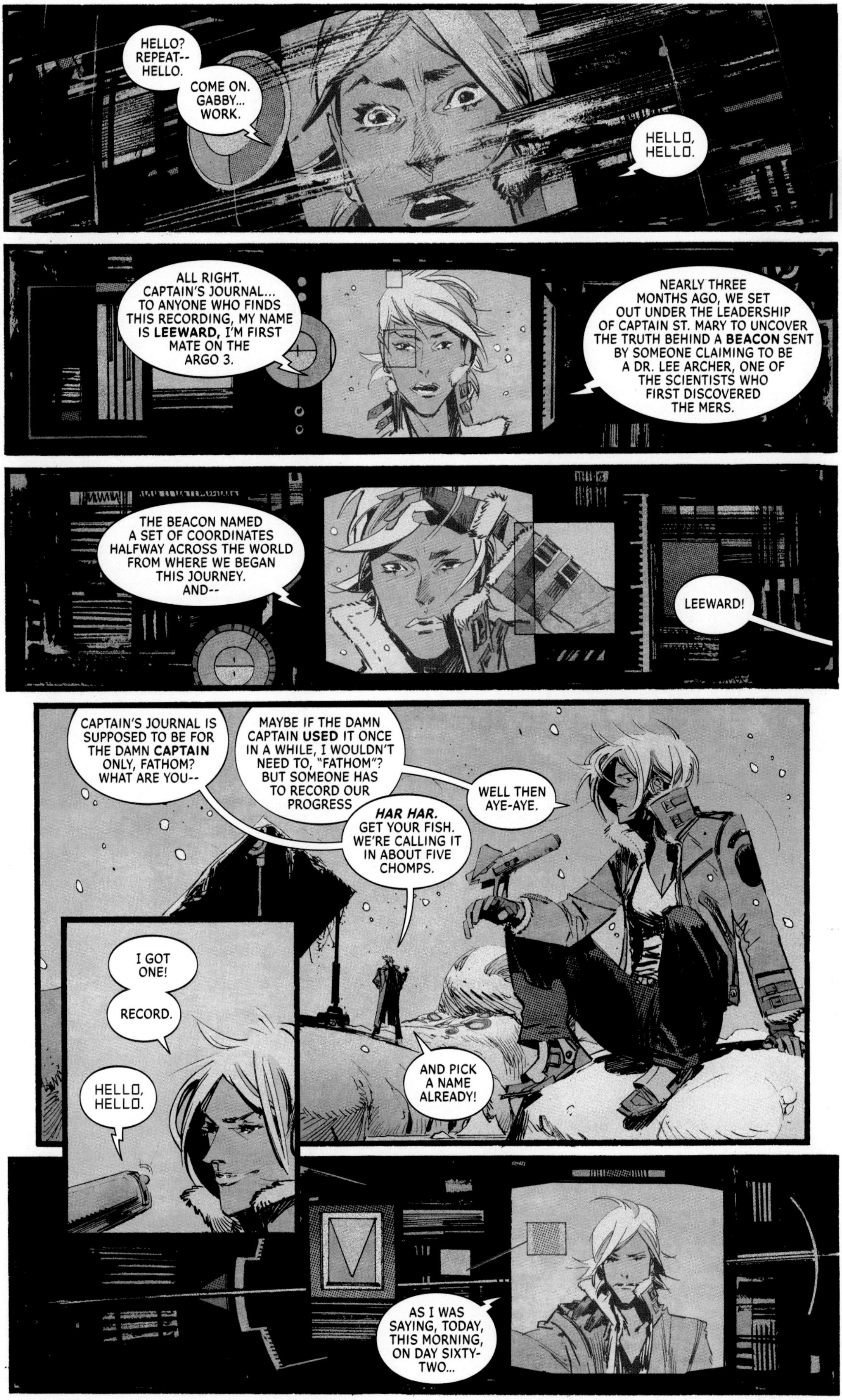

HELLO? REPEAT-- HELLO.
COME ON. GABBY... WORK.
HELLO, HELLO.
ALL RIGHT. CAPTAIN'S JOURNAL... TO ANYONE WHO FINDS THIS RECORDING, MY NAME IS **LEEWARD,** I'M FIRST MATE ON THE ARGO 3.
NEARLY THREE MONTHS AGO, WE SET OUT UNDER THE LEADERSHIP OF CAPTAIN ST. MARY TO UNCOVER THE TRUTH BEHIND A **BEACON** SENT BY SOMEONE CLAIMING TO BE A DR. LEE ARCHER, ONE OF THE SCIENTISTS WHO FIRST DISCOVERED THE MERS.
THE BEACON NAMED A SET OF COORDINATES HALFWAY ACROSS THE WORLD FROM WHERE WE BEGAN THIS JOURNEY. AND--
LEEWARD!
CAPTAIN'S JOURNAL IS SUPPOSED TO BE FOR THE DAMN **CAPTAIN** ONLY, FATHOM? WHAT ARE YOU--
MAYBE IF THE DAMN CAPTAIN **USED** IT ONCE IN A WHILE, I WOULDN'T NEED TO, "FATHOM"? BUT SOMEONE HAS TO RECORD OUR PROGRESS
WELL THEN AYE-AYE.
HAR HAR. GET YOUR FISH. WE'RE CALLING IT IN ABOUT FIVE CHOMPS.
AND PICK A NAME ALREADY!
I GOT ONE!
RECORD.
HELLO, HELLO.
AS I WAS SAYING, TODAY, THIS MORNING, ON DAY SIXTY-TWO...

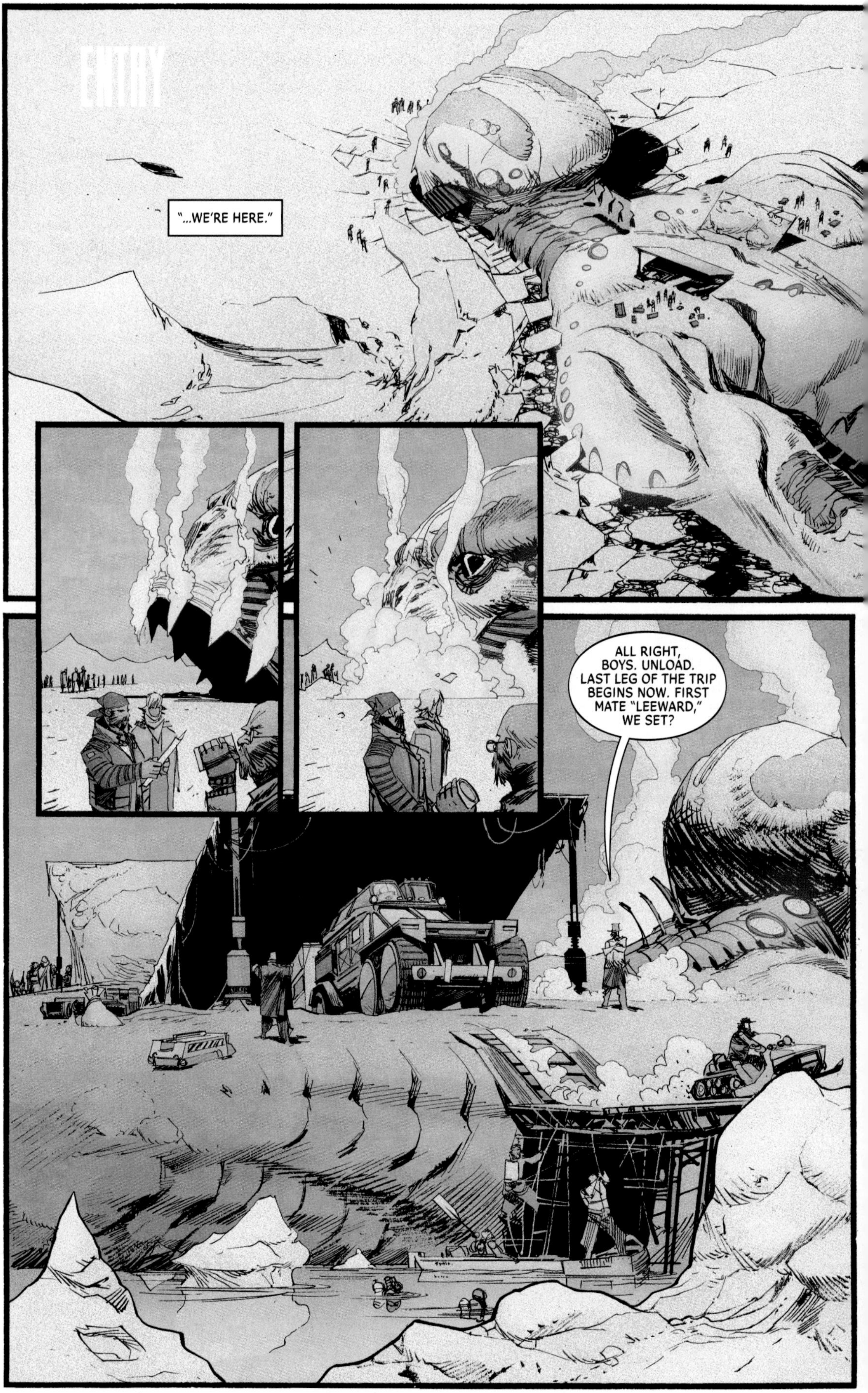
ENTRY
"...WE'RE HERE."
ALL RIGHT, BOYS. UNLOAD. LAST LEG OF THE TRIP BEGINS NOW. FIRST MATE "LEEWARD," WE SET?

THE WAKE
CHAPTER FOUR

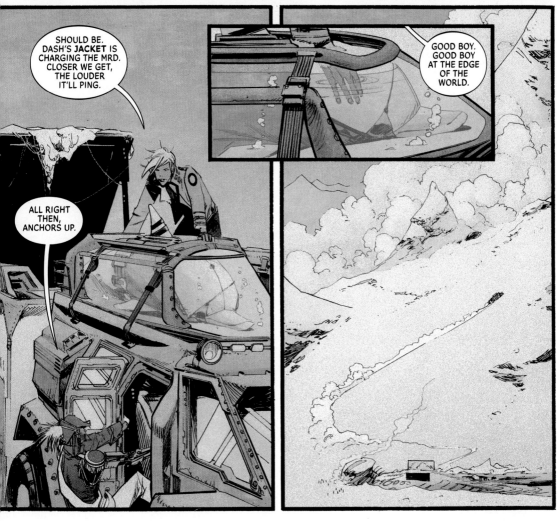

SHOULD BE. DASH'S **JACKET** IS CHARGING THE MRD. CLOSER WE GET, THE LOUDER IT'LL PING.

GOOD BOY. GOOD BOY AT THE EDGE OF THE WORLD.

ALL RIGHT THEN, ANCHORS UP.

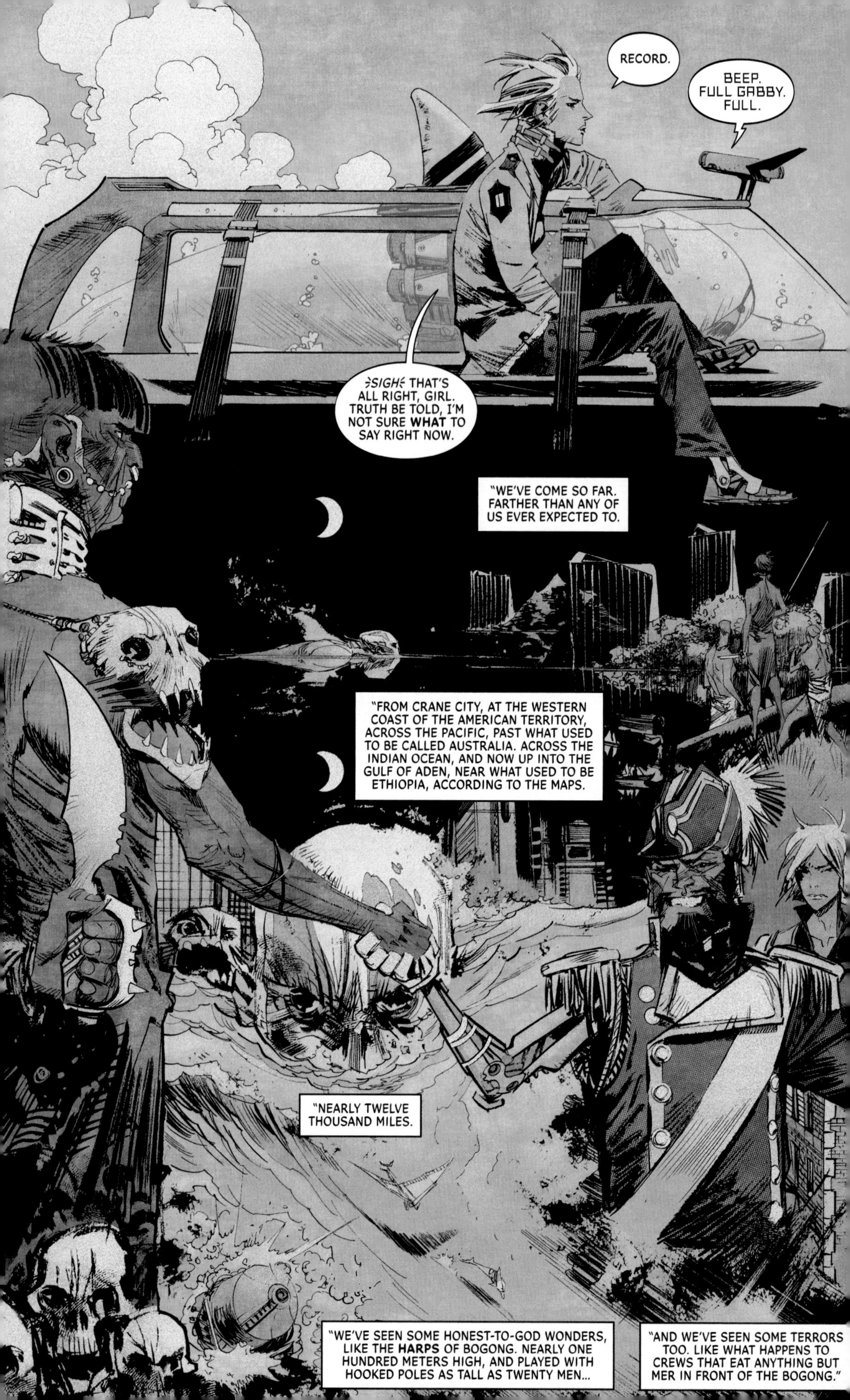
RECORD.
BEEP. FULL GABBY. FULL.
⋛SIGH⋚ THAT'S ALL RIGHT, GIRL. TRUTH BE TOLD, I'M NOT SURE **WHAT** TO SAY RIGHT NOW.
"WE'VE COME SO FAR. FARTHER THAN ANY OF US EVER EXPECTED TO.
"FROM CRANE CITY, AT THE WESTERN COAST OF THE AMERICAN TERRITORY, ACROSS THE PACIFIC, PAST WHAT USED TO BE CALLED AUSTRALIA. ACROSS THE INDIAN OCEAN, AND NOW UP INTO THE GULF OF ADEN, NEAR WHAT USED TO BE ETHIOPIA, ACCORDING TO THE MAPS.
"NEARLY TWELVE THOUSAND MILES.
"WE'VE SEEN SOME HONEST-TO-GOD WONDERS, LIKE THE **HARPS** OF BOGONG. NEARLY ONE HUNDRED METERS HIGH, AND PLAYED WITH HOOKED POLES AS TALL AS TWENTY MEN...
"AND WE'VE SEEN SOME TERRORS TOO. LIKE WHAT HAPPENS TO CREWS THAT EAT ANYTHING BUT MER IN FRONT OF THE BOGONG."

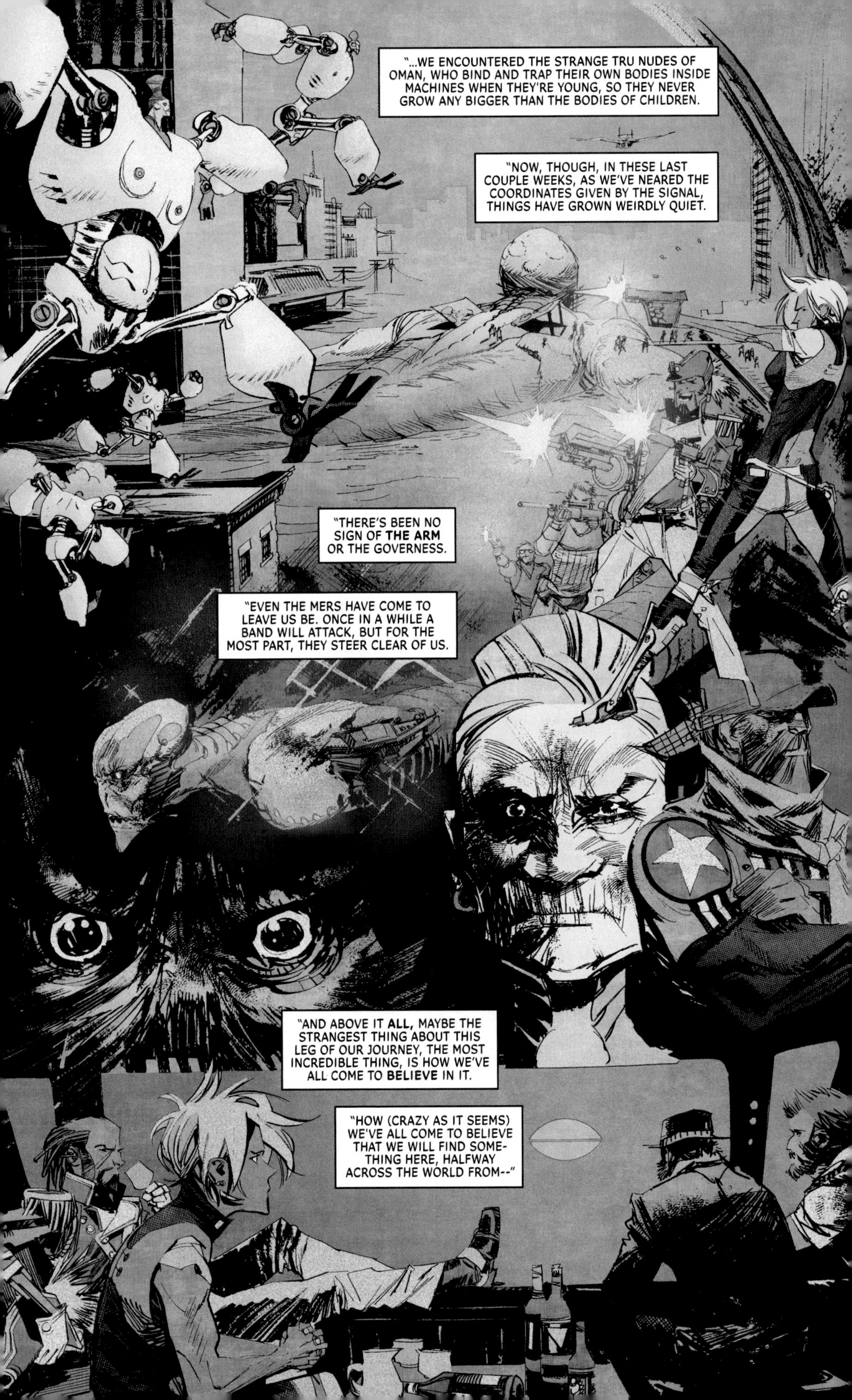
"...WE ENCOUNTERED THE STRANGE TRU NUDES OF OMAN, WHO BIND AND TRAP THEIR OWN BODIES INSIDE MACHINES WHEN THEY'RE YOUNG, SO THEY NEVER GROW ANY BIGGER THAN THE BODIES OF CHILDREN.
"NOW, THOUGH, IN THESE LAST COUPLE WEEKS, AS WE'VE NEARED THE COORDINATES GIVEN BY THE SIGNAL, THINGS HAVE GROWN WEIRDLY QUIET.
"THERE'S BEEN NO SIGN OF **THE ARM** OR THE GOVERNESS.
"EVEN THE MERS HAVE COME TO LEAVE US BE. ONCE IN A WHILE A BAND WILL ATTACK, BUT FOR THE MOST PART, THEY STEER CLEAR OF US.
"AND ABOVE IT **ALL**, MAYBE THE STRANGEST THING ABOUT THIS LEG OF OUR JOURNEY, THE MOST INCREDIBLE THING, IS HOW WE'VE ALL COME TO **BELIEVE** IN IT.
"HOW (CRAZY AS IT SEEMS) WE'VE ALL COME TO BELIEVE THAT WE WILL FIND SOME-THING HERE, HALFWAY ACROSS THE WORLD FROM--"

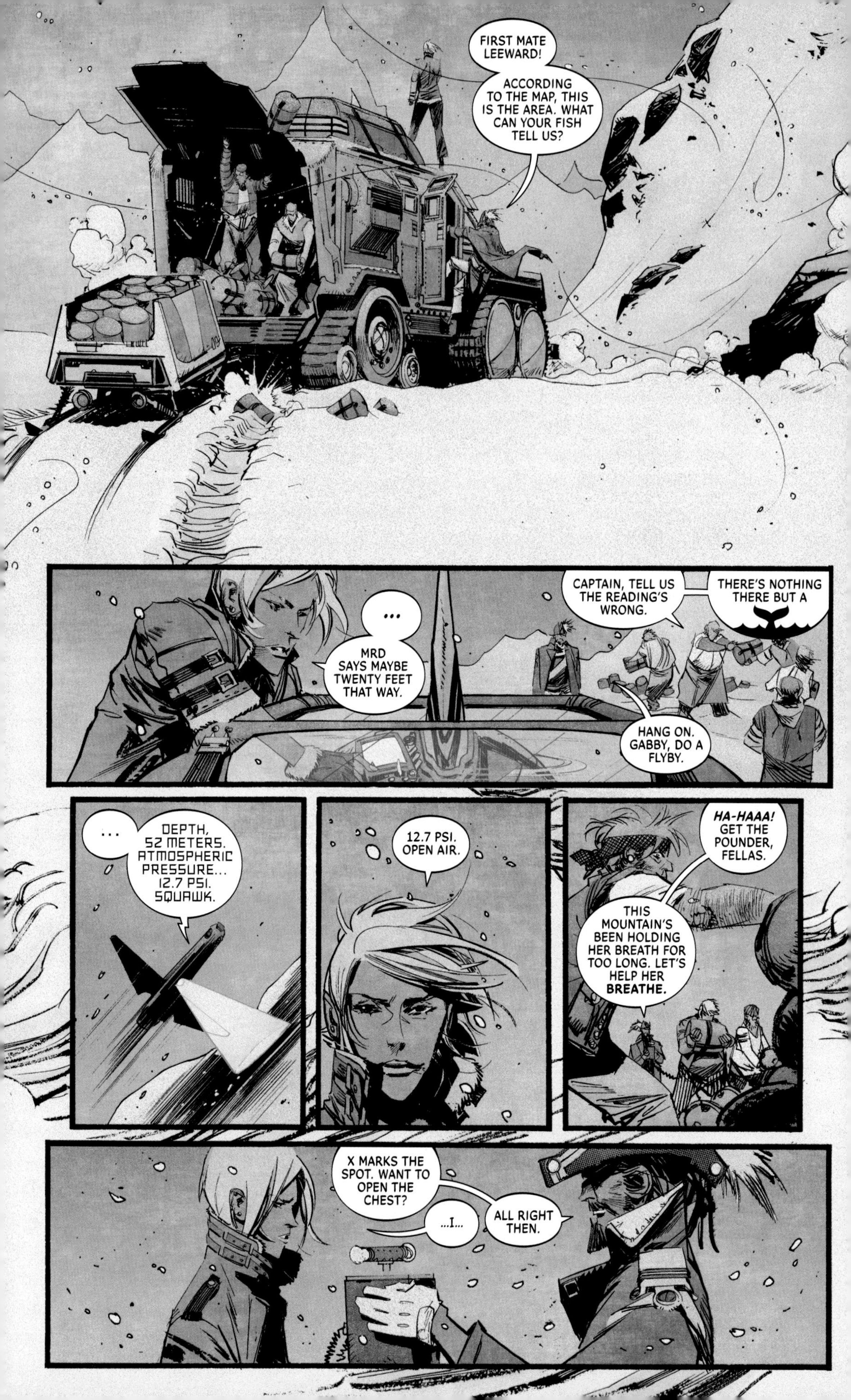
FIRST MATE LEEWARD!
ACCORDING TO THE MAP, THIS IS THE AREA. WHAT CAN YOUR FISH TELL US?
...
MRD SAYS MAYBE TWENTY FEET THAT WAY.
CAPTAIN, TELL US THE READING'S WRONG.
THERE'S NOTHING THERE BUT A
HANG ON. GABBY, DO A FLYBY.
...
DEPTH, 52 METERS. ATMOSPHERIC PRESSURE... 12.7 PSI. SQUAWK.
12.7 PSI. OPEN AIR.
HA-HAAA! GET THE POUNDER, FELLAS.
THIS MOUNTAIN'S BEEN HOLDING HER BREATH FOR TOO LONG. LET'S HELP HER **BREATHE.**
X MARKS THE SPOT. WANT TO OPEN THE CHEST?
...I...
ALL RIGHT THEN.

WAIT. CAPTAIN MARY.

I JUST... I WANT TO SAY THANK Y--

SHUT UP AND HIT THE DAMN BUTTON.

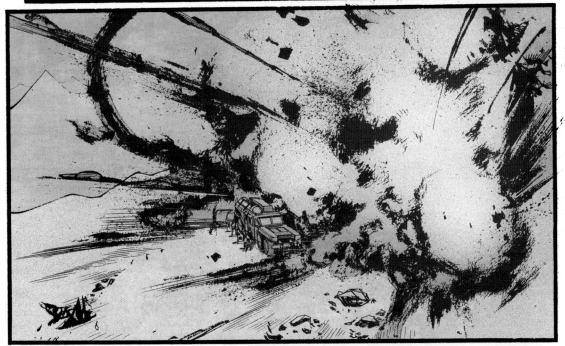

GO ON, GIRL.

LEAD THE WAY.

WHAT IS IT? WHAT DO YOU SEE?

...I.... SEE...

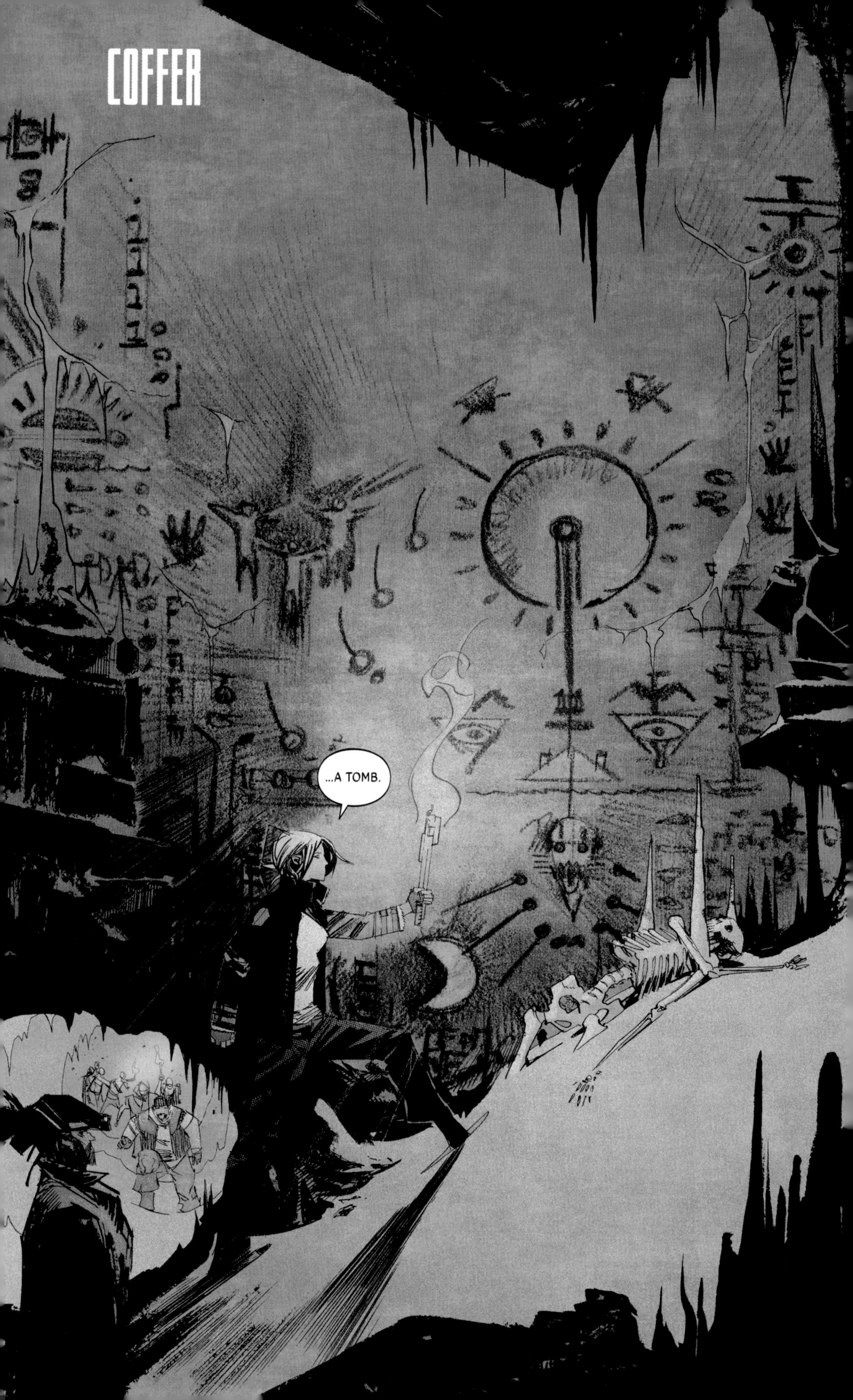
COFFER
...A TOMB.

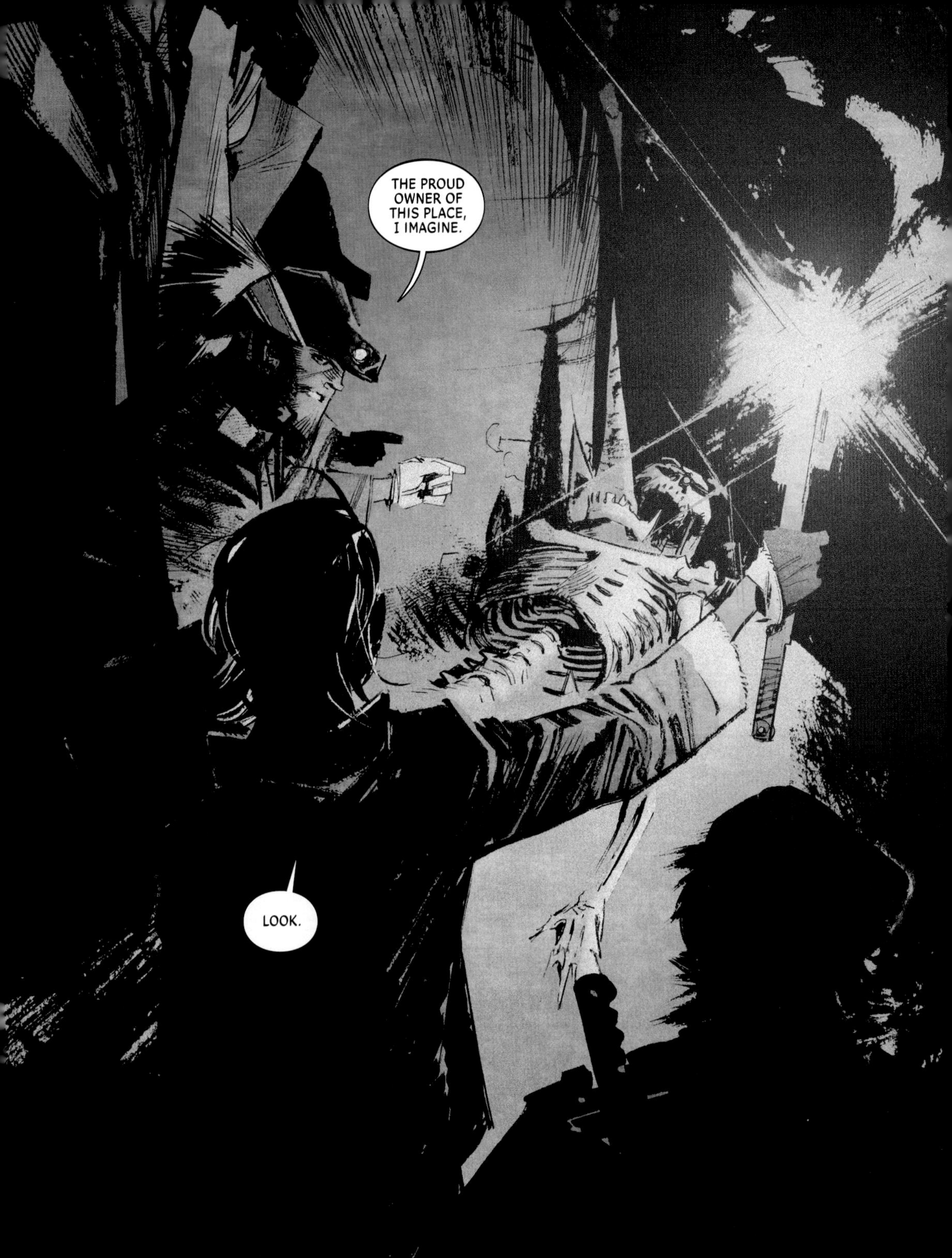
THE PROUD OWNER OF THIS PLACE, I IMAGINE.
LOOK.

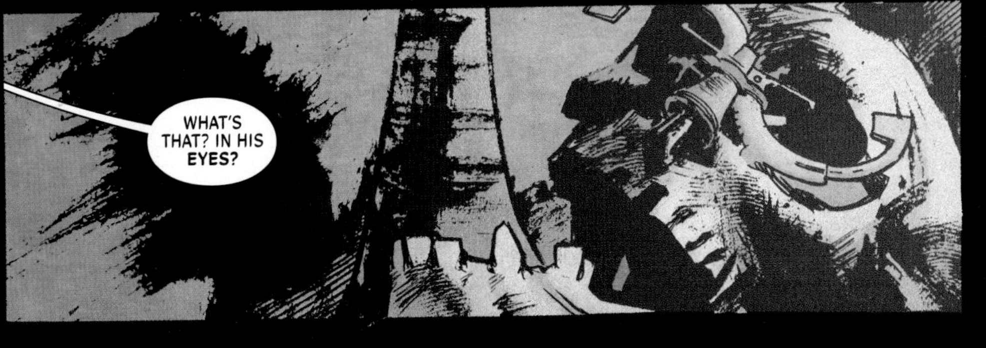
WHAT'S THAT? IN HIS EYES?

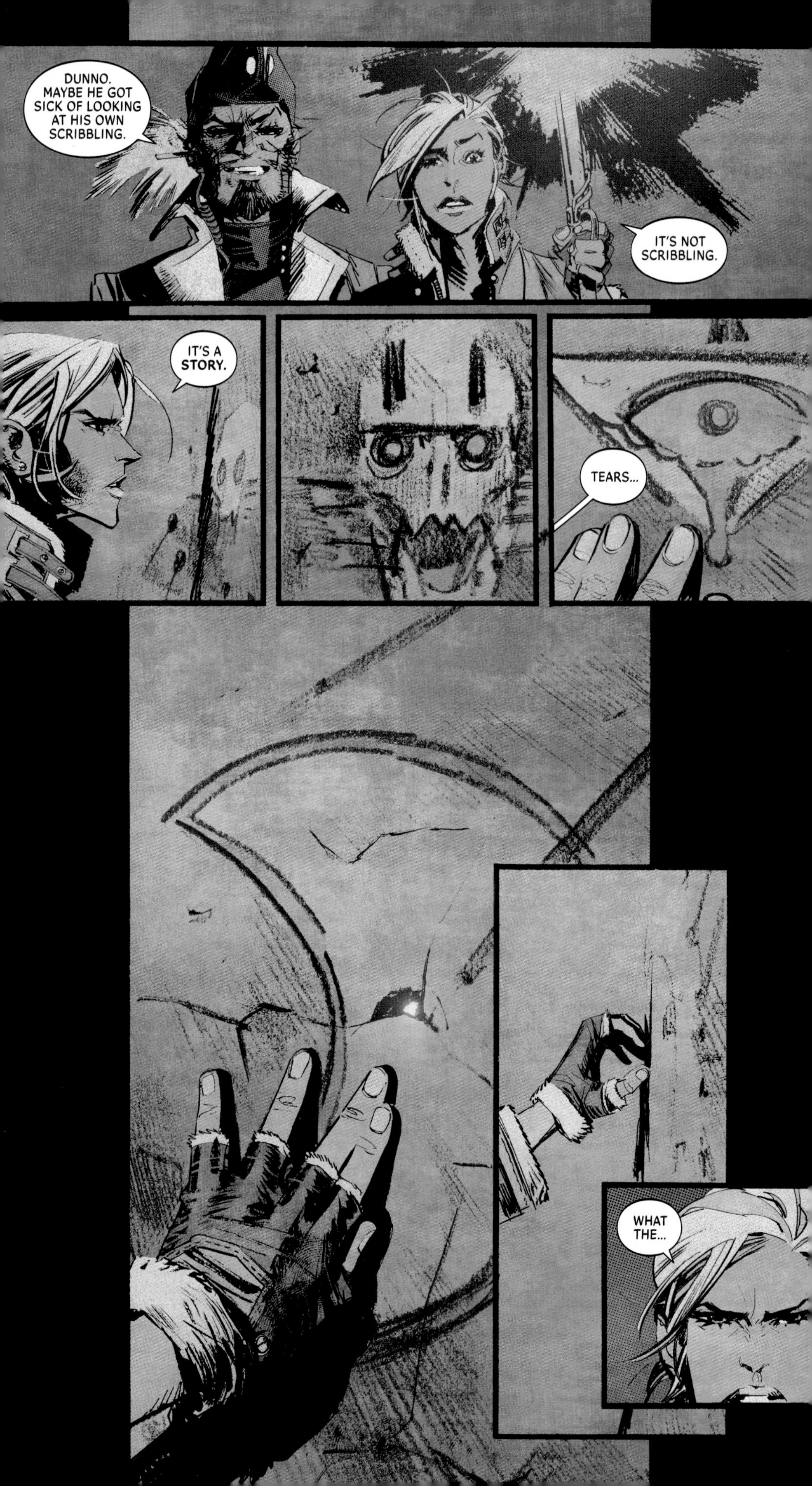
DUNNO. MAYBE HE GOT SICK OF LOOKING AT HIS OWN SCRIBBLING.
IT'S NOT SCRIBBLING.
IT'S A STORY.
TEARS...
WHAT THE...

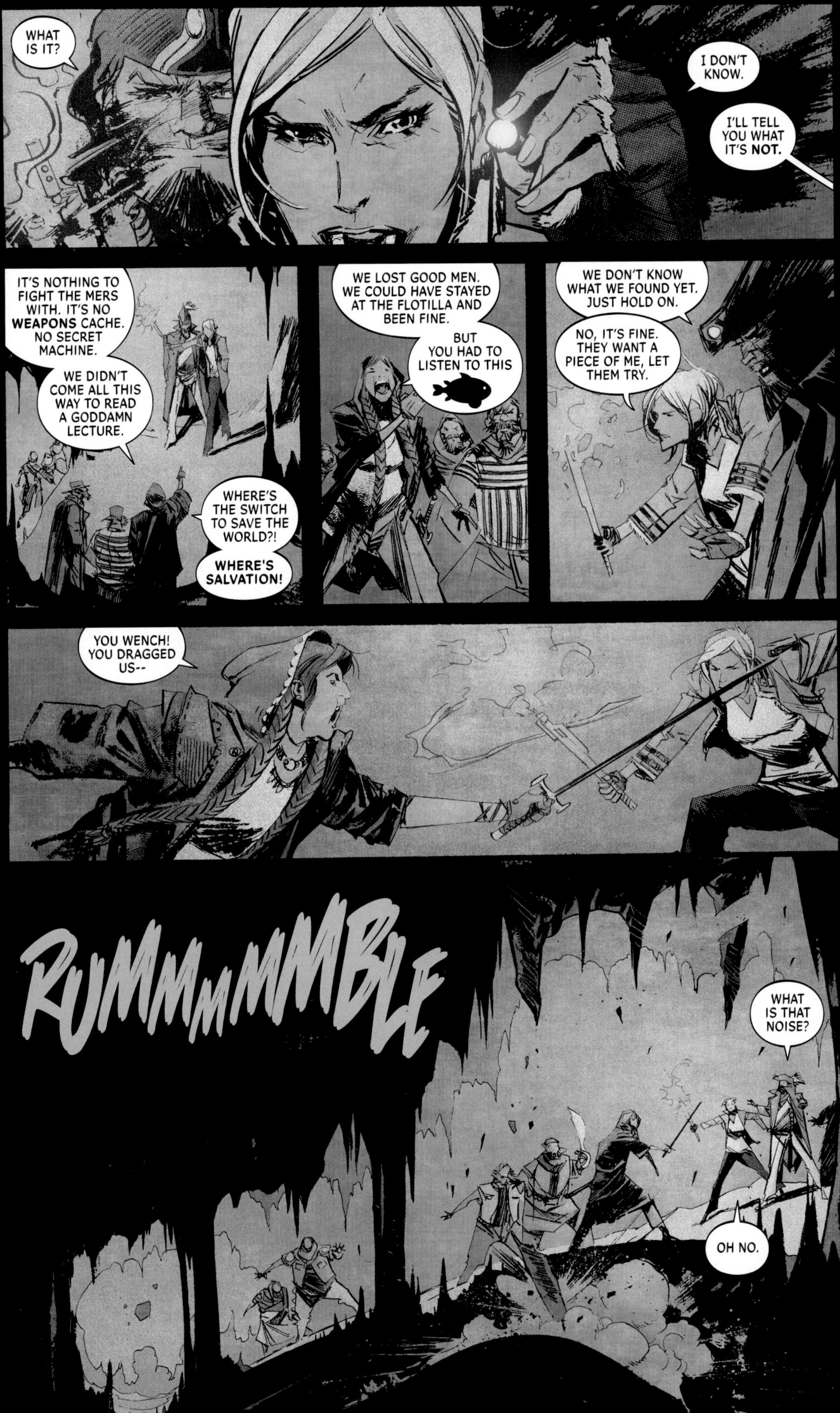
WHAT IS IT?
I DON'T KNOW.
I'LL TELL YOU WHAT IT'S **NOT.**
IT'S NOTHING TO FIGHT THE MERS WITH. IT'S NO **WEAPONS** CACHE. NO SECRET MACHINE.
WE DIDN'T COME ALL THIS WAY TO READ A GODDAMN LECTURE.
WHERE'S THE SWITCH TO SAVE THE WORLD?!
WHERE'S SALVATION!
WE LOST GOOD MEN. WE COULD HAVE STAYED AT THE FLOTILLA AND BEEN FINE.
BUT YOU HAD TO LISTEN TO THIS
WE DON'T KNOW WHAT WE FOUND YET. JUST HOLD ON.
NO, IT'S FINE. THEY WANT A PIECE OF ME, LET THEM TRY.
YOU WENCH! YOU DRAGGED US--
RUMMMMMMBLE
WHAT IS THAT NOISE?
OH NO.

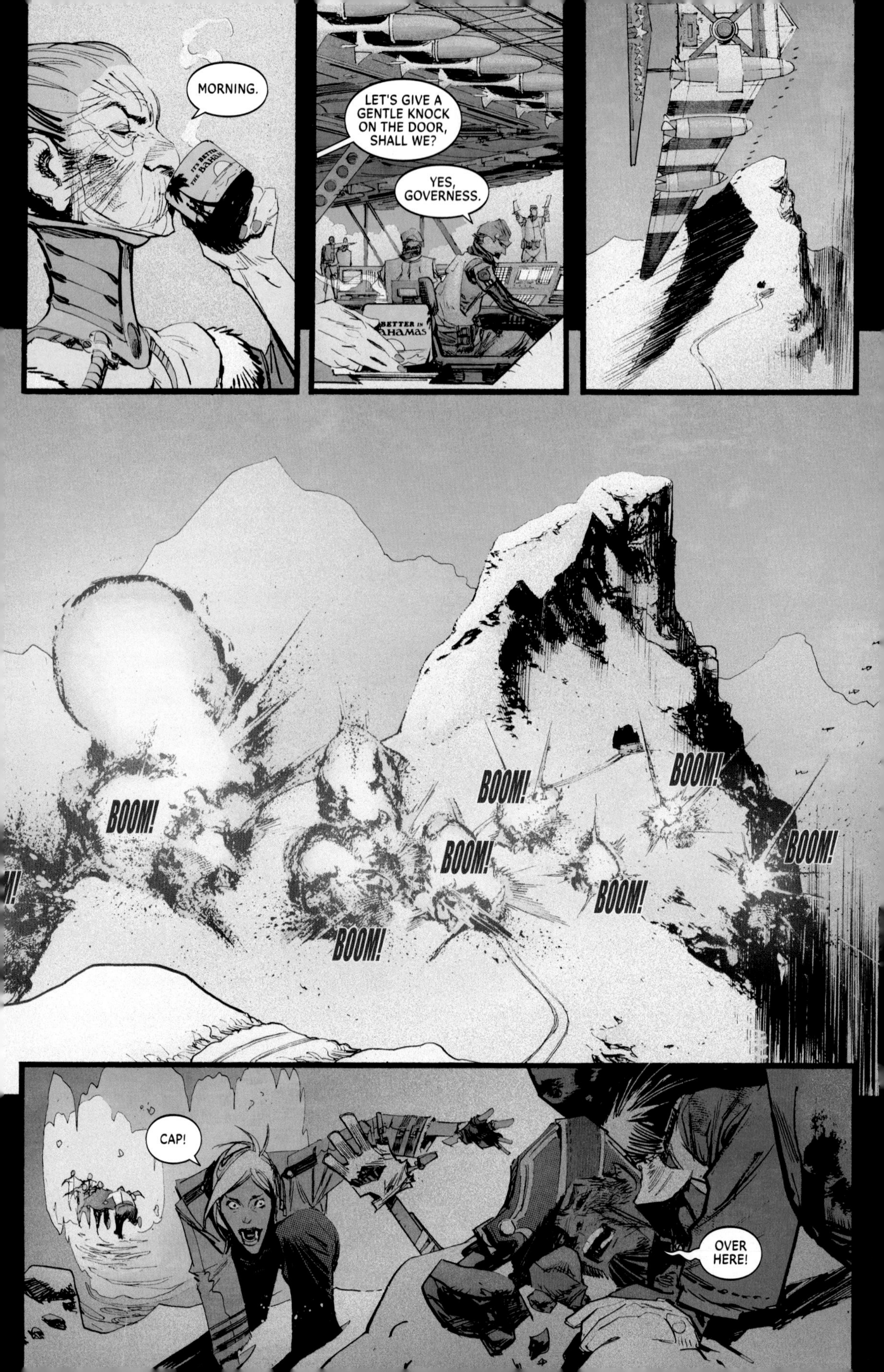
MORNING.
LET'S GIVE A GENTLE KNOCK ON THE DOOR, SHALL WE?
YES, GOVERNESS.
BOOM!
BOOM!
BOOM!
BOOM!
BOOM!
BOOM!
BOOM!
CAP!
OVER HERE!

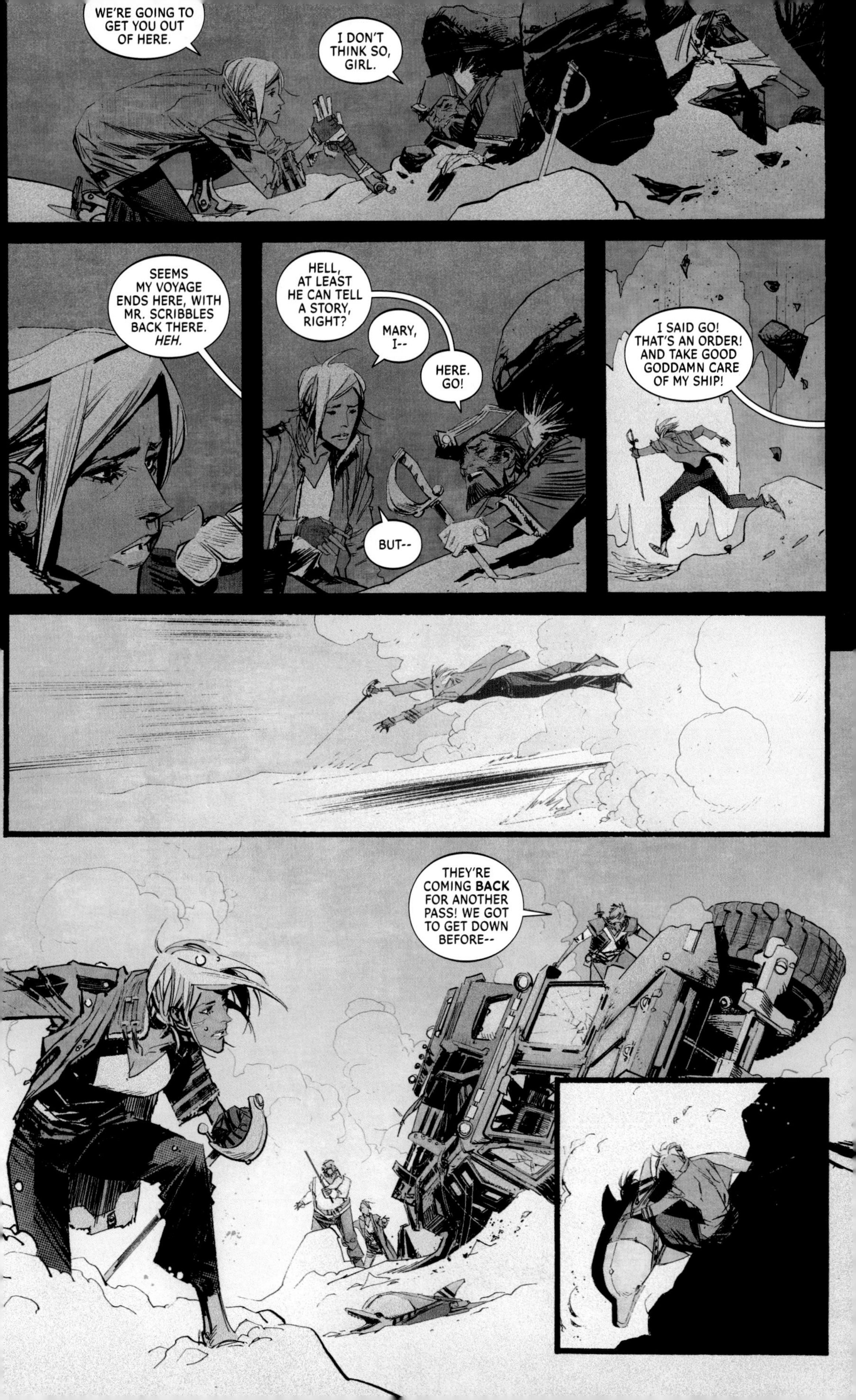
WE'RE GOING TO GET YOU OUT OF HERE.
I DON'T THINK SO, GIRL.
SEEMS MY VOYAGE ENDS HERE, WITH MR. SCRIBBLES BACK THERE. *HEH.*
HELL, AT LEAST HE CAN TELL A STORY, RIGHT?
MARY, I--
HERE. GO!
BUT--
I SAID GO! THAT'S AN ORDER! AND TAKE GOOD GODDAMN CARE OF MY SHIP!
THEY'RE COMING **BACK** FOR ANOTHER PASS! WE GOT TO GET DOWN BEFORE--

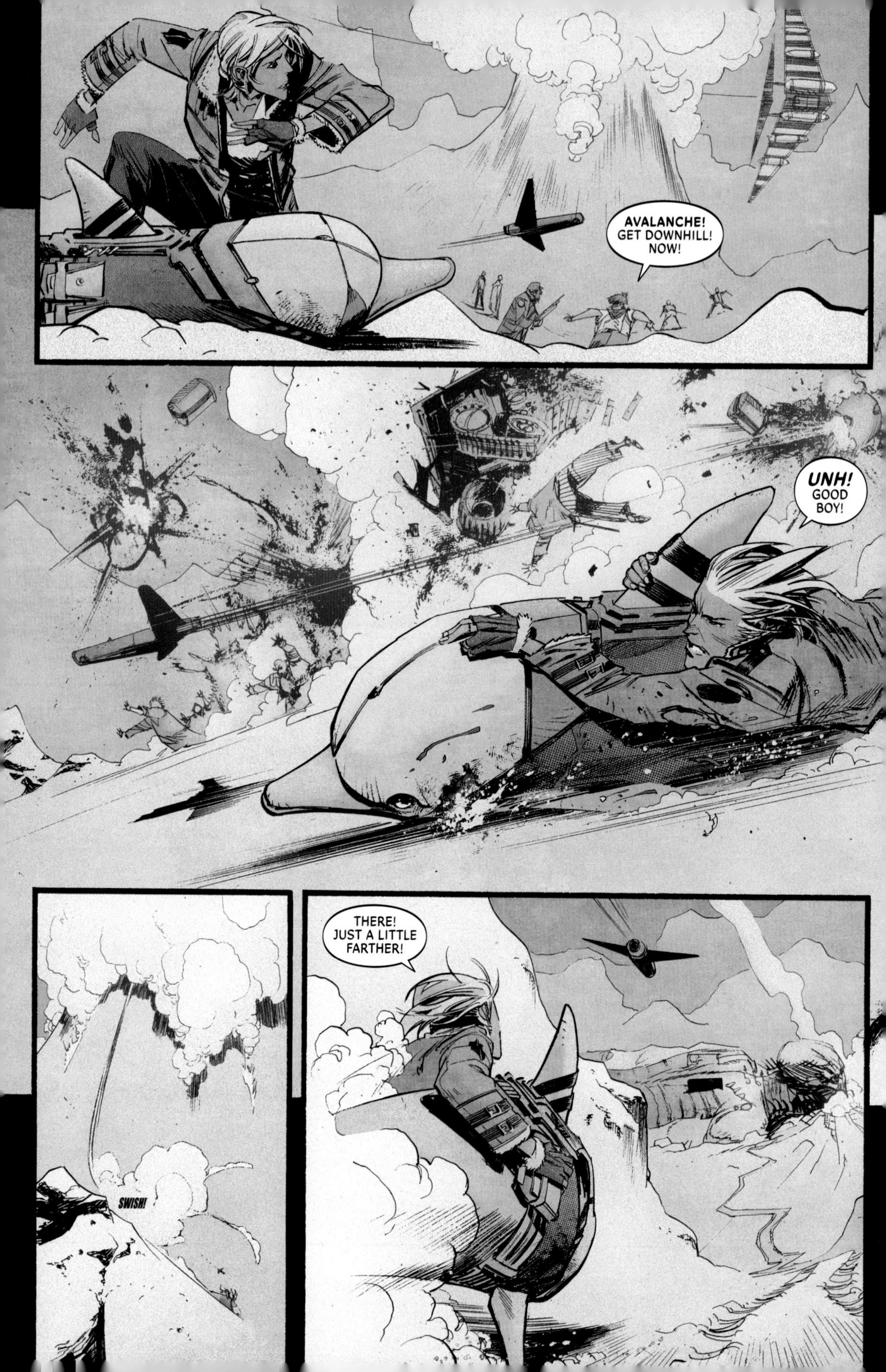
AVALANCHE! GET DOWNHILL! NOW!
UNH! GOOD BOY!
SWISH!
THERE! JUST A LITTLE FARTHER!

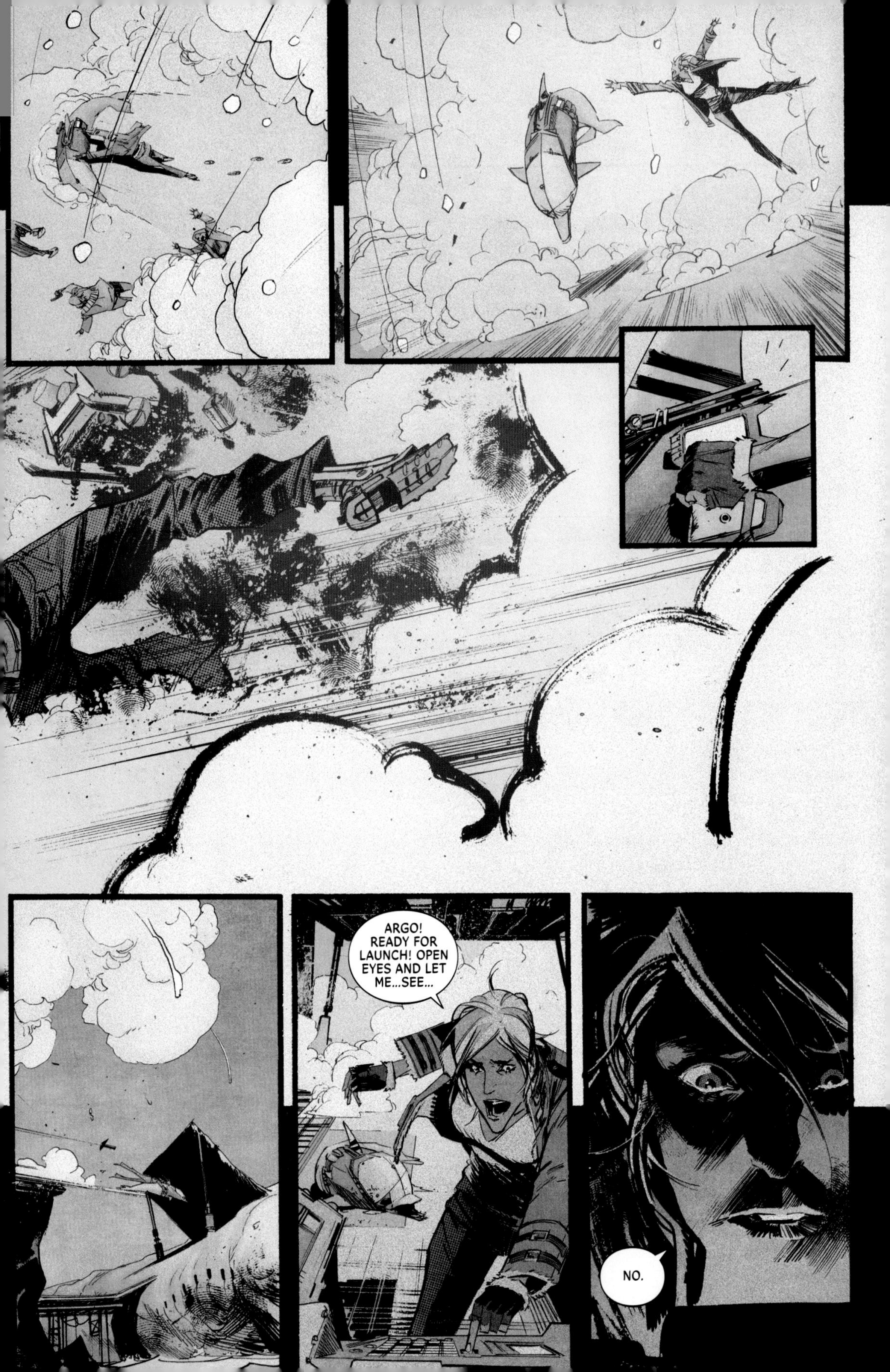
ARGO! READY FOR LAUNCH! OPEN EYES AND LET ME...SEE...
NO.

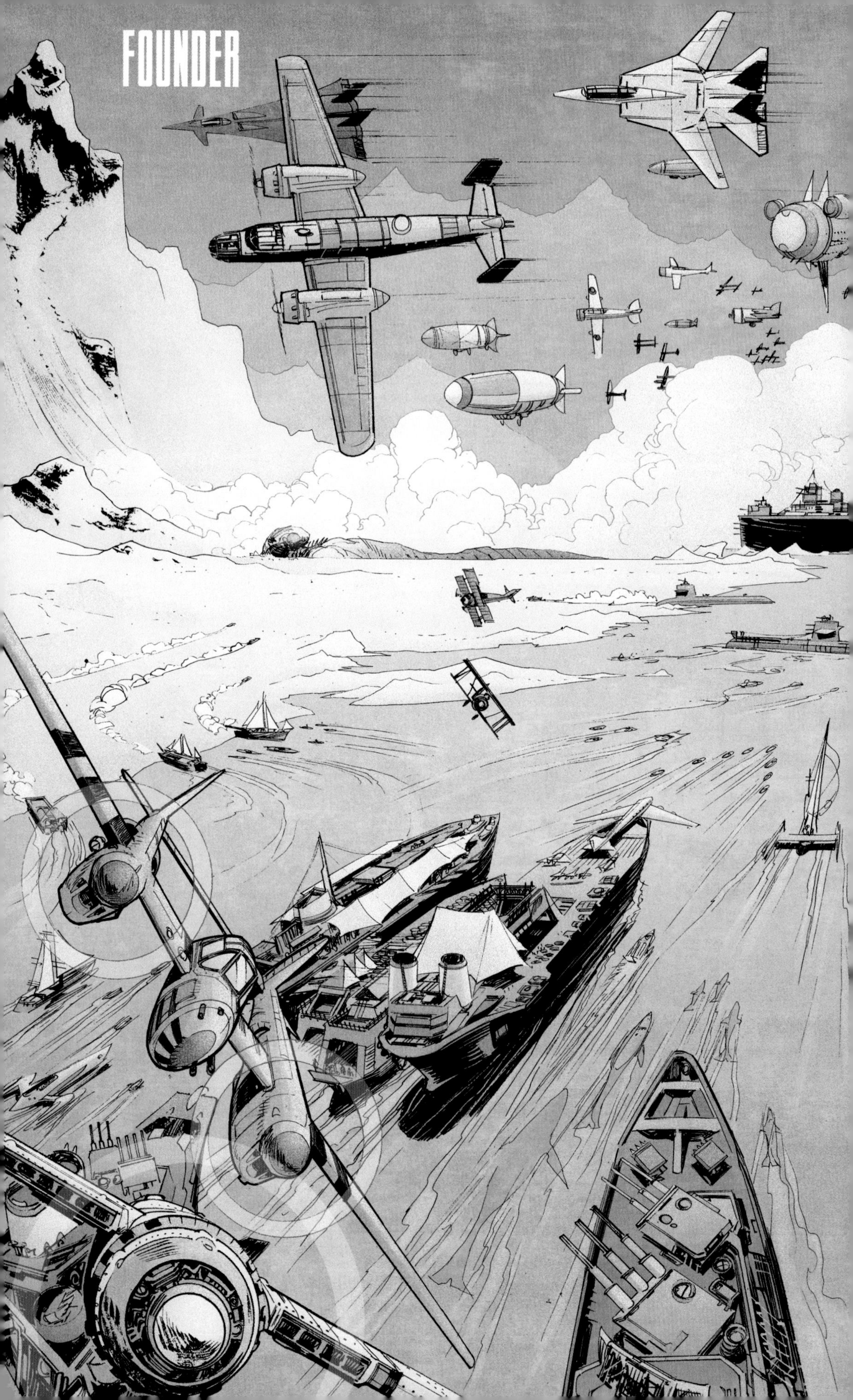
FOUNDER

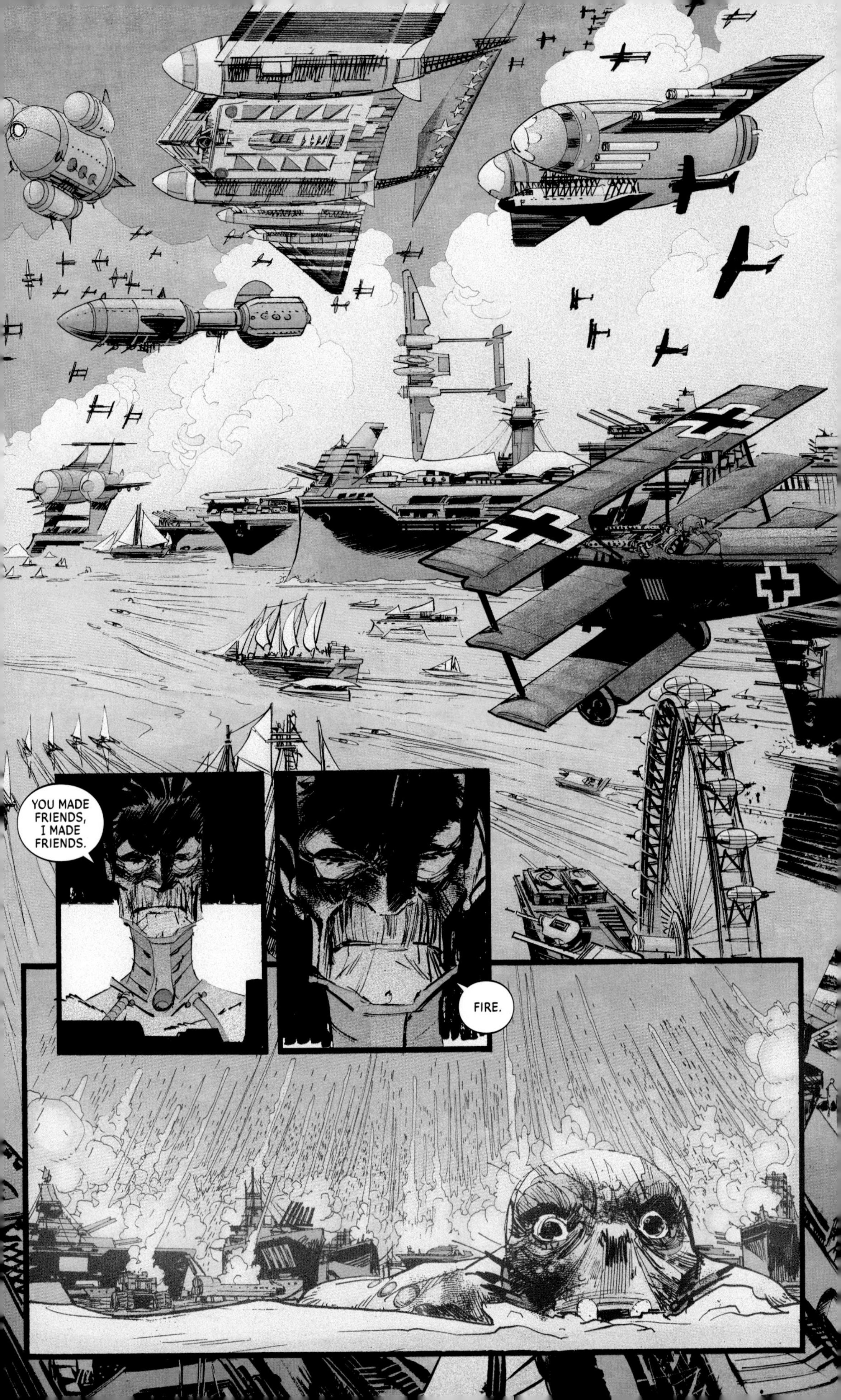
YOU MADE FRIENDS, I MADE FRIENDS.
FIRE.

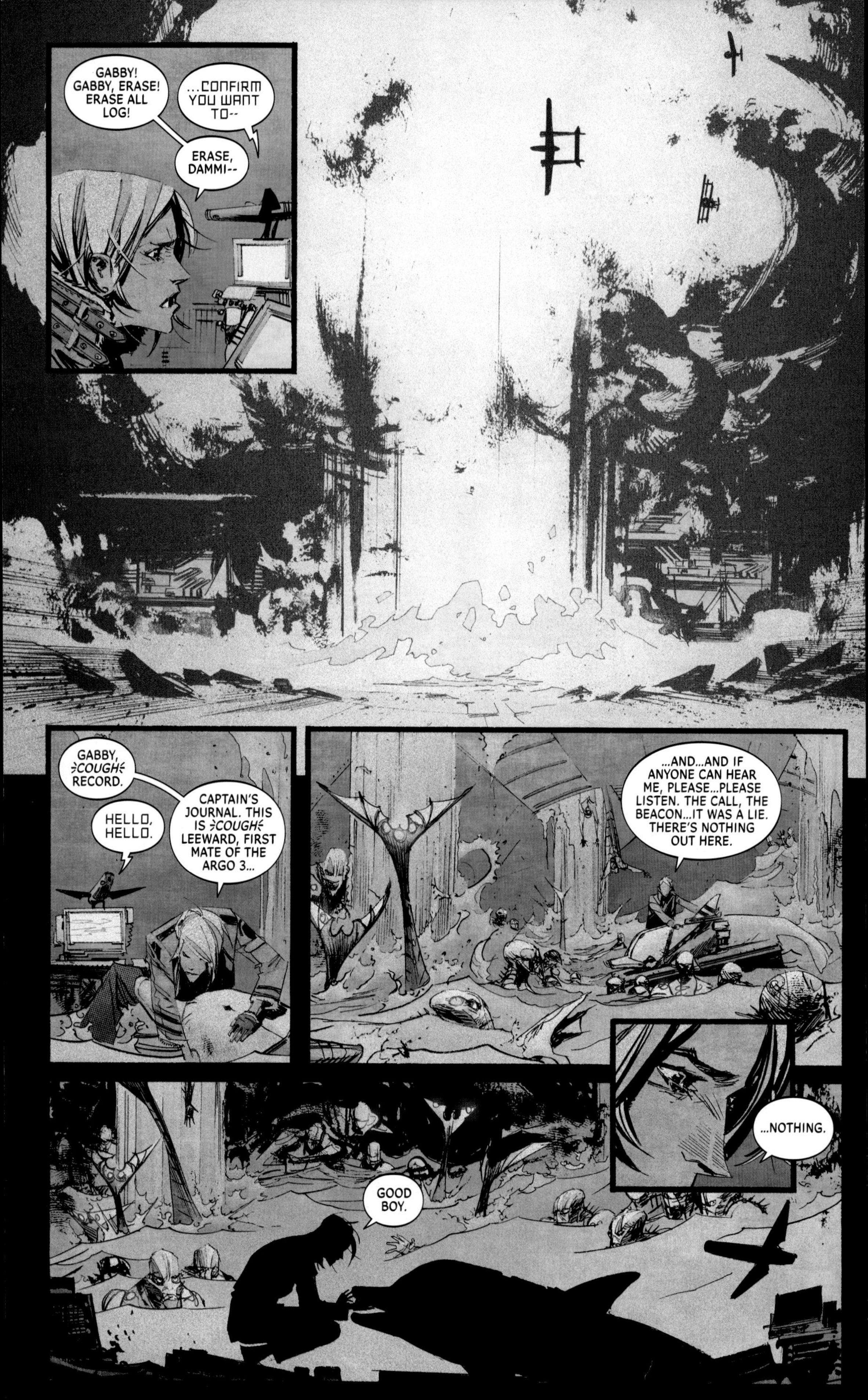
GABBY! GABBY, ERASE! ERASE ALL LOG!
...CONFIRM YOU WANT TO--
ERASE, DAMMI--
GABBY, ⸗COUGH⸗ RECORD.
HELLO, HELLO.
CAPTAIN'S JOURNAL. THIS IS ⸗COUGH⸗ LEEWARD, FIRST MATE OF THE ARGO 3...
...AND...AND IF ANYONE CAN HEAR ME, PLEASE...PLEASE LISTEN. THE CALL, THE BEACON...IT WAS A LIE. THERE'S NOTHING OUT HERE.
...NOTHING.
GOOD BOY.

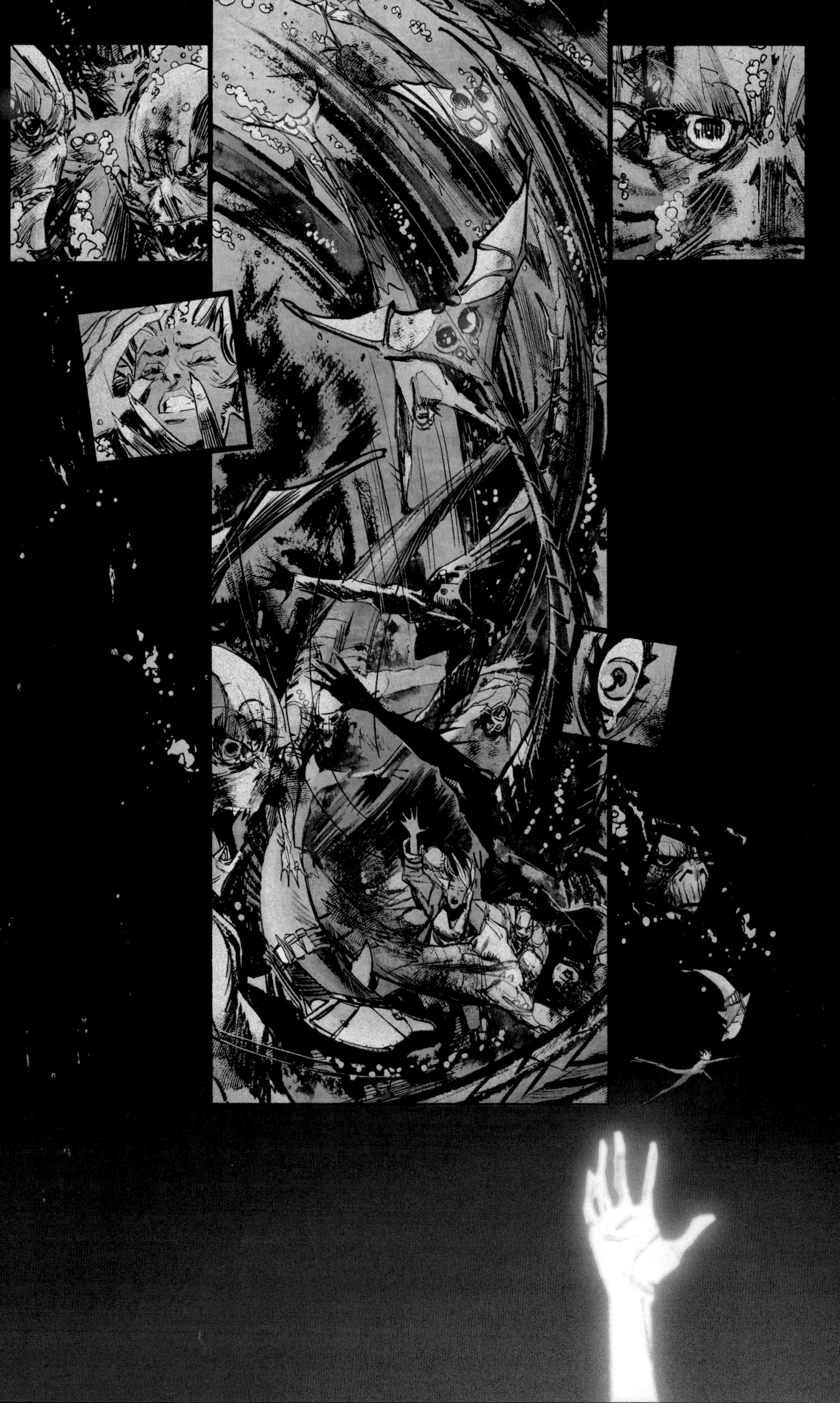

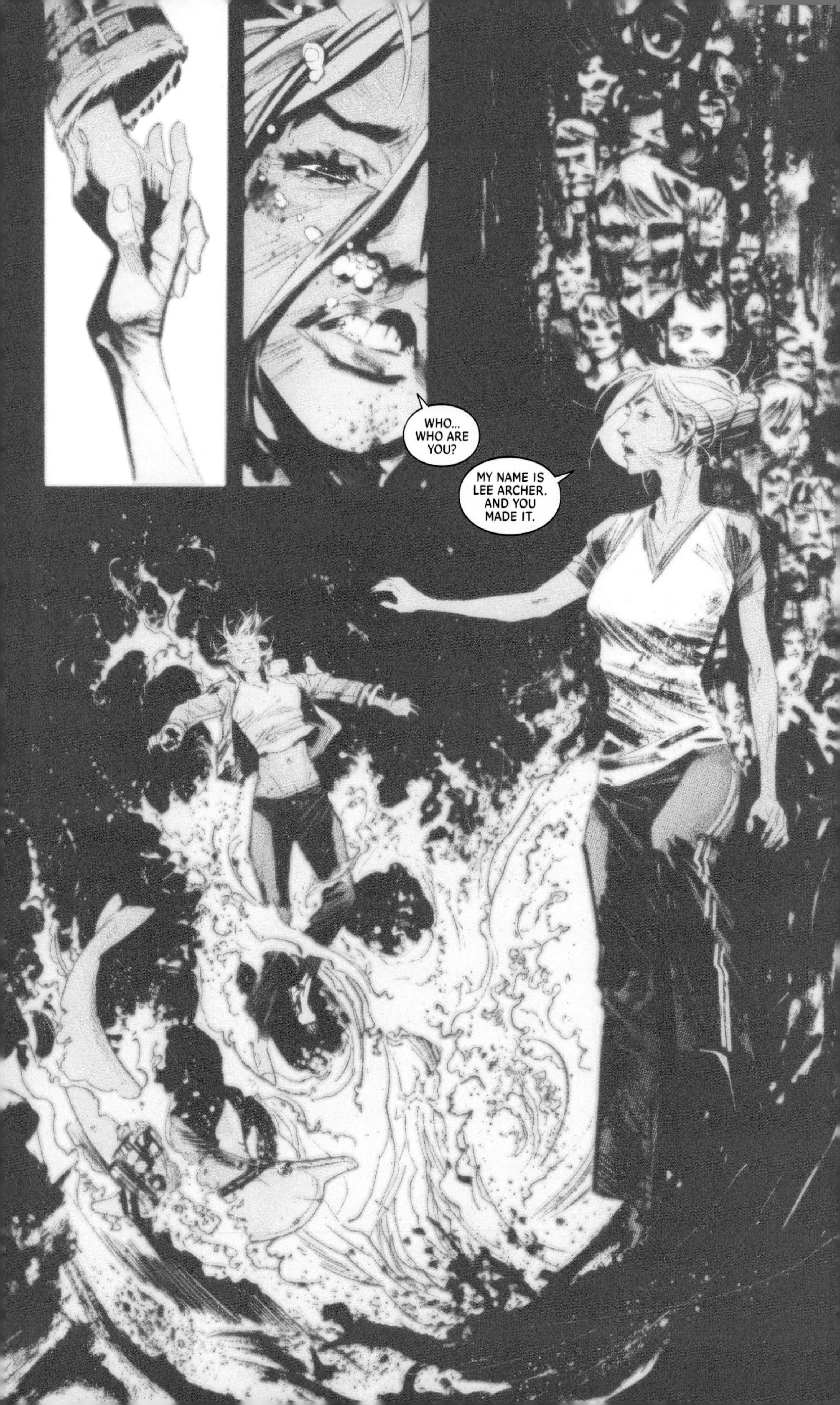
WHO... WHO ARE YOU?
MY NAME IS LEE ARCHER. AND YOU MADE IT.

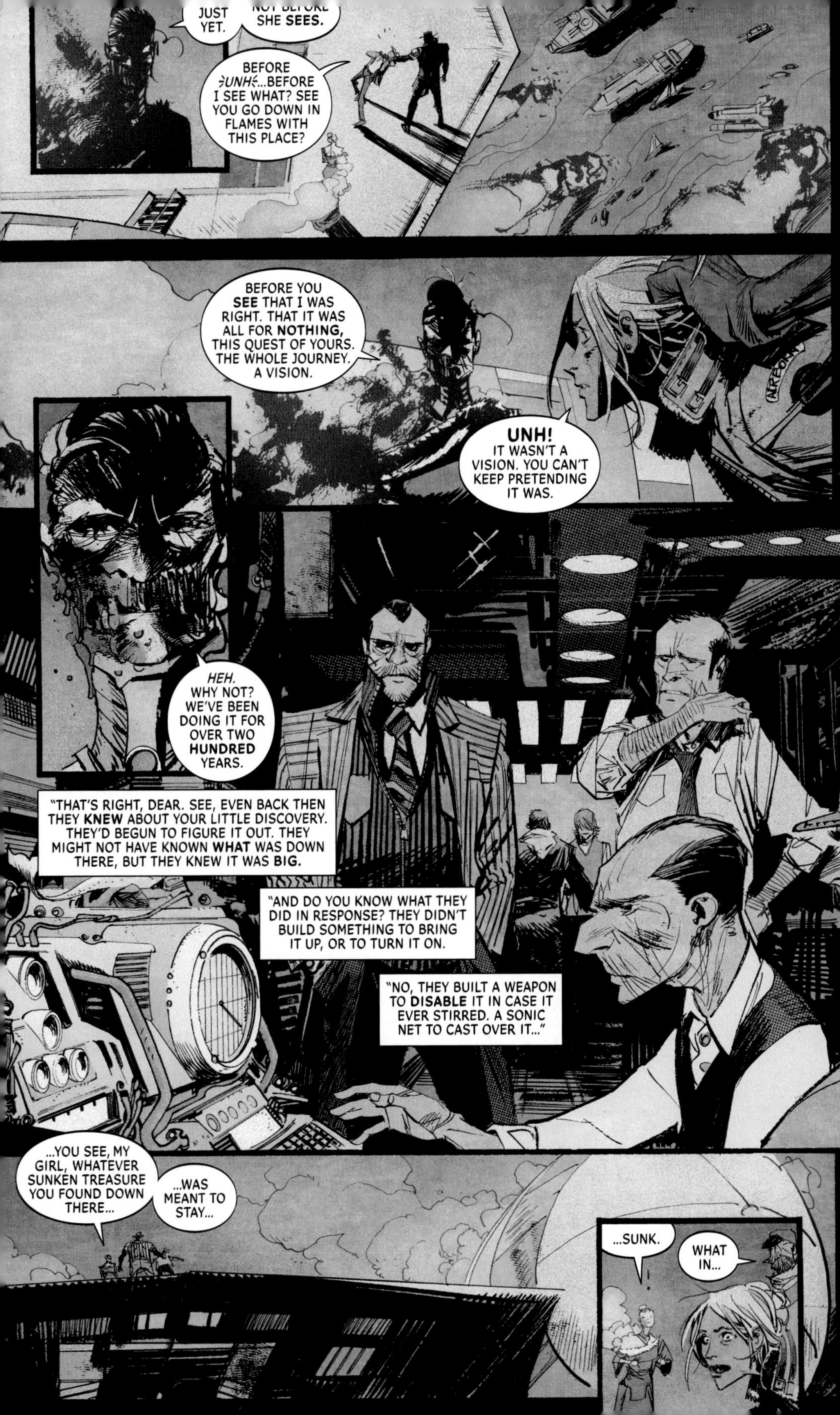
JUST YET.
NOT BEFORE SHE SEES.
BEFORE *UNH!*...BEFORE I SEE WHAT? SEE YOU GO DOWN IN FLAMES WITH THIS PLACE?
BEFORE YOU **SEE** THAT I WAS RIGHT. THAT IT WAS ALL FOR **NOTHING,** THIS QUEST OF YOURS. THE WHOLE JOURNEY. A VISION.
UNH! IT WASN'T A VISION. YOU CAN'T KEEP PRETENDING IT WAS.
HEH. WHY NOT? WE'VE BEEN DOING IT FOR OVER TWO **HUNDRED** YEARS.
"THAT'S RIGHT, DEAR. SEE, EVEN BACK THEN THEY **KNEW** ABOUT YOUR LITTLE DISCOVERY. THEY'D BEGUN TO FIGURE IT OUT. THEY MIGHT NOT HAVE KNOWN **WHAT** WAS DOWN THERE, BUT THEY KNEW IT WAS **BIG.**
"AND DO YOU KNOW WHAT THEY DID IN RESPONSE? THEY DIDN'T BUILD SOMETHING TO BRING IT UP, OR TO TURN IT ON.
"NO, THEY BUILT A WEAPON TO **DISABLE** IT IN CASE IT EVER STIRRED. A SONIC NET TO CAST OVER IT..."
...YOU SEE, MY GIRL, WHATEVER SUNKEN TREASURE YOU FOUND DOWN THERE...
...WAS MEANT TO STAY...
...SUNK.
!
WHAT IN...

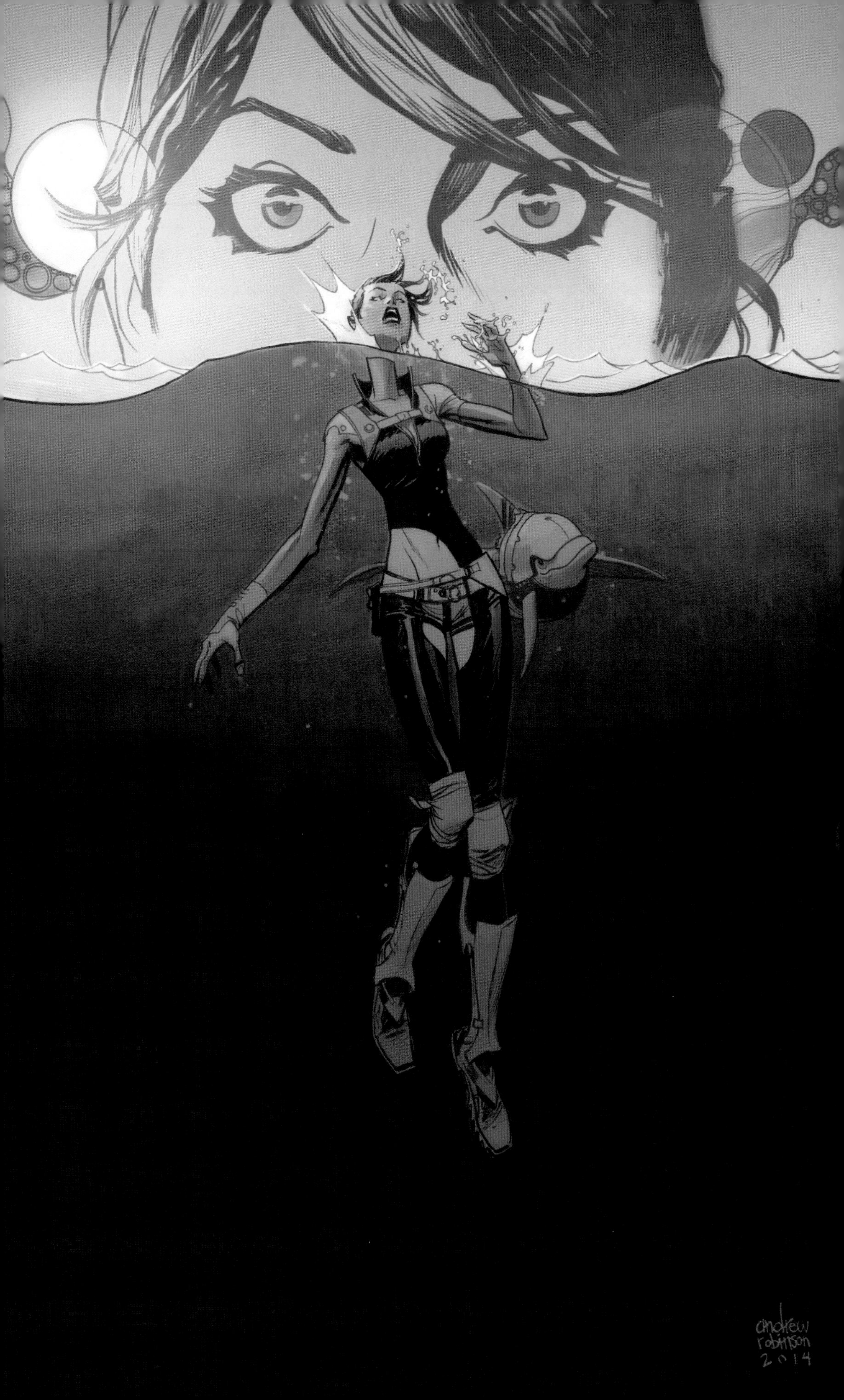
andrew
robinson
2014

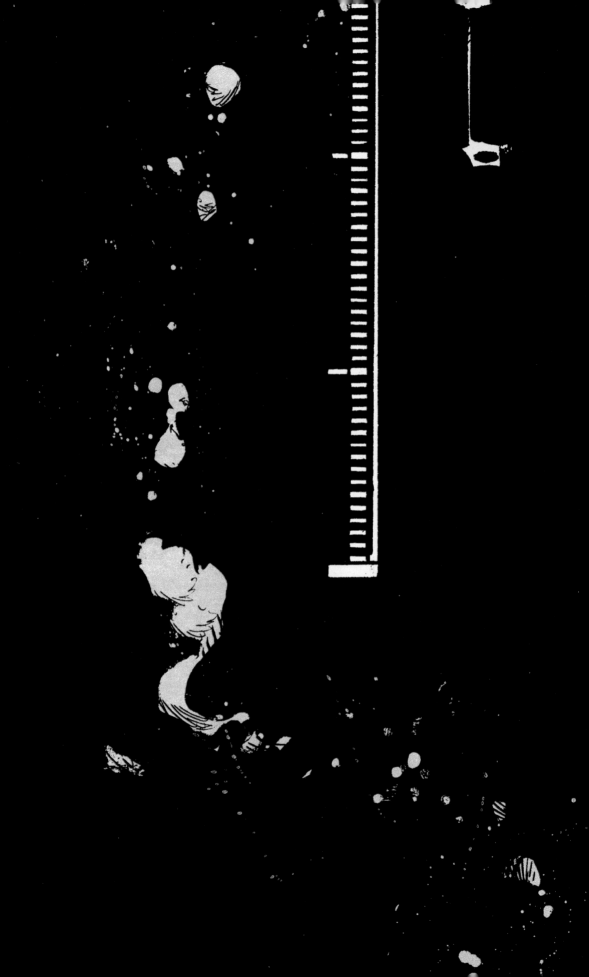

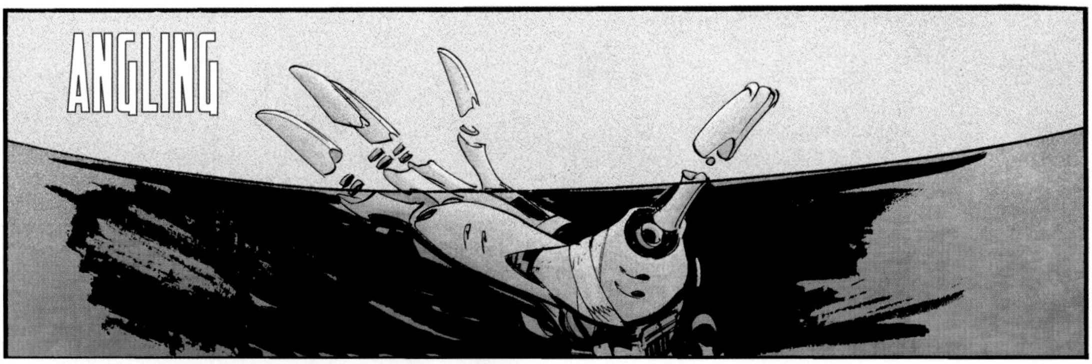
ANGLING

THE WAKE CHAPTER FIVE

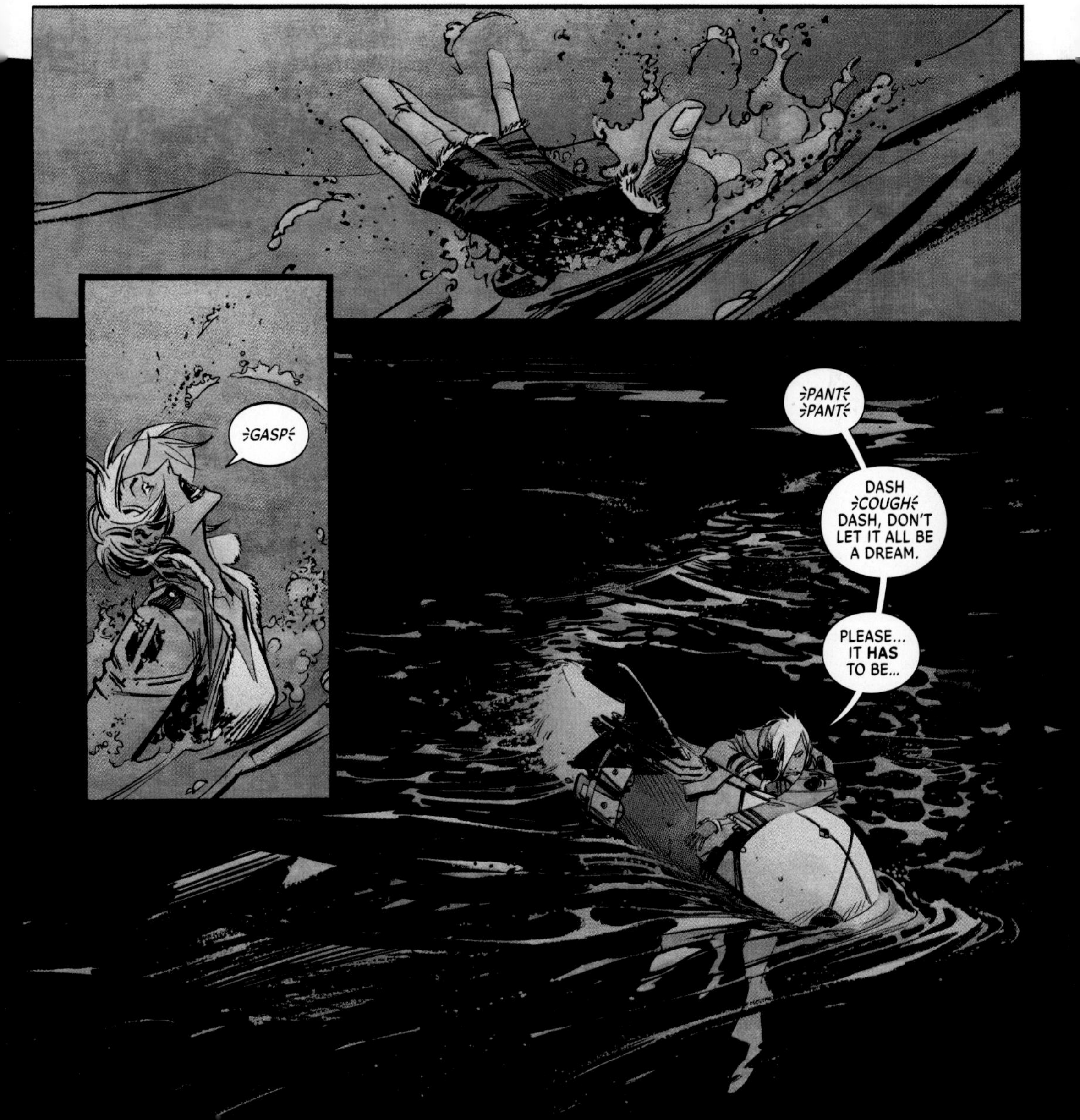
GASP
PANT PANT
DASH COUGH DASH, DON'T LET IT ALL BE A DREAM.
PLEASE... IT HAS TO BE...

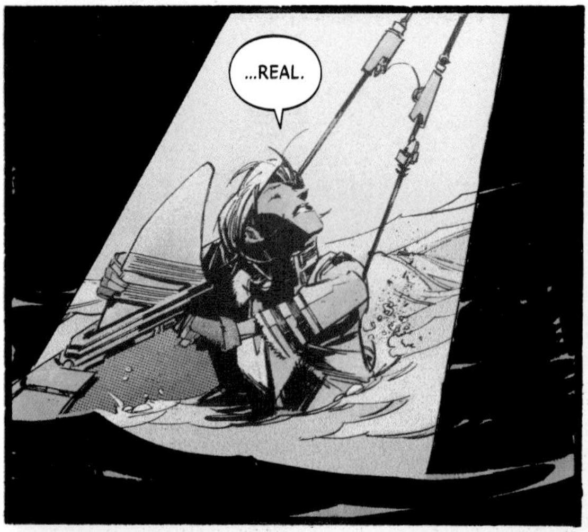
...REAL.

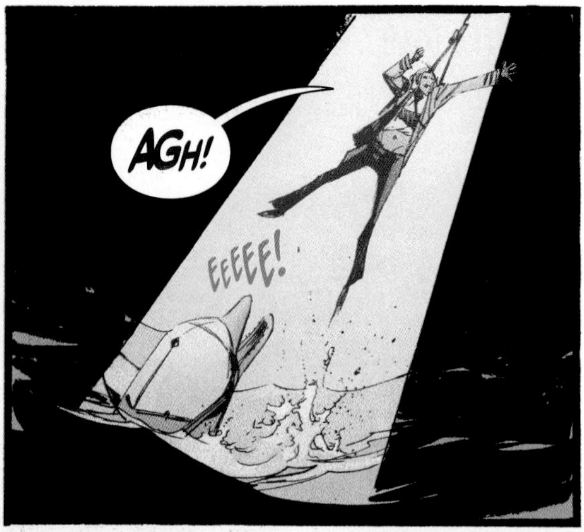
AGH!
EEEEE!

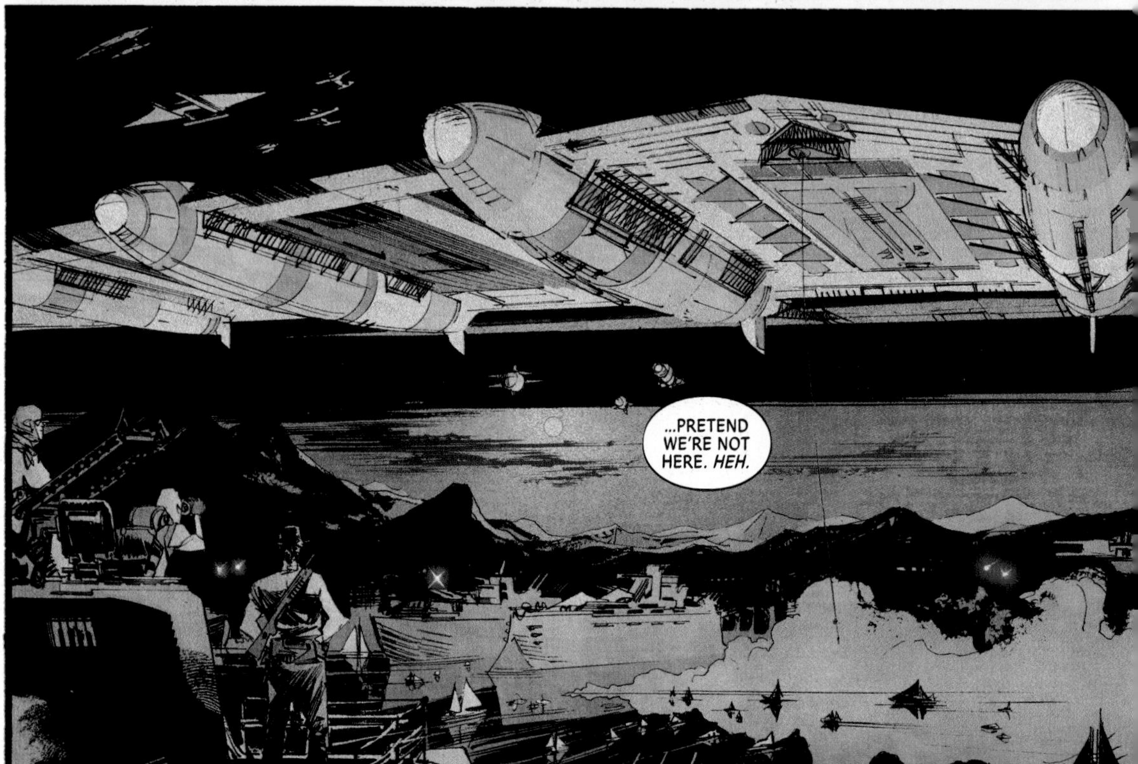
...PRETEND WE'RE NOT HERE. *HEH.*

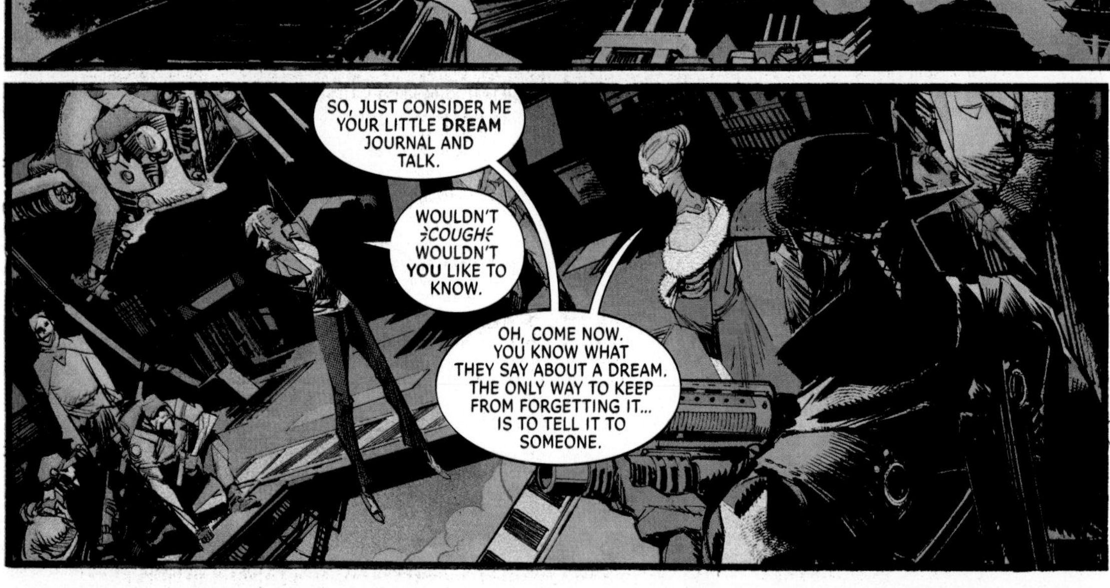
SO, JUST CONSIDER ME YOUR LITTLE **DREAM** JOURNAL AND TALK.
WOULDN'T *COUGH* WOULDN'T **YOU** LIKE TO KNOW.
OH, COME NOW. YOU KNOW WHAT THEY SAY ABOUT A DREAM. THE ONLY WAY TO KEEP FROM FORGETTING IT... IS TO TELL IT TO SOMEONE.

WELL, LOOK AT THIS! I'D HEARD THIS SPOT WAS PRIME ANGLING TERRITORY, AND IT SEEMS WE CAUGHT A REAL LUNKER! REEL HER IN, BOYS! BIG GAME ON THE LINE!

NOW THEN, DEAR! YOU WERE JUST ABOUT TO TELL YOUR LITTLE PET ABOUT THE VISION THOSE MONSTERS KISSED INTO YOUR HEAD DOWN THERE. I KNOW THE HOOK'S IN YOU, BUT GO ON. BY ALL MEANS, CONTINUE...

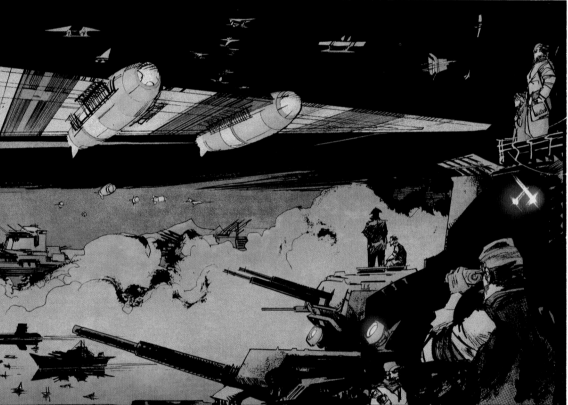

NOW OR THIS WILL GET...

COLORFUL.

SEE, BUT IT WASN'T A DREAM. IT WAS A MEMORY.

"LET IT OUT..."

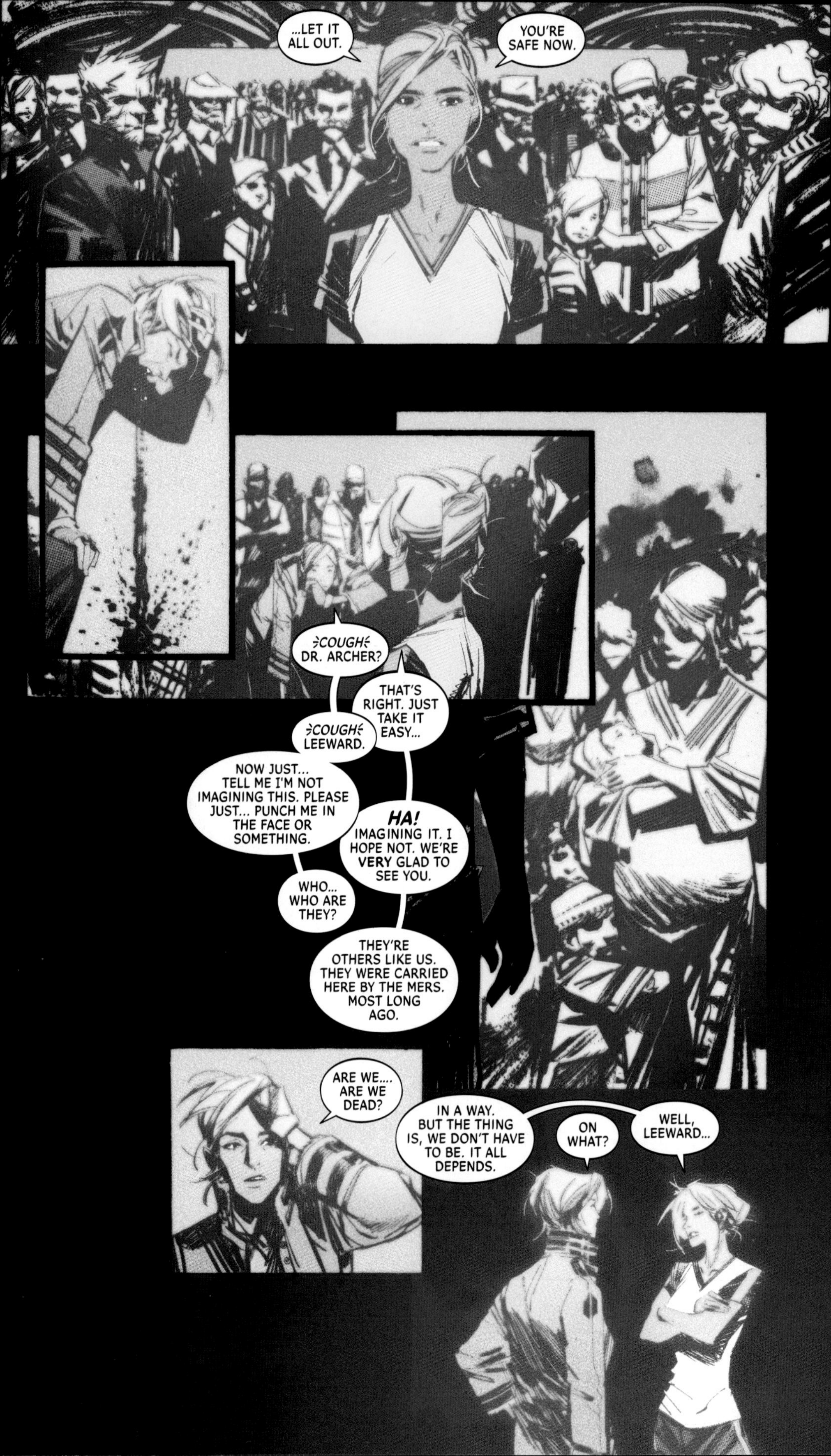
...LET IT ALL OUT.
YOU'RE SAFE NOW.
COUGH DR. ARCHER?
THAT'S RIGHT. JUST TAKE IT EASY...
COUGH LEEWARD.
NOW JUST... TELL ME I'M NOT IMAGINING THIS. PLEASE JUST... PUNCH ME IN THE FACE OR SOMETHING.
HA! IMAGINING IT. I HOPE NOT. WE'RE VERY GLAD TO SEE YOU.
WHO... WHO ARE THEY?
THEY'RE OTHERS LIKE US. THEY WERE CARRIED HERE BY THE MERS. MOST LONG AGO.
ARE WE.... ARE WE DEAD?
IN A WAY. BUT THE THING IS, WE DON'T HAVE TO BE. IT ALL DEPENDS.
ON WHAT?
WELL, LEEWARD...

"...ON YOU, ACTUALLY."

UNH!

JUST IMAGINE GENERAL MARLOW IS THAT PET DOLPHIN OF YOURS. SLICK AND SMOOTH. A LITTLE BLOWHOLE UNDER HIS CAP.

TALK, GIRL. YOUR DREAM...

≷COUGH≷ I TOLD YOU IT WASN'T A DREAM.

YOU KNOW, SOME PEOPLE BELIEVE THAT EVERY TIME WE SLEEP, WE DIE, AND WHEN WE WAKE WE ARE REBORN AS NEW SELVES. HERE I WAS SERIOUSLY HOPING YOU MIGHT WAKE FROM YOUR LITTLE UNDERWATER NAP AS SOMEONE MUCH SMARTER THIS GO AROUND.

BECAUSE WELL, IF THAT LITTLE MOUTH OF YOURS DOESN'T START WORKING A BIT BETTER VERY SOON...

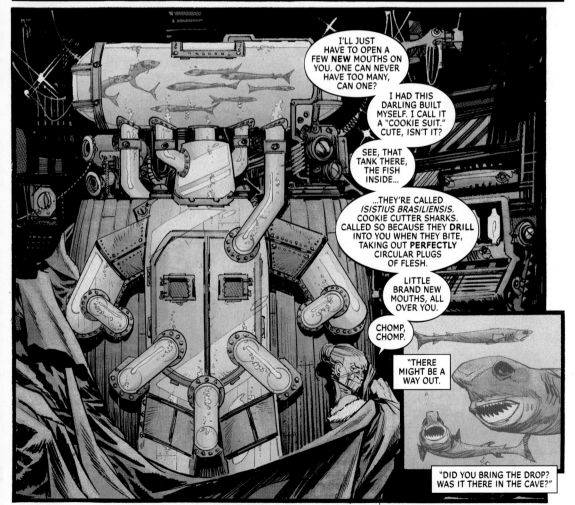

I'LL JUST HAVE TO OPEN A FEW NEW MOUTHS ON YOU. ONE CAN NEVER HAVE TOO MANY, CAN ONE?

I HAD THIS DARLING BUILT MYSELF. I CALL IT A "COOKIE SUIT." CUTE, ISN'T IT?

SEE, THAT TANK THERE, THE FISH INSIDE...

...THEY'RE CALLED ISISTIUS BRASILIENSIS. COOKIE CUTTER SHARKS. CALLED SO BECAUSE THEY DRILL INTO YOU WHEN THEY BITE, TAKING OUT PERFECTLY CIRCULAR PLUGS OF FLESH.

LITTLE BRAND NEW MOUTHS, ALL OVER YOU.

CHOMP, CHOMP.

"THERE MIGHT BE A WAY OUT.

"DID YOU BRING THE DROP? WAS IT THERE IN THE CAVE?"

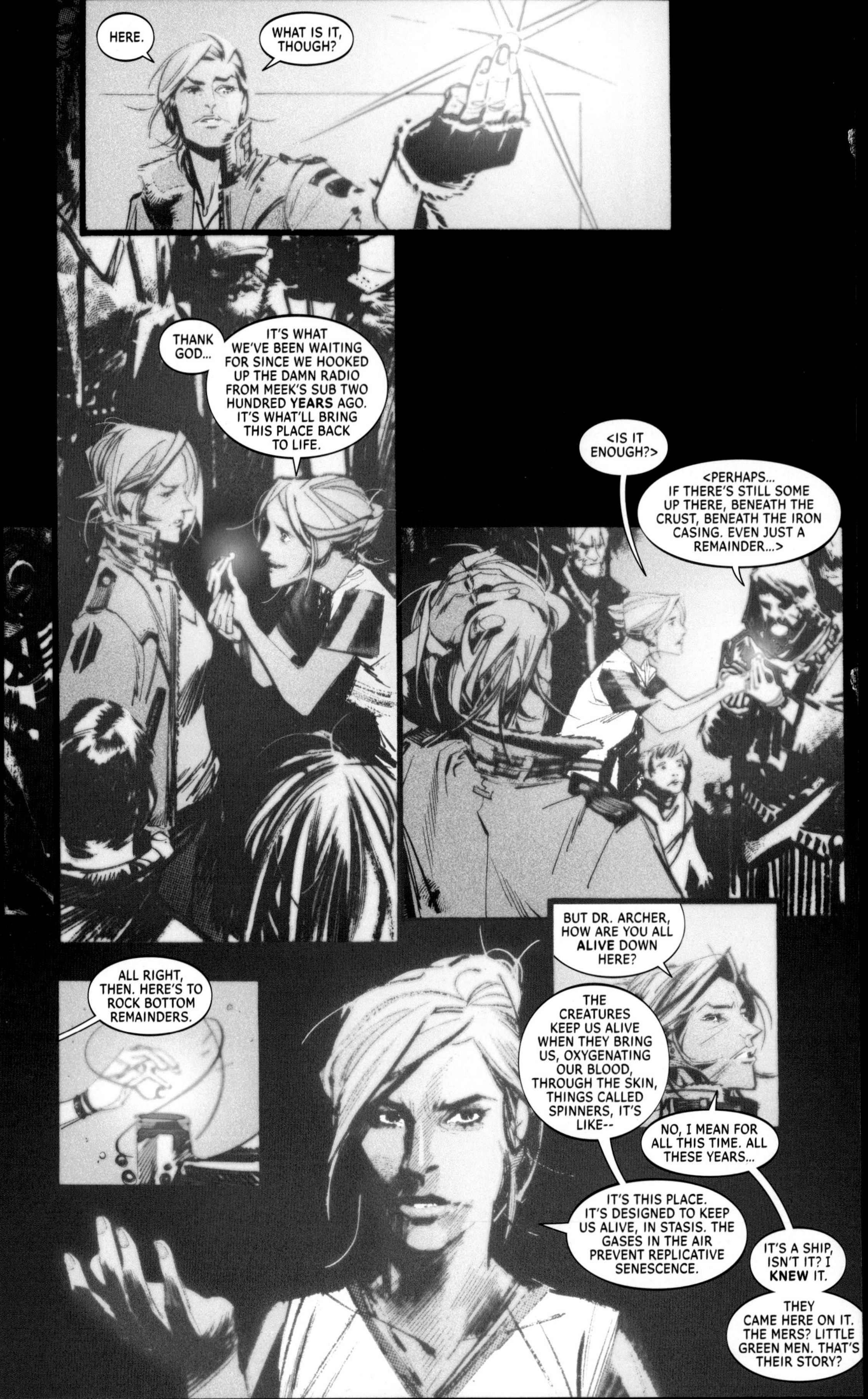
HERE.
WHAT IS IT, THOUGH?
THANK GOD...
IT'S WHAT WE'VE BEEN WAITING FOR SINCE WE HOOKED UP THE DAMN RADIO FROM MEEK'S SUB TWO HUNDRED **YEARS** AGO. IT'S WHAT'LL BRING THIS PLACE BACK TO LIFE.
<IS IT ENOUGH?>
<PERHAPS... IF THERE'S STILL SOME UP THERE, BENEATH THE CRUST, BENEATH THE IRON CASING. EVEN JUST A REMAINDER...>
ALL RIGHT, THEN. HERE'S TO ROCK BOTTOM REMAINDERS.
BUT DR. ARCHER, HOW ARE YOU ALL **ALIVE** DOWN HERE?
THE CREATURES KEEP US ALIVE WHEN THEY BRING US, OXYGENATING OUR BLOOD, THROUGH THE SKIN, THINGS CALLED SPINNERS, IT'S LIKE--
NO, I MEAN FOR ALL THIS TIME. ALL THESE YEARS...
IT'S THIS PLACE. IT'S DESIGNED TO KEEP US ALIVE, IN STASIS. THE GASES IN THE AIR PREVENT REPLICATIVE SENESCENCE.
IT'S A SHIP, ISN'T IT? I **KNEW** IT.
THEY CAME HERE ON IT. THE MERS? LITTLE GREEN MEN. THAT'S THEIR STORY?

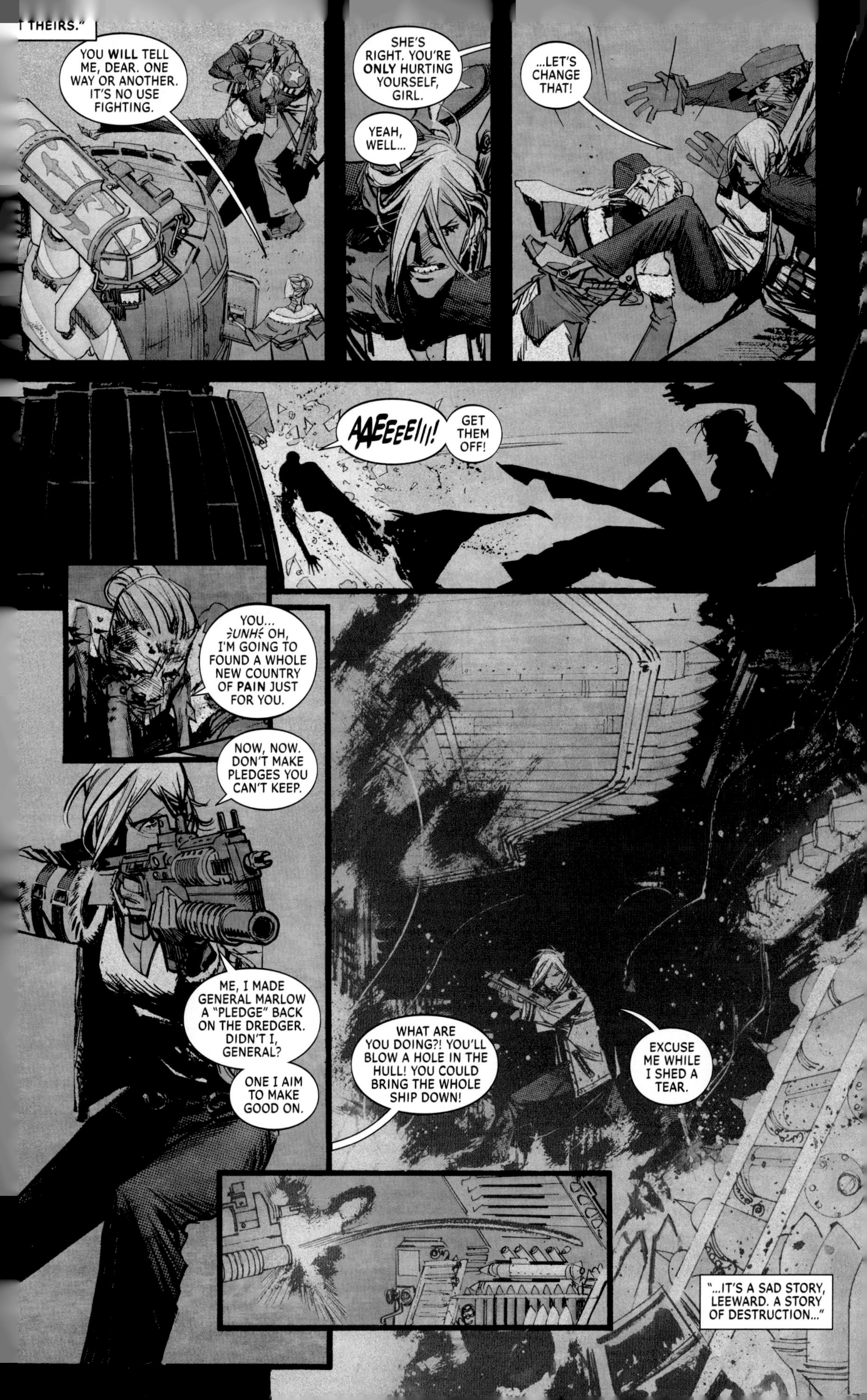
T THEIRS."
YOU WILL TELL ME, DEAR. ONE WAY OR ANOTHER. IT'S NO USE FIGHTING.
SHE'S RIGHT. YOU'RE ONLY HURTING YOURSELF, GIRL.
YEAH, WELL...
...LET'S CHANGE THAT!
AAEEEE!!!!
GET THEM OFF!
YOU... UNH OH, I'M GOING TO FOUND A WHOLE NEW COUNTRY OF PAIN JUST FOR YOU.
NOW, NOW. DON'T MAKE PLEDGES YOU CAN'T KEEP.
ME, I MADE GENERAL MARLOW A "PLEDGE" BACK ON THE DREDGER. DIDN'T I, GENERAL?
ONE I AIM TO MAKE GOOD ON.
WHAT ARE YOU DOING?! YOU'LL BLOW A HOLE IN THE HULL! YOU COULD BRING THE WHOLE SHIP DOWN!
EXCUSE ME WHILE I SHED A TEAR.
"...IT'S A SAD STORY, LEEWARD. A STORY OF DESTRUCTION..."

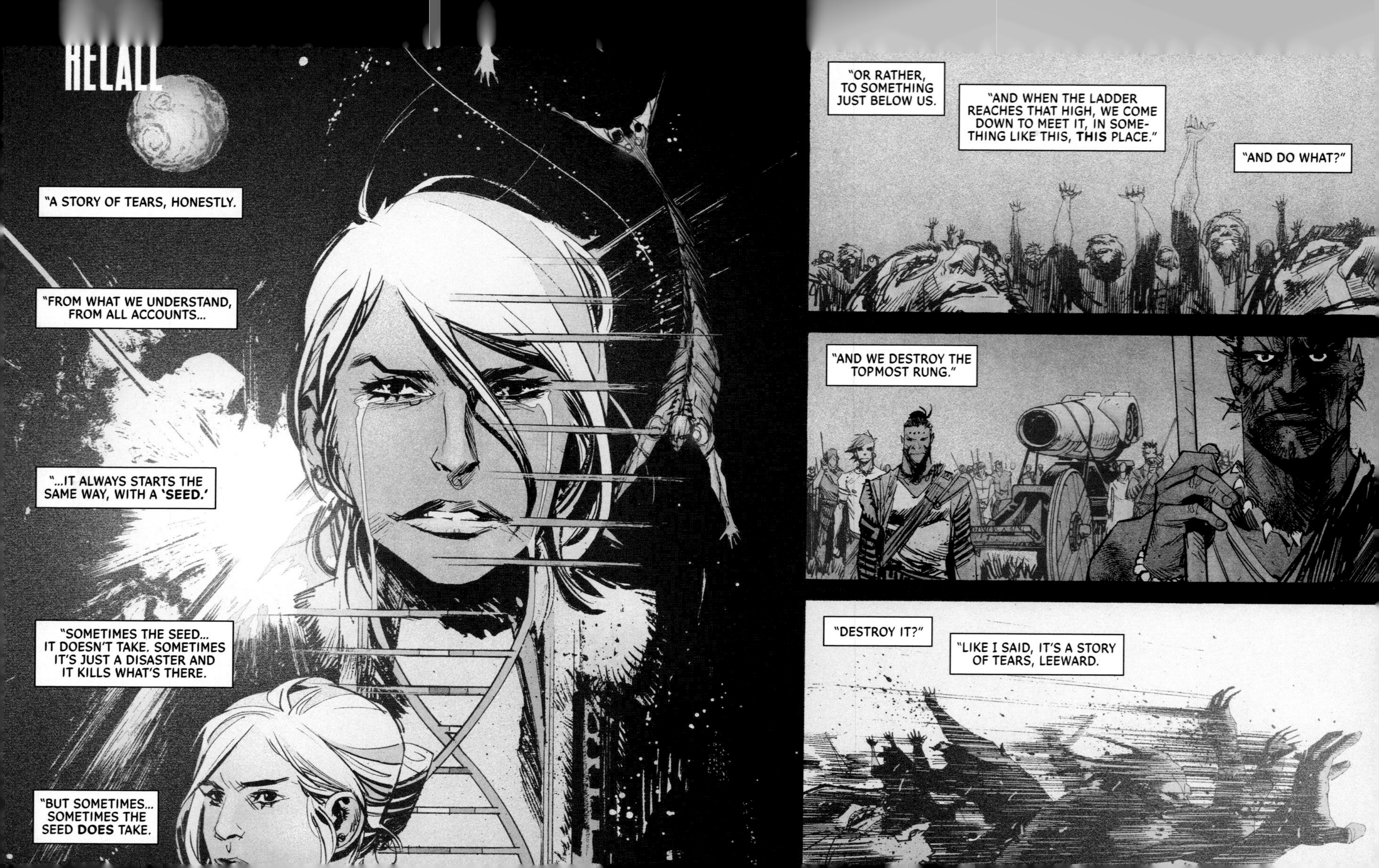
"A STORY OF TEARS, HONESTLY.
"FROM WHAT WE UNDERSTAND, FROM ALL ACCOUNTS...
"...IT ALWAYS STARTS THE SAME WAY, WITH A **'SEED.'**
"SOMETIMES THE SEED... IT DOESN'T TAKE. SOMETIMES IT'S JUST A DISASTER AND IT KILLS WHAT'S THERE.
"BUT SOMETIMES... SOMETIMES THE SEED **DOES** TAKE.
"OR RATHER, TO SOMETHING JUST BELOW US.
"AND WHEN THE LADDER REACHES THAT HIGH, WE COME DOWN TO MEET IT, IN SOMETHING LIKE THIS, **THIS** PLACE."
"AND DO WHAT?"
"AND WE DESTROY THE TOPMOST RUNG."
"DESTROY IT?"
"LIKE I SAID, IT'S A STORY OF TEARS, LEEWARD.

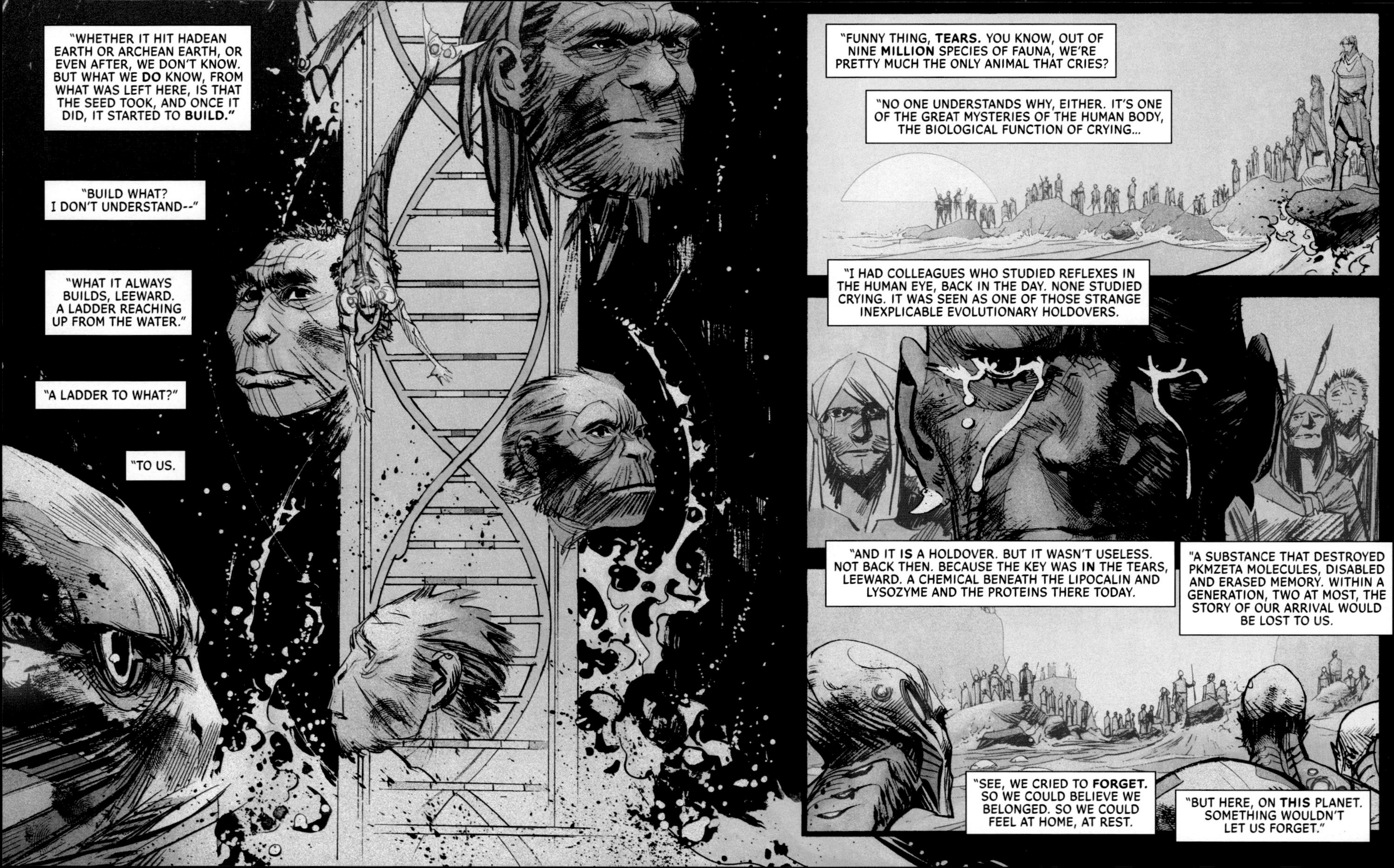
"WHETHER IT HIT HADEAN EARTH OR ARCHEAN EARTH, OR EVEN AFTER, WE DON'T KNOW. BUT WHAT WE **DO** KNOW, FROM WHAT WAS LEFT HERE, IS THAT THE SEED TOOK, AND ONCE IT DID, IT STARTED TO **BUILD.**"
"BUILD WHAT? I DON'T UNDERSTAND--"
"WHAT IT ALWAYS BUILDS, LEEWARD. A LADDER REACHING UP FROM THE WATER."
"A LADDER TO WHAT?"
"TO US.
"FUNNY THING, **TEARS.** YOU KNOW, OUT OF NINE **MILLION** SPECIES OF FAUNA, WE'RE PRETTY MUCH THE ONLY ANIMAL THAT CRIES?
"NO ONE UNDERSTANDS WHY, EITHER. IT'S ONE OF THE GREAT MYSTERIES OF THE HUMAN BODY, THE BIOLOGICAL FUNCTION OF CRYING...
"I HAD COLLEAGUES WHO STUDIED REFLEXES IN THE HUMAN EYE, BACK IN THE DAY. NONE STUDIED CRYING. IT WAS SEEN AS ONE OF THOSE STRANGE INEXPLICABLE EVOLUTIONARY HOLDOVERS.
"AND IT **IS** A HOLDOVER. BUT IT WASN'T USELESS. NOT BACK THEN. BECAUSE THE KEY WAS **IN** THE TEARS, LEEWARD. A CHEMICAL BENEATH THE LIPOCALIN AND LYSOZYME AND THE PROTEINS THERE TODAY.
"A SUBSTANCE THAT DESTROYED PKMZETA MOLECULES, DISABLED AND ERASED MEMORY. WITHIN A GENERATION, TWO AT MOST, THE STORY OF OUR ARRIVAL WOULD BE LOST TO US.
"SEE, WE CRIED TO **FORGET.** SO WE COULD BELIEVE WE BELONGED. SO WE COULD FEEL AT HOME, AT REST.
"BUT HERE, ON **THIS** PLANET. SOMETHING WOULDN'T LET US FORGET."

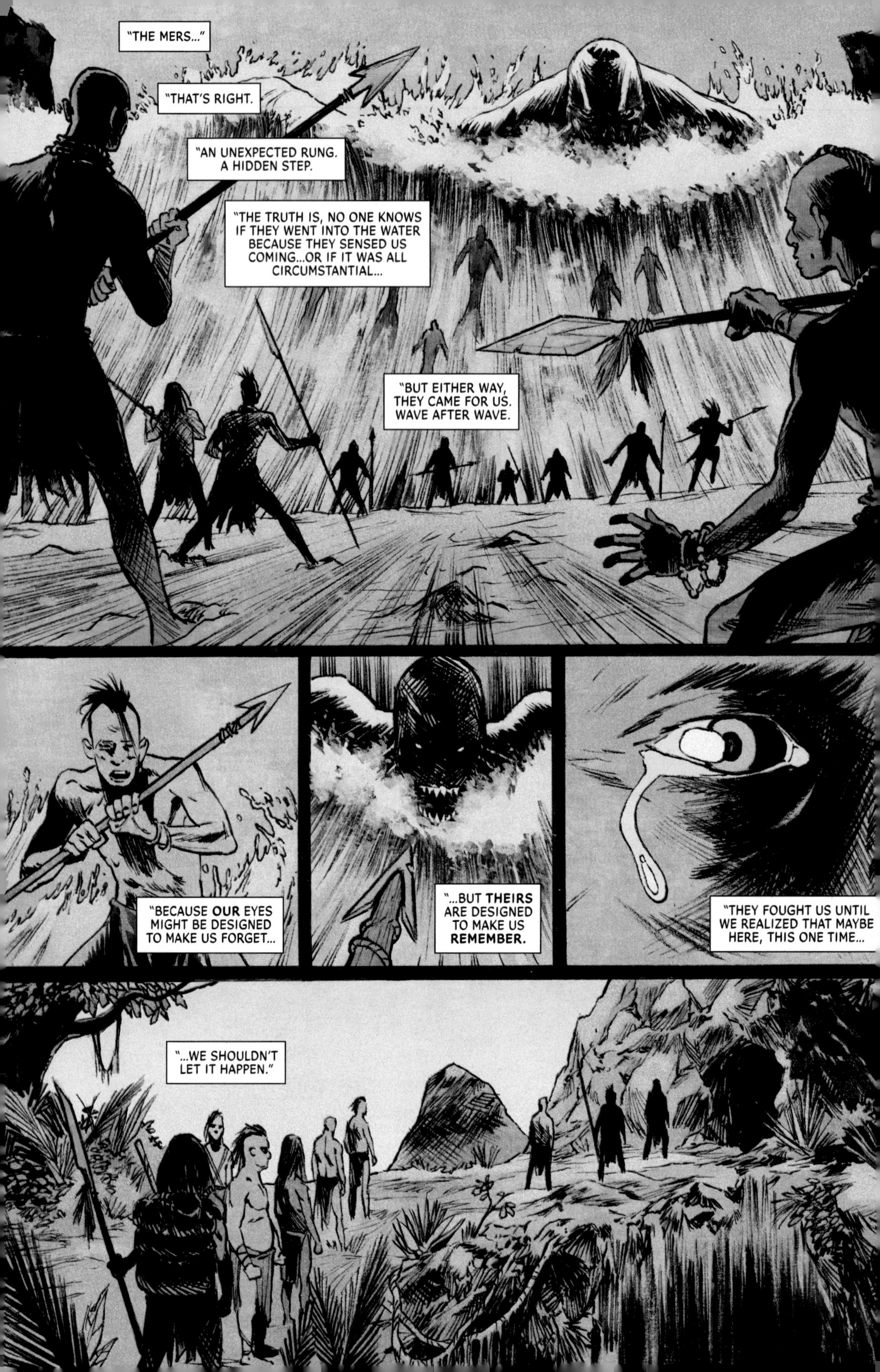
"THE MERS..."
"THAT'S RIGHT.
"AN UNEXPECTED RUNG. A HIDDEN STEP.
"THE TRUTH IS, NO ONE KNOWS IF THEY WENT INTO THE WATER BECAUSE THEY SENSED US COMING...OR IF IT WAS ALL CIRCUMSTANTIAL...
"BUT EITHER WAY, THEY CAME FOR US. WAVE AFTER WAVE.
"BECAUSE **OUR** EYES MIGHT BE DESIGNED TO MAKE US FORGET...
"...BUT **THEIRS** ARE DESIGNED TO MAKE US **REMEMBER.**
"THEY FOUGHT US UNTIL WE REALIZED THAT MAYBE HERE, THIS ONE TIME...
"...WE SHOULDN'T LET IT HAPPEN."

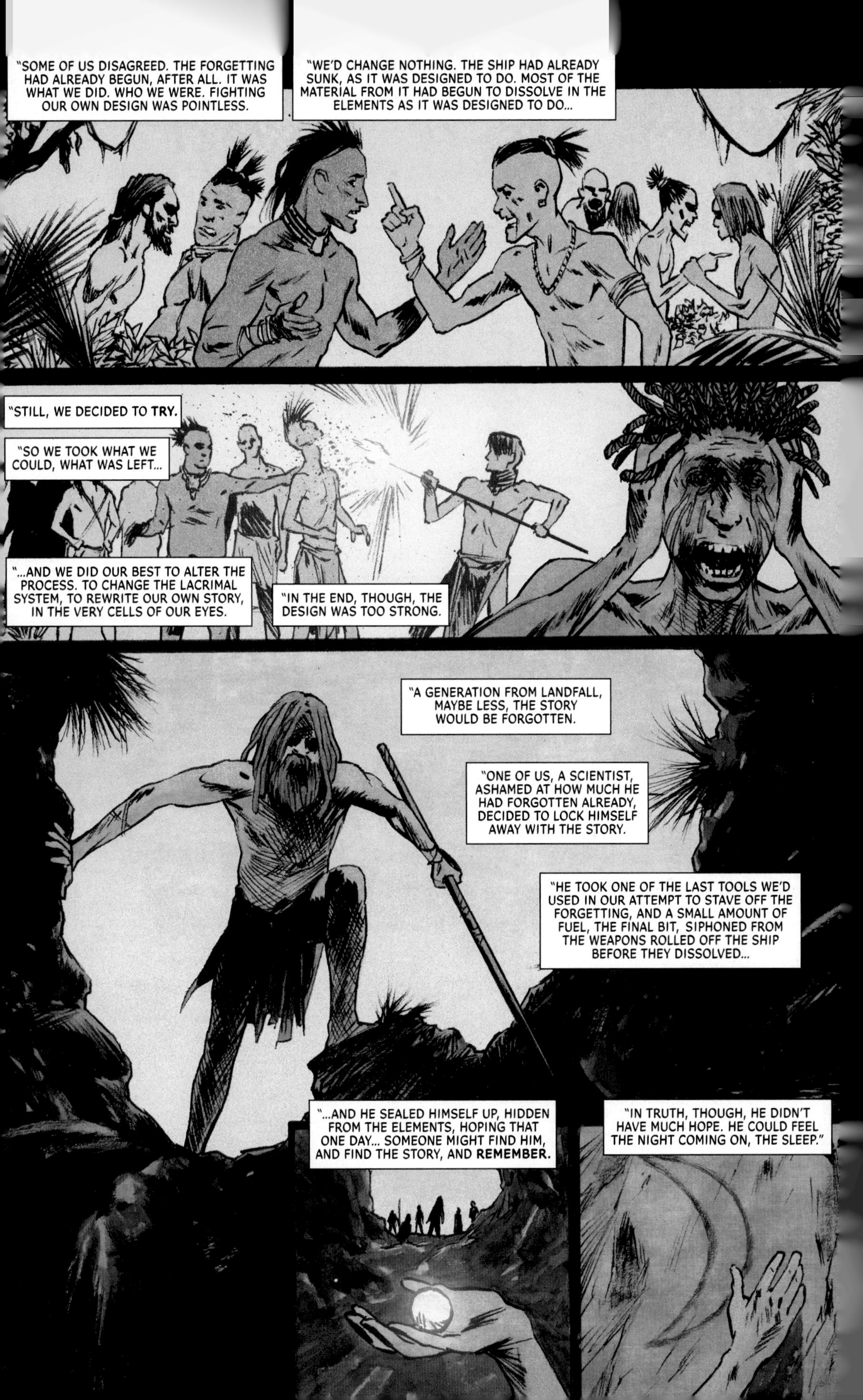
"SOME OF US DISAGREED. THE FORGETTING HAD ALREADY BEGUN, AFTER ALL. IT WAS WHAT WE DID. WHO WE WERE. FIGHTING OUR OWN DESIGN WAS POINTLESS.
"WE'D CHANGE NOTHING. THE SHIP HAD ALREADY SUNK, AS IT WAS DESIGNED TO DO. MOST OF THE MATERIAL FROM IT HAD BEGUN TO DISSOLVE IN THE ELEMENTS AS IT WAS DESIGNED TO DO...
"STILL, WE DECIDED TO **TRY.**
"SO WE TOOK WHAT WE COULD, WHAT WAS LEFT...
"...AND WE DID OUR BEST TO ALTER THE PROCESS. TO CHANGE THE LACRIMAL SYSTEM, TO REWRITE OUR OWN STORY, IN THE VERY CELLS OF OUR EYES.
"IN THE END, THOUGH, THE DESIGN WAS TOO STRONG.
"A GENERATION FROM LANDFALL, MAYBE LESS, THE STORY WOULD BE FORGOTTEN.
"ONE OF US, A SCIENTIST, ASHAMED AT HOW MUCH HE HAD FORGOTTEN ALREADY, DECIDED TO LOCK HIMSELF AWAY WITH THE STORY.
"HE TOOK ONE OF THE LAST TOOLS WE'D USED IN OUR ATTEMPT TO STAVE OFF THE FORGETTING, AND A SMALL AMOUNT OF FUEL, THE FINAL BIT, SIPHONED FROM THE WEAPONS ROLLED OFF THE SHIP BEFORE THEY DISSOLVED...
"...AND HE SEALED HIMSELF UP, HIDDEN FROM THE ELEMENTS, HOPING THAT ONE DAY... SOMEONE MIGHT FIND HIM, AND FIND THE STORY, AND **REMEMBER.**
"IN TRUTH, THOUGH, HE DIDN'T HAVE MUCH HOPE. HE COULD FEEL THE NIGHT COMING ON, THE SLEEP."

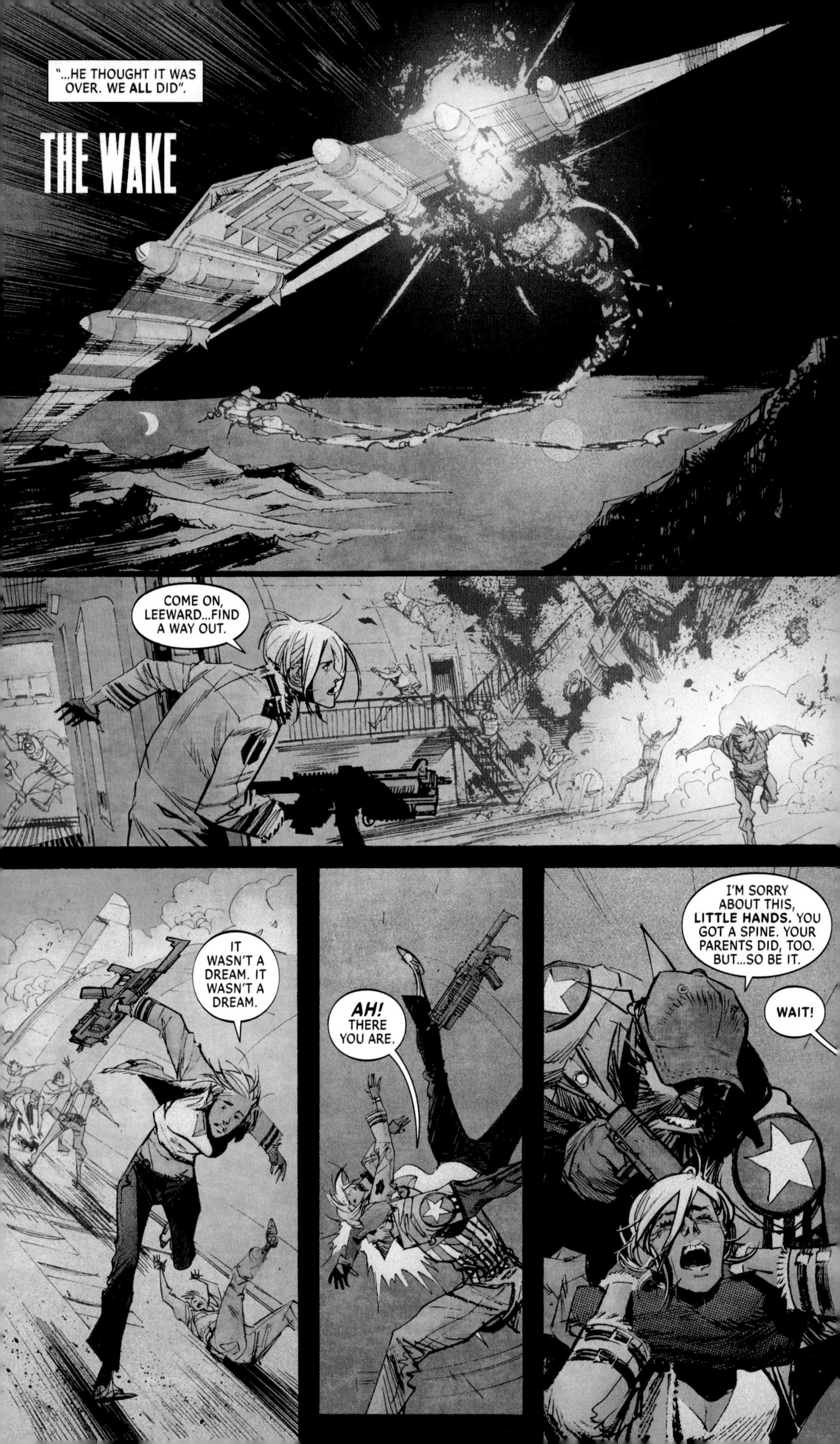
"...HE THOUGHT IT WAS OVER. WE ALL DID".
THE WAKE
COME ON, LEEWARD...FIND A WAY OUT.
IT WASN'T A DREAM. IT WASN'T A DREAM.
AH! THERE YOU ARE.
I'M SORRY ABOUT THIS, LITTLE HANDS. YOU GOT A SPINE. YOUR PARENTS DID, TOO. BUT...SO BE IT.
WAIT!

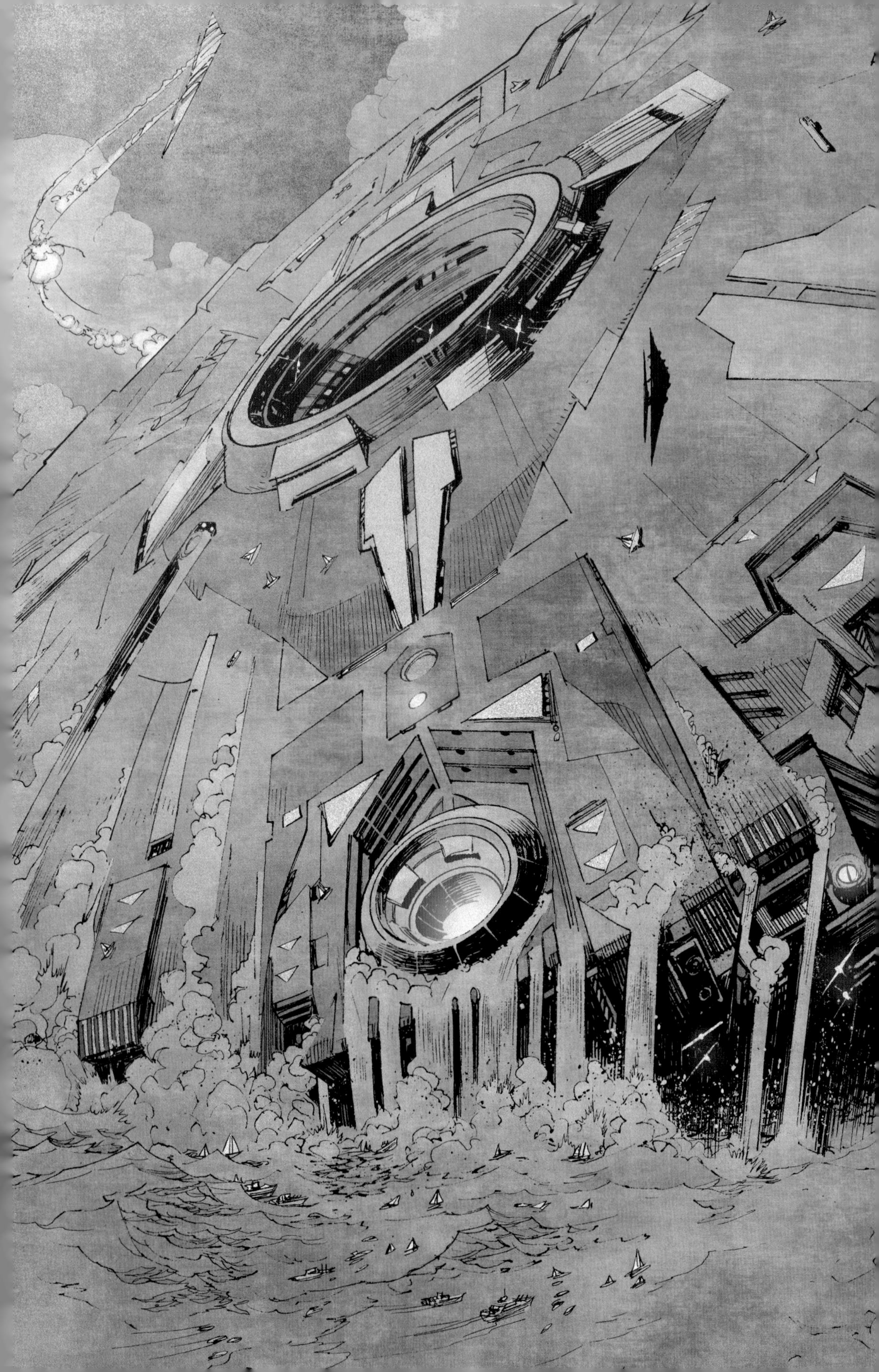

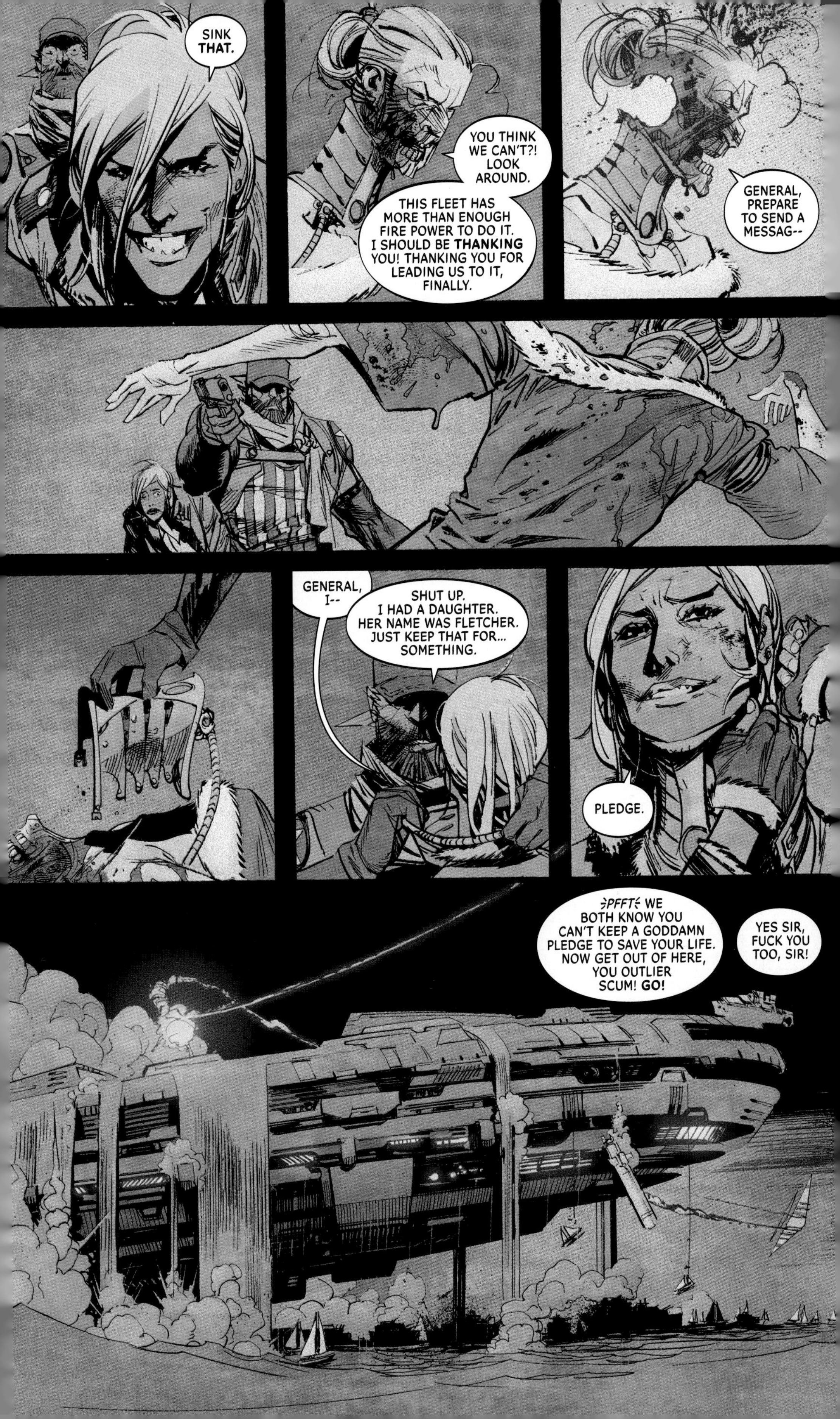
SINK THAT.
YOU THINK WE CAN'T?! LOOK AROUND.
THIS FLEET HAS MORE THAN ENOUGH FIRE POWER TO DO IT. I SHOULD BE THANKING YOU! THANKING YOU FOR LEADING US TO IT, FINALLY.
GENERAL, PREPARE TO SEND A MESSAG--
GENERAL, I--
SHUT UP. I HAD A DAUGHTER. HER NAME WAS FLETCHER. JUST KEEP THAT FOR... SOMETHING.
PLEDGE.
PFFT WE BOTH KNOW YOU CAN'T KEEP A GODDAMN PLEDGE TO SAVE YOUR LIFE. NOW GET OUT OF HERE, YOU OUTLIER SCUM! GO!
YES SIR, FUCK YOU TOO, SIR!

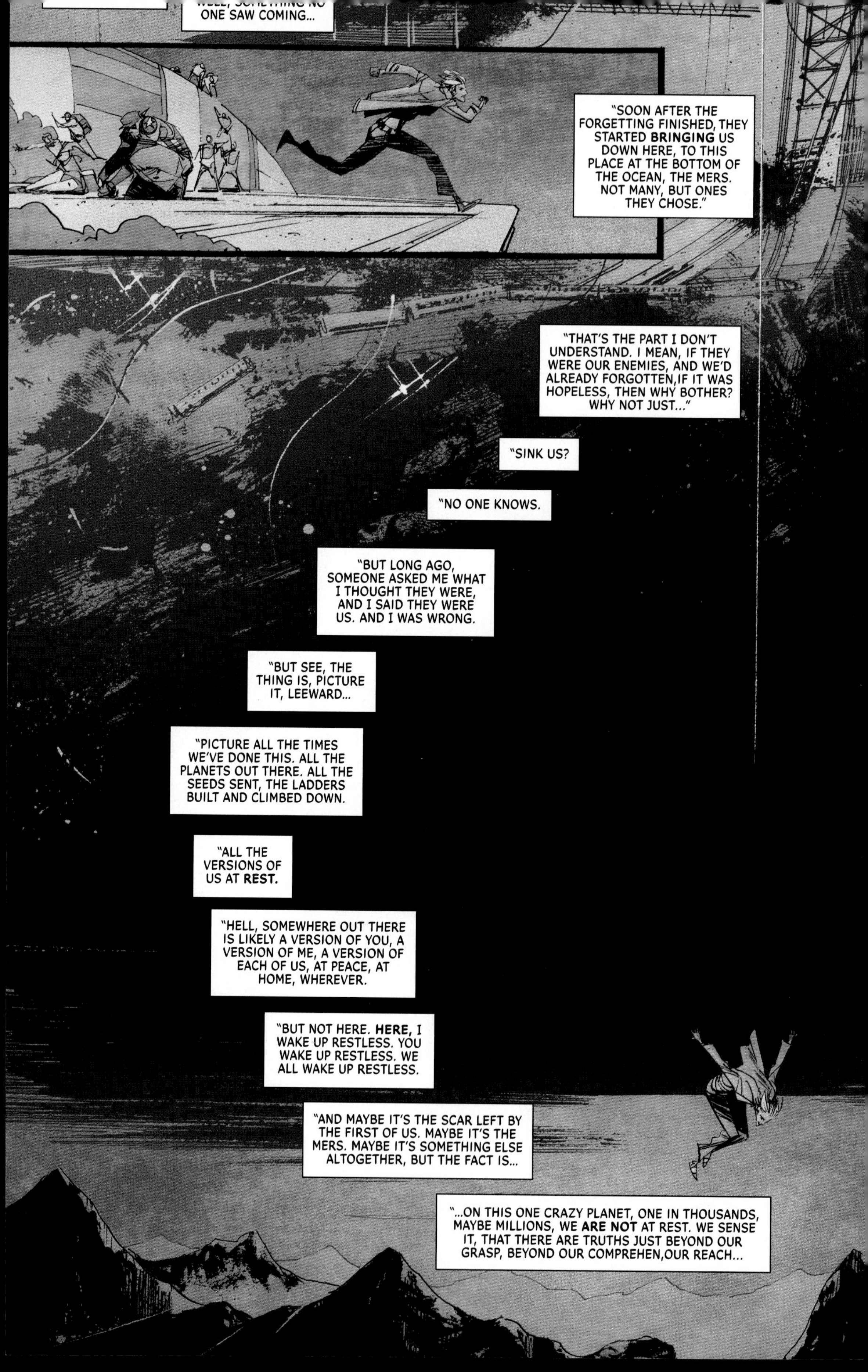
WELL, SOMETHING NO ONE SAW COMING...
"SOON AFTER THE FORGETTING FINISHED, THEY STARTED BRINGING US DOWN HERE, TO THIS PLACE AT THE BOTTOM OF THE OCEAN, THE MERS. NOT MANY, BUT ONES THEY CHOSE."
"THAT'S THE PART I DON'T UNDERSTAND. I MEAN, IF THEY WERE OUR ENEMIES, AND WE'D ALREADY FORGOTTEN, IF IT WAS HOPELESS, THEN WHY BOTHER? WHY NOT JUST..."
"SINK US?
"NO ONE KNOWS.
"BUT LONG AGO, SOMEONE ASKED ME WHAT I THOUGHT THEY WERE, AND I SAID THEY WERE US. AND I WAS WRONG.
"BUT SEE, THE THING IS, PICTURE IT, LEEWARD...
"PICTURE ALL THE TIMES WE'VE DONE THIS. ALL THE PLANETS OUT THERE. ALL THE SEEDS SENT, THE LADDERS BUILT AND CLIMBED DOWN.
"ALL THE VERSIONS OF US AT REST.
"HELL, SOMEWHERE OUT THERE IS LIKELY A VERSION OF YOU, A VERSION OF ME, A VERSION OF EACH OF US, AT PEACE, AT HOME, WHEREVER.
"BUT NOT HERE. HERE, I WAKE UP RESTLESS. YOU WAKE UP RESTLESS. WE ALL WAKE UP RESTLESS.
"AND MAYBE IT'S THE SCAR LEFT BY THE FIRST OF US. MAYBE IT'S THE MERS. MAYBE IT'S SOMETHING ELSE ALTOGETHER, BUT THE FACT IS...
"...ON THIS ONE CRAZY PLANET, ONE IN THOUSANDS, MAYBE MILLIONS, WE ARE NOT AT REST. WE SENSE IT, THAT THERE ARE TRUTHS JUST BEYOND OUR GRASP, BEYOND OUR COMPREHEN,OUR REACH...

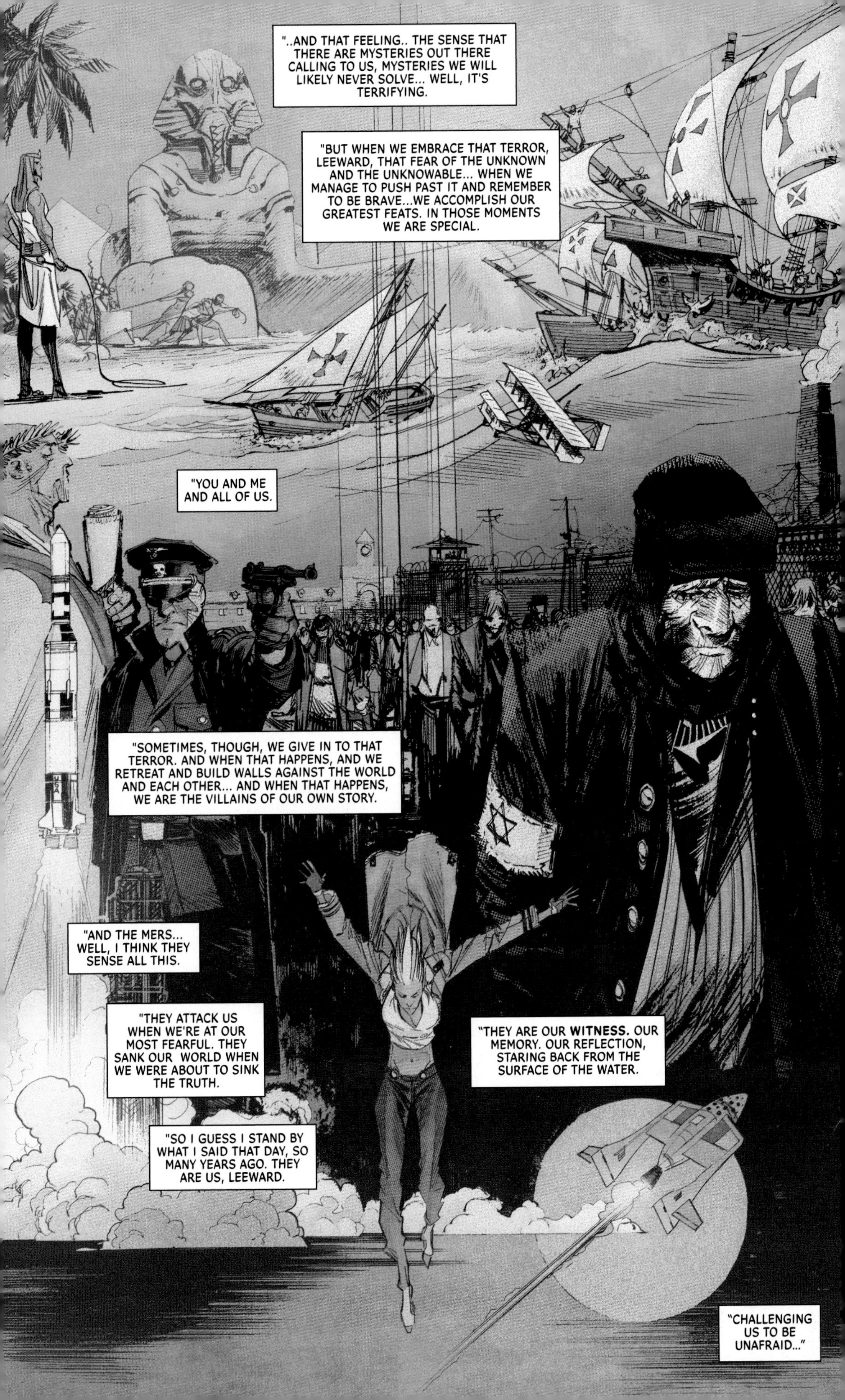
"..AND THAT FEELING.. THE SENSE THAT THERE ARE MYSTERIES OUT THERE CALLING TO US, MYSTERIES WE WILL LIKELY NEVER SOLVE... WELL, IT'S TERRIFYING.
"BUT WHEN WE EMBRACE THAT TERROR, LEEWARD, THAT FEAR OF THE UNKNOWN AND THE UNKNOWABLE... WHEN WE MANAGE TO PUSH PAST IT AND REMEMBER TO BE BRAVE...WE ACCOMPLISH OUR GREATEST FEATS. IN THOSE MOMENTS WE ARE SPECIAL.
"YOU AND ME AND ALL OF US.
"SOMETIMES, THOUGH, WE GIVE IN TO THAT TERROR. AND WHEN THAT HAPPENS, AND WE RETREAT AND BUILD WALLS AGAINST THE WORLD AND EACH OTHER... AND WHEN THAT HAPPENS, WE ARE THE VILLAINS OF OUR OWN STORY.
"AND THE MERS... WELL, I THINK THEY SENSE ALL THIS.
"THEY ATTACK US WHEN WE'RE AT OUR MOST FEARFUL. THEY SANK OUR WORLD WHEN WE WERE ABOUT TO SINK THE TRUTH.
"THEY ARE OUR **WITNESS.** OUR MEMORY. OUR REFLECTION, STARING BACK FROM THE SURFACE OF THE WATER.
"SO I GUESS I STAND BY WHAT I SAID THAT DAY, SO MANY YEARS AGO. THEY ARE US, LEEWARD.
"CHALLENGING US TO BE UNAFRAID..."

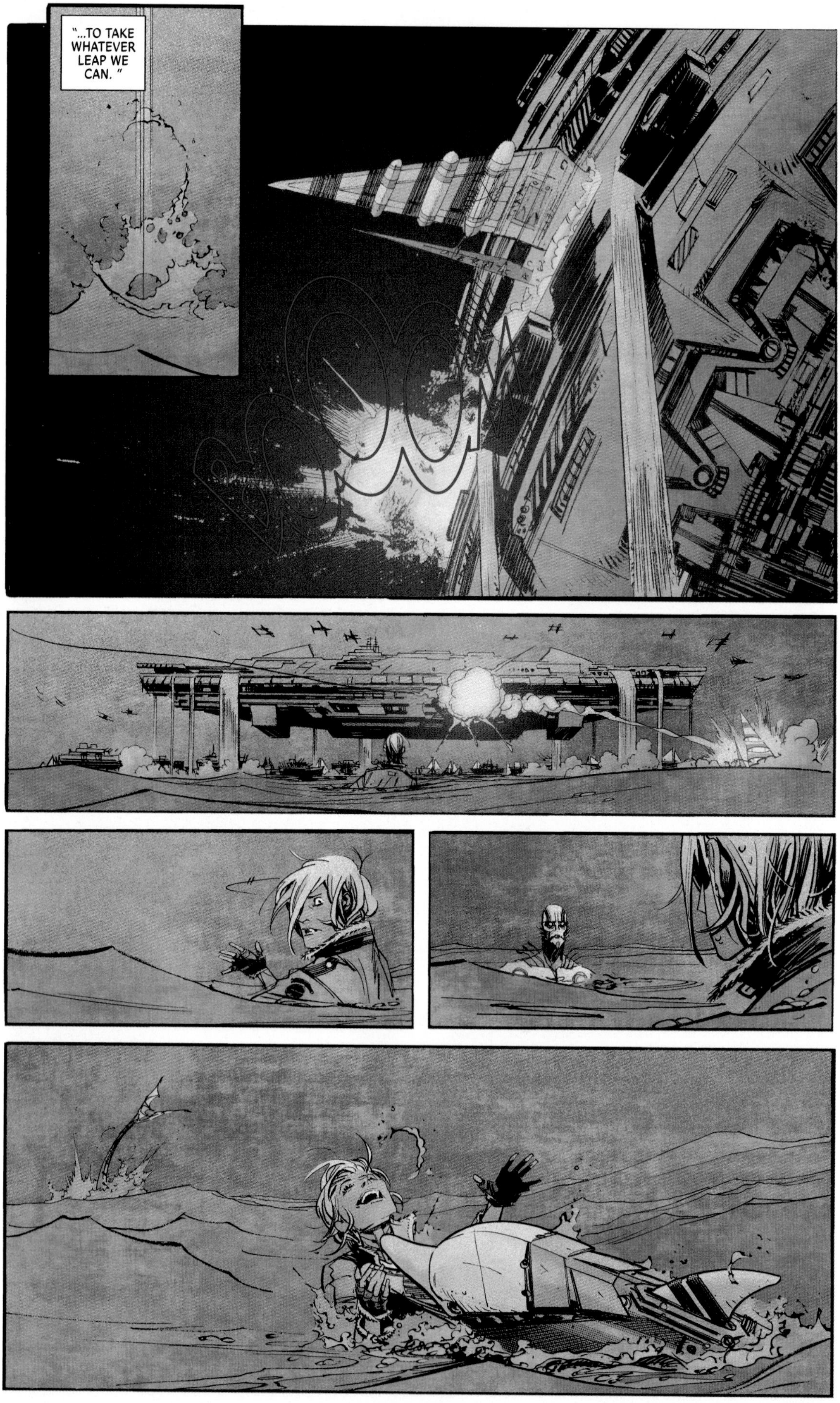
"...TO TAKE WHATEVER LEAP WE CAN."

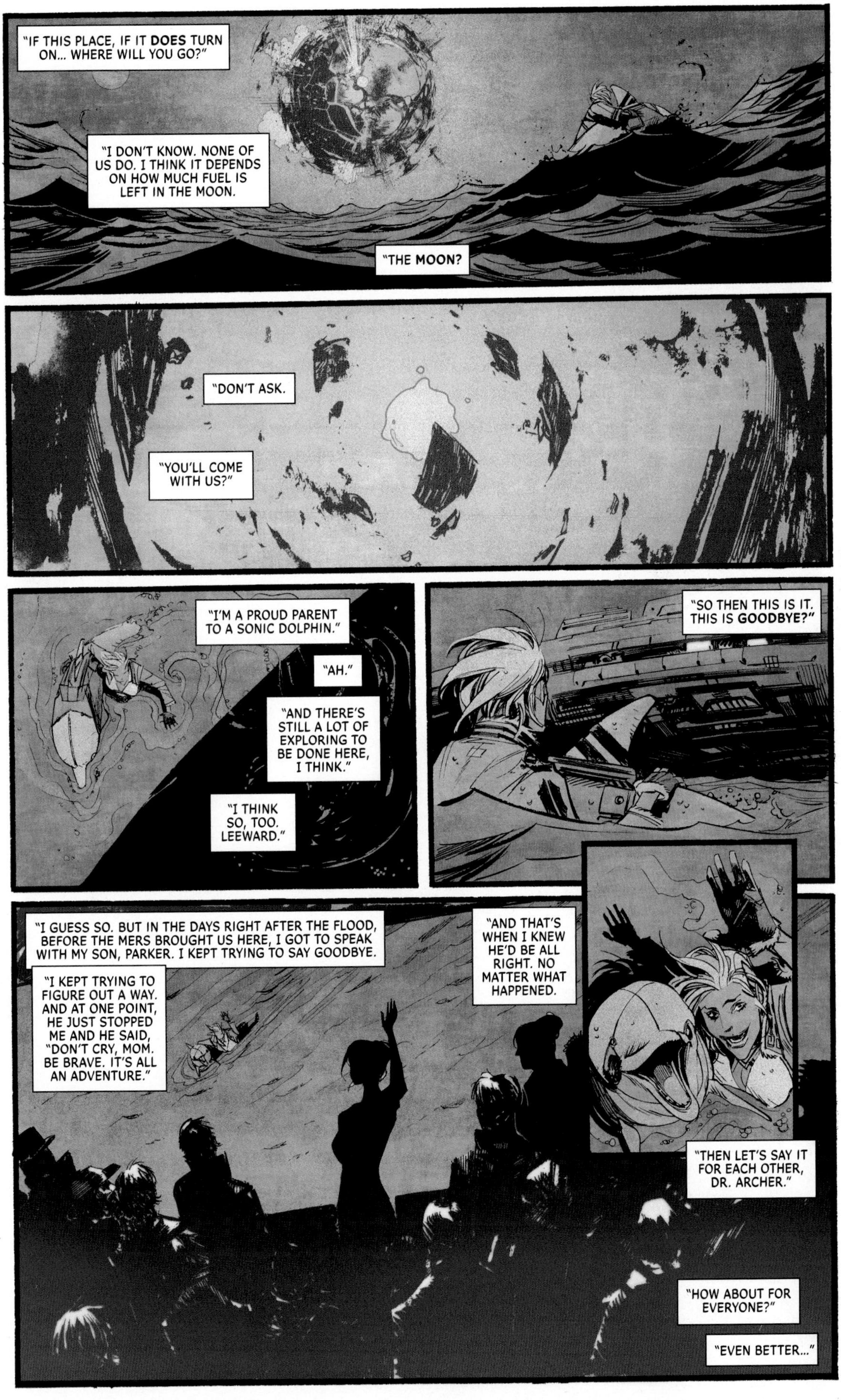
"IF THIS PLACE, IF IT DOES TURN ON... WHERE WILL YOU GO?"
"I DON'T KNOW. NONE OF US DO. I THINK IT DEPENDS ON HOW MUCH FUEL IS LEFT IN THE MOON.
"THE MOON?
"DON'T ASK.
"YOU'LL COME WITH US?"
"I'M A PROUD PARENT TO A SONIC DOLPHIN."
"AH."
"AND THERE'S STILL A LOT OF EXPLORING TO BE DONE HERE, I THINK."
"I THINK SO, TOO. LEEWARD."
"SO THEN THIS IS IT. THIS IS GOODBYE?"
"I GUESS SO. BUT IN THE DAYS RIGHT AFTER THE FLOOD, BEFORE THE MERS BROUGHT US HERE, I GOT TO SPEAK WITH MY SON, PARKER. I KEPT TRYING TO SAY GOODBYE.
"I KEPT TRYING TO FIGURE OUT A WAY. AND AT ONE POINT, HE JUST STOPPED ME AND HE SAID, "DON'T CRY, MOM. BE BRAVE. IT'S ALL AN ADVENTURE."
"AND THAT'S WHEN I KNEW HE'D BE ALL RIGHT. NO MATTER WHAT HAPPENED.
"THEN LET'S SAY IT FOR EACH OTHER, DR. ARCHER."
"HOW ABOUT FOR EVERYONE?"
"EVEN BETTER..."

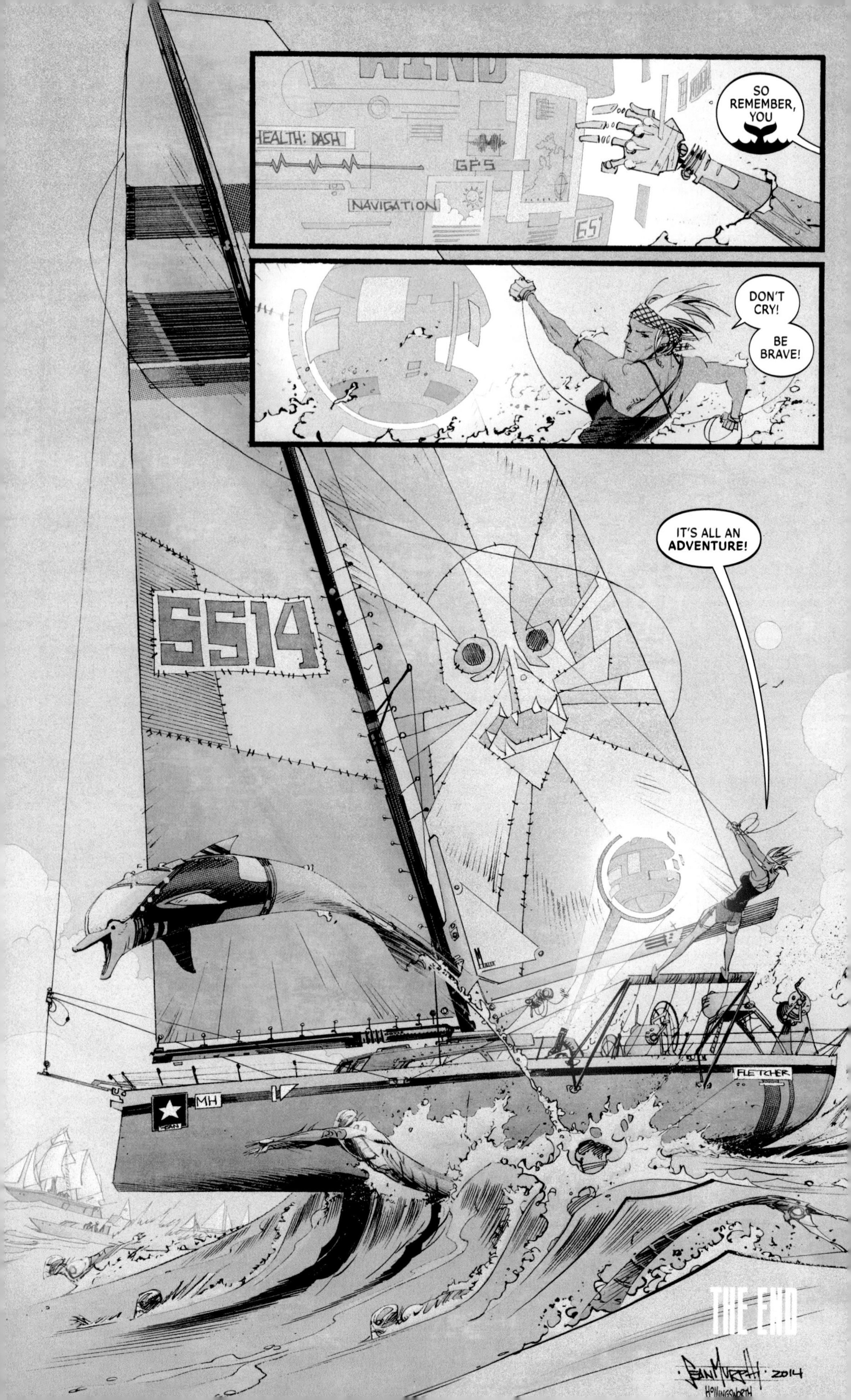
WIND
HEALTH: DASH
GPS
NAVIGATION
65°
SO REMEMBER, YOU
DON'T CRY!
BE BRAVE!
IT'S ALL AN ADVENTURE!
SS14
MH
FLETCHER
THE END
SEAN MURPHY 2014
HOLLINGSWORTH

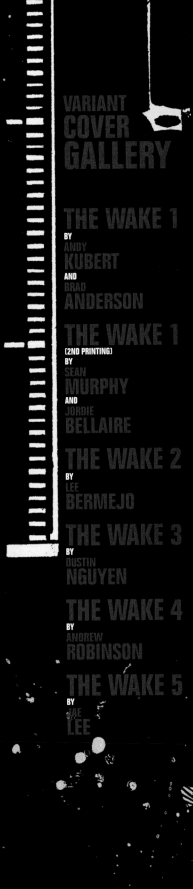

VARIANT
COVER
GALLERY

THE WAKE 1
BY
ANDY
KUBERT
AND
BRAD
ANDERSON

THE WAKE 1
(2ND PRINTING)
BY
SEAN
MURPHY
AND
JORDIE
BELLAIRE

THE WAKE 2
BY
LEE
BERMEJO

THE WAKE 3
BY
DUSTIN
NGUYEN

THE WAKE 4
BY
ANDREW
ROBINSON

THE WAKE 5
BY
JAE
LEE

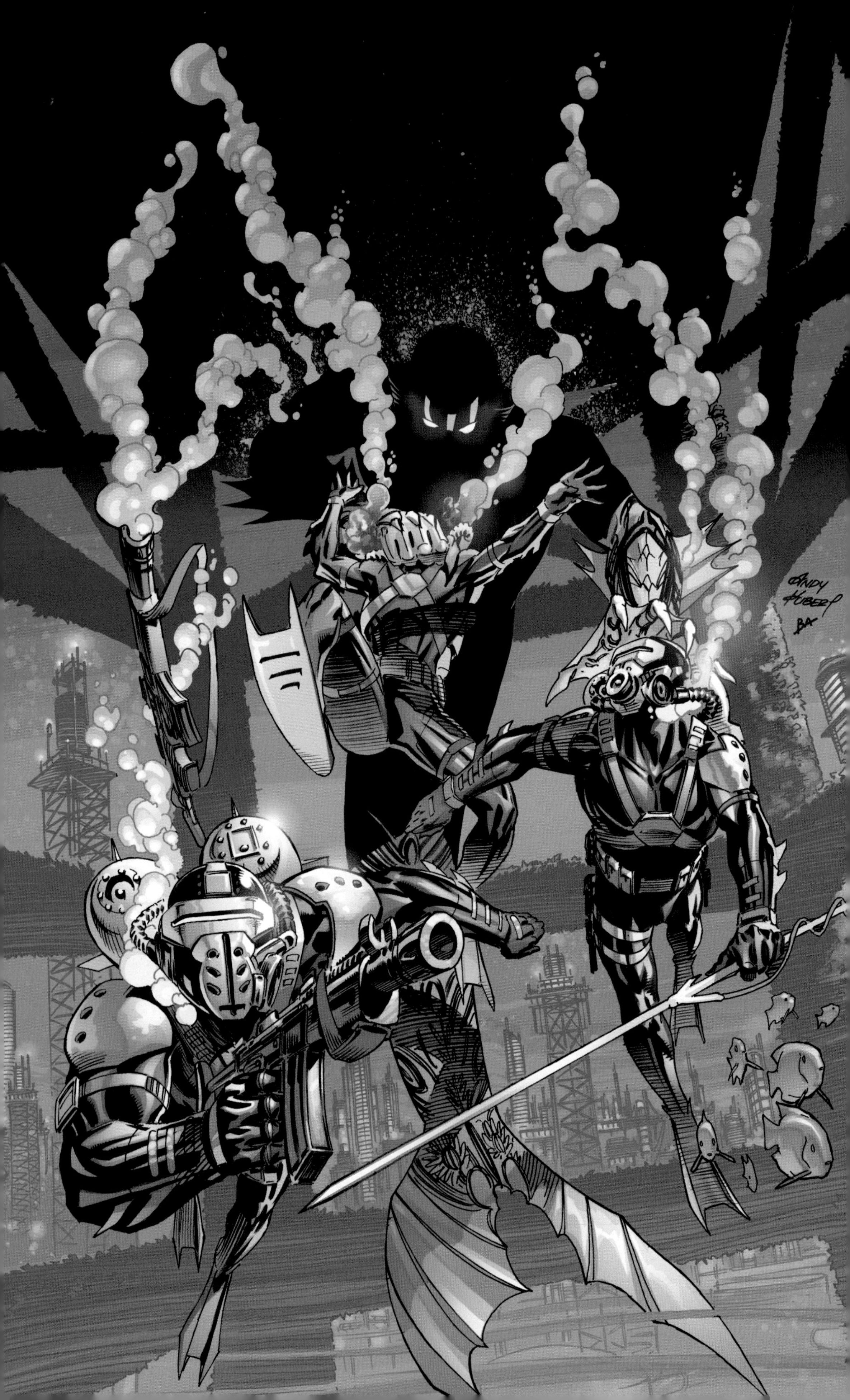
ANDY KUBERT
BA

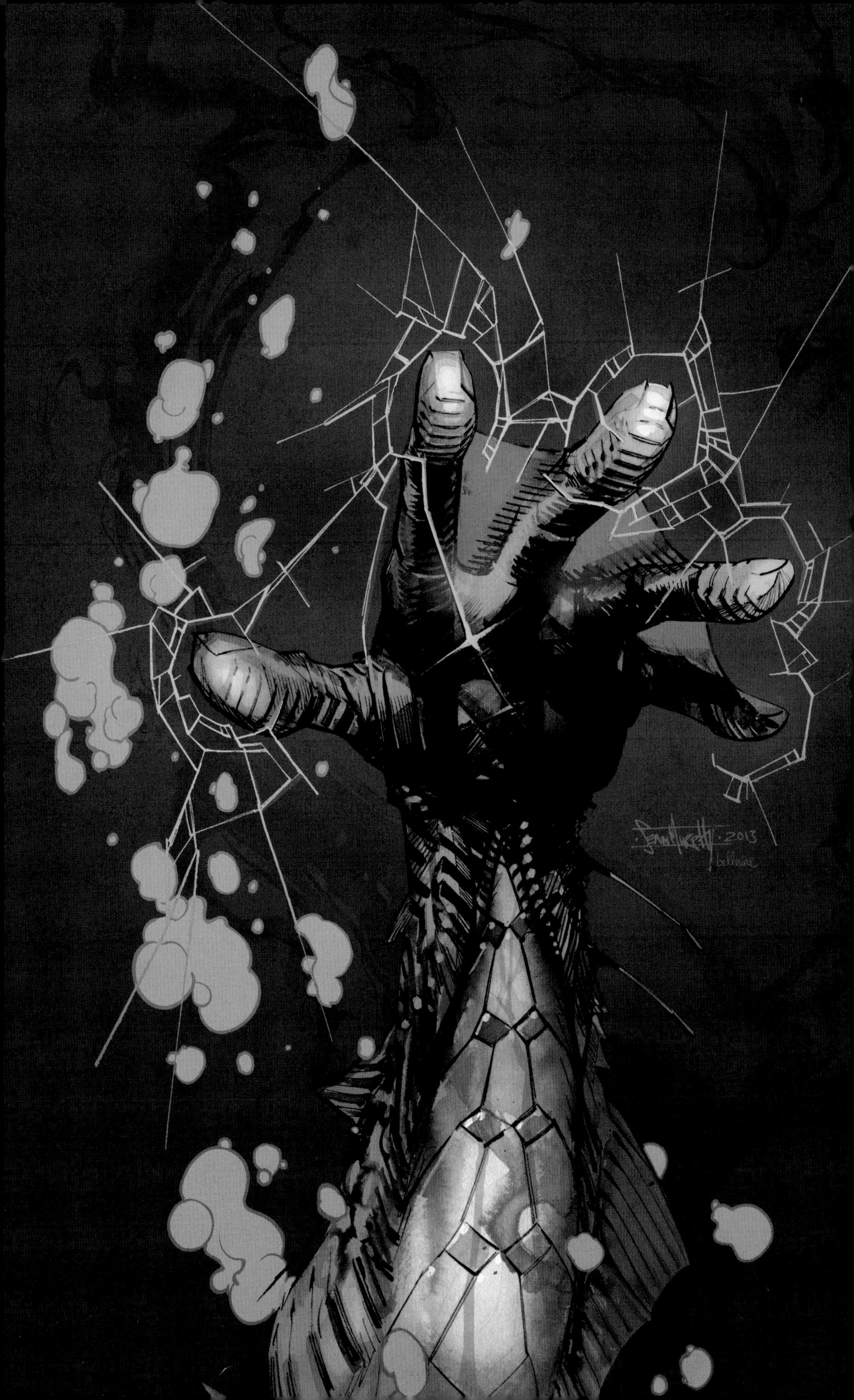

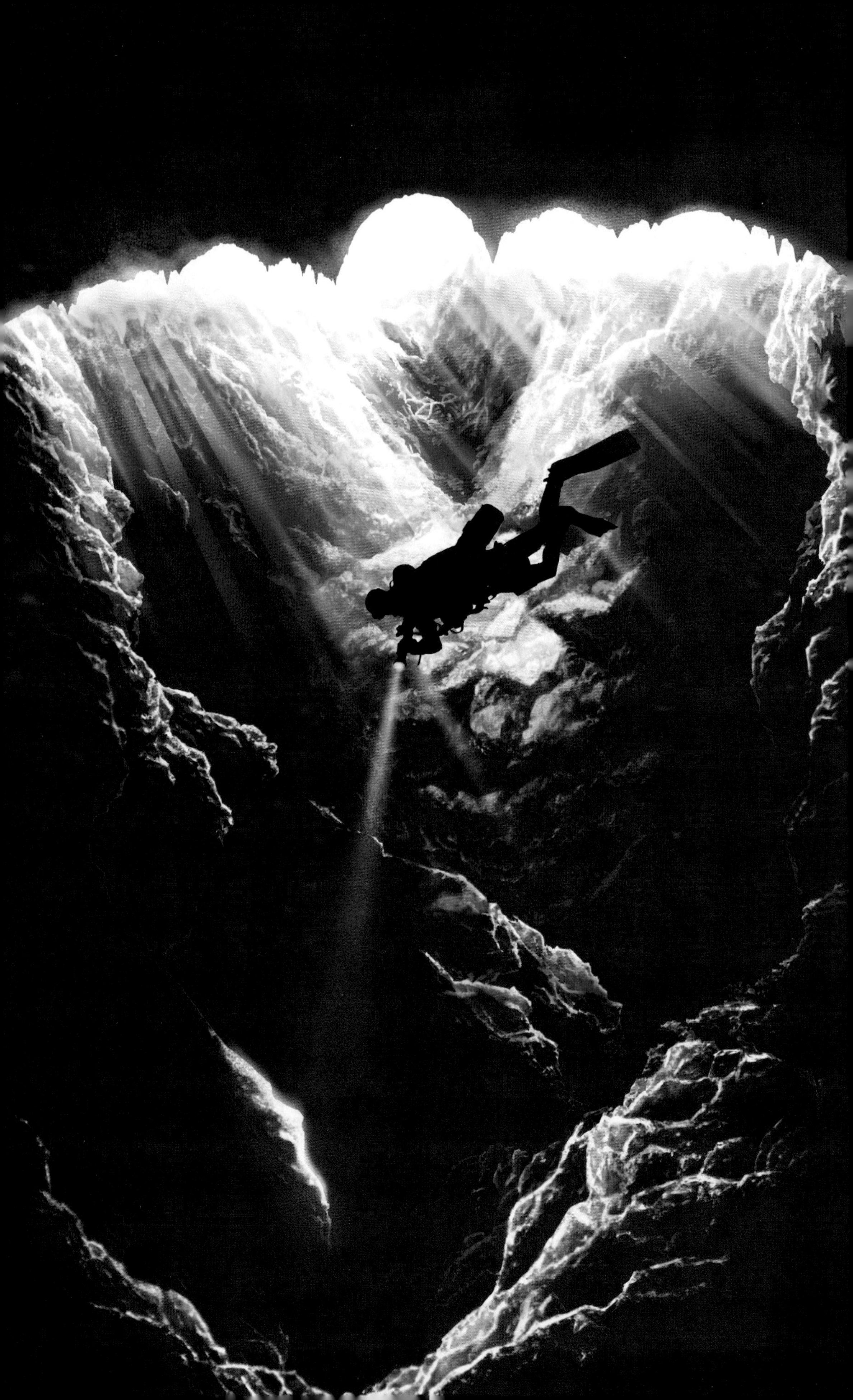

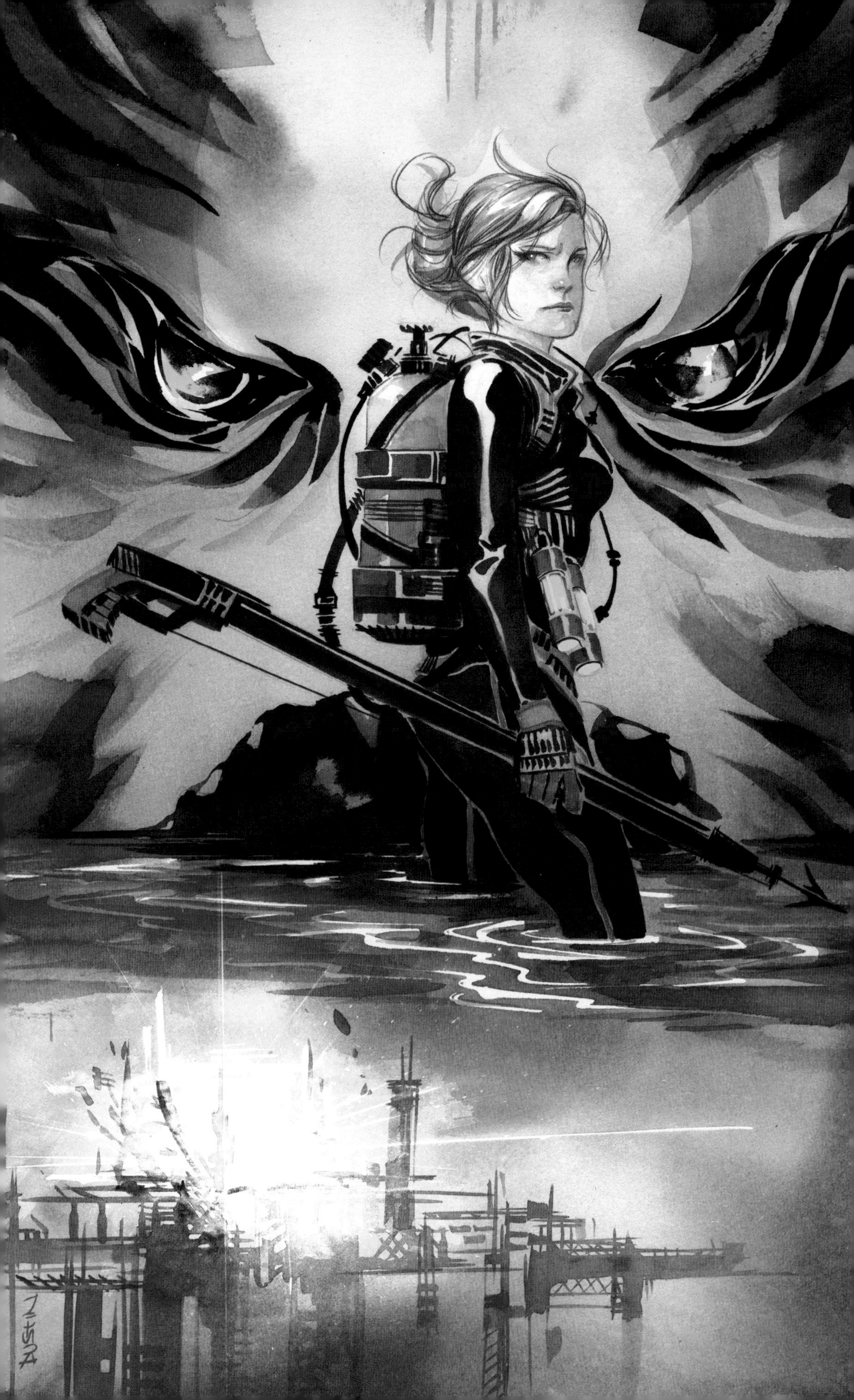

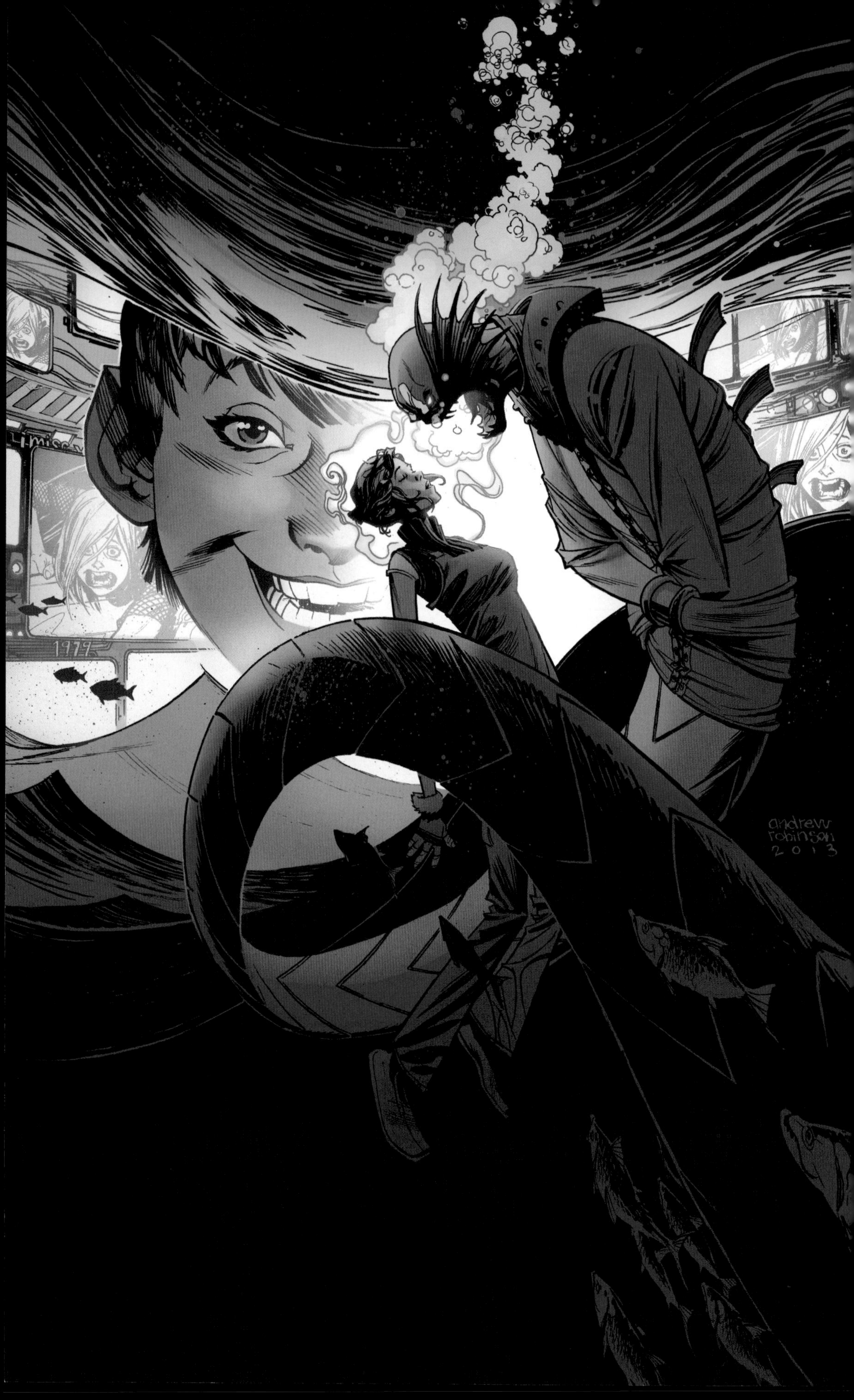
1979
andrew
robinson
2013

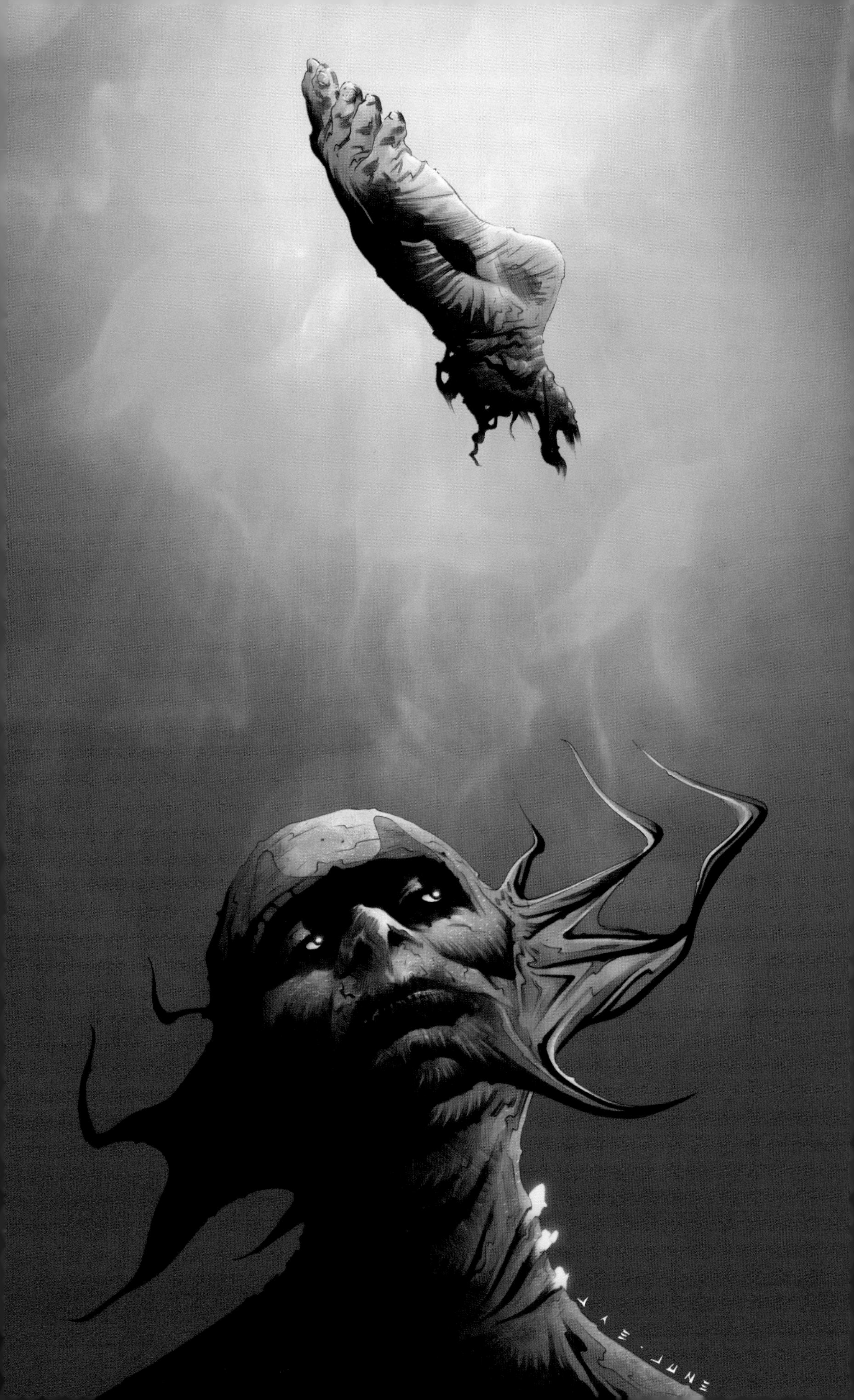

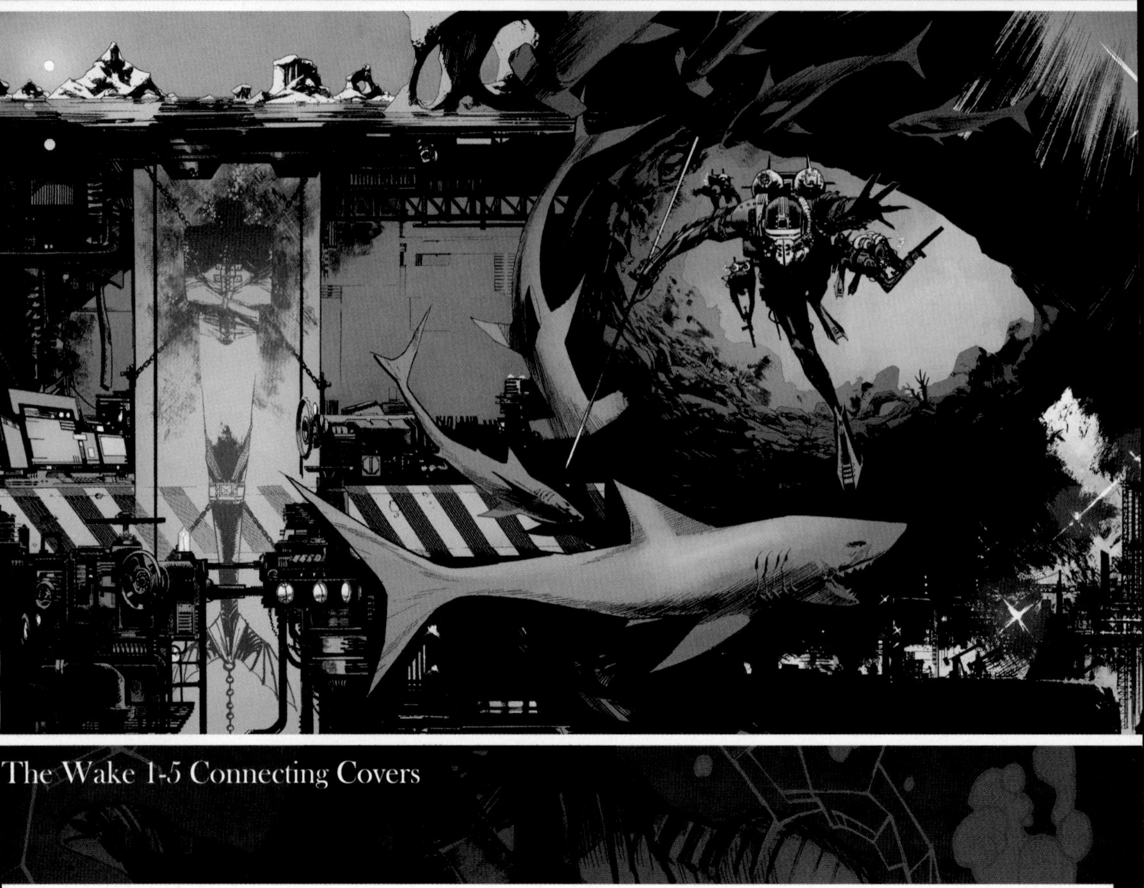

The Wake 1-5 Connecting Covers

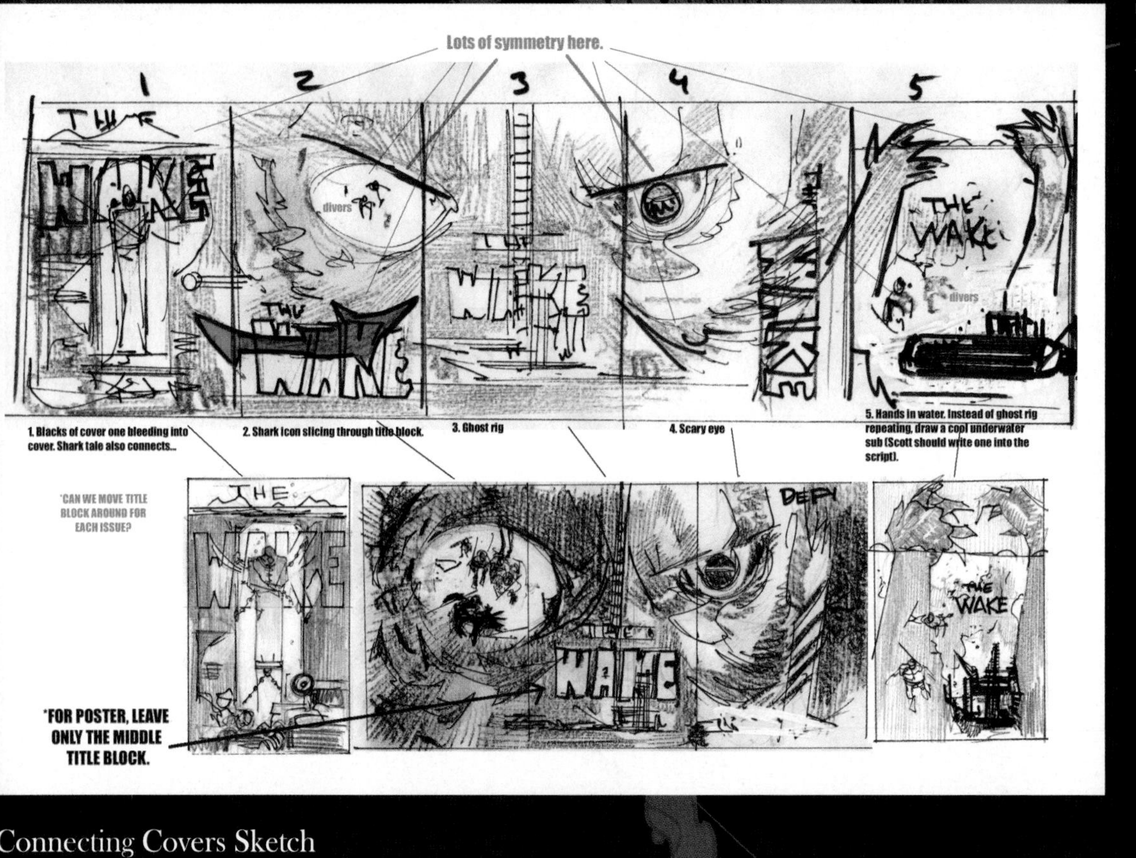

Lots of symmetry here.
1
2
3
4
5
THE
WAKE
divers
THE
WAKE
divers
1. Blacks of cover one bleeding into cover. Shark tale also connects...
2. Shark icon slicing through title block.
3. Ghost rig
4. Scary eye
5. Hands in water. Instead of ghost rig repeating, draw a cool underwater sub (Scott should write one into the script).
*CAN WE MOVE TITLE BLOCK AROUND FOR EACH ISSUE?
THE
WAKE
*FOR POSTER, LEAVE ONLY THE MIDDLE TITLE BLOCK.

Connecting Covers Sketch

We knew we had a big, epic series and Sean wanted to do a series of connecting covers to show the scope of this story.

Internally we called it the "Bond Poster" because it looked like a big, detailed illustrated poster for a James Bond poster in the '60s.

UNPUBLISHED PINUP
BY SEAN MURPHY.

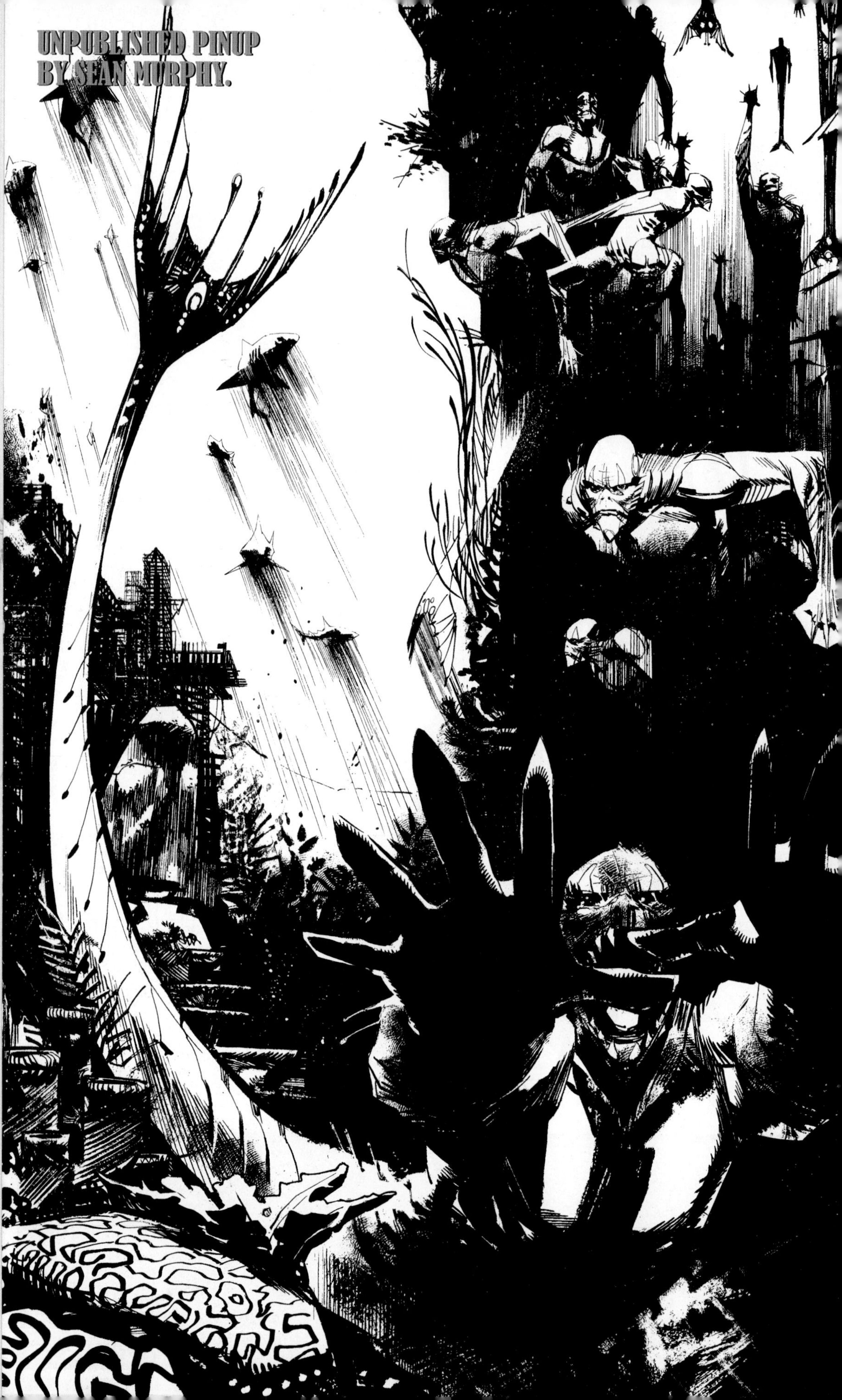

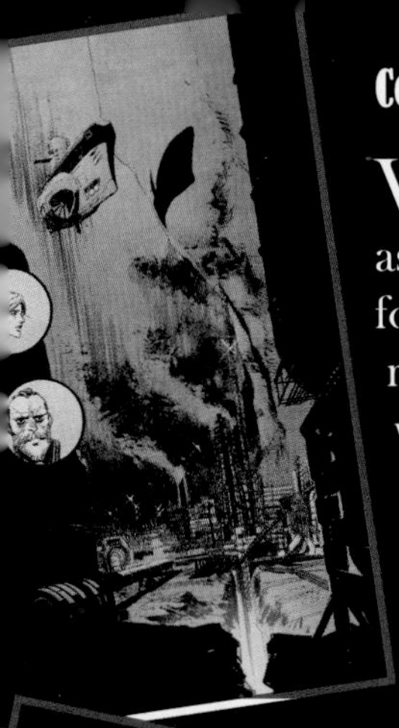

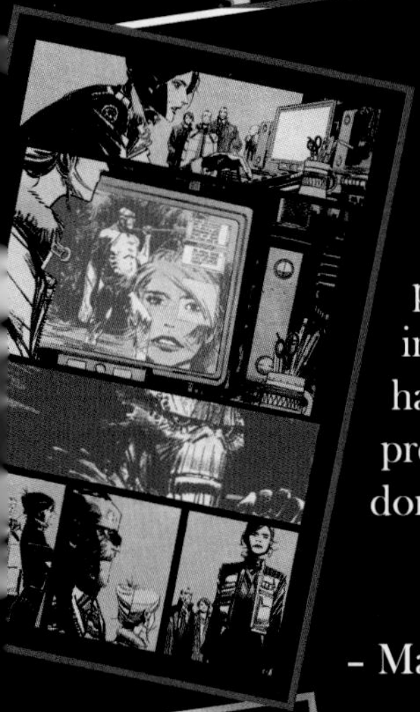

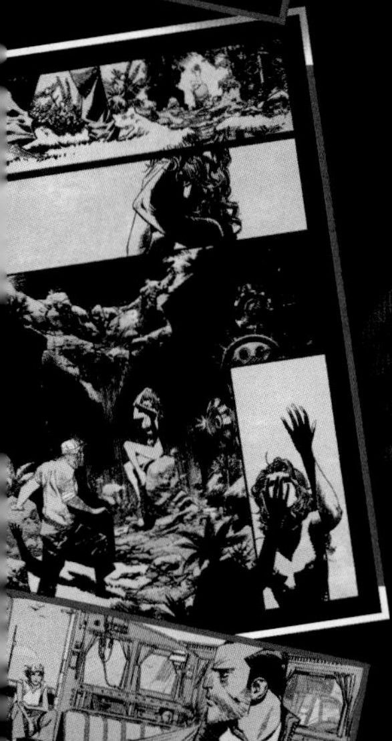

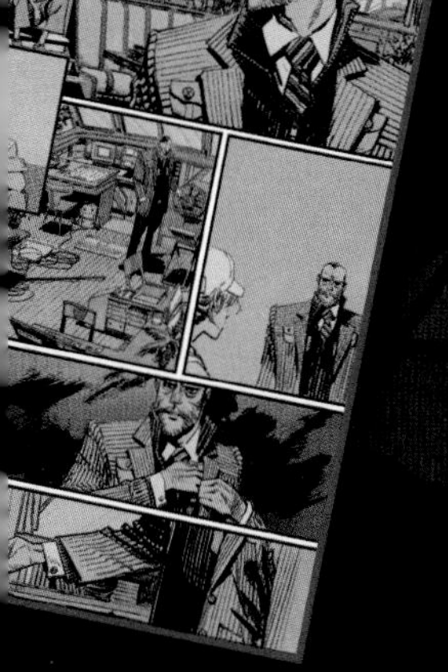

Colors By Matt Hollingsworth

When I first started talking with Sean about working on The Wake, he asked me if I liked Japanese woodblock prints and if I'd be willing to go for a similar look on the book. He sent me links to various pieces by Hiroshi Yoshida, which I loved. I looked and found more and more of his work and used it as inspiration. I would open a few pieces on my second monitor and leave them up while working. I wasn't copying them or their palettes, just drawing inspiration from some of Yoshida's amazing work. While I can't claim to have produced anything approaching the level of genius that Yoshida had, I'm glad that Sean turned me on to his work.

Another part of my approach on the book is that I color the entire book at one time. I keep all of the pages open and go back and forth on them, looking at the entire book and how it's fitting together as an overall design. It's important to me that the book works as a unified piece of storytelling rather than just having a bunch of pretty pieces that don't fit together.

- Matt

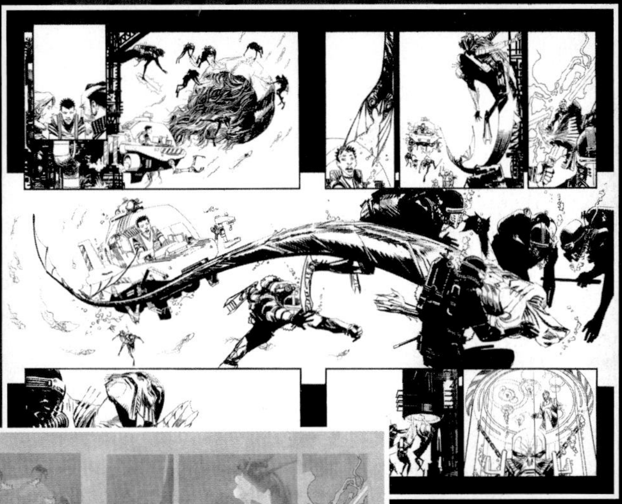

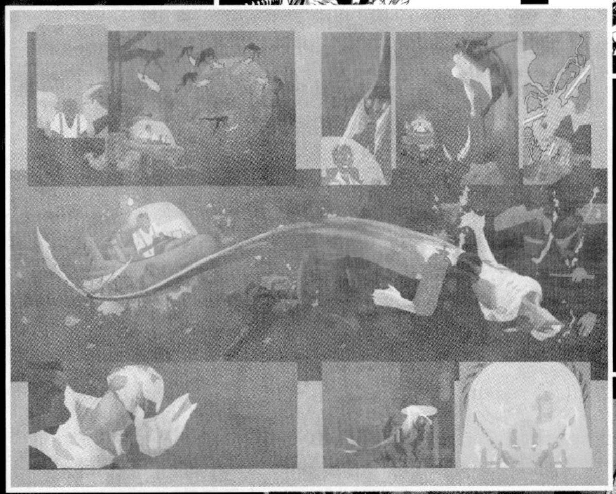

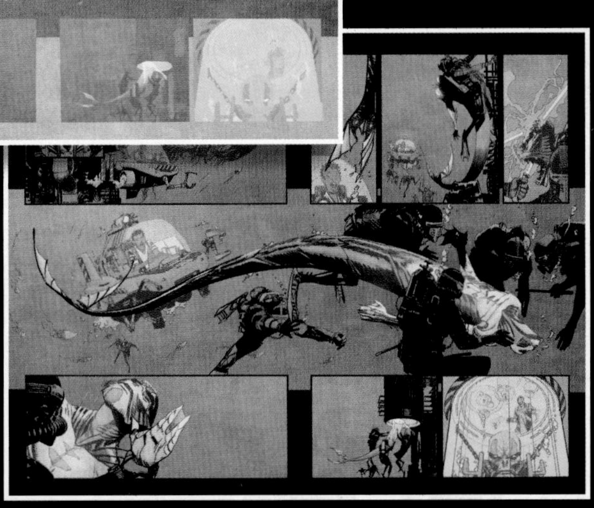

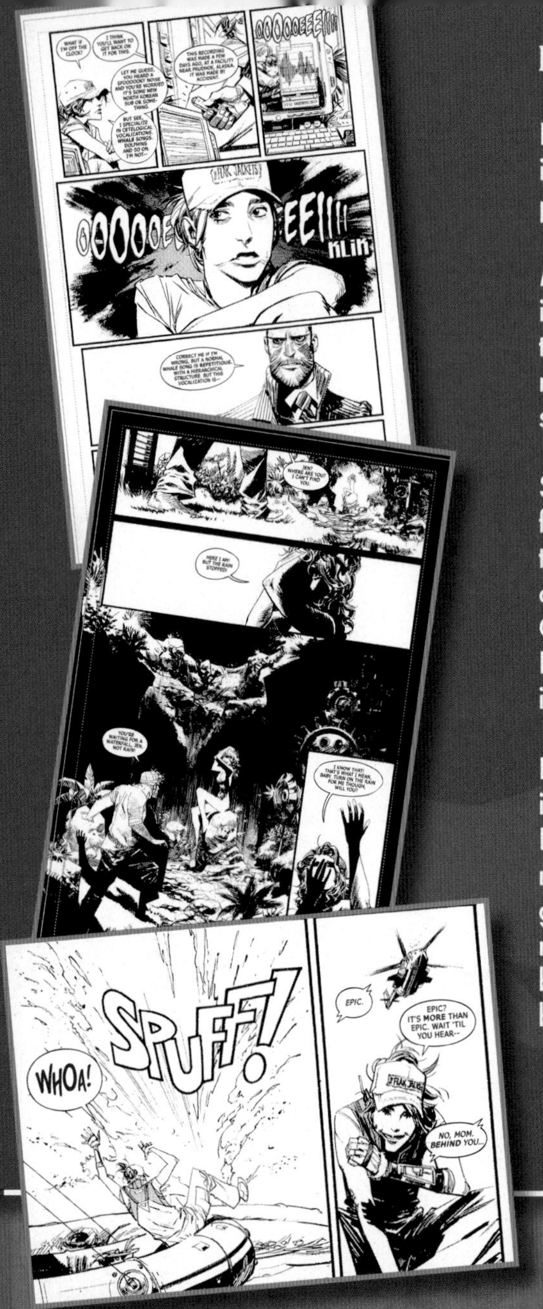
SPUFF!
WHOA!
EPIC.
EPIC? IT'S MORE THAN EPIC. WAIT 'TIL YOU HEAR--
NO, MOM. BEHIND YOU...

Letters by Jared K. Fletcher

Here would be my "process" if you could call it that. I always feel like my process is a damn process unto itself...

My entire approach to lettering comics like this is to try to make everything fit within the style of the artist. My style is that I have many styles. Or maybe no style. But I never teach the Wu-Tang style.

Since Sean's line is so thin, and a lot of the figures are on the taller side, I wanted a font that could match those qualities. Something clean with nice smooth lines. So I'm using a Comiccraft font called Legendary Legerdemain. It's crisp and doesn't draw too much attention to itself.

But the art also has a brush quality to parts of it. So I built a custom digital brush in Adobe Illustrator to stroke the word balloons with. It's normally just a flat uniform line weight. But this gives it some subtle variation to the lines that make up the balloons and help them better blend in with the art style. It takes a lot longer but I think it's been worth it so far.

The Mermaid balloons

Since the guy is seeing essentially a mirage of the woman, I wanted the balloons to be more of a mirage as well. I kept the font the same because he is still hearing a human voice. A change in that makes you think it's a creature he is talking to. So instead I changed the balloon shapes to tip it visually that this isn't quite what it appears to be. Now that I am working on a cintiq, I actually drew out all these balloons freehand with that. I'm using these digital tools with an analog method to try to get as much out of both as I can.

–J

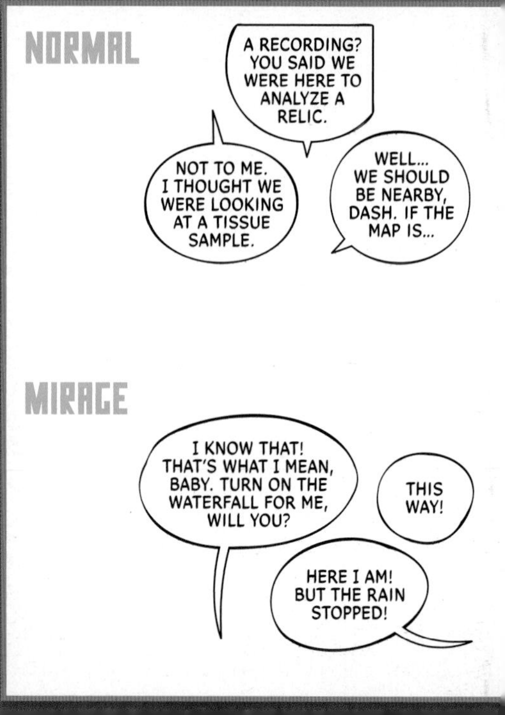
NORMAL
A RECORDING? YOU SAID WE WERE HERE TO ANALYZE A RELIC.
NOT TO ME. I THOUGHT WE WERE LOOKING AT A TISSUE SAMPLE.
WELL... WE SHOULD BE NEARBY, DASH. IF THE MAP IS...
MIRAGE
I KNOW THAT! THAT'S WHAT I MEAN, BABY. TURN ON THE WATERFALL FOR ME, WILL YOU?
THIS WAY!
HERE I AM! BUT THE RAIN STOPPED!

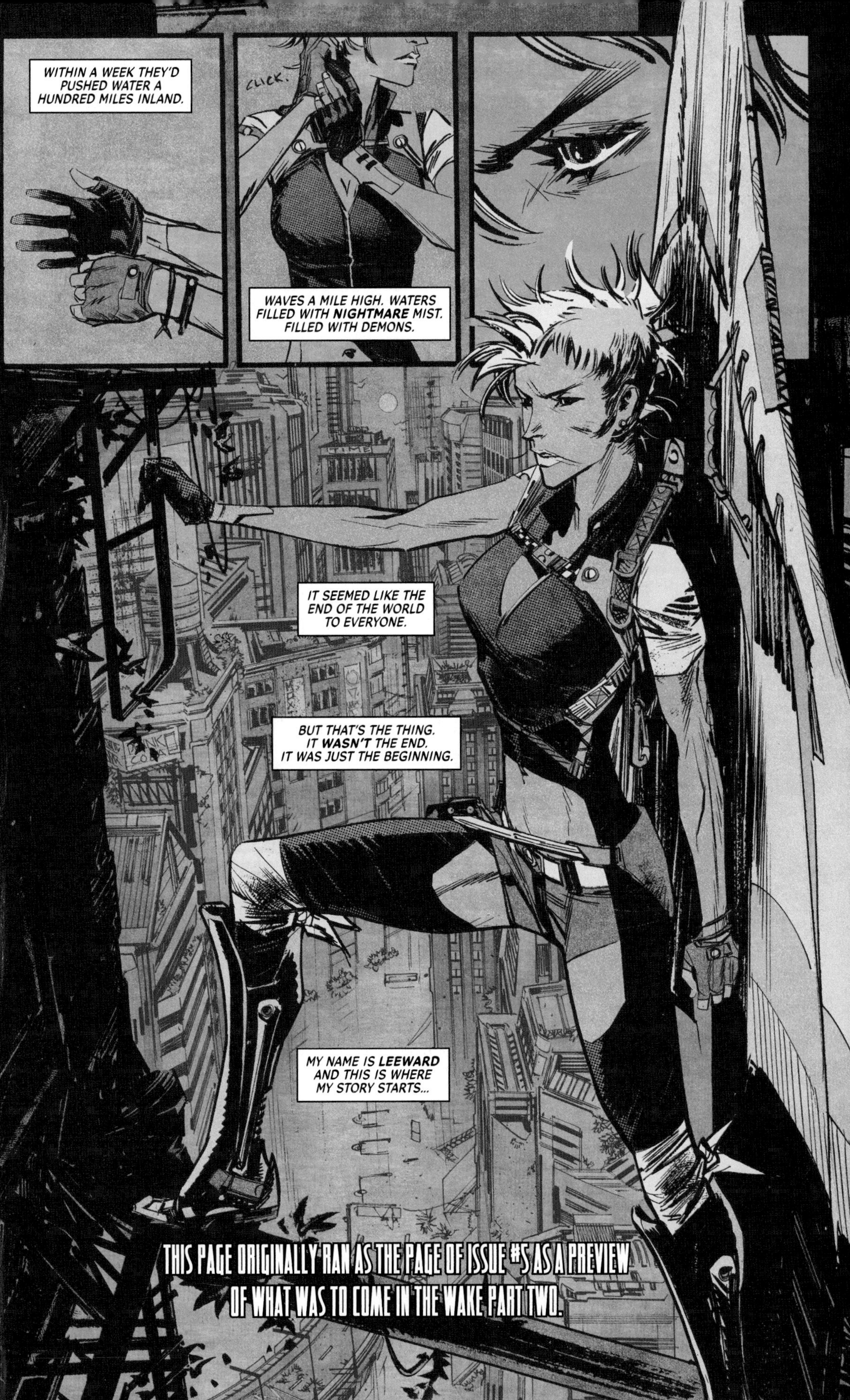
WITHIN A WEEK THEY'D PUSHED WATER A HUNDRED MILES INLAND.
CLICK.
WAVES A MILE HIGH. WATERS FILLED WITH **NIGHTMARE** MIST. FILLED WITH DEMONS.
TIME
IT SEEMED LIKE THE END OF THE WORLD TO EVERYONE.
BUT THAT'S THE THING. IT **WASN'T** THE END. IT WAS JUST THE BEGINNING.
MY NAME IS **LEEWARD** AND THIS IS WHERE MY STORY STARTS...

THIS PAGE ORIGINALLY RAN AS THE PAGE OF ISSUE #5 AS A PREVIEW OF WHAT WAS TO COME IN THE WAKE PART TWO.

SCOTT SNYDER

Scott Snyder has written comics for both DC and Marvel, including the best-selling series BATMAN and SWAMP THING, and is the author of the story collection *Voodoo Heart*. He teaches writing at Sarah Lawrence College and Columbia University. He lives on Long Island with his wife, Jeanie, and his sons Jack and Emmett. He is a dedicated and un-ironic fan of Elvis Presley.

SEAN MURPHY

After breaking into the industry at a young age, Sean Murphy made a name for himself in the world of indie comics before joining up with DC. In his tenure, he has worked on such titles as BATMAN/SCARECROW: YEAR ONE, TEEN TITANS, HELLBLAZER, JOE THE BARBARIAN and the miniseries AMERICAN VAMPIRE: SURVIVAL OF THE FITTEST. Sean also wrote and illustrated the original graphic novel *Off Road*, as well as his popular miniseries, PUNK ROCK JESUS.

MATT HOLLINGSWORTH

Matt Hollingsworth has been coloring comics since 1991. In that time, he's worked on such books as *Preacher*, Hellboy, Daredevil, *Hellblazer*, Death, *The Filth*, Catwoman, *Gotham Central*, Alias, Thor and Hawkeye. He also worked as a texture painter and digital artist on a number of feature films during a two-year stint at Stan Winston Studio, Rhythm and Hues and Sony Pictures Imageworks. He'd like to thank Hiroshi Yoshida, Moebius and Vincent van Gogh for continuing to inspire him. He moved to Croatia in 2006 where he continues to live with his wife Branka and their son Liam.

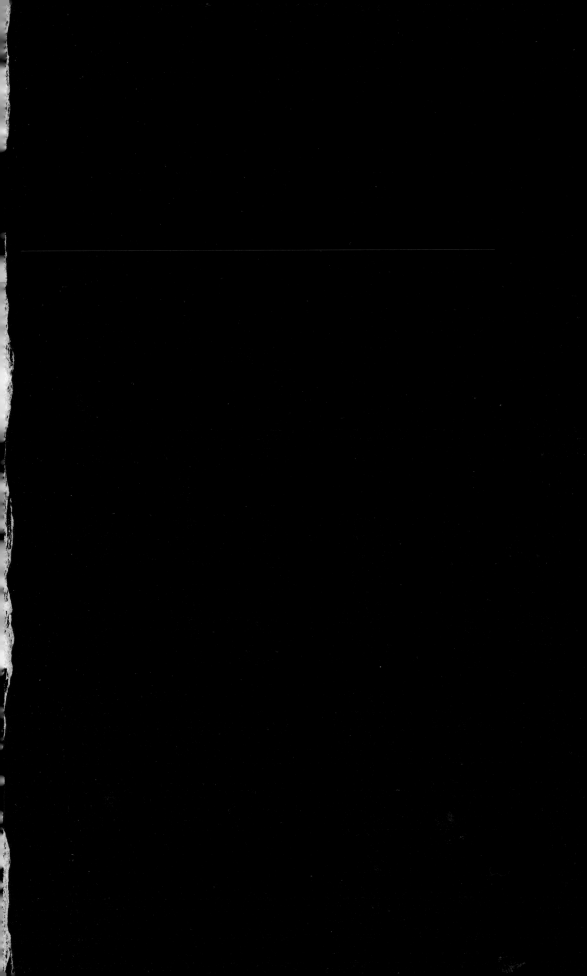